ABORTION!
PROS and CONS

Arguments, Views,
Facts & Information

By

Intecon

First published by AuthorHouse 04/19/04

ISBN: 1-4107-8106-2 (e-book)
ISBN: 1-4184-4268-2 (Paperback)
ISBN: 1-4184-4269-0 (Dust Jacket)

Library of Congress Control Number: 2003095760

This book is printed on acid free paper.

Printed in the United States of America
Bloomington, IN

Table of Contents

Preamble

Scholarly, analytical discussion of abortion. Provides facts, information, and opinions on abortion from a variety of sources. Discusses the problems that cause abortions, and offers new and innovative solutions for resolving the abortion conflict. Evaluates current developments on such issues as partial-birth abortion, breast cancer, Planned Parenthood funding, RU-486, CEDAW, SCHIP, ANDA, the elections, politics, the arrest of James Kopp for the murder of Doctor Barnett Slepian, the Laci and Connor Peterson murders, judicial nominations, and President Bush's influence.

Examines the arguments/views on both sides of the abortion debate, pro-life and pro-choice. Provides reference material, and help for crisis pregnancy and Post Abortion Stress Syndrome. Because this document has no organizational affiliations to promote, and contains numerous references to other web sites and sources, it is an excellent place to start a study of abortion. It has also evolved into a center for the best current thinking on the topic of abortion, including analyses of the health risks. It brings all the information together in one place. You should be able to find everything you need here. If you're a voter, make a difference by checking out the election section.

Some of the ideas presented here have been implemented since their original posting to the internet. However, I have no way of ascertaining for sure how influential these writings were to that implementation – although this tract has been widely distributed to those involved since its inception.

Preface

It was a nondescript but official looking envelope, from a sender I didn't recognize. I wondered why they would be writing me. I opened the envelope and stared with disbelief at the contents, trying to comprehend the implications.

Gradually I grasped that it was a letter of acceptance from the University of California. And not only had I been accepted, but they had offered me a full scholarship, making it possible for me to actually attend.

Of course I'd filled out the necessary forms and sent them in; but then I'd forgotten about it. It hadn't occurred to me that I might be accepted, or what the ramifications would be.

There seemed to be only one acceptable action to take. So that fall I turned in my active Teamsters Union card for an inactive one – just in case I should ever need it again. Then I loaded everything I owned into my car, pulled up my Midwestern roots, and headed west.

Fast-forward 30 years plus. I came off the project I had been working on in December of 1999. In January of 2000 I started looking for my next assignment. It didn't come as a big surprise that the market was not looking good. The technology skills that had sustained me for so many years seemed to be becoming more and more obsolete. After testing the waters for just two weeks, I came to a startling conclusion; and experienced that same feeling I had had when I opened that letter so many years ago. I was at another crossroads in my life; and decided to retrain myself in newer technologies – specifically in web related, and web site development, skills, which seemed to be a rapidly expanding field. So I bought some books, signed up for some classes, and essentially went back to school.

However, I saw more than just the technology. And I didn't see myself making a fortune on the internet. What I saw was a giant printing press, where almost anyone could publish just like Benjamin Franklin, Thomas Paine, or Martin Luther; and compete in the world of ideas worldwide at very little cost and without having to get past any gatekeepers. You didn't have to have significant capital, and you didn't have to spend decades trying to work your way up in an organization; or struggle to build your own organization. No boss or publisher could say I don't like you, or I don't like your work, or I don't agree with your idea, or I think you're a threat to me. You were free to compete unencumbered with these restraints, letting the response from your potential internet audience determine how well received and effective your message was, and how great your influence would be. And I had a cause very much in mind.

It took me about 4 months to get to the point where I thought I could build worthwhile, sophisticated web sites. And while I studied and attended classes I also began writing down notes on what I wanted to include and say on my website. Building the web site turned out to be relatively easy; but it took about 3 ½ months, working essentially full time, to create the content for the site. At the time I finally got it up and online it was about 90,000 bytes (alphanumeric characters). So then I went to a search engine, entered "abortion", and immediately discovered that there were 3,000 other web sites on the same topic ahead of my "great idea". If I had checked first, I probably never would have done it. So I went on to build other web sites, but as new events unfolded, I found myself going back to that original one to add to it.

Introduction

One advance requirement I set for myself was that I didn't want to just "rant and rave" on the topic. To the best of my ability I would try to give both sides of the controversy. Also, I would take a reasoned, logical approach, and support my contentions with facts and evidence as much as possible.

But it was with a certain amount of trepidation that I approached the task, because of the atmosphere I perceived surrounding the Clinton presidency. My assessment of the administration was that they didn't hesitate to use the power of the office – that is, intimidation and force – to play hardball with people who didn't share their outlook. But this feeling dissipated considerably when I actually started exploring the topic on the internet and found sites like "Abortion is Murder" that made mine look very mild and temperate in comparison.

Since it was written over a considerable length of time, you can also see my writing skills develop, from rather awkward at first, to eventually becoming more fluid. It starts out with what may seem obvious to some, then becomes more sophisticated as it goes along. For others, it may represent a first look, and understanding, of what lurks just below the surface of the debate.

As I mentioned, as time went by, I seemed drawn back to it by additional insights – even though I was focusing on other tasks at the time. But as spring of the first year approached – approximately 6 months into existence – I hit a peak of 44 visitors in one day and then tapered off to only having a daily audience in the single digits. The high day resulted mostly from my contacts with related organizations, and the lower days would have been even lower if it hadn't been for a few referrals from a like minded organization that didn't have a web site.

At first I suspected I might be being blocked. So I stocked up on blocking programs to check it out. But by following my trackers, and listening to my wife, who is a school teacher, I began to understand that my site was seasonal. That is, that not only were a lot of people on vacation in the summertime, but school was out, and a large portion of my visitors were students who found my site to be a valuable resource for writing reports.

But with such a small audience, I began to wonder whether it was worth the effort, and what role it might play. So I began to think in terms of what niche it could fill. But as I mulled it over I continued to add to the site, and came to some conclusions. First of all, I thought it was a worthwhile thing to be doing. And if students found it to be useful, I should try to cater to them somewhat.

Since I could see from my trackers that my student audience began at the grade school level, I would assume that they knew very little about the topic, just by virtue of not having been around very long. And my college audience would probably be largely scornful of religion – or so I thought – so I would be careful to keep my site secular. I didn't want to do the same thing other people were doing, and it seemed like the other web sites and organizations were mostly faith based. I hoped those faith-based organizations would appreciate that I could reach people they couldn't.

So I would try to spell everything out and keep the site non-religious. But what else? I had noticed that there didn't seem to be a whole lot of cooperation between the different organizations. In fact, there was actually some animosity that I could detect, in some cases. Plus there was no one place you could go to get a complete picture of what was going on. So I decided my site would be an aggregator of information. And what I didn't want to put directly on my site, I would link to and give a description of. Then people could find just about anything they needed in one place or at least where to find it quickly and easily.

I felt strongly that the day to day news was very important, but a lot of other places were already at least trying to do that; and I felt that I wouldn't be able to keep up with all of it. But it kept ending up on my web site anyway, because I placed such a high degree of importance in current events, and eventually it evolved into something different.

Here's the problem. The major media report as little as possible on abortion. To a certain extent this is a form of censorship, by excluding these events from their reporting. But it's probably also due to it being such a controversial subject; and that a lot of people don't want to either hear or see anything about it. I know how and where to go to get the news, but the vast majority of people wouldn't know that even if they wanted to. I know at least one source that specializes in that type of reporting, but they include a lot of things that I don't consider to really be abortion related (e.g., cloning, stem cell research, etc., etc.) Plus, a lot of people, especially younger people, don't follow the daily news. For them, it's as if the event never occurred.

So I decided I would only report what I considered to be important abortion related news, and I would use it to educate and make a point. Some times I just let the news articles make the point by themselves, and I don't feel any commentary is necessary from me. Other times I interpret and add to the reports to be sure the point isn't missed. I especially liked this approach because it's more authoritative than just me, alone, saying it. As you get deeper into the book you will find a lot of this going on in certain chapters. Rest assured, it's all there for a reason, it's not just filler. If it seems to drag a little, or be repetitive, you can be sure it's a lead in for something interesting and important. I also try to use a variety of sources to reenforce the veracity of the information.

Moreover, I see the book as being both contemporary, and a historical record of a pivotal time in our nation's history. As such, in addition to being organized by topic, there is a chronological sub-organization. Our daily news is here today, gone tomorrow, just one snapshot of a continuing occurrence. In my book you can get the complete picture of what's been going on over time, by bringing together related material from diverse sources, organizations, and events – in case you originally missed parts of it. Plus, in addition to being comprehensive, I provide analysis of what's been happening, and insights into why it's related and why it's important. I weave together this information from different sources to give you a clearer and more complete picture; so that at some point you will see not just the trees, but the entire forest. And you'll learn all the sources I use, so you can keep up on developments on your own, if that's what you choose to do.

So, ultimately, I created a niche that nobody else was serving. As the fall semester (or quarter) got underway, my traffic started to improve somewhat. Then, I got a break. Somebody at a much busier university web site found mine, liked it, and linked to me. I linked back, but decided not to contact them. I was afraid of doing or saying something that might upset my good fortune. It was a dependable source of visitors when school was in session. Marketing on the internet is a moving target, and as things continued to change, I decided to change, too. I would judiciously pay for inclusion in some search engines if I liked their plan. My choices made an immediately noticeable difference. I constantly followed where my visitors came from and how they found my site. A tracker (remote software for statistics on your visitors) that I had used when I started out and that I especially liked but had essentially self-destructed with a software change resuscitated itself providing me with better information on my traffic. At some point, with this additional information, I seemed to start to think like the search engines. I made changes to my web site that had what I thought were a major impact. Late to the party, nevertheless, suddenly, my web site was no longer insignificant. I had as much influence as a whole slew of college professors. I saw the importance of the 2002 elections early, and jumped in, following the key candidates early in the year, and high up in my web page, where it was more likely to be noticed. Election week, and election day, I had more visitors than ever before. I had visitors not just from public and higher education, but from house.gov and senate.gov and state governments and think tanks and corporations and every foreign country imaginable. I consider this book the best place to go for a thorough course on the abortion dilemma, and I think you will agree after you go through it. People new to the controversy will find it an invaluable resource, and everybody can, and will, learn from it. It includes a large amount of text that never made it onto the web site, simply because it seemed like too much work to do gratis. You can read this book and become an expert on the topic. Practically everything you need to know is either here or the book tells you where to go to get it. You will see most of the arguments here – and the counter-arguments. Then the book will tell you how to use the website to get the scoop on the latest developments (The website evolved into an entity where it is very difficult to find specific information. The book mostly solves that problem). Even if you think you know quite a lot about the issue, everybody will find things they didn't know here. For example, probably very few people know that Joe Lieberman was excommunicated because of his views on abortion. President George W. Bush attends the Methodist church. But did you know that while the Methodist Church officially condones abortion, the President is a Christian Conservative? You probably couldn't get the President to tell you that, but after reading this book that will be about the only conclusion a rational person could come to.

In short, this book is packed with information on the abortion issue. It's a treasure chest of facts and views, and certainly not just my opinions. I had one visitor tell me that she liked the parts I wrote best. That really puzzled me, because I think a lot of the sources I quoted say it better than I do. So I guess you'll just have to decide that for yourself. It also presents the evidence that backs up the conclusions, so that you can come to your own decisions. In fact, I present you with the information you need, and encourage people to do their own thinking on the subject. It's also a reference source. For example, if you or somebody you know are thinking about whether to get an abortion right away, it's hard to beat the Pregnancy Resources chapter. Or if you already have had an abortion, and it was a bad scene that you just can't seem to get out of your mind, there's the chapter called Healing After Abortion, with both pro-life and pro-choice resources – whichever you feel most comfortable with. The quotations are carefully selected to make and reenforce a point, impart information, bring together pieces of information to give a more complete picture, and to provide proof for assertions made. Everything is there for a purpose.

There are times when just the weight of the evidence makes the conclusion clear. And to keep a serious subject from getting too dull there are always more interesting lines not too far away. I also have a sense of humor; but if I didn't tell you that ahead of time you might miss it, so be on the lookout for it. And it's also a how to manual in case you should want to get more personally involved.

In addition, for the politically minded, it contains a very good series of chapters on the 2002 elections – at least on the candidates who were involved in the abortion controversy. It's information that you would probably have trouble finding elsewhere. I know I had some difficulty – especially the information after the election. Several weeks after the election was over I was still trying to fill in the blanks, but I finally found time to do it to my satisfaction. I said it was too much work to do again, but I'm starting to get 2004 campaign literature in the mail already, and maybe I'll just do it differently so it's not quite so much work, for the 2004 elections.

The chapters about my debate on about.com are kind of like a bonus exercise for the most serious students. It's very informative, and would be very worthwhile to read for someone who is planning to debate the subject. But it's also very drawn out, because of the way I approached it, and the way I approached it is part of what you learn from it. My opponents conceded very little, and you can't really have a good give and take exchange of ideas in that mode. I was more than willing to make some concessions, to give up some ground, for the purpose of reaching some agreements in some areas where I could see we did agree; but when I saw how my opponents approached it, I gave up on being Mr. Congeniality. I'd never really debated much until I got my web site up and running on the internet, and I went to the forums mainly in an attempt to attract more visitors to my site. But I eventually got pulled in to the action. Actually, I became the action. Far too late in life I learned I should have become a lawyer. As I perceived the general approach used, one person would give their arguments on a topic, the other would give theirs, and anybody else who wanted to could chime in. Then that would be the end of it. However, that didn't seem to be good enough for me. I was not content until I had destroyed my opponents comeback arguments too. Since they wouldn't concede anything, that meant we could be locked in a deadly embrace for some time. When one person eventually wimped out because they were starting to look too compromised, their handlers just sent in a replacement. But each time around, I developed new tactics, and that's why I believe that it was worthwhile to include so much of it, even though often times I was staring down the same arguments they had presented before. It's an interesting story in itself.

So now we come to the question of why you should buy a book that was built around a web site that you can visit on the internet for free. Well, one of the reasons, is that, for me at least, personal sacrifice doesn't seem to be the ultimate motivator. I had a lot of information just sitting on my hard drive that I thought was just too much trouble, just too time consuming, to put on my web site for free. Then when I started to think about publishing the book, I saw how much value that information could add to the book. So, as nearly as I can calculate, there's roughly 32% more material in the book than on the web site (not counting the graphic in a subdirectory there). But there's also another important reason. I approached the two undertakings from very different perspectives. In the case of the web site my goal was to get people to read the entire document, so I made very little effort to make it easy to find things there. It's basically one continuous tract, or I guess two tracts, of reading materials. On the other hand, when I first thought about doing the book, I realized right away that very few people would want to buy a book like that – and rightfully so. So, in addition to the new material, the book is all about organization and making it as easy as possible to find things. And with a book you don't feel like you have to read it all at one time because you might not be able to find your place again like you would feel on my website. So, a book you can read at your convenience. You can take it to lunch, you can read it on the train if you commute to work, you can read it in bed before you go to sleep (although I don't recommend this because it might be hard to put down). You can share it with friends, and refer back to it whenever you like; and if you're like me, put it on a shelf as an addition to your collection. Finally, I formatted parts of the book myself, and as I went along I added additional insights that I didn't bother to include in the web site version. Then I added an extensive index.

But why did I bother to write the book? To explain that, I have to go back to my personal odyssey. After about two years of study, in March of 2002, I felt I was ready to enter the brave new world of web site construction (for pay). So I started casting about for openings. What I soon discovered, of course, was the "tech wreck". There was a better chance of finding an opening with my old skills, by that time, than my new ones, and neither approach really worked. Even worse, I couldn't even get an interview. So I had read in my contractor magazine about a person who suggested finding another source of income, like the utility programs he had written and was selling. I didn't have any programs to sell, but it did start me thinking about what I might have that was saleable, and could generate some income. There was only one thing I could come up with. I'd thought briefly about asking for donations on my web site like charitable organizations do. Charitable organization or not, I was convinced that would never generate much of anything. So I decided to try to make the conversion from selfless moral crusader to petty capitalist and have a best selling book published. "Publish or perish" was beginning to have real life meaning for me.

Interestingly enough, I could never, never, never, have sat down and written this book without having first created the website. And I never would have even thought about writing the book if I had been able to find work in the fields I had trained for. So I can't help wonder if there's some divine providence at work, that I was supposed to do this. I feel like the night I worked until past 5 a.m. on my web site, and it was almost done, and the sun was coming up, and I cried. I cried because I no longer believed that I was doing it alone.

Over four years in the making. I invite you to take this journey with me. And here's my sales pitch – please buy this book. Not just for me, but if you've read this far, you owe it to yourself. I will try to price it so it's easily affordable. And it's grown from that initial 90,000 bytes, to over 2,500,000 bytes (alphanumeric characters).

Prologue

Posted 09/11/2000

Abortion Certainly a very controversial subject. It seems like I've been thinking about it forever. But how long? I can say with certainty that I was personally involved in my more idealistic days thirty years ago; before that time, although I'm sure there was concern, no guidepost exists. But even 30 years is a long time. Since then, other commitments have consumed my life earning a living, caring for my family, and other such routine pursuits. But the issue has never left my mind for long, returning to my ruminations time and again at each twist and turn in the conflict. Over time I have come to feel like the little boy who saw that the emperor had no clothes.

Now I've come to the stage where I have more time again, and no excuse for not speaking out and sharing my thoughts. I can not in good conscience continue to be a voice unheard, suppressing what I have to contribute to the debate. And so I am posting this to the door of the internet. No matter who you are, if you read this from start to finish, you will see things that needed to be said, but had never been heard or published before this document was produced; and had probably never entered your own thoughts on this matter but will enhance your understanding of the issue. As I go back and forth from one side of this debate to the other, you may find yourself first agreeing, then disagreeing, and vice versa, with what I have to say. But I hope I can lead you through this to the inescapable conclusions I draw; and to considering the solutions I advance.

The Problem

I've earned a living for over thirty years by solving complex problems. One of the first things I had to learn, was that you can't solve a problem until you understand what the problem is; however obvious that may sound now.

So let's begin by looking at a couple of typical cases that exemplify, or demonstrate, the problem. This is simply setting the stage so please bear with me.

For the first example, let's imagine a teenage girl, high school age, perhaps 15 or 16 years old. She had a boyfriend, but they broke up. She learned all about how to do sex in class, and didn't think it was a big deal. After all, grown ups do it all the time, just like smoking and drinking; and she sees herself as being grown up or at least she wants to be grown up. And at first she thought her boyfriend was such a neat guy, and they'd get married soon, and he was so insistent, and she kind of want to do it too. But now she's missed her period, and she knows enough to think she might be pregnant. She really didn't think very much about getting pregnant before, but now she does; and panic starts to set in. Will she have to miss school? Probably so. How can she face her friends when they find out? Won't people make fun of her when she walks around school, obviously pregnant? Probably so. And how will she be able to support and care for a baby? There's no chance of getting back together with the boy; and she's way too young to get married anyway. She was hoping to go to college, but will she still be able to? And how can she tell her parents? Will they be furious with her? What are the consequences there? Can she get an abortion without anybody finding out? Frankly, at this point she's probably also very scared. But let's leave her for the moment with all these thoughts racing through her head, and go on to the situation where the girl decides she has to tell her parents. What will their reaction be? Undoubtedly, some parents would embrace her and do everything they could to support her and get her through it. But this probably isn't typical, and I don't want to get into passing judgments on what the parents should or shouldn't do at this point. So let's look at the more likely reaction. They probably would have all the same reactions the girl had; or for sure think of those consequences and tell her about them if she hadn't thought about them herself. There might also be a physical reaction a quick slap to the head to send her head spinning, or worse yet a beating. The girl would probably know what to expect. But I have to believe this would be the exception. More likely, there might also be a string of verbal abuse. Anyway, she would survive this (I don't recall hearing of any murders over this, although I'm sure they are contemplated); and we can go on to the next step what additional reactions the parents may have. Well, they might feel that it would be a loss of face for them, too, among their friends and colleagues and acquaintances. Will people they don't even know be talking about them? And what does it say about their parenting skills. Have they failed as parents? There might also be a financial burden. There will be costly doctor visits, and time in the hospital. Will the burden of raising the child fall on them, and are they too old to accept that responsibility?

Now let's look at one more case, an adult single woman, to be sure we've touched most of the bases. She might already be an unwed mother, who can't afford to support and care for another child. Or she might be a career woman, ambitious and on the fast track, just testing the water sexually. Or she thought the father was the right person for her originally-but it didn't work out that way, and now she's pregnant. It would be really difficult for her just to tell her parents. But how would it go over at work? Would the men make fun of her behind her back? She'd be so embarrassed, and would it ruin her career there? Would she have to take time off, or quit; and then start over again someplace else?

If we've never been involved in an abortion type decision, we've certainly put ourselves in the other person's shoes. Obviously, we have some very real problems here; a situation of the utmost gravity. Also, some might say a life hangs in the balance. In many instances, expediency and panic take over at this point. But let's stop and consider the situation more carefully. Let's start by listing the problems an abortion might resolve: embarrassment, perceived humiliation, an interruption of one's education and participation in sports, a financial burden, an unwanted responsibility of caring for a child, a detour in one's career, and maybe some physical or verbal abuse. But at this point we don't have a single argument for not having an abortion listed; but there may be a, or some, argument(s) in the back of someone's mind that haven't been mentioned yet. We know there is a segment of the population that opposes abortion, for any reason; so let's examine what arguments they might offer. Their mantra seems to be the "Right to Life", and their organizations tend to call themselves this or that "Right to Life" group. An unfortunate choice of words, I think, because it can be interpreted to imply life at some future point in time; and words can be very important in a debate, as we shall see. But they're the underdogs at this point, so let's be generous and help them out by changing it to the "Right to Live". On the other side of the debate are the people who are in favor of abortion. Their slogan is "A Woman's Right To Choose". It's so completely awesome for its time probably one of the greatest slogans ever devised. They tried it out, it worked, they stuck with it over the years, and the idea has carried the day for them time and again. Very easy to understand, and the right to life people have never learned how to deal with it. It's a free country, and I ask you, how could anyone possibly be against it? I'm most definitely in favor of a woman's right to choose. But there is a problem with it, which nobody seems to notice, and that problem is that when a woman learns that she is pregnant there is another person in existence. Doesn't that person have that same right to choose? Are we going to say that just a certain privileged class of person has this right to choose to live or die and for other people? That doesn't sound fair. That can't be right. That's not freedom of choice-that's tyranny. Certainly the other person is not old enough to vote in an election, but doesn't that person have the same right to be protected by society as other children are protected? But wait, you say, it isn't really a person, it's a fetus. If you went to Planned Parenthood and were a little uncertain about getting an abortion, I'm sure that they'd probably reassure you that, yes, it was only a fetus. So would people at the abortion clinic. Anti-abortion people would probably engage in an argument over whether a fetus was a person; but as soon as they do that they accept the implied position that there is something different from a person that is called a fetus and they are probably wasting their breath because they have already compromised their position. So are you beginning to see how important language can be? S.I. Hayakawa talked about this kind of thing in his book "Language In Thought And Action"; but it's been so long ago, that the majority of people probably haven't read it. He went on to head a college in the California State College system, and later became the U.S. Senator from California.

IS IT THOUGHT?

In fact, a child is a child whether it's inside or outside the mother, whether it's one pound or ten pounds. Size doesn't determine humanity. I don't think the people who head Planned Parenthood or the National Organization for Women or Emily's List are stupid at all; and they would never go on television or to a public forum and argue that a child is not a human being while it's still inside the mother because they know they would be totally humiliated and lose the debate with any knowledgeable and equally prepared opponent. They don't want to look like fools; but believe me, they know. Instead they brilliantly talk only about a woman's right to choose, thereby avoiding the real issue and lots of people buy into it; especially young people who don't have the experience to make independent judgments. It allows people to rationalize their actions.

Still don't agree that a child inside its mother is really a child, and that that's not really at issue? Well, I got by that many years ago, but maybe I can help. Years ago, when Life magazine published the picture of a child in peaceful repose inside its mother on the front cover of the magazine, it was a stunning revelation for me, and it must have been for a lot of people; otherwise why would they have put it on the front cover? Today when a woman becomes pregnant it's commonplace to get an ultrasound of the baby to make sure there aren't any problems that need to be addressed, and to satisfy a natural, and perhaps pragmatic curiosity about what the baby's sex is. What do you suppose they're looking at? Ask to see somebody's ultrasound-they'll be proud to show you. And just think about it-does it make any sense at all to say a baby inside its mother isn't human, but the minute it pokes its head out it is? How totally, totally, absurd!

3

But if you still don't agree, ask your family doctor some very specific questions: At what point is it possible to hear a baby's heartbeat? When can you first measure brainwaves? How soon does a baby start to look like a person? If you don't get direct answers, if he's being evasive, try another doctor. If that seems like too much trouble, and you don't want to do you're own research, I can tell you that 6 days after implantation in the uterus the person has developed so rapidly that his heart, brain, spinal column, and nervous system are almost complete; after 8 days the person's heart has started to beat; and although still very small this individual has taken control of the pregnancy to try to assure it's survival and the mother probably doesn't even know she is pregnant yet. Sometimes I have observant individuals challenge the statistics I personally state. That's good, because I know they're paying serious attention. The difference is due to the fact that as long as two weeks can go by from the moment of fertilization until the placenta has completely attached itself to the uterus, at which time the woman "becomes pregnant"; and that's often when I begin counting.

The idea that a baby is born at the time it miraculously pops out of a woman is an archaic notion superseded by modern science. I've included links to other related sites at the end of this document that you can go to for more information. Of course there's another argument, that a child isn't a child until it can survive outside the mother. This is equally absurd. Did you ever hear of parents bringing a baby home from the hospital, and it got up, walked to the refrigerator, and fixed itself a sandwich? In fact, the child will be totally dependent on its parents and other adults for its survival for several years. When you bring the baby home from the hospital, please don't set it down in its room and forget about it and come back to see how it's doing in a week.

Here are some other facts about how rapidly a child develops inside its mother, taken from the American Life League publications "The First Nine Months" and "What They Never Told You About the Facts of Life": "DAY 30 At one month old, the embryo is 10,000 times larger than the original fertilized egg-and developing rapidly." "DAY 35 Five fingers can be discerned...". Keep in mind that mom probably doesn't even know she's pregnant yet. "WEEK 6 The mother is about to miss her second period and has probably confirmed that she is pregnant." "WEEK 9 Fingerprints are already evident...". "MONTH 4 The umbilical cord has become an engineering marvel, transporting 300 quarts of fluid per day and completing a round-trip of fluids every 30 seconds." Note, though, that the baby itself is completely separate from the mother, and not a part of her body in any way it is connected by the umbilical cord, which in turn is attached to the placenta, which is the part attached to the mother's uterus. The baby always has a separate blood system, which may even be a different blood type from the mother. At delivery, the placenta, and most of the umbilical cord, are simply thrown away. The placenta transfers nutrients and waste-not blood. The baby produces its own blood, just like we do. Floating in the amniotic fluid, the baby is something like an astronaut doing a space walk-actually swimming around, until it becomes too cramped close to the delivery time. "...feel pain for the first time...When your mom was 7 weeks pregnant". "By the time your mother found out she was pregnant, you were: A miniature human with arms, legs and a heartbeat". "When did you start using your brain? Fetal electric brain waves have been traced as early as the sixth week." "...babies as young as 22 weeks after conception, weighing only 14 oz., have survived premature birth." "...you'll continue to develop, just like you did in the womb, until you reach the...age of approximately 23 years!" Hardly just a mass of cells. The aforementioned publications can be had for the lofty price of .50 cents and .75 cents respectively.

"While giving an anesthetic for a ruptured ectopic pregnancy...I was handed what I believe was the smallest living human ever seen...This tiny human was perfectly developed, with long, tapering fingers, feet and toes...The baby was extremely alive and swam about the sac approximately one time per second, with a natural swimmer's stroke." Paul Rockwell, M.D. Well, perhaps that's an old quote, because they rather routinely observe babies grow within their mother's now but not first hand like that.

But the "Right to Live" people have found a truly bewildering array of ways to defeat themselves, shooting themselves in the foot, so to speak. For example, they talk about the "War on the Unborn", the "rights of the preborn", "killing the unborn", "the defenseless unborn", and so on. In other words they are telling people that they still subscribe to the antiquated idea that a child is born, or comes into the world, when the doctor delivers it at the hospital. This might have seemed to make sense in the Dark Ages, but we live in the 21st century, where they open people up, take out their defective heart, and put in a healthier model. We know what happens inside a woman every step of the way; how the child grows, develops, and matures. It should be obvious that a child is born when a woman becomes pregnant; depending on when you define the pregnancy as beginning; and I'll talk about exactly how I define that later. Again, the pro-lifers are defeated by linguistics; they unwittingly accept the language of their opposition. Then there's the "you shouldn't bring an unwanted child into the world" argument. The answer to this is also a no-brainer. Wouldn't almost everybody prefer to be unwanted to being dead! At least you have a chance to work at changing the situation. Also, I've noticed mothers tend to become proud of, and attached to, their children, once they have the opportunity to meet them face to face.

Let's take another look at how abortion advocates use mind games to come out on top in this debate. Say there is a public forum discussing the issue, or a group of friends sitting around debating it. It won't go on for long before one of the "liberal" debaters will ask, "and what would you do in the case of

5

rape?". If the people taking the pro-life side of the argument are new to the issue, they may be stumped by this. If it is somebody who has given the issue some deep introspection, they would most likely answer that it doesn't matter, they would still oppose abortion. Tricked again. Because people, and especially the ladies in the discussion, will begin rolling their eyes and saying "no-way!". All at once the pro-lifer, probably not realizing it, has been pulled into debating a very small side issue instead of the broad topic. Let's face it, he may be correct logically, but in today's climate he is so politically incorrect that he will never convince a majority of people. Let it go. The response should be that pregnancy resulting from rape is such an infrequent occurrence that we should ignore that circumstance for now and concentrate on making abortion illegal for the vast majority of other unplanned pregnancies. He can always come back and fight the rape battle after his goals of stopping the other abortions are achieved. So let me suggest, the next time somebody tells you they believe in a woman's right to choose; correct them "You mean a woman's right to kill".

The latest slogan I've heard bandied about is "A woman's reproductive rights". Here again, on the surface of it, it's hard to be against a woman's right to reproduce; although I think they mean "to not reproduce". This argument has the same shortcoming as "the right to choose", and is actually the same argument, just stated differently. The shortcoming is that once a woman discovers that she is pregnant, she has already exercised her right to reproduce, and now there is another person who has the right to start their own family someday-her child. This is just another right they have dreamed up for their own purposes. Certainly nothing exists in the Constitution or Bill of Rights about a woman's "reproductive rights". I think this reveals a disturbing trend the pro-abortion activists think that by attaching the word "right" to anything they can make it a constitutional right; and most of the supreme court justices follow this same methodology. Actually, the founding fathers of this country were very clear about the rights they held to be indispensable, in the documentary foundation they laid out and passed on to guide those who followed them. In the 2nd paragraph of the Declaration of Independence they clearly state their views on life: "WE hold these Truths to be self-evident, that all Men are created equal, that they are endowed by their Creator with certain inalienable Rights, that among these are Life, Liberty, and the Pursuit of Happiness—That to secure these Rights, Governments are instituted among Men, deriving their just Powers from the Consent of the Governed, that whenever any Form of Government becomes destructive of these Ends, it is the Right of the People to alter or to abolish it, and to institute new Government, laying its Foundation on such Principles, and organizing its Powers in such Form, as to them shall seem most likely to effect their Safety...".

Wise and visionary thoughts for their times, and I think it still rings true today. Although the pro-abortionists prefer to scoff at this; and many of our supreme court justices believe themselves to be above it; I value my heritage and don't intend to ignore it. Besides, when you stop and consider it thoroughly, you see that "a woman's reproductive rights" is more a statement of the problem, rather than the solution. In the view of the Christian Coalition of America, "...ignored the Founders' self-evident truth of a Creator-endowed priority of right to life. The liberal vision of a utopian society of sexual freedom and empowerment undermines the moral basis for a free society. A just society cannot be founded on the death of children. The 'choice' argument for abortion on demand also ignores the fact that a child in the womb is a separate individual with their own inalienable rights. 'Choice' is a diversion from a legitimate discussion of the fundamental issue: When does life begin?". So I guess I'm not the only one who "gets it", although I think that a world with no premarital sex may be another kind of unattainable utopian vision.

Abortionists like to point out that the Declaration of Independence is not a governing document. No matter, our citizenry deemed the views expressed there so important that they later put similar language into the Constitution through amendments. Section One of Amendment XIV (14) states: "...nor shall any State deprive any person of life, liberty, or property, without due process of law; nor deny to any person within its jurisdiction the equal protection of the law."

A lot of people also seem to be fooled by a purported need for population control. This is something that seems to come in and out of favor every few years, and organizations are formed to study and deal with it-until they realize that it's really not a problem at all. If you've lived all your life in the New York, Chicago, or Los Angeles urban areas, I can see why a person would think overcrowding is a problem; but if you've ever driven out of the city into the countryside-say on a trip to Florida-and seen the vast open spaces in this country; this becomes an obviously exaggerated concern. Why do you think farmers and ranchers have such a tough time making a living? It's because so much food is produced that it keeps prices at a level that is difficult to derive a profit from. Any perceived population problems are political problems-not biological ones. By this I mean the political structure of a country must be such that it encourages and allows people to provide for themselves; that is, creates conditions similar to what we have in the U.S. today. This is more a tactic to get big contributors to ante up for population control, so they think they're doing a good deed. Then the money is used, at least in part, to support abortion.

Then there is the argument about the health of the mother. This ignores the fact that an abortion is almost always fatal to the child; although I've heard of a girl who was aborted and survived and sometimes speaks before groups.

Unfortunately, a third of her generation wasn't so lucky. There's also a group of young people out in California who call themselves the "Survivors", for obvious reasons.

Even though people in this country profess to be of one religion or another, and go to church in varying degrees, we are still basically a secular society and religion is more of a social phenomenon of belonging than someplace people refer to to shape beliefs that may be in a state of conflict. The Pope is adamantly opposed to abortion; and yet Catholics seem to form their own opinions on this and a host of other issues. The Lutheran church has split into two branches: one opposes abortion; the other condones it. The Jewish faith is strangely quiet, considering their own holocaust in Germany. They don't seem to want to concern themselves with other people's holocausts-kind of like the world ignored what was happening in Germany during World War II.

To the many wonderful young Christian conservatives who are donating their time and efforts to fighting this battle; keep up the good work. But I would like to recommend that you leave your religion at home. People of other faiths often see this as an effort to convert them to your religious beliefs and it becomes a religious issue to them rather than a shared concern. I believe this issue transcends separate religions-it speaks to our very humanity.

The Solution

But I've gotten off task. I hadn't planned to get into all that quite yet, but it just sort of came out. I set out to try to solve some problems. We wanted to see if we could find any arguments against having an abortion, and if there were any other ways to resolve the problems spawned by an unplanned and unwanted pregnancy. Let's see what we have on the side opposed to abortion: A child is a human being irregardless of how small or how young, whether inside or outside the mother; and therefore has the right to choose to live. Since young children are unable to express their desire to live, at least until they learn to talk; it is reasonably certain that, like most of the population, they would prefer to live rather than be killed; and should be protected by the law and adult population until they become a legal adult at 18. This certainly appears to make sense: how could age or location be the determinant of whether a person is a human being, and therefore protected by the law? It seems much more accurate to apply a chromosome test to determine a person's humanity; even then there might be more than one correct result. So it looks like the "right to live" people are right; even though they've had their claims rejected by courts all over the country. On the other hand, before the Civil War, a large majority of people in the South believed that slavery was alright (some still do); so we see an example, not so long ago, in the annals of human history, of how a majority of people can be very wrong on an issue.

But this does nothing to do away with the concerns we discussed earlier; and faced by the people in an unwanted child predicament. But given the conclusions reached above, it no longer seems equitable to have our child killed to avoid embarrassment. Democrats criticize Republicans for wanting to stop abortion, but not being willing to vote for the funds and programs to deal with the problem. I think this is somewhat warranted, though it doesn't justify having an abortion. As the feminist movement has changed the way we regard premarital sex, society hasn't adapted to the resulting problems. I believe massive federal and state funding is needed to set up programs to deal with the problem of unplanned pregnancies; programs that don't include abortion. However, I don't believe a government bureaucracy is the answer either. I think these funds should go mainly to private and religious organizations to set up these programs. Many of the prototypes probably already exist in one form or another. Conservatives already advocate adoption; it just needs to be on a much larger scale; and obviously isn't going to reach that scale until some of the other problems are solved. Where there is financial difficulty, the government should step in and pay for the doctor and hospital bills without much questioning, except for proof of pregnancy and lack of sufficient income of the person pregnant and her spouse (if there is one). But once the mother is out of the hospital, I don't believe the government should continue its support, because this might encourage some girls to get pregnant.

This is where adoption can play a role, where there aren't other acceptable options; like parents of the girl becoming caretakers, or the girl quitting school and going to work to support the child. Additionally, alternative schools should be set up for girls who become pregnant, so they can continue their education without being subjected to the scorn of their peers, and maintain a degree of confidentiality; and this should be done on a scale sufficient to handle everybody who wants to get into the program. And boarding school capabilities should be provided for those who need it, until they can get on their feet again. Expensive, yes; but if you're going to put a stop to the scourge of abortion, you must provide viable alternatives. Further, I would like to propose that the major faiths opposed to abortion in this country set aside their differences to unite in common cause to form a National Committee Against Abortion to find what they can do in concert to eradicate this curse from our society forever, and help lead this country out of it's nightmare. Currently we have Catholics and Jews thinking Protestants are trying to convert them, and Protestants and Jews thinking abortion is a Catholic birth control issue. Get it together.

I would like to offer a suggestion that is sure to be especially controversial, but that I think is worthy of careful consideration and discussion. During a time when people have to import children from China to adopt, and dead baby parts are regularly marketed for profit, it seems we could allow, to some extent, the free market system to place a value on live babies, and allow people to purchase unwanted children in this country from single mothers; to encourage them to bear their children instead of having an abortion. Instead of having to pay for an abortion, girls could get paid for having their child. After all, not too long ago lotteries were illegal. We probably wouldn't want to encourage people to have children just to make money, but with 1.5 million abortions a year in this country I think there would be enough babies to go around and keep prices within reach for most people wanting to adopt. Scholarships might be a good means of payment for kids wanting to continue their education. Of course, there would probably need to be some rules and regulations; but not to the point that it would prevent this effort from being successful. Perhaps there would need to be a limit on the price that could be charged-after all we don't want to start a cottage industry. But we might want to let married women into the program if they can show that they would otherwise have an abortion because they can't afford to support another child. In addition to providing a free enterprise solution to the problem, if there turned out to be an oversupply, government could step in and pay for the surplus. They could then put the unneeded children in places modeled after Boys Town and Hershey. At Hershey they used to make the kids get up at daybreak to milk the cows.

So, what happens to unwanted children who are institutionalized like this? Well, at Hershey, an alumnus of the Hershey orphanage grew up to become the CEO of Hershey Foods. All he really needed was a chance-and to be alive. And guess what? The kids don't have to milk the cows anymore. But the reaction of the other alumni to the change was mostly opposition; apparently they had found memories of getting up early to milk the cows and felt it was a character builder. If you were to delve into this further, you would find many other success stories. From my own personal experience, years ago I worked with a distinguished gentleman who was an accountant, an especially hard worker, and a graduate of Boys Town. What I'm advocating, is a political, or structural, solution, instead of a biological one; that our society should be able to work out.

"Sadly, today adoption is chosen by less than two percent of the 1.3 million single women who unexpectedly become pregnant each year. This is tragic considering that there are over two million screened and qualified couples waiting to adopt these children." John C. Willke, M.D.

Nor do I think we should let the guys off the hook just because they're not the ones who get pregnant. They obviously played a part in this. Given today's DNA based identification techniques it should be easy to identify the father and hold him responsible for helping to support the child if the girl decides to keep the baby and she elects to pursue this course. Then if he fails to comply off he goes to a special facility for guys in the same predicament. Not because he's been bad, but because people have to be held accountable for their actions and we have to get a handle on this thing and stop the killing.

In sex education classes the emphasis should be taken off of "how to" and placed on "why not"; and the problems that can result, including the points I've mentioned above.

Establishment of the date of birth should also be changed by legislation making it the date that a woman and her doctor agree is the closest to the date the pregnancy commenced, or that science can determine. If no scientific test exists to establish the sex of the child at this early stage of development, this precludes choosing a name; however, in lieu of this, a social security number could be assigned as an identifier for the individual. This would then establish a legal existence, accountability, and equal protection under the law. In other words, if no delivery of the child was reported nine months hence, and there was no evidence or record of a miscarriage occurring at a hospital, a missing person investigation would have to be initiated. I realize this is a radical change in the way people think about a child being "born". But it really isn't that difficult. One of the definitions The American Heritage Dictionary gives for the word "born" is "Brought into existence; created". So, you see, it really does make sense.

Additionally, "fetus" is the Latin word for "young one" or "offspring". So something has been lost in the translation-or lack of translation. It would be clearer and less misleading to use the actual English terminology, rather than such a harsh sounding, impersonal, and confusing term as "fetus". "young (y¾ng) adj. young·er, young·est. 1. Being in an early period of life, development, or growth. 2. Newly begun or formed 3. Of, belonging to, or suggestive of youth or early life", from the American Heritage Dictionary, which is the one I happen to have on my computer. So, instead of saying "the fetus" in Latin, we would refer to "the young one", in English. Instead of talking about the "fetal stage of development", it would be more proper and easily understood to say "the younger stage of development"; unless the person happens to be an expert in Romance languages. "Youngest" would be quite proper, too. Try it, after a while it will come naturally and you'll start to like it. Problem is, right now, nobody else will know what you're talking about, so there has to be some kind of official transition. But it sure sounds a lot better than "fetus".

SEX

The media also needs to accept some responsibility and reevaluate their role in this, as an educator of our children; intended or not. The other night my wife rented a movie, and we watched "Home Is Where The Heart Is". It is a wonderful movie, and I encourage anyone who hasn't seen it yet to do so. It has a lot of good messages to convey, but I found myself wondering about the appropriateness of a bedroom scene toward the end of the movie. Not because I'm against bedroom scenes per se; I think they have their place. But this one seemed misplaced. Up until then the movie had painted Forney (despite his name) as someone who probably wouldn't know what to do if he had the chance; or wouldn't even want to out of respect for the girl. Not only was it out of character, but it wasn't even a "good" sex scene; as if they were following a formula that required them to put it in. I thought it would have been more effective and realistic if they had just embraced and kissed passionately, and he had blurted out that he loved her etc., and would she marry him, but she didn't have to answer just then. It got me thinking that the pendulum had swung too far from sexual repression to sexual liberalness. Then I started wondering about the episode where the two Christians kidnapped the baby...

"Even when sex isn't directly portrayed in the media, most kids will tell you that there's a constant implication that everyone does it, apparently without consequence." Psychologist Lynda Madison, writing for TV Guide, June 23, 2001 issue.

From the April 2001 Ryan Report: "Planned Parenthood spent more than $30 million in a single year on sex education programs...it is the sex education programs run by Planned Parenthood that historically spur its business growth ...the long term viability of the organization relies on sex education programs providing it new customers." "Without a viable sex education program, PP knows it is only a matter of time before its empire begins to collapse...should renew...efforts to put a halt to PP's access to our children."

The feminists so want to be the equal of men in all they do, and I have no problem with that. But they should also take pride in what they can do that men can't; which is to have children, the most important role in continuing our species.

A culture that encourages sex, and then leaves women to make this horrible decision on their own, is unfair to them, and a bonanza for the mass killers like Planned Parenthood.

I don't blame abortion on the girls and women who go to the abortion clinics. I think that in most cases we can assume that they don't understand that they

Intecon

are taking the life of their child and can't otherwise deal with the problems an unwanted pregnancy brings. Perhaps they are also encouraged by their parents (they've had children, they probably understand what they are proposing). Perhaps they know their clergy condone it. The society they live in seems to approve of it; it's thought to be legal by some, depending on how you interpret the law, and which law is applied, and whether you submit to bad laws. There are so many pressures, how can they withstand them?

The Law

That's why it's also essential that we not only offer the carrot, as I've done above, but also apply the stick, so that our society sends no mixed signals on this issue, but very clearly says to everybody that abortion is wrong, that abortion is against the law, and that abortion is murder. I also propose that any legislation passed to support the above programs, and any anybody else can come up with, include the following punishments for this offense. A year of incarceration in a facility designed for that crime for any woman convicted of having an abortion-3 months longer than the pregnancy would have lasted. As for the abortion doctors, they have no excuse. They see their handiwork every day. How could they not know? Greed has closed their eyes. They are serial killers, who should be tried as such, retroactively, with the expected outcome well deserved capital punishment. Over 1.2 million abortion-murders are performed in this country every year; the latest figure I have seen is 41 million since Roe vs. Wade.

And who is ultimately responsible for this atrocity? Yes, atrocity. And who knows how many worldwide? In the genocide in Rwanda, only 500,00 were slain. In our own Civil War, about 620,000 were killed. In Cambodia, 2,000,000. In Nazi Germany, 6,000,000 Jews and Gypsies and the handicapped were sent to their deaths (can you imagine a Nazi officer appearing before the Nuremberg war tribunal and saying "they weren't really people, they were Jews", like we are being told by today's society that children aren't human; or that the extermination of 6 million people was acceptable because it was legal), under Mao, in China, 20,000,000, and so on. We have surpassed all these milestones. And who do we have to hold responsible for saying this was legal, and opening the door to it? Obviously, the Supreme Court, who have upheld the "right" to abortion and cleared the way; who have had peaceful demonstrators and their priest, demonstrating in a pre-approved location outside the court, arrested, because they didn't want people to hear their point of view. The majority of justices (Steven Breyer, Ruth Bader Ginsburg*, Sandra Day O'Connor, David Souter, and John Paul Stevens) couldn't even find it in their hearts or minds to ban partial-birth abortion; a procedure where in an otherwise normal, full term, on time, delivery, a hole is poked in the baby's head, its brains are vacuumed out, and the remaining pieces sold according to prices on a parts list (you didn't know that?). There was a gulf so wide between these judges and their colleagues that the minority called the decision: "illogical" and "indefensible"; "in which the mere invocation of 'abortion rights' trumps any contrary social interest", "a particularly virulent strain of constitutional exegesis"; "inclination to bend the rules when any effort to limit abortion, or even to speak in opposition to abortion, is at issue"; "policy-judgmentcouched-as-law"; "visibly brutal means of eliminating our halfborn posterity is quite simply absurd"; and "Justice Scalia scoffed at the

15

idea that 'a 5-4 vote on a policy matter by unelected lawyers' should trump the will of 30 state legislatures". The Presbyterian Theological Seminary aptly called it "Supreme Arrogance". To make such a horrendous mistake is unjustifiable and inexcusable. They have brought disgrace to the Supreme Court and to the nation. They deserve contempt-not respect. The justices who voted this into being are obviously unfit to sit on any court; should be disbarred; and given the choice of resigning or being impeached. This is another way to change the makeup of the court, rather than just waiting for someone to retire. And it would help to insure that future justices act responsibly, professionally, and uphold the constitution; rather than just using their influence to forward the latest social scheme. Given the climate today, what better means of measuring a person's rationality, objectivity, and competence, than beginning with their views on abortion? Obviously, there is something amiss in the way we select Supreme Court judges. There are different kinds of intelligence, and being erudite and having a high IQ and political connections evidently doesn't guarantee that someone will make good decisions. *Ruth Bader Ginsburg-"Former counsel of the ACLU and as such was a consistent champion of the ACLU's extremist legal agenda". Alliance Defense Fund, February 2003. *"As an ACLU lawyer in 1977, Ginsburg had helped draft a legal report that recommended lowering the age of sexual consent nationwide to 12 years. Human Events was the first to report on her radical legal writings in support of legalized prostitution and pedophilia (see July, 1993 issue.)" Human Events, Week of May 26, 2003

So, this is the caliber of person President Clinton, and the Democrats, nominate to the Supreme Court. That's because, the only way they can get an agenda of abortion and pedophilia approved is through the courts. The Ashcroft Justice Department has cracked down on pedophilia, but can't do anything about abortion because the Supreme Court legalized it. Legalized prostitution is still on the agenda of international feminists. I'm not going to expand on that further, or make any effort to convince you of it, because it's a different subject. But I mentioned it to give you an insight into how these views are often associated. Abortion is the issue that most concerns me-because it kills people.

"Top UNICEF official calls for legalized and unionized prostitution On Tuesday, a high ranking UN Children's Fund (UNICEF) official called for the legalization of prostitution Speaking at the annual session of UNICEF's Executive Board, Urban Jonsson, UNICEF Eastern and Southern African Regional Director urged that UNICEF take actions to 'de-criminalise sex-work and facilitate the organisation of sex-workers.' Jonsson's comments are sure to fuel the growing suspicion that UNICEF has departed significantly from its central mission of protecting poor children from disease, hunger and death. There is a feeling among many that UNICEF has ventured more into promotion of what some see as a radical notion of women's rights, especially under Executive Director Carol Bellamy." Written by Douglas Sylva, Phd., for FRIDAY FAX June 6, 2003, Volume 6, Number 24, C-FAM (Catholic Family & Human Rights Institute), 866 United Nations Plaza, Suite 427 New York, New York 10017 Just so you don't think I'm making this stuff up.

Bill Clinton

And what of President Clinton, that stalwart defender of a woman's right to kill her offspring? He's no dummy, I think he knew the truth too, but thought his political advantage lay with the pro-abortion crowd. Frankly, I thought the whole impeachment business was pretty silly; trying to catch him on some technical violation of the law. What they should have been impeaching him for was using the federal government to support abortion. And what happens when somebody shoots up an abortion clinic or abortion doctor to try to save the children he is butchering? President Clinton sends out an FBI team to find the shooter, completely ignoring the serial killer/abortion doctor and the mountains of evidence in the filing cabinets. To the FBI I would like to say "Next time, just say no!". Or don't say anything and don't do anything. Don't put yourself in the same category as the Nazi SS. What should he do? He should pardon the person who did the shooting, bring him to Washington, pin a medal on him in front of the TV cameras, and give him (or her) a parade down Pennsylvania Avenue! And then we had Vice President Gore guaranteeing everybody he would continue the Clinton support of the abortion atrocity.

Bill Clinton contributed a history of poor judgements, like attacking American civilians with a tank because they were defending their 2nd Amendment right to bear arms ("the right of the people to keep and bear Arms, shall not be infringed"), and burning them up in their church! And even worse using the full power of the federal government in support of the abortion industry. Or using armed force with automatic weapons to return a small boy, whose mother died trying to bring him to freedom, to Cuba to be brainwashed by Castro's police state like his father and the rest of the Cuban populace (what a strange twist of fate). Or not responding when the Cuban government shot down two American planes in international waters. Or applauding when the Russian government shot up their own parliament building. Or creating a scandal that rocked the nation and distracted the government for months.

But I guess it's where you put the emphasis. The church people become a "cult" with "guns". They should apply those resources to get illegal guns held by criminals in our big cities off the streets. A friend of mine and his family put their mattresses on the floor and sleep there on New Years Eve because of all the wild gunfire; and there's somebody murdered every day. Just the other day there was a girl shot to death in her bed from the street while she slept. So why were they so bent on confiscating the guns of people with no criminal record who posed no threat to anybody if they were just left alone? Then they couldn't admit they made a mistake, and continued to make matters worse. It brought to mind the lynching of Joseph Smith in Carthage, Illinois, June 27th, 1884. Smith was the founder of the Mormon Church (Church of Latter-day

Saints); which was also founded in this country and has continued to thrive despite his premature death. More recently, I was reminded of it by the disturbing church burning scene in the movie "The Patriot". At least the people at Waco were having children, instead of killing them-which is the policy of the mainstream Methodist church; except in the case of partial-birth abortion. Have you forgotten "Thou shalt not kill?" They seem to think themselves above the ten commandments. The refugee case was presented as a custody case (Did Hillary or Janet Reno put that spin on it?). Why should Bill pay any attention at all to what Castro has to say about it? Or was Elian the victim of a movement to reestablish trade with Cuba? Castro certainly knew how to play it. Maybe it was a combination of these reasons. The planes shot down were piloted by "Cuban" Americans. The Parliament was filled with the bad guys, I guess; kind of like Republicans. And last but not least allowing our intelligence services to deteriorate to the point where we were vulnerable to the 9/11 attack on the World Trade Center and the Pentagon by terrorists who thought they had nothing to fear from our equally atrophied and immobilized armed forces.

So there is a pattern of poor judgment here, and an attack on our rights as a free people-both figuratively and literally: the sanctity of the church and people to worship as they see fit; the safety of our homes; the right of law abiding citizens to bear arms as a restraint to governments; even the sanctity of life itself, without which a nation can not be considered truly civilized. When something tragic happens, I always want to look for the root cause-not just at what is being currently reported. A lot of today's problems have roots in the past, if only we can make the connection. In both the Waco and refugee cases the situations should have just been left alone. Where there was only a minor problem at first, government intervention forced a major confrontation that had tragic consequences. Not only did a lot of people-women and children-die at Waco; but it was followed by the Federal Building bombing in Oklahoma City that caused even more fatalities. I know most people couldn't understand the connection; but the motive for the courthouse bombing was very, very, very clearly what happened at Waco. For instance, why do you suppose the bomb went off on the anniversary of Waco? It was the other shoe dropping. On the other hand, two wrongs don't make a right, and I want to make it clear that I am in no way condoning or supporting what occurred at Oklahoma City.

And it is quite possible that if Cuban Americans had been flying their planes over the waters between Cuba and Florida looking for refugees in trouble they would have spotted them and called for help and the drowning never would have occurred. That administration seemed to have to impose their judgments on others; and the most tragic and heartbreaking example of this is government support for abortion. Again, they could have just left it alone, and so many lives would have been saved. It bothers me how people dutifully fall in

line and accept things that need to be given more thought and questioned more
thoroughly.

Dick Armey, on Bill Clinton: "the most successful adolescent I have ever
known...(He) was basically like a prep guy saying:
'Where's the next Party? I love this job. Look at the parties.
What a great limo.'" From a column in Human Events by Marvin Olasky,
"The Week of December 23, 2002". On a more somber note:

Gary Bauer, on Bill Clinton: "For eight years Clinton ignored the danger that
was gathering around us. Now we face a very perilous situation today." CWF-
End of Day—February 19, 2003

Ronald Reagan

Lately I've noticed it's become fashionable to disparage President Reagan's intelligence. I'm not personally aware of any anecdotal evidence about anything he said or did, or any other kind of evidence, that would indicate this is true. I'm not sure how this got started-maybe someone just says something with the implied assumption that everybody knows that. Anyway, there were a couple of things about him that especially impressed me.

Early one Sunday morning I set out to get a Sunday paper. There seemed to be nobody else out and about at that early hour. When I reached the commercial thoroughfare from my side street, I looked to my right and there was a black limo parked about halfway down the block, in front of a small Republican campaign headquarters. Reagan had been running for governor of California, and I knew he was going around thanking the volunteers. Not particularly enamored of such things, I turned left and walked in the other direction. When I reached the middle of the block across the street from the store I was headed for, I turned to my right and looked to see if any traffic was coming. Standing just outside the headquarters, by himself, was the new Governor of California. For a split second our eyes met, as if he wanted to shake my hand too; and in that instance I understood what was meant by charisma. Later, after I had time to ponder it, I realized the Kennedys had had it too.

The other trait that President Reagan had that impressed me was that he always seemed to do the right thing, to make the right decision. President Reagan unified us and made us proud of our government. In his acceptance speech for the Republican presidential nomination, he showed he cared about people with his deep concern over the genocide going on in Cambodia. Ronald Reagan's son wrote, not too long ago, "I am reminded of a challenge issued by my father..., during his final week in office: '...When Roe v. Wade goes-as I have faith it must-the way of Dred Scott and 'separate but equal', a new debate will rise in...our land. And the voice that I believe must be heard and, in the end, shall be heard over all the others is the voice of life...'. Dad's challenge was that we prepare now to be part of that 'voice of life' in the great debate ahead, and he asked: 'Can I count on you?'". President Reagan knew that this was an issue which ultimately could have only one possible resolution.

President Reagan cared so profoundly about the abortion issue that while President he wrote a distinguished essay called "Abortion and the Conscience of the Nation", which was published in Human Life Review. More about that in a subsequent chapter.

I miss the days when I thought I could vote Democrat or Republican; but to say you are a Democrat today-to vote for a Democrat today-is tantamount to saying you favor infanticide; so closely have their positions on this issue become associated with the two parties. There are also some Republicans I can not vote for, for the same reason; and to straddle or try to ignore the issue raises serious questions about someone's qualifications to lead this country. But, as Mary Lou Gartner stated so well, writing for LIFEPAC of Pennsylvania, "The Republican Party was born on the principle that no human being should be considered the property of another, and on a repudiation of the Dred Scott decision by the U.S. Supreme Court. Abortion is the 'right-or-wrong' issue of our times. We should parallel the words of Abraham Lincoln today and say: 'The Republican Party looks upon abortion as a wrong and the Democratic Party does not look upon it as a wrong. That's the crucial difference between the two parties.'" I hope the Republican Party "stays the course", and I wish African Americans would pay a little more attention to history.

I had to become very knowledgeable about the abortion issue before I learned that not all Democrats are pro-abortion. They are so quiet and few in number that they are totally overshadowed and dominated by their noisier brethren. But they do have some influence in the Congress. Still, I like Ann Coulter's idea that the Democrats should change their name to the "Abortion Party". It better reflects the fact that the party is in the abortion industry's pocket; and totally under the control of radical leftists.

When Human Life Begins

I define myself as a conservative intellectual. Conservative, because that's how I think others would classify my views. Intellectual, because I develop my own ideas and opinions, and don't accept conservative dogma. I get a lot of Republican literature in the mail, because you have to register as something; and whenever they ask me my opinion, I'm very free with it, as you might guess. But when they ask me if I'm a Republican, I always check the no box, because I don't blindly accept whatever policy decisions they come up with. Well, you know, intellectuals, thinkers, are often thought to be strange, because they don't conform to society's norms; and I do some strange things. For example, I collect books, on the cheap, on things I'm interested in. What's even stranger, is that when the boxes of books pile up enough, I have no problem with letting my wife build me another barrister bookcase. I hope that someday I'll have time to actually read them.

Anyway, it's very interesting just to read the book club reviews, and one of my latest acquisitions is "The Monk In The Garden". More specifically, it's about peas, and the lifetime he spent raising them. Apparently, this wasn't much appreciated at the time, and there's even speculation he might have been excommunicated if he had been a more assertive type of person. Some time after his death, the ramblings he had recorded on his peas were rediscovered, and today he is regarded as the father of genetics. Here was someone I could identify with, because for many years I had been an avid gardener myself. It got me outside, tilling the soil was good exercise, I enjoyed planting a wide variety of seeds, nurturing and protecting the plants, and of course the harvest. It's kind of amazing, actually, how quickly the the plants grow once they spring from the seeds. By the time I no longer had time to garden, my fruit and nut trees were mature enough to give me a similar satisfaction. Sometimes trees are pollinated by the wind, sometimes by bees, and some are self-pollinating. I've had especially good luck with peach trees. In good years the trees are covered with blossoms, and once fertilized, the peaches develop quite rapidly. The fleshy part of the peach, that we eat, of course surrounds the pit, which contains the seed. The peach seed, like my garden seeds, and Gregor Mendel's peas, contains the complete genetic makeup, or code; the chemical blueprint, that developed after fertilization; and would be needed to grow a new tree (assuming that after fertilization it developed normally). So here's the point I've been leading up to: it's basically still a seed; a seed in an egg-like envelopment; nobody would argue that a peach is a peach tree. Please don't hate me Judie Brown, but I believe that a fertilized egg is only a seed until it is presented with the conditions that will stimulate it to start growing. In other words, I don't believe human life begins until the blastocyst plants itself, takes root, securely attaches itself to the womb; and begins to receive the nourishment that it has to have to grow. This position also makes it much easier to find common ground with people who believe in a variety of birth control methods, but have reservations about abortion.

Or, let's look at it using yet a another analogy. Let's imagine, for a moment, that I'm a neophyte research scientist trying to create human life outside the womb. I have very powerful microscopes, and very tiny instruments. With the left robotic arm, I pick up an egg harvested from my wife (in reality she would never let me do this experiment-maybe she has more sense than I do), and place it in a tiny petri dish. With the right robotic arm I pick up a sperm and place it in the same petri dish. I then pick up my miniature dish and tilt it so that the contents roll off into a miniature mixing bowl. Next, I turn on the blender and mix for ten minutes. All the elements are present that make up a human being; but at the end of this process, do I have a human being or do I have a scrambled egg?

Let's look at it from a third angle; an entirely opposite perspective. I'll be the experimentor, and you'll be the experimentee. I'll have you go stand in front of a wall, about six feet from me. Then I'll pull out a .357 magnum pistol, and shoot you through the heart. Would you then be a living person, or a dead person? "That's totally ridiculous", you say, "obviously I'd be dead. What's your point?" Then I would say "Everything is genetically present that defines you as a person, and that's what some people use to prove that a zygote, and then the blastocyst, are people, even though the blastocyst will never grow beyond about 100-150 cells if it never manages to attach itself to the womb; and there are a lot more cells than that still in your body even though you claim to be dead." "That's completely absurd", you say, not really picking up on my argument, "without my heart to pump blood to my brain I would be considered clinically dead in short order". "That's the point, I say, you would consider yourself dead when your heart and brain stopped functioning. Then how can you claim that a blastocyst that hasn't yet implanted in the uterus and has no trace of a heart or brain is a living person, on the other end of the spectrum?" Silence. You just sit there and ponder the turn of events. Then, it strikes you: "Yes, you say, but the zygote is potential human life, and that's not true of me, because I just died!" "Well, I say, the zygote, or even the blastocyst, is far from a sure thing. My wife was pregnant four times, and one of those pregnancies ended in a miscarriage. At the time, the doctor told us that 1 in 7 pregnancies ends in a miscarriage. <u>Potential human life is not the same thing as actual human life. Just because an egg is fertilized doesn't mean it will be able to attach itself to the womb</u>. It may just wash out, or not develop normally; and, as a result, the woman will never even become pregnant. However, even though you're clinically dead, doesn't mean that all possibility of being a living person has passed. I'll dial 911, we'll rush you to the hospital, and they should be able to salvage enough living cells to deposit in a tissue bank. Then, in a few years, we'll have you cloned. Why not, you probably won't even remember that I shot you! Despite this, I do agree with you, that you are a dead person, even though you could be reborn at some future time. But, by the same line of reasoning, I do not agree that a blastocyst is a living person, just because it might become one someday." Crazy, huh? But I think it helps show that this question of when human life begins is not as clear cut as some would have us believe. There's room for some compromise here. I think there may have to be some objectivity involved to get a consensus to eliminate abortion, and get a majority to agree on legislation to resolve this issue. We desperately need to get more agreement-more people on the same page. That's why I keep coming back to these paragraphs.

I know it's not good science, and that they're extreme examples. But I think it's sufficient reason to send some self-proclaimed ethicists back to their drawing boards.

For the sake of brevity in discourse I'll phrase it one more way. Every cell in our bodies carries our complete genetic code. But we don't call them people, because we know that they are only a very small part of the entire entity we call a person. They lack very important attributes, like a brain and a heart. On the other hand, once the blastocyst has completed its attachment to the uterus, which is necessary for a woman to know that she is pregnant, stem cell differentiation takes place with extreme rapidity. I've already mentioned how soon the heart and brain begin detectable functioning (they may be operating earlier, but we aren't able to measure it). Further down, I cite a reliable source, that states that "500,000 brain cells are forming every minute". If it weren't for the credibility of the source it would be difficult to believe something we can't possibly comprehend. But I did find an occurrence in nature that was more comprehensible to me. Last summer Cardinals built their nest right outside our dining room window. What colors! I instantly grabbed my camera, thinking I would be able to document this for several weeks. And of course the baby birds were so cute when they hatched out, and it seemed like they were about 50% outstretched jaw, begging to be fed. Again, it wouldn't count as good science, but it seemed like only a couple of days before they were physically full grown and had flopped out of the nest. I'll never know if mamma bird found her one chick. But it was a very visible, outside the body, demonstration of how quickly these developmental processes can progress.

I'm emphasizing this because I don't think pro-life forces should be squandering their time and resources trying to convince everybody that life begins at fertilization, or in opposition to blastocyst research-and this is the only way I have a chance of getting them to consider my views on this matter. It just hurts their future credibility when they are arguing against abortion in the more urgent, crucial, and winnable, pregnancy period debate.

We should structure our strategy around a top-down approach, from the least difficult goal to obtain to goals that will be harder and will take longer to achieve. For example, beginning with partial-birth abortion, then moving on to third trimester abortions, then parental and spousal approval, and so on. Each decision we can prevail in will save thousands of lives. Exactly when a human being's personhood begins is potentially a much more difficult issue to get agreement on, and intertwined with strong religious beliefs and practical considerations. We don't want them whispering in the halls of Congress "you know, they believe taking birth control pills is abortion". The opposition would love us for that, and I doubt the American public would ever buy into it; or there would be a huge black market in birth control pills, and a lot of very angry people. A lot of pro-life groups I follow and support, are, I believe, making this mistake. My concern, in this case, is also that the science follows the lead of Church doctrine. That's not bad if they're right, but they are human beings just like you and I. I'm well aware that because of this view several pro-life organizations don't consider me to be pro-life. Despite this, I haven't seen any arguments that would cause me to change my mind, and that continues to be my opinion. They seem to me to be a bit too doctrinaire and intolerant of the views of others. What do you think? Part of the value of this web site is its independence.

"Poll after poll shows women are more pro-life than pro-abortion." However, "Unless our efforts to stop abortion in America are coordinated—unless we all work together as a team—the carnage will continue unabated." Jane Abraham-President, Susan B Anthony List

Some legislation has been passed to only affect elective abortion. "'Elective abortion' is defined...as not including the use of drugs and devices intended for use as contraceptives...not including cases that necessitate 'the termination of the woman's pregnancy to avert her death.'" The Ryan Report, January 2001

This is one way of being sure laws don't apply to birth control. Another way to do the same thing is to pass laws against "abortion-on-demand"; because no one could demand an abortion without first being pregnant. Continuing on with this investigative reasoning, I think it is correct to say that all human life begins at the moment of fertilization, but that it is incorrect to say that a human being exists at the moment of fertilization. Let me explain further. The blastocyst journeys down the Fallopian Tube and into the Uterus and successfully attaches itself. It then develops very rapidly into a human being, who lives to be ninety years old. I would think it accurate to say that individual's life began at the moment of fertilization. But if the blastocyst just floats downstream, is unable to attach for some reason, and then flushes out, I would say that a human life never existed, or ever developed, and therefore can not be traced back to the moment of fertilization. Well, think about it. It's not an easy concept.

Furthermore, since a woman doesn't know she's pregnant until implantation occurs, and consequently wouldn't seek an abortion until then; the only purpose of defining conception as occurring at the moment of fertilization (some biology books define it at as being at implantation) in a Life At Conception Bill would seem to be an attempt to ban birth control and morning after pills according to Catholic teaching (either pill "might" prevent implantation)-and I find that disturbing.

Here, again, we see language playing an important role. The terms pregnancy and conception can have different meanings to different people. For instance, for someone not too into biology, or who has had a conservative Catholic upbringing, they don't think twice about the meaning of the word "conception"-it implies fertilization to them. However, since 1965, the American College of Obstetrics and Gynecology has held that "Conception is the implantation of the fertilized ovum." Out in California pro-abortionists are drafting legislation that specifically states that human life begins at implantation-not fertilization; which makes absolutely no sense from their point of view because it is an admission that what they want to kill is indeed a person-but they're too focused on their fear of losing their right to birth control pills to see the contradiction at this juncture. Likewise, the term pregnancy implies different things to different people. To me, the beginning of pregnancy logically occurs when the mother receives the chemical message from her child that says "I'm locked in mom", and her body begins to make changes to accommodate that presence; such as the cessation of ovulation that causes her to miss her period, changes in her breasts to prepare for feeding, and so on. Other people would consider the start of pregnancy to begin at the same time as fertilization, even though the mother has no way of knowing what has occurred at that point. So it's much more precise to talk in terms of fertilization and implantation. However, implantation, beginning perhaps 3 to 7 days after fertilization, is itself not very precise, because it can go on for a week from the time it begins until it is complete. And if fertilization occurs in the uterus, implantation will not occur at all. But at some point beginning during the implantation period an explosion of growth commences with such rapidity as to be difficult to comprehend as being possible for a living organism.

Likewise, "embryo" is another slippery and loosely used term. The American Heritage Dictionary, which is the one I happen to have on my computer, and also have confidence in, defines embryo thusly: "In human beings, the prefetal product of conception from implantation through the eighth week of development." In other words, under this definition, you couldn't have an embryo without a uterus to implant into, you couldn't have a person without an embryo, and all the talk about frozen embryos, embryo farms, embryonic stem cells, embryo research, embryonic people, and so on, becomes nonsense;

just as it does under my theory that the blastocyst is only the seed and can never be more than that until the placenta plants itself in the uterus and takes root there and begins to send nourishment to what now very quickly becomes the embryo. What is really being debated then, is what can be done with the pre-embryonic stage (blastocyst, or seed), and not what can be done with the embryo, or embryonic person. Without a uterus, the blastocyst isn't going to become a person under current technology, because the placenta is a marvel of engineering that we haven't been able to duplicate yet-as I understand it. I don't pretend to be an expert in these things, and I keep waiting, and looking for, the arguments that will undermine what I've said above, but it's going on three years now and I haven't found anything that would even begin to unravel my reasoning. That doesn't mean that I'm campaigning for "embryo" research though, because the advances that have been made so far with stem cells, and which are truly remarkable, have all come from adult stem cells, according to what I've seen; and for which it is claimed can be turned into any other type of cell. After all, that's the definition of what a stem cell is. What I'm searching for is truth.

But the truth about what constitutes an embryo is being ignored publicly by people I know know better. The reason for this dishonesty, I believe, is sometimes religious, and sometimes political. Religious to advance church teaching and curry favor within the church; and political to gain favor with voters who by large pluralities oppose and fear cloning. But I'm not sure these explanations cover the whole spectrum of reasons; I suspect there may still be factors involved that I don't yet understand.

As I approached the publication of my book, for which this web site will be the centerpiece (due out in the winter of 2003), I felt the need to be more scientific in my explanation, so that people wouldn't think this was just conjecture on my part. After three failed attempts to buy a used medical textbook on half.com, I was able to purchase the following book: "Williams Obstetrics", 20th Edition, by Cunningham, MacDonald, Gant, Leveno, Gilstrap, Hankins and Clark; a commonly used medical textbook first published in 1902 and updated on a regular basis since then. My edition was published in 1997. I chose this book because it was recommended by CBR (much more about them later). CBR uses it when somebody in the media, or otherwise, claim that their aborted embryo and fetus pictures are inaccurate or fake; by referring the person to the book and then threatening to sue them if the allegations are repeated. So far, they haven't had to sue anybody. Of course the book's objective isn't to make the same point I'm making, so I have to try to work around the medical terminology and pick out what's relevant to the issue I'm discussing:

"Early Human Development Definitions. The definitions that follow are taken from Moore (1973, 1988).

Zygote: The cell that results from the fertilization of the ovum by a spermatozoan.

Blastomeres: Mitotic division of the zygote (cleavage) gives rise to daughter cells called blastomeres.

Morula: The solid ball of cells formed by 16 or so blastomeres.

Blastocyst: After the morula reaches the uterus a fluid filled cavity is formed converting the morula to a blastocyst.

|According to this all you get without a uterus is a morula, and definitely not an embryo.|

Embryo: The embryo-forming cells, which are grouped together as an inner cell mass, give rise to the embryo, which usually is so designated when the bilaminar embryonic disc forms. The embryonic period extends until the end of the seventh week, at which time the major structures are present."

So my contention is that a ball of cells, apparently 16 in this example, does not constitute a person. Moreover, a study of blastocysts described in the book used samples taken from the uterine cavity-not grown outside it-although I won't say it would be impossible to do that. The caption for a picture in the book says "C. 107-cell blastocyst found in uterine cavity about 5 days after conception". The book seems to use the term conception rather loosely, depending on what it is talking about. The 107-cell blastocyst is then described in the text: "8 formative cells (embryo producing) were surrounded by 99 trophoblastic cells." So here we have 8 cells that some people would have us believe is a person. Well, I'm an adherent to a philosophy that says believe what you see with your own two eyes, and not what others tell you that you see, and I don't buy their contention. Moreover, it's not even an embryo yet, even though most laymen seem to think it is.

Next, "Implantation Just before implantation, the zona pellucida disappears and the blastocyst embraces the endometrial surface; this is the time of apposition, when the blastocyst is composed of 107 to 256 cells. The blastocyst becomes adherent to the endometrial epithelium; most commonly, implantation takes place on the endometrium of the upper part and, more often, on the posterior wall of the uterus. After gentle erosion between epithelial cells on the surface endometrium, the invading trophoblasts burrow deeper into the endometrium and the blastocyst soon becomes totally encased within the endometrium—specifically, the implanting blastocyst becomes completely buried in and covered over by the endometrium." So here we see the blastocyst completely buried in the lining of the uterus, but still a blastocyst-not an embrio.

"Biology of the Trophoblast Of all placental components, the trophoblast is the most variable in structure, function, and development. Its invasiveness provides for attachment of the blastocyst to the wall (endometrial surface) of the uterine cavity; its role in nutrition of the conceptus is reflected in its name; and its function as an endocrine organ in human pregnancy is essential to maternal physiological adaptations and the maintenance of pregnancy." So, we see why the blastocyst can't become an embryo outside the mother-it depends on the trophoblast attaching properly to the uterus to begin the flow of nutrients that will ultimately, and quickly, then become what I consider the first stage of personhood-the embryo. This will not change someone's opinion who wants to believe otherwise; but at least it makes me authoritative in my stance, rather than seeming speculative. If I were to be speculative, I would ask whether this process of "taking root" was an indication that the animal kingdom is descended from the plant kingdom.

The only way I can see to get an embryo for "embryo research" would be to remove it surgically from a woman. But I don't think you could have "embryo farms" because once detached from either the placenta or uterus, the child would die-so there really isn't any reason to be concerned about farms, that I can see. Or an abortion would produce an embryo, if done early enough, but usually not in pristine condition, to say the least, and very dead. An abortion is a form of surgical removal.

Of further interest, I think, is how long this adhering and integrating process (my own choice of words) goes on, before the actual child begins to form. The text book attempts to give a thorough explanation of this complex process, during which the reader needs to already have some knowledge of medical terminology to understand everything. The broad answer seems to be that child development doesn't begin immediately. So I've selected out some phraseology, based on ease of comprehension, that gives some sense of this process. Reading it more than once is helpful, too:

"Soon after blastocyst adherence to the endometrial epithelium, the cytotrophoblasts proliferate rapidly and the invasion of the surrounding decidua commences. The extravillous forward wave of cytotrophoblasts that ultimately form the anchoring cells in the decidua remain as individual cells or cytotrophoblasts. As the blastocyst and its surrounding trophoblasts, which are completely covered by decidua, grow and expand, one pole of this mass extends toward the endometrial cavity and the other pole remains buried in the endometrium/decidua. The innermost pole enters into the formation of the placenta...the enlargement and multiplication of of the trophoblasts in contact with the endometrium are alone responsible for the increase in size of the implanted blastocyst...As early as 7 1/2 days after fertilization, the inner cell mass, now referred to as the embryonic disc, is differentiated into a thick plate of primitive ectoderm and an underlying layer of endoderm. At 9 days of development (Fig. 5-5), the wall of the blastocyst that faces toward the uterine lumen is a single layer of flattened cells. The opposite, thicker wall is comprised of two zones, the troblasts and the embryo-forming inner cell mass. To illustrate the next stage of development, a thin section of a 9 1/2-day fertilized ovum (Fig. 5-6) is shown; the increase in size is from development of the syncytium". "The Embryo. The commencement of the embryonic period is taken as the beginning of the third week after ovulation/fertilization". So we see that apparently the child's development doesn't commence until the latter part of the initial attachment process, and the attempt of some religious groups to use science to point to fertilization as the defining moment of personhood doesn't hold up very well under close scrutiny-nor does the attempt to gloss over the fact that an embryo doesn't exist until at least 10 days after fertilization. What an embryo is not seems to be as important as what it is. An embryo is not a catchall for all the stages that come before. An embryo is a distinct stage that occurs after initial implantation; I say initial, because the attachment process and the growth of the placenta will continue after the embryo's growth begins. That makes sense, too, because the bigger the baby gets the bigger and more elaborate the infrastructure nourishing it will need to be.

A Civil War

There is a new Civil War going on in this country, much more violent than the first one, in the 1860's, and the fatalities are much higher. The violence is propagated almost entirely by the side called the "Abortionists", and its savagery is so intense that its defenseless victims are literally pulled apart while still alive, and the remaining pieces then butchered and sold for the highest price. The rules of engagement require that the defenders can only demonstrate at distances too great to save the victims, and if they themselves should in any way engage in violence or intimidation they are immediately arrested and thrown into jail or prison with no certainty that they will ever be released. By the time you finish reading this, I think that you will agree with what I have just said. Worldwide, abortion is the most catastrophic atrocity ever perpetrated by mankind.

What have we become? Is ours a sick society? We have turned on ourselves; we mutilate and murder our own children. Where have our values gone? As we destroy our most precious commodity, we destroy ourselves. Our leaders hide behind slogans and phrases like pro-choice and pro-life and refuse to debate or even discuss what is really going on! Can it be possible this is happening in America? Yes, it is possible, and it is happening, at the rate of 1.5 million abortion-murders each year. Who will be next, if this is allowed to continue? Ever notice the handicapped always seem to oppose abortion? Watch out, Stephen Hawking. Frankly, I'm a little nervous myself, with the Clinton administration, where might makes right. But maybe the cause could use a martyr. I'll probably be branded as mentally unstable. Maybe that's good, because I can take an insanity plea. But where could I find a psychiatrist who would lie? When will voluntary euthanasia go to mandatory for those swelling the social security roster? Well, it won't happen as long as the baby boom generation can vote. But that's the problem with our youngest citizens. They can't vote, or even say what they think, so they can't sway the politicians; who make decisions based on what they think the polls tell them the masses want; instead of trying to lead based on principles. They're obviously more interested in personal gain than what's right.

A couple of days after the 5-4 Supreme Court decision on partial-birth abortions I was in the barber shop and the national evening news was on the TV. They were doing a report on preemies, and the probability that they might have developmental problems. They showed several children that had been born prematurely and had disabilities. But guess what? Most people probably didn't think anything of it, but they didn't show any children who were born prematurely but were doing fine or even excelling; even though their own statistics showed that that was the case for the majority of premature births. So already the ultra liberal media was beginning to move up the ladder with their killing philosophy. I suppose a logical extension of this approach would be to include mothers who drank or smoked or took drugs while they were pregnant, and ultimately to deliver only perfect, no-defect, babies.

"My Silent Scream: My silent scream, My plea for life. This world unseen Sentences me to die. You say 'it's my body...It's my choice.' But I have no voice! So cry for me. And pray for me. Because humanity Has forgotten me. The love I have Is pure and true. This beating heart Cries out to you. You ignore my cries. You ignore the truth. Please God forgive them For they know not what they do." Joel Messener, 16. Dammit, where's the kleenex. Joel understands, do you?

There is a sadness and mourning in this land, for those who will never see the light of day, for those cut apart limb by limb, organ by organ; an eye, a cry; another eye, another cry; a spleen, a scream; a liver, another scream; a testicle, a brain, silence. Of course, the pieces are sold for profit and "research". I find it really difficult to imagine how horrible it would be to be cut up into pieces, how excruciating the pain must be. What kind of person could do this and feel no remorse; again, and again, and again? What kind of person could stand by and do nothing? Is there no outrage at this out there!

...we must be a voice for those who have no voice. You are that voice."— Bishop John F. Kinney

"...we're the only voice they have."—Erik Whittington

Well, I hope I haven't offended anybody. On the other hand, I've probably said something to make just about everybody mad. Perhaps that's a better state than complacency. If the FBI comes and drags me away, there may not be anybody to come to my defense. And if people can speak disparagingly about a man of Ronald Reagan's stature, they will probably have no mercy with me. I see a lot of my own criticisms as being constructive in nature, although they may not be taken that way. But keep this in mind-I am not at all important in the scheme of things. It is what I have said that is important, and that should be the focus of attention. If someone characterizes me as being "that", derides me about being "this", makes derogatory generalizations about what I have written, or dismisses it as unimportant, etc.; they are merely trying to distract you from what I have had to say. Don't succumb to these mind games. Think for yourself. There is much to discuss here. Ask yourself, are they addressing the content and the issues raised? Do your own evaluation. Decide for yourself. Don't just accept what someone else tells you is right. Keep in mind that just because you find something in here you disagree with, it doesn't invalidate the whole document; it should instead stimulate debate. There are a lot of specific things in here to agree or disagree with, and to expand upon. I don't have a monopoly on ideas, and it should spawn additional thinking on this topic, and how to best implement the ideas. Remember the central point here is that the child inside the mother is the same child outside the mother, and vice versa. And for God's sake, if someone starts talking to you about a woman's right to choose, don't be simple minded about it, look at the other side too, which is the child's right to choose; and at least say in your own mind "You mean a woman's right to murder her child.".

We're not talking beliefs or opinions here, we're talking facts that even the pro-abortion lobby has stopped debating. This is not just a minor disagreement in philosophy, this is an issue similar in magnitude to slavery, but which has already had much graver consequences. You always come back to the same fundamental question: Is it alright to kill the child; and there is only one possible answer-no, it is not. Only if you take a narrow, simplistic focus, such as the convenience of the mother, and don't look on the other side of the controversy, the inescapable humanity of the child, can you come away with a pro-abortion conclusion. And if there were even a shadow of a doubt in someone's mind about their pro-abortion stance, why would they go ahead with supporting an abortion decision when they might find out later that they had been wrong? Make no mistake, the building blocks of this child come from you-it is a part of yourself you are killing; but at the same time this child is a genetically unique person with their own separate body and their own separate rights. Above all, keep your eye on the ball, don't be distracted by new slogans. And when you go to vote, ask yourself, where do the candidates stand on the most important, and most basic right of all, without which there can be no other rights; by far the most important issue of our lives, the right to live. Society must be very clear on this issue, to give people the guidance they need in difficult circumstances.

There's also another dimension to who has "the right to choose". What about the father? It's just as much his child as hers. Shouldn't he have a say in this too? Doesn't he have an obligation to protect his child? And what about the maternal and paternal grandparents? It's certainly their grandchild, and they surely should have an interest in the outcome of this. And make no mistake here, it's the fate of the baby's body we're talking about-not the mother's. Now, I'm not advocating that all these people get together and hold a vote. It's still the responsibility of our society to apply the laws that protect all of us from murder. I'm trying to drive home the point that any woman who says she's "pro-choice" really isn't in favor of the right to choose at all. She's expressing a selfish, self-centered attitude-that she, and she alone, should be able to decide the fate of the child, without regard to the best interests of the child, the father, the grandparents, or society at large. And a lot of judges have taken this same nearsighted viewpoint, because they're not intelligent enough to get past the propaganda!

The radical left has a long history of accusing others of being what they are, thereby shifting the stigma to others in the minds of those who are easily manipulated. They will surely call me an extremist, and the simple minded will accept it without question. Are you simple minded? What could be more extreme than killing children; executing a third of our newborns every year, butchering them, and selling their parts? Jonathan Swift's satirical "A Modest Proposal" has become modern day reality.

I also realize some of the people I'm trying to help may say that I'm hurting the cause more than I'm helping it, because they have to be in control or disagree with some aspect of what I've said. But I feel compelled to speak out, to try to do my part, because, in the words of Congressman Henry Hyde, "Wherever and whenever you avert your eyes from a wrong, from an injustice,—you become part of the problem.". Edmund Burke expressed a sentiment similar to that when he said: "the only thing needed for evil to triumph is for good men to do nothing". On the other side of the issue, there are probably people who have a vested interest in continuing the myth that a child is not a human being, rather than having to admit they made a terrible mistake; they may even be subconsciously suppressing their feelings because of postabortion trauma or depression, and I give references at the end of this document that they can go to for help. On the other hand, some of the people fighting abortion the hardest, and trying to guide people away from it, and helping those for whom it is too late, are women who have had abortions themselves.

Did you know that the woman in the Roe vs. Wade case had her child and has come over to the pro-life side? A very lucky lady.

So I've just said what I thought. I'm just trying to help solve a very serious problem. When I ask myself is a child inside its mother a human being just the same as a child outside its mother, there is only one logical conclusion I can come to. I can have a different perspective from the politicians, because I'm not running for anything, and I'm not concerned about my popularity. I feel fortunate to be a loyal American, and when my country falls down, I hurt too; and I want to rush in and pick her up and set her back on the right course. And maybe, just maybe, the internet gives me the chance to do that. This is America. I believe that we will ultimately triumph in resolving this problem. And I hope that what I have had to say will open people's eyes to some things, will act as a unifying force, will begin a public dialogue, encourage differing theologies to find common ground and work together, and bring a swift conclusion to this deplorable episode in our history before many more lives have been sacrificed.

My wife and I have children of our own. For each of them, I've placed my hand on her uterus and felt them kicking and trying to punch their way out.

As our children grew from little waifs to adulthood, I've watched in amazement and awe at the things they've accomplished-things that I never could have dreamed possible.

A few years ago I was talking to a friend of mine about the movie "Forrest Gump". He said he didn't like the movie because he didn't think all those things could have happened to one person. Well, I didn't think of Forrest Gump as being a single person, but more of a composite, a vehicle for telling a story about an entire era; a story with many messages to convey. One of those messages, I thought, was that no matter how insignificant or unwanted a person may seem, he can still make a contribution to others. When Forrest met his son for the first time, and sat down next to him in front of the TV; and then when he saw him off to his first day of school; I felt great empathy with Forrest, because I had come to believe that perhaps my purpose in life, like Forrest, was to provide a link and a stable platform to launch my children's lives. Of course, some will accomplish more than others, but each is their own link to the next generation; I can hardly wait to get to know my grandchildren. So I have written this in part to encourage people to be this link-we can not foresee what good things may lie ahead, but we should not break this chain that is our human family and our humanity itself-especially in this country, where life is continually improving. When we kill our child, we kill a piece of ourselves, and we will never know what that child may have accomplished or meant to us and to others. And I hope I can also be the link to other generations for other families that won't mindlessly embrace this scourge that has gripped our nation for so many years. Like Forrest Gump said at the end of his speech before the peace rally in Washington, D. C., "And that's all I have to say about that".

This document becomes more and more informative as it unfolds; where other experts in the field do most of the talking, and you get a more complete picture. But it turns out I "lied" when I said I didn't have anything else to say-I just couldn't seem to shut up.

From Other Sources

My mind was wandering one day, and it dawned on me that it seemed to be primarily women who were advocating abortion. If this were true, I thought, and they were responsible for this tragedy, then had it been a mistake to give them the right to vote? This was not where I wanted to go, because I have the utmost respect for the women in my life; but if that was where my reasoning took me, I was not going to shy away from it. The next day I received a mailing from the Susan B. Anthony List, that showed statistics that the majority of women opposed abortion. What a relief! And as you will see from this list of references to other web sites, women are in the forefront of the fight against abortion. Let me quote to you some passages from the Encarta Encyclopedia about the woman this organization chose to name itself after: "Anthony, Susan B (Brownell) (1820-1906), outstanding American reformer, who led the struggle to gain the vote for women. She devoted 50 years to overcoming the nation's resistance to woman suffrage, but died before the 19th Amendment was adopted (August 26, 1920). Encouraged by her father, a onetime schoolteacher, Anthony began teaching school when she was 15 years old, and continued until the age of 30. A liberal Quaker and dedicated radical reformer, Anthony opposed the use of liquor and advocated the immediate end of slavery. From 1848 to 1853 she took part in the temperance movement and from 1856 to 1861 worked for the American Anti-Slavery Society, organizing meetings and frequently giving lectures. In 1863, during the American Civil War, she founded the Women's Loyal League to fight for emancipation of the slaves. After the end of Reconstruction she protested the violence inflicted on blacks and was one of the few to urge full participation of blacks in the woman suffrage movement. Anthony's work for women's rights began in 1851, when she met Elizabeth Cady Stanton. From 1854 to 1860 the two concentrated on reforming New York State laws discriminating against women. Anthony organized women all over the state to campaign for legal reforms. Anthony and Stanton became convinced that women would not gain their rights or be effective in promoting reforms until they had the vote, and nationwide suffrage became their goal after the Civil War. In 1869 they organized the National Woman Suffrage Association to work for a constitutional amendment giving women that right. Although the newly freed slaves were granted the vote by the 15th Amendment, women of all races continued to be excluded. From 1868 to 1870 Anthony and Stanton published a newspaper, Revolution, focused on injustices suffered by women. To dramatize her fight, Anthony defiantly registered and cast a ballot in the 1872 presidential election and, when arrested and convicted, refused to pay the $100 fine. She went to Europe in 1883, met women's rights activists there, and in 1888 helped form the International Council of Women, representing 48 countries. At the age of 80 she resigned as president of the National American Woman Suffrage Association, but she continued to be a regular speaker at its conventions until her death…".

"Her...achievement lay in her inspiration and perseverance in bringing together vast numbers of people of both sexes around the single goal of the vote." Wow. Quite a lady. And obviously someone who did her own thinking, and wasn't much influenced by the way people told her things should be. When asked her opinion on abortion, she replied "Child murder.". Don't let her down, ladies.

The Susan B. Anthony List, http:// www.sba-list.org /, is an organization to recruit and support anti-abortion women to run for Congress. They also support pro-life men running against abortion candidates. Click on the highlighted link to go to their web site; it includes an "Instant Advocacy" feature that allows you to email your Members of Congress directly from the site. "Supporters can write their own letters or pick from a list of pro-life legislation". They have been very successful in their electioneering, and run a sophisticated, growing operation. Address: 1800 Diagonal Road, Suite 285, Alexandria, Virginia 22314 "Training Pro-Life Women In The Political Arena" (and men).

If you're a pro-lifer, wanting to become politically active, there's also The Leadership Institute, Steven P.J. Wood Building, 1101 North Highland Street, Arlington, Virginia, 22201, (703) 247-2000, run by Morton C. Blackwell, President-from the Reagan era – that runs training and placement programs.

The American Life League, http:// www.all.org /, is a creation of, almost an extension of, Judith Brown. Whether it's the New York City subway system or the corporate halls of Benton, Arkansas, Judie Brown is an adamant and fearless defender of life. She's involved in many different aspects of the problem, from adoption to post-abortion trauma counseling. "Her passion for a pro-life America continues to light the lamp of truth about the moral and spiritual harm our country has suffered, since the legalization of abortion"- probably in her own words. Affiliate organizations include the American Bioethics Advocacy Commission; Crossroads; http: // www.crossroadswalk.org /; Dentists for Life; Rachel's Vineyard; Rock for Life, http:// www.rockforlife.org /; Stop Planned Parenthood International; Why Life; and the World Life League. In fact the word had gone around that Judie had been so effective that she had been added to the FBI VAAPCON data base of pro-life "subversives", and the FBI had been ordered to infiltrate her organization. I got this from more than one source, and think it's probably true. Of course, there's been no more talk of a FBI investigation since Janet Reno and Bill Clinton left town. Judie and her helpers recently received a blessing from the Pope, which probably doesn't mean too much to you if you're not Catholic-but hey, it can't hurt. I wonder if the Pope was on VAAPCON too, and they infiltrated the Vatican-I know he's said he's against abortion. I don't share her views on birth control and the point a human being first exists; but when did you ever agree with someone on everything? Unfortunately, I think she assigns it more importance than I do.

For quite some time I wasn't really sure how to classify ALL. What kind of an organization was it, overall? I think these words in the March-April 2002 issue of their Celebrate Life publication sums it up pretty well: "American Life League has an unwavering commitment to principle and truth...education is the core of our mission...ultimately the pro-life victory will come from cultural ...advances, and education...is the key to change". I quote them a number of times farther down in the document. American Life League, P.O. Box 1350, Stafford, VA 22555 Phone: 540-659-4171

"It was enough to bring ALL's Judie Brown to tears. Legatus, an organization of Catholic business leaders, has honored her with its 2002 Cardinal John O' Connor Unambiguously Pro-Life Award. Cardinal O'Connor was one of Mrs. Brown's heroes and mentors.

American Life League president Judie Brown is on her way to Rome for a meeting of the Pontifical Academy for Life. Mrs. Brown is serving her second five-year term on the papal advisory panel." From ALLNEWS, March 2003.

It would be difficult to overstate Mrs. Brown's importance to the pro-life cause over the years. Not only does she run an organization with a membership of several hundred thousand, but has probably educated many more than that through ALL's publications, and saved countless young lives. She's important enough within the Catholic Church to have talked directly to the Pope on more than one occasion, and I think that's rather unusual for a lay person. But on some issues, I think, it's necessary to differentiate between fact and faith.

I add things quite frequently, but I don't often take anything out, or change what's already there, because I see this as being partly a historical document, and you will sense that my understanding of events, evolves, too, as time goes by.

The Republican National Coalition for Life, http:// www.rnclife.org /, is run by Phyllis Schlafly. There is no more ardent, uncompromising defender of the Republican pro-life platform. Unquestionably brilliant, seemingly indefatigable, she possesses an incredible grasp of the politics involved. She eloquently demonstrates her staunch support in the following passage: "I wonder if a statement of tolerance for the views that slavery should be permitted, or that racism is O.K., or that handicapped people can be discriminated against, or that America should disarm, or that taxes should be raised, would be acceptable to those who want our Party to go on record as respecting the views of those who justify killing babies." Basically, she's the person most responsible for keeping the pro-life plank in the Republican platform. I would guess her views parallel Judie Brown's; although I don't think Judie is a Republican. Phyllis is involved in many different issues, more numerous than I have time to try to understand; so I just stick to abortion with her.

SURVIVORS of the Abortion Holocaust, www.abortionsurvivors.org:

"Unfortunately, over time, the Democratic Party decided to embrace every special interest group that hated God or the family…Now the Survivors are going to speak out against all the Democratic Party has become!…to speak out for the one-third of their generation murdered in the name of choice…

The Survivors made national news when they protested the movie Cider House Rules that portrayed abortion as a compassionate act…According to the LA Times Poll published on June 18, 2000, 67% of Americans believe abortion is murder. But on the other, 68% of Americans agree with the statement: 'No matter how I feel about abortion, I believe it is a decision that has to be made by a woman and her doctor.' This is scary. There are millions of Americans who believe it is okay to murder someone. Still there is hope even in those statistics. For years the pro-life movement believed we would win the war when we were able to convince America abortion was murder. The words 'Abortion is murder' were rarely used because some believed they were too radical. But we have won that contest and now even Planned Parenthood acknowledges abortion takes a human life. Our new hope is found in our past success. We defined abortion as murder. Now we must strip abortion of its compassionate face. The new rhetoric of the pro-abortion movement is found in the very question asked by the LA Times. The statement that abortion is a decision that has to be made between a woman and her doctor is rhetoric developed by the abortion industry. They had to surrender the humanity of the child and when they did they made the switch to proclaiming abortion a private and personal decision 'between a woman, her god, and her doctor.' …sharing about post abortion syndrome, the intense guilt felt by mothers who abort their child…unlicensed and licensed doctors who kill their adult patients because they are hurrying to kill as many children as quickly as they can in their quest for more money…And they will expose the latest lie of abortion as compassion. The Democrats have chosen to embrace child killing as a part of their national platform. The Democratic Party has declared war on the preborn child.

Now the Survivors of that abortion war are old enough to speak and fight for themselves and they will not be silent. The Survivors lost one-third of their generation in a war they didn't start, but they are giving their lives to finish it." Sage to the Survivors, Jeff White

"For those on the front lines of the peaceful pro-life movement, death threats are a way of life. Jeff White, who runs Survivors, a pro-life youth organization, received his first letter containing white powder more than two years ago. When I go for a while without receiving some kind of threat, I begin to question whether or not I'm being effective.' Mark Crutcher often is concerned for his family. 'Whenever I would go out of town, my wife received threatening phone calls so we knew we were watched constantly. Once we adopted a baby, we were more vigilant. After bomb threats my wife goes to hotels for safety.'" From "Anthrax, Abortion, and Other Abominations", Jane Chastain, World Net Daily, as reprinted in the November, 2001, "The Life Activist, Life Dynamics Inc., Post Office Box 2226, Denton, Texas 76202 (940) 380-8800,
www.lifedynamics.net.

"We did it!...the Campus Life Tours have made their goal of 200 campuses for the year. The Survivors College team members were arrested illegally over thirty times this year for courageously taking the truth of abortion to high schools and colleges. They handed out over 100,000 pieces of literature...But the team continues to work even as the school year comes to an end. They are preparing now for the summer training camp where hopefully a new group of young people will catch the vision for an abortion free America. '*The best tour experience...A young man, the captain of the speech and debate team... proceeded to use justifications for abortion such as poverty...the crowd turned against him...The students attending the school were primarily from poor neighborhoods and did not like the idea of having abortions because of the possibility of a child growing up poor. It was great to hear the crowd take over for me as they grew offended and impatient with his answers that were attempting to justify killing poor kids. It was amazing to see an entire crowd of people see the light simultaneously as to why the murdering of human beings is a horrible thing especially in the cases of the possibility of growing up in a poor neighborhood. Many minds were changed that day, and as a result many lives will be saved. Dan*'". From Jeff White, Founder of the Survivors, P.O. Box 332 Lake Arrowhead, CA 92352 Tel: (888) 813-9457 e-mail: info@survivors.la
http://www.survivors.la/

In a period of about 2 years, they went from doing demonstrations locally, in a fairly static pattern, to a nationwide footprint. Other organizations do school campuses too-but not nearly as many. The kids take a year off from school, and tour for the nine months of the school year. In addition to getting locked up, they have to sometimes endure abuse from the students they are trying to reach, and the school faculty and administration. They set out not knowing if there will be funds to pay for essentials, and the unexpected such as vehicle breakdowns; and keep a brutal schedule through all the adversity they encounter along the way. May, 2003

Concerned Women for America (CWA)-1015 Fifteenth Street, N.W., Suite 1100 Washington, D.C. 20005 Phone: 202-488-7000-www.cwfa.org.

"For more than 22 years, CWA has defended human life—in Congress, the White House, and on the state and local levels. We also have a leadership role in coordinating pro-family forces from the U.S. and abroad in opposing the pro-abortion agenda at the United Nations." Beverly LaHaye, Founder and Chairman, February 4, 2003. A large and influential organization of several hundred thousand-probably the largest membership for its kind of organization. Mostly made up of women, faith and family issues oriented, but they don't exclude men from membership, and it doesn't cost much to belong.

Traditional Values Coalition, P.O. Box 1882, Merrifield, VA 22116-8082, http://www.traditionalvalues.org/, headed by Presbyterian minister Reverend Louis Sheldon. Conservative Christian, with a lot of ongoing projects besides abortion, but they give abortion the emphasis it deserves; and not too good to march with the rank and file in the Washington, D.C, January 22, Roe v Wade anniversary parade.

Toward Tradition, http://www.towardtradition.org/", "Bring your love of God and Country. Bring your open mind and critical intelligence. Bring your family. Christians and Jews meet and work together." P.O. Box 58, Mercer Island, Washington 98040-9809 Seem to be sidestepping and de-emphasizing abortion in recent years; perhaps as being too controversial.

"We will continue encouraging Jews and Christians, who are united by common political, economic, and cultural values, to help restore America's greatness. Never in this nation's history has it been more urgently necessary to promote traditional, faith based, American principles of constitutional and limited government, the rule of law, representative democracy, free markets, a strong military, and a moral public culture. That is our mission,...to be the premier forum for communication and cooperation. Over the objections of critics we have diligently built bridges. We have passed by those who would sow dissension and have formed lasting and profound Jewish-Christian friendships between individuals, communities, and organizations. *We unapologetically promote this alliance because we believe it is essential to America's survival and prosperity.*" "Its purpose, then, is to effectively inject our vision into the opinion-making culture...further...my belief that the survival of Western civilization depends upon victory in the war of ideas between those who cherish America's moral, spiritual and economic heritage and those who vehemently reject it. It's up to you and to us to win this war of ideas." Rabbi Daniel Lapin President, Toward Tradition, 9311 S.E. 36TH Street, Suite 100, P.O. Box 58, Mercer Island, WA 98040-9809, December 11, 2002 www.towardtradition.org

"Some...are still bothered about their abortion(s) eight, 10, even 20 years after the fact...studies show that the longer a person is unaware of, or represses, the after-effects of abortion, the greater the impact on the psyche. Some women seem to have no problems after an abortion, while others struggle for years with the emotional scars of guilt, anxiety, anger and depression. Still others try to solve their problems with substance abuse, promiscuity, broken multiple relationships, or eating disorders...Unfortunately, post-abortion reconciliation and healing have become a necessary part of the abortion scene". Freelance writer Patricia V. Fogarty, published in Celebrate Life. If you think you might be experiencing post-abortion syndrome, one place you can call is Rachel's Vineyard, 877-HOPE-4-ME; or contact ALL, or go to the following link: www.rachelsvineyard.org. They are planning "180 retreats in 43 states and four countries" in 2003. By the time you read this it may be even more. Please also note that a whole chapter on PAS, or PASS, follows in this book. It's a little, or a lot, like many of the problems our soldiers brought home from Vietnam.

"...we call upon...people to love the least of their brothers and sisters...those still in the womb. Because of the legalization of abortion and the performance of some 3500 abortions daily in our country, the womb is literally the most dangerous place to be. In Biblical Hebrew, the word for 'womb' is the same word for 'mercy'...people...must show mercy and justice to those most in danger." Rev. Rob Schenck, President National Pro-life Religious Council (NPRC), http://www.nprcouncil.org/, June 10, 2002.

"Qui tacit consentire! He who is silent consents." Rev. Frank Pavone, in-coming President, NPRC, March 2003.

"Dr. Haskell brought the ultrasound in and hooked it up so that he could see the baby. On their ultrasound screen I could see the heart beat. As Dr. Haskell watched the baby on the ultrasound screen, the baby's heartbeat was clearly visible on the ultrasound screen. Dr. Haskell went in with forceps and grabbed the baby's legs and pulled them down into the birth canal. Then he delivered the baby's body and arms. Everything but the head.

The doctor kept the baby's head just inside the uterus. The baby's little fingers were clasping and unclasping, and his feet were kicking. Then the doctor stuck the scissors through the back of his head, and the baby's arms jerked out in a flinch, a 'startle' reaction, like a baby does when he thinks he might fall. The doctor opened up the scissors, stuck a high-powered suction tube into the opening and sucked the baby's brains out.

Now the baby went completely limp. He cut the umbilical cord and delivered the placenta. He threw the baby in a pan along with the placenta and the instruments he had just used. I saw the baby move in the pan. I asked another nurse and she said it was just reflexes. That baby boy had the most perfect angelic face I think I have ever seen in my life." Brenda Pratt Shafer, Registered Nurse, testifying before a Congressional committee, on a partial-birth abortion she witnessed in 1993.

"Babies are being slaughtered and dismembered and their bodies sold like so much livestock. How can God's people stand by and watch?". D. James Kennedy, Ph.d., Coral Ridge Ministries, PO Box 407137, Fort Lauderdale, Florida 33340-7137, on body parts sales.

National Right To Life Committee, 1-202-626-8800, 512 10th Street, N.W., Washington, D.C. 2004-1401, http:// www.nrlc.org /. Large national organization with branches in individual states that apparently works on pro-life legislation but doesn't make much of an effort to keep its members informed about what it's working on.

The American Cause, http:// www.theamericancause.org /, Pat Buchanan's organization. In his new book, "The Death of the West", Pat makes a case for the extinction of Western civilization because of inadequate birth rates (populations are actually declining in some European countries as a result of abortion; and one third of pregnancies here are aborted), and lax immigration laws.

Another new endeavor is the Save The Babies project. "The mission of our 'Save the Babies!' project is as straightforward as its name: inspire, organize and mentor college students to form active, visible, pro-life organizations on their campuses." "Each campus pro-life club chartered by The American Cause will be asked to do three things: Adopt a center that supports or counsels women facing an unexpected pregnancy, or a home for unwed mothers.

Choose an abortion clinic and join the sidewalk counselors, prayer vigils, or peaceful protests. Become a voice for the unborn on campus, using flyers, letters to the editor, speaking out in forums or bringing in speakers, getting the facts about abortion out in the open...to confront pregnancy and the life-and-death choice that pregnancy entails...they will be ready to step in and save the child of a confused coed, and in turn save the coed from a lifetime of the psychological and medical problems...I believe in, and am committed to, this project...must do what we can to not only, in the long run, change the law and the culture that permits abortion, but also to concretely, in the short run, help save lives...need to re-direct and re-energize the pro-life cause." Pat's sister, Angela "Bay" Buchanan, seems to be in charge of this project, helping to set up on-campus organizations and speaking on campus whenever she is invited. http://www.save-the-babies.org/

Legal Advocacy

The Alliance Defense Fund, http://www.alliancedefensefund.org /, seems to be an umbrella legal organization for a number of Christian denominations and groups. They sometimes speak in phraseology unfamiliar to most people, such as "the body of Christ", and "winning on your knees". If I could afford somebody to open my mail I would probably give them instructions to cut out all the references to "the body of Christ", and then give me the correspondence. But once I get past that, depending on what projects they are currently working on, I often end up sending a donation; because we share a lot of the same values.

They are very good at what they do. Alan Sears, their president and general counsel, is a very impressive guy, and probably a lot smarter than I am. They 've had as many as 7 cases before the Supreme Court at one time. I've been trying to get my daughter to do some work for them, but no luck yet. Their motto is "Winning the Legal Battle for Family Values, Religious Freedom, and the Sanctity of Human Life". They have a first rate web site, and you can learn a lot more about the organization and Alan there. PO Box 53007, Phoenix, AZ 85072-3007 From their newsletter:

"This day I call heaven and earth as witnesses against you that I have set before you life and death, blessings and curses. Now choose life, so that you and your children may live". Moses "God has called you and me to live in the world we have at this moment. We have no other choice. And what we do today—right now—will determine the future our children and our children's children inherit: life or death, blessings or curses. That is our duty to the future. Sadly, our opponents scoff at such sentiment. What you and I cherish, they disdain. What you and I honor, they denigrate. What you and I seek to preserve, they aim to destroy. And I cry out to God for our country and for my children". Alan Sears

In part, this reflects my view that nobody is isolated from what is going on. It affects everybody. I don't want to find out someday that one of my daughters, or granddaughters, had an abortion.

On May 13th, 2002, they had their 20th ADF-Assisted Supreme Court victory.

Overall, out of participation in 29 cases at the U.S. Supreme Court, they now have 22 victories; and hundreds of lower court victories. My impression is that they achieve this through funding, coordination, and input to the cases they become involved in; rather than always litigating the cases themselves. One way they expand their influence is through training attorneys in their National Litigation Academy and Blackstone Fellowship programs.

On the Supreme Court's partial-birth abortion decision: "As Justice Antonin Scalia said in his biting dissent, this 'method of killing a human child...is so horrible that the most clinical description of it evokes a shudder of revulsion.'

Justice Anthony Kennedy, in his dissent, declared that states ought to be free to 'forbid a procedure many decent and civilized people find abhorrent.'

And Justice Clarence Thomas called the majority's ruling 'indefensible'; it amounts to an endorsement of 'infanticide,' he said. Is partial-birth a 'widely accepted routine medical procedure'? 'Nothing could be further from the truth,' Justice Thomas stated. In fact it's 'so gruesome that its use can be traumatic even for the physicians and medical staff who perform it,' he pointed out. 'And the particular procedure at issue in this case, partial-birth abortion, so closely borders on infanticide that 30 States have attempted to ban it.'

Even the American Medical Association has disavowed this horrific, torturous form of death for babies! Why, then, do so many of our leaders still cling to partial-birth abortion as a 'right'? One reason is pro-abortion fanaticism that will not tolerate any restriction on any abortion. Another reason, sad to say, can be summed up in a single word: MONEY. Partial-birth abortion produces an almost entirely intact corpse—and there's a market for such a gruesome commodity. The sickening truth is, there's a growing demand for babies' body parts in this country...In fact, the middlemen who 'harvest' dead babies from abortionists and sell them to various customers make hundreds of thousands of dollars a year plying their unsavory trade! Furthermore, the older the pre-born baby is, and the more fully intact the corpse, the more money can be demanded for the 'body parts' market! This makes partial-birth abortion...the body-trafficker's favorite method for killing babies!...We cannot give in when the Supreme Court consigns babies to torture and death in all 50 states." The above quotes came from:

Jay Alan Sekulow, Chief Council, The American Center For Law & Justice, Post Office Box 64429, Virginia Beach, VA 23467-4429; is currently working to pass a veto proof national partial-birth abortion ban before the Congress adjourns for the pre-Election Day recess in mid-October. He also points out that "The American Medical Association's Council on Legislation voted unanimously to support a ban on partial-birth abortion. The council reportedly designated the procedure 'basically repulsive.'" Jay heads a team and organization that has also argued many cases and delivered many briefs before the Supreme Court defending innocent life, the family, and the freedom of faith. Additionally, they do legal research and offer opinions on points of law for members of Congress and the President; on a proactive basis. For example, they created a 36 page report on the legality and precedence of changing the filibuster rule by a simple majority vote; and defended the 2000 election result.

The American Anti-Persecution League comes to the aid of pro-life demonstrators who have been roughed up, arrested, or otherwise had their right to free speech impinged on. The perpetrators soon find themselves in a very uncomfortable legal position, and singing a different tune. You can reach them at 1-888-522-AAPL. They are currently suing the Supreme Court! Other pro-life legal help can be found at:

Legal Center for Defense of Life, 917-984-0725, 65 Madison Avenue Morristown, New Jersey 07960, legalctr@aol.com, http://www.legalcenternj.org/, a...non-profit organization founded in April, 1989, provides pro bono legal counsel and representation to those involved in litigation resulting from their peaceful defense of human life; defends the free speech rights of sidewalk counselors; helps pregnant women who are being coerced into abortion; gives advice to those setting up crisis pregnancy centers and shelter homes; and defends the rights of the elderly and infirm...LAWYERS DEFENDING LIFE".

Liberty Counsel-P. O. Box 540774, Orlando, Florida, 32854 407-875-2100 or 800-671-1776-Email:liberty@lc.org, http://www.lc.org/. The finest legal counsel money can't buy on issues of faith, family, and life.

Thomas More Law Center, 3475 Plymouth Road, Suite 100 Ann Arbor, MI 48105-2550, tel.: 734-827-2001, fax: 734-998-4778, info@thomasmore.org, http://www.thomasmore.org/. "...as the ACLU and other activist organizations continue to use the courtrooms of America to impose the Culture of Death on our society, the Thomas More Law Center will be there to confront them! You have my word on that." Richard Thompson, Founder, Chief Counsel, and President. This is the Michigan Prosecutor who went after "The Doctor of Death", Dr. Jack Kevorkian, when the other prosecutors were willing to just let it slide on by. He almost single handedly sent Kevorkian to prison, and that's part of why you don't hear as much about assisted suicide anymore. But It cost him his job as prosecutor, so he went out and started Thomas More-with financial help from Tom Monaghan's foundation. This is the public interest law firm that keeps the trucks rolling and banners flying for the Center For Bio-Ethical Reform (which you'll learn a lot more about if you keep reading). Along with a few other individuals in the pro-life movement, he's the kind of attorney people would prefer to settle with out of court.

"For example, according to the principal of Abington Junior High in Abington, Pennsylvania, the message on a student's pro-life t-shirt, 'Abortion is Homicide. You will not silence my message. You will not mock my god. You will stop killing my generation,' was equivalent to the *Swastika*. He, therefore, ordered the honor student to turn his t-shirt inside out. The student contacted the Thomas More Law Center. And Edward White III, one of the Law Center's attorneys, sent a four-page 'demand letter' challenging the principal's decision on constitutional grounds and demanding that the school take immediate action to provide assurances that the student would be permitted to wear the pro-life shirt back to school. Attorneys for the school district quickly agreed! Ed rightly noted that far too often public school officials forget that students don't lose their constitutional rights just because they enter a public school...the First Amendment does protect student pro-life messages." Part of a Memo from Richard Thompson, April, 2003. Attorneys like this have dedicated their lives to taking this kind of case-to defending our basic human rights.

The NPLA

National Pro-Life Alliance, 4521 Windsor Arms Court, Annandale VA 22003 1-703-426-8061: "Abortion Stops a Beating Heart". They are currently working at building a majority on partial-birth abortion in the U.S. Senate, and electing federal pro-life candidates. "Unless we thwart the abortion industry's electoral power grab, we could face a situation where the abortionists control all three branches of government. We already know they own the Supreme Court...our struggle to save the unborn faces disaster... important pro-life bills...would be deemed 'dead on arrival' by pro-abortion congressional leaders, who would pull out all the tricks in their playbook to guarantee they never have to cast a single unpopular anti-life vote. And when they do vote on the abortion issue it will be to expand the killing of unborn children." Robert Hughes, Legislative Director

From a newspaper ad run in local newspapers by the National ProLife Alliance against the candidacy of Senator Chuck Robb (he was defeated): "Killing late in the third trimester, Partial-Birth Abortion inflicts a violent death on thousands of babies every year...the ghastly procedure, where a baby is almost entirely delivered, but then killed, just inches and seconds before a live birth... thousands of partial-birth abortions take place in America every year. No one can justify delivering an innocent baby three-quarters of the way and then killing him instead. The procedure is so grotesque that polls show an overwhelming majority of the public agrees the practice should be outlawed. The American Medical Association is on public record saying the practice is never medically necessary and should be outlawed."

If you're writing a paper on abortion, listen up, because some of the other actions they are supporting would probably fit well into that framework:

"Pass a Human Life Amendment to the United States Constitution to overturn Roe vs. Wade and prohibit abortion, making all abortions illegal, except to save the life of the mother". I would wholeheartedly support such an action, but I think that approach has some drawbacks. First of all, it shouldn't be necessary-the law already exists against murder. Second, it would most likely be a lengthy process, and with 4,000+ children dying a horrible death from abortion in this country every day, we can't afford to wait.

First, a consensus would have to be built in the Congress-something we have not been able to do so far-except with regard to partial-birth abortion. I don't think a simple majority would be sufficient to pass a constitutional amendment, and this effort alone could take many years. Other exceptions would probably have to be agreed to; for example, in the case of rape, to get it passed. But, beyond this, it would have to be ratified by the states.

I think this would be especially difficult to do in extremely liberal states like Massachusetts (the only state to go for George McGovern in '72, and they keep returning Ted Kennedy to the Senate), California (their environmental regulations are so strict, and their price controls so tight, that they are running out of power; and they keep returning Dianne Feinstein and Barbara Boxer to the Senate), Vermont (same sex marriages, when 35 other states have passed laws against them), and so on.

"The elimination of all Federal (taxpayer-funded) abortions by Medicare, Medicaid, or other public health services, and the elimination of funding for any group which promotes abortions." This is one of the reasons I voted for Bush-please come through for the country on this George!

"Protect unmarried minors from being hustled through an abortion by requiring parental consent". It's sad to think that parental approval and authority can be so easily ignored! ["Using data supplied by the Centers for Disease Control, a *World* magazine study shows that the abortion rate among teenagers is declining much faster in states with strong parental consent laws… in states which require the actual consent of at least one parent, the teenage abortion rate plummeted by 55 percent." Life Dynamics News, February 2003]

"Prohibit the torture and murder of live, viable babies by partial-birth abortion". Personally, I think other kinds of abortion are just as horrible.

"Save the lives of viable babies by banning all abortions in the third trimester except to save the life of the mother." This is an excellent intermediate step, and should be achievable quickly.

"Ending research on aborted baby parts", to stop the trafficking and additional monetary incentive for doing abortions. There seem to already be laws on the books to do this that have been ignored and bypassed by the Clinton administration.

Pass "The Sanctity of Life Act—legislation which, under Article III, Section II of the Constitution, would remove from federal courts jurisdiction over the issue of abortion—thus overturning Roe vs. Wade". This is the first time I have heard of this option, and it sounds like an outstanding and potentially fruitful way to settle the whole issue quickly and for good. However, I don't know anything about the legalities or politics involved, and can't help wondering why it hasn't been raised before. But I think it should be enthusiastically pursued to see if it is a viable solution.

"The Life at Conception Act, which takes the Roe decision's own instructions to Congress to define exactly when constitutionally-protected life begins: the moment of conception?". These people have clearly done their homework, and put a lot of thought and research into this, and should be commended for it- this is an excellent approach also, and should be vigorously pursued. It is similar to my proposal to calculate a child's age beginning when a woman becomes pregnant. It would ultimately require an agreement on when to define the start of life for legislative purposes.

If you're a devout Catholic, or belong to the Christian Right block, this would probably be the moment of fertilization. My contention, that the fertilized egg is the seed, and life begins when it takes hold and begins to develop past that stage; that is, when the woman becomes pregnant; also has, I believe, the advantage of being more easily attainable, from a political point of view, because it does not rule out forms of birth control that many people subscribe to. Of course, that is going to be very difficult to do-even to get a majority to agree on that. But it's a lot easier than getting a Constitutional Amendment approved, where you have to get "two thirds of both Houses,...or...legislatures ...ratified by...three fourths...of the...states", and the dots are just to keep it simple so I don't have to type so much. It's from Article V of the U.S. Constitution. I regard that as nearly impossible in the current environment. On the other hand, the Court did say that if the Congress would decide when life begins, that would settle the matter. The politicians seem to prefer to avoid the issue:

"...unelected men and women on the Supreme Court have played God with innocent human life. They have invented laws that condemned to painful deaths without trial more than 40 million babies for the crime of being 'inconvenient'." "...the...Life at Conception bills declare unborn children persons as defined by the 14th Amendment to the Constitution, entitled to legal protection. This is the one thing the Supreme Court admitted, in Roe v. Wade, that would cause the case for legal abortion to 'collapse'. When the Supreme Court handed down its now-infamous Roe v. Wade decision, it did so based on a new, previously undefined 'right of privacy' which it 'discovered' in so-called 'emanations' of 'penumbrae' of the Constitution. Of course, as constitutional law it was a disaster." "Then the High Court made a key admission: 'If this suggestion of personhood is established, the appellant's case, of course, collapses, for the fetus' right to life is then guaranteed specifically by the 14th Amendment.' The fact is, the 14th Amendment couldn't be clearer: '...nor shall any state deprive any person of life, liberty or property, without due process of law, nor deny to any person within its jurisdiction the equal protection of the law.' Furthermore, the 14th Amendment says: 'Congress shall have power to enforce, by appropriate legislation, the provisions of this article.' That's exactly what a Life at Conception Act would do...Science is clear that human life begins at conception when a new human being, genetically neither 'part' of either parent, is formed; and Whereas The American people oppose abortion-on-demand and want innocent human life to be protected especially when it is most defenseless;…It belongs to Congress to resolve the question the Supreme Court said IT cannot resolve;…A Life at Conception Act, by declaring unborn children are persons entitled to constitutional protection, will rescue millions of unborn children from dying through abortion-on-demand".

"…the National Pro-Life Alliance is contacting hundreds of thousands of Americans…to mobilize a grass-roots army to pass a Life at Conception Act." Why, if there was even a smidgen of doubt in your mind, would you risk being wrong, and condemn all those people to die? The consequences were, and are still, mind boggling.

"Overturn the Clinton Administration's FDA approval of the manufacture and sale of RU-486."

"Protect pro-life medical personnel by making it illegal to fire or discipline any doctor, nurse, or medical assistant who refuses to assist with an elective abortion".

"Reduce hasty, ill-informed decisions by requiring a 48-hour 'cooling off' period after giving the mother mandatory counseling on the risks and consequences of abortion and explaining adoption alternatives" (informed consent).

"Promote alternatives to abortion by reducing the cost and needless, bureaucratic obstacles to adopt a child".

"Provide the father a say in the future of his offspring by requiring spousal consent prior to an abortion".

"Prohibit abortions to select the sex of the child".

"Fight against the appointment of federal judges who fabricate abortion rights".

"Flush out irresponsible judges by establishing term limits for federal judges".

"Treat as murder a criminal assault that results in the death of an unborn child" (I think this is done in some states now). Currently before Congress as the "Unborn Victims of Violence Act". ["This would be an important legal recognition that an unborn child is a living human being." Beverly LaHaye, CWA, 02/04/2003]

"Make it illegal to force any medical school or teaching hospital to teach abortion techniques".

"Organize boycotts of businesses that donate to Planned Parenthood and other abortion providers" (for example, through the United Way, although you may not want to use that example in your report and start another controversy. The Pro-Life Alliance probably had corporations and wealthy individuals in mind who contribute directly to Planned Parenthood).

"End research on aborted baby body parts".

Amen.

"President-Elect George W. Bush has vowed he will sign the Partial-Birth Abortion Ban, which Congress should pass this year". (I'm not so sure, with a filibuster a possibility, and more hysterical pro-abortion Senators this year than last). "The second major issue we're concentrating on is slashing taxpayer funding for abortion at home and abroad. The UN Population Fund finances the Planned Parenthood Federation and the radical forced-abortion policies of Red China-including abortions literally at gunpoint.

In a budget 'compromise,' Congress has put off the decision whether or not to fund overseas abortionists until February 15—a policy which President Bush can quickly end...you and I must be prepared to fight at each step in the budget process to completely shut off the flow of tax dollars to the abortion industry. Another major battle that will be a top priority in the coming year will be stopping the French Abortion pill-RU-486. Unfortunately, the Food and Drug Administration rushed through approval of the deadly pill last September 28. Your National Pro-Life Alliance is backing legislation to overturn this ruling, but we must act quickly, since the abortion pill has already hit U.S. markets. Of course, if we are to make any real progress in totally eliminating abortion-on-demand, ultimately we're going to have to do something about the federal court decisions. Arrogant judges have struck down or delayed nineteen popular state laws banning partial-birth abortion. That's why I plan to redouble our pressure for the 'Sanctity of Life Act'...Roe v. Wade would become a dead issue. New pro-life state laws could be passed free from judicial tyranny...Right To Life Act...votes on these two bills will clearly expose which politicians are for abortion-on-demand and which would protect the constitutional rights of the unborn". Martin Fox

What "kind" of an organization is NPLA? I would classify them as legislation and lobbying. An organization like ALL, which I think has a very large membership, would lose their tax exemption if they deviated from their educational mission and tried to directly influence legislation. But I know the two organizations talk. There's no law against that. Why don't they have their own web site, when they have the capability to contact hundreds of thousands of people through the mail? They refer people to this web site. But we've never

53

met. We've never even talked. They wouldn't know me if we passed on the street and I waved and smiled and said "Hi". If they wanted to, they could probably figure out what my name was, and where I lived. It would tell them nothing about me. If they know my name, they respect my privacy. They have no way of knowing what I will say next on this web site. I don't even know that. But I've known for many months, through my trackers, that they send me traffic, and it's much appreciated. Apparently, they liked this site so much, even a year or more ago, and our views are so similar and parallel, that they're not worried about what I'm going to write next. I take a little pride in that, but I'm fairly sure I couldn't do what they're doing. So it's probably the best arrangement-they do what they do best, and I do what I do best-without having to clear it with anybody.

"Under current federal law, as long as the baby's head is still in the womb, the abortionist can legally 'terminate' that child-just inches from birth…you and I must hold the pro-abortion politicians accountable as they face their constituents this November. Why are pro-abortion extremists so determined to hide the truth? Because they know most Americans, when told the truth, will demand Congress outlaw partial-birth abortions. Partial birth abortion is so grisly that even the most militant pro-abortion politicians…can't stand to talk about it—let alone defend it. They desperately want to avoid the subject. For the sake of every innocent baby marked for death, you and I must counter NARAL's attack and hold the politicians accountable for their pro-abortion votes. President Clinton may be willing to be remembered for defending these grisly abortions. But I doubt many members of Congress—hoping to be reelected this fall—want to be forced to defend such a gruesome practice. That roll-call vote will put the spotlight directly on politicians who voted to keep partial-birth abortions legal so they can't escape responsibility. Americans overwhelmingly agree with you and me that late-term, partial-birth abortions should be outlawed.

Now, you and I must KEEP the spotlight shining on the radical pro-abortion politicians – all the way to November. The weeks between now and November are our best opportunity. Every single member of Congress who votes against the Partial-Birth Abortion Ban is hoping that he can just get safely past November without too many of his constituents knowing about that vote. Your contribution…will help shine a bright spotlight on pro-partial-birth abortion politicians, all the way to November. I won't beat around the bush. The more you…give, the more I can make pro-abortion politicians sweat. And I really want to pour it on. I'm chomping at the bit." Martin Fox, President, National Pro-Life Alliance, August 12, 2002, http://www.prolifealliance.com /. Congratulations on your new web site, Martin. And thank you for sending that early traffic to me. During the slow summer months last year it probably gave me just enough in-centive to keep working on mine. And perhaps I even inadvertently helped you get yours.

Another intermediate step that I think would be helpful is legislation prohibiting counseling and abortion entities from having the same parent organization (like Planned Parenthood does). There is, obviously, at the very least, a conflict of interest here. Counseling at the separate agency, with a doctor's affidavit, could be required before a referral can be made and an abortion can be done.

"The Born-Alive Infants Protection Act ensures that any infant born alive will be treated as a person under federal law. With the erosion of moral law—particularly since the Supreme Court's Stenberg v. Carhart upholding partial-birth abortion in Nebraska—such a distinction becomes important. In Carhart, the high court didn't seem to care that the baby was alive and partly outside the mother's body when it was killed. The U.S. Court of Appeals for the Third Circuit went so far as to call it 'nonsensical' for lawmakers to base their view of abortion on whether the baby is inside or outside of the mother's body! The only relevant issue under the law, then, is whether the mother intends to kill the baby or not. Whether the baby emerges from the womb alive or dead is of no consequence whatsoever! The logical extension of this thinking is odious: A baby could be entirely delivered, not just partially, and then murdered—and it would all be perfectly legal.

So a new law protecting live babies—based on their location—is, quite sadly, needed now in this country! Two nurses from a Chicago area hospital testified that doctors sometimes induce premature labor, deliver live babies (between 16 and 23 weeks along), and then simply allow the baby to die". "Infants born at 23 weeks' gestation have an almost 40% chance of survival".

"Dr. Alexander warned that the Nazis' attitudes—for example, describing the patients they killed as 'useless eaters' – were also taking hold in the modern U.S. Dr. N. Gregory Hamilton, president of Physicians for Compassionate Care, observes that 'the value of each human life can be traded off in complex cost-benefit ratios. Members of the bioethics elite have quietly convinced many of our judges, hospital administrators and doctors that some human lives have relatively less value, and therefore less right to equal protection.'" "Some members of Congress have already come out strongly against any born-alive protection legislation. And Princeton's bioethicist Peter Singer goes so far as to argue that parents should have the option of killing disabled or unhealthy babies up to 28 days old. The life of a newborn human, he says, is 'of no greater value than the life of a nonhuman animal at a similar level of rationality, self-consciousness, awareness, capacity to feel, etc.' So 'killing a disabled infant is not morally equivalent to killing a person. Very often it is not wrong at all.'" Taken from **Rights Watch-A Publication of the Christian Coalition of America. http://www.cc.org/**

My father died when I was two years old. From his pictures I can tell that he was an impressive, dynamic guy. For two years he must have been my daily companion. But I have no memories of him or that period in my life. So if the logic stated above was adhered to, any two year old who was bad-or who's mother was having a bad day-could just be bagged and thrown out with the trash. Theologians like to argue that all human life has equal value. I think that premise can be easily dismantled, and don't want to be on their side of that argument. The point here is that to say that one person's life is more valuable than another's doesn't give the more valuable person the right to kill the less valuable one. That is infinitely unjust and a formula for chaos and tyranny. In this case particularly, who can say with certainty what a child's value to others will become? There are people who adopt only special needs children, and derive a great deal of satisfaction from doing so.

From Alan Keyes, Gary Bauer, and Mark Crutcher

Alan Keyes on Abortion:

"All that's left is to permit the murder of already born but rejected babies. With a judiciary run amok, believe me when I say that's not far off!!!" "...you and I can still vote for our representatives. But increasingly their power is being drained...by an IMPERIAL JUDICIARY that is usurping Congressional prerogatives and violating Constitutional principles. Action by the Supreme Court goes beyond the innocent children being murdered today—as horrid as that is. Because the logic of abortion is 'people are disposable property.' That is the same reasoning used to justify slavery! So now the principle that blasted the lives of my own ancestors looms over a new generation of Americans." "...the Court evidently sees no limit to use the laws IT can make! 'Separation of powers' is supposed to mean that laws are made by the legislature—by Congress—not by the Courts. Unfortunately, right now we have NATIONWIDE LAWS being made by an unelected group of 12 men and women!" "THE CHECKS AND BALANCES BETWEEN THE BRANCHES OF GOVERNMENT ARE BEING RIPPED APART BY UNELECTED JUDGES 'MAKING LAW' FROM THE BENCH." "...we must have a Congress that will assert its rights as the ONLY Constitutional body authorized to make law. And further, WHEN JUDGES BEGIN TO VIOLATE OUR MOST SACRED PRINCIPLES IT IS THE RESPONSIBILITY OF CONGRESS AND LEGISLATURES TO LIMIT JUDGES' POWERS AND EVEN REMOVE THEM BY IMPEACHMENT IF NECESSARY!!!" "...this judicial threat to our republican form of government." "keep Congress committed to actively opposing unconstitutional judicial activism. Likewise, A PRESIDENT IS NOT SUPPOSED TO ROLL OVER AND PLAY DEAD WHEN JUDGES ACT LIKE TYRANTS. He's supposed to defend the Constitution and the liberties of the people...can simply announce he will issue a pardon to every person who violates an unconstitutional 'law' forced upon the people by imperial judges."

"It is today's Godless and distorted notion of "rights" in America that has permitted the absurd and evil notion that the weakest among us, the unborn, have NO human rights at all." "It is time the leader of the most powerful nation in the world take to the bully pulpit on behalf of all human beings subject to such fatal moral confusion—including the innocent unborn!" "And I humbly suggest that our continuing wealth, and might, and stature as a leader of nations all utterly depend on our continuing to uphold what is right and true."

"We are an enormously diverse people, of every race, color, creed and kind. We have gathered folks here from all the four corners of the globe. We cannot claim a common ethnic stock, a common racial heritage; even, these days, it is unclear that common language will bind us. But one thing is clear-that we stand on common ground of our claim to human rights and dignity, which we have offered to all those people, from every corner of the globe. Not because it is our choice, but because it was understood by our Founders to be God's will." Alan Keyes, The Declaration Foundation. Added November 02, 2000.

"Today we have laws which make it a crime to kill spotted owls, some types of fish and even some insects, just to name a few. It's a black stain on our nation's character that we don't offer that same protection to the unborn." Sometimes, men and women…are called upon to act on…faith even when it seems as though their actions are doomed to failure. I have heard that call on behalf of our unborn children clearly and urgently, particularly over the last several months. And while I do not understand God's plan, I know that we must do everything in our power to stop partial-birth abortion before it takes another life. For the first time in at least 8 years, our nation is turning around. I believe we are on the verge of a great cultural renewal." "So today I am asking you to commit yourself, your family, your prayers and your resources to banning partial-birth abortion." Gary L. Bauer, President, American Values, April, 2001, http://www.ouramericanvalues.org/.

May, 2001-Here's something else that's going on now, where you might want to get involved. If not, you'll at least be up to date:

"President George W. Bush repeatedly stated throughout his campaign that, if elected, he would return America to a culture of life. That promise has become the rallying cry behind a new petition drive launched by Life Dynamics, Inc., a Texas based pro-life organization.

Since President Bush's election, the media has attempted to convince him that there is no public support for him to act on his pro-life campaign promises, said Life Dynamics President Mark Crutcher. There is also a misconception among many Americans that there really isn't anything the President can do about abortion. The First Step Initiative is intended to dispel both of those myths. Our goal is to show the President that there is actually widespread support for his pro-life vision.

This clear, concise, seven-sentence initiative asks the President to take two simple and innovative actions both of which are within his power to do.

THE FIRST STEP INITIATIVE

Dear President Bush,

During your Presidential campaign, you often stated that you wanted to help America embrace a culture of life. Like millions of other Americans, I totally support you in that effort. Toward that end, I am calling on you to immediately appoint a Presidential Blue Ribbon Committee whose sole mission is to provide you with a pragmatic strategy (including an implementation plan) for promptly returning legal protection to every unborn child from the moment of conception. This panel should include attorneys, judges, legal scholars, and public officials who are committed to the pro-life position, as well as selected individuals from the nation's pro-life leadership. As part of this initiative, I am also petitioning you to implement a National Abortion Education Program designed to encourage more Americans to adopt the pro-life position. This campaign should consist of radio, television, and print advertising and be modeled after the government's efforts to eradicate illiteracy, smoking, drug use, violence, and racism." Conservativepetitions. com To sign this petition go to: http://www.conservativepetitions.com/, or specifically-
http://www.conservativepetitions.com/petition.html?name=first_step_initiativ

Looking back, it was a good idea then, and still is. The petition also got a lot of signatures. But, just starting his new administration, I don't think that President Bush wanted to make waves. Perhaps it is something that could be revived for his second term.

What Famous People Say: Ronald Reagan, Jane Roe (Roe v Wade), et al

"Abortion and the Conscience of the Nation", by Ronald Reagan. You can read it online at the following link:

http://www.humanlifereview.com/reagan/reagan_conscience.html. To buy the book, with commentary and some other essays, go to the following link:

http://www.californiaprolife.org/reagan/reagan.htm. But, as I implied, it's an essay, not a book; although a very long and insightful essay. To make it a book they added writings from other people. There are three things I especially like about it. First of all, it shows that President Reagan, widely respected and very popular during his whole two terms in office, was unquestionably and unequivocally on the pro-life side; and looking for what he could personally do to stem the abortion tide. Secondly, the sophistication and clarity of his writing style puts to rest the Democrats' implications that he was somehow lacking intellectually. Third, it makes a very strong statement and case against abortion. I had planned not to use it in the book originally, but when I got to the part where I'm debating on about.com I saw that I had posted it to my opponent in that debate; so I just included it there after all. It's a historical document; in my opinion, right up there with Lincoln's Gettysburg address.

"What happens...to the moral fabric of a nation that accepts the aborting of the life of a baby without a pang of conscience?"—Jesse Jackson, 1977

John McCain, Boston Globe, page A9, Jan 31, 2000: "If Roe v. Wade is overturned and abortion outlawed, McCain said he believes doctors who performed abortions would be prosecuted. 'But I would not prosecute a woman' who obtained an abortion."

"Abortion is the ultimate exploitation of women." Alice Paul, feminist, author of the Equal Rights Amendment

"Women deserve better than abortion, and every child deserves a chance at life. Who can argue with our message? Women deserve better than suffering through three days of coerced labor in partial birth abortion, or witnessing their own abortions by swallowing RU-486. Certainly, no woman deserves to be abandoned by those she counts on the most. Although NOW and Planned Parenthood would have us believe otherwise, early American feminists such as Susan B. Anthony and Elizabeth Cady Stanton were vehemently anti-abortion." Serrin M. Foster, President of Feminists for Life, based in Washington, D.C. Her lecture, 'The Feminist Case Against Abortion,' has been included in an anthology on 'Women's Rights,' one volume in a series entitled, *Great Speeches in History*. She has presented her lecture at top colleges across the country and internationally at Oxford, Cambridge and other universities, at Senate and House briefings, and at the Parliament Buildings at Stormont, Northern Ireland." From Celebrate Life, May-June, 2003. FFL was founded in 1972. http://www.feministsforlife.org/

"When we consider that women are treated as property, it is degrading to women that we should treat our children as property to dispose of as we see fit." Elizabeth Cady Stanton, feminist, 1873

"Guilty? Yes. No matter what the motive, love of ease, or a desire to save from suffering the unborn innocent, the woman is awfully guilty who commits the deed. It will burden her conscience in life, it will burden her soul in death; But oh, thrice guilty is he who drove her to the desperation which impelled her to the crime!" Susan B. Anthony on abortion

"A PRO-LIFE ACTIVIST...Anthony wrote an essay in the publication she started, The Revolution, about the 'horrible crime of childmurder'. She was referring specifically to the tragedy of abortion. Anthony wanted to 'eradicate the most monstrous crime' but knew a law would not suffice. 'We must reach the root of the evil and destroy it.' SHE FOUGHT FOR MANY CAUSES... Susan B. Anthony stood against abortion and slavery. She thought that everyone-including the unborn-should be treated equally. SUFFRAGIST...In 1872, Anthony, three of her sisters, and other women were arrested in Rochester, NY for voting. From 1869 until her death in 1906, Anthony appeared before every Congress to ask for the passage of a suffrage amendment to allow women the right to vote. It wasn't until 1920 that American adult women received the right to vote with the 19th Amendment, also know as the Susan B. Anthony Amendment." From Jennifer Bingham, Executive Director, SBAList.

"Advocacy by women for legalized abortion on a national scale is so anti-women's liberation that it flies in the face of what some of us are trying to accomplish through the women's movement-namely, equality-equality means an equal sharing of responsibilities by and as men and women...What kind of future do we all have to look forward to if men are excused either morally or legally from their responsibility for participation in the creation of life...? To talk about the 'wanted' and the 'unwanted' child smacks too much of bigotry and prejudice. Many of us have experienced the sting of being 'unwanted' by certain segments of our society...". Chicana activist Graciela Olivarez, first woman graduate of Notre Dame Law School, charter member of the National Organization for Women, who "continued to practice a belief in the indivisibility of all human rights.". Feminists for Life, web site at: http://www.feministsforlife.org/.

On Gloria Steinem: "Ironically, after 30 years of marriage-bashing, Gloria married in the summer of 2000. Early in her career, she had said, 'You become a semi-nonperson when you get married.' She also talked about married women being 'part-time prostitutes' and called marital bedrooms 'settings for nightly rape.'

Steinem's own divergence from the values she lauded for 30 years should be a red flag to any person who looks for life's meaning in the principles she so adamantly and forcefully paraded before women." From the book "A Different Kind of Strength", by Beverly LaHaye and Janice Crouse.

I suppose Gloria realized time was running out to experience the closeness that can come with marriage and family. I remember her saying she had had an abortion. Now, unfortunately, it's probably too late for her to have children of her own.

Roe v Wade. Jane Roe v Wade. Actually her name was Norma McCorvey. One might suppose she was still savoring the victory and her role in it, even after all these years; and working tirelessly for the pro-abortion cause. So it might be instructive to check in with her to she what she thought about the way things turned out-sort of bring ourselves up to date. Here's what she has to say:

"Back then, I believed abortion was a woman's right to 'choose'. And, I was a fool." "Today, I oppose abortion. Because abortion is a lie. It always was. I know, because I told the lie that got it all started…

…I said I was gang raped. And I wasn't.
…I said I didn't know who the father was. And I did.
…I said I hated my baby. And I didn't.

And I said the Constitution protected my right to abortion. And it's nowhere to be found. I simply made it all up. And now, 41 million babies are dead, and counting…And abortion is legal in all 50 states because my great big lie took on a life of it's own, spinning wildly out of control and destroying innocent children in its path."

"…my lawyer (Sarah Weddington) never wanted to help me. She only wanted to use me by getting my name on that affidavit. She wanted me to help her legalize the violent slaughter of innocent babies in their mother's womb-just like she had killed hers…I never signed up to become a sacrificial lamb for anyone. I was desperate, scared and alone…I was just a young woman who needed help, and I turned to the wrong people."

"I have a new mission in life—to tell the horrible truth about abortion. And, to share God's love and forgiveness to those who suffer abortion's devastating aftermath. I'm not afraid to say abortion is murder, plain and simple. I know, because after Roe v Wade came down, I went to work in an abortion clinic. And I saw death firsthand." "I've seen the blood of a dead baby pour out onto the floor of the operating room. I've seen the tiny parts of babies (hands, feet, torsos, heads) pulled piece by piece from their mother's womb. I've heard the cries and blood curdling screams of women who just killed their own flesh and blood. And I've seen these same women call their mom on the phone and say… 'Mom, I just killed my baby. I'm so glad you didn't kill me!'"

"I knew most of the women…were never told the truth about abortion. They never knew that their babies had heartbeats, finger-prints, functioning organs, and a strong desire to live and grow…Instead, they were told it was 'tissue' or a 'missed cycle' or some other bald faced lie. I never thought people could be so gullible, and yet they were. But I knew better. And now, I'm tired of the lies. It's time for the senseless killing to stop."

"A few years ago I started my own pro-life group, Roe No More Ministry. My mission is to expose abortion for the lie that it is, and to tell the truth to the millions of Americans who think abortion is their 'choice.' Since founding Roe No More, I've tried my best to change the hearts and minds of Americans. My public speaking—telling the truth behind my story and exposing the lie of legalized 'choice'—has impacted hundreds of tiny, innocent lives." "I want to reach out to millions of vulnerable women and scared fathers, and tell them that abortion is murder. And Roe v Wade is a lie…I've spoken to thousands of students…all across America…I've set out to tell the horrible truth about abortion like no one else can…the landmark abortion case, 'Roe v Wade', is nothing but a lie seven powerful Supreme Court Justices simply invented in 1973…Life is precious. And it must be protected."

Like another insider, Dr. Nathanson, below, Norma has switched sides. She's also written a book, 'Won By Love', which she says: "…explains my 25-year journey from the poster child for abortion 'rights' to one of the most determined pro-life converts in America." You can contact her at Roe No More Ministry, PO Box 96451, Washington, DC 20090-6451; or P.O. Box 550626, Dallas, TX 75355, (214) 343-1069, or through her web site at http://www.roenomore.org

Norma recently filed an amicus brief to overturn Roe vs. Wade:

"Philadelphia, PA—The plaintiffs in the two landmark Supreme Court cases of Roe v. Wade and Doe v. Bolton, the two companion cases decided on January 22, 1973 which compelled legalized abortion throughout the nation, are appearing in Philadelphia on Thursday, May 31, 2001, to personally file Friend of the Court briefs with the United States Court of Appeals. In their briefs they tell the Courts why the decisions in their own landmark cases have proven to be harmful to the rights of women and why the decisions in their own cases should be overturned.

Norma McCorvey (Jane Roe in Roe v. Wade) and Sandra Cano (Mary Doe of Doe v. Bolton) are filing their Friend of the Court briefs in the case of Donna Santa Marie, et al v. Christine Todd Whitman, et al. The Santa Marie case is a federal class action suit brought by five women (three of whom had abortions that were performed without voluntary or informed consent) who argue that New Jersey's abortion laws violate the most important constitutional rights of women.

Harold Cassidy, lead counsel for the Santa Marie plaintiffs, known for his work advancing mother's rights (he was Chief Counsel, among other cases, in the famous Baby M surrogate mother case) stated that the underlying cases that prompted the Santa Marie plaintiffs to file the class action suit 'demonstrate how abortion laws are destroying the real rights of women.'"

And isn't it interesting that unless you have a connection to the pro-life cause, you would probably never hear about this? I stumbled across it on the About.com pro-life forum, where I sit in from time to time. It was posted by David A. Brown, who apparently is associated with Pro-Life Infonet.

"What does one do when 'the system' routinely injects propaganda to slowly and carefully transform something horrible into something tolerable..."

"In a representative democracy, freedom to choose is not absolute. System-regulated propaganda is so pervasive that individuals who initially support certain causes can eventually fall victim to the lies built within, with devastating consequences. Norma McCorvey is one example; she was deceived by the feminist pro-abortion propaganda machine. Let's not forget the many women who, seduced by 'choice', suffer from post-abortion syndrome later on."

"Women not initially receptive to the idea of legalizing abortion became involved in the feminist movement for other reasons. Marriage and childbirth were scorned and single women were encouraged to experiment sexually with a variety of sexual partners. The attainment of pleasure without consequences became a guidepost within the feminist movement. Demands for equal sexual rights with men, resulted in a rise in promiscuity. The pill was only an intermediate step to the 'Final Solution' that would end sexual repression, and establish liberation for sexually active women. It was not enough to control pregnancy by the easy evacuation of an unfertilized egg (i.e., preventing a baby from being conceived); the product of conception had to be stopped (i.e., the baby had to be exterminated). The activists' objective was to convince the public that 'choice' (abortion) was preferable to the alternative of 'forced slavery' (motherhood). If the tactics failed, they'd resort to the courts and establish abortion 'rights' via judicial fiat.

For abortion activists who were not comfortable enough to venture into this brave new world where unborn babies fell victim to sordid linguistic misrepresentations, there was the 'crisis' of overpopulation. If abortions were legal, we could eliminate world hunger, poverty, and the growing epidemic of welfare mothers and drifting fathers. From the vantage point of crimes against living children, abortion was being morphed even then into a necessary good... After 28 years, we've already learned to co-exist painfully and passively...".

"We are a far cry from those naive beginnings. That's why it's so important not to mince words. I'm not afraid to call partial-birth abortion 'infanticide', for that's what it is. I'm not ashamed to say that abortion degrades women, for that's what it does. As a Jew, I'm not wrong to refer to what supporters call 'choice' as an American Holocaust, for that's what it has become."

"Unless there is political intervention now to stop our progression into complacency...We'll be killing living children with resignation and acceptance, perhaps even glee, along with other members of our society deemed unfit or inconvenient. By then deformed thinking will be the norm and people will have so acclimated themselves that they will no longer be able to distinguish the difference in value between a living human being and a dead one."

"Maybe...fear will urge us to do what is right, and vote only for candidates who will end infanticide forever. Please, I beg you to remember the Holocausts. Both of them." Taken from "Between Two Holocausts", by Bonnie Chernin Rogoff. Bonnie is a freelance writer, and founder of Jews For Life. This was reprinted, in part, from ALL's monthly Celebrate Life publication. You can also read it, in its entirety, at Bonnie's web site, http://www.jewsforlife.org/.

Very cerebral stuff. It's an excellent depiction of what's taken place, but not quite, entirely adequate to explain why, in my view; for that you need to read what Dr. Nathanson has to say below, and other chapters in this book, to get more background, find the missing pieces, and eventually see the entire picture.

"Why have the radical feminist messengers been so celebrated when their messages have not stood the test of time?" From "A Different Kind of Strength", by Beverly LaHaye and Janice Crouse.

Rather than being "oppressed", women have been in the forefront of the battle against abortion. Would they be fighting to oppress themselves?

Dr. Bernard Nathanson

Confused by the pro-death crowd about which side is telling the truth in the abortion debate? Read the following statements. One of the favorite and most used tactics of the abortionists is to say that the pro-life people are lying. But what would the motive be? The statements below are well worth your time to read, and they're not very long. It will give you some invaluable insights into how abortion came to be legalized in America.

I consider Dr. Nathanson's own statement the most important and verifiable document in the abortion controversy. It's on numerous sites around the internet, he's a very erudite and professional man; he has written several books and made a couple of movies; and he's been a hospital administrator. Moreover, he's still around, speaks at pro-life functions, and is "on call" to the pro-life movement. Currently, he "is a clinical associate professor of obstetrics and gynecology at New York Medical College", and a member of the American Bioethics Advisory Commission. "He holds a premed degree from Cornell University, an M.D. from McGill University Medical College and a master's degree in bioethics from Vanderbilt, Nashville, Tenn. He is a member of the American Medical Association. He has held the position of director of gynecology at the Hospital of Joint Diseases in New York, chief of obstetrical service at St. Luke's Hospital Center in New York, and numerous other hospital staff appointments. He has published extensively."

CONFESSION OF AN EX-ABORTIONIST

By Dr. Bernard Nathanson

I am personally responsible for 75,000 abortions. This legitimises my credentials to speak to you with some authority on the issue. I was one of the founders of the National Association for the Repeal of the Abortion Laws (NARAL) in the U.S. in 1968. A truthful poll of opinion then would have found that most Americans were against permissive abortion. Yet within five years we had convinced the U.S. Supreme Court to issue the decision which legalised abortion throughout America in 1973 and produced virtual abortion on demand up to birth. How did we do this? It is important to understand the tactics involved because these tactics have been used throughout the western world with one permutation or another, in order to change abortion law.

THE FIRST KEY TACTIC WAS TO CAPTURE THE MEDIA

We persuaded the media that the cause of permissive abortion was a liberal enlightened, sophisticated one. Knowing that if a true poll were taken, we would be soundly defeated, we simply fabricated the results of fictional polls. We announced to the media that we had taken polls and that 60% of Americans were in favour of permissive abortion. This is the tactic of the self-fulfilling lie. Few people care to be in the minority. We aroused enough sympathy to sell our program of permissive abortion by fabricating the number of illegal abortions done annually in the U.S. The actual figure was approaching 100,000 but the figure we gave to the media repeatedly was 1,000,000. Repeating the big lie often enough convinces the public. The number of women dying from illegal abortions was around 200-250 annually. The figure we constantly fed to the media was 10,000. These false figures took root in the consciousness of Americans convincing many that we needed to crack the abortion law. Another myth we fed to the public through the media was that legalising abortion would only mean that the abortions taking place illegally would then be done legally. In fact, of course, abortion is now being used as a primary method of birth control in the U.S. and the annual number of abortions has increased by 1500% since legalisation.

THE SECOND KEY TACTIC WAS TO PLAY THE CATHOLIC CARD

We systematically vilified the Catholic Church and its "socially backward ideas" and picked on the Catholic hierarchy as the villain in opposing abortion. This theme was played endlessly. We fed the media such lies as "we all know that opposition to abortion comes from the hierarchy and not from most Catholics" and "Polls prove time and again that most Catholics want abortion law reform". And the media drum-fired all this into the American people, persuading them that anyone opposing permissive abortion must be under the influence of the Catholic hierarchy and that Catholics in favour of abortion are enlightened and forward-looking. An inference of this tactic was that there were no non-Catholic groups opposing abortion. The fact that other Christian as well as non-Christian religions were {and still are) monolithically opposed to abortion was constantly suppressed, along with pro-life atheists' opinions.

THE THIRD KEY TACTIC WAS THE DENIGRATION AND SUPPRESSION OF ALL SCIENTIFIC EVIDENCE THAT LIFE BEGINS AT CONCEPTION

I am often asked what made me change my mind. How did I change from prominent abortionist to pro-life advocate? In 1973, I became director of obstetrics of a large hospital in New York City and had to set up a prenatal research unit, just at the start of a great new technology which we now use every day to study the foetus in the womb. A favourite pro-abortion tactic is to insist that the definition of when life begins is impossible; that the question is a theological or moral or philosophical one, anything but a scientific one. Foetology makes it undeniably evident that life begins at conception and requires all the protection and safeguards that any of us enjoy. Why, you may well ask, do some American doctors who are privy to the findings of foetology, discredit themselves by carrying out abortions? Simple arithmetic at $300 a time, 1.55 million abortions means an industry generating $500,000,000 annually, of which most goes into the pocket of the physician doing the abortion. It is clear that permissive abortion is purposeful destruction of what is undeniably human life. It is an impermissible act of deadly violence. One must concede that unplanned pregnancy is a wrenchingly difficult dilemma, but to look for its solution in a deliberate act of destruction is to trash the vast resourcefulness of human ingenuity, and to surrender the public weal to the classic utilitarian answer to social problems.

AS A SCIENTIST I KNOW, NOT BELIEVE, KNOW THAT HUMAN LIFE BEGINS AT CONCEPTION

Although I am not a formal religionist, I believe with all my heart that there is a divinity of existence which commands us to declare a final and irreversible halt to this infinitely sad and shameful crime against humanity.

|Dr. Nathanson has since converted to Catholicism, being baptized in 1996.|

From: The Pro-Life Infonet Reply-To: Steven Ertelt Infonet@prolifeinfo.org
Source: WorldnetDaily; December 20, 2002

Former Leading Abortion Advocate Remembers Myths of Illegal Abortions

Washington, DC—'Women must have control over their own bodies. 'Safe and legal abortion is every woman's right.' 'Who decides? You decide!' 'Freedom of choice—a basic American right.' The 'pro-choice movement's' emotionally compelling slogans—fierce rallying cries of the most successful political marketing campaign in modern history, which made abortion-on-demand legal in the U.S.—have been powerful rhetorical weapons for fighting off efforts to reverse Roe v. Wade, coming up on its 30th anniversary next month. 'I remember laughing when we made those slogans up,' recalls Bernard Nathanson, M.D., co-founder of pro-abortion group NARAL, reminiscing about the early days of the pro-abortion movement in the late '60s and early '70s. 'We were looking for some sexy, catchy slogans to capture public opinion. They were very cynical slogans then, just as all of these slogans today are very, very cynical.'

Besides having served as chairman of the executive committee of NARAL—
originally, the National Association for the Repeal of Abortion Laws, and later
renamed the National Abortion and Reproductive Rights Action League—as
well as its medical committee, Nathanson was one of the principal architects
and strategists of the abortion movement in the United States. He tells an
astonishing story.

'In 1968 I met Lawrence Lader,' says Nathanson. 'Lader had just finished a
book called 'Abortion,' and in it had made the audacious demand that
abortion should be legalized throughout the country. I had just finished a
residency in obstetrics and gynecology and was impressed with the number of
women who were coming into our clinics, wards and hospitals suffering from
illegal, infected, botched abortions.' 'Lader and I were perfect for each other.
We sat down and plotted out the organization now known as NARAL. With
Betty Friedan, we set up this organization and began working on the strategy.'

What was the result of NARAL's brilliantly deceitful marketing campaign,
bolstered by thoroughly fraudulent research? In New York, the law outlawing
abortion had been on the books for 140 years. 'In two years of work, we at
NARAL struck that law down,' says Nathanson. 'We lobbied the legislature,
we captured the media, we spent money on public relations. Our first year's
budget was $7,500. Of that, $5,000 was allotted to a public relations firm to
persuade the media of the correctness of our position. That was in 1969.' New
York immediately became the abortion capital for the eastern half of the
United States. 'We were inundated with applicants for abortion,' says
Nathanson. 'To that end, I set up a clinic, the Center for Reproductive and
Sexual Health (C.R.A.S.H.), which operated in the east side of Manhattan. It
had 10 operating rooms, 35 doctors, 85 nurses. It operated seven days a week,
from 8 am to midnight. We did 120 abortions every day in that clinic. At the
end of the two years that I was the director, we had done 60,000 abortions. I
myself, with my own hands, have done 5,000 abortions. I have supervised
another 10,000 that residents have done under my direction. So I have 75,000
abortions in my life. Those are pretty good credentials to speak on the subject
of abortion.'

But something happened to Nathanson—something profound. Just as it
happened to countless other abortion practitioners, abortion facility owners
and staffers. Just as it happened to Norma McCorvey—the real name for
'Jane Roe,' the plaintiff in the Supreme Court's 1973 Roe v. Wade abortion
decision. These pioneers of the pro-abortion movement have all arrived at the
same conclusion—that abortion is the unjust killing of a human baby—and
have come over to the other side of the raging abortion debate—". I'm sorry to
say, Dr. Nathanson even aborted his own child.

"...lies are the only weapons the pro-abortion forces have. But those lies are entrenched in the minds of our young people." "We are fighting for our nation, rescuing today's college students from the intellectual gulag they are being held in." Jeff White, Campus Life Tours, Survivors, P.O. Box 332, Lake Arrowhead, CA, 92352, (888) 813-9457.

Places To Visit, Things To See

How Abortions are Done-http://www.w-cpc.org/abortion/methods.html

Stories about people who were aborted, but survived the procedure – http://www.abortiontv.com/AbortionSurvivors.htm

People Who Were Pro-choice But Are Now Pro-life: How They Changed Their View On Abortion- http://www.gargaro.com/choicetolife.html

Post Abortion: Regrets of Women Who Had an Abortion- http://www.gargaro.com/regrets.html

Abortion: The Number One Cause of Death In The United States http://www.sandh.com/keyes/deaths.htm

National Memorial For The Unborn-http://memorial-unborn.org/

"**many…in the pro-life movement know the healing effect a memorial…has on the mothers and fathers of aborted babies. Thousands of memorials to unborn babies, most without human remains, dot the landscape of our nation, many of them in cemeteries…with every abortion there is one dead and several wounded.**" Bradley Mattes, Executive Director, Life Issues Institute, Inc., 1821 W. Galbraith Rd., Cincinnati, Ohio 45239 (513) 729-3600, http://www.lifeissues.org-in Life Issues Connector, January 2003.

The Blackmun Wall-Adult women killed by abortion (that is, old enough to become pregnant). Named after U.S. Supreme Court Justice Harry Blackmun, who engineered and wrote the Roe v. Wade decision. http://www.lifedynamics.net/AboutLDI/index.cfm?fuseaction=BlackmunWall

Baby Parts Marketing-20/20 & The House Hearing Some people don't believe that this really goes on, or that it's illegal. They're just poorly informed on the subject. It's a very lucrative part of the abortion business – and well documented. The less damaged, and older, the baby is, the more its parts are worth. You might call it a "chop shop" business-pun intended. http://www.lifedynamics.net/Products/index.cfm?fuseaction=BabyParts

Got a beef about the abortion clinic you work for? Get help at: ClinicWorker.Com, http://www.clinicworker.com/. This is another LDI project, looking to get inside information on the abortion clinics. They're especially interested in insiders who have grown disillusioned. Optimally, they'd like to talk to every clinic employee who quits. Mark Crutcher, who heads LDI, bills himself as the person most feared by the abortion industry – based on their comments about him. He will know what to do with the information. There's more contact information below:

"For those women and their unborn babies coming into the abortion clinic, you are at ground zero." Life Dynamics Incorporated, Post Office Box 2226, Denton, Texas 76202 (940) 380-8800 http://www.ldi.org/. "Without Compromise Without Exception Without Apology We're not here just to put up a good fight. We're here to win, because winning is how the killing stops."

"An Open Letter To The American Abortion Industry From the President Of Life Dynamics, Mark Crutcher

If you think you can keep on butchering thousands of defenseless babies every day and not feel the sting of Life Dynamics you are seriously mistaken. Whether you work at an abortion clinic, or in the political process to keep abortion legal, what you are doing is a crime against humanity and Life Dynamics is going to use every legal means available to stop you. We will continue to drag you into court, and we will continue to discourage the medical community from being associated with you. And our undercover operatives will keep on infiltrating your death camps so that all your dirty little secrets will be exposed on our television show. As you know, the list goes on and on. And make no mistake there's more on the horizon. What I want to make absolutely clear to you is simply this: You can choose to see the light or you can be forced to feel the heat. But in either case, Life Dynamics will do what it takes to protect unborn babies and their moms from you."

Women Deserve Better (than abortion)-
http://www.womendeservebetter.com/

"Life's Greatest Miracle", from PBS Home Video and NOVA, $19.95 http://www.shoppbs.com/. "Swedish scientific photographer Lennart Nilsson brings this marvel to light…acclaimed inside-the-body story of life from conception to birth. The latest advances in imaging technology show, in awe inspiring detail, the making of a human life".

Also from PBS and NOVA, although not the bargain above, is "The Secret Life of the Brain". "The mystery begins in the womb: four weeks into gestation, 500,000 brain cells are forming every minute. Eventually, there will be billions of cells and trillions of links, with every cell finding its place and every link carefully organized." You can buy either video by clicking on the underlined link. Unfortunately, I don't get a cut. Perhaps I should look into that.

Gregg Cunningham's Center for Bio-Ethical Reform, P. O. Box 2339, Sante Fe Springs, CA 90670, has a "tough 8 minute abortion video" named "Harder

Truth" that it provides to pregnancy resource centers. "Choices Medical Clinic (CMC), a pro-life clinic which CBR helped found in Kansas, shared an encouraging e-mail report with us. They've used CBR's *Harder Truth* video to save babies since they opened in December 2000. Included in statistics from 2 years of operations was this tremendous news, 'Out of the 1300 patients seen in 2 years, 403 actually said 'if this pregnancy test is positive, I'm going to abort' or words to that effect. 335 actually were positive. 15 actually aborted. This is a success rate of 95.7%.'" I'm sure they would share it with you too. The CBR phone number is (562) 777-9117.

Joe Scheidler's Pro-Life Action League has at least two videos, "Face The Truth" and "No Greater Joy". You can call them at (773) 777-2900, or visit their web site at: http://www.prolifeaction.org/.

Concerned Women For America has a "powerful video *After the Choice* …brings the facts to women who have been systematically lied to by the abortion industry." 1015 Fifteenth Street, N.W. Suite 1100 Washignton, D.C. 20005, Phone: 202-488-7000, http://www.cwfa.org/

I don't get a lot of comments, and people who disagree usually don't leave their email address. However, when someone does leave a message, it usually results in a useful exchange of information, like what follows:

"Carol Everett wrote the book 'Blood Money' where she exposes the intentions of the pro-'choice' industry as being centered on profit. She talks about abortions' being performed on non-pregnant girls just to collect that chunk of cash. Carol herself ran 5 abortion clinics in the Dallas Tx. area. Focus On the Family did an interview with her that they saved to tape, available to the public. The tape is available upon request and of course they are assisted when a donation accompanies requests." J. Ezell

Buy the Baby Parts for Sale" video from Shop Net Daily, $24.95. "Join Marlin Maddoux, host of the nationally syndicated radio news talk program Point of View, for an investigation into the multi-million dollar a year baby parts trafficking industry, which is one of the most lucrative businesses in operation today. Yet most Americans are unaware of its existence."

What's an abortion like? Watch a movie of one. http://www.silentscream.org/ This is the first movie Dr. Nathanson produced, using ultrasound and an extensive dialogue. Requires a strong stomach. Later he produced a second one using an actual video camera. I'm not aware of the second one being on the internet. Later on in the book there's information on how to purchase them.

"In-utero surgery was new and rare, and therefore newsworthy…'The surgery on the child was over; they had to close the opening to the uterus and put the uterus back.'…'no one was near the uterus, but the uterus violently shook, so you knew this was being generated from inside. I was just in shock. The hand punched its way out the opening, all the way up to the elbow.' As the doctor reached over and put his finger to the palm of the baby's hand, the baby grasped on and squeezed the doctor's finger…'It changed my life to see the struggle, the struggle for life from inside the womb.'…In early fetal surgeries, the baby was not given anesthetic before surgery." Taken from a LDI interview with freelance photographer Michael Clancy, November 2001. The part about the anesthetic is important because people will argue that the baby couldn't have done it because he was anesthetized, along with a lot of other smoke they'll throw at you. But the picture of the baby's arm, and the baby's hand clearly grasping the doctor's finger outside the womb taken by the photographer above is on my website. And that's all you see of the baby, because the rest is inside the uterus. The doctor would have just put the arm back and sewed up the mother's belly. The child was about 21 weeks old, and the doctor corrected a condition known as spina bifida. Samuel Armas was later delivered normally-and six months later was developing normally. The picture originally appeared in USA Today, 5/2/00. I scanned in the picture, edited it, and put it on a separate page on my web site. You just click on a link and go to that page, then there's a link at the bottom of that page to bring you back to where you came from on the main page. I'm a hobby photographer and I've edited a lot of my own pictures, so I was able to get the baby's hand quite clear even though it's scanned. You don't hear about this kind of surgery today because there's a medical and media reluctance to talk about operating on someone who's not supposed to exist. Part of the "abortion distortion". They even call the operating procedure by a name that's not suggestive of what they're actually doing in some places. But the June 9, 2003, edition of Newsweek broke the taboo with an article on fetal medicine. Samuel Armas was 3 ½ by then, and made for a cute picture. It sounded like no more than 600 of these surgeries are being performed in the country each year. Dr. Joseph Bruner, of Vanderbilt University, has performed about 200 surgeries since 1997 for spina bifida, or myelomeningocele (the same doctor who operated on Samuel Armas). Even though some of Samuel's problems from spina bifida were fixed by the operation, he still has other problems related to the condition. But other types of fetal surgery being done today do completely resolve problems – many of them, unlike spina bifida, life threatening. Even more so, if the parents choose abortion instead.

Seen on a sign held by Ann Fontecchio in Fond du Lac Wisconsin:

"PLANNED PARENTHOOD DESTROYING A GENERATION ONE BABY AT A TIME".

"There's a sign on an office at ALL headquarters that reads, 'When God wants something done, He sends a baby—and waits.'"

Jim Sedlak: "…human beings are our ultimate resource".

RU-486

I received something written by Colleen Parro for RNC/Life, about the drug RU-486, that was so well stated that I feel obligated to pass it along.

"Oklahoma Congressman Tom Coburn was widely quoted as saying, 'Never before has the FDA approved a drug intended to kill people. The FDA's mission is to promote health, not facilitate the taking of life. Sadly, the FDA has approved a drug that will kill an unborn child and put mothers at grave risk.'

Arkansas Senator Tim Hutchinson said, 'Fast-track timetables are supposed to be reserved for drugs that will combat life-threatening diseases like cancer or AIDS. In this case, the Administration rushed a drug through that will take lives instead of saving them.'

In addition to the fact that RU-486 kills a developing baby within the first 7 weeks of life, the press has reported extensively on directions for its use and the dangers to the mother involved in drug-induced abortion. A report by Susan Willis for msnbc.com (10/2/00) reveals that excessive bleeding is common. Nine percent of women in U.S. trials bled for more than 30 days; one percent bled for over 60 days; Four women in U.S. trials (of about 2,000) required blood transfusions; 25 women were treated in emergency rooms or hospitalized for complications.

The steps for procuring a drug-induced abortion using RU-486 involve first, a visit to a doctor for an ultrasound to determine the stage of development of the baby and that an ectopic |tubal| pregnancy is not involved. The mother then receives the capsules containing mifepristone, an anti-progesterone drug that causes the lining of the uterus to break down, preventing the growing baby from remaining implanted in the uterine wall. Two days later, the mother must keep another medical appointment when she receives the drug misoprostol, a prostaglandin, which brings on uterine contractions. She remains under supervision for about 4 hours during which she may expel the baby. If not, she returns home, experiencing excessive bleeding and cramping, often accompanied by vomiting and diarrhea, until she delivers a dead baby. In two weeks, another medical appointment is necessary to make sure the abortion was complete. Otherwise, a surgical abortion will be necessary. This is not easy. This is dangerous."!

"In a statement issued on September 29, Patrick Buchanan said,…'the FDA's approval of RU-486 turns a new page in America's national tragedy. Millions more will perish, and their blood will stain our nation's soul. I say it is an affront to all that is right in America and an abomination before the God who authored these unborn lives.'"

"WASHINGTON-The RU-486 abortion drug that will be sold in the United States will be manufactured in a factory operated by the People's Republic of China, the Washington Post confirmed...the RU-486 produced in that factory and two others is now used for about one-half of the estimated 10 million abortions annually in China. Many of those abortions are forced on women under the government-enforced 'birth-quota' program. It is a public health issue because China is a major source of impure drugs-and the FDA cannot possibly monitor a Chinese factory effectively. It is a human rights issue because...of the Chinese Government's population control program which relies heavily on compulsory abortion." Source: National Right To Life Committee Press Release

"With the FDA's approval of the marketing of RU 486 in the United States of America, our young mothers will be subjected to chemical experimentation and our tiniest citizens subjected to chemical extermination. The abortion industry's never ending saga of seeking cleaner and quieter ways to kill children is reminiscent of another country's desire for a cleaner and quieter way to exterminate its citizens.

Nazi Germany sought and found its solution in a company by the name of I.G. Farben. I.G. Farben developed 'Zyklon B' which was the gas used to exterminate Jews. Incredibly, this is the same company that developed our present day RU486. Surprised! The name of that company today is Hoechst-Celeanse. Its French affiliate is Russeau-Uclaff, the 'RU' of RU486.

'History is a good teacher.' said Rev. Flip Benham, the National Director of Operation Rescue. 'The same company that developed a kinder and gentler way to kill our Jewish brothers and sisters has now developed a kinder and gentler way to exterminate our children.'" Source: Operation Save America

Historical note: It's not my understanding of history that the Nazis used the gas because it was "kinder and gentler", and Rev. Benham would probably agree. They used it to save ammunition, manpower, time, and to avoid an explosive situation where people were standing in line knowing the people ahead of them were being shot; plus the effect on the morale of the people doing the guarding and shooting could have resulted in discontent or a rebellion or a loss of secrecy. They went from something very clumsy and messy to something more efficient they called "The final solution to the Jewish problem" (Jews were not the only minority they were exterminating). Eventually they would execute 6 million innocent people this way-a drop in the bucket compared to what's going on around the world today! Today in America some people see abortion as the final solution to the pregnancy problem, and choose to ignore that they're killing millions of people to get there. Others see it as a way to get rich, and many politicians see it as the path to power by pandering to it. Does the truth hurt?

Similarly, feminists don't want RU-486 out of concern for the child they won't even admit exists; they want it because they think it will be more convenient and private for themselves (just like the Nazis didn't want to admit to the world what they were doing). This of course excludes Feminists for Life, http://www.feministsforlife.org/, an active pro-life organization.

I saw a cartoon. It was taken from the Akron Beacon Journal. A bottle was on a table. The label on the bottle read "Cabernet Red Table Wine...FDA Warning: May Cause Birth Defects". Next to the bottle was a box. The label on the box read "Smokes...FDA warning: Harmful To Unborn Children". Next to the box was a pill bottle. The label said "RU-486 FDA APPROVED". I didn't laugh.

"FDA Chief Fired Following Abuse of 'Accelerated Approval' Policy...Soon after taking office, President Bush dismissed Jane Henney, the controversial FDA director who...oversaw the fast-track approval of the abortion drug." (RU-486) "Previously, new presidential administrations usually held on to the incumbent FDA director, since the post was considered a scientific, not a political, position—a tradition Ms. Henney was all-too-ready to violate." National Pro-Life "Alliance Executive Director Mary King...cited numerous reports linking use of the abortion pill to cancer-a risk the FDA is required to study for virtually every new drug, yet bafflingly ignored its own standard procedures on carcinogenicity for this self-described human toxin! The long-term consequences of women who attempt another pregnancy after killing a first child by an abortion pill were also ignored. Independent studies have suggested a high risk of fetal deformation. Cases of uterine bleeding after ingesting the abortion pill have been commonplace. In Waterloo, Iowa, during the U.S. testing trials, one woman nearly bled to death, requiring emergency surgery and four pints of blood. Dozens of similar cases have already been reported." Taken from the Spring, 2001, LifeLine Newsletter.

"China Bans RU-486-The chemical abortion agent RU-486, currently being sold in the United States, is being manufactured in the People's Republic of China, but the Chinese government has banned its dispensation by pharmacies at home. The Beijing Youth Daily reported on October 10 that the State Drug Administration has banned the sale of abortion pills at pharmacies and said Beijing drugstores had already stopped selling the drugs. Specialists are saying unregulated use of the abortion drug could lead to incomplete abortions, major blood loss, infections and impotence." Republican National Coalition for Life FaxNotes-November 2, 2001

"'It's an amazing admission coming from a country where abortion is a government policy,'...The Chinese government has ordered the RU-486 abortion pill off the nation's pharmacy shelves, citing numerous reports of women who required hospitalization because of the drug's side effects. 'We have repeatedly called on President Bush and the FDA to take similar action in this country'...but thus far our pleas have been ignored.'" Judie Brown, in the Judie Brown Report

"New coercion in Chinese population campaign: Unhappy that cooperation with their one-child policy is not 100 percent, Chinese officials are cracking down even harder on the poor in the mountainous region of Guangdong. As many as 20,000 more abortions, some as late as nine months, are expected to be forcibly performed on women of the province, some as late as nine months, and all approved births will be followed by forced sterilization. Meanwhile, discrimination in access to education and health care against 'unofficial' children—those born without permission—continues throughout China.

"New Scientist magazine reported last year that a rising number of babies born with birth defects were being seen as attributable to RU-486 in developing countries. (See CNR vol. 2, no. 4, pg.4)" "Deaths related to RU-486 have been reported in the U.S. (on a Canadian citizen) and in France where the drug began." Source: Family News in Focus Press Release 10/25/01.

Canadian woman dies in abortion pill trials: A Canadian woman's death during the testing of the abortion pill RU-486 has prompted the suspension of the study..." The above two paragraphs were taken from the Issues Update section of Celebrate Life, November-December 2001.

Here's more from the Winter 2002 NPLA Lifeline: "Even Eduardo Sakiz, the CEO of RU-486's original manufacturer, has since admitted taking the abortion pill causes 'an appalling psychological effect' for many women." "...abortion pill...has been linked to fetal deformation and carcinogenicity in mother's milk when women who have taken RU-486 try to go through with a later pregnancy." I don't know whether sound scientific evidence exists to back up these statements. But even if they're only hearsay, and I was a woman considering taking the pill, I'd still like to hear about them.

Have I made my point on RU-486 yet?

From: The Pro-Life Infonet infonet@prolifeinfo.org
Reply-To: Steven Ertelt infonet@prolifeinfo.org
Subject: Family Research Council Responds to FDA RU 486 Report
Source: Family Research Council; April 18, 2002

Family Research Council Responds to FDA RU 486 Report

"Washington, DC—A new letter posted on the website of the Food and Drug Administration by the manufacturer of RU-486 raises serious questions about the drug's safety and the FDA's efforts to protect women's health. The letter contains information about six women who have had adverse health affects after taking the drug-two of whom died. Three of the women suffered bleeding after rupture of ectopic pregnancies, which are not aborted by the drug and can be diagnosed by ultrasound.

Dr. John Diggs, Jr., advisory board member for Family Research Council (FRC), sent a letter to the FDA Thursday calling for the agency to mandate ultrasound evaluation by a qualified examiner for ectopic pregnancy before prescription of RU-486.

In a Q & A section on the FDA's website, it says the 'FDA will approve a drug if it determines that the benefits exceed the risks for the approved use' and that 'when FDA approves a drug, the labeling includes information on benefits and risks and the appropriate dosing regimens...'

'What is the benefit of RU-486 that enhances women's health?' Dr. Diggs asked. 'Medications are used to treat illnesses. Then, we physicians make the assessment that the treatment, although risky, has great benefit over the illness. However, pregnancy is not an illness, but a natural, necessary, and healthy physiological state. Without a description of the illness, it is impossible to conclude that there is a benefit that merits the substantial risks to the mother. Obviously, the unborn child does not benefit in any fashion from this drug.'

Dr. Diggs also pointed out that the manufacturer's letter on RU-486 does not accurately describe and mandate the technology available to diagnose ectopic pregnancy. 'The standard of care to rule out ectopic pregnancy is pelvic ultrasound with the possible addition of transvaginal ultrasound. The vague terminology the FDA directs to practitioners using this regimen is inadequate and does not protect the health of women,' he said."

The RU-486 Files, http://www.ru486.org/-Articles and Newsclippings, Books, Related Resources, and Related Web Sites.

From: Jennifer Bingham, Executive Director, Susan B. Anthony List SBAList@DemocracyData.com Subject: Revisiting the Drug-Induced Abortion Pill—RU486! Date: 26 Aug 2002 16:30:41-0400 During the closing days of the Clinton administration, the drug RU-486, used for drug-induced abortions, was approved! Today, it is a common form of abortion and even worse, at least 180 schools nationwide have been discovered passing out this "medication" to young female students! This MUST be STOPPED! Not only is this drug destroying the lives of unborn children, it is detrimental to the health of the mother. Close examination by medical professionals tells another story as they describe the pill as a tremendous health risk for the pregnant woman. The FDA rushed to approve the drug-induced abortion pill, RU-486, in 2000 in a fashion that could have severe – even fatal-side effects for women. Not only is this destroying the lives of unborn children but it is also putting the life of the mother at risk.

From: The Pro-Life Infonet, Steven Ertelt infonet@prolifeinfo.org
Source: Cybercast News Service; November 21, 2002

"Bush Nominee for FDA Panel Says RU 486 Unsafe

Washington, DC—Dr. David Hager, a pro-life obstetrician chosen by President George W. Bush to head the Food and Drug Administration advisory committee that previously approved the dangerous RU 486 abortion drug, said Tuesday he opposed the drug because of safety considerations and inadequate testing.

The Christian physician is under consideration by the Bush administration to head the Food and Drug Administration's Reproductive Health Drugs Advisory Committee and has been the subject of opposition from abortion advocates who oppose his nomination. Even though the committee's most immediate task will be to consider issues related to hormone replacement therapy, Hager's pending appointment has drawn criticism from groups who claim he will try to hinder FDA approval of certain drugs and medical devices and make abortion more difficult to obtain. Speaking at a Capitol Hill forum hosted by Concerned Women for America, he made no secret of the fact that he thinks the FDA flouted its normal drug approval process in approving the abortion regimen RU-486, also known as Mifeprex, in September 2000. 'This certainly violated the general trend,' of drug approval, said Hager, who thinks the drug should be withdrawn from the market until further tests can be conducted to determine whether the drug is safe. Short of pulling the drug from the market, he said the FDA should amend RU-486 regulations to restrict its use to adult women and require that those prescribing the drug administer an ultrasound to determine whether there is a uterine pregnancy. If an ultrasound doesn't show a uterine pregnancy, that's a signal to check for an ectopic (fallopian tube) pregnancy. According to the FDA three women have died from using RU 486 in association with an ectopic pregnancy. Because RU-486 causes some of the same symptoms as do ectopic pregnancies, like bleeding and cramping, Hager and other doctors fear that the ectopic pregnancies will go untreated, causing injury or death. He and other critics of RU-486 say that the final FDA regulations do not track with precautions taken during the French and American drug trials. For example, the trials did use ultrasounds on patients, a practice that is optional under current FDA RU-486 regulations. And adolescents did not participate in the two trials, yet the FDA waived the so-called 'pediatric rule' that requires testing on children and adolescents before a drug is approved for their use. Concerned Women for America joined the American Association of Pro-Life Obstetricians and Gynecologists (AAPLOG), and the Christian Medical Association, of which Hager is a spokesman, in petitioning the FDA to halt all distribution and marketing of the RU-486. 'FDA, in approving Mifeprex, acted in a manner inconsistent with its statutory authorization, regulations and well-established policies,' commented Dr. Donna Harrison, speaking for AAPLOG. 'The approval of Mifeprex was ...arbitrary, capricious |and| an abuse of discretion,' said Harrison. 'It must be reversed.' Two groups most responsible for introducing Mifeprex to American consumers, Danco Laboratories and the Population Council, have both defended the abortion drug, claiming it safe and effective. 'Every aspect of the drug's manufacturing, marketing and distribution was reviewed by the FDA prior to approval,' a Danco spokesperson said in April. 'We fully stand behind the safety and efficacy of the Mifeprex regimen.'

The status of Hager's appointment was uncertain Tuesday. Hager himself declined to comment on it, referring such inquiries to FDA Deputy Assistant Secretary for Public Affairs Bill Pierce, who did not return calls seeking comment."

From: The Pro-Life Infonet Reply-To: Steven Ertelt infonet@prolifeinfo.org
Source: Associated Press; December 26, 2002

Bush Admin Appoints Pro-Life Doc to FDA Panel

Washington, DC—A physician who has been criticized by pro-abortion lobbyists for his pro-life views on abortion was named to a Food and Drug Administration panel on women's health policy. Dr. W. David Hager, a University of Kentucky obstetrician-gynecologist, was among 11 physicians appointed Tuesday by FDA Commissioner Mark McClellan to the agency's Advisory Committee for Reproductive Health Drugs. Hager has questioned the safety of the dangerous abortion pill RU-486 (mifepristone) and opposes abortion. Pro-abortion activists are concerned about Hager's appointment because he participated in a Christian Medical Association campaign this year that attempted to reverse the FDA committee's 1996 recommendation that led to RU-486 being approved. The National Organization for Women and six other abortion advocacy groups have called Hager's selection a conflict of interest in the name of ideology. The Planned Parenthood Federation of America issued a statement Tuesday calling the appointment of Hager and other doctors on the panel 'a frontal assault on reproductive rights that will imperil women's health.' But Hager, a part-time professor of obstetrics and gynecology, said his beliefs won't compromise his judgment. 'Yes, I'm pro-life,' he told the Courier-Journal of Louisville, Ky. 'But that's not going to keep me from objectively evaluating medication. I believe there are some safety concerns [about RU-486] and they should be evaluated.'

The advisory committee has not met for two years, and its entire membership had lapsed. Its job is to review and evaluate data-and make recommendations-on the safety and effectiveness of marketed and experimental drugs for use in obstetrics, gynecology, and related specialties. In addition to Hager and Giudice, the other physicians appointed were Leslie Gay Bernitsky, a urologist from Albuquerque, N.M.; Susan A. Crockett of the University of Texas Health Science Center at San Antonio; Nancy Dickey, chancellor of the Texas A&M College of Medicine; Scott Shields Emerson of the University of Washington, Seattle; Michael Furman Greene of Massachusetts General Hospital in Boston; Vivian Lewis of the University of Rochester Medical Center in Rochester, N.Y;. George A. Marcones of the University of Pennsylvania, Philadelphia; Valerie Montgomery Rice of the University of Kansas Medical Center in Kansas City, Kan.; and Joseph Barney Stanford of the University of Utah, Salt Lake City.—" It's very strange that they wouldn't want anybody on this committee that didn't share their viewpoint. They want to have the pro-life viewpoint completely suppressed, ostracized, scorned, and ignored. The fact is they just want abortion in any and every form and don't even care whether it's safe for the mother.

"Just before New Year's, President Bush appointed Dr. David Hager to the Food and Drug Administration's Advisory Committee for Reproductive Health Drugs. Said Wendy Wright, senior policy director for Concerned Women for America, 'The President's appointees represent diverse views and a variety of medical backgrounds. The FDA advisory panels are supposed to be places of open inquiry. One must carefully consider why Dr. Hager's critics wish to silence him.' Planned Parenthood and other groups opposed Hager because he has questioned the safety of the abortion pill, RU-486." Taken from "Human Events, The Week Of January 6, 2003". "Both *Good Housekeeping* magazine and *Ladies' Home Journal* have named Hager one of the country's best doctors for women." Life Dynamics News, February, 2003.

"As of 6:27 p.m. EST Monday, December 9, 2002 FDA Says Certain High-Risk Drugs Can't Be Imported By OTESA MIDDLETON Of DOW JONES NEWSWIRES WASHINGTON—Certain approved prescription medicines, including the abortion pill and Novartis AG's (NVS) schizophrenia drug Clozaril, will not be allowed into the U.S. from other countries and consumers shouldn't buy them on the Internet, the U.S. Food and Drug Administration said Monday. The FDA said these drugs are approved for use in the U.S. with certain restrictions, and if the products don't originate in America or are bought on the Web, the appropriate safety information may not be included."

The article above was taken from The Wall Street Journal Online, and identified ten drugs. I'll only quote the paragraph on RU486. "The agency doesn't want women taking Danco Laboratories' Mifipex, also called RU-486 or the abortion pill, without physician supervision." For more information you can contact: "Otesa Middleton, Dow Jones Newswires; 202-862-6654; otesa.middleton@dowjones.com".

From: The Pro-Life Infonet Steven Ertelt infonet@prolifeinfo.org
Source: Associated Press, Pro-Life Infonet; December 9, 2002

"Bush Administration Cracks Down on Illegally Imported Abortion Drugs

Washington, DC—The Bush administration is ordering 10 prescription drugs to be detained at the U.S. border if patients buy them abroad instead of through their doctors, calling the medications too risky for unsupervised use. Included in the FDA directive: the dangerous abortion drug mifepristone (otherwise known as RU 486 or Mifeprex). All of the drugs at issue can cause serious side effects and thus are allowed to sell in the United States only under severe restrictions, such as curbs on which doctors can prescribe them and what patients qualify. According to an FDA alert sent to the Pro-Life Infonet, the 'FDA has determined that unapproved versions of mifepristone manufactured outside the U.S. are being promoted in this country for use to end pregnancy. Due to the risks to the safety of the user in inadequately controlled settings, mifepristone should be considered inappropriate for release under the Personal Import Guidance.' The only approved company distributing the abortion drug is Danco Laboratories, LLC, of New York. The Clinton administration hurriedly approved the abortion drug, then known as RU 486. Pro-life groups have called on the Bush administration to review the approval process citing women's deaths and other severe medical complications following usage of the abortion drug. The Food and Drug Administration noticed Internet advertisements for some of the drugs that entice patients to order them directly, ignoring the safety restrictions. It is illegal to sell prescription drugs without a doctor's valid prescription, so the FDA is taking steps to shut those Web sites—and warned consumers Monday not to buy the drugs in question over the Internet. Because some of the Web sites are foreign, the FDA also asked U.S. Customs officials to seize shipments of the drugs from abroad. 'This is a loophole we're seeking to plug,' said FDA drug chief Dr. Janet Woodcock."

"Following the deaths of two women and hospitalization of at least twenty more, National Pro-Life Alliance Legislative Director Michael Muench has called upon President Bush to 'immediately revoke the government's approval of RU-486, the so-called 'abortion pill'. The two recent deaths and other incidents of serious side effects have forced even the U.S. Food and Drug Administration (FDA) and Danco Laboratories, the New York firm that distributes the abortion pill, to issue warning letters to physicians. By the FDA's own account, in addition to the two deaths, twenty-two other women required hospitalization or another 'intervention to prevent permanent impairment or damage.' Side effects suffered by women after taking the drug include hemorrhage and severe bacterial infections. One woman, age 21, suffered a heart attack three days after taking the abortion pill. She had no prior history of heart trouble. RU-486 is used in combination with another drug (prostaglandin) to carry out abortions. As still another sign of danger- Searle, the maker of the second drug-firmly disavows abortion as a legitimate use for its drug and has actively fought to prevent its label from sanctioning such a use. Searle has also written a letter of its own to physicians, warning against using the drug to provoke an abortion. President Bush has stated his opposition to RU-486 publicly." NPLA LifeLine, Winter 2003

Breast Cancer

Chicago Tribune-May 21, 2001: "Why all the silence about abortion and breast cancer? Dennis Byrne. Dennis Byrne is a Chicago-area writer and public affairs consultant...millions of women are being deceived about this risk, or denied the knowledge of important studies. Twenty-seven out of 34 independent studies conducted throughout the world (including 13 out of 14 conducted in the United States) have linked abortion and breast cancer. Seventeen of these studies show a statistically significant relationship. Five show more than a two-fold elevation of risk. In turn, the abortion industry says all those studies are trumped by one study, whose methodology, critics say, is seriously flawed. The biological hypothesis is that during pregnancy, a woman's breasts begin developing a hormone that causes cells—both normal and pre-cancerous—to multiply dramatically. If the pregnancy is carried to term, those undifferentiated cells are shaped into milk ducts and a naturally occurring process shuts off the rapid cell multiplication. An induced abortion leaves a women with more undifferentiated cells, and so, more cancer-vulnerable cells."

"The United Kingdom's Royal College of Obstetricians and Gynecologists became the first medical organization to warn its abortion practitioners that the abortion-breast cancer link 'could not be disregarded.' It said that the methodology of the principal ABC (abortion-breast cancer) researcher, Joel Brind, was sound. John Kindley, an attorney, warned in a 1999 Wisconsin Law Review article that physicians who do not inform their patients of the ABC link expose themselves to medical malpractice suits. He concluded that about 1 out of 100 women who have had an induced abortion die from breast cancer attributable to the abortion." "The American Cancer Society Web page lists induced abortions...among elements that may be related to breast cancer, and that the relationship is being studied. Earlier, Dr. Janet Daling and colleagues at the Fred Hutchinson Cancer Research Center, in a study commissioned by the National Cancer Institute, found that 'among women who had been pregnant at least once, the risk of breast cancer in those who had...an induced abortion was 50 percent higher than among other women.' The risk of breast cancer for women under 18 or over 29 who had induced abortions was more than two-fold. Women who abort and have a family history of breast cancer increase their risk 80 percent. The increased risk of women under 18 with that family history was incalculably high...'I would have loved to have found no association between breast cancer and abortion, but our research is rock solid, and our data is accurate. It's not a matter of believing, it's a matter of what is.'" "If you want to know more, look in on the Web page of the Palos Heights-based Coalition on Abortion/Breast Cancer", http://www.AbortionBreastCancer.com/; or to really get an in depth review of the various studies done, go to: http://www.etters.net/cancer.htm. An increasingly discouraging development is the degree to which pro-abortion advocates have taken over organizations that used to be widely respected, such as the National Cancer Institute, and most recently the American Medical Association-politicizing them.

"Let's look at two landmark studies, the first by Dr. H. Howe in in 1999. Using New York state official Health Department records, he found that aborting a woman's first pregnancy was associated with a 1.7 times increased risk of breast cancer under age 40. If she aborted her second or third pregnancy, her risk was increased four fold. Worldwide attention was focused on the second study in 1994 by Dr. Janet Daling. She has a reputation, worldwide, as an accomplished and highly respected epidemiologist. She found that an induced abortion increased the risk of breast cancer before age 45 by 50%. If done before age 18, it increased by 150%. If done after age 30, it increased by 110%. If she had a family member with breast cancer and aborted after age 30, her risk was increased by 270%. All 12 women in her study with such a family member, who aborted before age 18, got breast cancer before age 45…Dr. Joel Brind published a meta analysis in 1996 of the 28 legitimate studies available. His conclusion was that there was a significant independent risk for breast cancer associated with induced abortion. The reaction to these and other studies has been convincing enough to many people, including legislators who, in several states, have passed laws to require the abortionist to warn the prospective abortive client that this will increase her risk of breast cancer." Taken from an article in Life Issues Connector, April 2003 issue, by J. C. Willke, MD.

Also, see "Abortion Breast Cancer Link", by Dr. Joel Brind, Ph.D., http://www.abortioncancer.com/.

Another source of information is the book "Breast Cancer, Its Link to Abortion", and an associated pamphlet, by Dr. Chris Kahlenborn, which can be obtained through One More Soul, 1-800-307-7685.

"In August, the Ann Arbor-based Thomas More Center for Law and Justice, http://www.thomasmore.org/, announced that it had filed a lawsuit in California against Planned Parenthood Federation of America and its San Diego affiliate. The suit claims PP is in violation of the state's business code by failing to provide women with truthful information about the breast cancer related risks of abortion." STOPP International's Ryan Report, November 2001

"Mattson vs. Red River Women's Clinic: In North Dakota, Red River Women's clinic was brought to court September 11 on charges of false advertising. Brochures at the clinic claim that there is no evidence to link abortion with increased breast cancer risks." Issues Update, Celebrate Life, November-December 2001.

"British Study: Half of Expected Breast Cancer Cases 'Attributable to Abortion' London, England: British researchers from the Populations and Pensions Research Institution, an independent group of statisticians, reported that women who procure abortions double their risks of breast cancer, said The Age (England) on December 4, 2001. The incidences of breast cancer and abortion in Finland, Sweden and Great Britain were examined by the statisticians who concluded that the increasing frequency of the disease was directly related to a climb in the abortion rates. The statisticians determined that as many as one half of the cases of breast cancer in England and Wales between 1997 and 2023 'will be attributable to abortion.' Patrick Carroll, a statistician and author, revealed that breast cancer rates in England will surge from 35,110 in 1997 to 77,000 in 2023. This dramatic increase will occur because of the large number of abortions performed before first full term pregnancy. A woman who's never experienced a full term pregnancy unknowingly subjects herself to greater risks for the disease by having an abortion because her breast cells are in an immature state and are especially vulnerable to carcinogens at that time. Beginning at the outset of pregnancy, estrogen levels climb 2000% and cause a terrific multiplication of breast cells. When she procures an abortion, she is left with more cancer vulnerable cells than she had prior to the pregnancy. The maturing process known as "differentiation" only takes place in the third trimester and provides a woman with more cancer resistant cells.

Joel Brind, Ph.D., president of the Breast Cancer Prevention Institute, said, 'This implicates a risk factor that is a matter of choice. Simply undergoing |an abortion| once measurably increases the risk of breast cancer. We are talking about thousands of cases of breast cancer over the next twenty years. This is a very sobering statistic.'

Patrick Carroll asserted that, 'Breast cancer incidence has risen…in parallel with rising abortion rates. There is no doubt there is a causal relationship. Perhaps as many as 50 percent of these cases will be attributable to abortion and unless there is a major improvement in treatment, the number of women who die from the disease will rise alarmingly.'"

February 2002: "In December, British scientists found that women women who have abortions are up to twice as likely to suffer from breast cancer and reported that 'up to 50% of breast cancer cases in England and Wales over the next 26 years will be attributable to abortion.' These findings are scarcely the first of their kind. In 1986, four famed epidemiologists, including representatives from the National Institutes of Health and Centers for Disease Control, published a letter admitting, 'Induced abortion before first term pregnancy increases the risk of breast cancer.' The Coalition on Abortion/Breast Cancer reports that, 'Twenty-eight out of 37 worldwide studies published since 1957 have shown a positive association between abortion and breast cancer.' But women are not being warned of this lethal link—even though breast cancer is the greatest cancer killer among women aged 20 and 59. Nearly 46,000 women will die this year and 184,000 will be diagnosed. But just as Big Tobacco had an interest in suppressing information, so now the $3 billion a year abortion industry has a stake in enforcing silence... Research shows that a single abortion is comparable to the risk from lung cancer from long-term heavy smoking, but because the ABC Link touches an ideologically charged issue, the connection is ignored...4,000 American women unwittingly put themselves at risk every day. Louisiana, Montana and Mississippi now require that warning information be given to mothers considering abortion. The same should be true nationwide. Women comprise a far greater percentage of our population than smokers ever did...". "The American, a monthly publication of The American Cause". http://www.theamericancause.org/

"Despite all their talk about the 'constitutional right to choose,' pro-abortion forces do NOT want information like this to be aired in public, much less given to girls and women faced with an unwanted pregnancy. The simple fact is this: groups like Planned Parenthood have a vested interest in the abortion industry that is the biggest source of their funding-their lip-service to the idea of 'choice' is just that! The only choice they want women to make is to have abortions...and they desperately want to keep valid, medically proven information about the physical dangers that abortion presents away from them at all costs!" "We want them to know that their choice includes the choice to NOT have an abortion...". Bay Buchanan, March 2002 Here are some of the facts they present: "One in every nine American women will get breast cancer-the greatest female cancer killer between ages 20 and 59. An abortion raises a woman's chances of getting breast cancer by age 45 by 50%. For women under 18: Risk increases 150%. Abortion after 8 weeks raises the risk 800%. For women with a family history of breast cancer: Risk increases 80%. In a study by pro-choice Dr. Janet Daling, 12 women who had abortions before age 18, and had a family history, all 12 had breast cancer before age 45. The risk is 'incalculably high' for these teenagers, the doctor reported. A study at Howard University showed that an African American woman who has an abortion has a 50% increased risk of getting breast cancer by age 40, 180% increased risk in their forties, and 370% increased risk after age 50. Four states require doctors to warn women considering abortion about this cancer link; 12 more are considering legislation. If pro-choicers want women to make informed decisions, why don't they want us to have all the facts? They don't because they're not pro-choice. They're pro abortion."

"Scientist Says 'Abortion Explains Entire Rise in Breast Cancer since mid 1980's,' (Source: The Coalition on Abortion/Breast Cancer) November, 2002.

Last year an annual report on the state of cancer in the U.S. from 1973 to 1998 was published in the Journal of the National Cancer Institute (JNCI). |1| The National Cancer Institute, the American Cancer Society and the Centers for Disease Control collaborated on it. Breast cancer statistics revealed a more than 40% jump in incidence of the disease during that period.

The increase since the mid 1980's, however, was limited to younger women (not older women)-those young enough to have had abortions when the procedure was legalized in 1973. A similar disparity between age groups exists in Marin County, California which has the highest incidence of breast cancer in the nation. |2|

Joel Brind, Ph.D., the lead author of a 1996 paper which evaluated studies exploring the abortion-breast cancer (ABC) link |3|, told the Coalition on Abortion/Breast Cancer in November, 'Abortion can explain the entire rise in breast cancer since the mid 1980's, and it's not just because the rise is in women young enough to have had an abortion; it's also that the absolute numbers of increased cases fall within the range of the numbers we predicted in our 1996 meta-analysis.'

The JNCI report's chief author was Holly Howe. Yet, in 1989 she was also the lead author of an ABC study considered to have a superior design due to its reliance on medical records, instead of interviews. She and her colleagues reported a statistically significant 90% risk among post-abortive New York women. Statistical significance means that researchers are at least 95% confident that the results obtained were not due to chance or error.

Nevertheless, the 2001 report in the JNCI contains glaring omissions. Although it says, 'Prevention is a key strategy for reducing the national cancer burden,' nothing whatsoever is said about abortion or ways to prevent breast cancer. Moreover, no explanation is offered by Howe et al. for the huge disparity in incidence between the Roe v. Wade generation and older women.

Women are dying of the disease in increasing numbers. Taxpayers, health insurance policyholders, employers and breast cancer donors are unnecessarily paying billions of dollars in additional costs for cancer research, health insurance claims and Planned Parenthood funding because the nation's cancer watchdogs lack the necessary political courage to tell women that abortion causes breast cancer."

"Australian attorney Charles Francis has won the first-known set-tlement in a landmark case in which the plaintiff sued because her physician hadn't told her that researchers have associated abortion with breast cancer." From the January/February 2002 RNC For Life Report, by way of Australian women's group Endeavour Forum, http://www.endeavourforum.org.au/.

Angela LanFranchi, M.D., F.A.C.S. 515 Church St., Suite 1 Bound Brook, New Jersey 08805 732/356-0770 Diplomat of the American Board of Surgery Fellow of American College of Surgeons Statement to the Press Population Research Institute Conference Santa Clara, California April 5, 2002 Although I observed in my own practice in the early 1990s an inordinate number of 30 year olds with breast cancer who had no family history, but had abortions as teenagers, it wasn't until 1999 that I informed my patients of this risk. That was when a Harvard professor in charge of risk assessment at a well known Boston clinic told me she knew abortion was a risk factor for breast cancer and considered it in the evaluation of her patients. Although she chose not to publicly speak about this issue, she encouraged me to do so. I was reluctant at first to follow her suggestion. I depend upon referrals from obstetrician-gynecologists, some of whom do abortions, and I was worried they would stop sending me patients when they heard me give lectures on the abortion-breast cancer link. I lecture on the subject because it is unjust to withhold pertinent medical information from patients that is so well documented in the literature for over 20 years and that is in my textbooks. It amounts to child abuse to take a teenager in a crisis pregnancy for an abortion. At best, it will give her a 30% risk of breast cancer in her lifetime. At worst, if she also has a family history of breast cancer, it will nearly guarantee this. As a mother, I need to be informed of this to protect my daughter...There is overwhelming and convincing evidence that abortion and breast cancer are linked, along with a well described biologic mechanism. Twenty-eight out of 37 studies have been published and women still don't know. It's not only embarrassment and denial that cause doctors to ignore this data now. It is also the fear of malpractice. How can an abortionist not be held liable for increasing a woman's risk of breast cancer and not tell her? It is unfortunate, but it has become my belief that it will be lawyers who force the medical community to address this issue.

On May 24, 2002, the American Association of ProLife Obstetricians and Gynecologists released a paper on the Abortion-Breast Cancer Link which essentially reiterated and concurred with all the above statements. I have not included their research paper here because it would just be too repetitive. The reason I rehash as much as I do is because I know from experience that the pro-death people will always deny everything about anything pro-life ("It's all lies."); and, therefore, I feel the need to build an unshakable case-not just speculate.

"From: The Pro-Life Infonet infonet@prolifeinfo.org
Reply-To: Steven Ertelt infonet@prolifeinfo.org
Subject:Cancer Group Pulls Biased Web Page on Abortion-Breast Cancer

Source: Coalition on Abortion/Breast Cancer; July 2, 2002

Cancer Group Pulls Biased Web Page on Abortion-Breast Cancer

Chicago, IL—The president of a women's group, the Coalition on Abortion/Breast Cancer, reported today that the National Cancer Institute (NCI) has taken down an inaccurate web page discussing the abortion-breast cancer research. The NCI's fact sheet has been heavily criticized in recent months by this women's group, a prominent scientist |1|, at least three physicians and 28 members of Congress, including Rep. Dave Weldon, M.D. |2| They've objected to the agency's misrepresentation of the research, reliance on erroneous studies, confusion of the effects of miscarriage and abortion, inclusion of false statements and refusal to acknowledge the deleterious effects of abortion on the confirmed breast cancer risk factor-postponement of first full term pregnancy. Mrs. Karen Malec, president of the women's group, said, "We're delighted that the National Cancer Institute has pulled its web page discussing the abortion-breast cancer link. The web page misinformed women about research paid for by U.S. taxpayers and even contained lies about the findings reported in the medical literature." |3| Early last month, 28 members of Congress sent a letter to Secretary of Health and Human Services Tommy Thompson requesting a review of the NCI's fact sheet and calling its information "scientifically inaccurate and misleading to the public." They asked Secretary Thompson to check the web page "for accuracy and bias" and to take it down until after the conclusion of the review. The congressional representatives scored the agency for having suggested that "women who have had either induced or spontaneous abortions have the same risk as other women for developing breast cancer, "when in fact 28 out of 37 studies worldwide and 13 of 15 American studies report risk elevations. [Reference: http://abortionbreastcancer.com/ABC_Research.htm| They condemned the NCI for depending on a single study, Melbye et al. 1997, to deny a relationship between abortion and the disease, "although that study contains many significant flaws."|4| "In 1999, the agency was accused by a scientist of publishing an 'outright lie,'" reported Mrs. Malec, "because it said on its website that, 'The scientific rationale for an association between abortion and breast cancer is based on limited experimental data in rats and is not consistent with human data.' However, the NCI had paid, at least in part, for most of the 13 American studies done by that date, and all but one of them had reported increased risk." Mrs. Malec concluded, "We strongly encourage the NCI to come clean and to tell the truth. Tell women how many studies report risk elevations. Fully disclose the strong biological and epidemiological evidence which has been gathered since 1957 and which implicates abortion as a risk factor for breast cancer."

The Coalition on Abortion/Breast Cancer is an international women's organization founded to protect the health and save the lives of women by educating and providing information on abortion as a risk factor for breast cancer.

References:

1. "Latest Web Page from the National Cancer Institute: A well cooked bowl of factoids," by Joel Brind, Ph.D.; RFM News, March 23, 2002; http://abortionbreastcancer.com/Public_Policy.htm
2. U.S. Representative Chris Smith, et al. (June 7, 2002) Letter to Secretary of Health and Human Services Tommy Thompson
3. Press Release, Coalition on Abortion/Breast Cancer; March 20, 2002.
4. Melbye et al. (1997) New Engl J Med 336:81-5.

From: The Pro-Life Infonet Steven Ertelt infonet@prolifeinfo.org
Source: Coalition on Abortion/Breast Cancer; December 16, 2002

National Cancer Institute Still Biased on Abortion-Breast Cancer

Chicago, IL—The Coalition on Abortion/Breast Cancer reported today that the National Cancer Institute (NCI) has published new statements about research examining the relationship between abortion and breast cancer on a web page posted November 25, 2002. The page is entitled 'Early Reproductive Events and Breast Cancer.' This action comes after serious accusations of scientific misconduct were leveled at the agency during a four year period by more than two dozen members of Congress and six medical experts, including Congressman Dave Weldon, M.D. and former Congressman Tom Coburn, M.D. [1] After reviewing the NCI's new statements, Karen Malec, president of the women's organization, commented that: 'The NCI's failure to identify abortion among its list of risk factors for breast cancer and its continued omission of critical facts represent a form of gross scientific misconduct designed to mislead women about the safety of abortion. The agency continues to conceal the evidence that connects the delayed first full term pregnancy effect with abortion, an effect that has been universally recognized by medical experts since 1970. [2] Moreover, the biological and epidemiological evidence implicating abortion as an independent risk factor for breast cancer is staggering, but the anti-information NCI erroneously asserts that 'the data have been inconsistent.' What risk factor, other than abortion, could have as much evidence amassed against it, but still be excluded from the NCI's list of risk factors? Thousands of women will lose their lives because the NCI's uncaring bureaucrats evidently lack political courage.' 'It is heartening, however, that the spectacularly flawed study, Melbye et al. 1997, is not being used to disprove 29 studies reporting risk elevations,' continued Mrs. Malec. [3] 'It's encouraging that the NCI did not mislead women by confusing the effects of miscarriage with that of induced abortion which creates the false impression that these different biological events are one in the same. The agency also dropped its blatant lie that the study, Tang et al. 2000, found evidence of report bias.' [4] The lead author of the 1996 review and meta-analysis of the worldwide research [5], Joel Brind, Ph.D., reviewed the November web page and commented that, 'It's a step in the right direction, but it is clear that this is temporary until the agency convenes a workshop on this subject. It remains to be seen whether they will really put in information that is useful to the public about abortion and breast cancer.' Malec concluded that, 'The NCI's long-standing practice of lying and omitting crucial pieces of information makes it crystal-clear that women can't rely on the agency's self-interested bureaucrats, the nation's politicians and cancer organizations to protect their lives. This barefaced scientific misconduct will not stop until women demand to be told the truth. Women must become activists in order to stop the lies and protect their health, as well as the health of their sisters and daughters.' The Coalition on Abortion /Breast Cancer is an international women's organization founded to protect the health and save the lives of women by educating and providing information on abortion as a risk factor for breast cancer.

References:
1. http://abortionbreastcancer.com/Public_Policy.htm
2. MacMahon et al. (1970) Bull Wld Health Org 43:209-21.
3. Melbye et al. (1997) N Engl J Med 336(2):81-5.
4. Tang et al. (2000) Am J Epidemiol 151:1139-43.
5. Brind et al. (1996) J Epidemiol Community Health 50:481-96.

Some other organizations that recognize the Abortion Breast Cancer Link that I haven't mentioned before are the Breast Cancer Prevention Institute, the National Physicians Center for Family Resources, the Polycarp Research Institute, and the Catholic Medical Association. In addition, the 60 year old Association of American Physicians and Surgeons (AAPS) recently published two articles on abortion risk in its Journal of American Physicians and Surgeons Summer 2003, entitled: "The Abortion-Breast Cancer Link: How Politics Trumped Science and Informed Consent", and "Induced Abortion and Risk of Later Premature Births", which can be found on the internet at-http://www.jpands.org/jpands0802.htm.

Other Health Risks

"Abortionist Convicted of Manslaughter Phoenix, AZ—Abortionist John Biskind, 75, and his former administrator, Carol Stuart-Schadoff, 63, were convicted of manslaughter in the botched abortion death of LouAnne Herron three years ago. Herron, 33, bled to death April 17, 1998, after Biskind tore a two inch wide hole in her uterus during an abortion. According to medical assistant Teresa Jensen, Herron begged to know what was wrong with her as she lay bleeding to death in a Phoenix abortion facility. 'Is everything OK? What's wrong with me?' LouAnne Herron reportedly asked as blood collected under her body at the A-Z Women's Center abortion facility."

"Woman Hospitalized After Botched Abortion Phoenix, AZ—A 39-year-old woman was hospitalized with complications from an abortion and had to have an emergency hysterectomy." "The woman was taken by ambulance to St. Luke's Medical Center, where a surgery team apparently was waiting."

"Abortions at 28 weeks...involve the unpleasant business of dismembering a fetus measuring upwards of 14 inches" (read "child"). The preceding paragraphs were taken from the Care Net Report.

"In my book, 'Lime 5', published in 1996, I catalog 33 separate abortionists who have been arrested or disciplined by the medical board for sexual assault and misconduct...resulting in abortionists being put in jail, clinics closing, and babies and their mothers saved from the horrors of abortion." "...recent example. This past year a high profile abortionist Brian Finkel was arrested on 9 charges of sexual assault. In the weeks that followed, over 100 women came forward with stories concerning the type of treatment they received from this man. Where are the radical feminists screaming for justice? Abortion itself is apparently more important than the physical and psychological well-being of the women they say they represent." Mark Crutcher, President, LDI. "...we will not back down until the last American Death camp has been padlocked."

It seems that a lot of women have been led to think that because abortion is legal now, it's risk free to the mother. Nothing could be further from the truth. Christina Dunigan, the Guide to Pro-Life Views at About.com, posted a link to a list of mothers who had died from their abortions; it's kind of like a war memorial for moms. It will probably be a lot higher than you would guess. I decided not to count; there just seemed to be too many of them. Unfortunately, About.com changed, and that list is no longer there. However, I tracked down a piece of it, and you can go there, if it still exists, at url: http://prolife.about.com/cs/abortionmortality/index.htm. Hopefully, it will still be there.

"...more women are killed, physically injured, raped and psychologically traumatized under 'legal' abortion than before Roe v. Wade in 1973." "The truth is, abortion clinics want the highest possible number of abortions to keep the cash rolling in."

"...if you survey physicians on what they think about abortionists, virtually all of them—even 'pro-abortion' doctors—regard abortionists as losers—the dregs of the medical profession. Legalized abortion keeps them out of jail, but they're still regarded as scum by their fellow doctors!" Alan Keyes

"The CDC report also includes the troubling fact that in 1998, the most recent year for national data on abortion complications, nine women are known to have died as a result of abortion." These numbers are generally regarded as understated, because the cause of death may be altered to avoid problems. In California, a top state in the number of abortions performed, to the best of my knowledge, they don't report their statistics to the CDC-if at all. The quote came from The Pro-Life Infonet; December 17, 2002.

Driving back from the Washington, DC, March For Life, abortion was a common talk radio topic, given it was the 30th anniversary of Roe v. Wade. A woman was talking about the abortion she was practically coerced into getting when she was 19. In addition to not being able to put the regret out of her mind for many years; after she married and wanted to have children, she found that had become a difficult proposition. Her tubes had been blocked by the abortion, and the wall of her uterus had been damaged so that it was difficult for the placenta to attach. She eventually overcame her medical problems, and was able to have children. However, because she was still in her teens when she had the abortion, she pointed out that her risk of someday getting breast cancer had been increased by 600%. She had formed some type of pro-life organization, because of her experience; and seemed especially knowledgeable in the subject. She pointed out that for some reason, some women only had one child (based on her counseling activity). The implication was clear. If a woman had an abortion, she might be throwing away her one chance to have a child.

From: The Pro-Life Infonet Steven Ertelt infonet@prolifeinfo.org
Source: Elliot Institute; February 10, 2003

Abortion's Link to Premature Birth is No Mystery by David Reardon

[Pro-Life Infonet Note: David Reardon, Ph.D., is the director of the Elliot Institute in Springfield, Illinois.]

The March of Dimes has announced a major fund raising effort to understand and battle premature deliveries. March of Dimes medical director Dr. Nancy Green told Time magazine that the 27 percent rise in premature births over the last few decades 'is a mystery.'(http://www.time.com/time/magazine/article/0,9171,1101 030 210-418559,00.html)

Dr. Green's claim that the rise in premature birth rates is a mystery reflects either a distressing ignorance of the medical literature or a calculated case of selective recall.

At least 48 published studies have shown significantly higher risk of premature birth and low birth weight deliveries among women with a history of abortion. (1-48) One of the best, a Danish record based study (1), found the risk doubled after just one abortion. Multiple abortions increase the risk even more. A doubling of risk among an estimated one-fourth of delivering women who have a prior history of abortion would result in a 25 percent rise overall. The only real mystery surrounding the 27 percent rise in premature delivery rates among the post-Roe generation of women is why the March of Dimes has failed to call attention to this major risk factor. Their fact sheets downplay the risk of abortion, stating only that women are at higher risk of premature delivery if they 'have had more than three abortions or miscarriages.' Other risk factors such as drinking, smoking, and drug use are also elevated by a history of abortion. The March of Dimes professes that its position on abortion is one of neutrality. This is a good position to be in if one is trying to gather in donations from as large an audience as possible.

But the fact that the March of Dimes encourages prenatal screening for birth defects that can only be 'treated' by abortion does not support the claim that they are neutral. Instead, it supports the view that the March of Dimes is encouraging eugenic targeting of 'unfit' children that do not 'deserve to be born.' Their refusal to aggressively educate the public about the role abortion plays in heightening the risk posed to subsequent pregnancies is another sign that their claim of neutrality is a just a veneer over a pro-abortion, eugenic-minded 'charity.'

According to the March of Dimes, 'In 2000, hospital charges for 23,000 prematurity-related infant stays totaled $1.2 billion. The average charge was $58,000 per baby, compared to $4,300 for a typical newborn stay.' (http://www.marchofdimes.com/aboutus/791_6 775.asp) Treatment of these children through employer health plans is estimated at $4.7 billion per year. One fifth of these costs is attributable to extra cases of prematurity arising from abortion-related morbidity. Premature birth is the leading cause of neonatal death and is related to increased risk of cerebral palsy, vision and hearing loss, retardation and other lifelong health problems.

You can register your complaints about the March of Dimes coverup by calling 1-888-MODIMES. The list of 48 studies showing abortion's relationship to premature birth and low birth rate deliveries compiled by Brent Rooney can be found at http://www.vcn.bc.ca /~whatsup/APB-Major.html—". It's not too difficult to speculate that the cause of this would be a damaged uterus resulting in inadequate nourishment for the baby. Not scientific, but a common sense explanation, nevertheless; when you realize the instrument the abortionist is using, and can not observe, is capable of cutting up the infant-or poking a hole in the uterus.

People who claim to be pro-choice like to say abortion should be a decision between a woman and her doctor. The reality is that it becomes a decision between a woman and an abortionist-who may not even be a doctor. You don't have to be a doctor in every state to do abortions, and the woman who goes to an abortion mill for counseling probably wouldn't talk to the doctor even if there was one. Whoever counsels her there would most likely only be interested in selling her an abortion. Looked at another way, would your family doctor recommend an abortion as a "treatment" for pregnancy? If you're contemplating an abortion, you have options. Examine those options in the crisis pregnancy center below.

Actually, there is one aspect of the above argument I would agree with. I would support legislation that required a woman to consult with her family physician, or an obstetrician/gynecologist; to get their approval before having an abortion.

Some politicians like to straddle the issue by saying "I am pro-choice. I am not pro-abortion." Then they use that equivocation to justify voting against pro-life legislation. The fact is the results are the same; well over a million children murdered in this country every year. Abortion is the status quo-if you're pro-choice you're for it by default. "Pro-choice" when applied to abortion can only mean one thing-that you're in favor of letting mothers' choose to have their children murdered for their own convenience; despite the clever phraseology.

"Abortion clinic-now there is an oxymoron, if ever there was one. A clinic is a place that heals, but these establishments offer only one prescription to a woman with a crisis pregnancy: death for her young one and, for the mother, a painful memory that will last a lifetime. More often than not, she is rushed into the procedure by a 'counselor' whose only qualification is the ability to get her undressed and into the back room as fast as possible-a counselor whose only objective is to close the sale.

Often these counselors have had abortions themselves, and are trying to work through their pain by 'helping' others through this unpleasant and often unsafe experience in establishments that operate with the speed of an assembly line. An article in the American Medical Association in 1983 reported, 'Complications following abortions performed in free-standing clinics is one of the most frequent gynecologic emergencies...encountered.'

You would think that conditions would have improved in these establishments that now dot our landscape, but no. Pressure from feminist's groups has resulted in virtually no requirements and no oversight. As a result, these abortion mills have been left to police themselves.

Mark Crutcher, of Life Dynamics, verified 23 deaths from induced abortion in 1992-93 that were reported to state agencies. However, only two of these deaths were listed by the Centers for Disease Control, which has become highly politicized in the area of abortion. Bear in mind that most deaths resulting from induced abortion eventually are reported as something else: pelvic abscess, septicemia and hepatitis (from hemorrhage and blood transfusion). Crutcher, in his book, 'Lime 5', documented case histories of several hundred women badly injured or killed by abortionists. Only a fraction were reported." Jane Chastain, World Net Daily

Did you hear about the pregnant woman in England who was suffering from kidney failure, but went through with the pregnancy anyway, and was kept alive by her son's kidneys?

"Post-abortion trauma afflicts an estimated 560,000 women in America. Its symptoms are depression, suicidal tendencies, alcoholism, sexual promiscuity and repeat abortions"..."We can look back and see the trail of death and destruction, the countless souls doomed to eternal suffering, or we can look forward to a new century etched with the perseverance and integrity of the people of God. I prefer the latter". Judie Brown, American Life League (ALL)

The women who have the abortions are also its victims. For the women mentioned above, the problem didn't go away after their abortion-it got worse. If you think you might be suffering from the conditions mentioned above, you can call Rachel's Vineyard at 1-877-HOPE-4-ME.

"America, it is said, is suffering from intolerance. It is not. It is suffering from tolerance of right and wrong, truth and error, virtue and evil, Christ and chaos. Our country is not nearly so much overrun with the bigoted as it is overrun with the broadminded...In the face of this broadmindness, what the world needs is intolerance." Archbishop Fulton J. Sheen

From the January, 2001, Ryan Report: "...newspaper articles about the grue-some testimony PP abortionist Robert Crist gave during a trial in which PP challenged the legality of the partial-birth infanticide law in Missouri. The St. Louis Post-Dispatch wrote the following on May 25, 2000: 'In testimony Wednesday in St. Louis Circuit Court, Crist said that it is not uncommon for second-trimester fetuses to leave the womb feet-first, intact and with their hearts still beating. He sometimes crushes their skulls to get the fetuses out. Other times, he dismembers them.' Crist also cited cases when 9 to 10 week-old fetuses were unintentionally suctioned into the suction bottle intact, still alive with their hearts beating. The point PP was trying to make is that the law in question would not only ban a late term partial-birth abortion, but also the more routine procedures used earlier in the pregnancy which can cause the death of a baby after it is born or partially born (Post-Dispatch May 26, 2000)." STOPP International, http://www.stoppinternational.org/.

I got something in the mail from the "Survivors of the Abortion Holocaust" the other day. There was a picture of them with two large signs at a beach community in California. The signs were at least 5 feet tall, and 3-4 feet across. It was a distance shot, and I couldn't quite make out the details, so I got out a magnifying glass. One of the posters was of a smiling, healthy, well dressed baby. The caption said "LIFE". The other poster had a picture of an aborted baby-in pieces-it appeared to have been decapitated during the abortion procedure. The caption read "CHOICE". Another sign they carry has the message: "You Will Always REMEMBER The Child You Never Knew."

The following information was taken from an article entitled "After 30 Years of Abortion...Are Women Better Off?", by Kristen Panico, "Director of Education, National Organization of Episcopalians for Life", which was published in "Uniting For Life", Winter 2003-a publication of the National Pro-Life Religious Council:

"...after thirty years of abortion, we are now seeing the serious health consequences of abortion. Abortion can have a devastating impact on... emotional and physical health, fertility, and future pregnancies. Unfortunately abortionists and the medical community have downplayed the health risks of abortion. Endangering the physical and emotional health of millions of women, many we know and love. So as you read each...point below, try to make the data real. Think of the children who will lose their mother to cancer because of a choice she made while she was young. Think of the father who grieves for his miscarried child. Consider the women suffering from a... 'choice'.

43% of American women will have at least one abortion by age 45. We all have friends, coworkers, and neighbors who have had an abortion. Abortion is creating a women's health crisis.

In the US, over 140,000 women a year have *immediate* medical complications from abortion; problems such as: infection, uterine perforation, hemorrhaging, cervical trauma.

Abortion increases a woman's risk of breast cancer by 30%. A careful study of international literature shows a woman's risk for developing breast cancer has increased dramatically since 1960. According to the National Alliance of Breast Cancer Organizations, back in 1960, 1 in 14 women would develop breast cancer in her lifetime, currently 1 in 9 women have the chance of developing breast cancer.

After an abortion there is a higher risk of developing cervical as well as ovarian cancer. Childbirth actually protects against cancer of the reproductive system. The conclusion seems to be that if we can avoid abortion, some types of cancer may be preventable.

Abortion can lead to infertility, a long-term complication that often goes undetected for many years. Abortion can lead to infections (such as pelvic inflammatory disease), as well as uterine scarring. 'Single young women who have never carried a baby to term risk experiencing greater difficulty (than any other group) in conceiving and carrying future pregnancies to term.'

Abortion can lead to complications in future pregnancies including: miscarriage, premature birth, placenta previa, and ectopic pregnancy. How does this happen? During an abortion the cervix is artificially dilated, this can weaken the muscle and cause permanent damage leading to miscarriages and premature birth. The uterus may be perforated and sometimes it is scraped with a knife, both leading to scarring. When a woman gets pregnant the newly fertilized human embryo may have difficulty implanting in the womb because it can not attach itself to scar tissue. This can lead to placenta previa (when the embryo attaches itself to the lower part of the uterus near or over the cervix), and possible future ectopic pregnancy (when the embryo attaches itself to the fallopian tube) potentially fatal if not caught early. According to the Centers for Disease Control: 'From 1970 through 1989 more than one million ectopic pregnancies were estimated to have occurred among women in the United States. The rate increased almost fourfold from 4.5 to 16.0 ectopic pregnancies per 1000 reported pregnancies.'

In the twelve months following an abortion women have a death rate 4 times greater than women who continued with their pregnancies. This is a clear sign that women may be dying from abortion-related causes. It also suggests that there is a higher suicide rate for abortion than pregnancy. 'Although infrequently, women do die as a result of abortion, yet abortion-related maternal mortality is generally under-reported. One reason for this is that codes in hospitals report only the presenting cause of death, not the underlying reason which, for example, in the case of abortion-related death, might be hemorrhage, infection, embolism, or ectopic pregnancy.' Often staff may deliberately avoid citing a death as caused by abortion in order to protect the privacy of the woman. There are other causes of death as well: 'Approximately 14% of all deaths from legal abortion are due to general anesthesia complications.'

It is minorities who suffer the greatest number of serious complications and deaths after abortion. 'Death from legal abortion is more common among minority women than white women, women over the age of 35 and those who undergo the procedure during the second trimester.'

In a recent survey, post-abortive women who were seeking counseling reported: an increased use of drugs and/or alcohol to deaden their pain, reoccurring insomnia and nightmares, eating disorders that began after the abortion, suicidal feelings, and even attempted suicide. Sadly, many in the psychiatric community deny any serious emotional trauma after an abortion. Ironically, women who have undergone abortion often fit the psychiatric profile for diagnosing someone suffering from Post-Traumatic Stress Disorder.

This information is crucial because the right to choose is meaningless without the right to know."

"May 12, 2003 Study ties abortion to clinical depression By Sarah Marcisz THE WASHINGTON TIMES (http://www.washtimes.com/.)

Women who have abortions are 65 percent more likely to experience clinical depression than those who carry their pregnancies to term, according to a recent study. 'It has been frequently claimed that abortions have no negative psychological effects. This study shows this is clearly not the case,' said David Reardon, executive director of the Elliot Institute, a nonprofit, pro-life corporation focused on post-abortion research and education. The long-term effects of an abortion 'should be a high priority in federally funded research,' said Mr. Reardon, who co-wrote the study with Jesse Cougle, psychology professor at the University of Texas, and Priscilla Coleman, human-development director at Bowling Green State University.

In 1988, Surgeon General C. Everett Koop asked for a study on the issue of abortion complications. Congress denied the request. Mr. Reardon said it is past time for such a study to 'examine all interactions between women's physical and mental health, including not only reactions to abortion, but also to study PMS, postpartum depression, menopause and more.'

The Elliot study is based on data from an Ohio State University study funded by the U.S. Department of Labor that spans 21 years and annual assessments from 1,884 women. The research involved more precise methods compared with other studies, such as information on prior psychological state, nationally representative participants, consideration of sociodemographic factors and long-term assessments, Mr. Reardon said. But he said the study, the sixth in a series on the psychological effects of abortion, could be more precise. The data underrepresent the risk to women because 'the women most likely to conceal previous abortions are the ones most likely to experience clinical depression later on,' which is what Mr. Reardon says he believes happened with subjects in this study."

Additional risks-http://www.save-the-babies.org/risks.htm/.

The 2000 Al Gore, George Bush, Presidential Contest

Well, I've been very busy, and although I've been very concerned about the Al Gore, George Bush, never give up presidential contest in Florida, to the point that I've been having mood swings around it, I wasn't going to weigh in on the presidential race.

However, I see a chance to illustrate a point that a lot of people seem to be missing. That is, that the same strategy that's used to justify abortion is being used to justify the recount, whether or not you think it should go forward. First, a slogan has been chosen that everybody can agree upon: "All the ballots should be counted", and it is repeated over and over again like a mantra. But it doesn't reflect what is really going on. In fact, all the ballots have been counted, at least once, according to the rules established for the election by the legislature to ensure fairness to everyone. Then they were recounted, also according to the same rules for everybody. That's twice. But that's where applying the same fair standard to everybody ended. Since then there have been recounts (until today) only in predominantly Democratic counties. New standards for counting ballots were also applied in these counties, like reviewing ballots by hand, counting dimples, pregnant chads, and so on. Just rehandling these cards could cause changes in some-only in those counties. Plus, the Democrats, while saying they want to count every vote, were doing their utmost to get thousands of absentee ballots thrown out. So what they were really doing was trying to get Democratic votes recounted as much as possible to try to manufacture additional votes by making up new, exclusive rules as they went along. Dick Cheney called it vote manipulation. In the heartland, where we've had our share of vote manipulation behind the scenes in the past, lawyers call this out in the open outright vote tampering. It's just like when the Democrats twist abortion around into "A woman's right to choose", when it's really about a woman's right to kill.

Because the voters in the Democrat counties in Florida couldn't get the punched cards punched right, two years later they installed computers for people to vote on. Well, you probably heard what happened to Janet Reno in the primary, and this time they couldn't blame it on the Republicans. But, continuing:

Later, arguing before the U.S. Supreme Court, attorney David Boies would point out that his side had not requested a statewide recount of the undervotes; suggesting to me that they understood it was to their advantage, and they wanted to continue, to count only in heavily Democratic counties; and Justice Scalia would elicit laughter when he wise-cracked "You mean count every vote". Also, in my opinion, the Florida Supreme Court didn't cite any legal justifications for their decisions because they couldn't-there weren't any. It was a party line vote, plain and simple, especially the first time (the court was composed of 6 Democratic appointees and one Independent). In "the final analysis", as JFK used to say, Al Gore didn't fail to gain the presidency because he didn't carry Florida; he lost because he didn't win in his home state-Tennessee-where people knew him and his family best (his father was also a U.S. Senator). But why am I so critical of the Al Gore camp? Maybe I wouldn't have been so keenly interested and taken notice of the points mentioned above if he hadn't said in the first debate that he would only appoint Justices to the Supreme Court who would uphold Roe vs. Wade. That was a fatal flaw-both figuratively and literally.

Two years later, when he "tested the waters", he found he couldn't get the financial backing he needed for a second run, and dropped out of the presidential race. This suggests to me that even liberals were frightened by the "Constitutional crisis" he fostered. Years ago, in another close presidential contest, Richard Nixon, running against John Kennedy, opted to not challenge the results, even though there was ample evidence of voter fraud on a large scale in places like Chicago (since then they seem to have cleaned up their act). Richard Nixon was later able to get his party's support and run again, winning on his second try. He went on to end the draft and end the war in Vietnam, and was a very popular president until Watergate. Although it was never proven that he had knowledge of what happened at Watergate, the steady drumbeat of the media and Congress eventually was able to hound him out of office. The issue was never whether he ordered the break-in, but whether he found out about it later and didn't make that public, which would have been a violation of the law. Unlike Bill Clinton, he buckled under the threat of impeachment proceedings and resigned.

The recount was precipitating a constitutional crisis. Who was going to be in charge? People everywhere who were old enough to remember were saying that they understood now why Nixon didn't challenge the election results in his race with Kennedy, even though everyone knew there had been widespread vote fraud in Chicago that put Illinois in Kennedy's column-that Nixon was a wiser man than they had realized. The issue needed to be resolved, and not allowed to drag on until it threatened the stability of our democracy. People were beginning to wonder-is there going to be violence next? Fortunately, Gore finally acted in a responsible way, and conceded.

John Ashcroft, Planned Parenthood, and Mexico City

The confirmation hearings for former U.S. Senator John Ashcroft begin Tuesday, January 16. You can sign an online petition supporting him at the http://www.aclj.org/, the American Center for Law and Justice web site (you can currently sign a petition there against partial-birth abortion "murder during delivery, for filling body parts orders"). He is an excellent choice for Attorney General, and has served as attorney general and governor for Missouri. Liberal groups are saying he favors the criminalization of abortion. I am amazed that they would raise this issue publicly, which I had not even known how to verbalize before. Whether or not they are able to scuttle the nomination, they have introduced criminalization into the public arena. I have a lot of respect for John Ashcroft and his beliefs. Again, it is the liberals who hold the radical views, and accuse other people who oppose their ideas as being the extremists. I don't know what steps he would or could take as Attorney General.

Unfortunately, the Attorney General enforces the law-he doesn't make it. "Sen. Ashcroft is a man of impeccable integrity and fully committed to upholding the U.S. Constitution and the rule of law". Jay Alan Sekulow, The American Center For Law and Justice (a public interest law firm that focuses on constitutional issues). From Colleen Parro at RNCL: "His career has been a distinguished one and he is widely recognized as a Godly man whose integrity is beyond question. Pro-abortion groups are in a frenzy over the Ashcroft nomination. They will be spending vast sums of money to build public support against his confirmation. Already they have flooded the media with press releases attacking Senator Ashcroft, while at the same time praising the nomination of Colin Powell as Secretary of State because of his pro-abortion views."

He is also a honors graduate of Yale University and the University of Chicago Law School. My family has been involved with these schools, and I can attest to the fact that they only accept the very best and brightest students. Both President George Bush Sr. and President Clinton attended Yale, and the monetary theory that is used by the Federal Reserve Bank to manage the economy, and the science for the atomic bomb, originated from the University of Chicago. It is difficult for me to imagine how someone could be better qualified to be Attorney General than John Ashcroft. I find it especially discouraging that the people who oppose him because of his Christian background have proven themselves incapable of making their own independent moral judgments. Post-script: George Bush Jr. also attended Yale, as an undergraduate, but got his MBA from Harvard; where he developed his delegation management style. It seems that candidates don't see that kind of a background as being helpful when they're trolling for votes, but it shows the caliber of person who often achieves that pinnacle of success in politics. Even Al Gore, if I remember correctly, was a Harvard graduate; but probably wouldn't have included that fact on his resume when he was courting the labor vote. Jimmy Carter didn't have that kind of a background, but was elected at a time when people were looking for someone non-controversial after the Watergate scandal. Nixon and Johnson and Truman were vice-presidents first, but Eisenhower graduated at the top of his class at West Point and was the allied commander in Europe during World War II. John Kennedy, who I almost forgot because of his short tenure, graduated from Harvard, too, and probably got his law degree there. Gerald Ford, of course, was elevated to vice-president by Nixon after Spiro Agnew got into trouble. FDR was before my time. Perhaps the starkest contrast to the way things are today was the Iranians holding our embassy personnel captive for a year, during the Carter administration.

From watching the confirmation hearings, I would conclude that character assassination doesn't work well when the target of the accusations has a national forum on TV to reply from.

From the January, 2001, Ryan Report: "...Planned Parenthood was endorsing political candidates during the last election...via PP's political action fund, PPAF...should demand that such a politically-active organization be barred from getting any of our tax dollars. PPAF earmarked $10 million for a television and mail campaign in seven key battleground states...aimed at keeping George W. Bush from becoming president...PPAF said it would reach 2.2 million households...In addition to this national effort, state and local PP action funds in 46 states were involved in more than 700 races nationwide. PP action funds in California alone planned to spend $1 million on state, federal, and local races. One would hope that the politicians who were targets of PP's intense political involvement during the past election would have the good sense to oppose any future measure that would result in PP getting any more of our tax money...when the government gives $176.5 million to PP during one fiscal year (1998-99), PP doesn't have to rely on its supporters to come up with that amount of money to help fund PP's non-political activities. This political activity helps put more politicians in office who are likely to allocate even more of our tax dollars to PP. The way to break this cycle is to stop giving PP any of our tax money, period!"

"Planned Parenthood frequently causes restrictions on abortion to be held up or completely overturned by the courts. This has happened once again, this time in Tennessee...The court then struck down provisions in a 1997 state law, which required informed consent and a two-day waiting period. Also declared unconstitutional was a provision that all second-trimester abortions must take place in a hospital, not a clinic. PP has shown that its main concern is not for the welfare of women, but rather for making profits. PP, obviously, doesn't like any restriction that prevents PP from killing second-trimester babies at its own clinics. In his 38-page dissent, Justice Mickey Barker said, in part, 'Plainly stated, the effect of the court's holding today is to remove from the people all power, except by constitutional amendment, to enact reasonable regulations of abortion. Rather than leaving policy decisions regarding reasonable abortion regulation to the General Assembly, this court has converted itself into a roving constitutional convention, which sees itself free to strike down the duly-enacted laws of the legislature...is contrary to nearly 200 years of legal precedent.' Republican Tennessee state senator David Fowler, a lawyer, said he may propose that the legislature vote to remove the four 'judicial tyrants' by the two-thirds vote required by the Tennessee Constitution."

"According to a Los Angeles Times survey of 2,071 Americans this summer, only 43% surveyed support Roe, more than half say abortion should be illegal, and 57% consider abortion murder ('Americans Narrowing Support for Abortion,' Los Angeles Times, June 18, 2000)." The Ryan Report documents the activities of Planned Parenthood.

On January 22, 2001, President George W. Bush, on his third day in office, signed an Executive Order re-establishing the Mexico City Policy, so-named because it was first enunciated by President Reagan in 1984 at a Mexico City population conference. It bans U.S. aid to international groups that use their own money to support abortion counseling, surgery, or lobbying (Planned Parenthood). What an explosive political situation it could create if we were involved in killing their citizens-especially in Muslim or Catholic countries.

On the same day President Bush sent a message to the March For Life, gathered in Washington to protest the Roe v. Wade decision on its 28th anniversary, which was read to the crowd by Rep. Chris Smith, R-N.J.:

"The promises of our Declaration of Independence are not just for the strong, the independent or the healthy. They are for everyone, including unborn children...We share a great goal, to work toward a day when every child is welcomed in life and protected in law...to build a culture of life, affirming that every person at every stage and season of life, is created equal in God's image."

On February 1, 2001, John Ashcroft was confirmed by the Senate as Attorney General. Democrats claimed that his views were "outside mainstream America". But then why did polls show that a majority of Americans supported his confirmation? Why did the Senate vote 58-42 in his favor? I think the numbers tell a different story. Some of those Democratic senators have conservative constituencies.

"Ashcroft was sworn into office by Supreme Court Justice Clarence Thomas, a longtime friend." "A formal swearing ceremony will be scheduled for next week…" "Ashcroft…may be the most qualified person ever tapped for the post." (Sen. Orrin) "Hatch said he was bothered by the work of many of the outside groups that tried to influence the Senate's duty of advice and consent on presidential nominations, saying they had too much pull with too many Democratic senators…'it was disgusting'". CNN

If John Ashcroft was a racist, as the Democrats claimed, why would he be good friends with Clarence Thomas, an African American? Why would Clarence Thomas want to swear him in?

"'If that's the way you've got to send a message, by trashing a person's reputation, distorting his record…that's pretty pathetic'. Sen. Orrin Hatch 'I don't know that person' they're depicting.' Sen. Trent Lott". AP

Maybe what the Democrats are really concerned about is that a lot of laws that have been overlooked, or ignored for many years will get enforced now. I hope that's what happens. Prosecuting abortionists, for selling baby body parts; and killing, or allowing to die, children still alive outside the mother, would probably be sufficient to shut down most of the killing centers.

"Bush Slammed on Anti-Abortion Rule Thursday, March 08, 2001 By Patricia Reaney LONDON (Reuters)-Family planning experts accused President George W. Bush on Thursday of adopting a 'fascist approach' and creating a double standard by blocking U.S. funding for international groups that support abortion." "…the experts warned that Bush's decision will increase maternal deaths…". (There's no reason to believe that. But it should decrease infant mortality in the range of from 1 to 9 months into the pregnancy.)

"'We condemn this double standard,' Dr. Med Bouzidi, of the International Planned Parenthood Federation (IPPF), told a news conference."

"Bouzidi said Bush's decision to reinstate the so-called 'Mexico City Policy,' which bans financial support for organizations if any of their funding—even if it doesn't come from the U.S.—is spent on abortion, will make a deplorable situation worse."

"'The lack of control over a woman's body will lead to more unwanted pregnancies and death,' he said."

"'This is totally unacceptable in this day and age,' said Sandra Kabir of Population Concern, a group which promotes reproductive health worldwide."

Translation-reproductive health equates to abortion. Abortion leads to death, not pregnancy, which is a normal condition for a woman.

James Kopp and Barnett Slepian

Thursday, March 29th, 2001: James Kopp was arrested in France for the shooting murder of abortion doctor Barnett Slepian, in his Amherst, New York, home. I feel I must measure my words carefully in discussing this, lest they be quoted out of context and their meaning twisted. On the other hand, it would be the epitome of stupidity for anyone to publicly criticize this little known web site and drive traffic to it. To anybody contemplating a similar act, let me point out a few things. First of all, you are almost certain to be caught eventually, even if it takes over two years, as it did in this case. If successful, you would be saving the lives of only a few people, who you don't even know, and might not like if you did; in exchange for the doctor's life, and, potentially, your own. You would be vilified by the press, and declared mentally unstable; and after a while in jail and prison there's a strong possibility you would slip into depression, belatedly confirming that pronouncement. And the company you would be keeping there are the people society thinks it is best not to have around them-for good reason. You would also have pretty much destroyed your own life, and the chance of having a family and children of your own. The right to life people would trip over each other to disassociate themselves from violence in general, and you in particular. That having been said, let's get back to James Kopp. This was not a random act of violence, but appears to have been carefully planned over a period of time. I have to believe he knew the risks involved, and the consequences I described above. He managed his escape well, and stayed ahead of his pursuers for a remarkable period of time. Knowing nothing more about him, I would have to say I admire and respect the sacrifice he made. To indict him for murder, and not also indict Dr. Barnett Slepian for murder, would be the height of hypocrisy, a clear double and unfair standard, and a miscarriage of justice. This will probably be denied and papered over for years to come. That is not to say I condone his actions-one more death on top of the 40,000,000 that have gone before is too many. I do think he was fortunate to get caught now-I don't foresee the Bush/Ashcroft administration asking for the death penalty, and after watching Clinton in action we all know these things can be overturned or commuted-assuming he is guilty and convicted. It will be interesting to see how this plays out. It should put abortion back on the front burner; at least it will be harder for the press to ignore. I think it will be important how he projects himself. Will the media be able to stir up sympathy for Dr. Slepian, or slant or suppress news from the trial? Will abortionists be able to distort and capitalize on it? Stay tuned. My own opinion is that he should have been on the FBI's least wanted, not most wanted, list. Good luck, James, you're going to need it. And if it eases your mind any, I want you to know that there's at least one person out here who understands what you did, and why you did it, and is rooting for you, irregardless of what the other right to life people do or say. How many thousands did Doctor Slepian kill? "In the final analysis", I think justice was

done. It's the only logical conclusion a reasonable person can arrive at. If the laws against homicide had been enforced in the first place, there would have been no reason for this to occur. Now, how justice was dispensed, becomes the real issue.

I dropped the above paragraph into a forum at About.com. If you are interested in pursuing the debate that ensued, click on "Replies to Comments" below.

From: The Pro-Life Infonet
Reply-To: Steven Ertelt infonet@prolifeinfo.org
Subject:Kopp Admits Killing Abortion Practitioner, Pro-Life Advocates Condemn Killing
Source: Associated Press, Buffalo News; November 19, 2002

Buffalo, NY—A man who claims to be against abortion and is awaiting trial on charges of murdering an abortion practitioner admitted carrying out the deadly attack but said he meant only to wound the man and 'the bullet took a crazy ricochet.' 'The truth is not that I regret shooting Dr. Slepian. I regret that he died,' James Kopp said in a jailhouse interview in Wednesday's Buffalo News. 'I aimed at his shoulder.' Kopp, 47, said he shot abortion practitioner Barnett Slepian with a rifle on Oct. 23, 1998, because of his outrage over abortions. Pro-life advocates say his action mobilized abortion forces and did more to advance the pro-abortion cause. Slepian was heating soup at his home in this Buffalo suburb when he was killed by a bullet that came through a window. Kopp told the newspaper he was 'horrified' when he later learned that the bullet glanced off a bone and caused internal injuries that killed the doctor. 'The bullet took a crazy ricochet, and that's what killed him. One of my goals was to keep Dr. Slepian alive,' Kopp said, 'and I failed at that goal.'

Kopp became one of the FBI's most-wanted fugitives and was captured in France in 2001 after running from authorities. He pleaded innocent to a state charge of second-degree murder and is scheduled to go on trial on the state charge in February. If convicted of murder, Kopp could get 25 years to life in prison; the federal charge carries life without parole. District Attorney Frank Clark said he was not surprised by the admission. 'He didn't admit to anything that we didn't plan to prove by other means in the trial,' Clark said Wednesday. The FBI said it obtained a close match between DNA taken from a hair found in the woods behind Slepian's house and DNA from a toothbrush Kopp left with a friend months before the shooting. Investigators also said his car was seen in the neighborhood, and a map found in Kopp's belongings bore directions to a Tennessee pawn shop where the murder weapon-found buried behind Slepian's home-was bought. Kopp told the newspaper he decided to

113

make a public confession because he believes his supporters have been misled, and he wants them to know the reasons behind his actions. A few pro-life advocates claimed Kopp was innocent and attempted to discredit the police investigation. Kopp's lawyer, Bruce A. Barket, said he permitted the interview before trial because 'the sooner the truth is out the better.' He said the defense would be that Kopp is innocent of intentional murder because he 'just clearly didn't intend to kill the guy.'

Kopp said he feels sorrow for Slepian's wife and four sons. 'To pick up a gun and aim it at another human being and to fire, it's not a human thing to do,' Kopp said. His admission brought condemnation from pro-life advocates of all stripes. 'It is inconsistent for anyone in the pro-life movement to take a life. One can't in Catholic teaching go out and shoot doctors who perform abortions or anyone else. Our ways are not the ways of violence,' Bishop Henry J. Mansell said in reacting to Kopp's confession in Wednesday's Buffalo News. In Texas, Kopp's stepmother questioned why it took him so long to confess. 'He said he didn't mean to kill but that he meant to protect unborn children. Isn't that a contradiction?' Lynn Kopp said. 'If you did it, if you had such intense feelings, why hide from them after you've done the deed.'

In Canada, where Kopp, 47, is suspected of shooting and wounding three abortion practitioners, the leader of an Ontario-based pro-life organization said Kopp's action demonstrates disregard for life. 'He does not represent the pro-life movement or our philosophy. We have a commitment to nonviolence in defense of our pro-life position,' said Jakki Jeffs, president of Alliance for Life Ontario. 'I would state emphatically there is no room for violence.' 'We're condemning the violent act. We're glad he confessed. He needs to own up to it. He needs to repent and seek God's forgiveness,' said the Rev. Robert L. Behn, executive director of Last Call Ministries, a local pro-life group. People closest to Kopp said he was a hypocrite because of his actions, not pro-life. 'He went off the rails. See what happens if you don't do what Christ wants-the worst possible thing. How does Jimmy know that poor man (Slepian) wouldn't have repented the next day?' said Barrie Norman, a pro-life activist from Vancouver, British Columbia. The Rev. Flip Benham said Kopp 'betrayed the pro-life movement, unborn children and the Lord he proclaims to serve. You never overcome the problem of murder by murdering people.'

Kopp said he chose Slepian's name from a telephone book, that he had never read any news accounts about the doctor and that no one in the Buffalo anti-abortion movement had recommended Slepian as a target. He said he targeted Slepian largely because his home had a rear window facing a wooded area, where he leaned against a pine tree to steady his high-powered rifle. He said he scouted Slepian's neighborhood about six times over a year.

Well, it kind of played out like I predicted. I didn't come right out and say he did it, but I probably implied I thought so. I thought so because I could see his motivation-but I didn't want to be his accuser. Even his (step) mother seemed to disown him. I've already given a whole host of reasons why it's not a good idea to go around shooting abortion doctors, some of which we have already seen play out. I've had well over a year to think about it since then, but after rereading what I wrote, I don't see any reason to change it; but I will add to it somewhat. I like to follow people like John Ashcroft, and President Bush, and try to learn from them, and figure out why they do what they do and how they do it. They're adhere to the law people, and it makes sense because you don't want people running around making their own laws, even if they're morally right-that kind of thing can get out of hand in a hurry. Their approach is to first change the law and the decision makers. Most others wouldn't make the right decision about who and when to shoot, like James Kopp did. Yes, you heard me right, I don't consider what James Kopp did to be morally wrong any more than I would grieve over somebody shooting Osama Bin Laden. Both Barnett Slepian and Osama Bin Laden made it their business to kill innocents, with Slepian specifically targeting children. What Bin Laden has done pales in comparison to what the abortion industry has accomplished-killing over 40 million children in this country alone at a rate of 3,000-4,000 a day, equaling or exceeding in a single day the devastation of human life caused by the 9/11 attack. Deeply religious people are often, I believe, against abortion because that's what their church has taught them, along with their opposition to violence. But, if you know, I mean really know, with absolute conviction, that the child in the womb is just as much a human being as anyone else, how can you then fault the person who strikes out violently at the abortion industry? But the pro-life movement can not prevail through violence, because that just brings down the full force of law enforcement on our heads. We may not be patient, but it seems we must play a waiting game. Mr. Kopp, I feel you're doing just fine so far, I still understand why you did what you did and I respect you for it, and the sacrifices you are making; even though I don't recommend that others follow in your footsteps.

And while we wait, the killing continues.

"Kopp Convicted of Murder in Abortion Doctor's Killing

Tuesday, March 18, 2003

BUFFALO, N.Y.—James Kopp, was found guilty of intentionally killing (Doctor Barnett Slepian)…one day after (the judge) heard the case without a jury during an unusual single court session. Kopp waived his right to a jury trial last week. The judge set sentencing for May 9. Kopp faces a minimum of 15 years to life and a maximum of 25 years to life. Instead of hearing testimony, the judge was presented with a 35-page list of facts agreed to by both sides—including an admission by Kopp that he fired the shot…and then heard attorneys' arguments. In arguing for acquittal,…said Kopp believed in the use of force to prevent abortions, but meant only to wound the obstetrician to prevent him from performing abortions…Shortly after the shooting, Kopp fled to Mexico and then Ireland and was one of the FBI's most-wanted fugitives until his capture in France in 2001. Tuesday's verdict has no effect on Kopp's upcoming federal trial on a charge of interfering with the right to an abortion related to the Slepian shooting. A status hearing in that case was scheduled for Thursday. Kopp is also a suspect in the nonfatal shootings of four other abortion providers in Canada and Rochester between 1994 and 1997." Associated Press It's interesting that they refer to Slepian as an "Abortion Doctor", dropping the Ob/Gyn facade. Plus, since Kopp got his name out of the phone book, he had to have been advertising that he did abortions. So much for the apologists.

May 9, 2003: James Kopp was sentenced to 25 years to life today. It does not seem to be widely or prominently reported. The copyright message on the sole complete article I found was so draconian that I'll just put it in my own words-and his. They seem to think they have a monopoly on the event, although there was nothing so creative about what they wrote. The charge was second degree murder, and the least he could have gotten was 15 years. The judge didn't buy his argument that he didn't intend to kill Slepian. A youngish looking 48 years of age, with a worried, concerned countenance, he appeared somewhat missionary, and bookish, in large oval glasses. Judge Michael D'Amico's arguments for sentencing seemed lame and not very judicious, and I found myself disillusioned by their hollowness. In a rather lengthy statement before the judge, Kopp had his day in court, and secured his place in history. "I was innocent of murder then. I am innocent of murder now". "Why should the safety of Dr. Slepian be put over the safety of unborn children?" "I have separated murderers from their weapons of mass destruction. I wish I could do 10 life sentences or 10 death penalties to save them". Well stated. Move over, Patrick Henry. Vicki Saporta, president and chief executive of the National Abortion Federation, said "A strong message must be sent to anti-choice extremists that murdering an abortion provider is never justifiable". Au contraire, killing someone who performs abortions is always morally justifiable, to save other, innocent lives, just as it is in war; however, as I pointed out above, it is unwise and counterproductive, as demonstrated by this sentence. What could be more extreme than dismembering children? But ending it James Kopp's way obviously doesn't work. He even got very little press coverage, or even sympathy, at his sentencing, for what he did. Legality here overruled morality and gratitude. Justice will not be done until abortion is declared illegal and James Kopp is pardoned and set free. Especially so in New York state.

Norah Vincent, Beverly LaHaye, CWA, and Feminists

From: **Colleen Parro**
Subject:**Hitting the nail on the head**
Date: **March 29, 2001 2:05:16 PM EST**

Pretty amazing for the L.A. Times!

L.A. Times, March 29, 2001

"Feminists Have No Womb for Anyone Else

By NORAH VINCENT

Ours is a country in which you are ill-advised to be a fetus.

The highest court in the land has ruled that you're a parasite, disposable at will, even when you're almost out of the chute. You're just an extension of your mother's whim. She can do whatever she likes with you. Her court-instituted right to 'choose' trumps your right to live.

Now, taking a new leap, the courts have decided that her right to privacy trumps your right to a clean bill of health. If you're inconvenient, unaffordable or just plain unwanted, then you'll soon be a biohazard on your way to the town dump. If you're allowed to exercise your life, you may have to live it as a vegetable or a grotesque. In a stunning 6-3 decision, the U.S. Supreme Court ruled that hospitals may not test a pregnant woman for drugs for police purposes without either a search warrant or the woman's consent. Such tests were found to be a violation of the 4th Amendment protection against unreasonable search and seizure. 'The fact that positive test results were turned over to the police...provides an affirmative reason for enforcing the strictures of the 4th Amendment,' the court said.

Never mind that other rulings on the reasonableness of drug testing have allowed for the testing of a wide range of people, including government employees and high-school athletes. In these cases, the courts ruled, there was a 'special need.' The health of a fetus, however, apparently is not considered to be a special enough need to override the privacy rights of rogue mothers.

Naturally, this is considered another victory for feminism. And so it is. For it means that once again, the law has mandated that women need not be responsible for what happens in their wombs. The womb, after all, is the enemy. It must be kept in its place.

It cannot be allowed to control us. We must control it in every respect. The fact that we were born with wombs will never again be allowed to shackle us to them or to the progeny they grow. We, and we alone, are what matter now.

We can do anything. We can have as much sex as we want—as much wanton sex as some men do—and we need not be concerned with the consequences. If the unthinkable happens, if—surprise, surprise-nature actually takes its course and we become pregnant, well, we'll just do what we do after we binge on too many French fries. We'll purge. After all, if you want to stay thin after eating everything in sight, then it's the finger down the throat. If you want to stay barren but have as much protected or unprotected sex as you want, then it's the doctor in your business—but not too much in your business. Only as much as you want him.

What's more, when we're good and ready to have a child, we'll still be totally in control of our bodies. We'll smoke, we'll booze, we'll crack it up all night long if we take a mind to, and it'll be nobody's business. Because the Constitution protects us. We have a right to our privacy and our bodies, even though, when it comes to that seventh, eighth, ninth month of pregnancy, we're pretty sure we're not alone in them anymore.

But who cares, those babies are ours, and we can do with them what we like. We can smoke three packs a day. We can drink motor oil. And if that baby comes out with a brain that doesn't quite work right or that doesn't work at all, if it has an imposed mortal dependency on a narcotic, if it comes out with expensive special needs, well, the government will pay for it. That's what government is for: to safeguard my right to do what I like and pick up the tab when I've done it.

I can do anything, consequences be damned. Let freedom ring, because, by God, I am woman, and this is America."

Norah Vincent Is a Freelance Journalist Who Lives in New York City

Well, I like to be able to explain everything, but I'm not sure I can explain this. Maybe they thought it was humorous? My best guess is that the editors were out of town, or it was very early in the morning, and a staffer let it slip through, or a pro-lifer saw his or her chance. Here's why. I just had an experience where I was able to get a pro-life news release out, and they got a lot of complaints, and threats, and will probably never do it again. A big paper like the Los Angeles Times is going to get a ton of flack from a very large number of feminists and abortionists. It's not going to happen very often, so we should relish it when we can.

I received a letter from an anti-abortion women's group I hadn't heard of before. Of course I filled out their survey questions and joined up. I receive a lot of conservative mail, and I don't always take the time to read everything. But this particular evening I had allocated to catching up on my mail, and I didn't feel pressured to get on to the next thing. About halfway through I realized I was reading something written by someone who had a unique grasp of the political situation in Washington. Here are some excerpts:

"Liberals, feminists...ridicule, silence—even try to destroy anyone who would dare oppose them." They want us "to sit down and shut up. Any vocal opposition to their left-wing policies is increasingly being condemned as 'divisive' and 'mean-spirited,' 'extreme' and 'hate-filled'". "No matter how much we're scorned by the media or scolded by liberal politicians—no matter what sorts of names they call us—we must speak out...". "Federal courts, packed with Clinton appointees, have repeatedly overturned bans on the horrific procedure known as partial birth abortion."

"...America is at a crossroads. I believe our nation's destiny hinges on the combined prayers and actions of individual women and men like you and me. I also strongly believe that one person can make a difference...in this spiritual battle for the heart and soul and future of America." "One by one, the victories we win are holding the line against the forces bent on destroying the values you and I cherish." "I look forward to hearing from you soon." "Beverly LaHaye, founder and chairman of Concerned Women for America. CWA is the nation's largest pro-family women's organization, with over half a million members." http://www.cwfa.org/

Thank you, Beverly, for your insightful perspective. Hopefully, in the end, reason will prevail.

From the May 2001 Judie Brown Report: "'The truth is NOW is really history ...After years of being led by phony feminists, this once groundbreaking organization is all but dead and buried, suffocating beneath the weight of its hate-based gender politics.

And among American women, the most typical response to NOW's demise is 'good riddance, "said Tina Whittington." Also in the April issue were references to Planned Parenthood centers as "abortion mills", "killing centers", and "deadly little chambers of horror." Right on, Judie, I'm glad to see you're finally taking off the gloves and telling it like it is.

Unborn Victims of Violence and The Peterson Murders

"House To Debate Unborn Victims Of Violence Act By Jim Burns CNS
Senior Staff Writer April 26, 2001

(CNSNews.com)-The House Thursday is scheduled to debate the Unborn
Victims of Violence Act, a bill that would make it a federal crime to harm an
unborn baby in the process of attacking a pregnant woman. Rep.Lindsey
Graham (R-S.C.) is sponsoring the legislation, which has garnered 95 co-
sponsors. He says the bill would only apply to 'crimes committed under
federal or U.S. military jurisdiction and does not affect state laws.' The House
passed similar legislation last year but it never became law. President Clinton
and many other abortion supporters oppose the bill as a first step toward
defining an unborn baby as a person—with the ultimate goal being to outlaw
abortion.

The Bush administration, on the other hand, supports the legislation. In a
policy statement sent to the House Rules Committee Wednesday, the White
House said, 'The Administration supports protection for unborn children and
therefore supports House passage of H.R. 503. The legislation would make it a
separate federal offense to cause death or bodily injury to a child, who is in
utero, in the course of committing any one of 68 federal offenses.'

Graham believes that protecting the unborn is not a new idea. 'Unfortunately,
the laws covering federal crimes of violence such as bombings, car jackings,
and kidnappings are silent on the matter. The legislation holds criminals
accountable for their actions. It also protects the unborn while not wandering
into the divisive, highly-charged, emotional battleground of abortion. I think
it's a reasoned approach to a very serious problem.'

The American Life League said Thursday the Unborn Victims of Violence Act
is not a pro-life bill. League President Judie Brown said the measure grants a
'schizophrenic exemption for abortionists who kill the preborn.' 'Though the
intention of the bill claims to be protecting preborn persons from violence, it
exempts their greatest threat, the abortionists who butcher 4,400 little boys and
girls every day.'

Representative Joe Pitts (R-Pa.) supports the legislation because 'life is a
precious thing.' 'This is an uncontroversial bill that has passed the House
before by wide margins,' he said, noting that abortions—protected by Roe v.
Wade, are specifically exempted. 'Life is a precious thing. It was cited by
Thomas Jefferson as the very first right we should protect in the Declaration of
Independence. But in recent years, the law has gotten wrapped up in
technicalities and confused by radical interest groups bent on creating and

ensuring spurious rights the Constitution was not written to guarantee or even recognize. The right to live is no longer guaranteed. Congress is now taking an important step toward reestablishing that right for all of us, including babies,' Pitts said this week in a speech on the House floor."

April 26, 2001: The House of Representatives passed the Unborn Victims of Violence Act 252-172-legislation that has already been passed in 24 states. These bills essentially make it legally a homicide, or manslaughter, to kill a pregnant woman's child; although the federal bill sounds much more complicated than that. Although a White House statement referred to "unborn children", the media insisted on referring to the child as a "fetus". I think this terminology makes it an uphill battle for any such legislation, because there's no way you can make the word fetus sound like a human being. However, contrary to other news reports, I think the bill has a good chance of passage in the Senate. What we have here is one category of citizen, fiercely trying to deny any rights whatsoever, even the right to live itself, to another class of citizen, no matter what the circumstances. It's ugly-very ugly. This sort of thing was supposed to have gone out with slavery.

"Lawmakers who voted for the one-victim bill will have to explain why they voted to say that, when a criminal attacks a pregnant woman and kills her unborn baby, nobody has really died. These groups oppose any recognition that unborn children are members of the human family, even when their right to life is violated by criminal attackers". NRLC Legislative Director Douglas Johnson

"The success of this vote shows the far-reaching support this legislation gained. The American people expect justice to be done; they believe criminals should be held responsible for taking a life. Legislators should support this bill as a deterrent to violent crime". Michael Schwartz, vice president government relations, CWA.

"Violent assailants should not be given a pass for their crime because their victim was inside a loving mother's womb. A mother or father should not suffer a second assault of their child being ignored by our justice system." Wendy Wright, director of communications, CWA.

"The Unborn Victims of Violence Act provides defense for the defenseless, and follows the lead of several states that already give legal protection to unborn children for criminal acts of violence". Rep. Jo Ann Davis, (R-1st Va.)

"Those who do not respect the sanctity of life have built a legacy upon lies. They lied to us about the gruesome practice of partial-birth abortion, and now they are trying to tell us that there is nothing inside a mother's womb that ought to be protected from a murderer. This is wrong. We must stand up for mothers and their children". Rep. J.C. Watts (R-Okla.)

"The President does believe that when an unborn child is injured or killed during the commission of a crime of violence, the law should recognize what most people immediately recognize, and that is that such a crime has two victims." White House Press Secretary Ari Fleischer, April 25, 2003.

The pro-abortion strategy has always been to make no concessions. They believe that to do so would cause their whole position to unravel. Although each pro-life victory does weaken their defenses, by not being willing to concede anything they put themselves in untenable circumstances-such as unborn victims. At no stage do they want recognition of personhood, although in the later stages any idiot can just look at a woman's belly and tell that there is a second person there. So the legislation they will probably get, because they don't want to talk about it, is that that they least want-protection of the child during the entire nine months of pregnancy. They are well aware of this, but can't bring themselves to discuss the basic issue of when life begins, and where to draw the line-which could expand the debate to other circumstances. Colloquially stated, they have "painted themselves into a corner". What follows, about what was said above, is just one example of that. That is:

The Press Secretary's statement did not occur in a vacuum, but followed considerable media coverage of the Peterson murder case in California, which probably just about everyone has heard about by now. It's what might be called a "layered" occurrence of murder. In the first murder event you have the death of Laci Peterson, Scott Peterson's wife. But, nested within this murder, you also have the resultant death of the child she was carrying in her 8th or 9th month of pregnancy-certainly quite "viable". This occurred in a state where the legislature, the governor's office, and two U.S. Senators are firmly controlled by, and answer to, the abortion industry. On the other hand, California law clearly puts the death of the child in the second murder column. Because of the especially heinous nature of the crime, public opinion is probably behind the severest punishment possible being meted out for this crime, as are the prosecutors, who will likely charge Scott Peterson with a double murder. Because a second murder was committed, California law permits the application of the death penalty for the crimes. I have to believe that abortionists will use all there influence to prevent the child from being considered a murder victim, and thereby acquiring the legal status of personhood conveyed upon him by the process. But, if they do, they will face a very tough scenario, because I did not use the word "him" in the generic sense. The Peterson's knew he was a boy, and had even already named him-Connor. As if to make the point, for those who might doubt that they were two separate people, the bodies washed up on the beach separately. First, one was found, then the other.

"If this is murder, well, then any time a late-term fetus is aborted, they could call it murder". Morris County, New Jersey, NOW President, Mavra Stark. That's right, Mavra, murder is what it is. (As told to Jim Wasserman, Associated Press, April 22, 2003.)

Our legal system has become schizophrenic. If the child is not wanted, then our legal system tells us it's not a person, and can be killed. However, if it's wanted, our legal system, in at least 24 states, says that to kill the child is just the same as killing any other person, and is murder. The two interpretations can't coexist much longer, in my opinion, and we are going to have a federal law soon, too, that says you can't kill a "wanted" child.

What is more typical, and I have read several accounts of this, is that a boyfriend who doesn't want the child will punch his girlfriend in the stomach, or have someone do it for him, to cause her to miscarry. After all, if the abortion doctor can do it, he probably doesn't see why he can't do it too; especially since society sends the message that it's not a person and can be legally aborted. There are two cases in court, that I know of, right now, charging the assailants. If a woman suffers emotional trauma after, herself, having an unwanted child aborted, just imagine what the grief must be like for the woman who wanted the baby. And just think of the danger it puts women themselves in if they can be attacked with impunity to kill their babies. An other example: "Actor Robert Blake is accused of murdering his pregnant wife after she refused to abort his child." Life Dynamics News April 2003 In this case, the lack of regard for the life of the child has seemingly been extended to the mother.

"NOW also has an article posted on their website mentioning the leading cause of death among pregnant women is murder!!!! And they still don't even acknowledge the need for this critical bill." Jennifer Bingham, Executive Director, SBAList@DemocracyData.com

Subject: Unborn Victims of Violence Act Introduced in the House!
Date: 5 May 2003 21:48:15 –0400

"Peterson Murders Shift Debate on Unborn Victims Bill By Jeff Johnson CNSNews.com Congressional Bureau Chief May 08, 2003

Capitol Hill (CNSNews.com)-The murders of Laci Peterson and her unborn son, Conner, have refocused the debate on legislation intended to punish those who cause the death of an unborn child while committing another federal crime. The bill was reintroduced in the Senate Wednesday for the fourth time.

'No one should make this into an abortion issue,' said Mike DeWine (R-Ohio), the Senate author of the Unborn Victims of Violence Act (S. 146). 'No one looks at this tragedy in California and says, 'This is an abortion issue,' DeWine said, referring to the Peterson murders. 'There are two victims, and there should be two prosecutions. That's all we're saying.'

Scott Peterson, who was Laci's husband and Conner's father, has denied killing his wife or their son. He has been charged under California state law with two counts of murder. Had the crimes been committed under federal jurisdiction, he could only have been charged with murdering his wife.

Sen. Lindsey Graham (R-S.C.) said that most Americans, regardless of their beliefs about abortion, should 'come together pretty quickly' when a pregnant woman is attacked. 'About 90 percent of us say, 'Put the guy in jail as far as you can put him...and don't play this stupid game of ignoring the obvious,' Graham said. 'When the bodies washed up on shore, there were two people there: the little baby and the mother.'

The bill would exempt lawful abortions and deaths as the result of legitimate medical treatment from prosecution. The mother of a murdered child would be exempt from prosecution under the proposal. The proposal has passed the House twice by significant bipartisan margins but has yet to survive in the Senate.

Graham dealt with cases similar to the murders of Laci and Conner Peterson before first being elected to Congress. 'I was a prosecutor in the Air Force,' Graham recalled. 'We had situations on Air Force bases overseas and in other places where a pregnant woman would get attacked, and you didn't have a vehicle to deal with the loss of the unborn child.'

Laci Peterson's family-the Rocha family-has written DeWine and Rep. Melissa Hart (R-Pa.), the sponsor of the House version of the bill, voicing their support for the legislation and asking that it be named in Laci and Conner's memory. '[T]his bill is very close to our hearts. We have lost not only our future with our daughter and sister, but with our grandson and nephew as well,' members of the Rocha family wrote in their letter Monday. 'When we heard about this bill, we immediately thought of placing a request to have it named 'Laci and Conner's Law' in their memory.' DeWine was uncertain Wednesday morning if the legislation could be renamed after being introduced, but the change could be made during a conference committee if the bill is passed by both the House and Senate.

Bill predicted to pass, but Senate fight expected

Sen. Orrin Hatch (R-Utah), chairman of the Senate Judiciary Committee, said he is optimistic about the bill's chances in the Senate despite the fact that it has failed twice before. 'This time, I think, we will pass this legislation,' Hatch said, adding that reintroducing the bill while the public is attuned to the Peterson murder cases is important. 'I do think that what's happened there has electrified all of America against this type of violent conduct and abusive conduct,' Hatch added. 'I'd be shocked if it doesn't pass a hundred to zip.'

Douglas Johnson, legislative director of the National Right to Life Committee, said he appreciates Hatch's enthusiasm but doubts pro-abortion 'rights' groups will let the bill pass without significant opposition. 'They will say that this is a scorecard vote,' Johnson warned, noting that groups on both sides of life issues grade lawmakers on how they vote on significant pieces of legislation.

The National Abortion Rights Action League, which now calls itself NARAL: Pro-Choice America, has opposed the legislation each time it has been introduced in the past. 'This legislation is an attack on a woman's right to |abortion| disguised as an effort to protect pregnant women from violence,' the group wrote on its website. 'This legislation is part of a deliberate, coordinated anti-|abortion| campaign to undermine Roe v. Wade by endowing embryos and fetuses with 'personhood' rights.'

Graham disputed such claims, noting that California's version of the law has been in effect for 30 years with no effect on the availability of abortion in the typically liberal state. 'People have been prosecuted in California for attacking pregnant women and causing damage to the unborn child at the state level,' he explained. 'And abortion rights still exist in California.'

DeWine challenged the bill's opponents to come forward and clearly state their case. 'I have not heard anybody come on the TV and say that there should not be a prosecution under California law for the death of |Conner Peterson|,' DeWine said. 'I've not heard anyone offended in California saying that this was not a separate crime to kill this baby, who washed up on the shore. 'You're not going to hear anybody go to the Senate floor, I don't think, and say that California case shouldn't be prosecuted,' DeWine said. 'I would ask them |to| go to the Senate floor and say that.'"

"Dehumanization is always the first step in any planned massacre, which is why feminists stubbornly cling to the word 'fetus' and are panicked when an event like the Peterson killings puts the lie to their contention that the unborn child is somehow something less than human. Their defense of atrocities such as the abomination that is partial-birth abortion places them on the moral level of a concentration-camp employee.

125

Legality is not morality. It was legal to murder a black in 1840, a Jew in 1944 and it has been legal to murder an unborn baby in America for the last 30 years – in 50 more, perhaps it will be legal to murder a Christian, a Frenchman or a feminist. But morality is eternal, and regardless of the current state of the law, such actions will always be immoral.

As for the red-handed doctors, nurses and organizations that profit by stealing life from the unborn, better I say nothing. My thoughts regarding them are unprintable, and, I will confess, less than perfectly Christian.

But for once, a bright line has been drawn which prevents the supporters of 'a woman's right to choose' from hiding behind tortured definitions, incomplete phrases and naked appeals to selfishness, and forces the neutral majority to realize their complicity in America's greatest shame.

Indeed, I am grateful to those few abortionettes, like Mavra Stark of the Morris County, N.J., chapter of NOW, who are bold enough to publicly articulate what is the ultimate position of their pro-death camp – that a woman has a right to kill her child at any time.

Just this morning, I held a little girl in my arms, a beautiful little girl younger than Connor Peterson would be now, and when she smiled at me I was able to see the pure joy that was in her soul, even at such a young age. Wanted or unwanted, every child is precious and if a claim on privacy can be manufactured from constitutional penumbras and emanations, then surely an imperative to be born can be discovered in the inalienable right to life, liberty and happiness.

I hope that the sad and tragic fate of Laci Peterson and her little son, Connor, will help America wake up from its long, shameful national nightmare. Abortion is murder. Abortion must end."

Thanks to RNCLife for passing along the article these passages came from- "R.I.P. Connor Peterson", by Vox Day, in World Net Daily, Posted: April 28, 2003, 1:00 a.m., Eastern Standard Time.

As Congress is set to reconvene after its Memorial Day break, the bill is now being commonly referred to as "Laci and Connor's Law". May 31, 2003

"Jenny's Bill Connecticut's state senate has passed legislation that extends legal protection to preborn children. The bill, nicknamed 'Jenny's Bill' after Jenny McMechen, a pregnant woman murdered in 2001, provides a penalty of up to 25 years in prison for anyone found guilty of murdering a preborn child while assaulting the child's mother." Celebrate Life, May-June 2003, Issues Update

"Everyone agrees that the unlawful killing of a human being is murder. Everyone would further agree that soliciting, aiding, abetting or consenting to the unlawful killing of a human being is as wrong as murder. Murder in California and many other states is defined as 'the unlawful killing of a human being, or a fetus, with malice aforethought.' The pro-aborts had an exception added to the definition of murder in California to permit abortion. Under that provision, the definition of murder does not apply if, 'The act [killing] was solicited, aided, abetted, or consented to by the mother of the fetus.' The pro-aborts do not want you to closely examine these laws because you will discover within them their failure to fit in. Doesn't it seem strange that the language commonly used to identify a party codefendant in a murder is turned around to make abortion legal in California? For instance, in California, because of the 'exception to murder' language, a child or woman who did not consent to the abortion performed on her can seek an indictment for the murder of her child. The comparisons of these abortion laws across the United States could fill many pages. Suffice it to say that they just don't make sense...Regardless of how hard they try, the pro-aborts cannot make these pro-abortion provisions fit or make sense to rational people in our society." Ed Zielinski, General Counsel for Life Dynamics, in the May, 2003, issue of Life Dynamics News.

Dana Cody, of LLDF, refers to "the legal fictions that now govern American jurisprudence," and calls it "the 'abortion distortion.'"

Federal Judgeships, Chris Smith, and Excommunication

"Reuters:

**Bush Nominates 11 for
Federal Judgeships**

May 9, 5:15pm ET

By Steve Holland

WASHINGTON (Reuters)-President Bush on Wednesday offered his first 11 choices for federal judgeships with an appeal to Senate Democrats to 'rise above the bitterness of the past' and give them a fair hearing.

'I now submit these nominations in good faith, trusting that good faith will also be extended by the United States Senate,' Bush said as he made the nominations for appeals court judges in a White House East Room ceremony."

"'I urge senators of both parties to rise above the bitterness of the past, to provide a fair hearing and a prompt vote to every nominee,' Bush said. 'That should be the case for whoever lives in this house and whoever controls the Senate. I ask for the return of civility and dignity to the confirmation process.'

Bush was hoping to put a conservative stamp on the court, saying he picked nominees who know that 'the role of a judge is to interpret the law, not to legislate from the bench.'"

All that sounded very reasonable to me. So let's look at what the liberal party line was:

"In their first reaction, Senate Democrats said they would hold up at least of one of the nominees, a former aide to conservative Republican Sen. Jesse Helms of North Carolina."

In addition to being very partisan and hostile, that sounds very foolish to me. I assume that Jesse, one of the most powerful and influential senators, assured the president that he would see that the nomination passed.

"Senate Democrats vowed to hold up at least one nominee, U.S. District Judge and former Helms aide Terrence Boyle, because of concerns that the 4th Circuit Court of Appeals needs greater balance."

"Sen. Patrick Leahy of Vermont, ranking Democrat on the Senate Judiciary Committee, declined to offer any immediate assessment but said, 'The nominees who were selected for their qualifications are likely to be confirmed. Those who were selected primarily for their ideology are not likely to be confirmed.'"

I was stumped about exactly what was meant by the above paragraph at first. And those two paragraphs are contradictory. Balance equates to ideology. I think what Leahy's statement is really saying is that nominees who have the right philosophy have the right qualifications. I don't think Bush is going to submit unqualified candidates. Those don't seem like good faith, civil statements to me. They sound more like "mean spirited" grudges. But the following statement really capped it off:

"Judith Lichtman, president of the National Partnership for Women & Families, issued a blanket statement saying Bush's choices 'signaled that satisfying right-wing conservatives is more important to him than protecting the rights and freedoms of women, minorities, working people and others who rely on the courts for justice.'"

Well, first of all, my own personal opinion is that just about everybody in this country belongs to some minority. For example, Jewish Americans, Chinese Americans, Asian Indian Americans, and Irish Americans are all minorities; while women are a majority. But I'll accept Judy's "political" definition for the purposes of this discussion. Judy, how long had you had that statement prepared before President Bush made his announcement? Did you think about what you said at all? Because it makes no sense whatsoever. "Bush's 11 choices included three women, two African Americans and one Hispanic." That's a majority of the nominees, six out of eleven, from the very groups you implied in your statement! One of the nominees was a carryover from the Clinton nominations, and "…he included a few Democrats to make the group more palatable".

On the floor of the U.S. House of Representatives, May 16, 2001:

"I know that members of Congress are getting blitzed by Planned Parenthood and other abortionists…I appeal to you to resist. I ask you to stand with the victims, both mother and child, and against the victimizers. When we subsidize and lavish federal funds on abortion organizations, we empower the child abusers; and Planned Parenthood, make no mistake about it, both here and overseas, is 'Child Abuse, Incorporated.' Here in the United States, for example…Planned Parenthood has been given $2 billion and performed 2.6 million abortions since 1977. That is 2.6 million girls and boys who will never know the joys and challenges of living or the thrill of learning or marrying or playing soccer or raising their own families some day. That is 2.6 million

individual dreams and talents and creativity the world will never see…And if
that is not enough, Planned Parenthood both lobbies and litigates against
virtually every child-protection initiative, including parental notification,
women's right-to-know laws, abortion funding bans, partial-birth abortion,
and, again, most recently, the Unborn Victims of Violence Act."

"International Planned Parenthood Federation, which is based in London, is
leaving no stone unturned in its misguided, obsessive campaign to legalize
abortion on demand. If they succeed, millions of babies will die from the
violence of abortion. I urge members, please, let us not add to the body count
…Planned Parenthood's Vision 2000 strategic plan makes it very clear that
they want family planning organizations to bring pressures on governments to
campaign for abortion on demand. They do not cloak it, they do not disguise
it." Representative Chris Smith (Rep-N.J.)

The two paragraphs above were taken from a debate over an attempt to
override President Bush's Mexico City Policy. Of course, Congressman Smith
had no way of knowing how many abortion referrals Planned Parenthood has
been paid for.

"ALL president Judie Brown is among 2,000 notable Catholics who've signed
"A Canonical Petition to Excommunicate Culture of Death 'Catholics.'" The
petition mentions 50 political figures by name, including Sen. Edward
Kennedy, D-Mass., Sen. Tom Daschle, D-S.D., Sen. Patrick Leahy, D-Vt., Gov.
Gray Davis, D-Calif. and Gov. Tom Ridge, R-Pa."

"The petition cites Item 2272 of the Catechism of the Catholic Church:
'Formal cooperation in an abortion constitutes a grave offense. The Church
attaches the canonical penalty of excommunication to this crime against human
life.'" The Judie Brown Report, August 2001

It remains to be seen if the Church will act on principle or put self-interest
first. I don't know whether it would cause these people to modify their
positions to be less radical, or hurt them at the ballot box; but I think it would
make a point with rank and file Catholics about how seriously the Church
regards this offense. The petition is available for any Catholic to sign at: A
Canonical petition to excommunicate culture of death 'Catholics':
http://www.all.org/news/petition.htm.

Not a Catholic? Doesn't matter, you can go to the same site and click on the
link to the amicus curiae brief, and sign that.

Center for Bio-Ethical Reform

I copied the article below from about.com. I was going to just include a link, but I thought it was too important to risk that people might not go there to read it. It is the most incredibly well thought out, reasoned, lucid, rational, articulate, coherent, statement of policy on abortion that I have ever read. This is the rare instance where using outdated medical terminology works to the advantage of the pro-life cause. I was personally amazed that something technically called an embryo or "early fetus" could be so completely formed. But I didn't provide a link to their web site, because it is a little gruesome. However, this doesn't prevent you from copying and pasting their URL to your browser, if you personally want to go there. So I want to share this with you:

"Fetus Pics Hit the Road

Center for Bio-Ethical Reform Starts "Choice" Convoy

Dateline: 7/27/01

From the Center for Bioethical Reform

On Monday, June 25, 2001, the Los Angeles-based Center For Bio-Ethical Reform (CBR) launched its anti-abortion, Reproductive Choice Campaign (RCC). The project will involve the operation of a fleet of large, box-body trucks on whose sides will be displayed bill-board size, color photos depicting aborted human embryos and early fetuses. Several of these trucks can be viewed on the CBR Website at www.abortionNO.org. Initially, the trucks will be operated every business day on the Freeway system in Southern California. Routes will thereafter be added in Northern and Central California at times as yet to be determined. A nation-wide expansion will be undertaken before the end of the year. This is a long-term project which will continue indefinitely.

The purpose of the RCC is to make abortion impossible to ignore or trivialize. Public opinion surveys reveal that a large majority of Americans now oppose "pregnancy termination" in the second and third trimesters of pregnancy – especially if performed by "partial-birth" abortion. A smaller but still substantial majority support a right of abortion if it is committed in the first trimester of pregnancy. This fact is problematic from a pro-life perspective because The Centers For Disease Control report that some 90% of abortions are committed in the first three months of pregnancy.

These same surveys also disclose that public support for early abortion derives from the inaccurate perception that the first trimester baby is a mere "blob of tissue." In contrast, most Americans see the mid and late-term fetus as a real "baby" whose level of gestational development entitles it to rights of personhood. It is also clear that few Americans believe a suction abortion to be the moral equivalent of a "partial-birth abortion." We, therefore, conclude that it is vital to convince the public that the first term baby is as fully entitled to rights of personhood as a more mature fetus and that even an early abortion is as indefensible an act of violence as any "partial-birth" abortion. Extensive focus group research has proven conclusively that our pictures are the most effective means by which to achieve that goal.

RCC is a tactic which is consistent with mainstream campaigns of social reform. Shocking pictures have traditionally been used to dramatize injustice sought to be reformed in the areas of child labor abuses, civil rights for African Americans, U.S. military involvement in Vietnam, environmental causes, etc. What has changed is that for the first time in recent history, political conservatives are using this tactic in an effort to reform an unjust status quo which is being defended by political liberals.

It should also be noted that we believe it is important to protect children from exposure to disturbing photos, whether those photos depict aborted babies or any other shocking subject. That is why we base the trucks which exhibit our anti-abortion billboards in a location that is entirely industrial/commercial in its zoning. We will go out of our way to choose routes which minimize the time we must spend near residential neighborhoods. We will concentrate the truck routes on freeways rather than city streets. We will not knowingly drive past elementary schools, playgrounds, daycare centers, etc.

There is, however, no operating location in which we can guarantee that no child will ever see these painful images. The same risks to children exist every time the television is turned on. Sickening images are likely to appear, even during early prime time. The same is true with disgusting photos on the covers of magazines openly displayed at the checkout stands of supermarkets. Billboards are also increasingly likely to exhibit images inappropriate for young children.

When NBC Television broadcast Steven Spielberg's Holocaust movie, Schindler's List, in its early prime-time "family hour" slot (as PBS recently did again), then Congressman Tom Coburn, R-Ok., expressed concern over the large numbers of children who were exposed to the movie's extreme violence, profanity and explicit sexual content. His colleagues mocked him to scorn. UPI reported that Rep. Mark Foley, R-Fla., believed "the film belongs on television to educate children about one of the darkest chapters in human history." The article said "Foley agrees it was brutal, but truthful, telling of a 'demonic creature who was murdering millions of Jews...' But he says it is a story that should be told and remembered without any attempt to 'camouflage ...that evilness.'"

The New York Times quoted Rep. Tom Lantos, even more forcefully:
"...Lantos, a California Democrat who is the only Holocaust survivor in the
Congress, said Mr. Coburn should have been more concerned with the
children who were killed than with young viewers' hearing four-letter words."
The Tulsa World also covered the controversy. Lantos was quoted as
dismissing as "petty" Coburn's concerns about children seeing horrifying
violence. "He is dead wrong" Lantos said. He added "When you want 65
million Americans to watch...you don't start at midnight. These are such petty
and certainly misplaced priorities." Lantos even questioned Coburn's integrity.
"I think this is such a phony argument" he said. "It is such cheap political
grandstanding, my stomach turns." Rep. Martin Frost, D-Tx., also piled-on,
saying Coburn demonstrated a "lack of compassion" toward Holocaust
victims.

Now that children will be seeing our aborted baby pictures, will those who
savaged Rep. Coburn be as quick to defend our First Amendment rights as
they were to defend NBC's? We think it unlikely.

The Center For Bio-Ethical Reform will not submit to a two-tiered standard
for free speech: A permissive standard for the expression of liberal ideology
and a restrictive standard for the expression of conservative thought.

Our photos save unborn children and disturb born children everywhere they
are displayed. The question which must be answered by our critics is simple:
Do they care more about the feelings of kids than the lives of fetuses? If so, they
are not pro-life, they are "pro-feelings." We respectfully refuse to allow people
who are not pro-life to cover-up the truth about abortion. Those days are gone
and we will not go back.

Abortion is not exacting enough of an emotional toll on American society. The
culture is in massive denial about what abortion is and does. Social reformers
must always force-feed facts into the heads of people who are reluctant to
accept evidence of their own complicity in injustice. The Reproductive
"Choice" Campaign will be used to disturb the nation until the stress becomes
unbearable. Because the news media, entertainment media, education
establishment, clergy, etc. are suppressing the truth about what abortion is
and does, we will bypass these gatekeepers and take our message directly to
our target audience. The May 28, 2001 issue of U.S. News & World Report
featured a cover story about that audience. It was entitled "Traffic." The
article reported that:

Since 1982, while the U.S population has grown nearly 20 percent, the time
Americans spend in traffic has jumped an amazing 236 percent. In major

American cities, the length of the combined morning-evening rush hour has doubled, from under three hours in 1982 to almost six hours today.

Data compiled by the California Department of Motor Vehicles suggests that during rush hour, up to 50,000 people per hour will view the pictures displayed on each of our individual trucks. The freeway is the last place where viewers can neither turn the page nor change the channel. We have been presented with a vast captive audience and we will take full advantage of the fact that most will give our signs at least one curious glance. Once these pictures are in people's heads, they will never get them out. Every time viewers thereafter hear the word abortion, a disturbing picture will go off in their brains. Those with a functioning conscience will eventually change their points of view.

We understand that this project will not make us popular, even with many groups which call themselves "pro-life." We are losing the abortion battle precisely because so many "pro-life" organizations mistakenly believe they must be "liked" to be effective. But CBR is not trying to win a popularity contest. We are trying to effect social reform. Social reformers are never liked. We care less what people think of us than what they think of abortion. We are willing to have them hate us if that is the price which must be paid to have them ultimately hate abortion.

Those who retaliate against us with violence will only help focus public attention on our project. They will thereby unwittingly unmask the pro-abortion propensity for brutality. They will also inadvertently help us recruit staff and raise funds. As racists blamed Martin Luther King for creating a climate conducive to the riots he condemned, we expect to be accused of inciting similar unrest with our pictures. As was true of Dr. King, we also deplore violence but we will not be deterred by its threat against us. We are more determined to save babies than our adversaries are to kill them."

Postscript: "...our photos have reframed the abortion debate by exposing 'choice' as homicide. As she shouts 'It's my body,' Ms. Tomayo can no longer hide the presence of a second body-the one that has been dismembered, disemboweled and decapitated." "...the Centers For Disease Control say that 45% of women who abort have already had one or more previous abortions, post-abortive women are the women most likely to abort. This group is at such high risk for abortion that we certainly don't want them to 'feel good' about the 'procedure'." InPerspective, Winter 2001

"...how else are we to teach people who don't want to learn that abortion is an indefensible act of inexpressibly horrible violence? And even once they've learned, people often need to be bothered into acting against injustice. Shocking pictures change the minds of pro-aborts who still have a functioning conscience. Among pro-life viewers, these photos create a sense of outrage without which no one will ever be moved to take risks or make sacrifices to end injustice." "She had seen the same pictures we display on our trucks. Now she saw things from her baby's perspective." "'Everyone knows what an aborted fetus looks like. We don't need to see it.' Au contraire, Madame, you apparently do need to see it and we've got a long way to go until 'everyone knows what an aborted fetus looks like.' Even if 'everyone' knew that abortion is disturbing, many must see the pictures again and again before they become 'disturbed' enough to actively oppose the killing...photos which will change the course of history." "We'll make sure abortion bothers people when they head to work and even when they try to relax and we won't stop until they stop ignoring the plight of the unborn." Center for Bio-Ethical Reform

Gregg "Cunningham Communique" June 2002 Response to Airborne RCC is Sky High After five weekends of our Airborne RCC (Reproductive 'Choice' Campaign), we can safely say that the 30 x 100 foot banner with two labeled photos of a 10 week aborted baby is making a big impact. Beachgoers in Los Angeles, Miami, Boston, and outlying regions have viewed the truth about abortion-and most don't like it. The LA Times quoted Gregg's response. '...when Americans are killing children, they don't deserve a day at the beach.' ...Media coverage of Airborne RCC includes: The New York Times, The Associated Press, CNN, and Fox News. We FINALLY got the LA Times to do a story when they learned the NY Times was writing about Airborne RCC...a woman e-mailed us, 'I'm listening to Gregg on the *John and Ken Show* now. Terrific job Gregg!! You were articulate, calm and determined...' Karen also e-mailed us, '...he [Gregg] presented himself clearly & eloquently...he was kind to callers and CLEAR about his perspective...it was masterful to have researched the impetus for social change throughout history...' '...I heard part of the interview on the John & Ken radio show yesterday. Please keep the airplane and truck banners going. Sincerely, T.B.' This is typical of many letters we receive from people who are counting on us to do work that no one else in the world is doing." Nobody else has the incredible creativity, perseverance, common sense, smarts, organizational skills, temperament, and just plain guts, to do the unbelievable things this guy does! Here's some more of the same: "Unlike most pro-lifers, we believe that America won't reject abortion until America is forced to look at abortion. By covering-up the horror of abortion, the pro-life movement has helped the abortion industry make abortion relatively pain-free for most Americans. When the sewers of our cities are running with the blood of our children, we don't think America deserves a 'day at the beach'." You only think like that when opposition to abortion has become a dominating force in your life.

"...many are eager to learn from our research and to do what changes people's minds. One student told us, 'We want you to come to our campus, because what we're doing doesn't work.' Right now, a Hawaiian Reproductive 'Choice' Campaign truck is being prepared for action. Steve Holck, of Honolulu, decided Hawaii needed to see the truth about abortion, so he spent time with us learning how to develop a truck operation. Others from Florida to New Jersey have also begun efforts to get trucks on the road.

Lucas Lee, of Texas, contacted us to get a copy of the Reproductive 'Choice' Campaign video to show his church youth group. He'd been to our http://www.abortionNO.org/ website, and was impressed by the power of the imagery. He e-mailed us a report this Monday, 'This weekend went great. Between your video, the drama we had, and the message, I think 400 high school students went home this weekend knowing that abortion is murder.'" Lois & Gregg Cunningham in their *Communique*', Sept ember 2002. CBR phone number, (562) 777-9117. What I can't show you here is a new two part sign they have. On the left side of the sign is one of their standard body parts pictures with the caption "Would Jesus Use Bloody Pictures To Make His Point?" On the right side of the sign is a picture of Jesus on the cross with the caption "HE ALREADY DID."

"...A 27 year old Alabama woman who had just seen the photos told us 'I was in tears. I knew it was bad but I have never seen it.' A third Alabama woman (this one 20 years old) E-mailed us on the third to say 'I never saw an aborted baby before. I'm trying not to cry.'

Another E-mail came in on September 4th from a 19 year old female high school student from California. She said: 'The images prove that the media and pro-choice people lie. We are taught that babies 3-9 weeks are really not babies and have not yet begun to form. When I saw these pictures I was totally shocked to see that those babies are already little people.'" Gregg Cunningham, CBR, October, 2002

"Birmingham was a pivotal city for the civil rights movement, so it was only a matter of time before we took our truck campaign there. Sept. 2-6, 2002 was the week that Birmingham residents were challenged to consider the civil rights of unborn children. Two Reproductive 'Choice' Campaign (RCC) trucks traversed the highways around town. The trucks also spent three days at the University of Alabama campuses in Birmingham and Tuscaloosa, reaching thousands of students on their way to classes. NBC posted their telecast story on their website, opening with, 'A pro-life campaign began Tuesday on Alabama roadways. Abortion rights groups call the campaign a 'horror show'...' (September 2, 2002, nbc13.com) Pro-aborts don't realize how frequently they speak the truth". Cunningham Communique', October 2002

"An 18 year-old completed our http://www.abortionNO.org/ website survey on October 10, noting, 'I'm pregnant now and the thought [abortion] had crossed my mind, but I wanted to see what it looked like before I decided anything, and this changed my mind'". Gregg Cunningham, 11/21/2002

"'I saw 2 of your trucks this morning while dropping my 12 year old daughter off at school. This is the first time I've seen them. I have to say that my first reaction was shock, then disgust. At first I thought it was too 'in your face' & was shocked that it was right in front of a middle school. But the more I looked at the pictures the more I realized that that is exactly what the world needs to see. It's gruesome & disgusting, but it's reality. Abortion is a horrible, ugly, disgusting evil in our world today. This forces people to deal with the truth of what abortion is & decide which side they're on. When I was in 7th & 8th grade in Catholic school, we were shown pictures similar to the ones you have on your trucks. When I was 19 & pregnant with no husband, it was those images in my head that kept me from having an abortion. I pray that you'll have the same impact on millions of young women & older women alike. Thank you for taking a stand & God bless you & this campaign.' K.S. |E-mail| Our e-mail response to K.S. ascertained that her 12 year-old was the child spared from abortion." "The point of RCC is to force people to acknowledge the plight of the unborn-to help them consider their tiny neighbors." "There is no other pro-life project that has reached so many people in such a short time." From "A day in the life of the RCC", Cunningham Communique', December 2002. Also in that issue, "The perpetrators of genocide always dehumanize the 'inferior' class of 'beings' before they brutalize their victims." If you followed the news on Bosnia and Kosovo closely, you saw recent examples of that. Another thing that happens, is that "the perpetrators" get the laws changed so that what they are doing is legal and what others are doing in opposition is illegal. A good example of this is that if people are demonstrating too close to an abortuary the operators will call the police. When the police come, they will arrest the demonstrators, instead of the people inside who are killing the children. One more point on this most recent Communique'. There is picture of a GAP (Genocide Awareness Project) display on the New Brunswick Campus of Rutgers University. Although it is difficult to make out the detail, a large picture of a spotted owl is placed next to a picture of an aborted baby. The caption under the spotted owl reads "IF THIS IS WRONG", and the caption under the baby reads "CAN THIS BE RIGHT".

In CBR's glossy circular for December, 2002, there was a block of three pictures across the center of the first page. The first picture was of the attack on Pearl Harbor, in black and white-lots of smoke and ships sinking. At the top of the picture were the words "EMPIRE OF JAPAN". At the bottom of the picture were the words "PEARL HARBOR", and just below that "2,403 KILLED-DECEMBER 7, 1941". The picture next to it was of fire and smoke bellowing from the Twin Towers. At the top of this picture were the words "AL QAEDA-TALIBAN", below the picture "WORLD TRADE CENTER", and below that "2,937 KILLED-SEPTEMBER 11, 2001". The label atop the third picture reads "PLANNED PARENTHOOD", the picture is one of CBR's standard abortion pictures (in this case a severed leg and two feet transposed onto a quarter coin and covered in blood), underneath the picture says "1ST TRIMESTER (10 WEEK) ABORTED FETUS", and below that is inscribed "3,600 KILLED-EVERY DAY". Underneath the three pictures in bold type are the following sentences: "Despite news reports to the contrary, September 11 did not mark the worst single-day loss of life in U.S. History. Our Reproductive 'Choice' Campaign sign corrects this misconception." In sake of fairness and accuracy, I should point out that Planned Parenthood doesn't do all those abortions itself-just more of them than any other abortion provider in this country (and worldwide, for that matter). They go on to say: "We specifically chose the name Reproductive 'Choice' Campaign (RCC) so that every time our trucks with aborted baby photos roll through a town, everyone there knows exactly what 'choice' means to the unborn child."

"Upcoming events: Feb. 8, 2003—Legatus Annual Conference, Los Angeles, CA (Gregg Cunningham to receive the John Cardinal O'Connor Pro-Life Award)".

Tiny Tots, Some Common Sense, Title X, and September 11, 2001

"A week before Halea Maurer was born, her parents began preparing for her death. Told by doctors that their daughter was not getting adequate nutrition and oxygen, Anne and Ken Maurer of Elmhurst agreed to delivery at 27 weeks. Her only chance of survival was outside the womb, doctors said, but such an early birth would put her at great risk too. Halea weighed in at 12 ounces— even less than doctors had expected.

So her parents prepared a memento box of ultrasound images and cards from family and friends. They chose a name that is a variation of a Hawaiian word meaning 'fond remembrance'.

But Friday, Halea (which they pronounce HAL-ee-ah) was a thriving 4-month-old infant who tips the scale at 4 pounds, 6.5 ounces. 'We don't know what we did to deserve this,' said Ken Maurer, 31, cradling his tiny daughter as he and his wife prepared to take her home from Good Samaritan Hospital in Downers Grove Friday afternoon. 'We're so grateful.' Doctors credit Halea's survival to remarkable advances in neonatal care, scrupulous prenatal care by obstetricians and vigilance by the parents.

During a routine office visit, Anne Maurer's obstetrician noticed the fetus was not growing adequately. Consultations with neonatologists at Good Samaritan confirmed that the fetus was suffering from intrauterine growth restriction, which affects 3 to 7 percent of all deliveries. In this case, the placenta was not providing enough nourishment, and doctors still do not know why that happened. Based on the ultrasounds, doctors were expecting a baby of 500 grams, dangerously small but at the threshold for premature babies to survive, said Dr. Mike Fitzgerald, medical director of neonatology at Good Samaritin. But Halea was 340 grams when she was delivered by Caesarean section on June 25, nearly 13 weeks early.

'She was small, very small,' said Dr. Vihba Thaker, a neonatologist at Good Samaritin. 'But she was active, kicking around…and made some noises. I said she's a baby |who|, if we give her care, she will survive.'

According to the University of Iowa, Halea is the second smallest baby ever to survive in Illinois. She also ties for sixth place on the list of smallest babies ever to survive. Dr. Edward Bell, director of neonatology at the University of Iowa's Department of Medicine, said he composed the list of tiny babies based on reports by doctors and parents.

In the first few critical days after birth, doctors were amazed by Halea's vigor and the apparent normal development of her organs. But she has still undergone a flurry of medical interventions. She has been treated for hernias, suffered two infections, developed anemia because of the many blood draws to check her status, and had apnea, a typical problem in premature babies in which they stop breathing occasionally, Fitzgerald said.

Last week, though, Halea was taken off breathing support and was sent home Friday without any special care. 'Halea appears to be a totally normal baby,' Fitzgerald said. In fact, Fitzgerald said there is no indication she will suffer long term problems."

By Karen Mellen, Tribune staff reporter-taken from the front page of the Chicago Tribune, Saturday, October 27, 2001.

One of the kids in my extended family, I can't remember which one, was born with a double hernia, and he wasn't premature. There was a picture of Halea with the article. I don't normally go gaga over babies. But this was the most beautiful, most healthy looking, baby girl I've ever seen. Her parents looked pretty pleased too.

I've personally heard of babies surviving who were only 21 weeks old. Of course, they were probably about Halea's size. Note that the article refers to the baby as a fetus, but it was able to survive outside the mother.

"9.97 ounces at birth, 'miracle' baby finally goes home

ROME—A healthy 3 1/2-month-old girl who came into the world weighing only 9.97 ounces spent her first full day at home from the hospital Saturday, and her doctors said they believe she is the tiniest human on record to live so long. Doctors at Careggi hospital in Florence sent the 'miracle' baby home Friday weighing 4.4 pounds, saying she has a nearly 100 percent chance of a normal life. 'She really had the will to live, she was strong and lively,' said pediatrician Margarita Psaraki. Doctors said the unidentified baby and her parents live near Florence. The medical team nicknamed her 'Pearl.' The baby was delivered by Caesarean section in early February during the 27th week of pregnancy. At that stage of fetal development, some babies survive, but they have weighed much more at birth. The previous record was set in the 1990s by a baby in Japan who weighed 10.5 ounces at birth." From the Chicago Tribune, Sunday May 26, 2002, page 8.

"1 of tiniest babies ever beats the odds and lives By Deborah Horan Tribune staff reporter A healthy and relatively hefty Michael Despain was released Tuesday from the Oak Lawn hospital where he was born in October weighing only 12 1/2 ounces, unofficially the third smallest boy to survive premature birth.

Michael, whose twin died shortly after being delivered by Caesarean section, gave his parents a real scare only once in all the months he was developing and gaining weight—he suffered a collapsed lung. After four months, Michael weighs 4 pounds 9 ounces. 'I'm nervous and anxious,' said his mother, Janet. 'But I'm ready for him to come home.'

The drama surrounding Michael started when Janet Despain was told at 22 weeks into her pregnancy that she was having twins, but an ultrasound revealed trouble. The fetuses had stopped growing, their heartbeats were irregular, and their lungs were not completely formed. They weren't receiving adequate nutrition, doctors said, likely due to the possibility that they were sharing a placenta. They were not likely to survive for long inside the womb and they also were at risk for not surviving a premature birth, doctors said. After a month spent deciding what to do, Janet Despain, 28, and her husband Jeff, 31, of Monee, agreed to a Caesarean section on Oct. 18. After the births, doctors rolled Janet's bed into the neonatal care center, where she found Michael so tiny that she could have held him in one hand, she said. Jennifer was even tinier. Doctor's told the couple they doubted Jennifer, whose lungs were less developed, would live. The parents decided to take her off a respirator and together they held her while she died six hours after birth. 'We decided to let her go peacefully because she wasn't going to make it,' Janet Despain said.

Doctors said Michael defied the odds for boys and likely survived because he had few complications that normally plague premature babies, such as brain hemorrhaging, heart problems and frequent infections. He was half the size of a normal 26-week old fetus and required aggressive support on a respirator, said Dr. Charles MacDonald, a hospital neonatologist.

Boys are less likely than girls to survive a premature birth. Of 43 infants born weighing less than 400 grams (about 14 ounces) who survived, only six, including Michael, were male, according to Dr. Edward Bell, director of neonatal care at Children's Hospital of Iowa. 'We're still trying to unravel that,' said Bell, who keeps an unofficial log of premature babies, called the Tiniest Baby Registry". Chicago Tribune, February 12, 2003

"As of Monday, May 5, 2003 MEDIA & MARKETING P&G Targets Tiniest Preemies, 'Very Pre-Term' Baby Market By SARAH ELLISON Staff Reporter of THE WALL STREET JOURNAL

The target market for Procter & Gamble Co.'s newest diaper is small. Very small. Of the nearly half a million infants born prematurely in the U.S. each year, roughly one in eight are deemed 'very pre-term,' and usually weigh between 500 grams and 1,500 grams (one to three pounds). Their skin is tissue-paper-thin, so any sharp edge or sticky surface can damage it, increasing the chance of infection. Their muscles are weak, and unlike full-term newborns, excessive handling can add more stress that in turn could endanger their health.

Tiny as they are, the number of premature infants is increasing-partly because of improved neonatal care: From 1985 to 2000, infant mortality rates for premature babies fell 45%, says the National Center for Health Statistics. Increasingly, such babies are being born to older or more affluent women, often users of fertility drugs, which have stimulated multiple births."

"DEFEND AMERICA! DE-FUND PLANNED PARENTHOOD!

Homeland Security Problem: Every year, Planned Parenthood receives $142 MILLION in federal taxpayer dollars to abort nearly 200, 000 red-blooded American boys and girls.

Homeland Security Solution: Reallocate that $142 MILLION to the Homeland Security Department and use that money to protect American lives, instead of destroying them." (Title X and other federal programs.) An ad run in the Washington Times by The American Life League (http://www.all.org/news/defund).

"Mrs. Brown said…If those funds could instead be spent on the prevention of terrorism, America would reap the double benefit of saving thousands of Americans-both born and unborn. She suggested that even further savings could be realized by another practical suggestion: Remove the U.S. Marshals assigned to guard abortion clinics and re-station them aboard passenger flights." Taken from Action Notes, Celebrate Life, November-December 2001.

November 15, 2001: While visiting President Bush, Russian President Vladimir Putin remarked "Basically women are not treated as people in Afghanistan." That is also true of young children in the United States today.

"A hundred years from now the future may be different because I was important in the life of a child". Sandra Kuck

"Congress never intended to subsidize abortion. The law actually says that Title X money may not be used in 'programs in which abortion is a method of family planning.' …Title X grants comprise Planned Parenthood's second-largest source of revenue (after selling abortions)."

"Rep. David Vitter (R-Louisiana)...will offer an amendment (to an appropriations bill)...It will prevent any Title X funds from going to any 'private grantee, delegate, or clinic that provides chemical or surgical abortion.'" Family Voice-September/October 2001

"The rush to embrace 'bipartisanship'...forced Rep. David Vitter (R-La.) to withdraw an amendment that would have eliminated Title X funding of abortion providers such as Planned Parenthood." The Judie Brown Report-December 2001

On an abortion center in Appleton, Wisconsin: "A pro-lifer who lives in the house next to this clinic has placed two large signs in the back yard on billboards facing the Planned Parenthood parking lot and another large sign on the front lawn." From the Judie Brown Report, December 2001 The sign pictured read "It's Not Too Late To CHANGE YOUR MIND! WE CAN HELP ...Mother & Unborn Baby Care 733-7334 AAA Pregnancy Counseling Center 739-0039"

"The freedom of choice Planned Parenthood promotes is a choice to kill an innocent baby." James H. Garland, Bishop of Marquette, MI.

About a World Health Organization "abortion-related conference in Mexico City", by a spokesman for the Mexican Love Life Network, "these leaders have arrived as messengers of death under the pretense of public health".

"As horrible as this terrorist attack was, the number of people who died in all aspects of this horrible crime is only slightly less than the number of unborn babies killed every day by abortion, in the United States alone." Conrad Wojnar, reflecting on the terrorist attacks on 09/11/01, and expressing the realization unspoken by many of us in the pro-life movement.

"The victims of abortion are anonymous. The horror of abortion is invisible... it now seems likely that more Americans were killed by abortionists on September 11 (about 4,300) than were killed by terrorists (about 3,000)... Assuming 3,000 deaths among the 50,000 people who worked at the World Trade Center, about 1 in seventeen was killed. One in three unborn babies is killed by abortion every day. On September 11, it would have been six times safer to have been a worker in the Twin Towers than it is to be a baby in its mother's womb." "We will do for the public's perception of abortion what the press has done for people's understanding of terror." Taken from "In Perspective", Genocide Awareness Project, Center For Bio-Ethical Reform http://www.abortionno.org/.

"We are proud that our country, even as it experiences attacks from abroad, upholds our right to speak out for life. But we are also ashamed of our country, ashamed that we kill 1.2 million of our children each year. And we are grieved that America exports our ideas to the rest of the world under the guise of freedom, bringing death to children the world over. Survivors of the Abortion Holocaust, http://www.abortionsurvivors.org/. Of course, since then President Bush has cut off at least some of that overseas funding.

"In the past year...Courts across the land have continued to deny their protection to the unborn baby and those who speak out against abortion. Committed to protecting the sanctity of human life, The Rutherford Institute will continue to defend the free speech rights of those who oppose abortion— and to engage the public in a dialogue about the value of life." John W. Whitehead, Wednesday, January 9, State of the Nation, 2002, Rutherford Institute, Post Office Box 7482, Charlottesville, Virginia 22906-7482 http://www.rutherford.org

A New Pro-Life Leader, President George W. Bush, Emerges

"I will lead our nation toward a culture that values life—the life of the elderly and the sick, the life of the young, and the life of the unborn...and when Congress sends me a bill against partial-birth abortion, I will sign it into law." George W. Bush, August 3, 2000

In case you missed it. We like the company we keep here. President George W. Bush's declaration:

"National Sanctity of Human Life Day, 2002 by the President of the United States of America a Proclamation

This Nation was founded upon the belief that every human being is endowed by our Creator with certain 'unalienable rights.' Chief among them is the right to life itself. The Signers of the Declaration of Independence pledged their own lives, fortunes, and honor to guarantee inalienable rights for all of the new country's citizens. These visionaries recognized that an essential human dignity attached to all persons by virtue of their very existence and not just to the strong, the independent, or the healthy. That value should apply to every American, including the elderly and the unprotected, the weak and the infirm, and even to the unwanted.

Thomas Jefferson wrote that, '[t]he care of human life and happiness and not their destruction is the first and only legitimate object of good government.' President Jefferson was right. Life is an inalienable right, understood as given to each of us by our Creator.

President Jefferson's timeless principle obligates us to pursue a civil society that will democratically embrace its essential moral duties, including defending the elderly, strengthening the weak, protecting the defenseless, feeding the hungry, and caring for children—born and unborn. Mindful of these and other obligations, we should join together in pursuit of a more compassionate society, rejecting the notion that some lives are less worthy of protection than others, whether because of age or illness, social circumstance or economic condition. Consistent with the core principles about which Thomas Jefferson wrote, and to which the Founders subscribed, we should peacefully commit ourselves to seeking a society that values life—from its very beginnings to its natural end. Unborn children should be welcomed in life and protected in law.

On September 11, we saw clearly that evil exists in this world, and that it does not value life. The terrible events of that fateful day have given us, as a Nation, a greater understanding about the value and wonder of life. Every innocent life taken that day was the most important person on earth to somebody; and every death extinguished a world. Now we are engaged in a fight against evil and tyranny to preserve and protect life. In so doing, we are standing again for those core principles upon which our Nation was founded.

NOW, THEREFORE, I, GEORGE W. BUSH, President of the United States of America, by virtue of the authority vested in me by the Constitution and the laws of the United States, do hereby proclaim Sunday, January 20, 2002, as National Sanctity of Human Life Day. I call upon all Americans to reflect upon the sanctity of human life. Let us recognize the day with appropriate ceremonies in our homes and places of worship, rededicate ourselves to compassionate service on behalf of the weak and defenseless, and reaffirm our commitment to respect the life and dignity of every human being.

IN WITNESS WHEREOF, I have hereunto set my hand this eighteenth day of January, in the year of our Lord two thousand two, and of the Independence of the United States of America the two hundred and twenty-sixth.

GEORGE W. BUSH

For Immediate Release
http://www.whitehouse.gov/news/releases/2002/01/20020118-10.html Office of the Press Secretary January 18, 2002"

"President Bush has proven again that he will not be bent by the intellectual fashion of the day and will do what he believes right." The Claremont Institute, on a different issue, but in my opinion, appropriate here. http://www.claremont.org/

"Fetuses Are Children, Proposed Federal Rule Says Jan 31 6:19pm ET (2002) By Maggie Fox, Health and Science Correspondent

WASHINGTON (Reuters)-In a move that worried abortion-rights supporters, the U.S. government said Thursday it was proposing a rule that defines an unborn fetus as a child, saying it was meant to allow public money to be used to provide prenatal care for women. Both anti-abortion groups and groups supporting abortion rights said the proposed change in the State Children's Insurance Health Program (SCHIP), which would call a child a child from the moment of conception, would effectively give the unborn fetus a new legal status. 'The provision would enable states to make immediate use of the extensive funding already available under SCHIP to provide prenatal care for more low-income pregnant women and their babies, 'the Health and Human Services (HHS) department said in a statement. 'The proposed regulation, to be published in the Federal Register in the coming weeks, would clarify the definition of 'child' under the SCHIP program,' it added. 'At present, SCHIP allows states to provide health care coverage to targeted low-income children under age 19...The new regulation would clarify that states may include coverage for children from conception to age 19.' Abortion-rights groups have feared that President Bush, who opposes abortion..., could seek to erode abortion rights, and they worried that elevating the legal status of the fetus could make it easier to outlaw abortion. HHS Secretary Tommy Thompson denied the purpose of the rule change was to redefine the legal status of an unborn baby. 'I said what we are going to do is provide prenatal care,' Thompson told a news conference. 'What we are going to do is take care of poor women, to be able to provide prenatal care...'...both sides of the debate... 'We applaud this Bush Administration proposal to recognize the existence of an unborn child in order to allow the baby, and the mother as well, to receive adequate pre-natal care—a concept to which only the most extreme pro-abortion ideologues will object,' Douglas Johnson, legislative director for the National Right to Life Committee, said in a statement. But Regan Ralph, vice president for health at the National Women's Law Center, called it 'bad news.' 'It looks like cynical politics,' she said, accusing the Bush administration of using the rule as a way of effectively giving unborn babies a legal status they currently do not have, and thus attacking abortion rights. 'It obviously undermines the principle of Roe v Wade (the U.S. Supreme Court ruling that effectively legalized abortion) and suggests that women's health interests can be overridden by elevating the status of the fetus,' she added. 'And it turns the whole idea of prenatal health care on its head because prenatal health care is about the mother as well as the fetus.'...No one argues that prenatal care is a bad thing. Women who get proper prenatal care are much more likely to give birth to healthy babies. Earlier on Thursday the National Center for Health Statistics reported that the U.S. infant mortality rate fell by 3 percent from 1998 to 1999, in part due to more women getting prenatal care. HHS estimates that 10.9 million women of child-bearing age do not have health insurance. SCHIPS is a program aimed at filling that gap for children, as most people in the U.S. get health insurance through their employers." My browser is preset to start my internet sessions at Go2Net, because I like their arrangement of Reuters news. They select what is important, and I don't have to be grinding my teeth together as I read it, because Reuter's presentation of the news seems straightforward and unbiased. I didn't post this article at first, because I didn't think it was that significant, even though I understood the viewpoints. But, first of all, irregardless of it's motives, it has to be seen as an act of compassion, helping poor women, and their children, with important prenatal care. It's going to be very difficult for liberals to say, somehow, that they don't think we should give this to these women and children, and still look truly concerned about women's health. It's a flat out lie to say that women's health interests would be overridden-but the whole case for abortion is built on lies in the first place. So, is it really so important? My answer to this is-yes and no. It is because the whole pro-death movement is aimed at denying that children are people prior to the time they are delivered at the hospital (in some cases even after that). Therefore, their argument goes, because they are not "persons", they have no rights, as guaranteed by the 14th Amendment to the Constitution, the Ten Commandments (Thou shalt not kill), and common sense morality. I call this curious notion the "Inside Outside Theory of Life", or just plain "InsideOut" reasoning. Other times, I call it "The Global Positioning Theory of Human Life". No intelligent person should adhere to believing that the physical positioning of a child determines its humanity. But this is what the pro-aborts base their arguments on. SCHIP is just one of the ways I proposed changing our thinking about children the first day I uploaded this site to the internet-"specifically applied". That is, calculating a child's age from the moment a woman becomes pregnant. It's my understanding that Tommy Thompson is pro-life, although a lot of pro-lifers don't count him because he doesn't hew to their party line. I know President Bush is pro-life. So as for the motivation part, I leave you to draw your own conclusions. That's the, "Yes, it is important" part. The "No, it isn't important," part is that I don't think it will make any difference in any other areas right away. It's important to the pro-death people because they want absolutely no precedents set that suggest that a child has any rights while still being carried by its mother. Their purpose is to deny all rights to the child, while giving the mother all her rights plus special rights to boot. But, it is a first step, and, as they say, "The longest journey begins with a single step." Following are instructions, from Colleen Parro, in the Republican National Coalition for Life FaxNotes-March 12, 2002, about how you can personally help things along:

"SCHIP Comments Needed Now-Finally, the Department of Health and Human Services on March 5, 2002, published the regulation saying that the term 'Child' means an individual under the age of 19 including the period from conception to birth 'for the purpose of eligibility under the State Children's Health Insurance Program (SCHIP).' States are free to cover unborn children but can still choose not to. Please act now by taking advantage of the public comment period, which ends at 5 p.m. on May 6, 2002. Your comment can be as simple as this: It is simply common sense that unborn children are human beings who should be eligible for health care. That is what pre-natal care is all about. No fax or e-mail comments will be accepted. You must comment only via mail or hand delivery.

INSTRUCTIONS:
Please refer to file code CMS-2127-P.
Mail one original and three copies.
Send them to the following address only:
Centers for Medicare and Medicaid Services
Department of Health and Human Services
Attention: CMS-2127-P
P.O. Box 8016

Baltimore, MD 21244-8016

You may read the regulation as it appears in the Federal Register, March 5, 2002 (Volume 67, Number 43) |Proposed Rules| by visiting the Federal Register Online at (you can Copy and Paste-) http://www.access.gpo.gov/su_docs/fedreg/frcont02.html, or ask your Congressman to send it to you. How important is it that we all comment favorably on this new regulation? Here is what Kate Michelman had to say in a recent communication to the supporters of the National Abortion and Reproductive Rights Action League (NARAL): 'The Bush Administration recently proposed funding to recognize fetuses as children 'from conception' – a step toward making abortion illegal. This is a clear message to women: a woman's right to choose is not safe.' The abortion industry is pulling out all the stops to pressure the Bush Administration to withdraw the regulation. Please help now!" Note that she says "abortion industry". That's who's really concerned the most. But Colleen's still using the "unborn" terminology. I just have no influence. The letter that I wrote follows.

Centers for Medicare and Medicaid Services:

I am writing to comment on the new SCHIP regulation (CMS-2127-P) that says that the term "Child" should apply to an individual starting at conception. I favor the new regulation, because, obviously, the physical positioning of an individual shouldn't be a determinant of its personhood. That is, a person still being carried by its mother is just as much a person before it is delivered as after it is delivered. Good pre-natal care makes for a healthier baby, and will probably result in less cost to SCHIP over the long-term.

You could probably write one just as good. Or you could copy this one. The main reason I provided it is that I think the preventive medicine and probable cost saving factors are good points to make.

"Unborn Babies Now Covered By Federal Insurance Program

Thursday, October 03 @ 20:59:15 EDT

Summary: Under a new rule adopted by the Bush administration recently, states can extend health care coverage to unborn children through a federal program.

Under a new rule adopted by the Department of Health and Human Services (HHS), low-income pregnant women can now qualify for health care coverage for their unborn babies from the moment of conception. HHS head Tommy Thompson says the new rule 'represents a speedy new option for states that want to do more to ensure that women get critical prenatal care that will increase the chances that their children are born healthy.' He called this a 'commonsense, compassionate measure.'

The rules will impact the State Children's Health Insurance Program (SCHIP). States can add unborn children to their coverage if they wish. No woman or state is required to participate in this new health care option. Pro-abortionists are angry because they view this as a back-door way of deeming an unborn child to be a human being—something abortionists argue against. Douglas Johnson with the National Right to Life Committee has applauded the Bush administration for this effort, but he believes this new health care coverage will be blocked at the state level by pro-abortionists." Traditional Values Coalition

Animals, Rape, and Judicial Nominations

On the other hand, "The advocates of granting legal standing...have gained
support from constitutional scholar Laurence Tribe, a Harvard Law School
professor. Mr. Tribe argues that the leap isn't as great as it might appear:
Courts recognize corporations as juristic, or legal, 'persons'; that is, they enjoy
and are subject to legal rights and duties. 'The whole status...is what needs to
be rethought,' says Mr. Tribe. '...can certainly be given standing.' The push is
to extend the legal definition of 'persons' to Pan troglodytes...' In a speech in
Boston and a later law-review article, Mr. Tribe agreed, 'Clearly, Jerome was
enslaved.' But Mr. Tribe says there's no need for constitutional protections on
that score. The 13th Amendment already forbids slavery. Mr. Tribe notes that
nowhere does it state that only humans are covered; the status itself is
forbidden, he argues. Likewise, the Eighth Amendment bars cruel and
unusual punishment. Legal standing...could make it easier, not harder, for
courts to balance conflicting interests, he says." Mr. Tribe, of course, was
arguing for the rights of chimpanzees. But, if the arguments are good enough
for chimps, wouldn't they be good enough for humans, too? My source for the
quotes was The Wall Street Journal, April 25, 2002, and the columnist was
Wall Street Journal Staff Reporter David Bank.

But it's good to see the animal rights people getting involved, because it wasn't
always so. PETA (People for the Ethical Treatment of Animals) has filed a
brief before the Supreme Court in favor of the Pro-Life Action Network, which
has been accused of violating the RICO (Racketeering Influenced and Corrupt
Organizations Act) in NOW v. Scheidler; a ridiculous claim to compare pro-
life organizations to organized crime-but that's how these people think (if you
can call it thinking at all). According to the Life Legal Defense Foundation,
http://www.lldf.org/, NOW has painted themselves into a corner on this one,
because it's since been proved that NOW's witnesses lied, and got paid for it, in
a prior trial. It will be interesting to see how the Justices work around: "fraud,
perjury, and misconduct!"

"CBR's Genocide Awareness Project visited the University of Louisville (U of
L) April 10 and 11, 2002...students and professors...visited the exhibit. As
always, pro-aborts tried to confuse people by sidetracking them. But The
Courier-Journal (April 11, 2002) quoted CBR's Southeast Region Director
Fletcher Armstrong's response to the question of whether men should be
involved in a female issue, 'I assume people who owned plantations in the
1800's said people who didn't own plantations shouldn't have any say about
slavery'. 'What do you think about abortion in the case of rape?' was the
question of a disabled man riding a motorized chair posed to CBR Canadian
Intern Gillian Long. She initially thought this was another person seeking to
justify abortion in rape cases. She gave him our pro-life response and he

surprised her by replying, 'I am a rape victim baby. My mother had me and raised me.'"! Taken from the Cunningham Communique', June 2002.

"...we discussed abortion and euthanasia, and I noticed that many of the eight-graders who labeled themselves 'pro-choice' were horrified when they learned the truth about these practices. It made me realize how much the 'pro-choice' position is against human reason and how much it relies on tired rhetoric to succeed." Erin Campbell, Ave Maria Law School in Ann Arbor, Michigan, interning with the Life Legal Defense Foundation in Napa, California (707 224 6675), through ADF's Blackstone Fellowship program, published in the fall 2002 edition of "Lifeline".

"FOR IMMEDIATE RELEASE March 14, 2002 Charles Pickering Nomination Defeated Statement of NARAL President Kate Michelman

Washington, DC—'The Senate Judiciary Committee today rejected the nomination of Charles Pickering to the Fifth Circuit Court based on his activist opposition to...reproductive rights.' 'Pickering's defeat offers President Bush the opportunity to...nominate a judge for the Fifth Circuit who reflects... broad support for a woman's freedom to choose...As a Mississippi state legislator, Pickering called for a constitutional amendment to make abortion illegal. He also led Republican Party efforts to include the first anti-abortion plank in the National Party Platform, one that called for a constitutional amendment not only to reverse Roe v. Wade but ban abortion...NARAL will continue to closely monitor the records of all nominees and will continue to oppose those whose views threaten the right to choose.'" From the "NARAL Online Newsroom". So there you have it, "direct from the horse's mouth", so to speak-why the Charles Pickering nomination was defeated. Let me reiterate: "The Republican party was formed based on the principle that no person is the property of another person"; and I would classify that as a paraphrase, because I don't know the precise words or the original author-but the meaning remains the same.

"The Democrats claim no foul play here, but their arguments are shallow and transparent. Senator Daschle had the audacity to suggest that Justice Owen was 'unqualified'. Consider: she graduated top of her class from Baylor Law School, earned the highest possible score on the Texas Bar Exam, and received the highest rating-'well qualified'-from the liberal's own American Bar Association, the 'gold standard' for judicial ratings. And her record on the bench was exceptional! Truth simply has no meaning to the man!

Senators Leahy and Schumer insisted the nominee was 'too extreme' and 'way out of the mainstream'. How then, Senators, did the good judge garner 84% of the vote in her 2000 election to the Texas Supreme Court? And by the way, what would either of these guys know about mainstream?

The Feminists put a face on the real objection to the genteel judge from Texas, calling her 'an anti-abortion zealot.' So what exactly did this dignified lady do to bring such wrath upon herself?...the crime that sunk her nomination was that Priscilla Owen strictly interpreted a Texas statute requiring parental notification prior to minors obtaining an abortion. In short she applied Texas law as it was intended and as directed appropriate by the US Supreme Court. She did so with the support of over 80% of Texans, and over 80% of Americans.

It was the first time in history that the Committee rejected a nominee to this Court who had the ABA's highest rating. But the Committee Democrats knew they had to do the dirty work-just as they had to do it with an earlier nominee, Judge Pickering. The full Senate would have confirmed both these individuals. So much for 'extreme'!

And the President learned a nasty lesson. Last year, in the name of bi-partisan cooperation, President Bush gave California Senators Diane Feinstein and Barbara Boxer almost equal voice to the selection of federal district judges in their state. In return Feinstein personally met with Owen before the vote, commenting: 'I've met Priscilla Owen, I've talked to her, and I like her very much.' She then pulled the dagger from her purse and killed one of the President's top judicial nominees. So much for pacts with the devil." From: *The American*, September 2002

There was a lot more written about the Owen nomination from every source imaginable, and this was the most concise way I found to present it. But let me point out that the Texas law she upheld was about parental notification-not parental consent. The idea behind such legislation is-that if you have, for example, a 12 year old girl, going in for an operation, its a good idea for her mother to go in with her. Almost everybody agrees with that.

On "the liberal, left-wing leadership in the Senate...politicizing the judicial process and launching a...battle to block men and women appointed by President Bush to fill open federal judgeships. According to the Wall Street Journal, Leahy is 'already responsible for a judge shortage on the federal courts...' It also says that Leahy is obsessed with defeating President Bush's judicial nominees and that he has endorsed tactics 'even members of his own party assert are blatantly un-Constitutional.'...President Bush has publicly stated he intends to nominate judges who believe in following the law passed by our elected representatives-not in writing new laws themselves...the liberals have decided to pull out all the stops in defeating the President's nominees. They don't want any conservatives sitting as federal judges. The fact is, the liberals have decided to politicize the judicial process and get left-wing judges appointed who will make decrees from on high and force on us policies that were defeated by the voters. The hypocrisy of the liberals is disgusting. When the Republicans controlled the Senate, it was Senator Leahy who said in 1997, 'Those who delay or prevent the filling of these vacancies must understand that they are delaying or preventing the administration of justice.' He also said, 'I would like to believe that...no Senator is imposing an ideological litmus on judicial nominations.' But now that he's the Chairman of the Senate Judiciary Committee, he's bottling up President Bush's judicial nominees. And according to Senator Mitch McConnell, the liberals have established a litmus-test they are using against anyone they think doesn't support their radical left-wing agenda of abortion-on-demand and gay rights. Even the liberal Washington Post recently criticized Leahy. They wrote, 'delays are particularly objectionable when nobody will even come forward to make a case against the nomination...If there is no case, the Senate should move to a vote.' But in spite of that, Leahy continues to stall. It is commonly acknowledged that there is a vacancy crisis in the U.S. federal court system; Whereas, President Bush has nominated more judges and nominated them more quickly than any president in history-almost 100 in his first year in office...11 of the President's first nominees had to wait for over a year for a Senate vote, and many are still waiting...urge in the strongest terms that the members of the Senate Judiciary Committee stop playing political games and without further delay begin to give all nominees a timely and fair hearing." U.S. Justice Foundation, August 13, 2002

"Republicans last night filed a cloture motion to end the debate on Justice Owen and vote on her confirmation tomorrow. Though Justice Owen is widely thought to have the backing of a simple majority, her nomination lacks the 60 votes needed to end a filibuster.

Mr. Daschle's vow to block from a full Senate vote Justice Owen's nomination to the 5th U.S. Circuit Court of Appeals is another indication that 'the judicial confirmation process is broken,' said Sen. John Cornyn, Texas Republican. Mr. Cornyn, a member of the Senate Judiciary Committee, served on the Texas Supreme Court for three years with Justice Owen. Next month will mark the second anniversary of Mr. Bush's nomination of Justice Owen...Mr. Cornyn will mark the occasion next week by holding a hearing entitled 'Judicial Nominations, Filibusters and the Constitution: When a majority is denied its right to consent' to evaluate why five of the 11 people Mr. Bush nominated to the federal courts in May 2001 still haven't been confirmed. 'The U.S. Senate needs a fresh start,' Mr. Cornyn said. 'The process has become increasingly bitter and destructive and does a terrible disservice to presidents, senators, nominees and the American people.'

'The delays in the Senate confirmation process deter good people from seeking to serve on the bench and create a vacancy crisis in the federal courts that harms the American people,' Mr. Bush said. 'I call on the Senate to perform its constitutional responsibility to hold timely up-or-down votes on all judicial nominees, no matter who is president or which party controls the Senate.'" From a column by By Charles Hurt, THE WASHINGTON TIMES, 04/30/03.

"May 2, 2003 Bid to end filibuster of Owen falls short By Charles Hurt THE WASHINGTON TIMES http://www.washtimes.com/

Senate Democrats yesterday blocked a vote on the nomination of Texas Supreme Court Justice Priscilla Owen, the second of President Bush's judicial nominees to be filibustered. In a 52-44 vote, Republicans fell eight votes short of the 60 needed to break a Democratic filibuster against Justice Owen's nomination to the U. S. 5th Circuit Court of Appeals. Democrats already have a filibuster lodged against Washington lawyer Miguel A. Estrada, Mr. Bush's nominee to the U.S. Court of Appeals for the District of Columbia.

'This is unjustified obstruction,' said Majority Leader Bill Frist, Tennessee Republican. 'Our colleagues on the other side of the aisle are denying the Senate its constitutional right to give advice and consent.' 'This obstructionist tactic is an injustice and unfair to this good woman and unfaithful to the Senate's own obligations,' Mr. Bush said in a statement.

'Senate Democrats are now simultaneously filibustering two well-qualified nominees to the U.S. courts of appeals,' Mr. Bush added. 'The Senate has a constitutional responsibility to exercise its advice and consent function and hold up or down votes on all judicial nominees within a reasonable time after nomination.'

Mr. Bush first nominated Justice Owen to the federal bench two years ago this month. Her nomination was killed in the Judiciary Committee controlled by 11 Democrats last year, though she had the support from a majority in the full Senate. The president renominated Justice Owen in January after the November elections gave Republicans control of the Senate. Her nomination passed out of the judiciary panel in March on a straight party-line vote.

Democrats charge that Justice Owen is an extreme conservative unfit for the federal bench because of her rulings in favor of a Texas law requiring that parents be informed when their minor daughters seek an abortion. Sen. Charles E. Schumer, New York Democrat, rose on the Senate floor yesterday and spoke about the importance of blocking Mr. Bush's nominees. 'I'm proud of this moment,' he said. 'I think it's so important.'

Republicans found and released a long list of statements from Democrats who in the past argued against filibustering to prevent a vote on a nominee. 'I find it simply baffling that a senator would vote against even voting on a judicial nomination,' Minority Leader Tom Daschle, South Dakota Democrat, said on

Oct. 5, 1999, when President Bill Clinton was trying to get his nominees through.

House Majority Leader Tom DeLay, Texas Republican, went over to the Senate after yesterday's vote to lend his support to his fellow Texan, Justice Owen. 'The Democrats have imposed a glass ceiling over her,' said Mr. DeLay, who vowed to make a public issue out of what he called Democrats' obstructionism. 'We have a saying in Texas,' he said. 'It's 'Don't mess with Texas.'"

"Bush also named Dr. Elias Zerhouni…as his nominee to chair the National Institutes of Health…'Dr. Zerhouni shares my view that human life is precious and should not be exploited or destroyed for the benefits of others,' Bush said." Chicago Tribune, 3/27/02.

It's obvious President Bush would sign pro-life legislation, but we have to get it to him so that he can.

New York-Elliot Spitzer / Michael Bloomberg

In response to the New York Attorney General's ideologically and politically motivated attacks on, and harassment of, abortion alternative pregnancy centers in New York, in return for substantial campaign contributions by pro-abortion organizations, the following petition is being circulated by an affiliate of Expectant Mother Care; Spitzer Counter-Attack Response Center, 224 E. 237th Street, Bronx, NY, 10470-9916: "Whereas the topic of abortion has caused and continues to cause pain and division since the Supreme Court's 1973 Roe v. Wade decision; and, Whereas abortion proponents such as yourself claim to be in favor of 'choice' for women; and, Whereas the only alternatives to abortion in America are offered at pregnancy help centers such as you have targeted in your recent subpoenas; and Whereas these centers lack the financial resources to defend themselves thus giving the impression that the purpose of your subpoenas is to bankrupt them so as to close them down and remove alternatives to abortion in the state of New York; and, Whereas the lone complaint cited by your spokesman is scarcely grounds for subpoenas directed at (currently) twenty four organizations; and Whereas the allegations in your subpoena are more accurately applicable to abortion clinics in New York; Therefore, I PETITION you as the attorney general of New York to: Cease and desist from your one-sided partisan attack on these pregnancy centers. And, Subject abortion clinics to the same rigorous standard you claim to be impartially upholding in your attack on pregnancy centers." It's Gestapo tactics being used against charitable organizations offering free assistance to pregnant women and cutting into the profits at the killing centers.

"NYC mayor demands more abortion training Within days of entering office, New York City mayor, Michael Bloomberg issued a plan to make abortion training mandatory for OB/GYNs in the city's eleven public hospitals. National director for Stop Planned Parenthood International, Ed Szymkowiak, comments, 'You would think under the current conditions in New York City that he could find a better use for the city's money.' The National Abortion and Reproductive Rights Action League (NARAL) of New York applauds the proposal, which the group claims to have authored during the mayoral campaign." Issues Update, Celebrate Life, March-April 2002 That is, the mayor wants to train the doctors in how to kill their patients.

So we see pro-abortion organizations developing the perfect killing environment-mandated by government. Doctors forced to perform abortions, and women prevented from seeking alternative, and free, pregnancy counseling because it has been outlawed and shut down. Is this the environment, spread across the country, that you want to live in? It is for Planned Parenthood and NARAL-as many babies killed, and as much money made, as possible. No interference, and no opposing opinions. Is this your view of America? And if you decide to protest outside an "abortion clinic", you go to jail, just like in Monopoly. There's a Catholic priest, serving time in prison, for praying outside an abortuary in New York.

Planned Parenthood of New York City, Inc., alone, had $89,975,411 of income in 1998, according to the April 2001 Ryan Report, which gets its information from reports the various affiliates are required to file.

According to Chris Slattery, of Expectant Mother Care in New York City; NYC is considered the abortion capital of the world with 80 or more abortion centers/parasites (my descriptive terminology), and nearly half of all pregnancies ending in abortion.

"Fr. Norman Weslin was released from prison on April 3, 2002, after serving his entire five-month sentence for praying in front of an abortion facility in western N.Y...He was in excellent spirits and told Ed (Szymkowiak) his case would soon be up for appeal. He laughed when Ed asked him what would happen if he were to win the appeal, since he had already served the sentence. Ed joked that maybe they'll give him five months credit toward his next conviction...received over 1700 letters of support...Fr. Weslin was right back out at the scene of his 'crime' on April 6, 2002, praying outside a Buffalo abortion clinic...while Fr. Weslin was in prison the injunction that put him there was found unconstitutional by the 2nd Circuit U.S. Court of Appeals. When Father Weslin directly asked the local police on April 6 if his behavior was legal, the police replied, 'yes.'" Ryan Report June 2002 As I recall, the judge would not release Father Weslin despite the 2nd Circuit decision. How could he do that? You've got me on that one, I don't understand that either. Father Weslin must be a very dangerous man. My letter was one of the 1700 he received.

"Care Net is under attack by the National Abortion Rights Action League (NARAL). NARAL has even gone on record as saying they plan on publicizing, legislating, and litigating against Care Net with the intent of shutting us down. In NARAL's 60-page action kit for abortion activists, they explain how they plan on destroying us. There is no hidden agenda here. NARAL is very explicit about its priority: putting Care Net out of business. In the liberal bastions of California and Maryland, NARAL activists are filing their very own lawsuits against our pro-life centers simply because we're offering women a choice they don't: LIFE." Mike Reid, President, Care Net, in a January, 2003, letter. Care Net is a network of crisis pregnancy centers.

Partial-Birth Abortion Ban and Right to Life Act

From: Gary Bauer garybauer@mail.cwfpac.com
Subject: End of Day—5/23/02
To: Friends and Supporters of the Campaign for
Working Families, Gary L. Bauer, Chairman
Date: Thursday, May 23, 2002

The Poll You Won't Hear About

CBS News just completed a poll on America's attitude toward abortion, but
you won't hear Dan Rather talk about it. Why? Because the data once again
punctures the myth that American voters are "pro-choice." The poll instead
showed two voting blocks that are virtually identical in size. Thirty-one
percent of the country believes abortion should be generally available. Thirty
percent believes it should not be permitted. In the middle are 37% who believe
it should be available, but only under strict limits. CBS doesn't break down
this group any further, but we know from other data that many people would
permit abortions only for extremely rare circumstances. In short, there is a
working majority in the country composed of people who are either clearly
pro-life or who favor tighter restrictions.

From: Gary Bauer garybauer@mail.cwfpac.com
Subject: End of Day—6/20/02
Date: 20 Jun 2002 16:07:53-0400
To: Friends and Supporters of the Campaign for Working Families
From: Gary L. Bauer, Chairman
Date: Thursday, June 20, 2002

Partial-Birth Abortion On Agenda!

Congress has finally gotten around to addressing the horrific procedure of
partial-birth abortion. Rep. Steve Chabot of Ohio is introducing the Partial-
Birth Abortion Ban Act of 2002. The reason for the delay was that Rep.
Chabot and other pro-life members did not want to give moderates and liberals
a reason to vote against the legislation without addressing the issues raised by
the Supreme Court when it struck down Nebraska's partial-birth abortion ban
two years ago. The law Rep. Chabot is proposing will tighten the definition of
what constitutes a partial-birth abortion in order to answer the Court's
concern that the Nebraska law was "too vague." Rep. Chabot's bill will
include its own series of findings based on the extensive legislative hearings
held on partial-birth abortion and on the judgment of the American Medical
Association that the procedure is "not good medicine." Former Surgeon

General C. Everett Koop even testified that partial-birth abortions are "never medically necessary to protect a mother's health or her future fertility."

My friends, this is a battle we must win. Support for abortion on demand peaked in 1992 when 34% of Americans agreed with the statement "abortion should be legal in all cases." After the debates over partial-birth abortion, the level of strong pro-abortion sentiment fell to 22% by 1997. As the truth about abortion and the abortion industry is made known, the American people move our way. I will do everything I can to insure that this ban passes and we will keep you posted as the legislation moves forward.

From: "Jennifer Bingham, Executive Director" Executive.Director@sba-list.org Subject: The Partial Birth Abortion Ban was introduced yesterday!
Date: Thu, 20 Jun 2002 16:00:52-0400 DATE: June 19, 2002
FROM: Jennifer Bingham, Executive Director
SUBJECT: The Partial Birth Abortion Ban was introduced yesterday!

Yesterday, Congressman Steve Chabot introduced the Partial-Birth Abortion Ban of 2002 that prohibits the partial-birth abortion procedure unless it is necessary to save the mother's life. This bill also defines the process of partial-birth abortion.

To e-mail your Congressman to support this critical bill go to http://www.sba-list.org/BanPBA/. For more details on Partial Birth Abortion go to–http://www.sba-list.org/partialbirthban.

I'm sure you remember when former President Bill Clinton vetoed the federal ban passed by the 104th, 105th, and 106th Congresses—DESPITE THE FACT THAT THE MAJORITY OF AMERICANS SUPPORT A BAN! As you know, there is no medical or moral reason for any woman to ever have this procedure, or for any child to suffer such a cruel death. In addition to these medical groups, the overwhelming majority of Americans, both Republicans and Democrats, men and women, and many who consider themselves "pro-choice," agree that partial birth abortion is closer to infanticide than abortion, and has no place in our civilized society. Please e-mail your Representative to ask them to support a ban on this barbaric termination of a child which is minutes from their first breath. Americans must take a stand on this issue and get their Representatives to pass this ban! We need your help today. Please e-mail your Congressman. Thank you in advance for your help! Sincerely, Jennifer Bingham Executive Director Susan B. Anthony List.

From: "Jay Alan Sekulow, Chief Counsel" jaysekulow@aclj.net
Subject: I will NEVER give up!
Date: Tue, 23 Jul 2002 13:11:15 UT

You and I have a NEW WINDOW OF OPPORTUNITY to ban partial-birth abortion for once and for all...

This week the House of Representatives is voting on a new piece of legislation called the Partial-Birth Abortion Act of 2002-

Rep. Steve Chabot of Ohio has introduced H.R. 4965, the Partial-Birth Abortion Act of 2002 designed differently from the Nebraska state ban overturned by a slim majority of the Justices on the Supreme Court of the United States. I strongly believe that this well-written law COULD survive the legal challenge, and stand. Better crafted than the Nebraska bill, H.R. 4965 addresses some of the concerns of the high court. This could be the statute that wins a fifth vote from the Supreme Court...and finally OUTLAWS partial-birth abortion!

WE HAVE A CHANCE TO END THE INFANTICIDE-this most horrible form of baby-killing...in which the baby is allowed to be almost totally born (feet first, leaving only the head in the womb, in order to keep the operation technically "legal")...and then the abortionist punctures the baby's skull, suctions out the brains...and in many cases, sells the baby's dead body to a "harvester" who markets it to the scientific and academic research fields!

It is ghastly. It is an ABOMINATION. And yet it happens over and over and over again-entirely under the cloak of "legality"!

WOULD YOU JOIN ME TODAY IN DOING EVERYTHING POSSIBLE TO STOP IT?

Our legislative office and other attorneys from our staff have worked to provide Congress with thorough research, input and review of this new bill-and believe it will withstand any constitutional challenges. This is a strong piece of legislation-one that can be defended in the courts. In fact, we are already preparing for an onslaught of federal court challenges from the pro-abortion lobby that will come if the bill is passed by the House and the Senate and signed by the President. For the sake of unborn babies, we will defend it all the way to the Supreme Court if necessary!

"With babies dying every day, thank God we have another chance to save them. Dear Friend, Sometimes you just know what's right. It doesn't matter if it's popular, doesn't matter if others will ever agree with you. You just know. That's the kind of deep-down passion I feel about the horror that is still going on in this country—the torture-murder of babies as they're born—antiseptically known as 'partial-birth abortion.' I intend to keep on fighting for the preservation of life – opposing with every resource at my disposal the vicious dismemberment and destruction of babies in the process of being

161

born—and the outrage of calling it 'legal.'...we have a new window of opportunity—the Partial-Birth Abortion Act of 2002 pending in Congress...we have continued to work with members of Congress in an effort to craft new legislation that would...pass muster with the courts...The language of the bill will be a crucial factor in court...the real battle will come in the Senate. With much effort on our part, we could secure a majority in the Senate to pass the bill and get it to the President's desk for signing. In other words, America is poised for adoption of a nationwide ban on partial-birth abortion...I am praying that you are gripped by this outrage – and this opportunity!...You and I are the voice for millions of unborn children...I can't help but feel that it will be worth every penny...every hour of labor...every prayer prayed...if we can save the lives of unborn children and eradicate this evil from our land. Please help us today. Stand up for life...It's important that we have...petitions quickly on the desks of Congress as they return from their August recess. So your voice will be heard. Your heart for children, your commitment to commonsense morality, will be felt in Washington...we can't walk away from what has become a defining issue in our society. For the sake of unborn babies, we can't back down on partial-birth abortion—especially when we could see a federal ban passed into law! I do appreciate you...I thank God that He led you to stand with me and planted in you a deep-down dedication to what is right, no matter the odds, the difficulties, or obstacles. In the midst of a conflict like this, your friendship, support, prayers, gifts, and steadfastness encourage me. Thank you so much for your role in pro-tecting life...Your brother...Jay Alan Sekulow Chief Counsel" July 23, 2002, The American Center For Law & Justice, P.O. Box 64429, Virginia Beach, VA 23467-4429 http://www.aclj.org/

"EXECUTIVE OFFICE OF THE PRESIDENT OFFICE OF MANAGEMENT AND BUDGET WASHINGTON, D.C. 20503 July 23, 2002 (House Rules) STATEMENT OF ADMINISTRATION POLICY (This Statement Has Been Coordinated By OMB With The Concerned Agencies.) H.R. 4965-Partial-Birth Abortion Ban Act of 2002 (Rep. Chabot (R) OH and 152 co-sponsors) The Administration strongly supports enactment of H.R. 4965, which would ban a certain type of late-term procedure commonly known as 'partial-birth abortion,' except in cases where the life of the mother is endangered. Partial-birth abortion is a procedure that is not accepted by the medical community and that 30 States have attempted to ban. The Administration believes that enactment of H.R. 4965 is morally imperative and constitutionally permissible to prohibit this very abhorrent form of abortion."

From: "Jennifer Bingham, Executive Director"
Executive.Director@sba-list.org
Subject: House Passes Partial-Birth Abortion Ban Act tonight!
Date: Wed, 24 Jul 2002 21:45:55-0400

A PRO-LIFE VICTORY!

The U.S. House of Representatives passed the Partial-Birth Abortion Ban Act (H.R. 4965) on Wednesday, July 24 by a wide margin and with bipartisan support. The bill, sponsored by Congressman Steve Chabot (R-Ohio), passed by a vote of 274-151. Congress has approved national bans on partial-birth abortion before, but each time the bill was vetoed by President Clinton.

AND A CALL TO ACTION! WE NEED YOUR SUPPORT MORE THAN EVER!

Now that this commonsense ban has passed the House, we must encourage Senator Tom Daschle to bring the bill before the Senate!

With a pro-life President in the White House, the bill will surely be signed into law-but the bill much reach his desk first! That's where you can help. Please click the link below to e-mail Senator Daschle to ask him to bring the Partial Birth Abortion Ban before the Senate for a vote before the August recess.

http://www.sba-list.org/pbaban-http://www.sba-list.org/pbaban
Senate Majority Leader Tom Daschle (D-SD) is closely allied with the pro-abortion lobby, which vehemently opposes the bill. Daschle could prevent a vote on the House-passed bill.

That is why WE MUST keep the pressure on!

Thank you in advance for your help!

Sincerely, Jennifer Bingham Executive Director Susan B. Anthony List

The petition reads: "I am writing to express my strong opposition to partial-birth abortion and to urge you to bring the Partial-Birth Abortion Ban Act of 2002 up for a vote in the Senate. There is no medical or moral reason for any woman to ever have this procedure, or for any child to suffer such a cruel death. The American Medical Association, the 600-member Physicians' Ad hoc Coalition for Truth (PHACT) as well as our nation's highly respected former Surgeon General C. Everett Koop, all agree that partialbirth abortion is never medically necessary. In addition to these medical groups, the overwhelming majority of Americans, both Republicans and Democrats, men and women, and many who consider themselves 'pro-choice,' agree that partial birth abortion is closer to infanticide than abortion, and has no place in our civilized society. I urge you, in the best interests of women and their children, to vote in support of an immediate vote and end to partial-birth abortion. Please support the Partial-Birth Abortion Ban Act of 2002 (H.R. 4965) introduced by Congressman Steve Chabot and passed by the House. I would appreciate a prompt reply to my letter."

===

From: The Pro-Life Infonet infonet@prolifeinfo.org
Reply-To: Steven Ertelt infonet@prolifeinfo.org
Subject: New Partial-Birth Abortion Ban Receives Strong Bipartisan Vote
Source: Pro-Life Infonet; July 24, 2002

New Partial-Birth Abortion Ban Receives Strong Bipartisan Vote

Washington, DC (ProLifeInfo.org)—With another lopsided bipartisan majority, the House of Representatives approved a rewritten bill that bans partial-birth abortions. The House voted 274-151 for the partial-birth abortion prohibition and turned back 187-241 an effort by pro-abortion Rep. Tammy Baldwin (D-WI) to send the bill back to committee and add a health exception that would result in a ban on no partial-birth abortions. Nine Republicans voted against the ban and 65 Democrats voted for it. The pro-abortion motion to recommit to change the bill to a phony ban had 19 Republicans voting for it and 41 Democrats voting against it.

"We commend Congress for persevering in this long fight to protect the unborn from a monstrous death," said the Family Research Council in a statement.

President Bush supports the ban. He said in a statement it strongly supports the bill, saying it is ``morally imperative and constitutionally permissible to prohibit this very abhorrent form of abortion.'

However, the bill is unlikely to see the light of day in the Senate thanks to pro-abortion Senate Majority Leader Tom Daschle (D-SD). Daschle, who previously voted for the ban, signaled he would not support the bill that passed in the House, and is not likely to make any effort to find space on the legislative calendar to take it up in the Senate.

"If there was a clean up-and-down vote on the bill passed by the House, the Senate would approve it," said Douglas Johnson, legislative director for the National Right to Life Committee (NRLC). "If the ban on partial-birth abortion does not reach President Bush for his signature, the blame will rest squarely on the Senate Democratic leadership."

However, some pro-life members of the Senate may work to force the issue. "We do think that partial-birth abortion is a procedure that should not be allowed to stand," pro-life Senate Minority Leader Trent Lott (R-MS) said Wednesday.

Congressman Chris Smith (R-NJ), encouraged the House to pass the ban saying, "I believe it's time for a serious reality check and a serious compassion check."

Members who spoke in favor of the partial-birth abortion ban included pro-life members Myrick (R-NC), Barcia (D-MI), Linder (R-GA), Ros-Lehtinen (R-FL), Jo Ann Davis (R-VA), Hart (R-PA), Pickering (R-MS), Sullivan (R-OK), Cubin (R-WY), Forbes (R-VA), Pitts (R-PA), Barr (R-GA), Ryun (R-KS), Sensenbrenner (R-WI), Miller (R-FL), and Mark Foley (R-FL), who has a mixed record on abortion.

To see how your member voted on the Partial-Birth Abortion Ban, go to http://clerkweb.house.gov/cgi-bin/vote.exe?year=2002&rollnumber=343

To see how your member voted on the pro-abortion attempt to add a health exception, go to
http://clerkweb.house.gov/cgi-bin/vote.exe?year=2002&rollnumber=342

===

"The House voted overwhelmingly yesterday, 274-151, to ban the gruesome, inhumane practice of partial birth abortion. Sixty Democrats joined all but 7 Republicans to vote to end the procedure. No decent society can explain away a 'procedure' that allows an unborn child in the 7th or 8th month of development to have their skull punctured and brains extracted because someone 'chooses' it for them. And no word in our Constitution could possibly allow it. Let's hope Tom Daschle's Senate can also find the moral instinct to say 'no' to this hideous practice." Gary Bauer Thursday, July 25, 2002, Campaign for Working Families End of Day

----

From: The Pro-Life Infonet Steven Ertelt infonet@prolifeinfo.org
Source: Associated Press, Pro-Life Infonet; February 13, 2003

Partial-Birth Abortion Ban Re-Introduced, Chances Look Good

Washington, DC—On the heels of election victories in the 2002 midterm elections, pro-life lawmakers hope to pass several pro-life bills and send them to President Bush for his signature.

Ohio Congressman Steve Chabot (R-OH) has introduced a bill to ban partial-birth abortions with a bipartisan list of over 100 cosponsors. 'It's time for Congress to act and place this bill in front of the president so that we can finally end this national tragedy,' said Rep. Chabot. 'While I expect that some of the Senate's most zealous pro-abortion advocates will again attempt to block this legislation, I am confident that we will finally be able to pass this ban into law.' House Judiciary Committee Chairman, pro-life Rep. Jim Sensenbrenner (R-WI), said GOP leaders hope to get the bill passed by the full House before the Easter break.

The Supreme Court ruled 5-4 three years ago to strike down a Nebraska law banning the gruesome abortion procedure, saying the law did not adequately define the procedure and that its lack of a so-called health exemption imposed an unconstitutional 'undue burden' on women. John C. Willke, MD, president of Life Issues Institute, takes issue with the court's reasoning. 'When talking about the partial birth abortion procedure, we must remember: it's a very specific type of abortion done after viability. 80% of the babies killed have been normal. It is not needed to save the mother's life, or her physical health, and, from testimony of the abortionists themselves, we know that most of these abortions are purely elective,' Willke explained."

"The abortionists understand that passing the Partial-Birth Abortion Ban will give us momentum to pass other bills that are even more important…By expanding the visibility of our national campaign to stop the slaughter of partially-born babies, you and I will further reveal the sinister nature of the pro-abortion politicians who try to pawn themselves off as 'pro-choice.'" Martin E. Fox, President, National Pro-Life Alliance, March 5, 2003.

There are a lot of people who think nothing can be done about abortion. Each small victory helps to dispel that perception. Gregg Cunningham of CBR has written me more than once that he has had affluent visitors who are sympathetic to the pro-life cause, but don't really believe anything can be done about it; and are therefore reluctant to make donations.

"I was shocked when I first heard that it was legal in America to abort healthy, fully-developed children. I didn't want to believe it. But then I saw the facts. I've heard from hundreds of Doctors—Obstetricians—and they all tell me the same thing: 'This is never, never medically necessary.' Partial Birth Abortions are almost always performed on healthy babies of healthy mothers. It is barbaric. It is cruel. It is inhumane. It is murder, plain and simple…it needs to be outlawed now. I wrote the 'Partial Birth Abortion Ban Act.' And I took the lead in the Senate to BAN this barbaric practice. I have fought for years now to pass this ban.

I have taken a lot of heat over the years for speaking out so strongly against Partial Birth Abortion. Pro-Abortion special interest groups have pulled out all the stops to defeat me and drive me out of the Senate. Bill Clinton personally came to my state to campaign against me in 2000...

...these children can't speak for themselves. They don't have a chance to say, 'I would like to be born.' They do not get the chance to tell you how it feels to be brutally murdered seconds before their first breath. And unless you and I speak for them, they will be forgotten, along with thousands upon thousands of others. If a government deliberately allows this kind of barbarism to be inflicted on the most helpless and innocent, who among us will be spared in the end?" U.S. Senator Rick Santorum

"From: 'Legislative Alert!' SBAList@democracydata.com
Subject:Partial Birth Abortion Addressed in the Senate Today!
Date: 10 Mar 2003 16:55:56-0500

Today, the Senate will begin debating the Partial-Birth Abortion Ban Act. A vote is expected to take place by Thursday and both sides believe that the ban will be passed.

The pro-abortion groups are diligently working to portray this infanticide as a necessary form of abortion for the 'health' of a mother. According to the American Medical Association, partialbirth abortions are NEVER medically necessary.

We have a chance to FINALLY ban this horrific and gruesome procedure. But there is still a battle in the Senate."

"Partial-Birth Ban Passes Overwhelmingly

Early this morning the Senate passed the ban on partial-birth abortions by 64-to-33. Make no mistake about this, my friends: This vote would not have happened had the Democrats retained control of the Senate. Yet, it is also a clear example of the power of values issues to move votes. Nothing else in the Republican agenda is likely to come close to garnering 64 votes in the Senate.

But the fact is liberals are vulnerable on these issues and their radicalism needs to be exposed. Case in point: Senate Minority Leader Tom Daschle. Sen. Daschle voted for final passage of the ban, but he also voted for every attempt to gut, weaken and stall the ban over the past two days. Senator Daschle is up for reelection next year and when his back was against the wall, there was a line he dared not cross." Gary L. Bauer, Chairman CWF, 03/13/03

"After a heated and often trying debate, with pro-abortion Senators offering phony amendments to gut the bill, the Partial Birth Abortion Ban Act of 2003 (S.3) FINALLY passed the Senate! Congress has approved national bans with bipartisan support on partial-birth abortion twice before but both were vetoed by Clinton in 1996 and 1997. It is time for the House to take up this critical legislation!...support the passage of the Partial Birth Abortion Ban of 2003 (H.R. 760) as introduced on February 13th by Congressman Steve Chabot. Please know that most Americans support a complete ban on Partial Birth Abortion. We have a chance to FINALLY ban this horrific and gruesome procedure." "Legislative Alert!", SBAList@democracydata.com, 13 Mar 2003 16:29:11-0500

"The Senate yesterday passed a ban on partial-birth abortion, and both sides expect the legislation to be signed by President Bush this year, after a seven-year journey that included two presidential vetoes the Senate could not override.

'It is a victory for the innocents whose lives are brutally terminated by this procedure,' said bill sponsor Sen. Rick Santorum, Pennsylvania Republican, after his measure passed 64-33.

The measure would ban partial-birth abortions except when necessary to save the mother's life. In a partial-birth abortion—also known as dilation and extraction—the baby is partially delivered before its skull is pierced and its brain sucked out.

The House is likely to pass the ban by the end of April, predicted Rep. Steve Chabot, Ohio Republican and sponsor of the House bill. Mr. Bush has repeatedly urged its passage.

Sixteen Senate Democrats voted in favor of the bill,...Three Re-publicans opposed the bill—Sens. Olympia J. Snowe and Susan Collins of Maine, and Lincoln Chafee of Rhode Island.

Democratic presidential hopefuls Sens. Bob Graham of Florida and Joseph I. Lieberman of Connecticut opposed the ban, as both did last time the Senate considered it in 1999. Sens. John Kerry of Massachusetts and John Edwards of North Carolina did not vote yesterday, but both opposed the ban last time. Sen. Joseph R. Biden Jr. of Delaware also did not vote yesterday but supported the ban previously.

Opponents said the bill's passage was a major setback for abortion rights, and groups including NARAL Pro-Choice America plan to challenge the legislation in court as soon as it becomes law.

'It's a major strike, no question, against a woman's right to choose,' said Sen. Dianne Feinstein, California Democrat. Kate Michelman, president of NARAL, said it demonstrates how 'devastating' the 2002 elections were in giving Republicans control of the Senate, because 'now we have no firewall' to stop anti-abortion legislation. 'There is a war on women,' she said. 'And we are losing a major battle in the war on women today.'

A partial-birth-abortion ban twice passed both houses of Congress but both times was vetoed by President Clinton. The House overrode those vetoes, but the Senate could not muster the two-thirds majority required. In the last Congress, the House passed the ban, but the Senate—then controlled by Democrats—never considered it.

Mr. Bush plans to sign the bill. In a statement yesterday, the president called partial-birth abortion an 'abhorrent procedure that offends human dignity' and commended the Senate for voting to ban it. 'Today's action is an important step toward building a culture of life in America,' he said. 'I look forward to the House passing legislation and working with the Senate to resolve any differences so that I can sign legislation banning partial-birth abortion into law.'

Mr. Santorum's bill and Mr. Chabot's House bill are identical. During debate this week, however, the Senate added a Democratic amendment to the Santorum bill, stating support for Roe v. Wade, the landmark 1973 Supreme Court decision that made abortion legal. But Mr. Chabot said the House is not likely to include that language, and Republicans predict that it will be stripped out during conference and will not be part of the bill the president signs.

Mr. Santorum and Mr. Chabot said their bill provides a more precise definition of the partial-birth-abortion procedure, thereby addressing the justices' concerns that the Nebraska law also could have banned another abortion procedure in which the baby is dismembered in the womb. 'There is no vagueness here,' Mr. Santorum said. 'We are clear about this procedure.'

Those who support the ban are also gearing up for a court challenge. 'We will work aggressively to defend this law in court—a law that is not only necessary, but eminently constitutional as well,' said Jay Sekulow, chief counsel of the American Center for Law and Justice, a conservative civil-liberties group.

The last time the Senate voted on a partial-birth-abortion ban was Oct. 21, 1999. The measure passed 63-34, and after Mr. Clinton's veto the four further votes needed to override could not be found." Taken from "Senate OKs ban on late abortions", By Amy Fagan, THE WASHINGTON TIMES, March 14, 2003.

"From: Colleen Parro rnclife@swbell.net
Subject: Republican National Coalition for Life FaxNotes – March 14, 2003
Date: Fri, 14 Mar 2003 10:56:26-0600

Yesterday, the U.S. Senate passed the Partial-Birth Abortion Ban Act by a vote of 64-33. Once it passes in the House, differences in the bills will be reconciled in a Conference Committee. During the Senate debate, pro-abortion Senators tried to attach weakening amendments all of which failed with one exception, the Harkin Amendment. The Harkin Amendment reaffirms Roe v. Wade as 'appropriate,' securing 'an important Constitutional right,' and says that Roe 'should not be overturned.' This language must be deleted from the bill before it goes to the President's desk. Pro-life Senators voted for it on final passage because they were convinced it was the only way to win the necessary pro-abortion Democrats and Republicans who otherwise would have voted against the ban. They are counting on the House to pass a bill that does not contain this offensive amendment and the Conference Committee to remove it from the Senate version. All but five Democrat Senators who were present voted FOR the Harkin Amendment and nine Republican RINOs voted with them. Republicans voting to reaffirm Roe v. Wade are: Campbell (CO), Chafee (RI), Collins (ME), Hutchison (TX), Murkowski (AK), Snowe (ME), Specter (PA), Stevens (AK), and Warner (VA). The rest of the Republicans voted pro-life AGAINST the Harkin Amendment along with Democrat Senators Breaux (LA), Miller (GA), Nelson (NE), Pryor (AR), and Reid (NV)."

"Following Senate approval of the ban in March, NRLC Legislative Director Douglas Johnson commented, 'President Bush, 70 percent of the public, 64 senators, and four Supreme Court justices say there is no constitutional right to deliver most of a living baby and then puncture her head with a scissors. But five Supreme Court justices have said that partial-birth abortion is protected by Roe v. Wade. We hope that by the time this ban reaches the Supreme Court, at least five justices will be willing to reject such extremism in defense of abortion.'" National Right to Life Committee (NRLC) in Washington, D.C., Saturday, May 31, 2003.

"The Partial-Birth Abortion Ban of 2003 deals with Federal Court objections by maintaining that there is no circumstance in which partially delivering a baby, only to kill it in the birth canal, can possibly be necessary to preserve the mother's health. The ban is also very specific in outlining the partial-birth abortion procedure. Therefore, the looming Supreme Court battle over the Partial-Birth Abortion Ban will truly be a test of whether the Court takes its own words seriously when it wrote in the *Roe v. Wade* decision: '*If the State is interested in protecting fetal life after viability, it may go so far as to proscribe abortion during that period, except when it is necessary to preserve the life or health of the mother.*'" NPLA Lifeline, Spring 2003

The Partial Birth Abortion Ban passed the House June 4, 2003, apparently not until rather late in the evening, by a vote of 282 to 139, and authorizes a two year prison sentence for physicians who violate the ban. As I understand the process, the bill now goes to a House-Senate conference committee to work out the differences in language between the two versions, then has to be approved again by both houses. The President has encouraged the legislators to get it to him promptly so that he can sign it into law.

Opponents then plan to challenge it in court; but the bill has been crafted to meet previous court objections. Justices who have opposed it before have been given reason to let it pass inspection this time without altering their previous positions, and given the level of public support I would guess that at least one justice would change their vote. Another distinct possibility is that the makeup of the court could be more conservative by the time it passes judgement on the new law.

The issue that those who are pro-abortion cling to is that the bill contains no exclusion for a woman's health. But including that would completely nullify the effectiveness of the bill; because then a woman could claim mental health, spiritual health, stomach cramps, physical fitness, a non-healthy outlook on life, morning sickness, or maybe even financial health. It could be as broad as someone's imagination. "I don't feel good today, Doc-so could you do an abortion for me?" And you can be sure they would take advantage of it.

It's not a medical procedure. It's homicide. It's always fatal to the person being executed-in a horrible way. That's why it's not in the medical books. Pregnancy is not an illness or injury. And the child is being removed, precisely because it is healthy.

Some say there are worse forms of abortion. I agree with that. We need to outlaw those other forms too. Others say there will be just as many abortions-they will just be performed differently. I don't agree that there will be just as many, but it is true that some of them will be done using a different approach. But note that nobody who is pro-abortion is speaking out about what that other procedure might be. They dare not discuss it. Partial-birth abortion has been banned because it's so easy to see what's happening. No abortion supporter wants to discuss publicly what the alternative would be; because once that becomes common knowledge it will suffer the same fate as partial-birth abortion. Now here's what some others had to say about the bill's passage:

The president of the Family Research Council, Ken Connor, spoke of "a tide that is running against Roe v. Wade, which will eventually be dismantled." I agree with that prognostication.

171

Rep. Ileana Ros-Lehtinen, R-Fla: "Partial birth abortion is a gruesome and inhumane procedure and it is a grave attack against human dignity and justice. This practice must be banned".

When you recognize someone's name who's being quoted or photographed because of what they said, or did, that was pro-life; and you remember that it's someone you helped elect, even in a small way, it gives you just a little sense of satisfaction, and pride. Everybody should try it.

"After an eight-year struggle, a federal ban on partial-birth abortion is now in sight! But the battle won't end there. Predictably, a number of pro-abortion groups are already planning lawsuits. This very real life and death issue will likely be decided by the Supreme Court and who knows what the Court will do." Gary Bauer, Chairman CWFPac, End of Day—05 Jun 2003 17:23:14-0400 "Please feel free to pass on this 'End of Day' update to interested friends and family members."-garybauer@mail.cwfpac.com Campaign for Working Families 2800 Shirlington Road Suite 605 Arlington, VA 22206 Phone: 703-671-8800 Fax: 703-671-8899 Web: www.cwfpac.com
Join at: http://www.cwfpac.com/join_campaign.htm

Proponents of abortion are currently engaged in spreading the fiction that partial-birth abortions are only performed in the 5th and 6th months of a pregnancy, and as a trade-off procedure. The fact is that partial-birth abortions are performed in the 8th and 9th months of pregnancy because of the difficulty in killing the larger child by conventional means. This is why I believe that in many cases a decision will be made not to go ahead with the abortion, and the child will be spared. Not all abortionists do difficult late term abortions. For a lot of prospective clients it would likely involve having to travel a considerable distance, perhaps even flying. Just having an abortuary tell you that they don't do late term abortions would be enough to dissuade many people from taking their child's life. But I think the merchants of death will carry their argument all the way to the Supreme Court, so that those defending the ban will have to include a way to deal with this in their briefs to the Court, in order to win the case.

Those trying to block the ban, will also try to say in their briefs, where they don't have to discuss it publicly, that partial birth abortion is safer than some other means for the mother. So we must never lose sight of, or be distracted from the central issue-Is abortion safe for the child? As we proceed down this road the inconsistencies will become more obvious in the pro-abortion camp-in this case, that a child with its navel still inside its mother is not a person-but that one with its navel outside is. The more these issues are discussed publicly, the slipperier becomes the slope those profiting from abortion are on.

On the other hand, all the abortionists need is for one of the Judges to make their decision based on a lie they supply. Then the pro-life movement is confronted again by the argument they can't get the legislation past the Court, so what's the point in passing it in the first place?

"From: Colleen Parro rnclife swbell.net
Subject: Republican National Coalition for Life FaxNotes
Date: Fri, 21 February 2003 10:47:33

'Right to Life Act' Introduced in Congress – Congressman Duncan Hunter (R-CA) introduced 'The Right to Life Act of 2003' on February 5, 2003, in the U.S. House of Representatives. The legislation, H.R. 579, would provide constitutional protection to all unborn children from the moment of conception.

In his introductory statement, Congressman Hunter said in part; 'In 1973, the United States Supreme Court, in the landmark case of Roe v. Wade, refused to determine when human life begins and therefore found nothing to indicate that the unborn are persons protected by the Fourteenth Amendment. In the decision, however, the Court did concede that, 'if the suggestion of personhood is established, the appellants' case, of course, collapses, for the fetus' right to life would be guaranteed specifically by the Amendment.' Considering Congress has the constitutional authority to uphold the Fourteenth Amendment, coupled by the fact that the Court admitted that if personhood were to be established the unborn would be protected, it can be concluded that we have the authority to determine when life begins.'

'The Right to Life Act does what the Supreme Court refused to do in Roe v. Wade and recognizes the personhood of the unborn for the purpose of enforcing four important provisions in the Constitution: (1) Sec. 1 of the Fourteenth Amendment prohibiting states from depriving any person of life; (2) Sec. 5 of the Fourteenth amendment providing Congress the power to enforce, by appropriate legislation, the provisions of this Amendment; (3) the due process clause of the Fifth Amendment, which concurrently prohibits the federal government from depriving any person of life; and (4) Article 1, Section 8, giving Congress the power to make laws necessary and proper to enforce all powers in the Constitution.

'This legislation will protect millions of future children by prohibiting any state or federal law that denies the personhood of the unborn, thereby effectively overturning Roe v. Wade. I firmly believe that life begins at conception and that the pre-born child deserves all the rights and protections afforded an American citizen. The Right to Life Act will finally put our unborn children on the same legal footing as all other persons. I hope my colleagues will join me in support of this important effort.'

In the strongest terms, we urge every supporter of RNC/Life to get behind H.R. 579 by asking YOUR Representative in Congress to co-sponsor Rep. Hunter's bill. The Capitol Switchboard number is – 202/224-3121. Ask to be connected to the office of your Representative. If you wish to send a faxed message, you can find your Member's fax number by visiting our web site at:

http://www.rnclife.org and clicking on CongressMerge.com. Calls to the local district office are effective as well. District office numbers are usually found in the business white pages of the telephone book listed in the blue section under U.S. Government Offices under 'Congress.' Please do not send e-mail messages – they receive too many of them and they are not read in a timely manner. Regular mail is no longer efficient due to security concerns in the Capitol."

"By officially recognizing the personhood of unborn children, the Life at Conception Act is the basis for Congress to assume its responsibility…it simply applies the language already existing in the 14th Amendment, (and) would require only a simple majority of Congress. It is vital that Americans know that the people they elect to office not only have a moral obligation, but also the Constitutional authority to nullify legalized abortion. The Fourteenth Amendment guarantees the right to life to all Americans". LifeLine, Newsletter of the National Pro-Life Alliance, Spring 2003. Close, but not quite right. To say Americans implies citizenship, which it can be argued only applies to people "born" in America. The 14th Amendment makes no such distinction to require or acquire citizenship, but explicitly confers the right to life to persons: "…nor shall any State deprive any person of life, liberty, or property, without due process of law; nor deny to any person within its jurisdiction the equal protection of the laws."

In other words, it's not acceptable to kill someone just because he's, say, a French citizen-obviously-in America. But not so obvious in other cultures. For example, in some virulent strains of Islam, true believers are encouraged to kill Jews and Christians as a religious duty. Sad, but true. But the most important point that needs to be mentioned here is the "person" terminology; because that's what, and why, abortionists try to deny the personhood of the child still in the womb. Their argument is that if the child is still inside the mother it's not a person and can be legally killed because it's not covered by the 14th Amendment. Make sense? Of course not. And the NPLA is telling our representatives that they can't abrogate their responsibility for abortions occurring in this country by simply pointing to the Supreme Court decision and saying "Look, it's their fault", because Congress has the power and the obligation to resolve it themselves. Can't be much clearer than that! And it's certainly not necessary to amend the Constitution because the language is already there! The 14th Amendment also says: "Congress shall have the power to enforce, by appropriate legislation, the provisions of this article."

Hadley Arkes, Marvin Olasky, Born-Alive

"Hearings were held in the past week in the House on the Born-Alive Infants Protection Act, the bill that would preserve the lives of children who survived abortions. The committee went immediately into a markup, with the bill passing easily with a voice vote." Hadley Arkes, Ney Professor of American Institutions at Amherst College, July 17, 2001 8:45 a.m.

"'BORN-ALIVE INFANTS PROTECTION ACT' bill has just passed the U.S. House of Representatives, and is now before the Senate. Sponsored by Sen. Rick Santorum and other brave leaders in Congress, this bill will protect innocent little babies from being killed or allowed to die minutes after they are born alive. This inhumane procedure involves inducing labor and actually delivering a live baby, then deliberately allowing it to die by starvation or dehydration. This means that precious little babies are being...thrown into garbage cans...left to die from botched abortions...discarded as 'medical waste'...and abandoned to die shivering on cold hospital tables...President Bush...has promised to promptly sign the bill when it reaches his desk. We must work to quickly pass this legislation—because America has now crossed the line from abortion...to infanticide." Dr. Jerry Falwell, Liberty Alliance, P.O. Box 190, Forest, VA 24551

I heard what follows in a short clip on the radio. I said to myself, "Self, just go online and copy the story from there into About Abortions". Well, it wasn't that easy. I had to eventually go to an admittedly conservative news service just to find it; and even they didn't get it right. Oh well, I'll just quote the parts they did get right. It's a very important victory for the pro-life side, and maybe that's why it's being downplayed in the news. I wasn't even aware it had been brought up in the Senate-let alone passed. If they could get this through the Senate, I think it augurs well for the banning of partial-birth abortions as well-

"Bush Signs 'Born-Alive Infants Protection Act' Into Law By Jeff Johnson CNSNews.com Congressional Bureau Chief August 05, 2002 (CNSNews.com)- President Bush Monday signed...the 'Born-Alive Infants Protection Act' (H.R. 2175) during a trip to Pennsylvania, to mirror laws already on the books in more than 30 states. 'This important legislation assures that every infant born alive, including an infant who survives an abortion procedure, is considered a person under federal law,' he said. Attending the ceremony were Gianna Jessen, a young woman who survived an attempted saline abortion in 1977 and Jill Stanek, a nurse who alerted Congress about infants who were born alive but then allowed to die...'Today, through sonograms and other technology, we can clearly see that unborn children are members of the human family as well. They reflect our image, and they are created in God's own image,' Bush said.

'The Born-Alive Infants Protection Act is a step toward the day when every child is welcomed in life and protected in law. It is a step toward the day when the promises of the Declaration of Independence will apply to everyone, not just those with the voice and power to defend their rights,' he added. The bill was introduced in the 107th Congress by Rep. Steve Chabot (R-Ohio), chairman of the House Judiciary Subcommittee on the Constitution, in response to reports of infants being allowed to die...The law provides that 'In determining the meaning of any Act of Congress, or of any ruling, regulation, or interpretation of the various administrative bureaus and agencies of the United States, the words 'person', 'human being', 'child', and 'individual', shall include every infant member of the species homo sapiens who is born alive at any stage of development.' It defines the term 'born alive' as 'the complete expulsion or extraction from his or her mother of |a human being|, at any stage of development, who after such expulsion or extraction breathes or has a beating heart, pulsation of the umbilical cord, or definite movement of voluntary muscles, regardless of whether the umbilical cord has been cut, and regardless of whether the expulsion or extraction occurs as a result of natural or induced labor, cesarean section, or induced abortion.'"

One nurse, in one hospital (Christ Hospital, Oaklawn, Illinois), had the courage; against intimidation that would ultimately result in her firing, and seemingly overwhelming odds, to defend these kids-all the way to Congress. Thanks Jill, and congratulations on your victory! You made a difference, and a very important one!

"You might not have heard the news, for the Times and Post and the networks have not thought it something useful for us to hear: But for the first time since Roe v. Wade, the Congress will have enacted, and a president will have signed, a bill that marks a limit to the 'right to abortion.'...the Democrats in the Senate permitted the reading and the passage of the Born-Alive Infants Protection Act...no one except a crazed zealot would profess any doubt about the 'human' standing of the child at the point of birth...the bill planted premises that ran deep...prepares an even firmer ground for revisiting the bill on partial-birth abortion and insisting that the courts take a sober second look. The child marked for an abortion is recognized now as an entity that comes within the protection of the law. Congress surely has the authority to pronounce on the meaning of terms in the federal code, which Congress, and only Congress, can legislate...the term 'person,'...The bill is spare—and truly momentous. For it provides a predicate that can be built into the foundation now of every subsequent act of legislation touching the matter of abortion: that the child marked for abortion is indeed a 'person' who comes within the protection of the law. The irony, though, is that this bill could be enacted only on terms that barred its sponsors from proclaiming, or even explaining, the things that made it such a landmark. Congressman Jerry Nadler (D, N.Y.) had the wit to see that the Democrats would embarrass themselves by voting against the bill...the Democrats in the House and Senate clearly hated it. The Democratic strategy was just to go along—to avoid embarrassing themselves by voicing their opposition, and by giving the pro-lifers the argument that they evidently wanted. The price of passing the bill in the Senate was essentially to give the Democrats what they wanted. The bill was introduced for its formal 'readings' without explanation or fuss, by Harry Reid of Nevada, hardly a pro-lifer in anyone's reckoning. In this style, the bill was 'passed' late on a Thursday night, at the end of a cluttered legislative day, and just before the Senate would turn to a resolution honoring the musician and statesman Paderewski...there would be no roll call, and so no Democrat would be compelled to record a vote, either for or against. In fact, there were probably very few senators in the chamber when the bill was passed, in a perfunctory way, by a voice vote...no voice would be sounded to explain the significance of what was done." Reprinted from an article in the National Review by Hadley Arkes, July 31, 2002. I don't know that I'm ready to acknowledge that it was that significant; after all, the other side isn't going to just roll over and play dead because of this. But I do think, and hope, that it may mark a turning point. Thanks also to The Pro-Life Infonet for emailing me the above excerpt. See more on Hadley Arkes in the following article. It's neat to see the tie in, which I didn't notice at first. Otherwise, Hadley Arkes would have remained a mysterious person on this web site. It also certainly does add to and emphasize the significance.

From: The Pro-Life Infonet infonet@prolifeinfo.org
Reply-To: Steven Ertelt infonet@prolifeinfo.org
Subject: A Little-Noticed Pro-Life Victory
Source: TownHall; August 13, 2002

A Little-Noticed Pro-Life Victory by Marvin Olasky

Professor Hadley Arkes a dozen years ago made a terrific proposal to revive the faltering pro-life movement—and his efforts finally paid off last week, although hardly anyone noticed. In 1990, when many pro-lifers were still hoping for the home run—a constitutional amendment to ban abortion—the Amherst political philosopher proposed bunting for a single: Have Congress go on record as supporting the right to life of any child who is born alive following an "ineffective" abortion. That's what now has happened, and the Austin American-Statesman was typical in giving the result one paragraph in a roundup of the Aug. 5 news: "Bush Signs Fetus Status Law. President Bush signed a bill that declares a fetus that survives an abortion procedure a person under federal law." That description would be laughable were it were not so sad. Sometimes it's hard to avoid talking back to a newspaper: "The creature protected by that newly signed Born Alive Infants Protection Act could not

possibly be a fetus. The abortion procedure has expelled him from the womb.
He is born. He's a person. What else could he be?" But some judges in recent
years did not grasp that elementary fact, and some doctors and nurses sadly
left born-alive survivors of abortion to die in cold steel pans. Ironically, the
reluctance to come to grips with reality made passage of the Born Alive Act
possible: Democrats agreed not to oppose the bill, and Republicans agreed not
to give speeches about it. Democrats did not want to alienate their virulent
pro-abortion backers when a high-profile discussion of just-born life turned to
an examination of the same life several minutes earlier, but they also did not
want to go on the record for infanticide. For a time, it seemed that President
Bush might sign the bill into law without comment. He came through on Aug.
5, though, saying, "Today, through sonograms and other technology, we can
see clearly that unborn children are members of the human family...They
reflect our image and are created in God's own image. The Born Alive Infants
Protection Act is a step toward the day when every child is welcomed in life
and protected in law. It is a step toward the day when the promises of the
Declaration of Independence will apply to everyone, not just those with the
voice and power to defend their rights." The president also thanked by name
individuals who had made the act possible, including Arkes, who never gave up
on the idea. I remember Hadley speaking at meetings of pro-life leaders,
displaying his Jewish intellectual style amid a coalition of somber evangelicals
and Catholics. With a mischievous glint in his eyes, he would pepper his talks
with humorous, Damon Runyonesque remarks, and then arch his eyebrows
like Groucho Marx. The lines that could have come from "Guys and Dolls"
kept Arkes' arguments from becoming arcane. The force of his logic was hard
to dispute. He spoke then and has continued speaking about the "animating
principle" behind what Congress (even if through a silent scream) has
enshrined in law: "The child marked for an abortion is recognized now as an
entity that comes within the protection of the law." The next legislative step, of
course, is for Congress to extend protection from the fully born to the three-
fourths-born by passing a partial-birth abortion bill that will withstand
judicial challenge. That should happen soon, and President Bush will sign it
into law. Steps to help young women make better-informed choices between
life and abortion also are needed. The president referred to the power of
sonograms, and the administration and Congress should work together to help
pregnancy centers purchase the equipment that will allow more women to see
pictures of the babies they are carrying. So Arkes' content and style have led
to one victory and paved the way for bigger efforts. Unsurprisingly, none of
the nation's news pages (judging by a Lexis-Nexis check) mentioned him the
day after President Bush signed his bill into law, and most were like Austin's
newspaper in almost entirely ignoring the development. But future historians
should notice, and some abortion survivors certainly will.

The Pro-Life Infonet is a daily compilation of pro-life news and information.
To subscribe, send the message "subscribe" to: infonet-

Intecon

request@prolifeinfo.org. Infonet is sponsored by Women and Children First (http://www.womenandchildrenfirst.org). For more pro-life info visit http://www.prolifeinfo.org and for questions or additional information email ertelt@prolifeinfo.org.

Father's Rights, Child Custody, and Parental Notification

"Judge Reverses Self, Allows Woman to Proceed With Abortion By Jessica Cantelon CNSNews.com Correspondent August 05, 2002 (CNS News.com) –

The Pennsylvania judge who last week prevented a pregnant woman from having an abortion at the behest of the woman's ex-boyfriend has reversed himself.

The latest order, issued Monday by Luzerne County Judge Michael Conahan, effectively gives the woman the legal ability to proceed with her plans to abort her child. In his ruling, Conahan admitted that his previous order, blocking the abortion, had 'inflicted significant and extreme emotional distress' on Tanya Meyers, who is about ten weeks pregnant with ex-boyfriend John Stachokus' child. Conahan also cited several legal precedents in writing that 'neither an ex-boyfriend nor a fetus has standing to interfere with a woman's choice to terminate her pregnancy.' Stachokus' attorney, John P. Williamson, is 'currently working furiously to protect the life of the child and the mother,' according to a spokesperson for Williamson. The lawyer was busy Monday working on an appeal of Conahan's decision. However, any appeal would be moot if Meyers obtained the abortion before the appeal was filed. 'Unfortunately, it seems that the courts continually side with whoever chooses to terminate, whether it's destruction of human embryos |or| whether it's the destruction of an unborn child,' stated Serrin Foster, president of Feminists for Life, a group that describes itself as simultaneously 'pro-women and pro-life.' 'Whatever the scenario is, whoever wants to kill wins,' she added." "Erik Whittington of the American Life League said the Supreme Court's 1973 Roe v. Wade decision and other court precedents render the unborn child 'a slave to his or her mother's wishes regardless of the father.' Whittington said there is a lack of legal resources available to people trying to prevent abortion. On the other hand, abortions are a 'big money-making industry,' he said, that ensure an 'endless amount of cash' for pro-abortion activism. While he does not expect Stachokus to be able to file an appeal before Meyers goes through with her abortion, Whittington said the public debate over the issue would continue. 'You're going to see in the public how ridiculous abortion rights is because a father has no say in his child's life, and that's just totally ridiculous,' Whittington said. Fathers' rights organizations are weighing in as well. 'I think that this is just a good illustration of the enormous barriers that fathers have placed between them and the relationship with their children,' stated Dianna Thompson, executive director and co-founder of the American Coalition for Fathers and Children http://www.acfc.org/. She refers to 'the plight of the father' as 'the next civil rights movement.' 'Oftentimes fathers do try to be responsible, but they have no choices,' Thompson added. 'So therefore it makes it extremely hard for them to be the men and fathers they want to be.'"

"Nicholas DiGiovanni had done the same thing himself in 1999. A judge issued an injunction forbidding the abortion. But a higher court reversed the ruling, and DiGiovanni's girlfriend aborted his child. A high-powered pro-abortion activist group backed his girl friend in court. 'They were fighting ruthlessly to kill my child,' he said." The Judie Brown Report-September 2002

To my knowledge, these are the only two cases of fathers going to court to save their children. ALL recognized how special Nick was, and hired him to help run their youth programs while he attended college in the Washington, D.C., area. His example has also been an inspiration to me.

What follows isn't really about abortion, but it does have a human interest factor and a happy ending:

From: The Pro-Life Infonet infonet@prolifeinfo.org
Subject: Couple in Abortion Dispute Marry in Vegas
Source: Times-Leader; September 6, 2002

Couple in Abortion Dispute Marry in Vegas

Las Vegas, NV—A man and woman from Pennsylvania involved in a highly publicized court battle about abortion recently married in Las Vegas. A clerk in the Clark County Courthouse's marriage license bureau confirmed Thursday that John Stachokus, 27, and Tanya Meyers, 22, exchanged wedding vows Aug. 24. Reached at home Thursday, Meyers said she wondered why the media are so interested in her "love life" before hanging up on a reporter. Family members of the bride and groom declined comment. Meyers became pregnant during the couple's 10-month relationship. Stachokus argued Meyers had wanted the child, but changed her mind when they broke up. But, according to her mother, Meyers still was unsure if she would have the abortion. Soon after the ruling, Meyers miscarried.

What follows is not a happy ending:

"Father Kills Self In Front Of Planned Parenthood Clinic

Thursday, October 03 @ 19:43:13 EDT

Summary: A father who was grieving over his girlfriend's abortion of their baby boy, stood in front of the Planned Parenthood clinic in Overland Park, Kansas and killed himself on September 10.

Brad Draper, 44, shot himself in the head in front of the Overland Park, Kansas Planned Parenthood clinic on September 10. He died later in the hospital. Draper was grieving the killing of his unborn baby son by his girlfriend at the clinic. Draper published an obituary for his boy in the local newspaper in June, 2002. In his obituary, he said: 'Zachary Duncan Draper was beautiful as his mother, loved by God and others. My little baby boy didn't make it to his Daddy's arms. I never got to hold and kiss him, tell him stories or read him rhymes. I love you Zachary and look forward to seeing you in heaven.' According to the family, Draper had seen ultrasounds of his son and was very excited to be a father until his girlfriend had the abortion without telling him. Family members say he killed himself on what would have been his son's due date." TVC-Traditional Values Coalition

"From: Jennifer Bingham-Executive Director Executive.Director@sba-list.org Subject: Legislative Update Mon, 5 Aug 2002 15:36:51-0400 CHILD CUSTODY PROTECTION ACT (H.R. 476) Passed the House with bipartisan support! On April 17, 2002 the United States House of Representatives over-whelmingly PASSED the commonsense Child Custody Protection Act (H.R. 476) by a vote of 260 to 161! The Child Custody Protection Act would make it a federal offense to take minors across state lines in order for them to obtain abortions. Currently, more than 30 states have laws requiring consent or notification of at least one parent, before an abortion can be performed on a minor. Status: PASSED in the House of Representatives on April 17, 2002. Next stop will be the Senate! ACTION NEEDED Click here to e-mail your Senator to encourage support of the Child Custody Protection Act. http://www.sba-list.org/CCPA THE MURRAY AMENDMENT – STRIPS THE BAN ON ABORTIONS IN MILITARY HOSPITALS Passed the Senate! On June 21st, 2002 the Senate voted to allow military abortions at military hospitals not only abroad but in the United States too! Not only does it turn military hospitals into abortion clinics, but it also allows for federal funding to provide for abortions by subsidizing the cost of the building, properties, materials, etc. That means your tax dollars could be responsible for abortions in military facilities. The Susan B. Anthony List members generated over 11,000 letters to their representatives asking them to stop this amendment. Status: PASSED in the Senate. ACTION NEEDED Click here to contact your Congressman and Senators to ask them to support the continuation of this ban on abortion in military hospitals. http://www.sba-list.org/military ABORTION NON-DISCRIMINATION ACT (ANDA) (H.R. 4691) Introduced in the House On May 9, 2002 the Abortion Non-Discrimination Act (ANDA) was introduced. In July, the Health Subcommittee of the Energy and Commerce Committee conducted a hearing on the Abortion Non-Discrimination Act. ANDA addresses the need for comprehensive anti-discrimination protection for health care organizations that choose not to provide abortion. Currently, there are cases pending in courts around the country in which hospitals are being sued because they elected to stop providing abortion services at their hospitals. Status: Introduced in the House. ACTION NEEDED Click here http://www.sba-list.org/ANDA to contact your representative to urge them to support Abortion Non-Discrimination Act (ANDA)...The Partial Birth Abortion ban will resurface soon in the Senate".

"The National Pro-Life Alliance has drafted legislation to give parents the right to prevent an abortion from being performed on their teenage daughter. Congresswoman Marilyn Musgrave (R-CO) has introduced the bill, called the Parental Notification and Intervention Act [H.R. 1489] in the House of Representatives...would prohibit any physician from performing an abortion upon a minor or incompetent without giving four days notice to both parents. Either parent or a guardian would then have the legal right to stop the abortion from taking place at any time. Furthermore, no judge could bypass the parental notification without clear and convincing evidence of the danger of physical abuse from a minor's parent if they are notified. This bill builds on the success of states that have protected parental involvement and have seen a dramatic drop in the teen abortion rate.

Parental Involvement Laws Enjoy Massive Public Support The American people overwhelmingly support restrictions on abortion such as laws requiring parental notification for minors before obtaining an abortion. According to a 1996 Gallup survey, 74 percent of Americans were in favor...In a 1998 CBS/New York Times poll, 78 percent favored parental intervention. In a Los Angeles Times survey conducted in 2000 the figure rose to 82 percent. This trend has translated into legislation in many states nationwide. Roughly 41 states have passed laws...there is also a legal precedent for such legislation from the Supreme Court. In the 1992 case of *Planned Parenthood v. Casey* the Supreme Court upheld Pennsylvania's parental consent law...States that have enacted laws to protect parental involvement have experienced significant declines in the teen abortion rate".

"Currently, without a federal law in place, even in states with parental notification, parents are frequently left completely in the dark because a child abuser or offender will evade the law by simply taking the young girl to another state without such a law and obtain an abortion there. Also, state laws are many times struck down or rendered ineffective by judges who exploit a loophole by granting 'judicial bypass' to minors so routinely that the law is rarely actually enforced. According to Michael Muench, Legislative Director for the National Pro-Life Alliance, 'The Musgrave bill drafted by NPLA would ...close loopholes that exist in some state laws. The fact is, if you ask people if they think it's right that the same fifteen year old girl who can't even get her ears pierced without her parent's approval can walk into a Planned Parenthood clinic and get an abortion, the overwhelming majority of people take the pro-life side. This bill will stop judges from handing out judicial passes to children like candy, it will stop pedophiles and sex offenders from hiding their crimes by crossing state lines, and it will provide parents with the right to stop their daughters from killing their grandchild...Popular Support for Parental Intervention Makes Victory Achievable This bill is the next logical step to undermine *Roe v. Wade* until we can overturn it completely by passing a Life at Conception Act,...This is another issue on which the pro-abortion puppets of the death lobby find themselves at odds with the American people.' ...Making abortionists who violate this Act guilty of a felony. Providing a clear standard for granting the judicial bypass."

"Planned Parenthood Sues to Stop All Parental Involvement Making matters worse, Planned Parenthood is suing in states like Alaska to overturn parental consent laws which forbid abortions to be performed on minors without their parents approval. Martin Fox, President of the National Pro-Life Alliance was quick to point out that 'Not only do abortionists refuse to report sexual abuse of minors, they apparently do not believe that this abuse is of any concern to the parents of the child either. It's an abomination for Planned Parenthood to have unfettered access to minors while shutting out parents". National Pro-Life Alliance, Spring 2003 communications, all of the uncredited above.

License Plates

"Florida's 'Choose Life' license plate...Anyone can apply for a statewide specialty plate upon presenting a sufficient number of signatures, paying an application fee, and presenting a marketing plan. Over thirty specialty plates currently exist. The additional private fee paid over and above the cost for a standard plate goes toward supporting the sponsor of the plate. The additional private fee from the 'Choose Life' plate is distributed to organizations that promote adoption. The 'Choose Life' plate is the most popular specialty plate in Florida. It continues to break sales records. In less than two years, the private fees have generated over one million dollars that would be dedicated to promoting adoption." Taken from http://www.lc.org/, The Liberator-http://www.lc.org/newsletter/libindex.htm. There are a handful of other states that have similar laws, and abortionists don't like it one bit. Because of a precedent set in federal court by a win for Liberty Counsel's Mathew Staver on July 12th, 2002, it should be easier for pro-lifers in other states to move forward on this. Given it's success in Florida, I think this is worth pursuing in other states too. Does your state have a similar law yet?

"For years the side that wants to be described as 'pro-choice' has fought any attempt to promote the choice of life." Gary Bauer

"Louisiana Choose Life License Plate Ruling Appealed Again Baton Rouge, LA—The legal battle over Louisiana's plan to issue license plates bearing the motto 'Choose Life' is heading to the nation's top court. Two weeks ago, the 5th U.S. Circuit Court of Appeals refused to reconsider its March ruling throwing out a pro-abortion lawsuit that challenged the 'Choose life' legislation. Like other specialty plates, the 'Choose life' plate costs $25 more a year than a regular license plate. Money raised by the plate is earmarked for organizations that help mothers choose abortion alternatives. The 'Choose life' plate has a picture of a baby wrapped in a blanket in the beak of a brown pelican, the state bird. Now, attorneys for the abortion supporters who filed the suit are asking the New Orleans-based appellate court to halt the effect of its ruling while they try to persuade the U.S. Supreme Court to hear their case." Baton Rouge Advocate; August 23, 2002

"Eight states have already initiated the Choose Life plate with many others in the process of getting it approved. Recently Jill and Russ Amerling of Ocala, FL, originators of the concept, presented a seminar in Chicago on the merits and the process of bringing a Choose Life License plate to our state." Ed & Virginia McCaskey, Illinois Choose Life P.O. Box 586, Grayslake, IL 60030 http://www.choose-life.org/, Illinois Federation For Right to Life http://www.ifrl.org/, and CWA IL http://states.cwfa.org/illinois/ are involved too.

"Alabama Choose Life Plate Closer to Getting Approval Montgomery, AL—
Pro-life advocates are close to getting 'Choose Life' license plates displayed on
vehicles in Alabama. Through August, 897 motorists had put up $50 each to
order the tags. The state will start printing the yellow tags emblazoned with
'Choose Life' if a total of 1,000 orders is received by Nov. 30. 'We're on the
home stretch,' said John Giles, state president of the Christian Coalition. Giles
said proponents of the tags have sent posters and bulletin inserts to churches to
make sure the goal is reached. Florida became the first state to issue 'Choose
Life' tags in August 2000, and 34,000 have been sold so far, said Russ
Amerling, publicity director for Choose Life Inc., a Florida-based pro-life
group that promotes the tags. Legislatures in five other states have approved
the tags. The tags are on cars in Hawaii and Mississippi, have been held up by
court suits in Louisiana and South Carolina and have not yet gone into
production in Oklahoma, Amerling said." Associated Press; October 1, 2002,
via the Pro-Life Infonet. Supreme Court Justice Antonin Scalia denied a
request to overturn, or even to consider, a request to overturn the Louisiana
law, so Louisiana has the go ahead on its plates. I didn't at first think this
license plate issue was worth including here, but I've "changed my tune". It
works, it raises money for women with crisis pregnancies, it turns a car into a
moving billboard-I want to encourage people to push for this kind of program
in their states, and to buy the plates.

"The following states should have the Choose Life license plate bill before their
legislature in the 2003 session: Texas, California, Arkansas, North Carolina,
Pennsylvania, New Jersey, New Hampshire, Michigan, Ohio, Kentucky,
Georgia, and possibly West Virginia, Indiana, Illinois and Maryland." Ryan
Report Sept. 2002

From: The Pro-Life Infonet, Steven Ertelt infonet@prolifeinfo.org
Illinois Secretary of State Candidate Supports Choose Life Plate Source: RFM
News; October 8, 2002

Springfield, IL—The effort to make available Choose Life Adoption Specialty
Plates in Illinois received a boost when Kristine Cohn, the Republican
candidate for Secretary of State, announced she would endorse the initiative.
"We are fully behind the Choose Life adoption license plate program," said
Charlie Stone, Cohn's campaign manager. "It's a worthy effort. Everyone
knows someone who is adopted and when elected Cohn will do everything in
her power as Secretary of State to ensure the issuance of these plates will one
day become a reality."

Jim Finnegan, who has spearheaded the Choose Life Adoption Specialty Plates effort in Illinois, appreciates Cohn's support. "I was amazed how many people have an adoption story in their life. How sad it is some adoption agencies cannot meet the demand or financial responsibilities, in order to increase the number of children made available for adoption. This program could change the lives of so many," said Finnegan. "There are one million parents seeking to adopt from a group of slightly more than 50,000 children. Ms. Cohn's endorsement of this program makes sense." "Let me reiterate. This is not about abortion. It's about adoption and giving women greater choice," said Finnegan. "Anyone who attempts to make this into an abortion issue is mistaken and is not familiar with the pending legislation."

SB2426 has been pre-filed by state Senator Patrick O'Malley (R-18, Palos Park). One of the legislation's' co-sponsors is Peter Roskam (R-20, Glen Ellyn). The Choose Life Adoption Specialty Plates also has the support of influential community leaders, including Ed and Virginia McCaskey and Father John Smyth of Maryville.

Of course you don't have to wait to buy a pro-life license plate until your state approves one. If you're a demonstrative type of person you can buy one now from Victory Won http://www.victorywon.com/license_plates.htm, and then buy one from your state when they come out with them. If you're not sure how demonstrative you are, you can just buy the frame. I try to think of everything. I don't want to let anyone off the hook. If you don't happen to like their messages, you can design your own; and then buy both the frame and the plate. So many options! http://www.victorywon.com/license_frames.htm

Abortion Non Discrimination Act (ANDA)

From: "Legislative Alert-SBA List"
SBAList@DemocracyData.com
Subject: Pro-Life Victory Yesterday in the House!
Date: 26 Sep 2002 14:39:13-0400

The U.S. House of Representatives voted 229 to 189 in favor of the Abortion Non Discrimination Act (ANDA), rejecting opposition by a number of pro-abortion advocacy groups. This necessary legislation clarifies existing laws to protect health care organizations including hospitals, doctors, nurses, and health care plans that choose not to provide abortion, allowing these organizations or individuals to set their own abortion policies according to their organizational consciences.

"Still, 189 Members of Congress would allow hospitals, doctors, nurses, pharmacists and other medical institutions and personnel to be forced to be involved in abortions! Among them are 24 Republicans. They are: Bass (NH); Gilman (NY); Leach (IA); Biggert (IL); Greenwood (PA); Miller, Dan (FL); Boehlert (NY); Horn (CA); Morella (MD); Bono (CA); Houghton (NY); Ose (CA); Castle (DE); Johnson (CT); Shays (CT); Frelinghuysen (NJ); Kelly (NY); Simmons (CT); Gibbons (NV); Kirk (IL); Sweeney (NY); Gilchrest (MD); Kolbe (AZ); and Thomas (CA). 37 Democrats voted for the bill. The votes of pro-life Democrats are essential to the passage of pro-life legislation because they provide a counter-balance to the too-large number of RINOs (Republicans in Name Only) who support the agenda of the abortion industry." RNC For Life Report, September/October 2002-No. 46

"Mrs. Morella, who has led pro-abortion forces throughout her seven terms in Congress, was defeated by a pro-abortion Democrat. Penny Pullen, president of Life Advocacy Alliance, commented in her November 11 Life Advocacy Briefing that Morella's defeat 'and her absence from the Republican Caucus should provide both a salutary freshening and a useful lesson to those Republicans who think voting like a Democrat will spare them electoral problems.'" From: Colleen Parro Subject: RNC for Life FaxNotes-11/15/2002

About Abortions editor's note: This is important legislation because suits are being brought by pro-abortion advocates to force people and organizations to perform abortions. It still has to make its way through the Senate, and my gut feeling is that it won't get brought up this session. However, I have been following this issue, and if I decide it warrants more attention I will pull in more information on it from my hard drive.

"U.S. House to Decide: Should Hospitals and Other Health Care Providers be Forced to Perform Abortions Against Their Will? On or about September 25 or September 26, the U.S. House of Representatives is expected to consider a critical bill to protect the right of hospitals, doctors, nurses, insurers, and other 'health care entities' from being coerced into participation in abortion. The Abortion Non-Discrimination Act (ANDA), H.R. 4691, sponsored by Rep. Michael Bilirakis (R-Fl.) is necessary to clarify and strengthen a law enacted in 1996 (the Coats-Snowe law, 42 U.S.C. 238n) to protect the conscience rights of those who choose not to cover, pay for, or otherwise participate in the killing of innocent, unborn children.

Since Congress' enactment of the 1996 law, pro-abortion groups have been actively engaged in a concerted campaign to coerce hospitals and other health care providers, both religiously affiliated and secular, to provide, facilitate, or pay for abortions. Although the 1996 law was passed to prevent any 'health care entity' from being forced to perform, train, or refer for abortion, it has been attacked by pro-abortion activist groups and narrowly construed by the courts.

Stronger conscience protection is urgently needed. For example, the Alaska Supreme Court has demanded that a private, non-sectarian hospital perform elective late second-trimester abortions, despite the hospital's policy against performing elective abortions. At the behest of abortion rights groups, the New Hampshire attorney general derailed a hospital merger when it became clear that the hospital would no longer perform elective abortions. Pressured by a pro-abortion group, the Connecticut state government refused a certificate of need to a proposed outpatient surgery center because it declined to perform abortions." From a "Congressional alert from the National Right to Life Committee in Washington, D.C., issued September 16, 2002."

"This bill would protect hospitals and facilities from having to choose between killing babies and being shut down by an activist judge. That is exactly what is happening to an Alaska community hospital even as I write this!" Beverly LaHaye, CWA, Feb. 4, 2003

"...a bill that would allow hospitals and other medical facilities to exercise their conscientious objection to being involved in abortions on their premises. Currently, doctors, nurses and other medical personnel are protected under a 'conscience clause.' The bill described...would extend that protection to medical facilities and pharmacists as well." RNCLife, Tuesday, 24 Sept. 2002

For a more detailed discussion of the legal issues, you can go to a web site maintained by the U.S. Conference of Catholic Bishops-
http://www.nccbuscc.org/prolife/issues/abortion/facts2.htm

"The legislation states that the federal government should not discriminate against medical professionals or medical institutions that refuse to perform, participate in, support, or fund abortions. The Association of American Physicians and Surgeons (AAPS) supports this legislation as well as the Catholic Health Association, Catholic Medical Association, and other pro-family groups." Traditional Values Coalition, Friday, September 13, 2002 http://aapsonline.org/testimony/anda.htm

"Increasingly in recent years, pro-abortion groups have been actively engaged in a concerted campaign to coerce hospitals and other health care providers, both religiously affiliated and secular, to provide, facilitate, or pay for abortions. Typical of these efforts is the 'Hospital Provider Project' of the Maryland affiliate of the National Abortion and Reproductive Rights Action League (NARAL). As that organization explained, 'The goal of the Hospital Provider Project is to increase access to abortion services by REQUIRING Maryland hospitals to provide abortion...' (capitals added for emphasis) It appears that some organizations that call themselves 'pro-choice' are now reluctant to openly defend their coercive campaigns". NRLC, September 23, 2002 Also, "On its face, H.R. 4691 applies only to 'induced abortions.' The term 'abortion' has appeared in numerous federal laws (such as the Title X authorizing statute and the Hyde Amendment); the term has been consistently construed in federal law to apply to deliberate interruption of pregnancy after implantation. Therefore, the bill covers abortions whether induced by surgical means or by abortion-induced drugs such as RU-486, but it does not cover 'morning-after pills,' whether with respect to victims of rape or otherwise." Douglas Johnson, NRLC Legislative Director

----

From: The Pro-Life Infonet Steven Ertelt infonet@prolifeinfo.org October 15, 2002

No More Pro-Choice Movement by Richard M. Doerflinger

[Pro-Life Infonet Note: Mr. Doerflinger is Deputy Director of the Secretariat for Pro-Life Activities, U.S. Conference of Catholic Bishops.]

"Once there were basically two sides to the abortion debate. One side said that, whatever the moral status of unborn life may be, a woman and her physician must be free to make a choice about abortion. The other side said that, whatever value the struggle for greater freedom may have in other contexts, responsible freedom for women and physicians must stop short of destroying the life of an innocent child. Not surprisingly, these sides called themselves 'pro-choice' and 'pro-life' respectively.

Those were simpler times. For however useful these labels once were, it's becoming ridiculous to refer to abortion advocacy groups as 'pro-choice.' This was already clear to anyone following the debate on U.S. funding of the U.N. Population Fund (UNFPA) a few months ago. President Bush ultimately decided not to give this group any funds this year, because it helps the Chinese government implement a population program that uses coerced abortion and involuntary sterilization. His decision was greeted by howls of protest from pro-abortion groups, who ditched their commitment to women's 'reproductive freedom' to defend their allies in the population control movement.

More recently the coerced-abortion agenda has come home to guide domestic policy. When the House of Representatives debated a modest measure called the Abortion Non-Discrimination Act (ANDA) last month, the idea that each individual should have 'freedom to choose' whether to be involved in abortion was denounced as heresy by 'pro-choice' groups. ANDA builds on a law that Congress passed in 1996 to protect medical residency programs from being forced by government bodies to provide abortions or abortion training. It clarifies and extends that law to make sure that this protection covers the full range of health care providers, so everyone can make his or her own conscientious decision whether to participate in abortions. But to hear pro-abortion spokespersons talk, you would have thought that abortion was about to be declared a capital crime. If women can only get abortions from those actually willing to provide them, they seemed to say, there will be almost no abortions-an interesting comment on how widely accepted abortion is in the medical profession!

Pro-abortion groups opposed every aspect of this bill—including its effort to extend the conscience protection now enjoyed by doctors to cover other health professionals, such as nurses, who are mostly female. In opposing this modest step toward equal treatment, abortion advocates managed to promote an agenda that was anti-life, 'anti-choice,' and anti-woman all at the same time. Fortunately most House members ignored their tirades and approved the bill, which now goes to the Senate.

One bumper sticker produced by pro-abortion groups says: 'Against abortion? Don't have one.' That slogan always ignored the unborn child, who has no opportunity to choose not to 'have one.' But now women and doctors may join the child in having their choice disregarded, unless pro-life legislators are vigilant.

Against abortion? If you're in China, have one anyway. If you're a health professional in the U.S., perform one anyway. Oddly, that is now what being 'pro-choice' is all about."

"A 16-year-old asked a federal judge for a restraining order to prevent her from being forced to submit to an abortion that her parents wanted her to have, and suddenly we had silence from the people who call themselves 'pro-choice.' If people truly support 'the right to choose,' they would be rallying in support of this girl and others who choose life. The fact that they only support women who choose abortion shows the utter inaccuracy of them calling themselves 'pro-choice.' If they had the capacity for honesty, they would admit that they are pro-abortion." LDI News, May 2003

The Lame Duck 107th, McConnell, Shedd, the Military Ban, & Schumer

Of course, the Republican party regained control of the Senate in the 2002 midterm elections. For those who are more interested in the political dimension of the abortion controversy I will be updating the Election Section below with the details of those races as I have time to do so. The 107th Congress reconvenes on Monday, November 11th. Conservative Republican Trent Lott will be setting the agenda in the Senate; instead of radical Democrat Tom Daschle, the abortion industry, and the labor union bosses. I would imagine the Homeland Security bill will be the first issue to be dealt with, but between that and voting on the budget it seems there should be room for some pro-life legislation which has already been passed by the House-the Partial Birth Abortion ban & ANDA. The judicial nomination "logjam" should start to clear up too.

"Incoming Senate Majority Leader Trent Lott has already promised a vote on the Partial Birth Abortion Ban." Jane Abraham President SBA List-11/11/2002

"And what was the pro-life promise Lott had made? When asked about the partial-birth abortion ban that has repeatedly passed both houses of Congress by large bipartisan majorities, and that President Bush has vowed to sign, Lott said, 'I will call it up, we will pass it, and the President will sign it. I'm making that commitment—you can write it down.'" From Human Events, the week of November 18, 2002

As it turned out, the Republicans chose to wait for the 108th Congress to take control of the Senate, and Trent Lott stepped down as Senate Majority Leader.

"Senate Republican Leader Trent Lott continues to pass the word that he will quickly bring up for a vote a ban on partial-birth abortions. Good for him! Even though the usual 'nervous Nellies' are getting weak-kneed at the prospect, trust me, my friends. If there is a vote in the Senate next year to ban this hideous procedure, it will pass easily-at least 65 to 35!" Gary Bauer, Campaign for Working Families, Wednesday, November 20, 2002

"'This Republican Congress was elected because of the pro-life vote, and they need to heed that vote,' said (Family Research Council President Ken) Connor. 'We know the abortion issue was the number two issue that prompted voter turnout in Minnesota, the number three issue in Missouri, and we know 76 percent of self-identified religious conservatives in Georgia voted for Saxby Chambliss. In no small part, the favorable outcome of this election for

Republicans is a consequence of motivated pro-life voters who turned out to the polls.'

President Bush has indicated his support for all of the pro-life bills supported by leading pro-life groups." From: The Pro-Life Infonet Source: Washington Times, Washington Post; Nov. 12, 2002

"Democrats may be forced to shut down operations as a party and re-enter politics under a different name. *The party formerly known as 'the Democratic Party' will henceforth be doing business under the name 'the Abortion Party.'* That would have the virtue of honesty. Love of abortion is the one irreducible minimum of the Democratic Party. Liberals don't want to go to war with Saddam Hussein, but they do want to go to war to protect *Roe v. Wade.* In as much as George Bush rather than Barbra Streisand will be picking our federal judges, even now liberals are sharpening their character assassination techniques. People for the American Way—representing Americans up and down the Malibu beachfront—are already lining up lying Anita Hills... Liberals love to lie. The only moral compass liberals have is their own will to power." "What a miserable party. I'm glad to see their power end, and I'm sure they'll all be perfectly comfortable in their cells in Guantanamo. As Jesse Helms said on Ronald Reagan's election in 1980: God has given America one more chance." From a very hard hitting, sarcastic, and entertaining column "Party of Adultery and Abortion Takes a Hit", by Ann Coulter, in "Human Events The Week Of November 11, 2002"-Inside Washington. Read her new book "Slander".

"Senate Judiciary Cmte Approves Pro-Life Judical Nominees

Washington, DC—Democrats on the Senate Judiciary Committee yesterday did what they refused to do before on several occasions by sending two of President Bush's pro-life judicial nominations on for Senate confirmation votes despite strong opposition from pro-abortion groups. The committee, on voice votes, sent the appeals court nominations of U.S. District Court Judge Dennis Shedd and University of Utah professor Michael McConnell to the full Senate after having delayed the two men before the midterm elections. Shedd has been nominated for a seat on the 4th U.S. Circuit Court of Appeals in Richmond, Va., and McConnell is up for the 10th U.S. Circuit Court of Appeals in Denver. Approval of both is likely during the Senate's last-minute rush to clear pending nominations.

Kate Michelman, president of the National Abortion Rights Action League (NARAL), admits her group's opposition is based solely on McConnell's so-called 'extremist' view that unborn children deserve legal protection. In 1996, McConnell signed the 'Statement of Pro-Life Principle and Concern,' which said, 'We seek an America in which every unborn child is protected in life and welcomed in law.' Other co-signers include Dr. James Dobson, founder of Focus on the Family, and fellow academics Hadley Arkes of Amherst College and John DiIulio, Jr., of Princeton University.

In a nod to the Republicans, who won control of the Senate and the committee next year, outgoing pro-abortion Senate Judiciary Chairman Patrick Leahy (D-VT) did not call for a roll call vote on either of the nominations in the committee, which has 10 Democrats and nine Republicans. It was the first time he had not called for a roll call vote on an appeals court nominee since Democrats took over the Senate in June 2001.

Sen. Orrin Hatch (R-UT), the incoming Senate Judiciary chairman, called Shedd a 'decent, honorable, fair-minded person' and urged his confirmation as a nod to pro-life Sen. Strom Thurmond (R-SC). The 99-year-old Thurmond had asked for Shedd's confirmation before his January retirement after a 48-year career. Shedd is a former aide to the senator. Pro-abortion groups have denounced McConnell, who is pro-life, saying his lifetime of work for pro-life causes makes him too biased to be a judge. 'I trust that Professor McConnell will not seek to undermine women's reproductive rights,' Leahy said. Hatch said McConnell would make a fine judge on the regional courts that are one step below the Supreme Court.

'This is long overdue,' said John Nowacki, director of legal policy at the Free Congress Foundation. 'After 18 months, Senator Leahy has run out of excuses to keep stalling. Shedd and McConnell deserve an up-or-down vote in the Senate, but it's a shame that it took last week's election losses to prod the committee into action.' In a 1994 Michigan Law Review article, McConnell wrote, '…Abortion is an evil, all too frequently and casually employed for the destruction of life…'

The GOP gains power in the Senate when the 108th Congress begins in January, and plans to bring back appeals court nominees that the committee voted down this year. Pro-life Sen. Trent Lott (R-MS), the incoming Senate majority leader, said earlier that another Bush nominee, pro-life U.S. District Court Judge Charles Pickering, would be renominated next year. Sen. Kay Bailey Hutchison of Texas, the new Senate Republican Conference vice chairman, said Thursday that Texas Supreme Court Justice Priscilla Owen would be renominated by the White House as well. Owen drew praise from pro-life groups for upholding Texas' parental notification law by refusing to allow teen girls to have abortions without parental knowledge or involvement." From: The Pro-Life Infonet Reply-To: Steven Ertelt infonet@prolifeinfo.org Source: Associated Press; November 14, 2002 So we see that the Democrats are beginning to give second thoughts to automatically supporting the agenda of the abortion industry, as perhaps not being a winning strategy, in spite of the huge amounts of money donated to their campaigns by abortion supporters like Emily's List, Planned Parenthood, NARAL, NOW, People For the American Way, Catholics for a Free Choice, and so on; which again suggests that they're not really stupid-just immoral, unethical, and dishonest. McConnell and Shedd had already been reviewed by the committee, but apparently the Democrats thought it unwise to reject their nominations just before the elections. What I learned from this was that although the election of Jim Talent gives the Republicans a Senate majority, the makeup of the committees will not change until the 108th Congress convenes next year (2003); so we shouldn't expect any more judicial nominees to be released for confirmation until then.

"I hope the DNC will 'get it' and understand that their current stance on abortion is no way to run a majority party. Democrats For Life of America believes that a return to being a 'party of inclusion' and respecting 'the individual conscience of each American' may be the only way for the Democratic Party to make any gains in future elections." Kristen Day, Executive Director of Democrats For Life of America, http://www.democratsforlife.org/, November 14, 2002, via Infonet.

"White House Pressures Congress to Keep Military Abortion Ban

Washington, DC—Pressure from the Bush administration has prompted Congress to ditch an effort to remove the federal ban on performing abortions at military hospitals, all of which would be funded with taxpayer dollars. During consideration of the Fiscal Year 2003 defense authorization bill, pro-abortion Senators Patty Murray (D-WA) and Olympia Snowe (R-ME) offered an amendment to repeal the law that prohibits performance of abortions at U.S. military medical facilities. Pro-life groups opposed the amendment but it passed in June. National Right to Life legislative director Douglas Johnson told the Pro-Life Infonet, 'Secretary of Defense Rumsfeld threatened the entire bill with a veto unless the pro-abortion provision was dropped, so the pro-abortion senators dropped it.' The pro-abortion provision was removed from the final version of the military spending bill prior to Senate approval yesterday. Pro-abortion Senate Armed Services Committee Chair Sen. Carl Levin (D-MI) agreed in House-Senate negotiations to remove the provision following Rumsfeld's lobbying. The House in May voted 215-202 to reject a similar amendment. The updated bill, which authorizes $393 billion in spending for defense programs in 2003, was given final approval by the House on Tuesday and now goes to President Bush, who is expected to sign the measure now that the pro-abortion provision has been lifted." Source: Pro-Life Infonet; November 14, 2002-Steven Ertelt infonet@prolifeinfo.org

"Votes on Taxpayer-Funded Abortions Expected This Week-When the House Armed Services Committee Total Force Subcommittee Committee meets tomorrow, Wednesday, May 7, 2003, Rep. Loretta Sanchez will likely offer her usual amendment to allow elective abortions to be committed at taxpayer-funded military hospitals located on taxpayer-supported military installations." From: Colleen Parro, rnclife@swbell.net, RNCLife FaxNotes-May 6, 2003.

"A law since 1996, this ban on military abortion has protected the very nature of the military, to save life, not take it. When the Clinton administration lifted the ban on 'privately' funded abortions in military base hospitals in 1993, all military doctors refused to perform abortions at their field hospitals. Military doctors are not interested in taking lives! We cannot allow our armed services to be 'hostage to abortion politics'. From: Jennifer Bingham, Executive Director, SBAList@democracydata.com, Date: 12 May 2003 12:49:48-0400".

"On May 22, 2003, the House passed H.R. 1588, the National Defense Authorization Act for fiscal year 2004 by a vote of 361-68. As you know, Representative Loretta Sanchez (D-CA) offered an amendment to allow women in the military or dependents of armed forces members to obtain… abortions…I supported this amendment, although it failed to pass by a vote of 201-215." Representative Judy Biggert, (R-IL), May 23, 2003.

"The radical pro-abortion lobby is at it again. They are seeking to crush the pro-life movement in America by any means necessary, including using the full weight and power of the federal government. The latest attempt comes from New York Senator Charles Schumer, who during deliberations on the bankruptcy reform bill inserted language that specifically targets pro-life activists. Now, I support efforts to reform bankruptcy laws, but what exactly does abortion have to do with it? This is yet another attempt to twist federal laws against those involved in peaceful protests trying to save innocent lives. Thanks to pro-abortion Democrats, we have laws designed to protect access to abortion clinics that would have effectively prevented the sit-ins of the civil rights movement. Laws written to tackle the mafia are now brought to bear against pro-life activists. Yet, when evidence is presented that Planned Parenthood conspired to protect potential child molesters, nothing is done. My friends, this is why it is so important for people of faith to remain engaged in the political process. We must elect more pro-family, pro-life conservatives to public office who will defend the sanctity of life, preserve traditional marriage, and end government harassment of pro-family, pro-life activists." Gary L. Bauer, Friday, September 13, 2002 I haven't said anything about the bankruptcy bill language up until now, because it doesn't affect a lot of people-mainly little old ladies who are habitually addicted to praying outside aborutaries. That's not the real language in the bill, but they're a nuisance, I guess. "Laws written to tackle the mafia", of course, refers to RICO (Racketeering Influenced and Corrupt Organizations Act), in NOW v. Scheidler, currently, as I speak, before the Supreme Court. Do you see what I mean when I say these people have no, and make no, sense (defined in the dictionary as "A capacity to understand", or "Normal ability to think or reason soundly; correct judgment: *Come to your senses.*")?

"House Defeats Bill That Would Hurt Pro-Life Protestors

Washington, DC—A bankruptcy bill died in the House of Representatives on Thursday, as a group of pro-life lawmakers upset with how the law would apply to pro-life protesters led a bipartisan revolt against the measure. A group of pro-life lawmakers opposed the measure because of a provision aimed at preventing pro-life protesters from using bankruptcy to avoid paying court-ordered fines when convicted of unlawful protests. Pro-life Rep. Chris Smith, a New Jersey Republican who heads up the House ProLife Caucus, said a core group of about 45 pro-life Republican lawmakers refused to back the bill because of the controversial language. Others joined the opposition after seeing the measure was headed for defeat, he said. Smith said lawmakers could rewrite the bankruptcy bill minus the controversial provision—which was added to the measure by pro-abortion Sen. Charles Schumer (D-NY) at the request of pro-abortion organizations—when Republicans control both the House and the Senate in the next session of Congress. 'We'll be back next year and we'll do another one,' he said.

'(The Schumer amendment) effectively says, 'If you are a pro-life protester and you wind up with a money judgment against you for engaging in what we regard as constitutionally protected speech and activity, you are not going to be able to discharge that debt in bankruptcy,' Family Research Council president Ken Connor explained. 'The effect of that is to create a disfavored class for purposes of punishing politically incorrect speech, because the only group that is being singled out for this kind of treatment is pro-life protestors.' Peaceful pro-life protests are more often declared illegal than other political protests on other issues in part because of the FACE legislation passed by Congress during the Clinton administration. Although some labor unions also opposed the bill because of the free speech protest concerns, one Harvard legal analyst said the FACE bill makes the Schumer amendment most onerous for pro-life advocates. Pro-life advocates flooded the offices of Republican lawmakers with hundreds of phone calls in recent days expressing opposition to the legislation". November 14, 2002-Steven Ertelt, The Pro-Life Infonet

"2002 General Election analysts have attributed the success of Republican Congressional and U.S. Senate candidates to the fact that many of them are pro-life, many of whom are pro-life without discrimination against any babies for any reason. It should not go unnoticed that The Knights of Columbus bought full-page pro-life ads in major newspapers across the country, including USA Today, the week before the election. The ads featured a 4"x5" black and white photograph of a beautiful baby in utero on an otherwise blank page. Underneath the picture were the words, 'If you ever feel your vote doesn't count, remember someone's counting on you.' Below that, at the bottom of the page, appeared the words, 'Vote Pro-Life this election.'" From: Colleen Parro Subject: Republican National Coalition for Life FaxNotes-11/15/02

"Passage of Pro-Life Legislation Not Assured— Despite all the cheering from conservatives over the results of the election, and despite the fact that pro-life voters greatly influenced the outcome of a number of the most hotly-contested races in the country, and while there will be a Republican majority in the House and Senate in 2003, there will not necessarily be a pro-life majority.

In addition to the pro-abortion Democrats in the House, the number of pro-abortion Republicans is still uncomfortably large. And, too many Republican House Members justify abortion for one reason or another. In the Senate, it takes 60 votes to pass a bill. Republicans Arlen Specter (PA), Olympia Snowe and Susan Collins (ME), Lincoln Chafee (RI), Ted Stevens (AK), Ben Campbell (CO), and Pete Domenici (NM) usually vote against pro-life legislation. Because of that, it is essential that pro-life citizens keep in touch with their representatives, letting them know their views as pro-life bills are introduced and informing them of the reasons they should vote our way." Colleen Parro, RNC for Life FaxNotes-11/15/02

"Polls conducted even by liberal news organizations show that the country is behind the Republicans now because the majority of Americans share the basic values of the Republican Party. They expect Republicans to govern like Republicans. A *USA Today*/CNN/Gallup poll taken immediately after the election showed how deeply the conservative vision of public policy has taken hold in this country. Fifty-one percent of respondents said they believed the 'political views' of the Republican Party were 'about right,' while 10% said they were 'too liberal.' In other words, 61% believe the Republican vision is either right where it should be or *not right enough*." "Human Events, The Week of November 18, 2002" Put another way, most people don't agree with the radical, bizarre, unrealistic, viewpoints of most Democrats, and see through their efforts to twist the truth, the facts, and reality. I pine for an intelligent, honest exchange of ideas on what is best for our country; but other motives prevail.

More on the Courts, Assault, Bush on Abortion, Religious Charities

"Rep. Todd Akin of Missouri...took a tremendous step toward reigning in our out-of-control courts. Following the 9th Circuit Court of Appeals ruling banning the Pledge of Allegiance, Rep. Akin introduced legislation specifically prohibiting the federal courts from hearing any claim that the Pledge violates the First Amendment. This was a bold move to reassert the authority of the legislative branch over the judicial branch. Congress does have the power to limit the jurisdiction of the federal courts, but unfortunately it is rarely used." From Campaign Watch, Fall 2002

From: The Pro-Life Infonet, Steven Ertelt infonet@prolifeinfo.org
Source: Fox News Channel; November 21, 2002

"Michigan Court May Tackle Question of When Life Begins

Plymouth, MI-By the end of the year, the Michigan Supreme Court may take up a case that has already reignited the age-old debate of when life begins. The case involves Jaclyn Kurr, who was 17 weeks pregnant when she stabbed and killed her boyfriend, Antonio Pena, in October of 1999, after he punched her in the stomach. She later had a miscarriage. Found guilty of manslaughter, Kurr is now serving a prison term of five to 20 years. During her trial, Kurr's attorney, Gail Rodwan, argued that her client had the right to defend herself and her baby, under a statute in Michigan called the defense of others law. It says, in part, that a 'person has the right to use force or even take a life to defend someone else under certain circumstances if a person acts in lawful defense of another.' 'Mr. Pena struck her in the stomach with his fist and that was what prompted her defensive action-the fetus is not in a position to protect itself,' Rodwan told Fox News. But during Kurr's trial, the judge barred the jury from considering this argument after hearing medical testimony from a physician that a baby before birth isn't viable until 22 weeks, which Kurr's baby was not. The judge concluded that in order for Kurr to present a 'defense of others' theory, there had 'to be a living human being existing independent' of Kurr. Last month, a state court of appeals overturned Kurr's conviction on the grounds that the jury was not properly instructed on the 'defense of others' theory. The case has been appealed to the Michigan Supreme Court, which is weighing whether to take the case and delve into the controversy of when a baby actually becomes viable. 'It is going to open up the entire question of what is an embryo, what is life? When does it begin?' said John Mayoue, a Georgia attorney who specializes in rights of unborn children.

He said he's concerned that Michigan may set a dangerous precedent if the court decides a mother has the right to kill in order to protect the unborn.

But Kurr's attorney said the case has nothing to do with abortion. 'We are not addressing abortion questions,' Rodwan said. 'We are addressing a very narrow issue when a pregnant woman is assaulted, does she have the right to protect the [baby].' There is also a law on the books in Michigan prosecuting criminals who kill or injure an unborn child as a result of a violent crime against the mother. Congress has attempted to pass a similar pro-life law on the federal level. The House passed the bill, but it didn't make it out of the Senate. Michigan may soon reconsider this controversy if the state Supreme Court decides to hear Jaclyn Kurr's case. Until then, Kurr remains behind bars. Her fate, and the possibility of a new trial, are still up in the air."

President George W. Bush, in a letter to Deryl M. Edwards, The Liberty Alliance, November 26, 2002:

"I believe that all unborn children should be welcomed in life and protected by law. Over the years, I have championed compassionate alternatives to abortion, such as helping women in crisis through maternity group homes, encouraging adoption, promoting abstinence education, and passing laws requiring parental notification and waiting periods. Every child who is born is valuable and must have the full protection of our laws. I recently signed into law the Born Alive Infants Protection Act. I also support the Child Custody Protection Act, which would prohibit minors from crossing state lines to avoid their home state's laws and undergo an abortion. This legislation would protect the health and safety of minors and guard the rights of parents to participate in the medical decisions of their minor daughters. My administration strongly supports the enactment of H.R. 4965, which would ban partial-birth abortions, except in cases where the life of the mother is endangered. Partial-birth abortion is a late-term procedure that is not widely accepted by the medical community and that 30 states have attempted to ban. To prohibit this abhorrent and brutal practice, I believe that enactment of this bill is morally imperative and constitutionally permissible. My Administration also supports H.R. 4691, which protects hospitals and health care professionals from being forced to perform or otherwise participate in abortions. I am pleased the House approved this important legislation and call upon the Senate to follow their lead. People on both sides of this issue can agree that we should do everything we can to reduce the number of abortions in America. As President, I am committed to the goal of building a culture that respects life— the full spectrum of life, from the unborn to the elderly."

"Bush OKs funds for religious charities Executive order avoids Congress By James Gerstenzang Tribune Newspapers Philadelphia-Circumventing Congress, President Bush used his executive powers Thursday to make it easier for religious groups to obtain federal funds to perform charitable services. Bush's action puts into effect key elements of his faith-based initiative, a cornerstone of his agenda of 'compassionate conservatism' and a proposal he unveiled days after taking office. The initiative was blocked by Congress' failure to agree on the extent to which religious groups could mix their religious message with their charity work while accepting government money. Under Bush's new order, groups that hire workers based on the individual's religious beliefs will not be barred from receiving federal money, as they have been in the past. 'When the federal government gives contracts to provide social services, religious groups should have an equal chance to compete,' Bush said in a speech to several thousand religious leaders and other representatives of religious charities. 'When decisions are made on public funding, we should not focus on the religion you practice; we should focus on the results you deliver.'

In a setting that mimicked a bill-signing ceremony, Bush sat at a small desk behind a sign reading 'Compassion in Action' and signed an executive order he said would direct federal agencies 'to follow the principle of equal treatment' in awarding social service grants. Later, back in Washington, he also ordered such agencies as the Federal Emergency Management Agency and the departments of Housing and Urban Development and Health and Human Services to remove any regulations that might block religious nonprofit groups from qualifying for federal aid." "'I recognize that government has no business endorsing a religious creed, or directly funding religious worship or religious teaching,' the president said. But, he said, 'government can and should support social services provided by religious people, as long as those services go to anyone in need, regardless of their faith. And when government gives that support, charities and faith-based programs should not be forced to change their character or compromise their mission,' he said. Los Angeles Times", December 13, 2002

Perhaps I'm missing something here, because I haven't heard anyone else say anything about it, but I think this may open the door to government financial support of CPC's (Crisis Pregnancy Centers) and shelters for pregnant mothers. For example, the $61 million that goes to Planned Parenthood under one Title X program, of the Public Health Service Act, could be redirected to the CPC's and homes for pregnant women. It seems to be mostly faith-based groups that have strong enough moral convictions to run these programs, and it would surely fall into the family planning category-they just wouldn't be killing the children. The Vitter amendment would stop abortion providers from getting money from the program anyway. The CPC's just need to learn how to apply for the funds now.

On that same day, President Bush said "The founding ideals of our nation and, in fact, the founding ideal of the political party I represent, was and remains today the equal dignity and equal rights of every American". "This is the principle that guides my administration." Based on his past statements and actions, I feel confident he didn't mean to exclude the "unborn" from those "equal rights" he spoke of.

UNFPA, International, C-Fam UN NGO

From: Gary Bauer garybauer@mail.cwfpac.com
Subject: End of Day—7/22/02
Date: 22 Jul 2002 17:14:19-0400

To: Friends and Supporters of the Campaign for Working Families
From: Gary L. Bauer, Chairman

A Win For Life

According to numerous press reports, the Bush administration has decided to cut off funding to the United Nations Population Fund. Thirty-four million dollars had been appropriated for the fund this year, but federal law allows the president to withhold taxpayer dollars from any program of coercive abortions or forced sterilizations. The U.N. Population Fund has been complicit in China's policy of forced abortions for years, but the previous administration willingly turned a blind eye to the obvious. This is a victory for the pro-life cause. Denying taxpayer funding for pro-abortion programs overseas is precisely the kind of action we should expect from a pro-life administration. The President resisted intense pressure from pro-abortion lawmakers and the abortion industry in making this decision. And in doing so, President Bush took a clear step toward ensuring that not one dime of your hard-earned money is spent overseas promoting the destruction of innocent life.

From: The Pro-Life Infonet infonet@prolifeinfo.org
Reply-To: Steven Ertelt infonet@prolifeinfo.org
Subject: Bush Administration Withholds UNFPA Money
Source: Associated Press; July 22, 2002

Bush Administration Withholds UNFPA Money

Washington, DC—The Bush administration will not pay $34 million it earmarked for U.N. family planning programs overseas, an initiative aimed at controlling population but one that pro-life groups charge tolerates abortions and forced sterilizations in China. Administration officials, lawmakers and interest groups that monitor the issue said Sunday they have been told the decision is now final. One administration official, speaking on condition of anonymity, said an announcement is likely from the State Department on Tuesday, but added the timing could change. White House officials said privately that pro-life advocates have for months quietly encouraged the administration to permanently deny money to the United Nations Population Fund. The White House has kept the politically delicate decision a closely guarded secret. It has refused to divulge it even to allies in Congress, such as the Congressional Pro-Life Caucus. More than a dozen administration officials, inside the White House and out, declined to comment Sunday or did not return phone calls on the matter, so the reasoning behind the decision was not clear. The president has already signed into law the foreign aid bill that contains the $34 million. But when he did so in January, he noted in an accompanying statement that it gives him ``additional discretion to determine the appropriate level of funding for the United Nations Population Fund.' Two administration officials said Bush is now likely to channel the $34 million to family planning organizations run by the State Department's Agency for International Development that are not directly involved in abortion.

"…U.S. money being withheld by President Bush because of concerns about coercive abortions. President Bush last year signaled his intentions to withhold the U.S. contribution, said Michael Curtis, a spokesman for Nielson. The Bush administration announced its decision Monday, saying some of the U.N. money went to Chinese agencies that carry out ``coercive programs "involving abortion." From: The Pro-Life Infonet Source: Associated Press; July 24, 2002

From: The Pro-Life Infonet Steven Ertelt infonet@prolifeinfo.org
Source: Population Research Institute; December 6, 2002

"How Population Control Promotes Abortion in Pro-Life Countries By Steve Mosher

[Pro-Life Infonet Note: Steve Mosher is the director of the Population Research Institute.]

How does the international population control lobby impose abortion on sovereign nations? The case of Peru is instructive.

The British aid agency, known as the Department of International Development (DFID), and headed by an abortion activist by the name of Clare Short, recently offered Peru a $24 million dollar grant entitled 'Improving the Health of the Poor: A Human Rights Focus.' Belying its attractive title, the grant has little to do with either the 'health of the poor' or 'human rights', and everything to do with promoting population control and abortion. Even more troubling, the DFID grant would completely bypass the Peruvian Ministry of Health (PMOH). The funds would instead go to a private conglomerate set up for this purpose, a conglomerate that would include non-governmental organizations (NGOs) that collaborated with the politics of ex-president Alberto Fujimori, who launched genocidal sterilization campaigns in Peru throughout the 1990's. The DFID 'pre-selected' NGOs (Manuela Ramos, Flora Tristan, Demus, and Care Peru) promote the morning-after pill, a chemical that induces an abortion [an opinion, not a fact], and which is illegal in Peru. Health officials in Peru also note that these NGOs 'maintain an ongoing antagonism to the MOH.' The DFID itself has a history of promoting abortion in Peru. For example, DFID has funded a program to introduce Manual Vacuum Aspirators (MVA) into 27 hospitals and 15 health centers 'as a cost effective way of treating uncomplicated abortion.' Unfortunately, MVAs are used to perform abortions in poor regions, and are so substandard that they are not used in America for any purpose.

Peru's Minister of Health, Dr. Fernando Carbone, has quite rightly raised questions about DFID efforts to bypass his agency, which has a constitutional mandate to oversee all health matters in the country. He has asked DFID to direct its grant through the proper channels to ensure that the grant 'complies with Peru's national laws and government priorities.' Although Clare Short has yet to formally respond to Dr. Carbone's request, one of her allies, the so-called Center for Health and Gender Equity (CHANGE), which concentrates on promoting abortion under the guise of 'reproductive health,' has falsely accused him of rejecting the grant. For CHANGE, under the auspices of the 1994 International Conference on Population and Development (ICPD) in Cairo, 'reproductive health services—means providing women and men with information and means—to gain access to—abortion services' in Peru. According to CHANGE, 'Extremists in Peru' have undermined reproductive rights by refusing a five-year DFID grant 'intended to improve reproductive health services in the country.' CHANGE claims that Dr. Carbone, rejected the DFID project 'because it intended to promote health rights, including sexual and reproductive rights, and foster civil society participation in health programs.' If the DFID grant has not been rejected by the Peruvian Ministry of Health, why would CHANGE report that it had? The CHANGE report appears to be part of a systematic campaign designed to undermine the efforts of Dr. Carbone and others at the Ministry of Health to move Peru's public health sector towards a policy which recognizes basic health services as an integral component of public health, and away from the anti-natal and abusive policies of the past.

Throughout the 1990's, the Peruvian Congress recently reported, former President Alberto Fujimori's genocidal sterilization campaigns resulted in the involuntary tubal ligation of over 300,000 women. The United Nations Population Fund (UNFPA) provided instrumental technical support for the campaign. Peru's Health Minister, Fernando Carbone, recently told PRI that, while the PMOH does not oppose voluntary 'family planning,' its understanding of the term does not simply mean limiting family size but recognizing and caring for family health in its entirety of every person, from conception to natural death.

Intecon

It is unclear whether Clare Short will comply with Peru's request that her agency's grant respect the democratic and constitutionally established position of Peru's Ministry of Public Health to govern the public health sector in Peru. Short is known for aggressively promoting abortion rights worldwide and is publicly committed to increasing foreign aid for abortion and 'reproductive health services.' She has in the past sought to obliterate the sovereign rights of nations by establishing abortion as a basic human right at the UN at the expense of basic health care. Ms. Short has in the past accused PRI of making 'wild accusations' about the UNFPA's involvement in China's coercive population control program. We stand by our earlier remarks, which have been verified by the Bush administration's cut-off in funding to the UNFPA. And we ask Ms. Short to cease her attempt to undermine Peru's public health sector, not to mention its fledgling democracy, by promoting abortion in Peru in violation of Peruvian law."

These people are quite willing to bring down a government just so they can sell abortions (and sterilizations).

"Pro-life groups want the United States to send a strong message opposing abortions, but abortion supporters claim that view is detrimental to the reproductive health of women. Catholics for a Free Choice, an so-called Catholic pro-abortion organization that rejects the Vatican's pro-life stance, has led the campaign to drum up opposition and decry the Bush administration." "'Since the Bush administration came into office, we've seen a very programmed and strategic effort by the U.S. delegation to roll back the language of these agreements,' said Ellen Sweet, a spokeswoman for the International Women's Health Coalition…'We are expecting more of the same at this current meeting,' Sweet said. 'The United States is going to lead the attack on words like 'reproductive rights' and 'sexual rights.' These are all terms that the United States sees as adding up to abortion.'"

"An organization that supports the Bush administration's pro-life position and has applauded its efforts to stress abstinence over abortion downplayed Kissling's accusations. Austin Ruse, president of the Catholic Family and Human Rights Institute, said the agreement reached by 179 countries in Cairo was anything but unanimous in 1994, and deep divisions remain today in the United States and abroad. 'The Bush administration is not the Clinton administration and has no obligation to uphold the pro-abortion positions of the Clinton administration,' Ruse said. 'The Bush administration is not rejecting the entire Cairo document, only the parts of the document that endorse abortion.' In addition, he said more countries are following the lead of the United States under Bush's leadership, which is shifting the focus on population control from abortion to abstinence. 'A lot of governments all over

208

the world are rallying to the Bush administration for leadership on these issues'...Ruse said. 'The Bush administration will lead the negotiations and it will win.'" Something you probably wouldn't hear about elsewhere, that's going on. I quoted from The Pro-Life Infonet, which got it from Cybercast News Service; December 11, 2002, "Abortion Advocates Bash Bush Admin at Population Summit". Austin Ruse heads a NGO (Non-Governmental Organization) at the UN; which is apparently based in Canada. They seem to be able to participate in a lot of what goes on, and hear about, first hand, what they're not allowed to be included in. So they're in a good position to monitor, report on, and influence event outcomes.

"From: 'Austin Ruse—C-FAM' c-fam@c-fam.org
Subject: Friday Fax/UN Committee Calls for Unfettered Access to Contraceptives for Children
Date: Thu, 12 Jun 2003 18:29:47-0700

Dear Colleague,

Today we report on how out of control UN committees are. The UN Committee on Children has called for complete unfettered access for children to all manner of contraceptives, with the rights of parents completely ignored.

Spread the word. Yours sincerely, Austin Ruse President

FRIDAY FAX June 13, 2003 Volume 6, Number 25

UN Child Rights Committee Calls for Child Access to Contraceptives

Last week, the United Nations Committee on the Rights of the Child sought to weaken parents' authority to guide their children's access to contraceptives and other sexual and reproductive services and information.

At the conclusion of its current session in Geneva, the Committee released a general comment on adolescent health in which it asserts that all countries that have ratified the Convention on the Rights of the Child (CRC) should 'strictly respect the right to privacy and confidentiality, including confidential advice and counselling on all health matters,' and 'that access to information on sexual and reproductive health be accessible regardless of prior consent from parents or guardians.'

The Committee exists to guide nations' implementation of the Convention on the Rights of the Child, a document that has now been ratified by every country on earth except Somalia and the United States. After a country ratifies CRC, it must submit periodic reports to the Committee, which then determines if the country is in compliance with the Convention. The Committee has the ultimate power to interpret the CRC document, and to establish what legal obligations the Convention creates for ratifying nations.

Many scholars of international law worry about the broad interpretive powers possessed by the Committee. For instance, Brigham Young University law professor Richard Wilkins has frequently charged that the Committee, through its radical interpretation of the CRC document, has in effect created new legal obligations never imagined by nations when they ratified the original Convention. In this case, the CRC document nowhere mentions that children have a right to such reproductive and sexual services without their parents' knowledge or consent.

The current general comment builds upon other controversial Committee interpretations of CRC. For instance, in a general comment on HIV/AIDS issued in 2002, the Committee said that states are responsible for providing children with 'confidential sexual and reproductive health services, free or low cost contraception, condoms and services.' The Committee also showed 'particular concern' for '...taboos or negative or judgmental attitudes to sexual activity of girls, often limiting their access to preventative measures and other services. Of concern also is discrimination based on sexual orientation.' Free contraceptives and sexual orientation are not mentioned in the original document.

The Committee has also informed individual nations that they must comply with these interpretations. For example, the Committee has told Grenada that it should increase '...its efforts in promoting adolescent health policies and counselling services, as well as strengthening reproductive health education, including the promotion of male acceptance of the use of contraceptives.' The Committee has told Djibouti to '...provide access to information about sexual and reproductive health, and that services in this area be user friendly and address the concerns and need for confidentiality of adolescents.'

Austin and Douglas didn't seem to think it was necessary to explain what I would guess is as obvious to them as it is to me. But since I don't know how sophisticated my audience will be, I will elaborate. Pro-abortion groups have taken control of this UN Committee and are using the UN to mandate worldwide reproductive health services (abortion), and creating the conditions that will make it seem "necessary". They couldn't care less about the welfare of the children, or their parents. They want to eliminate parental authority so that they can perform the maximum number of abortions on the children. Forgive me, Austin, for stealing you're thunder.

Catholic Family and Human Rights Institute http://www.c-fam.org/— (CEDAW Information, or the "Convention on the Elimination of All Forms of Discrimination Against Women", a new vehicle for promoting abortion world-wide-including in the U.S., if it is ratified by the Senate. At this writing it has already been ratified by a Senate committee.)

"Since President Carter signed CEDAW in 1979, President Bush has no authority to veto it. The Senate vote will be the final word on CEDAW. If CEDAW passes, this UN document will become US law, superseding all current US laws that conflict with it. Ratification requires a two-thirds majority, and informal headcounts in the Senate suggest that CEDAW may be approaching the 67 votes necessary for passage." Further information can be found at: Eagle Forum, http://www.eagleforum.org /, Concerned Women for America, http://cwfa.org/library/nation/2000-09_pp_cedaw.shtml, Focus on the Family, http://www.family.org/cforum/research/papers/a0020975.html, and National Right to Life, http://www.nrlc.org/Federal/LegUpdates/july152002letter.html.

"FRIDAY FAX December 27, 2002 Volume 6, Number 1

Douglas A. Sylva, Ph.D. now writes every issue. He has taken the Friday Fax to a whole new level of professionalism. Today we report on the UN negotiations on 'family planning' recently completed in Bangkok, Thailand, where a wonderful effort was once more turned in by the Bush Administration. Spread the word. Yours sincerely, Austin Ruse President

US Attacked for Pro-life Stance at UN Conference in Bangkok

According to a US State Department official, the US delegation at last-week's UN population conference in Bangkok was confronted by a 'horrendous disinformation campaign' about its positions and motives. Eugene Dewey, US State Department Assistant Secretary for Population, Refugees and Migration, said that 'It disturbs me, the disinformation campaign which has been perpetrated by some participants of this conference.' Most of the administration's critics have claimed that the US sought to undermine the worldwide consensus achieved at the 1994 International Conference on Population and Development (ICPD). International Planned Parenthood Federation (IPPF) Director-General Steven Sinding stated that he was 'deeply frustrated that a single country can hold up consensus in reaffirming a fundamental international commitment to women's health.' However, Dewey asserted that such statements spread 'the lie that the US is trying to pull back or to overturn the ICPD plan of action. This is absolutely false.' Instead, in

Bangkok, the US attempted to align itself with the many serious reservations placed in the original ICPD document by pro-life countries that feared that some language in the document could promote abortion. The US officially supports some aspects of ICPD, including its commitment to the idea that all family planning programs must be voluntary. Many critics also argued that the US administration possesses an unfounded fear that phrases such as 'reproductive health services' are euphemisms for abortion. UN Population Fund (UNFPA) Executive Director Thoraya Obaid bluntly stated that 'The phrase 'reproductive health services' is not code for the promotion or support for 'abortion services.' But, when the US attempted to include such a clarification in the Bangkok document, in order to resolve the issue, it was defeated. And, although Sinding asserted that ICPD 'does not promote abortion,' he also admitted that 'It is heartening to learn that 17 countries in this region have reviewed their abortion laws' in order to provide 'safe and legal abortions.' An observer present at the negotiations in Bangkok told the Friday Fax that the conference, officially called the Fifth Asian and Pacific Conference, appears to have been orchestrated by UNFPA, its chief nongovernmental partners, and members of other national delegations, in order to embarrass the Bush administration and to call into question its commitment to the well-being of women. For instance, the pro-abortion group 'Catholics' for a Free Choice (CFFC) placed advertisements in newspapers in Europe, Asia and the United States showing a woman and infant underneath a headline stating that 'The Bush administration has picked its next target.' The US was not cowed by this criticism. It supported calls from some developing countries for natural family planning, and argued for abstinence training as one of the strategies to slow the HIV/AIDS epidemic. Dewey told the conference that 'The United States supports the sanctity of life from conception to natural death,' a statement that closely mirrors recent remarks made by President George W. Bush.

"From: 'Austin Ruse—C-FAM' c-fam@c-fam.org
Subject: Friday Fax/Internal UN documents show financial mismanagement at UNFPA
Date: Thu, 02 Jan 2003 11:15:11-0800

Dear Colleague,

I am happy to announce the release of a new C-FAM report that is sure to help all those around the world who seek to stop UNFPA from its harmful mission.

'The United Nations Population Fund: Assault on the World's Peoples' is the most thorough investigation of UNFPA ever published. C-FAM research director Douglas A. Sylva spent six months looking closely at all aspects of UNFPA, and was even able to analyze internal documents that show widespread financial mismanagement. If you are in your government and seek to defund UNFPA, order this report from us today. If you are a journalist, radio talk show host, whatever, you will want to report on this new White Paper. All activists will also want copies. Spread the word. Yours sincerely, Austin Ruse President

Action item: Order a copy, or ten or twenty, of this new blockbuster report. The cost is $5.00 per copy (please add $2.00 for shipping and handling. Send your check or money order to C-FAM, 866 UN Plaza, Suite 427, New York, New York 10017. We also accept credit card orders.

FRIDAY FAX January 3, 2002 Volume 6, Number 2

Internal UN documents show financial mismanagement at UNFPA

An investigative report just released by the Catholic Family and Human Rights Institute (C-FAM) and the International Organizations Research Group (IORP) has found widespread financial and programmatic mismanagement within the United Nations Population Fund (UNFPA). 'The United Nations Population Fund: Assault on the World's Peoples' reports that internal UN audits show that UNFPA does not monitor the quality or reliability of the reproductive goods it ships to poor countries. The report also unveils little known internal UN audits that accuse UNFPA of failing to account for up to 50 per cent of its funds for the years 1998 and 1999.

UNFPA is the chief organ of population control and abortion promotion at the United Nations and has come under severe criticism from the United States, one of UNFPA's chief donor countries. In recent months UNFPA was accused by the US government of aiding and abetting forced family planning programs in China and subsequently lost all US funding. Efforts to defund UNFPA are ongoing in the British House of Commons and House of Lords. This new report is expected to fuel efforts to strip UNFPA of its funding, which has decreased almost $200 million over the past ten years.

Report author Douglas A. Sylva, C-FAM research director and director of IORP, reports that 10 million condoms sent by UNFPA to Tanzania were later discovered to be faulty by the AIDS-beleaguered nation. Sylva uncovered UN reports that showed UNFPA could not account for its money because it did not follow the routine book keeping practices necessary to keep track of it. UN auditors also discovered that, during the same period of time, 75 per cent of the UNFPA programs investigated 'failed to deliver all of their planned outputs,' while 25 per cent 'fell significantly short.' There were numerous cases of fraud, and frequent breaching of United Nations financial regulations at both UNFPA headquarters and at numerous UNFPA county offices. The UN auditors concluded that these problems of mismanagement have grown worse over time.

The C-FAM report, the second in C-FAM's White Paper Series of investigations, also establishes how UNFPA secretly promotes abortion. UNFPA distributes crude medical devices called manual vacuum aspirators, devices that UNFPA's nongovernmental partners use to perform illegal abortions throughout the developing world. The report also chronicles how UNFPA integrates its activities with pro-abortion NGOs, including the International Planned Parenthood Federation, and how these organizations have developed strategies to allow for UNFPA to help them increase access to abortion.

The report corroborates accounts of UNFPA involvement in coercive population control programs in China, Vietnam and Peru. In fact, documents written by one of UNFPA's population control allies and acquired by C-FAM show that UNFPA provided essential demographic expertise to the Chinese government, even setting up a population research center affiliated with the Chinese Family Planning Commission, the agency that is responsible for implementing China's forced-abortion and forced-sterilization program.

Copyright – C-FAM (Catholic Family & Human Rights Institute). Permission granted for unlimited use. Credit required.

Catholic Family & Human Rights Institute 866 United Nations Plaza, Suite 427 New York, New York 10017 Phone: (212) 754-5948 Fax: (212) 754-9291 E-mail: c-fam@c-fam.org Website: www.c-fam.org"

"From: "Austin Ruse—C-FAM" c-fam@c-fam.org
Subject: Friday Fax/UNFPA Competence Challenged by UNFPA Board
Date: Thu, 19 Jun 2003 11:25:09-0700

Dear Colleague,

We report today on trouble for UNFPA at their Executive Board meeting this week. Five months ago, C-FAM and our International Organizations Research Group issued a White Paper on UNFPA that exposed massive accounting and program tracking irregularities at UNFPA. These charges, though based on UN documents, were hotly denied by UNFPA and her allies in the EU [the EU even established a permanent office to debunk C-FAM's charges]. It seems the exact same questions that we raised in our report are now vexing UNFPA's Executive Board.

Spread the word. Yours sincerely, Austin Ruse President

Action Item: Many of you have asked for a copy of our UNFPA White Paper called "Assault on the World's Peoples." I am happy to report it is now available on our website at http://www.c-fam.org/iorg.htm Down load it, translate it, get it around everywhere, especially to your elected leaders.

FRIDAY FAX June 20, 2003 Volume 6, Number 26

UNFPA Competence Challenged at Executive Board Meeting

United Nations Population Fund Executive Director Thoraya Obaid faced a series of pointed questions this week at a meeting of the UNFPA Executive Board, many of them from the population control agency's most loyal allies. Obaid's top donor countries were concerned with the adequacy of UNFPA's management and financial reporting. The United Kingdom, Sweden, Benin, Denmark, the United States, Ireland and Canada all questioned whether UNFPA had the analytical ability to determine if its programs were successful.

As an example of UNFPA's continuing oversight problems, a major UNFPA statistical document released this week at the meeting contained a serious mistake, a mistake acknowledged by Obaid in her comments to the Executive Board. According to the document, UNFPA spending on reproductive health and family planning in 2002 had dropped significantly, from $119 million to $104.9 million, when in reality such spending rose to almost $130 million. The document, which relied on the incorrect figure for its analysis of UN FPA activities, was thereby rendered largely useless.

Issues regarding financial and programmatic mismanagement at UNFPA were first raised by C-FAM and the International Organizations Research Group (IORG) in their investigative white paper on the agency, 'The United Nations Population Fund: Assault on the World's Peoples.' Citing UN audit documents, the paper reported that UNFPA had lax quality control standards, even shipping 10 million faulty condoms to Tanzania, and that it possessed little capability to measure the outcomes of its programs.

At the time, some officials within the European Union showed hostility towards the report. In February, Claus Hougaard Sorenson, a high ranking member of the European Commission's office for Development and Humanitarian Aid said, 'these allegations have very little factual basis and in many cases have

distorted information or used it out of context...The UNFPA Executive Board
has dealt with the allegations on financial issues appropriately and decisively.'
However, these appear to be the same allegations now raised by a number of
EU member states.

At the Executive Board meeting, the European Commission (EC) continued to
exhibit a desire to protect UNFPA from criticism. In a statement to the Board,
the EC representative claimed that, 'In the last 12 months, the Commission has
become the target of a campaign aimed at...discrediting the EC and our
partners such as UNFPA.'

This 'campaign' appears to be a reference to the presentation of the C-
FAM/IORG paper to the European Parliament, which seemed to draw the ire
of the EC. In an internal memo obtained by the Friday Fax, the EC even
declared that it had established an office to monitor the activities and
publications of C-FAM and IORG.

This renewed debate regarding UNFPA's financial competence comes at a
critical juncture for the population control agency, as its allies in Washington
DC gear up for a major push to have its US funding restored.

Copyright – C-FAM (Catholic Family & Human Rights Institute).
Permission granted for unlimited use. Credit required."
(It's hard to ignore accounting fraud, because then you become culpable too.
And, yes, some members of Congress are trying to get funding restored to the
UNFPA from the U.S. This is definitely Dead On Arrival if they can't explain
where the money is going. Colloquially speaking, no one in their right mind
would touch it with a ten foot pole.)

From: "Austin Ruse—C-FAM" c-fam@c-fam.org Date: Fri, 10 Jan 2003

"Dear Colleague,

We report what may be good news today. The United States Agency for
International Development (USAID), one of the largest aid agencies in the
world, is moving tentatively away from population control and fertility
reduction as means to development. This could mark a seismic shift in the
international debate. Spread the word. Yours sincerely, Austin Ruse
President Action item: To view the report itself, go to
www.usaid.gov/NatsiosReport

New USAID Program Takes Tentative Steps Away from Population Control At a Washington D.C. press conference on Tuesday, Andrew Natsios, the head of the US Agency for International Development (USAID), announced what may be a major shift in USAID policy away from promoting fertility decline as a chief means to achieve international development. According to 'Foreign Aid in the National Interest,' 'As far back as the mid-1980s, it was reported that demographic factors such as fertility decline and population growth play a role in economic development – but that good governance, adequate resources, sound economic policies, and lack of corruption are even more important... The conclusion, then, is that good economic policies do more to reduce poverty than fertility and family planning programs.' Since USAID is the main US foreign aid agency, distributing about $10 billion every year, this report promises to have profound implications for US funding priorities.

The report asserts that, for the majority of developing countries, health care programs should expand beyond a reproductive health mentality in order to address the needs of all members of a family. 'Global health programs can shift their focus from women of reproductive age and children under 5 to entire families, including income earners and elderly dependents,' the report states. This shift is deemed essential for sustained development, since 'If both aging dependents and productive breadwinners are chronically ill, a family's future is bleak. Hence the importance of health strategies that aid economic growth.' The report also concludes that 'The near-term challenge is to learn more about families – their problems, their aspirations, and how they are adapting to changing living patterns and health status. How are they allocating their resources to meet changing demands, and how can foreign assistance help that process?'

'Foreign Aid in the National Interest' reflects the Bush administration's broader foreign aid principles, principles enumerated in the administration's 'Millennium Challenge Account.' For example, the USAID report asserts that countries that engage in authentic political and economic reforms should be rewarded by increases in US funding. This approach, it is believed, will make US international aid substantially more efficient, help reforms become permanent and encourage other nations to embrace their own policy changes. The report states that 'Levels of foreign assistance must be more clearly tied to development performance and to demonstrations of political will for reform and good governance. Good performers must be tangibly rewarded...' At the same time, 'If there is no political commitment to democratic and governance reforms, the United States should suspend government assistance and work only with nongovernmental actors.' USAID's staff includes holdovers from the Clinton administration who may be reluctant to adopt such dramatic changes. However, to date, the Bush administration has shown an unwillingness to compromise its core beliefs in the realm of international relations.

"U.N. GUARDS VIOLENTLY ATTACK AMERICAN CITIZEN"
"Congressman Demands Investigation!"
"Rep. Ron Paul Seeks Probe After Mawyer Assaulted"

You didn't see those headlines in your local or national paper, or hear them on
the evening news, because your media either didn't know about it or deemed it
to not be news you should hear about. But they are headlines about events that
did occur, as reported in The Washington Observer, "a publication of THIS
NATION, a Project of Christian Action Network…a national grassroots pro-
family organization with a membership of 250,000." Martin Mawyer is the
president and founder of THIS NATION (www.christianaction.org).

"The incident began…when Mawyer arrived at the U.N. to deliver 60,000
petitions to the U.N. from American citizens. The petitions to the U.N.
addressed a variety of issues of concern to citizens…Not only did the U.N.
agree to accept the petitions of our supporters in advance, said Mawyer, but
they assured us that we would be met on the steps of the U.N. and may
possibly be able to meet personally with a U.N. official who would listen to
some of our concerns.

When Mawyer arrived, U.N. Security officers refused to accept the petitions.
They then threw him to the ground, dragged him down the steps of the U.N.,
And tossed him roughly onto the sidewalk. Badly bruised and cut, with his
clothes torn and dirtied by the violent treatment, Mawyer was stunned".

There's no doubt that this occurred, because Martin had "…my staff and my
wife and son looking on in shock", who got some very good pictures of the
incident.

"Because the U.N.s treaty with the United States requires the U.N. to abide by
the laws of the United States, Mawyer had a right to deliver petitions…That
obviously falls within the First Amendment guarantee…'to petition the
Government for a redress of grievances.'"

218

Keyes, Lott, Frist, Time and Newsweek, CounterAttack

"This country is coming to the climax of the greatest moral crisis of its existence,...The terrorist movement we are fighting against disregards the worth of innocent human life...For us to be morally consistent in that fight against terrorism, we ourselves must adopt a principle of respect for life and reject the idea that it is ever justified, with malice aforethought, to take the life of another human being." Alan Keyes, Sarasota, FL, by way of Bradenton Herald and The Pro-Life Infonet, December 8, 2002, in a fund raising address to the Manasota Solve Crisis Pregnancy Center, founded by Helen Cadoret "26 years ago".

"To: Friends and Supporters of the Campaign for Working Families From: Gary L. Bauer, Chairman Date: Friday, December 20, 2002

Lott Throws In The Towel

After days of endless apologizing, Trent Lott has thrown in the towel and resigned as Senate Majority Leader. Late last night he began making phone calls to GOP colleagues to let them know his decision. Also over night the White House began a more concerted push to replace Lott with Senator Bill Frist who will now emerge as the 'frontrunner.' Frist is a savvy media personality, but he angered many conservatives by interfering in Republican primaries around the country, virtually always in favor of the moderate candidate over the conservative. And he was a staunch supporter of former Surgeon General Satcher who was pro-abortion. I hope a more reliable conservative-Nickles or Santorum will throw their hat in the ring." To me, this doesn't sound good. We've gone from a man who promised to pass the partial-birth abortion bill to one from the "moderate" wing of the party; where "moderate" may well mean liberal and RINO (Republican In Name Only). Senator Lott, of course, resigned because of a remark he made that was seized upon by the liberals and media as being "racist" and "segregationist".

"Back when they supported segregation, Lott and Thurmond were Democrats. This is something the media are intentionally hiding to make it look like the Republican Party is the party of segregation and race discrimination, which it has never been. In 1948, Thurmond did not run as a 'Dixiecan,' he ran as a 'Dixiecrat'—his party was an offshoot of the Democratic Party. And when he lost, he went right back to being a Democrat. This whole brouhaha is about a former Democrat praising another former Democrat for what was once a Democrat policy. Republicans made Southern Democrats drop the race nonsense when they entered the Republican Party." "Thurmond went on to reject segregation, become a Republican, and serve his country well as a U.S. senator." Ann Coulter writing for Human Events, "The Week of December 23,

2002". Today, Democrats seem to accomplish segregation through pushing welfare.

Someday, soon, I hope, support for abortion will be considered just as reprehensible as slavery and segregation; or even more so.

Will President Bush's desire to hold the political middle ground hurt the anti-abortion cause? Bill Frist seems to be his man.

"Several members of the Senate quickly lined up behind Tennessee Sen. Bill Frist, a doctor who normally votes pro-life but received significant criticism from the pro-life community for backing the confirmation of a doctor who performed abortions as Surgeon General during the Clinton administration. According to National Right to Life, in a 1998 letter to constituents, Senator Frist wrote, 'As a physician, my professional ethics are grounded in preserving life, and I am opposed to abortion.' Tennessee Right to Life PAC Director Sherry Holden said Frist had told her organization he was pro-life. 'He said he's against abortion, period'". The Pro-Life Infonet Source: Associated Press December 20, 2002

"*Time* magazine (Nov. 11, 2002) ran a 10-page cover story 'Special Report: Inside the Womb,' featuring beautiful pictures of babies in the womb at all stages of development." "*Newsweek* magazine (Dec. 9, 2002) ran a cover story about the 'New Virginity.' Chastity and virginity are starting to catch on. And now the new Miss America, Erika Harold, is speaking out strongly for total abstinence before marriage." Joseph M. Scheidler, Dec. 23, 2002 Then the June 9, 2003, issue of Newsweek had a cover story "Should a Fetus Have Rights? How Science Is Changing the Debate". I got a copy of this one from the drugstore. Journalistically, I would consider it a courageous thing to do, although I don't know that you can say they're on a crusade for either side. I'll probably comment on it eventually, to give my perspective, since I didn't get interviewed for it (humor intended). But I won't want to sound critical, since it's great any time the topic gets mainstreamed in an ostensibly neutral way, and it's not easy to give an unbiased account if you have a strong opinion. They wrote quite a lot, most of which I've read once, and I think an assessment would take more time than I have to give before I send my book to the publisher. But it will probably be done by the time the book comes out, so if you happen to be interested in what my opinion was, you'll need to come to the web site for it.

From: The Pro-Life Infonet Reply-To: Steven Ertelt infonet@prolifeinfo.org Source: Focus on the Family; January 1, 2003

Roe v. Wade: 30 Years Of Lies by Tom Neven

[Pro-Life Infonet Note: Tom Neven is editor of Focus on the Family magazine.]

Hoist by your own petard—an old literary expression that means blown up by your own bomb. In 1973 the ACLU and feminist lawyers dropped a bomb on American culture by asking the Supreme Court to legalize abortion on demand. But the two women they used as pawns are now doing something explosive—trying to take their cases back to the Court to have them overturned. And according to Rule 60 of the Federal Rules of Civil Procedure, there's nothing the pro-abortionists can do about it. Rule 60 states that 'Upon such terms as are just, a motion can be made by a party and the judgment will be set aside.' Basically, the plaintiffs say they know things now that they didn't know before, such as the fact that Roe v. Wade and its companion case, Doe v. Bolton, were based upon lies, the fact of post-abortion trauma suffered by millions of women and the well-documented link between abortion and breast cancer.

Taken advantage of

Norma McCorvey, the Jane Roe of Roe v. Wade, and Sandra Cano, the Mary Doe of Doe v. Bolton, are now pro-life Christians. While McCorvey's case was about abortion, even though she lied to her lawyers, Cano's was not remotely associated with the gruesome procedure. In 1970 Cano was a homeless mother of three children who had been taken away. Cano approached the local legal-aid office seeking custody of her children and a divorce from her husband. What she received was something she never requested: the legal right to abort her child. Cano admits she was young, uneducated and naïve. 'I never wanted an abortion. I just wanted my children back,' she says. Her legal-aid attorney, Margie Pitts Hames, however, filed the case under false pretenses. Cano says that either Hames forged her signature on the affidavit, or she slipped it in among other papers Cano was told to sign for her divorce. Cano never saw the affidavit that was filed with the Supreme Court, but she says unequivocally, 'The facts stated in the affidavit in Doe v. Bolton are not true.' 'Before my court date, I was instructed not to say anything and just be there,' Cano says. 'This is the only time I ever made an appearance in court before the Doe decision—and I never spoke a word.'

The deception went further. Cano says that a TV interview was basically faked. 'They set up the cameras facing my back, and then Margie did all the talking like she was me. It wasn't even my voice.' Years later, when Cano tried to have her court records unsealed, she was fought by, of all people, her former attorney, Hames. 'At first I couldn't understand why; she knew it was me. But now I understand.' The affidavit said that she had applied for an abortion, had been turned down and had therefore sued the state of Georgia. 'According to the records, I had applied for an abortion through a panel of nine doctors and nurses at [statefunded] Grady Memorial Hospital,' she says. 'This is a lie. I contacted the hospital and tried to get my records. At first they said they were there, but when my attorney sent for them, the records disappeared, if they ever really existed.'

In fact, Cano was against abortion. When told she had 'won' her court case, Cano says, 'It was like a whole bunch of bricks were put on my shoulders, and it has been that way ever since. I never wanted an abortion. Regardless of the worst state of misery or depression, it would never cross my mind to take the life of a child.'

Another pawn

In 1969 Norma McCorvey was a self-described hippie and often unhappy. 'I'd been on the streets since I was 9 or 10,' she says. 'I often told my mother, 'I wish I could find the person who invented life. I'd slap 'em.' 'She was pregnant for the third time—the second time out of wedlock—and looked into getting an abortion. The illegal abortion clinic she was referred to was, in the mildest of terms, disgusting.' There was dried blood all over the floor and on the side of this makeshift table,' McCorvey says. 'There was a grip hanging from the ceiling. I guess that's what the girls would hold on to. This was before they could give them anesthesia. I saw the conditions of the place and went outside to get ill.'

Eventually, McCorvey was recommended to two young women fresh out of law school, Sarah Weddington and Linda Coffee. She lied to them, saying she had been gang-raped. 'They said, 'Well, you know, women have the right to vote,' McCorvey says. 'I'm sitting there and thinking, Well, I may live part time in the streets and part time at my dad's, but I'm not stupid, okay? They were treating me like I was stupid, and I resented that. 'Then they said, 'Well, Norma, don't you think women should have rights to their own reproductive organs?' And I'm going, like, yeah. I wasn't real sure what they were talking about, but then you have to understand that I stayed stoned a lot.' They told McCorvey that the case was only about Texas' abortion laws. (Ironically, because the case dragged out in the courts, McCorvey never got an abortion. She gave up the baby for adoption.) When she found out that the case had gone all the way to the Supreme Court and resulted in legalizing abortion in all 50 states, she was stunned. 'I sat in the dining room that night and just kept rereading the newspaper story and drinking—drinking and thinking,' she says. 'It made me sad to know that my name, even though it was a pseudonym, would always be connected to the death of children.' McCorvey got a straight razor and started cutting her wrists a little at a time. 'That didn't work, so I went out and I got as many pills as I could. I took all of them and chased it with a quart of Johnny Walker, thinking I would die, and I wouldn't ever have to talk to Sarah Weddington or Linda Coffee again. But that was not God's plan for me.'

Silent no more

Both women now are in a position to take away some of that shame, particularly since McCorvey became a Christian in the mid-1990s and Cano two years ago. With the help of the Texas Justice Foundation, they are asking the Supreme Court to rehear their cases. (The Foundation is also representing Donna Santa Marie, a 16-year-old girl whose parents forced her to get an abortion—after her father allegedly punched her in the stomach to try to induce a miscarriage.) Allan Parker, president of the Foundation, says, 'They were willing to listen to Norma the first time; they ought to be willing to listen to her again.' He is launching a three-phased strategy called Operation Outcry: Silent No More. (See http://www.HelpAfterAbortion.com) 'We have filed a Friend of the Court brief on behalf of Norma and Sandra, and thousands of women who have signed our Friend of the Court form, saying they don't agree with Roe v. Wade.' In Parker's second phase of litigation, he has sued the Texas Department of Health for not adequately protecting women's health as it relates to abortion. 'While this suit can't overturn Roe v. Wade, we want women to be told, 'This is a human life that you're taking. You still have the choice under Roe, but you may suffer severe psychological consequences.' The third phase of Operation Outcry will be filing the motion to reopen Roe v. Wade and Doe v. Bolton, based on the fact that false testimonies were used in both. 'I believe that the Supreme Court will take and hear the case,' Parker says. 'It's a unique, historic opportunity in America where two people who won landmark Supreme Court decisions want to go back.'

From: The Pro-Life Infonet Steven Ertelt infonet@prolifeinfo.org
Source: NBC, Fox News Channel; January 12, 2003

"New Senate Majority Leader Frist Promotes Pro-Life Legislation

Washington, DC—The pro-life community has waited with baited breath to find out how Tennessee Sen. Bill Frist would handle pro-life legislation now that he, and not pro-life Sen. Trent Lott (R-MS), is the Senate Majority Leader. Frist provided his first glimpse when speaking on several talk shows Sunday morning. He said he would work toward a ban on partial-birth abortions and on human cloning research. When asked about potential abortion-related legislation on NBC's 'Meet the Press,' Frist said, 'We are just beginning sort of all the planning in terms of what particular bills. I think things like partial-birth abortion—and I can tell you as a physician who has been in the operating room for thousands of days and hundreds of thousands of hours, the whole concept of partial-birth abortion offends the sensibilities of me as a physician. It's a rogue procedure. It's not in the medical textbooks. Something like that where we've got not consensus but broad, broad support among the American people, I can see that coming very, very quickly.' He added, 'It's an abhorrent, abhorrent procedure that offends the civil sensibilities of every, I think, just about every American.'

Meanwhile, on the question of President Bush's pro-life judicial nominations, Frist said he will support Bush's renomination last week of U.S. District Judge Charles Pickering to serve on the 5th U.S. Circuit Court of Appeals in New Orleans. Pickering has been criticized by many pro-abortion organizations and because of his opposition to abortion. The Senate Judiciary Committee last March voted 10-9 along party lines to reject Bush's original nomination of Pickering. 'There are many people who think he did not get a fair hearing before,' Frist said, adding, 'So I receive his nomination gladly…I plan on supporting Pickering.'"

March For Life Month and Pressure on the 108th Congress

"Life Proclamation President Bush, continuing a tradition we began in the Reagan Administration, has declared this Sunday National Sanctity of Human Life Day. The life issue will predominate in the next week as the country marks the 30th anniversary of Roe v. Wade. Demonstrators from both sides will fill the streets here in Washington, D.C. But, the bottom line hasn't changed in 30 years. We continue to exploit women and destroy several thousand pre-borns every day. America is better than this." Gary L. Bauer, Chairman Campaign for Working Families Wednesday, January 15, 2003

The March For Life will be on Wednesday, January 22 (as it is each year), and this one may mark a historical turning point in the struggle. I believe it starts around noon, and the marchers are going to assemble at the Washington Monument.

"In a recent report conducted by the Alan Guttmacher Institute (the research arm of Planned Parenthood), it was reported that Partial-Birth Abortions have tripled in the last four years! This is a devastating tragedy and something must be done! The majority of the American people agree that partial birth abortion is infanticide. In many cases, babies old enough to survive outside the womb are murdered in the birth canal, when the baby is almost delivered. The study showing this number increasing is an alert for fast action! Obviously, something MUST be done to stop this brutal practice. The 108th Congress MUST pass a ban on partial birth abortion and end this atrocity!" Jennifer Bingham, Executive Director SBAList 15 Jan 2003 13:48:20 Actually, about 80% agree.

From: The Pro-Life Infonet Steven Ertelt infonet@prolifeinfo.org
Source: Washington Times, Cybercast News Service; January 16, 2003

New Poll Shows Americans are Pro-Life

Washington, DC—Nearly 70 percent of Americans say they favor 'restoring legal protection for unborn children,' according to a new poll that pro-life groups say shows public opinion is swinging their way on the abortion issue.

'This is the new, big change in this country,' Sandy Rios, president of Concerned Women for America, said yesterday as she and other leaders of pro-life groups released the findings of a Wirthlin Worldwide poll taken last month.

Some 1,000 adults were asked whether, in light of medical advances that reveal the unborn child's body and facial features in detail, 'are you in favor of restoring legal protection for unborn children?' Sixty-eight percent of the randomly surveyed adults said they were in favor of legal protection, with 44 percent in strong agreement of such action. Only 25 percent opposed such pro-life action. Almost the same number—66 percent—said they favored nominees to the Supreme Court 'who would uphold laws that restore legal protection to unborn children.' Only 28 percent said no.

These polls reflect a growing pro-life attitude, said Janet Folger, president of Faith2Action, a new outreach organization for pro-life and traditional family issues. 'We have the American people standing with us.' 'The bottom line is, 30 years of chanting 'choice' cannot overshadow what it is that's being chosen,' Folger said. 'A child, even the child of an abortion supporter, can recognize that that being in the womb is a human being, that being is a baby.'

'We are stronger. We are more united. We are standing with truth, backed by technology,' Folger continued speaking about the condition of the pro-life movement, 'and the vast majority of the American people.'

The grassroots leaders praised President Bush and his administration for their pro-life positions, including proclaiming Sunday as National Sanctity of Human Life Day. 'He's done more, practically speaking, than any other president,' said Rios.

Thomas Glessner, president and founder of the National Institute of Family Health and Life Advocacy (NIFLA), said that new ultrasound technology can both persuade women to opt against abortion and persuade the American public that the developing child before birth is a unique human being worthy of legal protection. NIFLA research indicates that up to 90 percent of women who see their unborn child using new '3-D' ultrasound technology choose to carry the baby to term.

Pro-abortion activists have called providing access to such ultrasound equipment 'intimidation,' and have taken legal measures to block such access. Glessner's group provides legal representation and helps pregnancy health centers become licensed health care facilities to avoid legal problems.

In response to the new polling data, NARAL Pro-Choice America said the pro-life message was out of step with the beliefs of many Americans. 'A majority of Americans believe that women should have the right to choose and that decision should be between a woman and her doctor,' the group said in a statement.

The polling data comes at a time when a new study by the pro-abortion Alan Guttmacher Institute, affiliated with Planned Parenthood, shows the number of abortion facilities across the U.S. has decreased significantly. The number of abortion facilities decreased by 11 percent in 2000 to 1,819. Of those, 46 percent were abortion-only facilities, 33 percent were hospitals and 21 percent were private physicians' offices. Only 13 percent of U.S. counties had an abortion facility, as did only 86 of the nation's 276 metropolitan areas.

'Just as we now look back at our nation's history and ask how decent men and women could have tolerated and defended such horrors as slavery, segregation and discrimination,' Rios said Wednesday, 'so the next generation will ask how decent men and women could tolerate and even welcome such abominations as abortion.'"

"Unborn Babies Gain Support A new poll by Dick Wirthlin was released yesterday during a press conference I spoke at along with Sandy Rios of Concerned Women for America and Janet Folger of Faith2Action. Sixty-six percent of the public wants Supreme Court nominees 'who would uphold laws that restore legal protection to unborn children.'" Gary Bauer, End of Day—1/16/03

"Every child is a priority and a blessing and I believe that all should be welcomed in life and protected by law. Through ethical policies and the compassion of Americans, we will continue to build a culture that respects life."—George W. Bush, January 15 2003, Human Events Quote of the Week, January 20, 2003.

I thought President Bush's economic stimulus package had a lot for just about everybody, after I heard his speech on the radio. Of course the media just wanted to talk about the dividend tax elimination, and ignore all the other measures. Tom Daschle called it "obscene". Initially I attributed that to a limited vocabulary or poor command of the English language. But I've since concluded that it was blind partisanship rooted in stupidity. The Democrats are most interested in opposing anything and everything the President proposes, because they believe it will somehow help them recapture the White House and Senate; rather than finding solutions to the nation's problems. They don't want an economic recovery now, because it would take away a big campaign issue for them. They believe that two years from now the economy can still be trying to recover; which is a long shot, at best, in my opinion. To keep things in perspective, they're also not so interested in tax cuts because a significant portion of the people that vote for them don't make enough to have to pay any, or only very little, taxes. They want to tax more so that they can send more to their constituency in the form of federal programs; that is, transfer payments. To them, *anyone* who pays taxes is "wealthy".

"I want to thank you very much for including me in the celebration of life... you've made great sacrifices to come to Washington today. I admire your perseverance and I admire your devotion to the cause of life. The March for Life upholds the self-evident truth of our Declaration of Independence—that all are created equal, given the unalienable rights of life and liberty and the pursuit of happiness. And that principle of America needs defenders in every place and every generation. In our time, respect for the right to life calls us to defend...all who are weak and vulnerable. And self-evident truth calls us to value and protect the innocent children waiting to be born. You and I share a commitment to building a culture of life in America...We support abstinence education, and crisis pregnancy programs, and parental notification laws. We offer compassionate alternatives to abortion by promoting adoption...My hope is that the United States Congress will pass a bill this year banning partial-birth abortion, which I will sign. Partial-birth abortion is an abhorrent procedure that offends human dignity. For 30 years, the March for Life has been sustained by constant prayer and abiding hope that one day, every child will be born into a family that loves that child and a nation that protects that child. When that day arrives, you will have the gratitude of millions—especially those who know the gift of life because you cared and you kept faith. May God bless you all". President George W. Bush addressing the thousands gathered on the Washington Mall by telephone, from St. Louis, Missouri, 01/22/03.

I attended the January 22nd, 2003, March For Life, in Washington, D.C. I walked from the Washington Monument, to the steps of the Supreme Court; but before the march began, because I wanted to be there when the march arrived, so I could take pictures and get a feel for things. I found about 100 "pro-choice" demonstrators protesting in favor of Roe, and playing the media prior to the main event composed of thousands of demonstrators; and a media personality putting his own peculiar spin on the event. There was a line of police between the pro-choice demonstrators and the Court, and on a day when the temperature was in the teens they rotated every few minutes with police inside the building to keep warm. Actually, there were police everywhere; on motorcycles, in squad cars, and on foot. Almost as many as the pro-choice people. There was even a policeman taking pictures of the crowd with handheld video and still cameras, while I was obliviously taking pictures of the police activity. If he took my picture, I don't mind-I was proud to be there. As the marchers flowed down the street like an invading army of Roman Legionnaires, the media personality disappeared and suddenly there were three lines of police behind the barricades in front of the Court building, even though I had heard someone on the radio say there had never been any violence at the marches.

I thought: What you have here is a judiciary so obsessed with its own power that it feels it needs an overwhelming show of force to intimidate peaceful school children, the elderly, Catholic parishioners, and God fearing Christian Conservatives from middle class America into submission to its arbitrary will. Any court decision so unpopular, evincing so much protest, that generates so much fear of the populace among a majority of the Supreme Court must be rotten to the core. It's the Court's guilt and fear from a decision that deep down they have irreconcilable doubts about that I saw reflected in those police lines January 22nd. A more peaceful crowd than what marched past me that day is difficult to imagine. I literally laughed at the police, with their long billy clubs across their thighs, in riot gear; and my sense was that they were embarrassed to be there. The ones I looked in the eye looked away, and the ones I asked for information were as helpful as they could be. The ones on the streets even seemed protective of the marchers. I saw one policeman get off his motorcycle and run after a man on a sidestreet. At first I was a little startled, but then I realized he was chasing the man because the man had fallen and he wanted to make sure the man wasn't hurt. However, my impression was that 2 or 3 floaters was all that was needed to shoo people away who wandered behind the barricades. It reminded me of scenes from Montgomery, Alabama, when the schools were desegregated down South (in the 60's?). Yet another parallel to slavery and oppression.

The reporters were all over doing interviews with anybody willing. One rather unassuming lady had a yellow lined pad that she was writing statements from people on. I assumed she was from a local paper or pro-life organization or church. Since it was relatively quiet before the marchers arrived, and she was standing close to me, I asked her what organization she was from. "The New York Times, sir", she replied. But, when Reverend Louis Sheldon, the only pro-life leader I recognized, marched by; and tarried for a moment in the area they were working, the reporters seemed to evaporate. I later found out, however, that there had been speakers at the Washington Monument. One gentleman, dressed as George Washington, marched by and seemed so out of place that I wondered whether he was some kind of nut or grandstander. But as I began to leave I saw him again, posing for photos with a pro-life sign in each hand, and giving interviews. I couldn't resist taking pictures of him, and it turned out that he was a very articulate fellow with a flair for promotion, who was recounting to people what George Washington had had to say that was relevant to the abortion crisis today; and it made sense.

There were many slogans that I had never heard of before, but they went by so quickly that it was difficult to remember more than a few. One I especially liked was "One killed, one wounded". Another was "I am an American!", next to a picture of a baby. There was "Women deserve better", and "Abortion is the exploitation of women"-something that Susan B. Anthony understood too.

There was also a sign with a drawing of a box of kleenex and the words "This is tissue" next to it; and alongside it a picture of a baby with the words "This is baby" that I thought was especially innovative. "A boy in a tree held a 'Jesus was a fetus' sign." CNS 01/22/03

It was a lot like the Rose Bowl Parade, but with fewer floats and more people. The people interviewed by the media seemed to agree that there was a shift in sentiment to the pro-life side (with which I concur), and that there were more young people there than they had ever seen before. The police estimated 50,000, not counting those along the route cheering on the marchers. That's 50,000 compared to 100 on the other side. Seems like there should be a message there of some kind. Like a no-brainer. What will it take to wake up a majority of the judges on the Supreme Court that they've made a horrible mistake? That evening about 20 women from Silent No More held a candlelight vigil with signs saying they regretted their abortions. Quotes from two of the featured speakers at the Washington Monument before the march follow:

"Because of all of you, and millions of Americans you represent, abortion is in steep decline in America today. Abortion is less available, less legal, and less morally acceptable than at any time since 1973. You alone have exposed the empty promises of the left, who offer choice but deliver only heartache and disappointment and a national conscience seared by pain'"—Rep. Mike Pence (R.- Ind)

"Every one of you is part of the most important human rights movement in the world today."—Rep. Chris Smith (R.-N.J.)

"Today, January 22nd marks the 30th Anniversary of Roe vs. Wade! Since this remarkable decision that made abortion legal at any time for almost any reason. And since this time, over 42 million babies have been killed by abortion. No one knew what a profound change that would be! With this decision came a culture of death in which we murder our own children in the name of choice." Jennifer Bingham, Executive Director, SBAList, January 22, 2003

"In the 30 years since the U.S. Supreme Court decriminalized abortion, millions of children have been brutally slain; millions of hearts have been broken in their grief and sorrow; and, yes, millions of people in this great land simply don't care. The apathy is discouraging; the child killing is appalling; the misery is heart wrenching. I want to talk specifically about the mothers, fathers and grandparents of aborted children. It never occurred to me to think about the depth of their agony until the weekend I spent at a Rachel's Vineyard retreat. Honestly, I will never be the same again. I heard with my own ears how mothers were led to believe that aborting a child was nothing but a 'choice.' No sooner was the money collected and the deed done then these

230

same mothers were abandoned to face—alone—the undeniable reality that aborting a child is a horror beyond telling. I wept with them, prayed with them…". Judie Brown, President, ALL, in Celebrate Life, January-February, 2003.

"Adolph Hitler, Joseph Stalin, Pol Pot-they would have been proud of the United States of America on January 22, 2003 as we marked thirty years of legalized killing in our country. Even with all their evil efforts, these three butchers were never able to equal the body count that we have amassed in this country through abortion. The toll is over 40 million dead babies." Conrad Wojnar, The Women's Center, Chicago, IL February, 2003

But PP continued to blow smoke. Here are excerpts from a "Speech by Gloria Feldt, President Planned Parenthood Federation of America January 2003 This year we celebrate the 30th anniversary of Roe v. Wade…That historic ruling helped improve the health and lives of women all across America. And you know, when you improve the lives and health of women, you improve the lives and health of children, and families, and our whole community. And most importantly, in gaining control of our bodies we gained control of our destinies, and our dreams. As U.S. Supreme Court Justice Harry Blackmun said, 'Roe was a necessary step for the full emancipation of women'. But 30 years after that monumental decision, a vocal and virulent minority is working nonstop to deny women our constitutional right". Taken from PP's Save Roe web site. Excuse me, I think I'm going to be sick.

"Pro-life democrats from around the country joined together to hear Ambassador and former Mayor of Boston Ray Flynn rally the troops before the March for Life. Ambassador Flynn says pro-life Democrats face two choices: Leave the party, or stay and fight. We choose to stay and fight!" Democrats For Life of America, http://www.democratsforlife.org/.

"Rove Speaks Karl Rove, President Bush's chief strategist, gave a rare interview with reporters yesterday during which he made some very encouraging statements. Specifically, Rove said that banning partial-birth abortions and human cloning are high items on the President's agenda. Calling these two issues part of 'the immediate tasks at hand,' Rove indicated the White House is prepared to offer more than just moral support, but political muscle as well in the legislative battles on Capitol Hill." Gary Bauer, Chairman, Campaign for Working Families, January 23, 2003.

"NARAL went 1-for-20 in its congressional election picks in November. That is, all but one of the 20 House and Senate candidates it chose to support and endorse—all Democrats—lost. The abortionists' fundamental problem is that they don't have truth on their side. They aren't even honest about their real agenda, which is why they are forever playing semantic games". David Limbaugh, TownHall; January 25, 2003

"The President and majorities in Congress are dedicated to ending legal abortion. Since 1995, Congress has voted 148 times on reproductive rights and health legislation—pro-choice Americans lost all but 25 of those votes. During that same period, states have passed 335 anti-choice laws, 34 last year alone. Not surprisingly, not a single of the President's appellate court nominees has demonstrated any hint of support for freedom of choice...are depending on pro-choice Senators to ensure the federal courts will continue to serve as a defense against hostile legislatures...warrants the use of every available political, persuasive and procedural tool." NARAL President Kate Michelman, January 27, 2003

"We must not overlook the weakest among us. I ask you to protect infants at the very hour of their birth and end the practice of partial-birth abortion." President George W. Bush in his State of the Union speech, Tuesday, January 28, 2003.

"Bush, undaunted by the Democrats and unfazed by the political pundits, rejected the easy road and instead reappointed both Pickering and Owens! It was unbelievable-bold, decisive, and said boatloads about the man. It was President Bush's 'I paid for this mike' moment. Everyone in this awful city suddenly knew who was in charge. Bush defied the press, the pundits, and the pollsters, stuck it to the Democrats, and instructed Republicans to get ready for the fight. And, he let pro-lifers know they were welcomed members of his team.

Of all his accomplishments I believe the greatest to date is that he has changed the dialogue in the country from one of choice to one of life. And as the unborn are gaining the respect they so deserve, more and more Americans are feeling a need to legally restrict abortions. With George W. Bush as President I believe the unborn have a true friend in the White House." Bay Buchanan, in The American, January/February 2003, an American Cause publication.

"Yesterday, Congressman Steve Chabot (R-OH) introduced the Partial-Birth Abortion Ban Act of 2003 in the U.S. House of Representatives. This bill would make the gruesome practice of partial-birth abortion illegal. It is crucial that this legislation move swiftly so that we can get this before President Bush who is ready to sign the bill into law! As you may know, in a recent report released by the Alan Guttmacher Institute (the research arm of Planned Parenthood), it was announced that Partial-Birth Abortions have tripled in the last four years! This is a devastating tragedy and something must be done! That is why I need you to take action today! Please take a moment to encourage your Con-gressman to SUPPORT the Partial Birth Abortion Ban so that this horrific practice can FINALLY be stopped!" Jennifer Bingham, Executive Director, SBAList@democracydata.com http://www.sba-list.org/ 14 Feb 2003 16:55:35

Women's Right to Know, RICO, and Feeling Pain

"Indiana's Women's Right to Know Law Upheld by Federal Court Indianapolis, IN—A federal appeals court Monday revived a pro-life state law requiring women to be presented abortion information in person from an abortion practitioner at least 18 hours before an abortion. Women seeking an abortion in Indiana currently are allowed to get information about abortion and its risks beforehand over the phone. Women in Indiana will now get the information, as well as facts on fetal development, in person.

'This is a major victory for women,' states Indiana Right to Life executive director Mike Fichter. 'The information required by Indiana law is basic, common sense information that any woman seeking an abortion has a right to know, and there is no other way to deliver this information properly than by face-to-face interaction.'…a 1995 law…required women in Indiana to make two trips to the abortion facility—the first to receive the required information and the second to undergo the abortion.

The law requires women seeking an abortion, except in the case of a medical emergency, to be counseled about the risks and alternatives to abortion. They also are to be offered the chance to see pictures or drawings of a fetus at the same stage of development as their own. The person performing the abortion, a referring physician, physician's assistant, nurse or midwife can provide the counseling, which includes information of adoption alternatives. Similar laws in other states have significantly reduced the number of abortions. About 16 other states have Women's Right to Know laws." Source: Indianapolis Star, Pro-Life Infonet; September 17, 2002

"Liberty Counsel NEWS RELEASE Contact: Mat Staver Date: February 6, 2003 For Immediate Release Physician Associations Argue That Women Considering Abortion Have The Right To Be Fully Informed West Palm Beach, FL-Today the Catholic Medical Association and the Christian Medical Associations filed a brief in defense of a Florida law which requires that women have the right to know about the consequences of undergoing an abortion. Together, the two associations represent over 20,000 physicians. Last year, a state trial court judge ruled that the informed consent law violates Florida's right to privacy contained in the state constitution. The case of Presidential Women's Center v. State of Florida is now pending before the Fourth District Court of Appeal in Palm Beach Florida County, Florida. The Associations are represented by Teresa Collett, professor of law at South Texas College of Law, along with Mathew D. Staver, President and General Counsel of Liberty Counsel.

The brief first argues that the abortion clinic and its doctors have no standing to challenge the law, because their position as medical providers is in direct conflict with the rights of women considering an abortion. The abortion providers have an obvious profit motive. It is not in their best interest to inform women of the consequences of abortion. The interest of the abortion providers is not the interest of women who have the right to know about the procedure. While physicians have been allowed to represent women seeking an abortion, it is a different matter when a physician argues that the patient should not know of the consequences of the procedure.

The brief also argues that women make better choices when they are fully informed. The brief criticizes the trial judge who struck down the law, stating: 'The order of the trial court reflects a failure to recognize that a right exercised in ignorance is not freedom. It's just tyranny once removed.'

Staver commented, 'Abortion providers arguing that they should not be required to inform women about the consequences of abortion is akin to the fox guarding the hen house. Abortion doctors have an incentive to spend as little time with their patients as possible in order to increase their profit margin. Although abortion providers claim they act in the best interest of women, their actions are to the contrary. The best interest of women, and for that matter the best interest of any patient, is to be fully informed of the impending medical procedure. Women have a right to be fully informed.'" In case you might be wondering how this is going to turn out; based on past performance Mat is almost a certain winner at some point in the litigation.

Yahoo News-"Health-AP Supreme Court clears way for abortion restrictions Mon Feb 24, 8:34 PM ET By ANNE GEARAN, Associated Press Writer WASHINGTON-The Supreme Court cleared the way for an Indiana state law that places some of the United States' most severe restrictions on abortions, including requirements that a woman be counseled face-to-face about the risks and offered pictures of what her fetus might look like. The high court on Monday turned down an appeal from abortion clinics in Indiana...Mike Fichter, executive director of Indiana Right to Life, an antiabortion group, said, 'For the first time abortion providers in Indiana will be required to give women information about the risks. We're glad that the court battles look like they're finally over.'

The high court action means that Indiana may begin fully enforcing a law passed eight years ago that requires in-person counseling and an 18-hour waiting period before a woman can get an abortion.

Nearly every state places some restriction on the availability of the procedure, including requirements that women wait a day or so after requesting an abortion and that they receive certain medical or legal information

235

beforehand. The high court has allowed a variety of restrictions…Mississippi and Utah…Louisiana and Wisconsin also have similar in-person counseling requirements.

Waiting periods and laws requiring women to get information ahead of time are not new, but Indiana's law goes further than most states in combining the two restrictions."

"According to the (Indianapolis) *Star*, fewer women had abortions in Mississippi and Utah after in-person counseling became mandatory in those states." CNSNews.com

"Abortion proponents are fighting a new Michigan law that prevents abortion providers from charging women for abortions before a 24-hour waiting period. The waiting period begins when a woman receives counseling about abortion. Abortionists' practice of making women pay for abortions before they've had the 24-hours to think about their options is a clear case of coercion. Abortionists know that once a woman has paid for an abortion, they've got her because she is under financial pressure to go through with the procedure. The pro-abortion Center for Reproductive Rights has filed a lawsuit asking a federal court to enjoin the new law. This demonstrates once more that abortion advocates don't care what's best for women. They care about doing as many abortions as possible in order to maximize their profits." Life Dynamics News, May 2003

"Informed Consent Act, a (Federal) bill that will place Ultrasound machines in crisis pregnancy centers nationwide…one abortionist on Long Island said, 'The bottom line is no woman is going to want an abortion after she sees a sonogram'…

Gloria Feldt, president of Planned Parenthood has decried the bill, saying pro-lifer's are 'using medical technology as political propaganda.' You see, the radical abortionists are scared to death of the Ultrasound machine and its ability to dissuade any rational woman from choosing abortion. Bottom line: the Ultrasound machine provides women with a picture of their baby in the womb showing them the real choice they must make." Congressman Rick Renzi, (R-AZ), one of the people the pro-life movement helped to send to Congress in 2002. He and Care Net are working together to pass H. R. 195, the Informed Choice Act. "To authorize the Secretary of Health and Human Services to make grants to nonprofit tax-exempt organizations for the purchase of ultrasound equipment to provide free examinations to pregnant women needing such services". What a concept.

"Protesters Aren't Racketeers, Supreme Court Rules By Susan Jones and David Thibault CNSNews.com Staff February 26, 2003

(CNSNews.com)-Pro-life groups Wednesday cheered a U.S. Supreme Court ruling that prohibits the use of federal anti-racketeering law to be used in the prosecution of pro-life protesters or any other protesters. The 8-to-1 ruling is considered a victory for protesters of all stripes, although the case involved members of the Pro Life Action Network and Operation Rescue who were convicted in 1998 under a racketeering law known as RICO (Racketeer Influenced and Corrupt Organizations). According to wire reports, the Supreme Court ruled that pro-lifers' political activity could not be considered the type of extortion that RICO prohibits. The original case dated all the way back to 1986. The 1998 convictions occurred after numerous delays. The case ended up in the Supreme Court because the trial court had allowed prosecutors to link various violent acts committed by other anti-abortion protesters to the demonstrations conducted by members of the Pro Life Action Network and Operation Rescue. The Seventh U.S. Circuit Court of Appeals upheld the trial court decision. The case was then appealed to the Supreme Court.

Writing for the majority of the high court, Chief Justice William Rehnquist agreed that the pro-life protesters interfered with abortion clinic operations. 'But,' he wrote, 'Even when their acts of interference and disruption achieved their ultimate goal of 'shutting down' a clinic that performed abortions, such acts did not constitute extortion.'

The American Center for Law and Justice (ACLJ) provided legal services to Operation Rescue in the case. The RICO law was 'designed to combat drug dealers and organized crime,' the center stated in a news release, and 'was wrongly used against the pro-life movement.' 'The decision removes a cloud that has been hanging over the pro-life movement for 15 years,' according to the ACLJ.

The Rutherford Institute, which also argued in favor of the pro-life movement in its friend of the court brief, called it 'the most significant pro-life protest case to come before the court in years.' 'The Supreme Court's near-unanimous decision gives breathing room for the First Amendment-protected speech of many political groups that have been virtually shut out of public debate because of threats of huge fines like those imposed on these protesters,' according to institute president John W. Whitehead.

Concerned Women for America president Sandy Rios also praised the high court's ruling, declaring that, 'pro-life activists are not mobsters.' 'The Supreme Court has set the record straight on the time-honored American tradition of the right to protest,' Rios said.

Family Research Council president Ken Connor said 'acts of violence directed at abortion clinics, abortionists or women seeking abortions are wrong and already against the law.' As a result, Connor said, the RICO law should not be targeted at pro-lifers. 'What NOW (National Organization for Women) and other pro-abortion groups want to do is threaten pro-lifers with financial ruin in order to silence debate,' he added.

Gloria Feldt, president of Planned Parenthood Federation of America, expressed disappointment at the verdict, but vowed to 'not allow it to be a green light for anti-choice terrorists.'" Truly amazing that it took so long or got this far. Any idiot could see that racketeering laws weren't written to persecute pro-life protesters. Justice Paul Stevens dissented.

"N.O.W. expressed 'shock' at the decision. In fact, despite their loss, N.O.W. *continues* accusing me of orchestrating a 'violent campaign to close abortion clinics nationwide.' Fay (Clayton) indicated to me that our fight isn't over. N.O.W. has already stated publicly that it may try to use the Patriot Act against pro-lifers. I wouldn't put anything past Fay. Enough is enough! I've been on the defensive for 17 long years. The baby killers have felt free to slander and libel me as a violent terrorist, and they continue to do so. This has to stop. It's now time to take the offense with appropriate legal action. N.O.W. must be stopped, and so must Fay. I'm conferring with my attorney to determine what kind of action to file against those who've so abused the legal system with this malicious and frivolous lawsuit. Let me assure you that we'll file something that will call Fay and N.O.W. to account for their outrageous defamations and for their incredible abuse of the legal system. N.O.W.'s goal was always to bankrupt the Pro-Life Action League and me. Their preposterous racketeering lawsuit failed. Let's make sure they never succeed." Joseph M. Scheidler, March 31, 2003. This is a very drastic step for Joe. He's a love and pray for your enemy, and build bridges between people, type of person. What pushed him to do this was Fay's behavior after the decision, which I didn't feel necessary to relate in further detail here. What has somehow gotten lost in the moment, is that the real violence goes on *inside* the aborturies.

There's been another legal development, that you probably won't hear too much about right away, but that I consider a very important first step:

"South Carolina Abortion Regulations Upheld by U.S. Supreme Court – South Carolina's health authorities may now implement a 1995 law that requires abortion clinics to open all files, including patient medical records, if requested by state investigators. The law was challenged by a Greenville, S.C. abortion clinic on the basis of patient confidentiality but the state argued that the new regulations will improve state oversight of abortion providers, improve standards at abortion clinics making the procedure safer, and are part of ordinary state record keeping. Currently, South Carolina is the only state whose law allows regulators to see, copy and store abortion patients' medical records without stiff requirements that the information be kept confidential. (AP, 4/29/03)

The regulations consist of 37 pages of requirements for any facility that would perform five or more first trimester abortions per month, or one second trimester abortion per month, and sets fines of up to $5,000 per day for some violations. Dr. William Lynn of the Greenville Women's Clinic said he had to close two of his offices in the state because of the economic impact of trying to comply with the regulations. We expect that South Carolina will be joined by many other states!" Thanks to Colleen Parro, RNC/Life FaxNotes, for passing this along, Thur, 8 May 2003 07:01:39-0500.

The reason I believe this is so important, is that it will give authorities a tool for enforcing the laws that every state has for reporting underage girls having abortions; plus those brought across state lines by older adults to avoid their own state's laws. I don't believe, even for a moment, Dr. William Lynn's statement.

It apparently excludes those abortions done by doctors who are legitimately family or Ob/Gyn practitioners who occasionally fill a request from a regular patient. I think if we could get to that point, where those are the only abortions done, that it would represent substantial progress. Much more follows in a subsequent chapter on underage, or minor, pregnancies-by adult males.

"From: The Pro-Life Infonet Steven Ertelt infonet@prolifeinfo.org
Source: Helena Independent Record, Pro-Life Infonet; February 27, 2003

Montana House Reverses Itself on Fetal Pain Bill

Helena, MT—In a rare move, a narrow majority of the state House of Representatives reversed itself and voted against a pro-life bill mandating that abortion practitioners offer painkillers for the unborn children of women seeking abortions past the 16th week of pregnancy. House Bill 460, sponsored by pro-life Rep. Penny Morgan, R-Billings, passed the House on a preliminary vote of 52-47 Wednesday. Representatives Dan Hurwitz, Joey Jayne and Paul Clark switched their votes and the House defeated the bill Thursday 46-51. Gregg Trude, executive director of Montana Right to Life, told the Pro-Life Infonet Rep. Jayne indicated she felt unborn children would be harmed by receiving the anesthesia. The legislation would have made it a felony for an abortion practitioner not to offer the pain relief for the baby.

'There is scientific evidence to show unborn fetal pain at 12 weeks,' Morgan told her colleagues on the House floor. 'Compelling evidence in the House Judiciary committee proved that babies feel pain in their mother's wombs,' added Julie Millam, director of the Montana Family Coalition.

Opponents of the bill said the Legislature has no right to tell doctors how to do their job. They also said the state would be requiring doctors to perform an experimental procedure, since unborn children are not usually given painkillers before they're aborted in Montana. The measure 'is absolutely inappropriate for this body,' said pro-abortion Rep. Eve Franklin, D-Great Falls.

Proponents said the legislation would affect a very small number of abortions, about 135 of the 2,300 abortions performed yearly in Montana. Most women seek abortions before they are 16 weeks pregnant, proponents said. 'You should have some compassion for the child inside you that you're about to get rid of,' said pro-life Rep. Jeff Pattison, R-Glasgow.

Morgan said certain medical journals demonstrate an unborn child's ability to feel pain early in its development. The abortion procedure, which involves dismembering the baby in the womb, is painful and she said painkillers administered to the woman don't reach the baby before the abortion is performed.

The final vote on the bill can be viewed at http://data.opi.state.mt.us/legbills/2003/Votes/h044006.txt ".

An unbelievable discussion in that they're admitting that the person is being dismembered while alive and awake, and that he or she feels pain, but they can't decide whether to give the person a painkiller. And how would the baby be harmed more by the anesthesia, than by being cut up and pulled apart? Of course states can regulate the practice of medicine. Hopefully, some of the legislators will have to find another line of work.

The Estrada Nomination and The Michigan Five

"A struggle for the soul of America is under way, a struggle to determine whose views, beliefs and standards will serve as the basis of law." Pat Buchanan

----

From: The Pro-Life Infonet Steven Ertelt infonet@prolifeinfo.org
Source: Associated Press; January 30, 2003

Senate Judiciary Committee Approves Pro-Life Judicial Nominee

Washington, DC—Senate Republicans, breaking a Democratic blockade against President Bush's key pro-life judicial nominees, put Miguel Estrada a step closer Thursday to becoming the first Hispanic on the U.S. Court of Appeals in the nation's capital. On a 10-9 vote strictly along party lines, Republicans used their new majority from last fall's election to make Estrada, 41, the first pro-life appeals court nominee to clear the Senate Judiciary Committee since Bush took office. 'The committee has spoken, progress is being made, the logjam in the Senate is now breaking,' White House spokesman Ari Fleischer said. Aware that the appeals court often is a steppingstone to the Supreme Court, Democrats had waited 16 months after Bush nominated Estrada to give him a confirmation hearing last October. Afterward, they refused to schedule a vote on him, complaining that Estrada had evaded their questions about his legal views. The Washington lawyer, who came to the United States as a teenager from Honduras, graduated from Harvard Law School in 1986. He has practiced constitutional law and argued 15 cases before the high court."

"Take Action! Urge Your Senators to Oppose the Nomination of Miguel Estrada The Senate is expected to vote on the nomination of Miguel Estrada to the District of Columbia Circuit Court of Appeals this week. Join us in urging your Senators to block his confirmation today. Planned Parenthood Federation of America opposes Miguel Estrada based on his refusal to state that he believes the Constitution guarantees a woman's right to choose. Both in his hearing before the Senate Judiciary Committee and in written questions, Estrada was asked specifically about his views on privacy and reproductive issues and he failed to declare his support for a woman's right to choose and therefore must be rejected." Planned Parenthood Federation of America: http://www.ppaction.org/campaign/estradaFullSenate

"But perhaps most outrageous of all is the attack underway in the Senate against Bush nominee Miguel Estrada for the U.S. Court of Appeals.

Democrats are conducting a filibuster against Estrada, who was born in Honduras and educated at Harvard. He is accused of no wrong doing, no ethical problems and is obviously well qualified. (He earned the American Bar Association's highest rating-the "gold standard" of judicial nominations, according to liberal Democrat Chuck Schumer of New York, now one of Estrada's leading critics.) He is being blocked for one reason-Senate liberals fear he is a social conservative, a religious man who they fear may vote pro-life and pro-family on the court." Gary L. Bauer, Chairman of the Campaign for Working Families, February 13, 2003.

"A Crack In The Wall? Tuesday, Washington's leading liberal newspaper, the Washington Post, did something rather unusual: The Post sided with President Bush and joined the growing chorus of media outlets coming to the defense of embattled judicial nominee Miguel Estrada. While the Post may be a liberal paper, it is not dominated by vicious ideologues and it actually maintains a fairly balanced sense of how the system should operate. In an official editorial entitled 'Just Vote,' the Washington Post castigated Senate Democrats in very harsh rhetoric. The Post blasted Democrat arguments against Estrada as ranging from 'the unpersuasive to the offensive.' The Post went even further, calling racial charges lobbied by Senate liberals 'as repugnant as they are incoherent.' The editorial board summed up the Democrats' obstructionism by saying 'the Estrada filibuster is a step beyond...deplorable games.'" Gary L. Bauer, CWF, Thursday, February 20, 2003

FOXNews.com

"Fox News' Major Garrett contributed to this report.

WASHINGTON—History was made in the U.S. Senate Thursday, but it wasn't the kind that Republicans or the Bush administration wanted to confront. Senate Majority Leader Bill Frist decided to call a procedural vote to break a Democratic filibuster against U.S. Court of Appeals nominee Miguel Estrada. The filibuster against a judicial candidate was historical in itself.

The decision to call for a 'cloture' vote on an appellate court nominee overturned more than two centuries of Senate precedent and rewrote the constitutional definition of 'advise and consent.' Never before has a nominee been caught this deep in the web of Senate politics. Republicans need 60 votes to break the filibuster and they know they don't have them. The move toward a defeat on the floor next week could doom Estrada, one of Bush's lawyers in the Supreme Court case that determined his presidency.

So far, Republicans are only guaranteed 55 votes to confirm Estrada, who would be the first Hispanic on the Circuit Court for the District of Columbia. If there was no filibuster, that would be enough to get him confirmed.

'The last thing we want to do is to raise the bar for this particular nominee to 60 votes. Obviously, we can't stay on this issue forever,' said Sen. Rick Santorum, R-Pa., speaking with a tone of defeat already expressed by several Republicans.

'Miguel Estrada could lose,' said Senate Judiciary Committee Chairman Orrin Hatch, R-Utah. 'I feel sorry for his family. I feel sorry for him. I only hope that if they succeed in denying him this, that he will not assume that we are like that,' said Sen. Pete Domenici, R-N.M.

Frist told Fox News that he had no choice but to call the Democrats' bluff on the filibuster. A vote is scheduled for next Tuesday. 'I would think the battle is just beginning. At that juncture, we would know who we need to talk to. I've got a feeling, I've got a sense that Democrats are entrenched, and our goal is to pull them out of those trenches. It may take a few days. It may take a few weeks—it may take months—but it's my goal to pull them out of those trenches.'

Democrats said they would drop their filibuster if Estrada would answer more questions about his judicial philosophy. The Justice Department also turned over internal memos Estrada wrote as a deputy solicitor general in the Clinton Justice Department. Every living solicitor general—seven total—opposes turning over working memos.

Democrats also denied that their actions are in any way hindering the work of the Senate."

"To: Friends and Supporters of the Campaign for Working Families
From: Gary L. Bauer, Chairman Date: Friday, February 28, 2003

Washington is buzzing about a Robert Novak column that exposes the secret plan developed by Ted Kennedy to block all of President Bush's appellate court nominees. The current controversy centers around Miguel Estrada, who is being filibustered to death by Senate liberals. But the plan is much broader and goes back to a secret meeting that took place on January 30th in the office of Senate Minority Leader Tom Daschle. At that meeting Daschle, Kennedy and six other Judiciary Committee Democrats endorsed a strategy that will result in filibusters against any conservative nominee. How serious is the situation? George Will asserts today that if allowed to succeed, this tactic would effectively amend the Constitution by requiring a supermajority to approve judicial nominations. It would put Kennedy, Daschle and Clinton in charge of judges, instead of President Bush. The President's ability to appoint conservative judges is important because liberal activists are exercising raw political power to remake America in their image by judicial fiat."

"SUBJECT: Judiciary War Continues over Pro-life Judge! The President of the United States has the constitutional power of his office to appoint federal judges! But the Senate is intervening with this very important constitutional function! In fact, pro-abortion Senators are blocking repeated attempts to vote for the President's Judicial Nominations…And the massive pro-abortion lobby is behind this fight and working hard to energize their pro-abortion supporters …stands in the way of the American ideal of Democracy!" Jennifer Bingham, Executive Director, SBAList@democracydata.com, 4 Mar 2003 14:03:44 –0500

"To: Friends and Supporters of the Campaign for Working Families
From: Gary L. Bauer, Chairman Date: Tuesday, March 4, 2003

Vote On Filibuster Senate Republican leaders disclosed today they would move for a vote on 'cloture,' a legislative term that means there will be a vote to end the filibuster on Miguel Estrada's nomination to the federal bench. Cloture requires 60 votes and will likely fail, but Republican leaders argue this will force every senator to go on the record one way or another. This does not mean the Estrada nomination is lost. It only means that debate will continue later. And Republican leaders are prepared to bring up cloture again and again and again until this nominee gets an up-or-down vote on confirmation." Time: 17:27:07 –0500

"Miguel Estrada holds extreme positions that are outside mainstream America." Tom Daschle on CBS News radio, March 6, 2003.

"Democrats want Estrada to divulge whether or not he agrees with specific Supreme Court rulings on controversial issues such as abortion and states' rights. He has refused to do so because those issues could come before him on the bench in the future as an appeals court judge.

'In the judicial process, judges are not expected to give opinions until there is a case in controversy, until there are facts, until briefs are submitted, until there is oral argument, until there is deliberation among the judges-and then a decision is made,' said Sen. Arlen Specter (R-Pa.), 'not to answer a wide variety of hypothetical questions that are posed in nomination proceedings.'

Additionally, Democrats want unrestricted access to all of the confidential memoranda Estrada wrote during his tenure as assistant to the solicitor general in the Clinton and George H.W. Bush administrations. The Justice Department has refused to grant what Senate Judiciary Committee Chairman Orrin Hatch (R-Utah) called a partisan 'fishing expedition.'

'In spite of an almost nine-hour committee hearing, in spite of having all of his briefs and his oral arguments before the Supreme Court in 15 cases, in spite of the fact that he has the unanimously well-qualified highest recommendation or the 'gold standard' from the American Bar Association, in spite of the fact that they have numerous other documents and records,' Hatch explained, 'they're saying they don't know enough about Mr. Estrada, so they have to go into the highly privileged matters concerning...some of the most privileged documents in the history of the country in the Solicitor General's office.'

All seven living former solicitors general, including four Democrats, have written the Senate to oppose the Democrats' request for access to the documents. In their letter, they warned that allowing the legislative branch of government to view deliberative materials of the executive branch would cause irreparable harm to the separation of powers and make it impossible for the Justice Department to fairly represent the United States government before the Supreme Court in the future.

Hatch noted that the transcript for Estrada's nearly nine-hour hearing consumes almost 300 pages and that-although all members of the Judiciary Committee had the right to submit written follow-up questions to Estrada afterwards-only two Democrats did so.

'...let us follow the constitutional process we have followed for two centuries and vote 'yes' or 'no' to advise and consent on the president's nominee. For my colleagues who have concerns about Mr. Estrada's answers, or if you didn't like the things that he didn't answer, vote against him,' Coleman insisted. 'But give him a vote.'

Frist offered Democrats another chance to question Estrada before the Judiciary Committee if they would agree to set a date and time for a full Senate vote on Estrada's confirmation. Democrats refused...Frist filed a second cloture motion Tuesday afternoon to end debate on the confirmation vote. At least 54 senators now support Estrada's confirmation.

Republicans have vowed to keep the Estrada nomination on the Senate calendar until it receives the constitutionally mandated 'up or down' vote. Frist said Monday evening that he will also add other judicial nominees opposed by ultra-liberal Democrats to the Senate calendar, potentially forcing Democrats to choose which nominees they will devote their resources to blocking and which they will allow to come up for a vote.

Although Frist has not yet forced Democrats to maintain an actual physical filibuster, he does have the option of doing so at his discretion. If Frist chooses that option, Democrats would have to keep a member of their party speaking

on the Senate floor 24 hours a day and refuse to yield to any Republican or
Democrat who supports Estrada. Democrats would also have to be available at
all times to object to any unanimous consent request to bring the confirmation
up for a vote and to vote against cloture motions to end debate on the
confirmation." Extracted from "Senate Dems 'Not Going to Yield' on Estrada
Filibuster", By Jeff Johnson, CNSNews. com Congressional Bureau Chief,
March 12, 2003

"In a procedural vote yesterday to end debate and vote on Mr. Estrada's
nomination, the opponents held onto all 45 senators who have blocked voting
on the nomination—enough to prevent a vote by the full Senate, which would
almost surely confirm Mr. Estrada.

'Talking for a month was a mistake,' said Mr. Lott, who was quick to add that
he thought the nomination could still make it. He said he had thought of a
strategy that could put Mr. Estrada up for a confirmation vote needing only 51
votes as opposed to the 60 now required to invoke cloture. He declined to
elaborate, warning that his idea is 'nuclear.' Sen. Rick Santorum, Pennsylvania
Republican and party conference chairman, said for now Republicans are
content holding occasional cloture votes to portray Democrats as
obstructionists. No date is set for the next cloture vote. After Easter, he said,
party leaders would roll out a new strategy that would place greater pressure
on Democrats, but declined to say what the new strategy would entail. Sen.
Lindsey O. Graham, South Carolina Republican and member of the Judiciary
Committee, also said Republicans have been discussing ways to force a simple
majority vote on Mr. Estrada. Judge Robert H. Bork, whose nomination to
the Supreme Court was killed by committee Democrats in 1987, happened to
be in the Capitol yesterday on unrelated business. 'They have changed the
constitution to a 60-vote requirement,' said Mr. Bork. 'I think it's a
disgrace.'" Charles Hurt, THE WASHINGTON TIMES, March 19, 2003.

Sometimes, I think, the Republicans go too far to take the high ground, be
gentlemen, and try not to offend anyone. I think the Democrats want to put on
a good show for their abortion backers, but they will fold when their bluff is
called.

Remember Daschle saying Estrada held 'extremist' positions?
Here's another of Daschle's own many recent extremist positions:

"Here in the U.S., overnight polls show a spike up in the support for the
President's Iraq policy, with over 70% of the public saying, 'Let's Roll!' Even
polls in England have moved dramatically in our favor.

Where in the middle of all this is the head of Senate Democrats?

Minority Leader Tom Daschle spoke to a government union last night and shared this nugget with his audience:

'I'm saddened, saddened that this president failed so miserably at diplomacy that we're now forced to war. Saddened that we have to give up one life because this president couldn't create the kind of diplomatic effort that was so critical for our country.'

So, to Senator Daschle American soldiers will die because of President Bush, not Saddam Hussein. Diplomacy failed because of President Bush, not Saddam Hussein or Jacques Chirac. The bottom line is that Senator Daschle prefers the foreign policy of France, which seeks to tie America in knots, versus the foreign policy of America, which seeks to eliminate a brutal dictator. Senator Daschle needs to hear what his constituents think about his comments." Gary Bauer End of Day—3/18/03 18 Mar 2003 17:31:06

The people I talk to say what a disaster it would have been if Gore had gotten elected, that he wouldn't have known what to do; and how well President Bush has stepped up and handled the situation. Personally, my guess is that had Gore, or Daschle been president, they'd still be trying to negotiate with Yasar Arafat and Osama Bin Laden, and never could have conceived of a pre-emptive strike in Afghanistan or against Saddam Hussein. We'd be just as impotent and ineffectual as France, and a much bigger target. Another disaster waiting to happen.

"Michigan Senators Block Five Bush Judicial Nominees By Jeff Johnson CNSNews.com Congressional Bureau Chief March 24, 2003

Capitol Hill (CNSNews.com)-Michigan's two Democratic senators have registered objections to all five of President Bush's judicial nominees from their state, effectively killing their chances for confirmation by returning negative 'blue slips.' Conservative legal experts said Friday that the action proves the judicial confirmation process must be reformed.

Senators Carl Levin and Debbie Stabenow notified the Senate Judiciary Committee Wednesday of their negative recommendations for 6th Circuit Court of Appeals nominees Richard Griffin, David McKeague, Susan Bieke Neilson and Henry Saad. The pair also objected to the confirmation of Thomas Ludington to the U.S. District Court in Eastern Michigan.

Phil Kent, president of the Southeastern Legal Foundation in Atlanta, worked for former Sen. Strom Thurmond when he was chairman of the Senate Judiciary Committee. Kent has long disapproved of the blue slip process, which allows a nominee's home state senators to effectively veto their confirmation.

'I think we need to do away with it,' Kent said. 'I think the blue slip thing is archaic, and I also think, in this day and age, when there's ideological litmus testing that it's just another weapon liberals can use or, for that matter, Republicans or conservatives could use.' It will be difficult to bypass the Senate tradition of blue slips, explained John Nowacki, director of legal policy for the Free Congress Foundation, even when the process is being abused as he believes it is in this case. 'This isn't a case where home state senators have some unique insight into why every Michigan nominee should not get a hearing and a vote,' he argued. 'Instead, it's an attempt to keep a court with six judicial emergencies vacant while Levin and Stabenow play petty political games.' Nowacki noted the contrast between President Bush's handling of the judicial nomination process-including re-nominating several of former President Clinton's nominees-and the treatment afforded Bush's nominees by Democrats in the Senate.

'George W. Bush is the only president to nominate a failed court of appeals nominee of a predecessor from another party,' he recalled. 'He's shown a willingness to reach out to the other party but-as Levin and Stabenow, once again, have demonstrated-he can't expect the same consideration from the Democrats.'

The blue slip process was originally created, Nowacki explained, in a time when nominees were more likely to be known to senators from their home state than to other senators and when thorough background investigations were not always possible. Kent believes that time no longer exists. 'I think the FBI background check is far better than anybody 'knowing somebody,' Kent said. 'I'm not concerned about anybody slipping through if somebody didn't know [a nominee].' Kent notes that, in addition to the FBI background probe, investigators from the Senate Judiciary Committee thoroughly examine the qualifications and background of every nominee. He's optimistic that, especially as the 2004 presidential elections approach, a bipartisan agreement can be reached to set new rules for judicial confirmations. 'Nominees should get a hearing, there shouldn't be any blue slips involved, and once a hearing is held, you get an up-or-down vote on the floor of the Senate,' Kent said. 'And I think Republicans and conservatives have to agree to that if there's a Democrat...a liberal in [office].'

Calls to Sen. Stabenow's office seeking comment on this story were not returned. A spokeswoman for Sen. Levin acknowledged to CNSNews.com that the senator had returned negative blue slips on all five nominees but could offer no explanation as to why."

As usual, the Democrats show contempt for our democratic system, and look for ways to circumvent it. They opt for short term political advantage, instead of fair play-in this instance a fair hearing for nominees from their own state. Their short sightedness only hurts them at election time. The judicial nominations of Pickering and Owen that they opposed hurt them in the South in the 2002 elections, but they don't seem to have learned anything from it. Take Owen, for example. A very popular jurist in her home state. Not giving her a fair chance at approval surely hurt them at election time not only in her home state, but among Southern women in general; partly accounting for the Democrats' poor showing in the South-just as a rejection of Miguel Estrada will hurt them with Hispanics-a voter group still in play. The Republicans don't have to get a majority of the Hispanic vote to be helped by this. They just have to make a good showing there.

"May 2001. A small bite in time, but one that also featured another event worth noting: the nomination of Miguel Estrada to the federal appeals court for the District of Columbia.

There is a growing and ever-more important Hispanic populace in the United States that surely must be coming to grips with the fact that one of their own is held to a higher standard by Senate Democrats. Why else the filibuster?

Mr. Estrada has met with 10 high-ranking Democrats to propel his nomination forward with propriety and candor. But the filibuster persists.

Sen. Edward Kennedy, Massachusetts Democrat, is on record from 1998 saying that if senators don't like a judicial nominee, they should 'vote against them. But give them a vote.'

Sen. Richard Durbin, Illinois Democrat, said nearly the same thing in 1998, too, to 'vote the person up or down.'

Democratic Sens. Dianne Feinstein of California and Joseph Biden of Delaware are on record largely proclaiming the exact same thing.

And Sen. Patrick Leahy, Vermont Democrat, opined in 1998: 'If senators are opposed to any judge, bring them up and vote against them. But don't do an anonymous hold, which diminishes the credibility and respect of the whole U.S. Senate. |Let| the Senate do its duty. If we don't like someone the president nominates, vote him or her down.'

I ask you, where are those voices now? How could they all have said one thing so short a time ago and done something so completely different today? Evidently, they've learned how to talk the talk but not walk the walk.

Here's what we know since way back in May 2001 when President Bush nominated Miguel Estrada to become a judge for the D.C. Circuit Court of

Appeals. Democrat after Democrat in the Senate have done all they could to trash his nomination. They've planted innuendo via a compliant major media suggesting this man is not fit for the appointment. And yet, we know he is qualified enough to have been selected by a sitting president, to have served as a law clerk under Justice Anthony Kennedy at the Supreme Court, that he has argued 15 cases before that august body and been a federal prosecutor in New York. As if that weren't enough, Mr. Estrada, a self-defined specialist in constitutional law, has garnered the highest award offered by the American Bar Association. The Honduran native, who came to our country knowing little of our ways or even how to speak our language, has since graduated two Ivy League universities with honors, Columbia College and Harvard Law School. To say Miguel Estrada isn't at least qualified for this opportunity is ridiculous. That's not confusing whether one agrees with the nominee, only that if ever there was a person who should be qualified, it's Miguel Estrada.

There are many, many vacancies on our federal courts. They cause needless backlogs, frustration and an obvious delay of justice. The president has seen fit to nominate Mr. Estrada because he believes him to be well qualified. All the president asks—all the people of the United States deserve, and all that the 60 Plus Association demands on behalf of seniors everywhere—is a simple vote, up or down." From "Picking judges judiciously" by James L. Martin president of the 60 Plus Association in Arlington, Va. March 26, 2003, News World Communications.

Fairness isn't an approach the Democrats feel is necessary for them to adhere to. It only applies to people being fair to them, and their supporters.

"Owen Re-nomination Passes Senate Judiciary Committee By Jeff Johnson CNSNews.com Congressional Bureau Chief March 28, 2003 Capitol Hill (CNSNews.com)-The Senate Judiciary Committee passed the nomination of Texas Supreme Court Justice Priscilla Owen to the 5th U.S. Circuit Court of Appeals Thursday on a 10-to-9 party-line vote. Democrats, objecting both to Owen and to previous procedural maneuvers by Chairman Orrin Hatch (R-Utah), were unable to stop the vote.

Sen. John Cornyn (R-Texas) supported Owen's nomination. 'As Justice Owen goes from the Judiciary Committee to the floor of the Senate, I'm hopeful that she will get the bipartisan support that she deserves,' Cornyn said after the vote. 'She's a highly qualified and experienced judge, and she understands that a judge's role is not to advance a political or social agenda.' Cornyn, who served with Owen as a justice on the Texas Supreme Court, (said) 'I can testify from my own personal experience, as a colleague and fellow justice, that Justice Owen is an exceptional judge who works hard to follow the law and to enforce the will of the legislature'.

John Nowacki, director of legal policy for the Free Congress Foundation, believes Owen is finally getting the consideration she deserves now that voters have returned control of the Senate to Republicans. 'I know that, just as it was last year, there's going to be a majority in the Senate who want to see her confirmed, who will vote for her confirmation,' he predicted. 'The real question is whether the Democrats are going to try to filibuster her nomination as well.'"

"The Democratic filibuster of Miguel Estrada's nomination to the U.S. Circuit Court of Appeals for the District of Columbia hit its 51st day yesterday. Other nominations have been stacking up behind his." THE ASSOCIATED PRESS, March 28, 2003, via Newsday and NewsMax.

"To: Friends and Supporters of the Campaign for Working Families
From: Gary L. Bauer, Chairman Date: Wednesday, May 7, 2003

Is Frist's Finger On 'The Button'?

Now that five cloture motions have failed to end debate on Miguel Estrada and with Democrats simultaneously filibustering a second nominee, Priscilla Owen, frustrated Senate Republicans are reportedly considering a 'nuclear option' to break the stalemate on confirming the President's judicial nominees.

The Senate's Byzantine rules evidently provide one exception to breaking a filibuster that does not require the usual 3/5th or 60-vote majority, but this procedure hasn't been used in almost 30 years and only once prior to that. The scenario is complicated and there's division within the Republican ranks as to whether or not it should even be tried.

Comity and process rule the Senate and some Republicans are afraid to break with tradition out of fear that some day the Democrats will use this maneuver on them. But, the fact that Democrats are now filibustering two judicial nominees proves they know how to play hardball and they aren't afraid to use any maneuver necessary to achieve their political objectives. If this situation were reversed, is there any doubt that Democrats would hesitate to 'push the button?' Senate liberals have so politicized the confirmation process with pro-abortion, anti-religious litmus tests that something drastic must be done.

Restoring balance to our federal courts is so important, I believe Senate Republicans must use every option at their disposal. If we don't start playing by the same rules, we'll continue to lose time and time again." Amen.

"A few Senators are working to rewrite the Constitution. They are saying 'no' to the President's nominees by keeping his well-qualified nominees for the federal judiciary from coming to the Senate floor for a vote-in direct violation of their duty under the U.S. Constitution to vote on the President's choices! The nominees coming under attack now are highly-qualified candidates. These are men and women who will uphold the law and the Constitution.

But while the Senators are blocking confirmation votes through the use of a 'filibuster,' the federal courts remain OUT OF BALANCE with liberal judges who reject religious liberties and respect for the unborn. And our judiciary is incredibly OVER-BURDENED. In many courts there's a backlog of cases-simply because there are too many judicial vacancies! The filibuster rule is enabling a minority to STOP these nominations and override the Constitution! While the Senators stall, our freedoms and constitutional guarantees are falling victim to judges who do not fully understand the Constitution!

What is happening now is only a WARM-UP to the debate that will unfold when a vacancy occurs on the Supreme Court of the United States and President Bush puts forth a well-qualified nominee. We must stand strong now-or the President will face even more opposition when the stakes are higher!" From: "American Center for Law and Justice", Date: Fri, 9 May 2003 14:31:25 UT

"Judicial Nomination Process Is Broken, Bush Says

(CNSNews.com)-The U.S. Senate is failing to live up to its constitutional obligation to hold up-or-down votes on judicial nominees, President George Bush said Friday. 'Today we are facing a crisis in the Senate and therefore a crisis in the judiciary,' he said in remarks at the White House. Judicial nominees should not have to wait 'years' for up or down votes 'while partisans search in vain for reasons to reject them.' President Bush said the tactics are those of a small group of senators, and he accused them of setting a pattern that threatens judicial independence. Meanwhile, he said, vacancies on the bench are hurting citizens seeking justice. 'The judicial confirmation process is broken, and it must be fixed for the good of the country,' Bush said. Every person nominated to the federal bench deserves a timely vote, Bush insisted, noting that he's sent 42 federal appeals court nominees to the Senate, and 18 are still waiting for a vote. Of those 18, eight have been waiting for more than a year. 'This is not business as usual,' Bush said. 'This is an abdication of congressional responsibility, and is hurting our country.' He said the men and women he has nominated are a historically diverse group, and he mentioned some of their names and accomplishments. He urged Americans to help him by letting their senators know that 'obstructionist policies' hurt all of us." So its the same old story of the Abortion Party trying to get around the will of the majority for their abortion clients and contributors. The Republicans need to give them a way out so that they can tell PP and NARAL and NOW and Emily's List that at least they tried.

"Frist Moves to Change Rules, End Judicial Filibusters By Jeff Johnson CNSNews.com Congressional Bureau Chief May 09, 2003

Capitol Hill (CNSNews.com)-Senate Majority Leader Bill Frist (R-Tenn.) introduced a resolution Friday that would end the filibuster against two of President George Bush's judicial nominees by Senate Democrats. The move came just before a Rose Garden appearance with the president at the White House.

Bush expressed his displeasure with the delay in voting on his nominees during that meeting. 'Exactly two years ago, I announced my first 11 nominees to the federal appeals court,' he said. 'I chose men and women of talent and integrity, highly qualified nominees who represent the mainstream of American law and American values. 'Eight of them waited more than a year without an up-or-down vote in the United States Senate. As of today, three of that original group have waited two years,' Bush continued. 'Their treatment by a group of senators is a disgrace.'

Later, Frist stressed to reporters that he is not telling people how to vote. 'As majority leader, I don't want to tell people how to vote, but I do want to respect that basic tenet of the Constitution of 'advice and consent' that gives every United States senator that right, that ability to give advice and consent,' Frist said as a light rain began to fall on those attending a press conference outside the Russell Senate Office Building in Washington.

'As long as you have Democrats filibustering in this unprecedented way,' he continued, 'our Senators are being denied...that opportunity to give that advice and consent. Why? Because they're being denied that opportunity to vote.'

Earlier this week, Sen. Charles Schumer (D-N.Y.) tried to blame Bush for the filibusters. 'Yes, we're sort of at a deadlock, but this was not started by Democrats in the Senate,' Schumer claimed. 'This was brought on because President Bush, as he said it in his campaign, he said he chooses to nominate people in the mold of Scalia and Thomas...Bush's nominees have had a hugely ideological caste, and we have had no choice.'

Frist proposes up to 13 days of debate, then a vote

The Frist plan would guarantee that a minority of senators could force up to 13 days of debate on any judicial nominee. If they chose to filibuster, 61 votes would be required to invoke cloture-the term for breaking a filibuster-on the first attempt. The first cloture motion could not be filed until the nomination has been pending before the Senate for 12 hours. If that motion failed, each successive cloture motion would require three fewer votes to end debate,

dropping the requirement to 57 three days later and then 54 after three additional days. If, after 13 total days of debate, three cloture motions had failed, a final vote to end debate and bring the nomination up for a vote would require only 51 senators or a simple majority of the senators present and voting, whichever is less.

Frist's resolution is modeled after a proposal introduced in March by Georgia Democrat Zell Miller. Miller's plan was based on a resolution originally introduced in 1995 by Democrats Tom Harkin of Iowa and Joseph Lieberman of Connecticut. Unlike their proposals, however, Frist's resolution includes the initial 12 hours of debate and applies only to presidential nominees, not legislative proposals.

'We're here to say they're dead wrong'

Bush nominated former U.S. Assistant Solicitor General Miguel Estrada and Texas Supreme Court Justice Priscilla Owen two years ago Friday. Sen. John Cornyn (R-Texas), a former colleague of Owen's on Texas' high court, said Democrats' strategy of 'delay in hopes of surrender' is destined to fail.

'The obstructionists are hoping that over time, we will grow tired and just go away,' Cornyn said. 'The Democrats' leadership thinks that they can get away with blocking these well-qualified nominees, but we're here today to say they're dead wrong.' Cornyn was backed by representatives from more than a dozen organizations supporting Estrada, Owen or both.

C. Boyden Gray, former White House counsel to President George H. W. Bush, noted that a partisan filibuster has never been used to block judicial nominees until now. 'If the Senate, in its wisdom, does not like any of these nominees, it can vote them down in an up-or-down vote,' he said. 'The filibuster…is a brand new, unconstitutional device, and it ought to be terminated right now.'

Groups launch ad campaigns to oppose filibusters

Gray is chairman of the Committee for Justice, which released a cartoon Friday depicting Democrat senators Patrick Leahy (Vt.), Edward Kennedy (Mass.), Charles Schumer (N.Y.), Hillary Clinton (N.Y.) and Senate Minority Leader Tom Daschle (S.D.) as missiles under the headline 'Weapons of Mass Obstruction.' The advertisement in which the cartoon appears sarcastically quotes terminology from Daschle's recent criticism of President Bush's foreign policy and urges the quintet to 'Let our judges go!'

The Committee for Justice is not the only group supporting the president's judicial nominees to purchase advertising or to turn Daschle's own words against him. The Center for Individual Freedom (CFIF) has distributed an ad entitled simply, 'Hypocrite!' that quotes some of Daschle's past Senate floor statements on judicial nominees. 'I find it baffling that a senator would vote against even voting on a judicial nomination,' Daschle told his colleagues on October 5, 1999. 'Hispanic or non-Hispanic, African American or non-African American, woman or man, it is wrong not to have a vote on the Senate floor,' the South Dakota Democrat said on October 28, 1999.

Jeffrey Mazzella, CFIF's senior vice president of legislative affairs, challenged Daschle to be true to his own word. 'Tom Daschle is a leader in the United States Senate. It's about time he start acting like one,' Mazzella said. To oppose a judicial nominee is one thing, but to deny all 100 senators their advice and consent role in the process is unconscionable. 'For Daschle,' he concluded, 'it's blatantly hypocritical.'

Democrats claim Frist's resolution would require a two-thirds majority to pass because Senate Rule XXII-the filibuster rule-includes a provision mandating that majority. Republican staff in the Senate have found supporting precedent to argue that all rule changes require only 'a simple majority of the Senators present and voting.' If Democrats object to the rules change, Senate observers predict their objection will merely be ruled out of order."

"If this change had been in effect at the beginning of the year, Miguel Estrada would have been confirmed in March, when a third cloture motion received 55 votes. As it currently stands, we just lost a sixth cloture vote on Estrada yesterday as well as a second vote on Priscilla Owen. This is a balanced approach that preserves the traditions of the Senate, while protecting the right of the President to make appointments and the obligation of the majority to govern.

Ironically, Frist's rules change is modeled after a plan originally proposed by leading Senate liberals, Tom Harkin of Iowa and Joe Lieberman of Connecticut! The difference is that Frist's plan only applies to executive appointments, whereas the Harkin/Lieberman proposal was sweeping and would have also applied to regular legislation. Nine currently serving Senate Democrats supported the Harkin/Lieberman change to the filibuster. I am going to go out on a limb here and bet that they won't support Frist's more narrowly crafted measure." Gary Bauer, End of Day—5/9/03 17:29

"May 12, 2003 Politicizing the judiciary Tom Bray

The Democratic war against judicial nominees who dare to disagree with liberal dogma is reaching laughable proportions—if it were not so serious. For several centuries, it has been the assumption that a sitting president should be allowed to name judges to his liking, as long as they met certain basic requirements of competence and character. But the Democrats have made it clear that nominees will have to measure up to their ideological liking as well. To bottle up other nominations, Democratic senators are using the so-called blue-slip process.

Democrats say that Mr. Bush is trying to pack the court with right-wing ideologues. But packing the court usually refers to Franklin D. Roosevelt's unconstitutional effort to expand the number of judges on the Supreme Court so that he could appoint more Democrats. Mr. Bush isn't proposing any such thing. He is simply trying to fill existing vacancies in the court system, which is any president's duty.

Lastly, say Democrats, too many of Mr. Bush's nominees are outside what left-wing interest groups are pleased to call the mainstream of American politics— by which they mean anybody who dares to disagree with them about abortion, racial quotas and gay rights. False again. A wide majority of the public opposes gay 'marriage,' racial quotas and unlimited abortion rights, according to most polls. Ultimately, of course, the Democrats have dug themselves into a losing position. Americans understand that there will be a certain amount of politics involved in appointing judges. But it's doubtful they want to see the kind of open—and extreme—politicization of the judiciary that is the logical outcome of the current Democratic abuse of the nomination process. Tom Bray is a Detroit News columnist." From "COMMENTARY" on www.washtimes.com.

"The Committee for Justice, a group that opposes abortion rights, yesterday released a nationwide poll of 800 Hispanic adults indicating that 88% of them want the Senate to vote on Estrada's nomination (Washington Post, 6/12)." Source: Kaisernetwork Publish Date: June 12, 2003

"Nine Abortion-Rights Groups Form Joint Not-for-Profit Group Devoted to Judicial Issues

(Kaisernetwork) Nine abortion-rights groups, including NARAL ProChoice America and the Planned Parenthood Federation of America, have formed a joint not-for-profit organization aimed specifically at opposing a potential Supreme Court nominee who does not support abortion rights, Roll Call reports.

The group—officially called the Joint Emergency Campaign but referred to by the group as the 'G-9'—was initially formed 18 months ago when an imminent Supreme Court vacancy seemed possible. However, because an opening did not occur immediately, some of the group's initial $5.5 million has been spent on advocacy regarding controversial circuit court nominees over the past 16 months. However, the group's fund has since been replenished, and it plans to

mount a $5 million media campaign once a vacancy opens up on the Supreme Court. According to Roll Call, the campaign idea is to mount a "quick, broad strike" at any nominee who opposes abortion rights (Kane, Roll Call, 6/11).
Source: Kaisernetwork Online at:
http://www.kaisernetwork.org/daily_reports/rep_index.cfm?DR_ID=18217 ".

Margaret Sanger, Planned Parenthood, and African Americans

THE REPACKAGING OF MARGARET SANGER, Wall Street Journal, May 5, 1997, by Steven W. Mosher-
http://www.prolifeinfo.org/fact9.html

I was personally offended when Planned Parenthood recently announced plans to give its Margaret Sanger Award to the BBC documentary "The Dying Rooms."

Don't get me wrong: The documentary is a wonderful and courageous piece of work. An undercover camera crew managed to gain entry to China's state-run orphanages and videotape the mistreatment and murder of the girls there. I appeared in the documentary, testifying that this tragedy is a direct consequence of the country's one-child policy.

It was the award, named after Planned Parenthood's founder, to which I objected. For Sanger had little but contempt for the "Asiatic races," as she and her eugenicist friends called them. During her lifetime, she proposed that their numbers be drastically reduced. But Sanger's preferences went beyond race. In her 1922 book "Pivot of Civilization" she unabashedly called for the extirpation of "weeds…overrunning the human garden"; for the segregation of "morons, misfits, and the maladjusted"; and for the sterilization of "genetically inferior races." It was later that she singled out the Chinese, writing in her autobiography about "the incessant fertility of [the Chinese] millions spread like a plague."

There can be no doubt that Sanger would have been wildly enthusiastic over China's one-child policy, for her "Code to Stop Overproduction of Children," published in 1934, decreed that "no woman shall have a legal right to bear a child without a permit…no permit shall be valid for more than one child." As for China's selective elimination of handicapped and abandoned babies, she would have been delighted that Beijing had heeded her decades-long call for exactly such eugenicist policies.

Indeed, Sanger likely would have turned the award on its head, choosing to praise publicly rather than implicitly criticize China's government for its dying rooms. Even the inhuman operators of Chinese orphanages might have gotten an honorable mention, in order to underline the importance of their front-line work in eliminating what she called the "unfit" and "dysgenic." Sanger was not one for subtlety in such matters. She bluntly defined "birth control," a term she coined, as "the process of weeding out the unfit" aimed at "the creation of a

ABORTION! PROS and CONS
Arguments, Views, Facts & Information

superman." She often opined that "the most merciful thing that the large family does to one its infant members is to kill it,", and that "all our problems are the result of overbreeding among the working class."

Sanger frequently featured racists and eugenicists in her magazine, the Birth Control Review. Contributor Lothrop Stoddard, who also served on Sanger's board of directors, wrote in "The Rising Tide of Color Against White World-Supremacy" that "We must resolutely oppose both Asiatic permeation of white race-areas and Asiatic inundation of those non-white, but equally non-Asiatic regions inhabited by the really inferior races." Each issue of the Birth Control Review was packed with such ideas. But Sanger was not content merely to publish racist propaganda; the magazine also made concrete policy proposals, such as the creation of "moron communities," the forced production of children by the "fit," and the compulsory sterilization and even elimination of the "unfit."

Sanger's own racist views were scarcely less opprobrious. In 1939 she and Clarence Gamble made an infamous proposal called "Birth Control and the Negro," which asserted that "the poorer areas, particularly in the South...are producing alarmingly more than their share of future generations." Her "religion of birth control" would, she wrote, "ease the financial load of caring for with public funds...children destined to become a burden to themselves, to their family, and ultimately to the nation."

War with Germany, combined with lurid tales of how the Nazis were putting her theories about "human weeds" and "genetically inferior races" into practice, panicked Sanger into changing her organization's name and rhetoric. "Birth control," with its undertone of coercion, became "family planning." The "unfit" and the "dysgenic" became merely "the poor." The American Birth Control League became the Planned Parenthood Federation of America.

Following Sanger's death in 1966, Planned Parenthood felt so confident that it had safely buried her past that it began boasting about "the legacy of Margaret Sanger." And it began handing out cutely named Maggie Awards to innocents who often had no inkling of her real views. The first recipient was Martin Luther King-who clearly had no idea that Sanger had inaugurated a project to set his people free from their progeny. "We do not want word to go out that we want to exterminate the Negro population and the Minister is the man who can straighten out that idea if it ever occurs to any of their more rebellious members," Sanger wrote Gamble. Had Dr. King known why he may have been chosen to receive the award, he would have recoiled in horror.

The good news is that Sanger's-and Planned Parenthood's-patina of respectability has worn thin in recent years. Last year Congress came within a few votes of cutting a huge chunk of the organization's federal funding. The

1995-96 Planned Parenthood annual report notes that it has closed up shop in Mississippi, and that the number of its staff and volunteers has fallen by 4,000 over the previous year.

Perhaps the next time the Maggie Award is offered to someone of character and integrity-and more than a passing knowledge of Sanger's bigotry-he will raise an indignant cry of refusal. He will have ample grounds.

Mr. Mosher, author of "A Mother's Ordeal: One Woman's Fight Against China's One-Child Policy," is vice president for international affairs of Human Life International in Front Royal, Va. Michael W. Bird, a writer living in Minneapolis, helped with the research for this article.

Portions © 1995-2002 Women and Children First.

Discussion of Margaret Sanger, the founder of Planned Parenthood-http://www.lancasterlife.com/NurembergFiles/.

More on Sanger-http://www.hli.org/search/content_search.asp (enter "Sanger" in the search field).

"Jim Sedlak of ALL's Stop Planned Parenthood International division… related a history of Planned Parenthood, emphasizing its racist and eugenics roots. 'I made sure to mention her so-called "Negro Project" of the 1930s, which was aimed at trying to stop large numbers of black babies from being born…the basic philosophies espoused by Margaret Sanger are still motivating the organization's activities today. PP promotes uninhibited sex, birth control and abortion.'" "PP's interference with lines of communication between parents and their children…PP even calls girls' homes using a prearranged code name so parents won't know it is PP…PP is interested in sex education, birth control, and abortion, and these are the products by which the organization brings in income. Every year since 1987 PP has made a profit of at least $6 million. Over the last 14 years, PP has accumulated $415 million in profits, and it is continually seeking even more money from taxpayers." That's from the federal and state governments. This information was excerpted from the November 2001 Judie Brown Report, and the March-April 2002 issue of Celebrate Life.

"For the last complete fiscal year, 30% of Planned Parenthood's income came from U.S. taxpayers". May 2002 Judie Brown Report (PP also manages to procure funds from the states.)

From: Colleen Parro rnclife@swbell.net
Subject:Abortion Statistics for Each State
Date: Wed, 29 May 2002 16:59:54-0500

To: Friends of RNC/Life

This is excellent information for you to have and use in your own states.
Thanks again to John Cusey of the House Pro-Life Caucus for providing it to
us.

"Alan Guttmacher abortion statistics for each state

Dear Pro-life Groups: I am not in the habit of sending out information from
the Alan Guttmacher Institute, but these charts on what percentage of unborn
children are aborted in each state are so disturbing I thought you should see
them. Once you look past their rhetoric, the horror of the numbers is striking.
For instance, in the District of Columbia 50% of unborn children are killed
through abortion and only 37% are born alive. In some states, like New York
and New Jersey, the teen abortion rate is around 50%, while the statewide rate
is closer to 30%. Utah and the Dakotas have the lowest abortion percentages
with 7% and 9% respectively, which means even in the most pro-life states
roughly 1 in 10 unborn children are killed through abortion. This link also has
information on how many family planning clinics are in each Congressional
District and how many of them are run by Planned Parenthood...Thank you to
Maureen Kramlich for finding this disturbing information." (Which can be
seen at the following web site-
http://www.agi-usa.org/pubs/state_data/index.html).

The Alan Guttmacher Institute is the "research" arm of one of the pro-death
organizations-Planned Parenthood. Contact information for the Congressional
Pro-life Caucus is John Cusey 202-225-7669, Fax 225-7768, 2373 RHOB.

"'...the public school system...has ceased being an educational place so much
as an indoctrination place' 'a former PP birth control patient who became
pregnant and had an abortion. She didn't need her parents' permission and
received no education about abortion,' 'but they took my money and ended my
baby's life. I was young and stupid and must live with this memory and
decision forever.'" Taken from Dr. Laura Schlessinger's radio show.

I walked into our family room the other night, and there was yet another
program on TV about Afghanistan. I was pretty satiated with that kind of
thing by then, so I was just half listening. A woman reporter was doing a
special on the country. She was interviewing a high ranking Taliban official
about why the soccer stadium that had been built with international aid was
being used instead for executions. His reply was that "If you would build us a
stadium for executions, then we could use this one for soccer". The scene then
changed to the reporter back in her office, where she said: "You see, they don't
think like we do!" That same statement could be aptly applied to Margaret

Sanger and the hierarchy at Planned Parenthood. Once you comprehend that, it's much easier to understand what's going on.

Here are some other, more recent examples: Gloria Feldt, the president of Planned Parenthood, offered free abortions to the women widowed by the attack on the World Trade Center. Planned Parenthood of Blue Ridge, Virginia, also seeing a marketing opportunity, and not to be outdone, offered free red, white, and blue condoms. PP, and the American Red Cross, teamed up to hand out condoms to children as young as 12 years old at the Winter Olympics Games in Salt Lake City, even going into restaurants to distribute-until they were embarrassed by demonstrators.

"'Believe it or not, Planned Parenthood ran a Mother's Day campaign that included the option of making a donation to Planned Parenthood in someone's honor. Planned Parenthood will exploit anything for a buck.'…in 2000 alone, Planned Parenthood killed 197,070 children through surgical abortion… 'Planned Parenthood has done more to deprive children of their mothers than perhaps any other organization on earth, thus making its very existence an affront to what Mother's Day represents,' said Ed Szymkowiak."
The Judie Brown Report-June 2002

"Planned Parenthood knows no bounds when it comes to advocacy of the wanton killing of unborn children. The latest evidence is its 'Choice on Earth' campaign – just in time for the Christian celebration of the birth of Jesus Christ and its biblical call for 'peace on Earth.'…sales of holiday cards and T-shirts with the 'Choice on Earth' slogan". Taken from "Choice on Earth? Christmas Cards That Offend" by Joseph Farrah, World Net Daily, via ProLife Infonet, December 2, 2002. He went on to say: "…the international Planned Parenthood organization has held up China's population control policies as a model for the rest of the world. That's the kind of 'choice' Planned Parenthood supports. 'Choice' means one thing to Planned Parenthood and one thing only – abortion.", and "Is that choice? Well, yes, it's the kind of choice Planned Parenthood believes in – which is to say no choice at all. Choice means only one thing to the ghouls at Planned Parenthood – abortion whenever possible, abortion on demand, abortion for profit, abortion at all costs." plus "The slaughter of the innocents – that's what Planned Parenthood advocates…It's not about choice. It's about death. It's about force. It's about rebellion against God. It's about manifest evil so unspeakable the only way we can talk about it today is by employing euphemisms – like 'choice.'" That last especially hit home, because I have a difficult time getting my wife, a very kind and caring person, to talk about it at all. She just can't even bare to think about it, so her way of dealing with it is to shut it out of her consciousness.

"Then they have the gall to wish recipients of these cards a 'peaceful holiday season'! Planned Parenthood doesn't get it. Tearing innocent unborn babies limb from limb; puncturing their skulls and sucking out their brains; ignoring the emotional devastation that often results in women is NOT peaceful. The next time they are looking for nominations for the 'Lecherous Parasite on Society' award, I have a suggestion for them." Bradley Mattes, Executive Director, Life Issues Institute, Inc., January, 2003.

Not content to rest on her laurels, here are some gems from Gloria Feldt's May 8, 2008, Mother's Day column on the Planned Parenthood web site: "In 1926 Margaret Sanger published the book Motherhood in Bondage...Much has changed...The reproductive freedom movement has ushered in an era of motherhood in freedom...Anti-choice forces with allies from the White House to the state house are thwarting motherhood in freedom and forcing women into the role of mother...Or, take the abortion ban, which is barreling through Congress to a certain signing by the president. This is not a ban on one rarely used abortion procedure. Rather, it is a stealth statute that will ban many commonly used abortion procedures without regard for a woman's health. (The partial-birth abortion ban.) But as we celebrate Mother's Day, let us pledge that we will never allow anti-choice zealots to take us back to the days of motherhood". So she still hasn't learned to just shut up. What a ditz. I assumed for many years that PP gave condoms away free. Not so. When you look at the financial reports they are required to file, you find that condoms, and other birth control devices, are a major source of income. Why does PP need to sell condoms when you can buy them at the local drugstore? It seems to many informed observers that they want to encourage kids to become sexually active so that they can sell more abortions. They know that once that happens the kids won't always use the condoms, and pregnancies will go up. How can anybody believe that? It's so farfetched and outlandish! You bet your boots it is. But I reject a lot of things from this site that I don't think have a firm factual basis. Despite that, I do share the above view-that it's unannounced policy at the top. PP is profit driven. "In its 2000-2001 fiscal year, the Planned Parenthood Federation of America showed...income for the period was more than \$670 million...was responsible for 197,000 surgical abortions..."! That comes from the March 2002 Judie Brown Report. They got it from "the just-issued Planned Parenthood Federation of America 2000-2001 Annual Report."

"In December, the Texas Supreme Court voted unanimously to uphold a state law prohibiting Medicaid funds from being used for abortions. In an eight to zero vote, the court said that the ban on funding abortions for Medicaid women does not violate the state's Equal Rights Amendment. The ruling overturned a decision from Austin's Third Court of Appeals, which had ruled in favor of a group of abortionists and lawyers. The abortionists initially sued the Texas Department of Health, arguing that the state should pay...It is estimated that had the initial ruling stood, taxpayers in Texas would have been forced to pay a cost of $8 million." Taken from Life Dynamics News, February 2003.

"PP makes millions of dollars selling contraceptives and abortions. Comprehensive classroom sex ed programs encourage sexual promiscuity by teaching kids about such contraception and abortion. Thus, comprehensive sex programs ultimately bring lots of money to Planned Parenthood...Planned Parenthood depends upon classroom sex education programs to provide new customers for its contraceptive business". STOPP International's Ryan Report, October 2001 "A few years ago PP opened up a new front on its assault against children and parental authority—its web site for kids—teenwire.com. The utterly disgusting nature of this web site is difficult to even talk about much less describe in detail in print. It is a cesspool of perversion aimed directly at children. No longer do parents just have to worry about whether PP is in the schools. Now parents need to be vigilant about PP reaching their kids online, even in the sanctuary of their own homes." The Ryan Report, April 2002

"Granite City, IL—A mother who tried to enter an abortion facility to see her 16-year-old daughter was stopped by abortion facility officials and local police." "Abortion facilities have faced increasing scrutiny from many who believe they prey on teen girls and encourage them to get around parental notification laws. The Child Custody Protection Act pending in Congress would prohibit abortion facilities from conducting abortions on minors without parental consent." Source: St. Louis Post Dispatch; 2/23/02

"As everyone knows by now, a school can't even give an aspirin to a student without the parents' consent. But in most states a schoolgirl can sneak into an abortion mill and undergo major surgery without the parents' knowledge or consent. Many mothers and fathers would support their daughter through her pregnancy if only they knew about it." Joe Scheidler, November 25, 2002

"SUBJECT: Parental Consent Not Required? Did you know that your child cannot get a tattoo, her ears pierced, or attend a school field trip without your permission BUT she CAN get an abortion?! This just DOESN'T make sense! Many states have parental consent laws to protect children but states that don't are a haven for young girls, subjected to statutory rape, being taken across state lines by the very men who are responsible for these crimes! A law before Congress—passed in the House and stalled in the Senate—would change this. Parental Consent Laws are designed to protect our children! Help us get the Child Custody Protection Act (H.R. 476) passed!" Jennifer Bingham, Executive Director, SBAList "Our children need protection! This bill would make it a crime to transport a minor across state lines to avoid state laws requiring parental or judicial consent before a child can have an abortion. Again, I encourage you to take action to ensure the safety of children. Your action will not only make a difference to an unborn child but also to young girls who are being taken advantage of." DATE: November 25, 2002

"On October 14, Newsday published a story by Roni Rabin in which she described the expectant mothers whose husbands were killed in the vicious attack on the World Trade Center. Danielle Salerno and her husband John were expecting their first child. Although he desperately wanted children, Danielle did not. She didn't want to be tied down. But then, she had a change of heart. She got pregnant immediately and was almost four months along when John was killed by the terrorists. "It's a miracle," Salerno, 30, a native of Port Washington who lives in Westfield, N.J., said of her pregnancy. "I consider myself very lucky. I don't think I could have been able to handle all the years we've had together and having really nothing left, only photographs." "I just wish he'd had a chance to see his child...Nobody wanted a child more than John."

At Cantor Fitzgerald alone, Newsday reports, the number is staggering: 60 wives of missing employees are pregnant, a spokesman said. Numerous firefighters' wives are also expecting, along with unknown numbers of others. They face raising their children alone. Many of those expecting their first child were in the process of securing life insurance and drawing up wills. If their husband was the primary provider, they may have to sell their home, buy health insurance, and make financial decisions on their own. Yet, not one of the expectant mothers interviewed by Newsday said they regret being pregnant. Their pregnancies harbor little nuggets of the person they loved, and they can't wait to hold their newborns."

Taken from Republican National Coalition for Life FaxNotes-October 23, 2001.

"Congresswoman Loretta Sanchez tried to add an amendment to emergency anti-terrorist legislation that would have allowed women in the Armed Forces to receive free abortions in overseas military bases—paid for by your tax dollars!

And while President Bush and members of Congress were doing their best to safeguard our nation and be united, the radicals at EMILY's List vowed to 'disagree with the President and his administration'...". Jane Abraham, President, SBA List, November 7, 2001.

"...those—who are not just of another opinion—but are the mortal enemies of everything we believe in, from the dignity of the human person to the nature of a just and protective society and government." Temple University scholar Franklin M. Little

Why do so many large corporations and "charitable" foundations controlled by wealthy people give to organizations like PP and NARAL? Could it be that the Sanger attitude toward Africans and Hispanics still lives on behind closed doors? Sometimes you have to ask the right question to get the right answer. How do you explain it? We have to assume these people have above average intelligence, to have accomplished so much in the material world.

"Class-Action Malpractice Lawsuit Filed Against Planned Parenthood

St. Louis, MO—A major class action lawsuit has been filed in U.S. District Court in St. Louis against Planned Parenthood Federation of America and Planned Parenthood of St. Louis. The suit contends Planned Parenthood has systematically committed fraud by failing to inform women about the risks, both physical and emotional, associated with abortion. Further, it says Planned Parenthood has been engaged in the systematic targeting of low-income and minority women for abortions. According to Planned Parenthood, 42.7% of the abortions are performed on minorities, which is three times more than on whites as a percentage of their respective populations. Department of Health and Human Services reports African American women made up 43% of abortions and account for approximately 11% of the female population. In many predominantly African American communities, abortions outpace live births 3 to 1. Another indicator is the fact that the overwhelming majority of Planned Parenthood's clinics are located in or near minority neighborhoods." Source: Agape Press; 01/22/02

"Editor's Note: Margaret Sanger enrolled in a nursing program but left before completing her training. According to George Grant, author of a biography of Sanger, the Planned Parenthood founder called herself a trained nurse but her status more closely paralleled that of today's orderlies. It never ceases to amaze us that Margaret Sanger is revered as a hero, even though she promoted a racist agenda. For more on this topic, read our indepth paper, 'The Negro Project: Margaret Sanger's Eugenic Plan for Black Americans.' Visit http://fv.cwfa.org/sanger, or call 1-800-323-2200 to request your free copy." Taken from Family Voice May/June 2002.

Planned Parenthood doesn't even do very well at dodging the bullet. They don't seem to see anything wrong. I took the following from a May 06, 2002, column by Jason Pierce in CNSNEWS.COM Cybercast News Service: "PPFA continues to use Sanger's name at its awards dinners...still honoring Sanger by giving awards in her name." On PP's web site they acknowledge "Marget Sanger clearly identified with the issues of *health* and *fitness* (emphasis added) that concerned the early 20th-century eugenics movement...Sanger believed there should be 'incentives for the voluntary hospitalization and/or sterilization of people with untreatable, disabling, hereditary conditions,' that there should be 'stringent regulations to prevent diseased and feeble-minded immigrants into the U.S.' and that 'illiterates, paupers, unemployables, criminals, prostitutes, and dope-fiends' should be placed on farms and in open spaces' as long as necessary". Sounds pretty open ended to me. And the article quotes Ed Szymkowiak: "They claim that's not what they think anymore, but I think there is a contradiction there, when you are honoring the person who promulgated the eugenics movement here in the U.S. to a large degree."

"On October 19, 1939, Sanger outlined a plan for stopping the growth of the Black community. She predicted that 'the most successful educational approach to the Negro is through religious appeal. We do not want word to go out that we want to exterminate the Negro population and the minister is the man who can straighten out that idea if it ever occurs to any of their rebellious members.' (Elasah Drogin, Margaret Sanger: p. 33) Her planning, which included being careful to make it appear that handpicked Blacks are in control, is followed with success even today."

Taken from "Who Was Margaret Sanger?", a publication of the American Life League. It's a difficult thing for Blacks to do anything about, because abortion proponents help to elect, and thereby control, the liberal senators who block anti-abortion legislation and judicial nominations, and also happen to be the same politicians most African-Americans get conned into voting for. But the African-American community is not totally unaware of this threat, as indicated by the following excerpts from one of their pro-life web sites:

"ABOUT L.E.A.R.N., INC. (Life Education And Resource Network) L.E.A.R.N. INC., http://www.learninc.org/page/about.php is the largest, African-American, evangelical pro-life ministry in the United States. Rev. Johnny Hunter is President. L.E.A.R.N. INC. publishes extensive data and research information on the racist origins of Planned Parenthood, it's founder, Margaret Sanger, and the American Eugenics movement. As an expert on Planned Parenthood's involvement in the black community, Rev. Hunter and other members of the network are available as speakers. L.E.A.R.N. INC., P.O. Box 6357, Virginia Beach, VA 23456 Phone#: (757) 495-0720 Fax#: (757) 495-1279"

I heard Akua Furlow, one of their original founders, speak, and she gives a very nice presentation on the careful investigative work she performed on Margaret Sanger to confirm her suspicions. After all, it is something that is hard to believe when you are first confronted with it. The most accessed page on their web site seems to be on Erma Clardy Craven, a "pioneer and champion of the pro-life movement" http://www.learninc.org/articles/mainframe.html.

Pastor Clenard H. Childress, Jr., the Northeast Director of L.E.A.R.N., maintains a more sophisticated web site called "Black Genocide". He says it as well as anyone: "Abortion is the greatest deception that has plagued the black church since Lucifer himself. Pro-Choice? This carefully devised phrase was contrived to provoke our inward zeal for freedom and the civil right to make choices freely. I am all for freedom of choice, except when it comes at the expense of innocent lives. Women who have been deceived into wrong choices and children who were never given any choice at all are the victims of pro-choice America." http://blackgenocide.org/

"The most merciful thing that the large family does to one of its infant members is to kill it."
Margaret Sanger, Woman and the New Race, 1920

"Blacks, soldiers, and Jews are a menace to the race."
Margaret Sanger, Birth Control Review, April 1933

"Sanger was closely tied to Ernst Rudin, who served as Hitler's director of genetic sterilization. An April 1933 article by Rudin entitled 'Eugenic Sterilization: An Urgent Need' for Sanger's monthly magazine, The Birth Control Review, detailed the establishment of the Nazi Society for Racial Hygiene and advocated its replication in the United States. A subsequent article by Leon Whitney published the following June by Sanger, entitled 'Selective Sterilization,' praises and defends the Third Reich's pre-holocaust 'race purification' program." Source: World Net Daily; May 30, 2002, Planned Parenthood on the Run, by Joseph Farah.

"There is a striking kinship between our movement and Margaret Sanger's early efforts...Our sure beginning in the struggle for equality by nonviolent direct action may not have been so resolute without the tradition established by Margaret Sanger and people like her." Planned Parenthood, www.plannedparenthood.org/about/ thisispp/sanger.html, in April 2002

"The only difference between Sanger and Hitler is that Sanger got away with it because her victims were invisible". Nick DiGiovanni Reality Check, April 2002

Another organization that you'll hear promoting and defending abortion is the National Abortion Federation. Who are they? I just read that they're an association of abortion doctors. So NAF has the same financial incentive to protect abortion that PP does. Don't be lured into believing that they're doing it just on a philosophical, benevolent basis. They're protecting their businesses. Emily's List, as I understand it, was founded by a Hollywood movie producer who wanted to make dirty pictures unencumbered by legal restrictions. I don't think NOW has a monetary motivation. More than likely they started out as a bona fide women's organization and got taken over by left wing radicals-based on things I've heard. Call it speculation based on knowledge.

"One Survivor met a young lady who was very upset with them for holding the signs of the aborted babies. She explained that she had an abortion and she knew that they didn't perform abortions when 'it' (the child) was so developed. She had asked Planned Parenthood what week of pregnancy she was in when she had her abortion and was told she was in her 2nd week! The Survivor she was speaking with quietly told her that Planned Parenthood doesn't perform abortions before the 5th week." Taken from Survivors Action News, June 2002, Dan McCullough, Director.

"On June 23, 1940, an African-American couple from Tennessee was expecting their 20th child. This family was financially unstable; they could barely feed or clothe the 19 children they already had. The child might suffer from a variety of illnesses including polio, which could leave her in leg braces. Many would consider her race, poverty and risk for crippling diseases too many strikes against her and suggest abortion. Would you abort? If you said yes, then you'd have chosen to abort Wilma Rudolph, the first female Olympic gold medallist. With the help and love of her family, Wilma became a world-class runner, a crusader against segregation, and a constant model of perseverance." Martha Nolan, Reality Check, April 2002

"Chris Klug started life prematurely, and was not expected to live. He survived, but with a series of health problems-including severe asthma. Chris is not like most people. He is a fighter who looks at every obstacle as a new challenge. Chris grew up loving sports, especially snowboarding. When that sport was made an Olympic event, Chris dreamed of competing for the United States. Then one more tragedy struck. In 1993, Chris was diagnosed with a rare and deadly liver disease. He lost much of his strength before an organ donor was finally found for a life-saving liver transplant in 2000. Incredibly, just 19 months after this major surgery, Chris won a bronze medal for the U.S. at the 2002 Olympic Games!"—Lloyd D. Ward, Chief Executive Officer, United Sates Olympic Committee

"About 30 years ago, feminists believed they were ensuring women a more powerful place in the world by establishing a right to legalized abortion on demand. It's only now, after half a billion or so worldwide abortions, that we're starting to see the ugly irony evil had in mind all along. Instead of making women more prominent, legalized abortion is actually working overtime to give women a smaller and smaller presence on the world stage. There's now indisputable evidence of a growing global trend to abort female babies in favor of male babies. This pattern of gender-based abortion had its beginning in third-world countries like China. But the anti-female practice soon spread to India, Japan and Europe. And now, right here in America, some abortionists admit that the fastest growing part of their business is aborting girl babies for parents who prefer boys. Officials in Japan are expressing fears of impending social disaster, as they anticipate a future in which women make up barely more than one-third of the population. It's an unprecedented condition of female oppression that could soon become worldwide—all thanks to the discernment of 20th century feminism…". Judie Brown, president, American Life League, in the May, 2002, The Judie Brown Report.

Suspected Sexual Abuse of Minors Must Be Reported

"Life Dynamics Targets Planned Parenthood In May, Life Dynamics headed by Mark Crutcher issued report on an undercover investigation it conducted on Planned Parenthood's involvement in covering up statutory rape crimes committed against girls by adult males.

Planned Parenthood personnel helped girls avoid reporting statutory rape crimes against them. The media has been following this story, and we have compiled a list of links to show you how differently the liberal media has been spinning this story. Some news outlets portray Life Dynamics as the guilty party instead of applauding the group for exposing these statutory rape cover ups.

FOX: Pro-Life Group Launches Undercover Sting
Lincoln Journal Star: Group says clinics abide statutory rape
Lycos: Abortion Foes Reveal Deceptive Tactic
Miami Herald: Abortion foes reveal their covert tactics
New York Times: Abortion Foes Reveal Deceptive Tactic
Newsday: Anti-abortion group accuses clinics of telling girls to
Northern Lights: Abortion Foes Reveal Deceptive Tactic
Star Telegram: Abortion Foes Entice Clinics to Break Law
World Net Daily: Abortionists mum on concealment charges
World Net Daily: Planned Parenthood concealing crimes?
World Net Daily: Planned Parenthood on the run
Yahoo: Abortion Foes Reveal Deceptive Tactic

Life Dynamics also will air a one-hour special on its investigation. 'Who's Protecting Child Predators,' a 1-hour special will air on the Cornerstone Television Network this Monday, June 3, at 10 PM/ET. Learn how the culmination of a 9-month investigation exposes the criminal partnership between Planned Parenthood, the National Abortion Federation, and men who sexually abuse underage girls. This report will detail evidence showing how tax dollars are being used to pay for a massive cover-up of child sexual exploitation. On this television program you will hear portions of actual conversations where clinic employees tell LDI's undercover team how to avoid legal reporting requirements and demonstrate their willingness to conceal the predator's identity. If you would like a VHS copy of this TV special, call 1-800-800-LIFE and order the June 2002 edition of the television show LifeTalk. A copy of the pro-gram will cost you $3.50, which includes shipping and handling. A printed 23-page synopsis of Life Dynamics' investigation is available at no charge by calling 1-940-380-8800.

From: 'TVCNews' tvcnewscp@norm.nmailer.com, Vol. 5, Issue 23, Fri, 7 Jun 2002 01:18:08-0400 TRADITIONAL VALUES COALITION NEWS, http://www.traditionalvalues.org/. This email goes out to nearly 500,000 people each week."

"Suspected Sexual Abuse of Minors Must Be Reported – When a minor requests condoms, birth control pills, a chemical or surgical abortion or any other 'reproductive health' service, the clinic, agency, nurse, doctor, teacher, counselor, etc. must report instances of suspected child abuse to child protective services or other governmental authority designated by state law. Minor girls seeking such services are often the victims of statutory rape perpetrated by adult males. Planned Parenthood, the National Abortion Federation, school-based clinics and others are in apparent violation of the law when they fail to report suspected sexual abuse perpetrated on minors who seek their services." From: Colleen Parro, rnclife@swbell.net, Republican National Coalition for Life Fax Notes-May 24, 2002.

Links to news coverage on Life Dynamics', http://www.lifedynamics.com/ special report Child Predators, http://www.childpredators.com/:

World Net Daily news report: Planned Parenthood concealing crimes? http://worldnetdaily.com/news/article.asp?ARTICLE_ID=27687

Investigation says sex by men with underage girls 'epidemic' CBN: Planned Parenthood May Be Charged with Cover-up Crime http://www.cbn.org/cbnnews/news/020524d.asp

CCN: Abortion providers fail to report child abuse CWA: CWA Blasts Abortion Providers for Helping Sex Offenders Cover Their Crime http://www.onlinearchive.org/article.php?sid=292

FOX: Abortion Clinics Look the Other Way http://fox61.trb.com/wtic-052202-abortion.story?coll=wtic%2Dhome%2D1

Agape Press: Abortionists Implicated in Alleged Rape Cover-up http://headlines.agapepress.org/archive/5/242002a.asp

World Net Daily, by Joseph Farah: Planned Parenthood on the run http://wnd.com/news/article.asp?ARTICLE_ID=27780

American-Republican: Profits before predators http://www.rep-am.com/

Newsday: Anti-abortion group accuses clinics of telling girls to keep sex abuse secret http://www.newsday.com/

Associated Press: Clinics accused of agreeing to keep sex abuse secret
http://www.ctnow.com/

"The Law is Clear Failing to report child abuse is a crime in all fifty states. Abortion facilities present themselves to the community as a health care provider, and the law requires that health care providers must report suspected child abuse. Outrageous as it sounds, Planned Parenthood of Greater Northern New Jersey actually produced a book called *Unequal Partners, Teaching About Power and Consent in Adult-Teen and Other Relationships*. The book, in its second edition, is part of their sex-ed curriculum. In the forward, authors Sue Montfort and Peggy Brick write, 'The first edition of *Unequal Partners* was developed in response to research indicating that a large number of 'adolescent' pregnancies and births involve men older than 20.' The authors readily acknowledge considerable research that indicates serious problems for young girls who are sexually active with adult men. Even in the face of conclusive research, the authors make this alarming statement. 'It is important for users of *Unequal Partners* to know that this manual promotes healthy relationships regardless of the sex or age difference of the partners.' Truth never seemed to be an obstacle too big to overcome for abortion clinics all over the country. It also became clearly evident that circumventing the law was a routine task for many facilities. Some readily admitted that it was a common occurrence...in Hartford, Connecticut...the...*Associated Press* reported that 'Assistant State's Attorney Steve Sedensky said just the fact that a 13-year-old is pregnant is evidence of abuse, without even mentioning a boyfriend in his 20s.'...Life Dynamics released this statement. 'Planned Parenthood and the National Abortion Federation have made a conscious decision to conceal the sexual exploitation of children and protect the men who commit these crimes.'

It would not be unreasonable to require that recipients of tax dollars follow all state and federal laws. It is also possible that if past funding was fraudulently obtained, it may need to be returned. The number of potential victims of sexual abuse could number into the millions. This widespread problem may also have the potential for a huge class-action lawsuit. Many schools have Planned Parenthood come into the classrooms where underage girls and boys are funneled into a system that facilitates a crime. School districts throughout the nation may want to make reviewing their relationships with these organizations a priority...this sexual abuse, which has reached epidemic proportions,...demonstrates that the desire to make more money for the abortion industry tramples the rights and well being of women and young girls ...Contact Life Dynamics, PO Box 2226, Denton, TX 76202 http://www.lifedynamics.com/. Phone 800.800.5433 or http://www.ChildPredators.com/" Article by Bradley Mattes, and taken from a reprint in Phyllis Schlafly's RNC For Life Report, "A Publication of the Republican National Coalition for Life July/August 2002-No. 45", http://www.rnclife.org/. I didn't reprint the whole article. This web site doesn't need to be any bigger. So if you want to read all the examples, etc.; go to one of the above mentioned links. I will make this comment, though: It's been my observation that people who brazenly flout the law are often brought down by it-especially in child molestation cases.

"Life Dynamics fields calls every week from legislators, prosecutors, and law enforcement officials from both the state and federal level...in all 50 states healthcare providers are required by law to report to the state when a minor seeks birth control, an abortion, treatment for a sexually transmitted disease, or a pregnancy test...the overwhelming majority of America's family planning facilities openly and routinely violate these laws. When the public hears from individual young girls what we have heard—when they see the damage that was done to very young girls because an abortion employee refused to obey the laws that require them to report suspected child abuse—then the truth will come out. The judges and juries, pro-life or not, will punish these abortion clinics." Mark Crutcher in The Life Advocate, Sept. 2002

People, in general, don't want to hear or talk about abortion, but they'll follow sex scandals for weeks and months on end.

"The last line of defense for an unborn child is the pro-lifer who counsels moms as they walk into the abortion mill. After reading about LDI's Child Predator Report, several sidewalk counselors have begun calling the police when they see an underage girl enter the clinic. The response of police departments varies widely, but in every case thus far, the call to police has been a legitimate reporting of a potential crime. To help sidewalk counselors put the Child Predators Project to use in their area, LDI is creating a new sidewalk counselor training kit. This kit will explain in detail how, why, and when to involve local law enforcement. The law is on our side, but you need to know how to convey that to your local police officers. This kit will include a new video, a manual, an on-site checklist, reporting forms, and material to give to law enforcement personnel. This new LDI sidewalk counselor kit is $7.50 plus $2.50 for shipping...call 1-800-800-LIFE". Taken from The Life Activist, September 2002.

"Since the war in Iraq has begun, people's attention has been drawn away from issues here in America. At the same time there is a battle still being fought here in America. As the nation faces this time of uncertainty, there is no question that the future of thousands of babies has already been decided. We cannot allow that future to go unchanged. Our projects and initiatives are making real progress in dismantling the abortion industry and returning protection to the unborn. Projects like Child Predators, which was launched less than a year ago, is picking up steam. Initiatives based on this project have begun in over thirty states and are aimed at the abortion industry's bottom line. In addition, lawsuits are being prepared that will hold the abortion industry accountable for the lives they have destroyed." "From the Desk of Mark Crutcher President, Life Dynamics Incorporated April 2003".

Dana Cody, "...attacking the lie that abortion was promoted in the face of opposition only from selfish and chauvinistic males-when, in reality, selfish and chauvinistic males are only too happy to have abortion available as an easy escape from the demands of fatherhood...the abortion culture has actually empowered the abusers of women, made the lot of women more precarious, and reduced any chance a woman might have to resist exploitation. Can anyone really pretend that, of all the 4,500 abortions done daily in this country, only a very few involve pressure on the aborting mother?...in reality, selfish and chauvinistic males will resort to abortion by assault if the more covert kind doesn't materialize quickly enough...essentially the same crime is committed in abortion mills around the country—and all the time...what the abortion culture had long promised—an easy escape from paternity...attacking the lie that abortion is a benefit to women—that there must be perpetual enmity between a mother and her unborn child." Executive Director, Life Legal Defense Foundation, P.O. Box 2105, Napa, California, 707.224.6675, 11/22/2002.

"Planned Parenthood is the single biggest abortion provider in the United States...its international arm has long been involved in coercive population control, and...it was founded by a eugenics enthusiast and Nazi sympathizer whose theories (if you want to dignify them with the name) encouraged forced sterilization in occupied Poland, among other places. It's as if the Hitler Youth were to succeed in repackaging themselves as some kind of Campfire Girls... the biggest abortion advocacy group that ever dragged itself out of the primeval ooze...Planned Parenthood's involvement in the childkilling industry—it's hard, really, to imagine a more outrageous crime than that...we live in a society whose values are profoundly corrupted by propaganda—so that Planned Parenthood's most culpable crime is not recognized as such by people in general.

What you may not know—unless you're really savvy about the Planned Parenthood scam—is that Margaret Sanger's gift to the death culture has recently been caught defying laws still very much in effect. There was no doubt: Planned Parenthood nationwide was engaged in a systematic coverup of child abuse.

Planned Parenthood receives millions and millions of dollars every year for providing 'birth control' and 'sexuality education' to young people—mostly in the public schools...distributed through state and federal programs...these funds constitute a third or more of Planned Parenthood's operating budget...it all goes, in one way or another, to the biggest abortion provider—the biggest childkiller—in the country.

There's only one problem with the way Planned Parenthood is currently running this racket. It depends heavily on public school districts that allow Planned Parenthood access to young people—and even funnel them into PP's programs...Because school districts themselves are as liable as Planned Parenthood itself—if they direct sexually abused children toward secrecy and away from mandatory reporting! We Can Pry This Monster Out of the Nation's Schools!...the school districts are liable—and they know it. If they let Planned Parenthood into their institutions and Planned Parenthood fails to report clear evidence of statutory rape...then the school districts are in real legal trouble.

Planned Parenthood is like a gigantic tentacled beast...about as cute as a monster from a gross-out sci-fi flick. Those tentacles go so deep into so many crevices, and under so many rocks, that, before the Child Predator Project materialized, it seemed impossible to pry the abomination loose...help us to pry the nation's number-one pro-abortion monstrosity loose—and to starve it of the funds it needs to corrupt and slaughter more of America's children...help us to get Planned Parenthood out of the schools-and out of the lives of America's schoolchildren!" Dana Cody, Executive Director, LLDF, 04/24/03, P.O. Box 2105, Napa, CA 94558

"Planned Parenthood...led the charge to break down all sexual 'barriers' and encouraged and promoted young people to experiment with and practice sex whenever they felt like it. They were taught that they could do this 'safely' and without guilt, because it was normal and 'everyone was doing it'. They did this from within the schools, social organizations, and churches, while infiltrating the homes and minds of families across the U.S. and around the world. Along with this came an increase in sexual activity, STDs, pregnancies outside of marriage, and untold mental, emotional, spiritual and psychological problems. PP helped create these problems, but now they will help solve them—for another fee. Go back to PP and get your STDs treated...have a surgical or chemical abortion if your pregnancy test comes back positive. And for sure, come back for more birth control once this 'problem' is taken care of. The very organization that helped to proliferate these 'problems' now is seen as being helpful when it treats the problems it has created. How absurd is that? And remember this, all of these services are fee-based. Even if they are 'free' to the customer, PP receives taxpayer funding (30 percent of their funding is from taxpayers) and will bill the government (you and I) instead. PP profits from higher sexual activity by selling...contraceptives, doing pregnancy tests, STD tests, and checkups. Then when 'problems' come up from sexual activity, PP is there to charge for STD treatment, chemical abortions and surgical abortions as 'backup' birth control (197,070 surgical abortions in the year 2000 alone). All this results in generated profits of over $38,000,000 in FY 2001, and total profits of $454,000,000 in the last 15 years. This is profit generated by this 'non-profit' machine. The cycle is endless when the PP way is followed: promote sexual activity as normal and safe, sell contraception, sell testing, sell treatment for associated problems, go out and keep doing what you're doing, 'See you next time!'" Marty Leenhouts, Mankato, Minnesota

"Abortions Outpace Adoption 80-1 at Planned Parenthood By Jason Pierce CNSNews.com Staff Writer May 08, 2002 (CNSNews.com)-When it comes to pregnant women deciding between abortion and adoption, more than 98 percent of those women seeking counsel from Planned Parenthood Federation of America ended their pregnancies with abortion in 2000, according to data collected by the organization. Meanwhile, the number of adoption referrals by PPFA fell for the fourth consecutive year in 2000, to fewer than 2,500. During the same year, Planned Parenthood clinics around the country performed almost 200,000 abortions, according to statistics available on the organization's Internet website. Stated another way, Planned Parenthood abortionists performed almost 80 abortions for every adoption referral the organization made in 2000, the data show. According to Planned Parenthood, there were 9,200 adoption referrals in 1997, but that number had dropped to 2,486 by 2000."

"According to their 2001 annual report, Planned Parenthood referred one pregnant woman to an adoption agency for every 109 abortions performed at its clinics. Ed Szymkowiak, national director of the pro-life organization STOPP International, said, 'For the fifth straight year, Planned Parenthood's adoption referrals have decreased. It is plain to see that all Planned Parenthood cares about is making big bucks by aborting babies, not humane alternatives like adoption.'

"For the past three decades, Planned Parenthood and the rest of the abortion industry have waged a quiet but successful war against adoption." John C. Willke, M.D., President Life Issues Institute, Inc., May 5, 2003

Szymkowiak said, 'Americans need to realize that Planned Parenthood is funded, in large part, by their tax dollars—nearly a quarter of a billion dollars for Planned Parenthood's fiscal year 2002.'" Taken from Life Dynamics News, March 2003. "National News From the Front Lines of the Pro-Life Battle".

From: The Pro-Life Infonet Steven Ertelt infonet@prolifeinfo.org
Source: Family Research Council; December 2, 2002

Planned Parenthood Pays Teens to Educate Their Peers

Washington, DC—"Using taxpayer dollars, Planned Parenthood is embarking on a new strategy aimed at increasing the number of teens using its services. In Morrow County, Ohio, Planned Parenthood has inked a deal with the school system there to pay teenagers $100 to be trained as 'outreach workers.' They would then be paid an additional reward for every teenage client they recruit as a new Planned Parenthood customer. The money the abortion business will use to pay its teenage workers will come in part from federal and state grants via the Temporary Assistance to Needy Families program. 'Under no circumstances should taxpayers be forced to subsidize Planned Parenthood's efforts to promote teen sex,' said Ken Connor, president of Family Research Council. 'The idea of paying teens to recruit other teens into Planned Parenthood's grasp is unconscionable; doing it with taxpayer dollars is outrageous.' According to the U.S. Government Accounting Office, Planned Parenthood received more than $137 million in federal money during the 2001 fiscal year. 'This week's cover story in Newsweek, which details a significant rise in abstinent teens, shows the Bush administration is on the right track by promoting abstinence-only education,' Connor said. 'Why then are we using tax dollars to promote Planned Parenthood's culture of abortion and so-called 'safe sex'? 'This latest scheme is more evidence, as if more were needed, why the 108th Congress should act decisively to de-fund Planned Parenthood,' Connor said."

"In order to flourish, the abortion industry needs people to be having sex and getting pregnant so that the stream of abortion customers will sustain the cash flow they have grown accustomed to. Planned Parenthood (PP) is not about to sit on its laurels and let the cash registers go silent. They are leaving no stone unturned in their campaign to aggressively pursue every possible customer. Here is an example. Planned Parenthood worked out a cozy business arrange-ment with the school system in Morrow County, Ohio. They will pay teenagers $100 to train them as 'outreach workers'. This is a fancy term for teenage sales people promoting PP's products to their peers. They will then be paid a bonus for every teenage customer they bring in. What is equally outrageous is where they are getting the money to pay their young sales staff. The funds will come from the Temporary Assistance to Needy Families program. Does this mean that fewer needy families will be getting crucial financial assistance for the basic necessities of life to feed Planned Parenthood's aggressive marketing plan? In 2001, PP received more than $200 million in government dollars a lone. Their total income was over $672 million. After expenses, they had a profit of nearly $39 million. Does this sound like a needy family to you?

Because Planned Parenthood has hundreds of millions of dollars to throw around, they can buy their way into communities. Here's a case in point. A confidential financial agreement between PP of Central Texas and the city of Waco has made it possible for them to promote their radical pro-abortion agenda in the public library system. An undisclosed amount of money (reported to be less than $10,000) was paid by PP to put their 'specialized collection of books, periodicals, pamphlets, videos, curricula and teaching aids' into, as PP says, 'a branch of the Waco-McLennan County Public Library System.' This collection of pro-abortion propaganda is opportunistically called 'women's health care' materials." By Bradley Mattes, Executive Director, Life Issues Institute, Inc., 1821 W. Galbraith Rd., Cincinnati, Ohio 45239 (513) 729-3600, in Life Issues Connector, January 2003, http://www.lifeissues.org/.

Religion and Abortion

Earlier I mentioned that some churches inappropriately fail in giving their membership moral guidance by seemingly embracing abortion; without giving any supporting evidence for that. What follows reinforces that assertion: "Say what? *'It's important to have a religious voice for choice.'*—Rev. Monica Corsaro Washington state chaplain Planned Parenthood With a lot of fanfare, Planned Parenthood recently announced the appointment of a state chaplain in the state of Washington. Rev. Monica Corsaro is a Methodist. Her bishop made the position her official ministerial assignment. The *Seattle Times* notes that the Methodist church 'is generally considered friendly to the pro-choice position.' The *Seattle Times* interview with Rev. Corsaro leaves no doubt about her own views: 'Corsaro said she was raised with the belief that God believes in each person's ability to make choices.'" How profound. But I guess that's the caliber of person that philosophy attracts. The quoted material was taken from the May 2002 Judie Brown Report.

"Columbus, OH—The Presbyterian Church (U.S.A.) assembly has reaffirmed support for abortion if the baby is too young to survive outside the womb. After that, it said, abortion is acceptable only to save a woman's life, avoid fetal suffering or in cases of rape or incest." Source: Associated Press; August 17, 2002

"*Lifewatch*, a publication of the Task Force of United Methodists on Abortion and Sexuality, reported in its December, 2001 issue that the Religious Coalition for Reproductive Choice (RCRC) 'is flatly opposed to any restriction on any abortion, including any partial-birth abortion.'.

First, on April 29, 1996, the Religious Coalition for Reproductive Choice sent a letter to the members of the United States House of Representatives. The first sentence of the RCRC letter states:

'As mainstream religious leaders, we write to express our Agreement with President Clinton's veto HR 1833, the so-called 'Partial-Birth Abortion Ban,' and urge Congress not to override that veto.' This letter is signed by these United Methodists: Ms. Lois Dauway, Women's Division, General Board of Global Ministries; Dr. Thom White Wolf Fassett, Executive Secretary, General Board of Church and Society; Rev. George McClain, Executive Director, Methodist Federation for Social Action; Dr. M. Douglas Meeks, Dean Wesley Theological Seminary; Bishop Susan Morrison; and Rev. Philip Wogaman, Foundry United Methodist Church, Washington, DC.

The second piece of information was a letter from RCRC, dated Sept. 17, 1998, to members of the United States Senate. It begins with this sentence: 'As national religious leaders and leaders of religiously affiliated organizations, we write to express our support of President Clinton's veto of the so-called Partial Birth Abortion Ban Act of 1997, HR 1122. We respectfully urge the Senate to sustain the veto.'...the Religious Coalition for Reproductive Choice, it must be admitted, engages in political activism...notified the press of its letter-writing campaign...organizational activity clearly establishes that the Religious Coalition for Reproductive Choice...is strongly committed to working to keep partial-birth abortion legal in our society." Taken from an article by Rev. Paul Stallsworth on the front page of *Uniting for Life*, A Christian Pro-Life Newsletter, Spring 2002, National Pro-Life Religious Council, 109 2nd St. NE, Washington, DC 2002.

Wait. There's more here than is immediately evident. First of all, I didn't receive it until the Fall of 2002, and it has "Address Correction Requested" hand written on it. Somebody managed to get my name and address and thought I should see this six months after it was published. First, I'd like to congratulate them on identifying me, because I don't make it easy to do, and say I'm flattered you went to all that trouble. Thanks for sending it, too. But this is like a "first contact", and I'm pretty ignorant of what is actually going on inside the Methodist Church. That leaves me with a "hot potato", that I'm not sure how to interpret.

But I'll try to point out to my readers what's obvious, and what's not, and hope to get some clarification later in the mail. First, there are some big names in the Methodist Church that are very supportive of abortion, and I think that's the Church's official position too. But let me point out that Rev. Stallsworth is the editor of Lifewatch, he also wrote the article, and he's Methodist himself. So there appears to be a "guerilla underground" so to speak. But the NPRC that he was published by does not appear to me to be a Methodist organization. So I'm going into this mainly for my Methodist readers. If you're Methodist, you only have two choices, in my view; vote with your feet and leave the church, or work from within to change it. If you want to work from within, I've given you a way to find others who are already doing that.

Later, from the December 2002 issue of Uniting For Life, http://www.nprcouncil.org/, "The National Pro-life Religious Council (NPRC) is a Christian coalition which...works to encourage every Christian denomination to affirm and witness to the biblical standard of the value, dignity and sanctity of human life, and to foster ministry to those vulnerable to the violence of abortion or euthanasia. Member Organizations Alpha Omega Life Conservative Congregational Christian Conference (CCCC) International Communion of the Charismatic Episcopal Church (CEC for Life) Lutherans for Life (LFL) The Lutheran Church-Missouri Synod (LCMS) National Clergy Council (NCC) National Organization of Episcopalians for Life (NOEL) Presbyterians Pro-Life (PPL) Priests for Life (PFL) Religious Outreach

National Right to Life Committee Task Force of United Methodists on Abortion and Sexuality (TUMAS) United Friends for Life (UFL)". So we see that support within the denominations that endorse abortion is not monolithic, but that there is growing opposition to that policy.

One of the strategies of the pro-abortion forces has been to take control of influential organizations, where the general membership may be unaware of what the real purpose is; witness the NCI, NIH, CDC, and AMA. There now appears to be a movement afoot to retake the churches from control by the abortion industry; just as leadership in Washington is changing bureaucratic appointments of heads of government agencies.

"...65 members of the US House of Representatives and the US Senate...are also members of The United Methodist Church", so this potential shift in church doctrine does at least pose the possibility to change some minds there. President Bush also attends the Methodist church, and at the same time is an influential pro-life leader. But:

What do all the following people have in common: Patrick Leahy, Ted Kennedy, Christopher Dodd, Tom Daschle, Joseph Biden, John Kerry, Richard Durbin, Jack Reed, Patty Murray, Mary Landrieu, Barbara Mikulski, and Tom Harkin? You're right, they're all members of Congress, and they're all U.S. Senators. They're also all Democrats. They're all Liberals, too, although they might prefer to be called Progressives. The word liberal seems to have picked up some negative connotations, so they're in the process of renaming themselves. Personally, I would describe them as radical socialist leftists. In addition, they're all Catholics. And they're also all strongly pro-abortion. Add to that pro-abortion Republican and Catholic Senator Susan Collins. Without these people's support, and others like them, legalized abortion would cease to exist in this country. So, if you vote for these people because you know they're Catholic and assume they're pro-life, you should change your method of selection. I got these names through the Catholic American Life League, which ran an ad in the *Washington Times* newspaper on January 22, 2003, with a picture of each Senator labeled "Openly pro-abortion 'Catholic'"-with one exception.

That one exception is Dick Durbin, who was included in a previous ALL list, but not the ad. I know he meets the qualifications, so I racked my brain as to why he wouldn't be included. I came up with an explanation that satisfied me, but you can always contact ALL if it doesn't satisfy you. They ran the pictures in three rows, four pictures to a row, which they designated "THE DEADLY DOZEN". To run Durbin's picture they would have had to create a fourth row with just one picture-a poor use of the space. Durbin would have been a good candidate to drop because he's from the Midwest, and the ad ran in an East Coast paper-the coast where most of those included live. He doesn't have to run again for six years, and the ad would have little impact on him personally. Plus, I'm sure they had their own good reasons not to include him, but to keep Harkin, Murray, and Landrieu. The initial impetus for this tactic was apparently provided by an insight from Dr. Bernard Nathanson, who seems to have acquired some influence in the pro-life movement since converting to Catholicism; and sits on the American Bioethics Advisory Commission, together with 19 other M.D.'s, Ph.D.'s, J.D.'s (Doctor of Jurisprudence, or lawyer), a college professor and a Priest (Fr. Joseph Howard).

"Mrs. Brown wrote to each senator's bishop. Sen. Tom Daschle's bishop, Bishop Robert Carlson of Sioux Falls, reports Daschle seldom attends Mass, but when he does, he does not receive Holy Communion. Thus far, no other bishop has responded.

Just prior to the ad's publication, the Vatican issued a special statement reminding those in public office they have a duty to fight against legislation that attacks the dignity of human life

'Those who are directly involved in lawmaking bodies have a grave and clear obligation to oppose any law that attacks human life.' according to the statement, which adds that laws 'must defend the basic right to life from conception to natural death.'"
Taken from ALLNews, February 2003, Vol. 9 No. 2.

So it appears Daschle is a "Catholic in Name Only" (CINO).

"...three other members of the Senate who claim to be Catholic are pro-abortion. They are: Maria Cantwell (D-WA) Debbie Stabenow (D-MI), and Lisa Murkowski (R-AK)". From: rnclife, 1/23/2003.

As for Durbin, true to form, he voted against the ban on partial-birth abortion and against the nomination of Miguel Estrada. Very cleverly, preceding the vote, he proposed a pro-life amendment. If it had passed it would have killed the bill. However, he knew it had no chance of passage. But now he can play both sides of the issue and appear to be pro-life. He also voted for the amendment discussed below, so don't be confused by his obfuscation.

"14 Senate Catholics say Roe v. Wade must stay in place Before the U.S. Senate voted on the partial-birth infanticide bill, it tacked on an amendment. This amendment says the Roe v. Wade ruling that opened the abortion floodgates 'secures an important constitutional right' and 'should not be overturned.' Fourteen senators who claim to be faithful Catholics voted yes."
ALL NEWS, April, 2003. That's everybody named above except Debbie Stabenow.

Now then, according to what follows, they were complicit in a "gravely immoral", "serious sin", a "crime" under Canon Law, punishable by excommunication. Very serious charges, and I would imagine that anyone who voted for them knowing this would be complicit also. I can't accompany you into the voting booth, but you know who you are, and I would suppose God knows too.

It's not church policy that's at fault here-it's enforcement; and it's the people who keep reelecting them that are at fault. It's your country, and your religion. Read what follows, and then retake control of your country from the pretenders to your faith:

"Canon 1398 of the Catholic Church's Code of Canon Law says, 'A person who procures a completed abortion incurs an automatic excommunication.' The excommunication, Pope John Paul II said in his 1995 encyclical Evangelium Vitae (n.62), 'affects all those who commit this crime with knowledge of the penalty attached and thus includes those accomplices without whose help the crime would not have been committed.'

In his 1990 pastoral letter The Obligations of Catholics and the Rights of Unborn Children, Bishop John Myers of Peoria, IL, clearly stated the Church's position:

'One who supports legal abortion cannot avoid formal complicity by maintaining that he or she wills not abortion as such, but only the freedom of others to choose abortion. Anyone who supports legal abortion seeks to remove from one class of human beings a basic protection afforded to others. By helping to make abortion available, a person becomes formally complicit in its basic injustice whether or not he or she would actively encourage anyone else to have an abortion. From the ethical point of view, there is no distinction between being 'pro-choice' and being 'pro-abortion'...All formal cooperation in abortion is gravely immoral.'

In 1998, the American Catholic Bishops issued 'Living the Gospel of Life: A Challenge to American Catholics' in which they urged 'those Catholic officials who choose to depart from Church teaching on the inviolability of human life in their public life to consider the consequences for their own spiritual well-being, as well as the scandal they risk by leading others into serious sin.' (n.32)". Thanks to Colleen Parro, rnclife@swbell.net, for passing this along in the Republican National Coalition for Life FaxNotes November 22, 2002.

The American Life League also points out in its ad: "'Those who...obstinately persist in manifest grave sin are not to be admitted to communion.'" I think you share in this sin if you vote for the people you know to be pro-abortion-the people who vote against pro-life legislation; that is, legislation that attempts to restrict, defund, and criminalize abortion.

"Catholic Representatives Who Vote Pro-Abortion

Republicans: DE – Mike Castle; FL – Ginny Brown-Waite (new); and NY – Sherwood Boehlert.

Democrats: AZ – Ed Pastor; CA – Mike Thompson, George Miller, Nancy Pelosi, Ellen Tauscher, Anna Eshoo, Dennis Cardoza (new), Xavier Becerra, Diane Watson, Lucille Roybal-Allard, Grace Napolitano, Linda Sanchez (new), Joe Baca, Loretta Sanchez; CT – John Larson, Rosa DeLauro; IL – Luis Gutierrez, Lane Evans; IN – Peter Visclosky; MA – Richard Neal, James McGovern, Marty Meehan, Edward Markey, Michael Capuano, William Delahunt; MI – John Dingell; MN – Betty McCollum; MO – William Clay, Karen McCarthy; NJ – Frank Pallone, Robert Menendez; NY – Carolyn McCarthy, Joseph Crowley, Nydia Velasquez, Charles Rangel, Jose Serrano, Maurice Hinchey; OH – Marcy Kaptur; OR – Peter DeFazio; PA – Robert Brady; RI-Patrick Kennedy; TX – Nicholas Lampson, Ruben Hinojosa, Silvestre Reyes, Charles Gonzalez, Ciro Rodriguez; VA – James Moran; and WI – Jerry Kleczka, David Obey." National Right to Life Committee Scorecard – 107th Congress Contact: Colleen Parro – Phone: 972/387-3830 – Fax: 972/387-3830 – E-Mail: rnclife@swbell.net RNC for Life FaxNotes-January, 31, 2003

"The 'Doctrinal Note on Some Questions Regarding the Participation of Catholics in Political Life' recently issued by the Vatican has caused quite a stir among faithful Catholic pro-lifers and members of the media who follow such things. The document reminds Catholic Bishops, politicians, and voters alike of the Church's 'constant teaching,' reiterated once again by Pope John Paul II, 'that those who are directly involved in lawmaking bodies have a grave and clear obligation to oppose any law that attacks human life.' It further states that, 'what is at stake is the essence of the moral law' and points out that laws concerning abortion and euthanasia 'must defend the basic right to life from conception until natural death.' In addition, it points out the necessity to 'recall the duty to respect and protect the rights of the human embryo.'

In an unexpected move apparently motivated by the Vatican statement, the Bishop of Sacramento, CA, William K. Weigand, at a mass commemorating the 30th anniversary of Roe vs. Wade, denounced Governor Gray Davis' support of pro-abortion policies and called on him to renounce them or refrain from receiving Holy Communion. 'As your Bishop, I have to say clearly that anyone – politician or otherwise – who thinks it is acceptable for a Catholic to be pro-abortion is in very great error, puts his or her soul at risk, and is not in good standing with the church,' Weigand said. The Bishop added, 'Such a person should have the integrity to acknowledge this and choose of his own volition to abstain from receiving Holy Communion until he has a change of heart.' [Catholics believe that Jesus Christ is truly present in the Blessed Sacrament (Holy Communion) and that one must be free from sin (in the state of grace) in order to receive it. To be denied the Sacrament is a VERY big thing for a Catholic.] As expected, Governor Davis re-stated his support for 'a woman's right to choose.' What does it say about a public figure who rejects the central aspect of his faith?" Colleen Parro, RNC for Life FaxNotes-12/31/2002

"Davis Blamed for Cancelling Pro-Life Group's Use of Statehouse By Lawrence Morahan CNSNews.com Senior Staff Writer May 08, 2003

(CNSNews.com)-A pro-life organization is slamming California Gov. Gray Davis for cancelling the group's use of a room at the statehouse for a Wednesday news conference criticizing the governor and other elected officials over abortion, but blame is being passed around between offices connected with the event.

According to the American Life League (ALL), a Virginia-based pro-life organization, the Democratic governor's office pulled the plug on using the statehouse in Sacramento for a news conference Wednesday to unveil an advertisement critical of the state's lack of support for pro-life legislation. The apparent last-minute reversal came even though ALL claimed it had received permission to use the venue almost a month ago. At a news conference held in an alternate location Wednesday, ALL officials denounced the cancellation, claiming it was politically motivated. 'I wish I could honestly say I'm surprised by the actions of Gray Davis' office, but I am not,' said ALL President Judie Brown in a statement.

'I'm sure he'd have us believe this decision was an objective one that came at such a late time out of necessity, but that's as believable as his claim to be a faithful Catholic while openly supporting the murder of pre-born children through legalized abortion,' Brown said.

The pro-life group had scheduled the statehouse news conference to unveil a new ad being run in state newspapers that features what it calls 'California's Deadly Dozen'-a reference to Davis and 11 other elected officials from California who are Catholic but also support abortion 'rights' in one way or another. The Roman Catholic Church opposes abortion.

Among those listed in the ad along with Davis are Lt. Gov. Cruz Bustamante, U.S. Reps. Nancy Pelosi, Loretta and Linda Sanchez, and Diane Watson. 'These 12 California politicians claim to be Catholics, but their public support for the deadly practice of legalized abortion is scandalous in the eyes of the church,' the ad reads." She reminds me somewhat of Joan of Arc on a crusade.

"Even as a minister I am careful what I presume Jesus would do if he were alive today, but one thing I know from the Bible is that Jesus was not against women having a choice in continuing a pregnancy...Jesus was for peace on earth, justice on earth, compassion on earth, mercy on earth, and choice on earth." "'Reverend' Mark Bigelow of The Congregational Church of Huntington, United Church of Christ, in Centerport, New York, on the O'Reilly Factor on December 2, 2002, who serves on the Planned Parenthood Federation of America's Clergy Advisory Board". "...on FreeRepublic.com's forum...One...participant wrote, 'Someone should ask this pseudo-Rev...this question'What would Mary do?'" All the above was courtesy of the December 2002 Center for Bio-Ethical Reform glossy circular put out by Gregg Cunningham, where everything is nicely referenced with Roman numerals to its source.

You probably won't see what follows in the headlines:

"A rabbinical court in Brooklyn has taken the unusual step of excommunicating Senator Joseph I. Lieberman, the democratic vice-presidential hopeful, over his stances on homosexuality and partial birth abortion. Cybercast News Service reported on 10/24/00 that a specially-convened New York Torah Court said Mr. Lieberman had caused 'grave scandal' for Judaism. 'While claiming to be an observant Jew, Lieberman has been misrepresenting and falsifying to the American people the teachings of the Torah against partial-birth infanticide...' the news service quoted the court as saying." Source: Republican National Coalition for Life

To put it succinctly, Christians and Catholics who support or ignore abortion are no better than the Germans who turned their backs on the extermination of Jews during World War II; and Jews who support, or do, abortions, are no better than the Nazis who gunned down and gassed their relatives. Are you listening, Joe Lieberman? Because you wear your religion on your sleeve like it makes you special, while in fact you are a disgrace to your religion and people. That's why they excommunicated you.

"Many rabbis and devout Orthodox Jews asked me to cry out...I don't care if Joe Lieberman mentions God's name 13 times in 90 seconds, or speaks biblically and in Hebrew. He is diametrically opposed to Orthodox Judaism's uncompromising stands on life and decency. And he remains excommunicated. Excommunicated. No matter how many political rabbis he may trot out, the only kind of orthodox Joe Lieberman is, is an orthodox liberal." Rabbi Yehuda Levin, speaking on the Washington Mall, to the March For Life participants, on the 30th anniversary of Roe v Wade, 01/22/2003.

Intecon

From: The Pro-Life Infonet Steven Ertelt infonet@prolifeinfo.org
Source: Cardinal Newman Society; December 9, 2002

"Catholic Universities Under Fire for Promoting Abortion, Planned Parenthood

Washington, DC—Seven Catholic universities and colleges in the United States which promote Planned Parenthood on their websites are coming under intense scrutiny. Recently, San Francisco University received criticism for links on its student health web site promoting Planned Parenthood and a facility that performs abortions. After receiving letters from pro-life Catholics, the university pulled the links temporarily to review them. Following the decision, pro-life Catholics have focused on other Catholic university web sites that include links to Planned Parenthood or abortion facilities. DePaul University in Chicago, founded in 1898 by the Vincentians, boasts of being 'The largest Catholic university in the nation.' However, DePaul not only links to the pro-abortion Planned Parenthood but goes even further offering its students internships with the pro-abortion organization. (See links verifying DePaul's Planned Parenthood internships: http://condor.depaul.edu/~soc/undergraduate_descriptions.htm)

Georgetown University in the nation's capital prides itself on being 'founded in 1789' and 'the nation's oldest Catholic and Jesuit university.' Nonetheless, the Georgetown website links to the Planned Parenthood Federation of America, it also suggests the use of the morning after pill in case of rape. (See Georgetown's sexual health site: http://www.georgetown.edu/student-affairs/healthed/sex.htm)

Loyola University in Chicago is one of the largest of the 28 Jesuit universities and colleges in the United States. Besides linking to Planned Parenthood, the university's women's studies website links to the pro-abortion political group National Organization for Women.
(See: http://www.luc.edu/depts/women_stu/links.html)

Santa Clara University in California, founded in 1851 by the Society of Jesus, not only links to Planned Parenthood on its Medical Assistance website, but explains clearly that 'Planned Parenthood provides services including family planning, pregnancy testing, prenatal care, cancer screening, surgical sterilization, abortion.'
(See:http://www.scu.edu/SCU/Projects/SourceBook/Medical/content.htm)

288

Seattle University in Washington links to Planned Parenthood for 'wellness' services, the students are urged to 'activism' with groups such as the pro-abortion "National Organization for Women."
(See: http://www.seattleu.edu/wismer/links.htm and
http://www.seattleu.edu/student/wellness/Resources2001v2.html)

Two other Catholic institutions, Boston College and John Carroll University in Cleveland also offer their students links to Planned Parenthood offices from the university websites.
(See: http://www.bc.edu/bc_org/svp/house/offcampus/phone.htm and
http://www.jcu.edu/studentl/HealthServices/information.htm)

Patrick J. Reilly, president of the Cardinal Newman Society, dedicated to the renewal of Catholic identity in Catholic higher education, criticized the Catholic schools links to abortion agencies. 'In Ex Corde Ecclesiae, one of the requirements of a Catholic university is that all official actions and commitments must be in accord with the university's Catholic identity,' said Reilly. 'Anything that would appear or be announced or promoted by the university's website or professors is an official action. By promoting Planned Parenthood or taking any step that might drive students towards Planned Parenthood for an abortion is not only a violation of Ex Corde Ecclesiae but a scandal and a terrible crime against these young women. The Society, which is backed by ten U. S. bishops and archbishops and counts among its spiritual advisers, Rev. Benedict Groeschel, and Rev. Richard John Neuhaus, works towards the faithful implementation of Pope John Paul II's 1990 constitution Ex Corde Ecclesiae 'On Catholic Universities'. All Catholic colleges and universities are encouraged to provide web site links to local crisis pregnancy centers, national CPC web sites such as www.pregnancycenters.org or to pro-life groups."

And I certainly concur, that to help someone in any way to get an abortion is to implicate yourself in the crime. I checked out the college web sites mentioned above, on 01/04/03; and Georgetown, Santa Clara, Boston College, and John Carroll, had shown some class by cleaning up their web sites. However, Loyola, DePaul, and Seattle, didn't seem to have found it necessary to make any changes-so I suppose they must be "special".

"It is clear that university centers that do not respect the Church's laws and the teaching of the Magisterium, especially in bioethics, cannot be defined as Catholic universities." Pope John Paul II, The Vatican; December 5, 2002; at the conference on "Globalization and Catholic Universities".

"Cybercast News Service Abortion Supporters to Speak at Catholic College Graduations By Steve Brown CNSNews.com Staff Writer May 09, 2003

(CNSNews.com)-A collection of pro-Catholic and cultural conservative groups are complaining about the speakers who have been invited to Saturday's commencement ceremony at Los Angeles' all-female Mt. Saint Mary's College. A protest is planned for the appearance of U.S. Reps. Loretta and Linda Sanchez, sisters and ardent abortion rights defenders.

'Mt. Saint Mary's claims to be a Catholic college, and one would think, given that if they want to call themselves Catholic, they might invite people who reflect Catholic values,' Joseph Starrs, director of the American Life League's (ALL) Crusade for the Defense of Our Catholic Church, told CNSNews.com. The protest is scheduled for Saturday from 2-3:30 p.m. at the Mt. Saint Mary's College-Chalon Campus.

Since 1999, Loretta Sanchez has voted 100 percent of the time with pro-abortion or abortion rights advocates such as Planned Parenthood and the National Abortion Reproductive Rights Action League, and zero percent with the pro-life National Right to Life Committee, according to the self-described 'unbiased' non-profit group Project Vote Smart.

Sibling freshman Congresswoman Linda Sanchez, while not having had the chance yet to vote on an abortion-related issue, did work for the National Organization for Women (NOW) Legal Defense and Education Fund-an organization with an established pro-abortion stance. In an article for Women's Enews, an online news publication funded by NOW, Linda Sanchez was quoted as saying, 'With the House, Senate and White House all in Republican hands, I am very concerned about women's reproductive health and a woman's right to choose. 'Over time, we have seen a subtle but pernicious erosion of Roe v. Wade,' Linda Sanchez said in the article, referring to the 1973 U.S. Supreme Court decision that legalized abortion during all nine months of pregnancy.

'You cannot be both Catholic and pro-abortion,' Judie Brown, president of ALL, said in a release. 'These women have built their careers on a platform that flies in the face of what the Catholic Church teaches on the sanctity of life.'

'Their ongoing assault on the unborn and on traditional values make them not only ineligible to be speakers at a Catholic college, it's an outrage that they would even be invited to a Catholic college to speak,' Starrs said. 'One would think that they would want to invite speakers who would uphold the dignity of women, but instead, they invite two people who are doing everything they can to degrade women and make sure that fewer women are born.'

The Mt. Saint Mary's controversy is part of a trend of Catholic colleges inviting pro-abortion legislators to speak at commencement, according to the Cardinal Newman Society, one of the organizations participating in Saturday's protest of the Sanchez sisters' appearance.

In a May 7 release, the society said it had identified 16 Catholic colleges that had invited 'inappropriate' speakers for commencement ceremonies, including New York City Mayor Michael Bloomberg, slated to speak at the College of Saint Rose in Albany, N. Y., and MSNBC's Hardball host Chris Matthews, invited to address graduates of the College of the Holy Cross in Worcester, Mass. Both have argued in favor of abortion rights.

'It's shameful that 16 Catholic colleges and universities would invite scandal by honoring abortion-rights advocates and other inappropriate speakers and nominees,' said Patrick Reilly, president of the society, in the release. 'Certainly, they realize that there are thousands of upstanding, admirable people out there who deserve these honors.'"

"Athlete Chooses Life, is Thrown off Team Tara Brady, 21, is an athlete, but her son comes first. Her decision to give birth to the baby she conceived out of wedlock resulted in dismissal from Sacred Heart University's basketball team, revocation of her scholarship and being forced out of school. Brady has filed a civil rights lawsuit against Sacred Heart accusing the school of violating Title IX. As a school that receives federal funding, Sacred Heart is subject to a Title IX regulation that forbids discrimination based on pregnancy in school programs.

Brady is astonished that Sacred Heart University, a Roman Catholic school, punished her for choosing to complete her pregnancy. 'I have been against abortion since the first time I learned about it,' she said. 'This may sound stupid, but the way I look at it is God will forgive the premarital sex more than he would killing my child. But if I had an abortion, I'd still be on the team.' Brady appealed the school's decision and her scholarship was reinstated and she was allowed back on the basketball team.

Her pride and joy, Sean, is now 14 months old and is a chronic smiler. 'My son is absolutely amazing. He's the cutest thing ever,' Brady said. 'He's the happiest person I ever met. I can come home and basketball can be going badly or I can do badly on a test, but I see him and everything is fine.'" Life Dynamics News, May 2003

Good reasoning, and a good decision not to have an abortion, Brady. But I can kind of see the school's possible point of view too, on getting pregnant in the first place-team discipline, training rules, bad example, poor behavior, and so on, is how it might go. And the coach not being able to finish the season because all her players are pregnant.

"Abortion: A Religious or a Political Issue? Some say that opposition to abortion is a religious issue and because of the Constitutional separation of church and state it doesn't belong in the political process. This is, of course, nonsense. First, the term 'separation of church and state' appears nowhere in the Constitution. Second, it is a scientific reality that the unborn child is a living human being, and a person doesn't have to be religious to conclude that he or she shouldn't be murdered. Just because the pro-life position is embraced by people of faith does not make abortion a religious issue. The fact is that abortion is a civil rights and a human rights issue. The 'separation of church and state' rhetoric is an example of how our society applies a different standard to abortion than to any other issue. There is a Biblical Commandment, 'Thou shalt not steal,' but no one is screaming that laws against theft are religious. There is also a Biblical mandate to take care of the poor, but you don't hear welfare being called a religious issue and none of the government's business. And when people of faith demonstrate against the death penalty, war or racism, or speak out for animal rights or environmental causes, you don't see a lot of hand wringing about the separation of church and state. At the same time that politicians are telling us abortion is a religious issue and doesn't belong in politics, preachers are telling us that it's a political issue and doesn't belong in the church. Meanwhile, the little bodies keep piling up." Taken from Life Dynamics News, February 2003.

Gianna Jessen, Carol Everett, and Generation Y

From: The Pro-Life Infonet Steven Ertelt infonet@prolifeinfo.org
Source: New Hampshire Union Leader; January 22, 2003

Abortion Survivor Tells her Story of Struggles and Triumph

Some kids don't know when to quit. Gianna Jessen never learned how. By her own account she came into this world under extraordinary circumstances, having already suffered brain damage due to oxygen deprivation. She was diagnosed with cerebral palsy by doctors who would later be amazed that she could sit up, much less walk. At 25, she walks with a pronounced limp and admits to frequent and unexpected falls. She doesn't mind telling audiences she has gotten rather good at it over the years.

"After 25 years of falling, you learn how to fall," she said at St. Joseph Cathedral in Manchester, where she was anything but a "flop." The talented singer and songwriter from Nashville, Tenn. sang some devotional songs, then told her story as the keynote speaker during a pro-life rally that was part of a weekend-long "Triduum for Life" sponsored by the Respect Life Office of the Roman Catholic Diocese of Manchester.

"This will not be a sad story, this will be a story of triumph and victory," she said early on in her narrative. She has been on the speaking circuit since her early teens, telling her story with, literally, a missionary zeal. But for the grace of God, she might be counted in the world only as a number, one of the 40 million or so infants who have been aborted since the Supreme Court's Roe v. Wade decision was handed down 30 years ago today. Jessen was, indeed, aborted. But stubborn and determined soul that she is, she lived anyway. A quarter of a century later, she is still going strong. "And still talking about it," she said, suggesting a possible title for a sequel to the biography that was published several years ago: "Gianna: Aborted and lived to tell about it."

Her mother was 17 years old and 7½ months pregnant when she had a saline abortion at a Planned Parenthood clinic in Los Angeles. In the saline method, a highly concentrated salt solution is injected throughout the abdominal wall into the amniotic fluid surrounding the baby. The solution poisons the infant, causing convulsion and, in about an hour's time, death. In most cases, the woman goes into labor 24 hours later and delivers the dead baby. The solution usually burns the skin off the infant, resulting in the delivery of the "candy-apple baby" often seen in pro-life literature.

That photograph is accompanied by a remarkable understatement on a page published by the Society for the Protection of Unborn Children. Concerning the level of pain likely suffered by the saline-aborted fetus, the society suggests the following: "The contortion on the face of this baby, after the burning of the skin by the salt solution, may be an indication of what the infant has endured."

Somehow Jessen was spared that fate. Her mother went into labor well ahead of the expected delivery time, though long after her baby was supposed to be dead. Gianna was born alive, weighing slightly more than two pounds. The abortionist had gone home for the night and the nurse on duty took the newborn to a hospital where she was placed in an incubator.

"If the abortionist had been there, he would have ended my life, either though strangulation, or he would have left me there to die," said Jessen, who counts it a miracle that she survived the saline treatment. "I should be completely burned, I should be blind, I should be dead."

She spent her infancy with a foster mother named Penny, a rather remarkable woman in her own right. "Over the course of her life she's cared for 56 children considered unadoptable. Eventually, Penny's daughter, Diane, adopted Gianna. It was Diane who found the child's natural mother and learned the details of Gianna's birth.

Jessen was present when President Bush signed the Born Alive Infants Protection Act into law in Pittsburgh last summer. So was Jill Stanek, the nurse who was fired from Christ Hospital and Medical Center in Oak Lawn, Ill. after testifying before Congress about an aborted infant left to die in the hospital's laundry room. Jessen has also told her story at congressional hearings, before church groups, youth outreach programs and on college campuses. She has even begun to get speaking engagements in public schools, where she seems likely to create some controversy, and even legal battles over church-state separation, by her vocal witness to the "loving power of Jesus Christ."

She is, however, familiar with struggles, in her own life and those she has read about in the Bible. Like Jacob, the patriarch of Israel, she recalls a time in her own life of a spiritual wrestling with God and of saying, "I will not let you go until you bless me." Jacob, too, walked with a limp.

"From: The Pro-Life Infonet Steven Ertelt infonet@prolifeinfo.org
Source: Lewisville (TX) Newspaper; February 22, 2003

Former Abortion Facility Director Reveals Abortion's Inside Scoop By Bob Weir

|Pro-Life Infonet Note: Bob Weir is a Texas-based syndicated columnist and author of four books.|

On a bitter cold Sunday morning, my wife and I went to Lakeland Baptist Church in Lewisville to pay our respects to God and to hear another motivating sermon from our pastor, Dr. Ben Smith.

However, on this day Brother Ben relinquished his pulpit to a woman named Carol Everett. Ms. Everett is the author of 'Blood Money,' an expose of the abortion industry. For more than 20 minutes, this former abortion provider electrified the congregation with the true stories of tactics used and lies disseminated by the pro-choice cartel that has systematically robbed our country of the moral and spiritual fiber that kept us united for more than 200 years.

Tearfully explaining that she was involved in about 35,000 abortions, she chokes up when revealing that she aborted one of her own 30 years ago. 'That was, and always will be, my daughter,' she cried. 'I still celebrate her birthday each year.'

Painting a horrifying picture of the greed, cynicism, and coldblooded preoccupation with selling abortion as a lucrative product, Ms. Everett admitted her role in gaining the confidence of girls as young as 12, in order to separate them from their most important support group, their parents.

'First, I established myself as an authority on sex, explaining to them that their parents wouldn't help them with their sexuality. Second, our doctors prescribed low-dose birth-control pills with a high pregnancy rate, fully aware that they needed to be taken very accurately at the same time every day or pregnancy would occur. This ensured the teens would be my best customers, as teenagers typically are not responsible enough to follow such rigid medication guidelines on their own. I knew their sexual activity would increase from none or once a week to five or seven times a week once they were introduced to this contraception method. Then I could reach my goal: three to five abortions for each teenager between the ages of 13 and 18.'

Ms. Everett spelled out in grisly detail the despicable system of encouraging promiscuity among teenagers in order to trick them into unplanned pregnancies then scare them into having abortions, while doctors and their partners in the avaricious enterprise split up the profits. And huge profits they are: thousands of dollars per hour, according to the author/lecturer.

295

Operating like a homicidal assembly line, the medical team aborts a child in room A, then scurries across the hall to room B, where their staff has prepared the next pitiful victim of a country that has lost its way. We're often told that the pro-choice movement is based on a political philosophy of female empowerment. What kind of female seeks power by snuffing out the life of a child? The very idea that the only route to power for the women of America is the power over their ovaries is extremely demeaning. Some of the most successful leaders in the history of the world were also mothers.

I'm afraid we have been sold a bill of goods by the multibillion-dollar abortion industry, which has become, in many instances, a scheming, crafty, organized group of hustlers dedicated to enriching the bank accounts of the 'blood money' practitioners. Ms. Everett's personal experiences puts the lie to the appellation 'pro-choice.' Using the innocuous-sounding metaphor is merely another deliberate obfuscation masking the true intent, which is pro-death. Thirty years ago, the Supreme Court legalized abortion, but they never intended it to be a substitute for conscientious birth control or a license for degenerate behavior.

The steady erosion of values in the last three decades cannot be viewed as coincidental. When the heart and soul of a nation becomes so callous that a living, growing fetus struggling to be born, can't rely on the protection of its mother, why should we be surprised at the devaluation of human life in other instances? How can we consider ourselves to be a proud and just people, if we refuse to stand up for the most helpless among us? Furthermore, how can we stand by and allow people to become wealthy by encouraging pregnancy to our children, then tearing the results from their womb and discarding it like a glob of human waste?

If Ms. Everett can have the courage to turn her life around, there is still hope for the rest of the country."

"'Generation Y' are America's youth currently between the ages of 7 and 22. They are the children of the Baby Boomers. And, get this, there are 60 million of them. That's nearly four times the number of 17 million Generation Xers. The opinions they form on crucial social and political issues will influence our nation's leaders…Over the last couple of years, research from various sources is showing that Generation Y kids are fundamentally pro-life and conservative regarding family values. The most recent was a study by UC Berkeley (never known for its pro-life leanings). They interviewed over 1,000 randomly chosen Americans nationwide. The result regarding abortion was not what they expected. 44% of Generation Y kids responded pro-life…There's more. In just two years, at the time of our next presidential election, 30 million of them will be voting age. Who would have thought that children, growing up watching M-TV and other sex-saturated television-youth who have seen many

of their older predecessors treat sex as a casual recreational activity—would seemingly take a stand against abortion and for family values. Some researchers believe that these latchkey kids who have grown up in broken homes are searching for a more stable life for themselves and their children. This data and other encouraging research have shaken Planned Parenthood and the rest of the abortion industry." John C. Willke, M.D., President Life Issues Institute, "Serving The Educational Needs of the Pro-Life Movement." 11/22/2002
http://www.lifeissues.org/

Kids growing up are quick to see the hypocrisy and mistakes in what their parents and older siblings do-and learn from it. And I can't help but believe that any study done at UC Berkeley would be slanted against getting the results they got; which means the true percentage is probably higher than what their study showed. And isn't it interesting to see the different factions competing for 7 year olds? These are not just casual philosophical differences we're talking about, but a deadly serious business.

"'Abortion isn't a rights issue; it's become for increasing numbers of young people a moral, ethical issue,' said Henry Brady, a professor of political science and public policy at the University of California at Berkeley who has conducted surveys on the topic." From Life Dynamics News, May, 2003. Like "Thou shalt not kill."?

"A Zogby International poll taken this past December found that 32 percent of Americans changed their opinions on abortion during the last decade, with 21 percent becoming more pro-life. And among those surveyed, more than two-thirds said that they would strongly advise any pregnant woman not to have an abortion. In more good news for the pro-life movement, the strongest opposition to abortion came from people in the youngest age groups." Life Dynamics News, February 2003

"'Midge & Baby' is part of Mattel's 'Happy Family' line of dolls. The Midge doll has a nine-months-pregnant belly that comes off to reveal a removable baby. Midge is in a maternity dress and comes with a variety of miniature baby care product toys...doll became so embroiled in controversy that Wal-Mart pulled it off the shelves...Some women's rights extremists whined that Midge might encourage girls to get pregnant by glorifying motherhood. Since these are the same people who are getting rich doing abortions on teens, that was obviously not their real motivation. So what's the real problem with Midge? Well, you see, the baby in her removable tummy is the same one she also carries in her arms. And abortion enthusiasts find that intolerable. After all, if girls learn that pregnancy goes hand-in-hand with babies and motherhood, America's abortionists might lose some future customers." Life

Intecon

Dynamics News, February 2003. The perfect toy for the little girl whose mother is expecting.

Jill Stanek, Lisa Madigan, and Peter Fitzgerald-Illinois

Jill Stanek, for Illinois State Representative from the 81st District. This is the nurse who persevered in her fight against live birth abortions being performed at Christ Hospital in Oak Lawn, Illinois, until, and after, she was fired from the hospital. This race will be decided by the mid-March primary. She is running against a staunchly pro-abortion, and well funded, opponent, who sits on the governing council of Christ Hospital. Jill's testimony to the U.S. House Judiciary Committee "led to the introduction of the Born-Alive Infants Protection Act." Jill Stanek 2002, 20017 S. Wolf Road, Suite 1 North, Mokena, IL, 60448, (708) 479-8230. http://www.jillstanek2002.com/

"I was told about an aborted baby who was supposed to have spina bifida but was delivered with an intact spine...an aborted baby who came out weighing much more than expected—almost two pounds...baby was accidentally thrown into the garbage, and when they later were going through the trash to find the baby, the baby fell...onto the floor...After the death of babies who briefly survive live-birth abortion, their remains are taken to the hospital morgue—where all our dead patients are taken...Something is very wrong with a legal system that says doctors are mandated to pronounce babies dead but are not mandated to assess babies for life and chance of survival...We look the other way and pretend that these babies aren't human while they're alive but human only after they are dead...I felt like the only sane person in an insane asylum ...I wondered how no one else could see this the way I saw it. I could never get past the thought that if I quit...I would be leaving babies to die". Jill Stanek "As Jill continued to speak out, she just blossomed...courage and fearlessness ...cost her a job she loved...What started out for Jill as a scary thing became one of the greatest adventures of her life". Sandy Rios, CWA

"Meanwhile, the Born-Alive Infants Protection Act of 2001 passed both houses of Congress by overwhelming margins. During the first session of the 107th Congress, it was inserted into the Patients' Bill of Rights, which now awaits Negotiations...Sen. Ted Kennedy (D-Massachusetts) could possibly scuttle the bill". Jonathan Imbody "I give Jill so much credit...Even when she found out there were no laws prohibiting the practice, she worked to get laws on the books...If it weren't for that one woman, we wouldn't have this legislation today." Wendy Wright, Family Voice Jill was unable to unseat her 20-year entrenched incumbent opponent, "...who, during the last two weeks of the campaign claimed to be 'pro-life' even though her record clearly showed her pro-abortion stance. This created great confusion among the voters." RNCL PAC (With Jill's testimony, the Born-Alive Infants Protection Act was passed by the Congress, and signed into law by President Bush. One person can make a difference.) People had been trying, unsuccessfully, to get that legislation passed for years. To use a football analogy, when Jill picked up the ball, she had blockers ahead of her all the way to Congress. Locally, in Illinois, Patrick O'Malley played a crucial role, but there were people in the U.S. Congress, too, who saw that she got to give her testimony. It became an idea whose time had come. I believe the Peterson murder case in California will play an equally effective role in getting legislation passed.

Joe Birkett is running for Illinois Attorney General against a blatantly pro-abortion opponent. Citizens to Elect Joe Birkett, P.O. Box 792, Wheaton, IL 60189-(630) 690-7100 http://www.joebirkett.com/

From: The Pro-Life Infonet infonet@prolifeinfo.org
Reply-To: Steven Ertelt infonet@prolifeinfo.org
Source: Chicago Tribune; September 17, 2002

Illinois Atty General Race Focuses on Abortion

Springfield, IL—The issue of abortion took center stage in the Illinois attorney general's race Sunday as pro-abortion Democrat Lisa Madigan accused pro-life Republican Joe Birkett of "exploiting breast cancer for political purposes" because he backs a state study to examine whether a link exists between abortions and breast cancer. But Birkett, who opposes, contended further study is warranted because "it's a legitimate issue that should be resolved." With the two candidates in a close race, Madigan's campaign believes the contenders' sharp differences on abortion could translate into votes for her among women who live in the suburbs, which is Birkett's geographical base of support. Abortion opponents have stepped up efforts to gain legislative support on the state and national level for physician warnings and government studies on abortion and breast cancer. Pro-abortion groups have countered that those pushing such efforts are more concerned about frightening women than protecting their health. The American Cancer Society and the National Cancer Institute consider as suspect any linkage between abortion and breast cancer. However, the groups' positions are fraught with politics as most of the decision makers support abortion. Madigan said Birkett, in response to a candidate questionnaire from the Illinois Federation for Right to Life, answered "yes" when asked by the group if he would "support legislation that would establish a task force to study the link between abortion and breast cancer." That answer, she said, shows Birkett is out of touch with the mainstream and with scientific research. "I will be an active attorney general who will defend and protect women's reproductive rights against all of its attackers," she said at a news conference at Planned Parenthood's offices in Chicago.

"Illinois Atty General Race is a Virtual Tie With just 11 days until voters go to the polls, the race to become Illinois' top law enforcement officer is a toss-up, threatening to be a nailbiter right up to election night. After months of

300

campaigning, pro-abortion candidate Lisa Madigan was leading pro-life candidate Joe Birkett 43 percent to 42 percent in the attorney general's race—a statistical dead heat, according to a Chicago SunTimes/Fox News Chicago Poll." Pro-Life Infonet; October 27, 2002 Madigan is totally unqualified for the position. Birkett has a wealth of experience. But Madigan's father is one of the most powerful Democratic politicians in the state, and people recognize the connection. Machine politics still runs Chicago and turns out the voters. It's not a question of whether that's good or bad; it's just the way things are, and that's the background.

From: The Pro-Life Infonet infonet@prolifeinfo.org
Reply-To: Steven Ertelt infonet@prolifeinfo.org
Source: Illinois Leader; October 28, 2002

Illinois Atty General Candidate Pledges to Attack Pregnancy Centers

Springfield, IL—The Northside Women's Center, a crisis pregnancy center, will be targeted by pro-abortion candidate Lisa Madigan if she becomes the next Attorney General.

But one CPC leader says she won't back down if Madigan follows the lead of pro-abortion elected officials in California and New York and attacks her center. "I will be Lisa Madigan's worst enemy on this," Sue Davinger, executive director of Pregnancy Aid South Suburbs said today as she stepped out of her role at the Tinley Park facility to speak out against Madigan. Madigan faces pro-life candidate Joe Birkett, who is backed by numerous pro-life groups. The two are locked in a tight battle.

Madigan pledged to "go after phony crisis pregnancy centers that don't offer abortions," following the lead of New York Attorney General Elliot Spitzer, who used his office in an attempt to shut down crisis pregnancy centers. Pro-abortion candidates for attorney general are increasingly agreeing to take part in a campaign by the pro-abortion group NARAL which has enlisted their help in an attempt to shut down as many pregnancy help centers as possible. These centers have been responsible for providing women with practical resources to choose abortion alternatives and, ultimately, are in competition with the hundreds of abortion facilities across the country.

"Lisa Madigan is not 'pro-choice,' she is 'pro-abortion,'" Sue Davinger said today. "She wants to eliminate a woman's right to have a choice to be informed and to protect her health. Madigan wants to promote abortion and the killing of unborn babies." "Her goal is to suppress knowledge of alternatives to abortion to these women in crisis pregnancies," Davinger said.

"She has failed women and I am taking her on right now, I will be her worst enemy."

Davinger said Madigan's threat to pregnancy crisis centers should be taken seriously by people who care about unborn children and the promotion of adoption in Illinois. Madigan's commitment to begin an all-out attack on pregnancy crisis centers is confirmed by Illinois' most well-funded radical pro-abortion group called Personal PAC, a group that fully supports Madigan. Personal PAC has listed on its website several issues that will be affected by whoever is elected attorney general. Personal PAC says that the new Attorney General will "enforce laws on behalf of the state, including punishing fake abortion clinics established by anti-choice activists to intimidate women out of having abortions."

Madigan says, "Every year, anti-choice forces try to roll back the protections afforded to women under our Constitution. And every year, Personal PAC works with pro-choice leaders to uphold our constitutional right to reproductive choice." "I am proud to stand with Personal PAC in defense of a woman's right to choose," Madigan is quoted on the Personal PAC website as saying, "...I deeply appreciate the assistance of Personal PAC in making sure that [her pro-life opponent Joe Birkett] is defeated..."

"Nothing surprises me that comes from Lisa Madigan on the abortion issue," Bonnie Quirke, president of Illinois Federation for Right to Life said. "Pro-lifers in Illinois have every reason to be afraid of what Lisa Madigan will do if she is elected as Attorney General." "If she plans on taking on pregnancy crisis centers throughout Illinois, she is taking on the crown jewels of the pro-life movement," Quirke said. "Pregnancy crisis centers serve women in crisis with positive alternatives at a crucial time in their lives."

Former Illinois State Representative Penny Pullen explained further that "the abortion lobby's definition of 'phony' is anybody that won't commit abortions." "Illinois citizens still have an opportunity to head off a similar search-and-destroy mission in their state's chief law enforcement office," Pullen said. "The contest between Miss Madigan and her pro-life GOP opponent Joe Birkett is rated a 'dead heat.'"

"Lisa Madigan is touting Planned Parenthood and NARAL rhetoric. She hasn't familiarized herself with the work that goes on at crisis pregnancy centers throughout the state," Davinger said. "She has betrayed the 15 to 20 thousand women a year who seek help and find help at the pregnancy crisis centers throughout Illinois."

Lisa Madigan was the winner in that race. For Joe Birkett it was a matter of not having enough campaign funds to counter the distortions in her advertising. I think it's a tragedy. Joe Birkett had been a prosecutor for 21 years, and was the State's Attorney for Dupage County, one of the "collar counties" adjacent to Chicago. Madigan had worked for only four years at a law firm where she had never even argued a case in court. She lacks the experience, judgement, and temperament to be the state's top law enforcement officer. I would guess she will be a figurehead, making the political decisions. She will also make unnecessary mistakes. One of the first mistakes she will make is to try to shut down the crisis pregnancy centers in the state. Some of the finest lawyers in the country will trip over each other to get to represent the CPC's. There will be a different team for each organization, and she will soon find herself tying up a large portion of her staff on an unpopular campaign that she has no chance of winning.

Even people who are pro-abortion aren't opposed to the free services offered by these organizations. After all, that's truly having a choice. Plus, it's poor planning from a personal point of view. She's 36, engaged, and running out of time to have a family. She's not even going to be there because she's going to be on maternity leave part of her tenure. My oldest daughter's pregnant too. But she's been realistic about it and made arrangements for someone to take her place at work; and she's not in charge. Lisa should have waited four years, had her kids, and then run. Like I said, I expect her to be a figurehead, and to make more mistakes.

"While the elections earlier this month bode well for the Congress and many state legislators, the situation in Illinois has turned ugly, at best. The victor in the Attorney General's race here in Illinois is a vehement abortion supporter who had vowed before the election to 'crack down' on pregnancy centers that did not offer abortion or abortion referral". Conrad Wojnar, Executive Director The Women's Center, 5116 North Cicero Avenue, Chicago, Illinois 60630 (773) PRO-LIFE or (773) 794-1313, e-mail: wc@womens-center.org. Conrad manages several locations in the Chicago metro area. http://www.womens-center.org/

"I hope that you accept my best wishes for a happy and blessed New Year. I say I hope you accept my best wishes because I'm not sure that you would want to accept the sentiments of a 'phony' like me. I founded and have run a 'phony' crisis pregnancy center for 19 years, so I figure that makes me a phony. At first, I was a little uncomfortable with that terminology because it was assigned to us by the incoming Attorney General for the State of Illinois, Lisa Madigan. Ms. Madigan has labeled pro-life crisis pregnancy centers like The Women's Center, 'phony centers' because we don't perform abortions. If that makes the Women's Center and me 'phonies,' I'm very pleased to accept her label as a compliment of the highest order! *Attorney General Madigan has said publicly that she's gunning for organizations like The Women's Center-she wants to put us out of business. In her warped view, it should be illegal for people to offer women in crisis pregnancies any answer other than abortion.* But what can we expect from a politician who is 'owned' by the liberal elites from NOW, Planned Parenthood and NARAL? It is a sad situation when a 'practicing Catholic' seems to have sold her own soul for temporal earthly aggrandizement...what really matters to me is the well-being of our clients and their babies. That concern holds true not only for me but for all of our staff and volunteers." Conrad Wojnar, Executive Director, The Women's Center, in a letter, January, 2003. Easy Conrad, you have more friends than Lisa realizes. Good luck with your new center serving Northwestern University. Conrad's parting shot: "*The phonies can be found at those abortion mills that don't care about a pregnant woman's problems, just the color of the money in her pockets...abortion is never the answer-it just adds to a woman's anguish.*"

Conrad recently returned from Australia. A group setting up a CPC down under flew him in (through Europe to save money) to help them get started, because The Women's Center has such a fine record (about 2,000 lives saved per year). Apparently not all CPCs are equal. It's one thing to have a woman come to you because she wants to continue her pregnancy, but quite a different matter when she wants an abortion. So it's quite obvious why the abortion providers would like to shut Conrad down-$500 X 2,000 = about $1,000,000 in business he takes from them each year-probably a lot more than they put into Lisa's campaign. He charges each one of his clients zero dollars, figures out what he can do to help them; with supplies from his storeroom, with advice, with references for whatever other services they might need, to find work, and spiritually, too, if they're so inclined. His signature is as good as money some places. Ideally, they'll try to straighten out relationship problems for the girls, too; and plan for the future. And this is only one Illinois CPC organization.

"I view partial-birth abortion as a particularly inhumane procedure. Partial-birth abortion, also referred to as intrauterine cranial decompression, is truly gruesome." Illinois Senator Peter G. Fitzgerald, October 9, 2002

"In the name of common decency, humanity, and hope for a better nation, I implore my colleagues not to allow partial-birth abortions to continue in America." Senator Peter G. Fitzgerald, February, 2003

Dred Scott

I strongly believe that "those who fail to study history are doomed to repeat its mistakes". Now I imagine that's a paraphrase, and although I have a strong interest in history, I can't tell you whom I'm paraphrasing. I had this same problem when I first read President Reagan's "Abortion and the Conscience of the Nation", http://www.humanlifereview.com/reagan/reagan_conscience.html, when he compared the Dred Scott decision to Roe v Wade-I didn't recall exactly what Dred Scott was all about, although I knew it had something to do with slavery. Later, debating on the About.com forum, I would realize that it was necessary for me to familiarize myself with it. Here's some of what I found out:

"In March 1857 the court ruled in a 7 to 2 decision that Scott was still a slave and therefore not entitled to sue in court. For the first time in history, each of the nine justices on the court wrote an opinion in the same case, explaining their various positions on the court's decision.

Chief Justice Taney's 54-page majority opinion of the court had wide-ranging effects. In it he argued that free blacks-even those who could vote in the states where they lived-could never be U.S. citizens. At the time some or all adult black males could vote in Maine, Massachusetts, New Hampshire, Rhode Island, Vermont, and New York, and blacks had held public office in Ohio and Massachusetts. Nevertheless, Taney declared that even if a black was a citizen of a state "It does not by any means follow...that he must be a citizen of the United States." Taney based this unprecedented legal argument entirely on race. Although he knew that some blacks had voted at the time of the ratification of the Constitution of the United States in 1787, Taney nevertheless argued that blacks "are not included, and were not intended to be included, under the word 'citizens' in the Constitution...On the contrary, they were at that time (1787) considered as a subordinate and inferior class of beings who had been subjugated by the dominant race, and...had no rights or privileges but such as those who held the power and Government might chose to grant them." In words that shocked much of the North, Taney declared blacks were "so far inferior, that they had no rights which the white man was bound to respect." Taney concluded that blacks could never be citizens of the United States, even if they were born in the country and considered to be citizens of the states in which they lived. This also meant that Dred Scott had no right to sue for his freedom in a federal court.

Taney discussed the constitutionality of the Missouri Compromise and the debate over slavery in the territories. His goal was to finally settle the status of slavery in the territories in favor of the South. Ignoring the plain language of the Constitution, Taney argued that Congress did not have power to pass laws to regulate anything, including slavery, in the territories.

Taney also argued that any law that prohibited a master from taking a slave into the territories violated the Fifth Amendment, which protected the right to private property. Taney wrote that "the right of property in a slave is distinctly and expressly affirmed in the Constitution."

"Dred Scott Case", Microsoft(R) Encarta(R) 98 Encyclopedia.

I think most rational, unbiased people would see strong parallels here with Roe v Wade; and some of the subsequent Supreme Court decisions. Today we look at those opinions as virtually unthinkable. Some day we will think of the Supreme Court's decisions on abortion that same way-or at least future generations will. Some of us already do look at it that way-just substitute Blackmun for Taney and you have the reincarnation of the Dred Scott folly in the Roe v Wade decision. The opposition to the Dred Scott decision in the North resulted in the formation of the Republican Party, and catapulted Abraham Lincoln into the Presidency. Unfortunately, nobody of Lincoln's stature and vote getting ability has come to the fore yet on the issue of abortion; although I think we have people of the right ideological bent-for example Alan Keyes and Senator Bob Smith. You can pursue this line of thought further at the following web site: "Abortion: Slavery Reincarnate"- http://rlbm.home.tripod.com/lincoln.html. Of course, slaves were seldom killed; in part because they had monetary value. Since I wrote this several years ago, a quieter standard-bearer has seized the stage – President George W. Bush. He can still fulfill this role if he wins a second term.

"The *Dred Scott v. Sanford* decision was one of the precipitating events of the Civil War and resulted in over 600,000 dead Americans by 1865.

...what the U.S. Supreme Court says is not written in stone. This court has reversed its rulings in the past and will in the future.

(Editor's note: In my opinion, that's what recently happened in NOW vs. Scheidler.)

...the Constitution...is not meant to be re-written every time the political breezes shift. The amendment process is how changes in the 'law of the land' come about.

The Constitution is clear that the authority not given to the federal government belongs to the states. Nowhere does the Constitution regulate the practice of medicine.

...the most infamous Supreme Court justice who ever lived, Justice Harry Blackmun, talked about the pregnant woman's privacy rights existing in the penumbra, or shadow, of the Constitution. None of the majority justices were concerned with the child's rights.

The State of Texas stood for the protection of life in the womb because even in 1973, simple biology made it clear that life begins at conception.

The dissenting judges in *Roe v. Wade* and *Doe v. Bolton*, Justice Byron White and Justice William Rehnquist, did not find any constitutional basis for these decisions. They stated, '...nothing in the language or the history of the Court's judgement...|the majority| fashioned and announced a new constitutional right for pregnant mothers...The Court |majority| apparently values the convenience of the pregnant mother more than the continued existence and development of the life...that she carries.'" Taken from "A Primer on Legalized Abortion", by Ed Zielinski, General Counsel for Life Dynamics, Inc., in the March, 2003, Life Dynamics News.

Ed continued his Primer in the April edition. Here's some of it: "The very same day and without the fanfare or visibility of the Roe v. Wade decision, Doe v. Bolton was decided. The Doe v. Bolton decision...allows for abortion any time in the pregnancy based on the opinion of a single doctor...stated essentially that a physician may exercise 'his best clinical judgement' and perform an abortion at any time he deems necessary 'in light of all factors— physical, emotional, psychological, familial, and the woman's age—relevant to the patient's well-being.' In plain terms, this decision made abortion available in every pregnancy at the patient's demand.

Beware of the consequences Keep in mind these prophetic words spoken by Senator Jesse Helms in 1975 when he proposed an amendment to extend equal protection and due process to the unborn, in response to the logic and decisions of the Supreme Court: '...if an innocent human being can be defined as a non-person |therefore not entitled to constitutional rights| because he is too young ...there is no reason in principle why he cannot be defined as a non-person because he is too old, or too retarded, or too disabled.'

Compare the U.S. Supreme Court's decision to the German Constitutional Court in 1975. The German Court struck down a law making abortions more readily available: the German Court relied on the protection of life in the German Constitution. Apparently the Germans learned from their historical experience. Once in German history, people were categorized as non-persons / untermenschen, and this precipitated wholesale slaughter in the Nazi death camps of World War II. The remaining question is: What will we learn from history? Permission to slaughter young Americans was given to pregnant women and abortionists in January 1973 and remains unless we legally remove that permission to kill children."

This also tends to confirm what I have assumed for quite some time now-that it was legal to kill the disabled, the mentally ill, those with Down's Syndrome, the elderly, those with incurable diseases (Multiple Sclerosis, for example, comes to mind), Gypsies, Jews, and so on-in Nazis Germany. That is why it is difficult for me to understand why anyone Jewish, with this history in their background, and almost certainly aware of it, could be a supporter of abortion. Wake up.

"...just because the law allows something—the massacre of Jews in Nazi Germany, slavery, segregation, abortion-it can still be wrong." Life Dynamics News, May 2003. This might be a good time to point out what happened to the Nazis who committed "legal" crimes in the 1940s. After the German defeat they were brought before war crimes tribunals, convicted, and hung (depending on the circumstances, they may instead have received very long prison sentences-including life in prison).

Pro-abortion people are fond of claiming they gained a Constitutional right to abortion from the Roe v. Wade decision. Not so. It is important to make the distinction that the Court's opinion conveyed a "legal right" to an abortion, but not a "Constitutional right". The only way to change the Constitution is through the amendment process. Legal findings are just interpretations of existing laws, most of which we have no reason to question. In the case of Roe v. Wade, the Court sent down a decision that abortion could not be prohibited, invalidating laws in a majority of states.

Seeing is Believing

I found a web site that has pictures of a child's development in the womb on a month by month basis. Not photos, but graphic representations, that become fairly large when you click on them. I don't know the source, or how scientifically accurate they are. I think they probably give a ballpark depiction, and that's good. I have a big problem with them, however, and my jaws locked down tighter and tighter as I went through them, because no matter how big the baby was, they insisted on calling the child an embryo or fetus, and that's why I put this way down here. But the people are well intentioned-they sell baby products! To look at them, go to-http://www.babycenter.com/fetaldevelopment.

The latest information I have is that the above site has been taken over by Johnson & Johnson, so the science must be okay. But even before J&J swooped in, they won a 1998 and 1999 Webby Award. This is probably the most educational site of its kind that uses graphic representations; in terms of clarity, ease of use, and the amount of information it provides.

"Pro-aborts like to use words like 'fetus' to dehumanize the child in the womb; but…'fetus' is just the name of one state in human life—just as infant, teenager and adult are other stages."

"…point out that the human being is a person with full rights at every stage of his existence—our looks may change over the years, but our personhood and human dignity do not."

"In all cases, the person is still the same person."
The Judie Brown Report—February 2001

"America may be winning the war against Islamic terrorists, but the terror of abortion continues to rip apart our nation's soul". Judie Brown and Father Joseph Howard, Jr., September 4, 2002

The University of California Medical Center maintains a web site that goes into such great detail about early development that it is probably only suitable for the very studious individual. It is called the "Visible Embryo", if you want to visit it at: http://www.visibleembryo.com/.

Take the Stand Up Girl Contact Embryoscopy In Utero Tour:
http://www.standupgirl.com/inside/embryoscopy/index.html.

Colorado Right To Life Pictures: 8-20 weeks, page down at site:
http://www.coloradorighttolife.org/.

Another excellent source, if you happen to be in California, is the Alfred Shryock Museum of Embryology, Loma Linda University School of Medicine. They have a very large collection of specimens of actual "fetuses and embryos" and the museum's url is: http://www.llu.edu/llu/medicine/anatomy/museum.htm.

However, when you go to their site you will see a picture of the large museum room where they are housed and the glass cases – not the individual specimens.

So it occurred to me that probably not everybody could just jump in the car, after school or work, and drive over to Loma Linda University to see this marvelous exhibit. And what good is a resource like that, if it's mostly inaccessible to the vast majority of people? What to do? Well, I decided to put in a little extra effort, and create a substitute display, even though I've never been there:

http://www.aboutabortions.com/EmbFetal.htm. Armed with the idea and inspiration obtained from Loma Linda, and coached by one of my brighter kids, I created my own online museum. It's not nearly as good or extensive as the real thing, but I think you'll be pleasantly surprised. However, it's graphics intensive, so if you have a slow connection you'll need to have some time and patience. Even if you have a fast connection it will take a little while for everything to be rendered. The main motivation for the site was to drive people to my primary abortion site. They would look at the pictures, then click through to the abortion site from the bottom of the page. Or so I thought. In actuality, almost no one does that. It turned out to be an entirely different audience. I don't know if it's med students, or biology students, or morticians, or what; and I don't really care. Before long it was getting twice as many hits as my abortion site. And there's a lot to find wrong with the site, because it's good enough that probably everybody who goes there wishes it was better. Yes, it's probably the best of it's kind if you judge it on the basis of "actual specimen" photos, photo quality, number of photos, amount of information, quality of graphic design, variety, and unquestionable authenticity. But I'm not improving it. So there.

Basic Embryology Review Program University of Pennsylvania School of Medicine (BERP): http://www.med.upenn.edu/meded/public/berp/.

University of New South Wales Embryology-Department of Anatomy: http://anatomy.med.unsw.edu.au/cbl/embryo/embryo.htm.

The First 9 Months (Requires Flash 5 and time to watch the video): http://www.parentsplace.com/first9months/main.html.

Just the facts, life before birth-your first nine months:
http://www.justthefacts.org/continue.asp.

Fetal development pictures from conception to birth:
http://www.gravityteen.com/prenatal/ninemonths.cfm.

Pregnancy Help Now-Fetal Development:
http://www.geocities.com/pregnancyhelpnow/fetalDevelopment.html

Here are some things you probably don't want to see. I know I don't. But, for somebody in medical school, planning a career in abortion, it might be their cup of tea (almost nobody actually makes that plan today):

"'The Silent Scream' A first trimester suction abortion shown by ultrasound, with a running explanation of the procedure provided by former abortionist Bernard Nathanson, M.D. This video reveals abortion in all its graphic and gruesome horror. Video, 28 minutes. Order # AB30, $15.00", producer Dr. Don Smith.

"'Eclipse of Reason' Produced by former abortionist Bernard Nathanson, M.D., this film documents the termination of a five-month-old boy as seen by a camera placed inside the mother's uterus. Video, 27 minutes. Order # AB31, $25.00" Call 866-LET-LIVE

And finally, for those with a strong stomach, who want to see what it looks like in the abortion room, compared with other forms of terrorism, go to The Christian Gallery, http://www.christiangallery.com/. Although it's quite gruesome, it's the best presentation of this aspect of the evidence that I've seen.

To the abortionists out there (I use the term generically to mean anyone who favors abortion), I say, Hello? Of course they'll continue to attempt to divert people's attention from the facts, and the real issue. Their most potent weapon seems to be subtly saying things with the implication you know its true, thereby simultaneously disparaging their adversaries; so you need to be aware of this tactic when you watch them on TV. And right away they'll switch the topic from abortion to something else-like birth-control. You want to say in response: "Stopping abortion is the topic I'm concerned about." And once we agree to do that, then we can hammer out whether the law will define human life as beginning when the egg is fertilized, or that the child is born when the blastocyst splits and the placenta attaches itself to the uterus, or wherever in that range (probably a time period from 0 to 2 weeks).

Campaign Section

Bob Smith, New Hampshire, a key opponent of abortion in the U.S. Senate, "faces a tough GOP primary". "Under the Fifth and the Fourteenth Amendments, it is clear that human life is to be protected. And finally, on the moral side, the thought of taking unborn children and discarding them down sinks and trash cans is so abhorrent that any legitimate system of morality must find it totally unacceptable. We've basically discarded 43 million of our own children since Roe v Wade in 1973...What I want people to say about Bob Smith after I leave the Senate is that 'he led' on this issue. I took the floor on the Right to Life Act. I took the floor on the issue of covering unborn children with Medicaid other than just the mother. And I took the floor on the selling of body parts. I led. And when people said that [the selling of body parts] didn't happen, I said that it did. And I proved it...I'm passionate about stopping it (abortion). I don't make any apologies for it, and never have." Senator Bob Smith, excerpted from a Celebrate Life interview in the May-June 2002 issue. "No person shall...be deprived of life, liberty, or property, without due process of law". Amendment V to the U.S. Constitution.

Senator Smith on: "...this murderous act known as Partial Birth Abortion... these children can't speak for themselves. They don't get a chance to say, 'I would like to be born.' They do not get the chance to tell you how it feels to be brutally murdered seconds before your first breath. And unless you and I speak for them, they will be forgotten...I hope you will be brave enough to stand right beside me...Please help me save these innocent lives." The Democrat in the race is "Jeanne Shaheen who supports all abortions, all the time." NPLA Newsletter, Summer 2002 "In New Hampshire, pro-life Congressman Bob Sununu defeated incumbent pro-life Senator Bob Smith. With 85 percent of precincts reporting, Sununu had 63,711 votes, or 53 percent, while Smith had 53,466 votes, or 45 percent. Sununu will now face pro-abortion Governor Jean Shaheen in a close election race." Source: Pro-Life Infonet September 10, 2002 So a pro-life champion went down to defeat in the primary. He will be sorely missed, but since Sununu also appears to be pro-life, not all is lost. He will not lead on the issue like Smith did, and purists questioned whether he was pro-life enough; but hopefully we'll have his vote in our column for the most important pro-life bills. I don't get to see first hand what goes on in New Hampshire, but I get a lot of mail from Bob raising funds and promoting other issues. In my own mind I questioned the political toll it would take to support issues like right to work legislation. There wasn't much chance of getting that kind of a bill passed, so you would probably just be making the labor union bosses mad. My personal hope is that President Bush will find him an influential position in the executive branch of the administration, like he did for John Ashcroft. As a footnote to this, John Sununu's father was chief of staff in the Bush Sr. administration.

"A recent poll in the New Hampshire Senate race shows Shaheen in a statistical dead heat with her Republican opponent, Rep. John Sununu (Hotline, 9/20)." Taken from the Insider News, EMILY's List, Week of September 22, 2002. If you're wondering where the name EMILY came from, here is the explanation they give on their web site: "EMILY stands for 'Early Money Is Like Yeast' (we help the 'dough' rise)." Is that corny, or what? But "EMILY's List has raised $26 million." Jennifer Bingham, Executive Director, SBA List- Fortunately, they don't always spend it wisely.

"New Hampshire Abortion Advocate Gets NARAL Support Pro-life advocates in New Hampshire have no reason to vote for pro-abortion Gov. Jeanne Shaheen in New Hampshire's key U.S. Senate race. The extreme pro-abortion group NARAL is coming out in full force for her campaign against pro-life Rep. John Sununu, who has a 100% pro-life voting record. Kate Michelman, president of the National Abortion Rights Action League, said New Hampshire is one of 10 states where races will determine control of the Senate. NARAL is going all out to boost Shaheen over Sununu, she said. 'If we lose the (U.S.) Senate, if it returns to Republican conservative leadership, women may lose the right to choose,' she said." Election 2002 Updates From Across the US-Pro-Life Infonet; Oct. 15, 2002

"GOP Sen. Bob Smith...Rep. John Sununu...differed on relatively little... Sununu life-time American Conservative Union rating 94%". Human Events, The Week of October 21, 2002. What I got from the preceding article was that Sununu was practically an ideological copy of Smith; but younger, more handsome, and perhaps more politically savvy. Looks do matter in politics. Shaheen is also very politically savvy. That's why she is where she is. But she's also very liberal and very pro-abortion. There's no reason not to vote for John, which Bob Smith agrees with. (Team Sununu, P.O. Box 500 Rye, N.H., O3870; 603-625-5585) Sununu victory was an early call.
It turned out the White House had favored Sununu because they believed he had a better chance of defeating Jean Shaheen, and that paid off for them in the end. Sununu 51%, Shaheen 47%.

Ray Clatworthy for U.S. Senate, P.O. Box 96539, Washington, D.C., 20090-6539, running in Delaware. "...a U.S. Naval Academy graduate...He became one of the most privileged Marine aviators, earning the opportunity to fly the F-4 Phantom...At the time...one of the fastest planes in the world. It is a privilege Ray has not forgotten...Ray understands the importance of utilizing every technological advantage we have in order to win the War on Terrorism ...a successful small businessman, devoted father and man of unshakeable faith...As an Admiral I take the defense of our nation very seriously. I know you do too. Please, help me protect it...For America, Rear Admiral Perry 'Mike' Ratliff, U.S. Navy (retired)"

Intecon

"As a former Marine aviator, this race for the United States Senate has taken on a new meaning since the tragic events of last year. I want to make absolutely certain we immediately reverse the eight years of deterioration our armed forces suffered under ex-president Bill Clinton. I firmly believe more funds must be allocated to bring our military technology up to speed to win the next battle to protect our nation. That's why I will push to streamline the federal government, to cut billions in fat and waste. And because I believe in the sanctity of the family, I will push for programs that restore traditional values in America—not undermine them—unlike Joe Biden—I will vote for the President's nominations to the U.S. Supreme Court who recognize that the U.S. Constitution is not a document to be re-written at will by a simple majority of the court...not...the three-ring circus Joe Biden directed during his chairmanship of the Senate Judiciary Committee...Joe Biden is part of the problem in Washington. And with President Bush's agenda hanging in the balance, it's time for Joe Biden to go...even now, with President Bush's approval rating near 70%, dozens of his appointments remain bottled up in the Democrat-controlled Senate. From important matters like the judiciary, to national missile defense, to protecting the right to life of the unborn, Joe Biden and I are miles apart on the issues. As a former Marine officer who spent nearly a decade of my life serving our country at the Naval Academy and in the Marines, my view of the world is far different than Joe Biden's viewpoint. This campaign will come down to a few thousand votes. My radio and T.V. ads are up and running, Joe Biden's record is being exposed, and thousands of voters are making up their minds on who they are going to vote for every week. I simply cannot afford to let up now...with this election so close, and...control of the U.S. Senate at stake...please help me contrast my views with Joe Biden's record." Ray Clatworthy, August 23, 2002

"Joe Biden has made it clear he will stand in the way of any Supreme Court nominee he believes is 'too conservative'." 09/11/02 "Joe Biden is on record a month after September 11th proposing that American taxpayers like you and me send $200,000,000 to the radical government of Iran. His proposal was nothing short of outrageous. Because Joe Biden knows that Iran is on the official State Department list of state sponsors of terrorism. Why he would propose sending a terrorist state like Iran $200,000,000.00 has never been adequately explained to me. And it makes no sense to anyone I've talked to." Ray Clatworthy, Friday September 20, 2002

"For over half his life, Joe Biden has been nothing but a professional politician. And like all too many Democrats in the Senate, he has not served one day in the U.S. Armed Forces. Yet Joe Biden holds one of the most powerful positions in the world—Chairman of the Senate Foreign Relations Committee ...I intend to change that on election day....Joe Biden...voted to allow the continued desecration of the American Flag...He has also co-sponsored 'The

314

Freedom of Choice Act' which allows abortion on demand until birth. He is the most liberal Senator ever elected from Delaware. Joe Biden votes the liberal line…nearly every time. The good people of Delaware have too much common sense to elect hard-core liberals…Joe Biden gets re-elected because only a few people in Delaware know his true voting record…I'm going to make sure they know how far to the left Joe Biden votes in Congress. With our nation still waging a War on Terrorism and poised to go into Iraq, I know my voice will have an impact in the U.S. Senate from day one." Ray Clatworthy, Monday September 30, 2002 This was one of the contests that demonstrated a military background and a gung ho attitude didn't guarantee election-Ray Clatworthy lost, 58% to 41%.

Senator Tim Hutchinson, Arkansas, "has co-sponsored several…pro-life bills" and "is in a tough race" against a pro-abortion candidate. "Arkansas Senate Race a Dead Heat, Survey Shows Incumbent pro-life Sen. Tim Hutchinson and pro-abortion challenger Mark Pryor are in a dead heat in their Senate race, according to a poll commissioned by the Arkansas Democrat-Gazette. The newspaper reported Sunday that Hutchinson garnered support from 45.2 percent of those polled and Pryor, the state's attorney general, received 45.4 percent. Zogby International conducted the telephone survey of 500 randomly selected, registered, likely voters." Election 2002 Updates From Across the US; Pro-Life Infonet, Oct. 15, 2002 The Tim Hutchinson race was about the only Senate race disappointment of the evening for the Republicans. Mark Pryor won 54%-46%.

"…in Arkansas, which incumbent Republican Sen. Tim Hutchinson lost to Mark Pryor (D), the vast amount of the vote cast on the abortion issue went to Hutchinson. It just wasn't enough to overcome voter resentment over the divorcing his wife of 29 years to marry a 35-year old member of his Senatorial staff." From "The Pro-Life Advantage At The Polls", Cybercast News Service and The Pro-Life Infonet; November 18, 2002, By Paul M. Weyrich. Apparently Pryor switched his position to oppose abortion (Human Events).

Wayne Allard won his Colorado Senate seat by just 51% of the vote 6 years ago, has voted 100% pro-life, and is up against an opponent who receives pro-abortion support. Allard won 51%-45%. This year (2002), "The right to life issue was decisive in both Colorado and New Hampshire, where incumbent U.S. Senator Wayne Allard (R) and challenger U.S. Rep. John Sununu (R-NH) won their respective races with 51 percent of the vote." (Same source as Hutchinson results above).

Congressman Saxby Chambliss, with "a 100% pro-life voting record", is running against "incumbent Democrat Max Cleland", who has always voted in favor of partial-birth abortion, but tries to "deceive his constituents". This is the U.S. Senate race in Georgia.

"Georgia Pro-Lifers Favor Chambliss Over Miller Although Senator Zell Miller is widely regarded as one of the few moderate Democrats in the U.S. Senate, he nevertheless supports abortion. As a result, pro-life advocates, encouraged by national pro-life groups, are supporting the candidacy of pro-life Congressman Saxby Chambliss. Chambliss holds a 100% pro-life voting record as a member of the House of Representatives." Source: Pro-Life Infonet; September 17, 2002

"Georgia Senate Race Now Very Close A recent poll shows pro-abortion Georgia Senator Max Cleland with a small 45 to 41 percent lead over pro-life candidate Saxby Chambliss. Cleland has a 0% pro-life voting record and Chambliss a 100% pro-life voting record as a member of the House of Representatives." Pro-Life Infonet; October 2, 2002, Election 2002 Campaign Updates

Chambliss won 53%-46% in one of the biggest upsets of the night. "The preliminary tally from the Secretary of State's office gives Senator-elect Chambliss a margin of 140,000 votes. Nine percent of the electorate listed abortion as the 'One issue that mattered most.' Of the 182,000 votes that were cast on the abortion issue, Chambliss received 73 percent or over 133,000 votes. Clearly being pro-life was a help to Chambliss." Dr. Wanda Franz, the president of National Right to Life

Catherine Davis, US House 4th District, and Phil Gingrey or Cecil Staton, for US House 11th District, are also endorsed by Georgia Right to Life, which issued the following statement:

"Our society, our government, and our unborn children suffer when Georgia's prolifers decide not to vote or when they vote for politicians that don't respect the sanctity of human life. The power that we have is taken away and given to politicians who see nothing wrong with abortion on demand. We should feel privileged to have this right and feel obligated to use the power of our vote to protect those who cannot speak for themselves. Turnout is expected to be low, and your vote will count more than ever. Your vote will make a difference (remember November, 2000 in Florida)! Legalized abortion is the most important single issue facing Americans today. The right to Life for all members of our human family is the most important right guaranteed by our founding fathers. Vote as if your life depended on it, because someone's does."!

Bill Salier is the pro-life candidate for the U.S. Senate in Iowa, but faces pro-abortion opponents in both the primary and general elections. Harkin, who ended up running against Ganske, won Iowa for the Democrats, 54%-44%.

In Louisiana, "Democrat Senator Mary Landrieu, a defeatable pro-abortion incumbent, is the first openly pro-abortion Senator to represent the state in recent memory...won narrowly in a disputed election in 1996. Two announced Republican challengers, Suzanne Terrell and State Rep. Tony Perkins, have taken solid pro-life stands."

But not according to RNCLife FaxNotes on October 4, 2002:
"Susanne Haik Terrell who served as honorary co-chairman of a Planned Parenthood event held in New Orleans in 1994. A fine candidate, state Senator Tony Perkins who is a solid pro-life conservative who has been endorsed by RNC/Life PAC is running for the seat, and so is Rep. John Cooksey...you can mail your contribution to Tony Perkins at Perkins for Senate – P.O. Box 36 – Baker, LA 70704." I think Louisiana has a strange primary system.

"Voters in Louisiana will choose between incumbent Democrat Senator Mary Landrieu, Republican Tony Perkins, Suzanne Terrell, and Rep. John Cooksey. Landrieu earned an "F" from the National Taxpayers Union on her voting record. Terrell is the commissioner of elections in Louisiana. She claims to be pro-life but hosted a Planned Parenthood event. Rep. Cooksey is a supporter of homosexual adoption and special rights for homosexuals in the workplace. Perkins is a member of the Louisiana House of Representatives and authored the nation's first Covenant Marriage law in 1997. He is a graduate of Liberty University and served in the U.S. Marine Corps. TVCPAC endorses Perkins."
TVC, Thursday, October 24, 2002

"I just returned from Louisiana over the weekend where I campaigned on behalf of State Representative Tony http://www.tonyperkins.com/. Tony is running for the United States Senate and I can tell you he is exactly the kind of conservative we need in the Senate. Tony's commitment to our values is unquestioned. He is perhaps best known for authoring Louisiana's Covenant Marriage law, but he has 'fought the good fight' for faith and family in Louisiana on every issue you and I care about most. He is pro-family, pro-life and pro-Israel. He is articulate and a great debater. In a year when we are losing conservative stalwarts like Jesse Helms, Phil Gramm and Bob Smith, we need this former Marine in the Senate to go toe-to-toe with Tom Daschle, Ted Kennedy and Hillary Clinton!

Now, some of you may know that they do things a bit differently in Louisiana. In Louisiana all candidates for the same office, Republicans and Democrats, run on one ballot on November 5th. If the top vote getter receives an outright majority, they win. However, if no candidate receives a majority, the top two vote getters, regardless of party, go into a December run-off. There are at least half a dozen candidates running this year against incumbent Democrat Mary Landrieu. It is very possible, given the close nature of most of the Senate races this year, that control of the United States Senate could come down to this one race being decided in a December run-off. It is assumed that Republicans would benefit from this scenario as pro-family conservatives would likely turnout in greater numbers. Control of the Senate-and our federal courts and President Bush's policy agenda-could literally come down to this one race in a post-Thanksgiving special election. I can't tell you just how important this race really is! But don't just take my word for it.

My good friend, Dr. James Dobson, rarely endorses candidates for public office, but he has made an exception for Tony Perkins! Here are a few comments Jim made about Tony in a recent letter:

'Tony's strong commitment to protecting the rights of preborn children and his unwavering stand on a host of other topics relating to the family make him the obvious choice for those who care about the values upon which our nation was founded.

'Louisiana is a conservative state and Tony is the clear conservative choice. His accomplishments include authoring the nation's first covenant marriage law and legislation to protect the preborn and guarantee children the right to pray in schools. We need this man in Washington!'

We do indeed need Tony Perkins in the United State Senate. This race is not about 'choosing the lesser of two evils.' As Jim Dobson said, Tony is the clear conservative choice." Sincerely, Gary L. Bauer, CWFPAC, Wednesday, October 23, 2002

Landrieu (incumbent), 563,400, 46%, 98% of precincts reporting; Terrell 327,975, 27%; Cooksey 166,545, 14%; Perkins 115,242, 10%; Brown 23,453, 2%; Landry 10,266, 1%; Lemann 3,862, 0%; Robbins 2,577, 0%; Skillman 1,644, 0%. Well, that's how they do it in Louisiana. Now there will have to be a run off, in December, between Landrieu and Terrell because nobody got 50% of the vote. It was also strange how the Republicans approached this contest, because even the pro-life people couldn't agree on who to support. The RNC sent Terrell $500,000, which enraged conservatives; but she was also supported by the SBA List and NPLA. On the other hand, CWFPAC, and the Life and Liberty PAC supported Tony Perkins. The runoff will not affect the balance of power in the Senate, which has already been decided. But it should still be a hard fought battle.

"Terrell said her pro-life position is crystal clear. 'I am a practicing Catholic, and I abide by the tenets of my church,' she said. 'And while I respect other churches and other religions and other feelings and other positions, I am pro-life, I am a Catholic and it's as simple as that.' 'I have always been and will always be pro-life,' she said. Terrell was faced with a situation that prompts some women to have abortions when a physician told her that she was pregnant with a child who could have birth defects. She chose 'to have the child that God gave me.' Terrell said the pro-life movement needs her in Washington, because there is only one other pro-life woman in the Senate. America's pro-choice culture won't change without 'pro-life women making the case,' she said." Source: Pro-Life Infonet; November 10, 2002; Steven Ertelt

"Suzanne Terrell—a strong Pro-Lifer who has been endorsed by the SBA List Candidate Fund—is locked in a neck-and-neck battle with Pro-Abortion incumbent Mary Landrieu. The winner will be decided in a special election on December 7." Jane Abraham, President, SBA List-11/11/2002

"Pro-Life Candidate Leads Louisiana Senate Race Washington, DC-The Susan B. Anthony List commissioned a survey on the Louisiana Senate race, which shows that pro-life candidate Suzanne Terrell currently enjoys an eight point advantage over incumbent Senator Mary Landrieu. The two are facing a run-off election for the U.S. Senate on December 7th. 'Suzanne Terrell supports the reasonable pro-life measures that Louisiana, and the majority of America also supports,' said Jane Abraham, the President of the Susan B. Anthony List. 'We believe this is to her advantage, and that it will be demonstrated in the run-off election.'

Findings from the survey include:

* If the December run-off were held today, Suzie Terrell would garner 48% of the vote and Senator Landrieu would receive 40%. The 8 point Terrell advantage is outside of the 4.4% margin of error.

* Terrell performs much better with her party base than does Landrieu. Among registered Republican voters, Terrell acquires 72% of the vote compared to just 16% for Landrieu. With registered Democrats, though, Landrieu nets only 51%, while Terrell receives 42% of the vote.

The survey was conducted by Wilson Research Strategies for the Susan B. Anthony List on November 10-12th." From: The Pro-Life Infonet, Steven Ertelt, at infonet@prolifeinfo.org, 11/14/2002

DATE: December 6, 2002 FROM: Jennifer Bingham, Executive Director SUBJECT: Update-LA Senate Run-off "THE SENATE RACE IS CLOSE! The latest polls show the race is very close – within the margin of error. A Mason Dixon poll released yesterday shows Landrieu ahead of Terrell by 2 points-47% to 45%. The SBA List and our Candidate Fund have made a HUGE impact in Louisiana! In fact, we were featured in the following article about our involvement in the Louisiana Senate Run-off Race: http://www.politicsla.com/

Intecon

DATE: December 8, 2002
FROM: Election Update, SBA List Candidate Fund
SUBJECT: Suzie Terrell Puts Up a Great Fight in LA!

"Unfortunately, pro-life Suzie Terrell was unable to defeat pro-abortion
Senator Mary Landrieu yesterday in the Senate run-off race in Louisiana – but
the race was close and Suzie put up a great fight. This was a valiant effort! The
results were 48% Terrell to 52% Landrieu, with a vote differential of
approximately 40,000 votes. Thanks to you and the rest of our membership
our Candidate Fund raised over $60,000 for Suzie Terrell. And our voter
identification efforts were in full force. The Susan B. Anthony List identified
57,000 pro-life women voters in Louisiana from an untapped universe. The
Susan B. Anthony List and our Candidate Fund sent two postcards to each
identified voter and made two Get-Out-the-Vote phone calls to each. The SBA
List also ran educational radio ads throughout the state. We also had an
internet GOTV program targeting an additional 54,000 registered voters in the
state. We are pleased at our efforts and the efforts of the members of Susan B
Anthony List. We will continue to work to fight to protect the lives of the
unborn by urging our representatives to pass legislation that will do just that.
I can assure you that every action counts! We will continue to step up our
efforts as the new Congress convenes on January 7, 2003. Thank you for all of
your assistance! Jennifer Bingham Executive Director http://www.sba-list.org"

"To: Friends and Supporters of the Campaign for Working Families
From: Gary L. Bauer, Chairman Date: Tuesday, December 10, 2002

A Bad Night On The Bayou

The media spin on Saturday's Louisiana elections further proves Napoleon's
observation that in politics stupidity is no handicap. Far from being a
repudiation of the President and his policies, it is clear to the serious and
informed observer (the liberal media is usually neither) that purely local issues
dictated the results. For starters, turnout in Louisiana was low and, according
to conventional 'wisdom,' that should have benefited the Republican
candidate. However, according to our sources, December 7th was opening day
of deer hunting season and last weekend also just happened to coincide with
training duty for National Guard members. When you factor in the loss of
votes from these two conservative constituencies with the traditional Democrat
emphasis on turnout among African-American bloc voters, it becomes obvious
that Democrat Mary Landrieu benefited from the low voter turnout.
Furthermore, Landrieu successfully exploited local economic fears, mainly
sugar imports from Mexico, in a way that appealed to some conservatives.

While the Senate race captured all the attention, the 5th Congressional District should have been a slam-dunk for the GOP. Again, local issues dominated. The Republican Party never recovered from its brutal primary. Two of the leading primary candidates refused to back the GOP nominee due to the tactics employed in winning his campaign. Additionally, the Democrat in the race was a pro-family social conservative. Disaffected Republicans could have easily felt comfortable voting for him to protest the primary campaign tactics."

This was one the Republicans thought would be a win, so the loss hurt. Terrell also said she thought the acrimonious primary hurt her in the runoff. Personally, I don't think the issues and party allegiance always determine the winner. Sometimes people vote for candidates just because they "like" one person better than another. Physical appearance, personality, charisma, how a person "carries" and projects themselves, all can be important factors. And, afterall, Landrieu was the incumbent. And some people probably voted for her because they had liked and voted for her father, who was the mayor of New Orleans at some time in the past. Plus, a special effort was made to bring out African American voters, and Landrieu seemed to be successful in blurring the distinctions between the two candidates on the issues.

"Radically pro-abortion Democrat Senator Paul Wellstone is either trailing or has a slight lead, according to a series of polls, against pro-life St. Paul Mayor Norm Coleman. Senator Wellstone is a cosponsor of legislation that would force private insurance companies to pay for abortion drug coverage, and has a 0% pro-life voting record." Even if you're pro-abortion, keep this in mind when you get down to the section on RU-486. The above quote, and all the Senate race quotes, are taken from the "Winter 2002 Newsletter of the Pro-Life Alliance". Contact Coleman Victory Committee, 425 2nd Street NE, P.O. Box 97224, Washington, D.C., 20077; or 1410 Energy Park Drive, Suite 11, Saint Paul, MN 55108. "...my opponent's unbending partisanship has been a constant obstacle to getting anything done...we need to rebuild our economy, defend our nation, educate our children, and provide for our seniors. During 2001 alone, Paul Wellstone voted for higher taxes 218 times." That's Norm Coleman speaking.

"Minnesota Pro-Abortion Senator Holds Small Lead Pro-abortion Sen. Paul Wellstone has taken a narrow lead over pro-life challenger Norm Coleman, according to a poll released Saturday. The random telephone survey of 1,048 likely voters found 47 percent supported Wellstone, while 41 percent favored Coleman. Coleman's campaign disputed the results. 'Our numbers do not show a Wellstone lead of six points,' said Coleman spokesman Tom Mason. 'We see it as a dead-even race and we feel confident. Any 12-year incumbent who is polling under 50 percent is in jeopardy.' The Pro-Life Infonet, Steven Ertelt infonet@prolifeinfo.org, Oct. 20, 2002

"Minnesota Dems Choose Mondale for Senate, Leads in Poll Minnesota Democrats Wednesday night chose pro-abortion ex-Vice President Walter Mondale to replace Paul Wellstone as the Democratic nominee for the Minnesota senate seat. The Minneapolis Star Tribune shows a recent poll has Mondale leading pro-life candidate Norm Coleman by 47 percent to 39 percent—close to where the race stood two weeks ago when Wellstone led Coleman 47 to 41 percent.

Minnesota Poll Shows Pro-Life Candidate Leads Gov Race Pro-life state Rep. Tim Pawlenty holds a small lead in the latest poll out by the Minneapolis Star-Tribune in the state's governor's race. Pawlenty is favored by 33 percent over pro-abortion state Senator Roger Moe (with 29 percent) and pro-abortion ex-Congressman Tim Penny, who polled 19 percent. Pawlenty is up and Penny is sharply down since the last poll; Moe is unchanged. Pro-life advocates in the state feel good about the race." Pro-Life Infonet; 10/30/2002 The death of Paul Wellstone in a plane crash has made the Minnesota Senate race especially hard to call. Will people turn out? "Minnesota Pro-Life Group Offers Numerous Election Resources Minneapolis, MN—With a close senate and gubernatorial race, Minnesota is one of the top targets for both sides of the abortion debate in the 2002 elections. Minnesota Citizens Concerned for Life has all the information you need to make the best choice for life.

MCCL's Pro-Life Voting Guide for All Races is located at
http://www.mccl.org/votersquide.pdf

Guide to the MN Governor Candidates Can be found at
http://www.mccl.org/gov_elec_singlepg.pdf

Walter Mondale's Pro-Abortion History can be found at
http://www.mccl.org/mondale.pdf

Comparison B/t Mondale and Coleman Can be Found at
http://www.mccl.org/mondale_coleman.pdf

(These are PDF files that require Adobe Acrobat to read. They are great for printing out and distributing.)" From the Pro-Life Infonet; October 30, 2002; Steven Ertelt, infonet@prolifeinfo.org

Tim Pawlenty won the governor race. The polls weren't a very good indicator of the outcome of the Senate vote. When I went to bed at 4:00 A.M. it still hadn't been decided, but I awoke to hear Walter Mondale, a relic of the Carter era, concede. The margin of victory for Norm Coleman, personally recruited by President Bush to run for the Senate, was 50% to 47%, with 98% of the precincts reporting. Minority parties got the rest of the vote.

"Howard Fineman of Newsweek, Rush Limbaugh and a few others said the Dems lost the election partially because of their loutish behavior at the Wellstone memorial service. Just recently, former New York Mayor Ed Koch agreed. That event will live in political infamy. It will rank right up there with the 1968 Democratic convention in Chicago and the New York State Democratic convention where Hillary was nominated. Like its crass and clueless predecessors, the Wellstone 'memorial rally' evolved into a raucous radical left-wing high-fiving partisan frat party. Boorish behavior was the norm. The conduct and demeanor of the participants at the Wellstone event would have been more suitable on a college campus where leftist students and professors gather to bash conservatives like David Horowitz or Ann Coulter.

Minnesota Angst and Anger

The booing of Jesse Ventura and Republicans at the Wellstone fiasco was the last straw for Independents and disaffected Minnesotans. Before that the Independent vote could have gone either way. In addition, many conservative and religious Republicans could have stayed home. But as one Independent Duluth businessman stated as he viewed the event on TV, 'They [the Democrats] just slit their throats.' Suffice it to say if the rally/memorial service had not turned ugly, both inside and outside the University of Minnesota's Williams Arena, Mondale probably would have won Wellstone's Senate seat.

The debate between Coleman and Mondale was the other revealing and disastrous event for the Democrats. Mondale came off as a 'grumpy old man' without the charm of Walter Matthau and Jack Lemmon. Mondale's finger waving and crotchety gracelessness completed the picture begun at the Wellstone Memorial Rally. The Democrats came across as a party comprised of classless bullies who embarrassed a majority of the people who live in Minnesota. They showed themselves not as the party of the 'little guy' and the working man, but as the party of the little minds and hearts, with the attendant mindless mob behavior patterns of the radical left. Several statewide Minnesota polls showed that 70 percent of Minnesotans believed the Wellstone rally and the Coleman-Mondale debate hurt Democrats tremendously.

As it was, Minnesota had a record voter turnout of over 65 percent. Centrist issues were not a factor in Minnesota. Bona fide conservative issues brought conservatives out in force. In addition, the perception that the Democrats were churlish radical ideologues finally hit home to this basically populist state. In fact, it may have hit home to the voters in the rest of the nation as well." Diane Alden, Friday, Nov. 15, 2002, at NewsMax.com

"In Minnesota, we worked hard and saw Norm Coleman squeak by Walter Mondale. (Helped, I admit, by the backlash to Sen. Wellstone's memorial service-turned-political rally-a sickening spectacle I can only describe as 'Clintonian'.)" **Linda Chavez**

"With 79 percent of the electorate voting, Norm Coleman prevailed over former Vice President Walter Mondale. The margin was 49.53 percent for Coleman and 47.26 percent for Mondale. With over 2.2 million voters participating, the vote total for Coleman was just over 51,000 more than for Mondale. According to Fox News, the abortion issue was decisive for over 315,000 voters of which 81 percent, or 255,000 votes, went to Coleman. That amounts to five times his winning margin." **Dr. Wanda Franz, the president of National Right to Life**

In Missouri "The pro-life backlash against Senator (Jean) Carnahan will likely bring her down." Not so fast. This has turned out to be a very tight race, as you will see below.

In the South Dakota Senate race: "Pro-abortion freshman Democrat is already trailing the state's lone U. S. Representative, John Thune, who votes 100% pro-life. Pro-lifers may make the difference." **John Thune-U.S. Senate http://www.johnthune.com/**

"Aberdeen, S.D.—Addressing a well-bundled crowd in the Northern State University gymnasium on a frigid South Dakota morning, the president, with great fervor, touted the candidacy of Rep. John Thune, who is running neck-and-neck against incumbent Democratic Sen. Tim Johnson. This campaign has acquired something of a personal tone; South Dakota is the home of Senate Majority Leader Tom Daschle, the chief voice of the Democrats in Washington and Johnson's mentor. Aberdeen also is Daschle's hometown. The president considers this race so important, he is returning to South Dakota on Sunday. Nearly every poll has shown the South Dakota race to be within the margin of error, and it is expected to go down to the wire on Tuesday." Excerpts from a column by Edwin Chen, Tribune Newspapers, via the Los Angeles Times, Friday November 1, 2002. As I sit here at 3 A.M. Friday morning, the 8th of November, three days after the election, it still hasn't made it to the wire. Tom Daschle campaigned side by side with Johnson, and it seems like every prominent Republican has been there at least once. With 100% of precincts reporting the tally is 167,481 for Johnson, 166,954 for Thune. Very little, if any, news has been coming out of South Dakota. It's like the two parties have agreed to just not talk about it. Apparently there is a recount going on. It may be mandated by law when it's this close. Whether or not that's true, the Republicans have been enforcing the election laws, something that hasn't been seen since Clinton took office, because of his, and his party's, "anything goes" approach to politics. The FBI was in South Dakota even before the election, investigating widespread Democrat vote fraud; so I assume they're still doing that, and not willing to accept the results at face value. It will probably be awhile.

I had to go to the Sioux Falls Argus Leader newspaper online to get the story. It appears that Tim Johnson won. John Thune could legally request a recount, but is waiting while "county auditors recheck the votes as part of a routine review", before making a final decision. So there's no recount yet. It seems that Thune is leaning away from requesting one. But according to the National Review, "a team of Republican election experts is in South Dakota, looking into the circumstances". So a recount is still possible, but seems unlikely, unless they find something blatant at this late date (11/11/02). President Bush doesn't like to make waves. Tim Johnson won by about 527 votes, some of which were probably fraudulent votes from people whose identity had to be verified verbally because there isn't a written version of the Indian language so that the votes couldn't be traced. Other people probably voted for Johnson hoping to keep native son Daschle Senate Majority Leader. See how important a few votes can be?

John Cornyn is the pro-life Senate candidate in Texas. Despite early reports that he was in a tougher race than he had expected, John Cornyn won easily 55%-43%. http://www.cornyn2002.com/

More recently, from National Pro-life Alliance Legislative Director Robert Hughes-"In Colorado, State Senator Marilyn Musgrave, who has sponsored every major piece of pro-life legislation, including the state's Partial-Birth Abortion Ban, is seeking to take her pro-life leadership to the U.S. House, but faces a wealthy pro-abortion lawyer in the primary. Democrats controlled redistricting in North Carolina, jeopardizing pro-life Reps. Robin Hayes and Charles Taylor...'In competitive contests in dozens of races like these, pro-life support can make the difference'...Membership support of NPLA-PAC is essential to help elect strong pro-life candidates like...John Hostettler (IN-8) and Ernest Istook (OK-5). NPLA-PAC supported winning candidates in 21 of 25 congressional races in the last election. 'We expect 2002 to be even more successful, with twice as many candidates supported, if we raise the funds necessary. The future of our struggle to end abortion-on-demand and save millions of yet-to-be-born babies is at stake.'" Marilyn Musgrave, John Hostettler, and Ernest Istook all won.

"Running in the Indiana Second Congressional District is Chris Chocola, who has answered his National Pro-Life Alliance survey 100% in favor of saving the unborn...the race will likely come down to the wire." In Minnesota's "Second Congressional District, pro-life challenger John Kline...is considered a slight favorite". In Montana, "State Senator Mike Taylor, who answered his National Pro-Life Alliance survey in favor of ending abortion-on-demand, is

challenging U.S. Senator Max Baucus, who has a 0% pro-life voting record."
Summer 2002 / Newsletter of the Pro-Life Alliance

"Indiana Congressional Candidates Differ on Abortion Chris Chocola,
candidate for congress in Indiana's new second district, proudly announced his
support for the Sanctity of Life during a Monday night debate in Logansport.
Chocola stated he believes, 'Life begins at conception, and taking life any
moment before natural death is the wrong thing to do'. Long-Thompson called
abortion a private matter that should not be decided by Congress. As a former
congresswoman, however, Long-Thompson supported congressional measures
to expand taxpayer funding of abortion-supportive overseas 'population
control' programs and supported allowing abortions at overseas military
bases". Election 2002 Updates From Across the US—Source: Pro-Life Infonet;
October 15, 2002 Chocola, with encouragement from President Bush, won by
50%-46% to represent a newly created district, defeating Thompson.

Andrew Raczkowski is the pro-life candidate in the race for the Senate in
Michigan: c/o Raczkowski for U.S. Senate, PO Box 988, Royal Oak, MI 48068-
0988. Congressman Raczkowski says "when Vice President Cheney was here
in Michigan on his most recent stop he made…a strong personal statement of
support for our campaign." "I do want to thank…the one I hope to swear in
next January as the next United States Senator, Rocky Raczkowski"—Vice
President Dick Cheney, June 20, 2002 "Believe me, when the Vice President
made these statements I knew without a doubt that my race not only had the
full support of the White House-but that it was at the very top of their target
list as well. They desperately want me to become the 51st Republican vote in
the U.S. Senate. That's why Vice President Cheney is so encouraged about my
race. Vice President Cheney knows that I am currently an Infantry Officer in
the United States Army Reserves and a Paratrooper who will greatly aid his
pro-defense agenda in the U.S. Senate…one of the leading Republican
Representatives in…Michigan…I have the organization and conservative
message…My father told me…one of the best ways to restore our nation's
Judeo-Christian morality was by defending innocent human life at all stages…
need to defend the U.S. Constitution from the ACLU and other far-left liberal
groups that seek to destroy its original meaning…by contrasting my pro-
family, pro-life, pro-taxpayer, pro-freedom agenda against Carl Levin's 24-
year liberal record…race for the U.S. Senate is a pivotal race, and one that is
needed to restore GOP control…President Bush's approval ratings are
through the roof in Michigan…winning this race for the U.S. Senate is a
must." Andrew Raczkowski lost. "Although I did not win my race for U.S.
Senate—please know that I gave it my all. And…I received tens of thousands
more votes than the last two previous challengers did!" Thursday, December
26, 2002 Levin 61% to 38%.

"As we look ahead to the 2002 elections, there are 34 members of the United States Senate whose terms expire in 2002. Listed below is the name...of each of these senators along with Planned Parent hood's rating of them. A 100% rating means the representative supports Planned Parenthood's programs all the time. A 0% rating implies their voting record shows that they never supported Planned Parenthood programs. As you review this list, please remember that it represents the degree to which each of the senators supports Planned Parenthood. Just because a senator has a 0% rating from PP does not mean that he or she is 'Pro-life'. It does mean that they do not support PP...". STOPP International Ryan Report, November, 2001. On the other hand, at least in my opinion, a 70% to 100% rating would indicate a pro-death Senator.

100%: Carl Levin, Paul Wellstone, Max Cleland, Max Baucus, Robert Torricelli, Tom Harkin, Richard Durbin, John Kerry, Susan Collins, Jack Reed, and John Rockefeller (all Democrats).

80%: Mary Landrieu, Democrat.
71%: Joseph Biden, Democrat.
33%: Ted Stevens, Republican.
29%: John Warner, Republican.
14%: Pete Domenemici, Republican.

0%: Tim Hutchinson, Mitch McConnell, Thad Cochran, Robert Smith, Chuck Hagel, Phil Gramm, Jeff Sessions, Larry Craig, Pat Roberts, Gordon Smith, James Inhofe, Michael Enzi, Wayne Allard, and Fred Thompson, all Republicans.

Together with the fact that President Bush is having a very difficult time getting the Senate to even consider his judicial nominations, this suggests to me that a vote for a republican Senator in 2002 would be well spent.

Jean Carnahan was not rated, but is strongly pro-abortion. Strom Thurmond and Jesse Helms, of course, will not be running again, which makes it even more important to elect pro-life Senators.

Anne M. Northup For Congress, PO Box 7313, Louisville, Kentucky 40257-9874. http://www.northupforcongress.com/ "Thank you for supporting my congressional campaigns in the past. I know you must have a national perspective when it comes to politics, otherwise why would you ever have contributed to a Member of Congress for whom you can't even cast a vote? I suspect the answer is that you are as interested as I am in keeping the Democratic Leader, Dick Gephardt, from becoming Speaker of the House of Representatives. Unfortunately, Mr. Gephardt knows that in order for him to become Speaker, he most likely has to beat me. Here's why he thinks he can:

In the Third Congressional District of Kentucky (Louisville), Democrats outnumber Republicans by a two-to-one margin. Before I was elected in 1996, a Democrat held this seat for 28 years. The Mayor of Louisville and all 12 City Council members are Democrats. The Governor of Kentucky is a Democrat, for whom my opponent worked for over five years. All of my previous races have been very close. I've won 50, 52 and 53 percent of the vote. I lose about 50 precincts in the city by overwhelming numbers. For example, in 2000, I lost one precinct 356 to 5, another one 824 to 34 and another 199 to 6! Former President Clinton carried my congressional district in 1992 and 1996 and President George W. Bush lost it in 2000. When I think about it, I sometimes wonder if it is worth the effort it takes to keep this district in Republican hands. After all, it takes an incredible effort, including people like you who don't even live in my state. But if President Bush is going to have any legislative accomplishments in the next two years, we must keep the House of Representatives under Republican control. It's that simple and that important! In 2000 we raised and spent over $2.8 million. It Took that amount of money because my opponent joined with the AFL-CIO, the Teamsters, the League of Conservation Voters, the Sierra Club and others to spend over $3 million against me. This year will be no different. As a matter of fact, I anticipate that I will need to raise and spend $3.1 million to survive. And of course, there are only so many people in Kentucky who can help me raise that kind of money. So I am looking once again for help...I have enclosed a couple of articles about my campaign from 'National Journal', one of the most respected news organizations in Washington, D.C."

"Kentucky 03: Last week, Vice President Cheney came out of his undisclosed location to attend a fundraiser for GOP Rep. Anne Northup, who faces Jack Conway, a former aide to Gov. Paul Patton. Conway has no primary competition and already has nearly $500,000 in the bank. This is as bellwether a race as they get when it comes to figuring out if Democrats can take back the House. If the Democrats win this seat, it will say a lot about the national turnout landscape. Northup is a survivor, though, so nothing can be assured." National Journal's Congress Daily AM, Thursday, February 14, 2002

"Money and attention are pouring into Kentucky's 3rd District House race, an election shaping up as one of the most competitive House races in the nation." "'It's going to be a competitive race,' said Stu Rothenberg of the *Rothenberg Report*. 'The Democrats in DC are really hyping it, talking about the big money being raised by Conway. But I think Northup is a strong candidate,' Rothenberg said. '...this is an area politically that is very polarized. I'm expecting a close race.'...No other Democrat challenging an incumbent but running in a primary has raised more, said the Democratic Congressional Campaign Com-mittee...Conway is walking a fine line in his attacks on Northup." National Journal's Congress Daily AM, Wednesday, February 27, 2002 Anne Northup won, 52%-48%.

Melissa Hart, People With Hart Committee, Fourth District, Post Office Box 435, Wexford, PA 15090-9954, (724) 779-4750.
http://www.PeopleWithHart.com/

"Seventeen months ago, your support helped carry me to victory in my first race for Congress. We surprised more than a few observers that year, as I was elected as a Republican in a district that had been regarded as safely Democratic since the early years of the Eisenhower Administration."

"While I remain confident of my prospects for reelection, the Fourth Congressional district has over 55,000 more Democrats than Republicans. More than a quarter of the district's voters were added in re-districting, and have never seen my name on the ballot as a candidate for Congress. Despite a year marked by several bipartisan achievements, too many in Washington still place partisan politics ahead of the national interest...Two years ago, the national Democratic Party and their liberal groups spent hundreds of thousands of dollars on misleading, negative television advertisements to defeat me, and as we plan for this year's campaign, we must assume that they will do so again. The only way I can hope to overcome that kind of campaign, based on distortions and outright deception, is to take my positive message directly to the people of the Fourth District. I cannot do that without your help. Two years ago, we had to raise $1.7 million to wage an effective campaign, and this year will be no different."

"Congresswoman Hart has been an active champion for the unborn. She has co-sponsored numerous important pro-life bills. For example, she sponsored the Safe Havens Act, a bill that protects women in crisis pregnancy situations who want to leave their newborn babies in a safe location like a hospital without prosecution." From SBA List Candidate Profiles-April 2002. Melissa Hart won, 65% to 35%.

Dave Rogers for Congress, c/o Friends of Dave Rogers, P.O. Box 96545, Washington, DC, 20090-6545, running in Rhode Island's 1st Congressional District. Dave, as a U.S. Navy SEAL, was "deployed to the Republic of Panama during 'Operation Just Cause.'", and received the U.S. Navy Commendation Medal With Bronze Combat "V" for his actions there in 1989- 4 men in his unit died there, and two more were later killed in Afghanistan. Dave also "served my country as a SEAL on the U.S.S. Saratoga Aircraft Carrier during the Persian Gulf War.", and is still in the Reserves. He says "Remember, U.S. Navy SEALS are on the front lines of the battle to protect America. They deserve your support as they put their lives on the line to protect you and your family. Please show your support...by helping me go to battle for them in Congress...what happened on September 11th shook America to its very core. Now it's time to fight back with all we have. No one wants to help President Bush rebuild the military and win this war as badly as I do...Won't you please help me restore real leadership to Congress...Your support...will show you are a proud supporter of America's military heroes now fighting to protect you and your family". And, Dave is just as direct in his stand on abortion, as he shows in the following quote: "I'm for protecting innocent human life."

"U.S. Navy SEAL-'Sea, Air, Land,'...all volunteers for hazardous duty... proficient...trained in foreign languages...trained as 'school teachers'... training a six-month, grueling course...Dedication to completing his mission... is the hallmark of the individual SEAL...He is a patriot, he is dedicated to the precepts and principles of the United States...The Navy SEAL will look forward to giving his very best under any circumstances. He will accomplish his mission under the most arduous conditions...seeks to perform 'above and beyond the call of duty' on every mission...A faith in the correctness of his country, the legitimacy of his superiors, and the faith of the American people come together to produce one of the most dedicated servicemen our country can produce...'Many are called but few are chosen', ...are...involved in Afghanistan...and continue to perform Special Operations missions for the country around the world, today." Taken from "What Makes A SEAL-My Perspective", by Rear Adm. George Worthington (USN Ret.)

"I've been campaigning to defeat Patrick Kennedy for well over a year now ...just a few months ago Patrick Kennedy declared that he has 'a high probability' of being elected Speaker of the House. As things stand, I'm steadily closing the gap in my race against Democrat Patrick Kennedy—Ted Kennedy's liberal son! With Kennedy's polling numbers in the 40%'s, they're right to be afraid of how vulnerable he is...my victory will shatter the liberal Kennedy mystique in Congress once and for all!...I'm not going to promote big government social welfare programs at the expense of our military. Frankly, I think our entire federal budget deserves a top to bottom review. I have been fighting the liberal Kennedy Democratic machine for years. Defeating Patrick Kennedy is within our grasp." Dave Rogers, September 13, 2002 Kennedy, of course, has no military experience. Can Dave Rogers win in this David vs. Goliath contest? I don't know. I'm too far removed from it to even guess. But he's going all out, giving it his best shot, and I think he deserves our support. I'm shoulder to shoulder with you, Dave, and I know you'll be fighting right up to election day!

"Getting through SEAL training was the single toughest accomplishment of my life. Frankly, I don't know if I could ever do again what I had to do to become a SEAL. But what I do know is that being a SEAL made me who I am today. It defined my character, it pushed my endurance, and it broadened my horizons.

My campaign against Patrick Kennedy is about much more than the contrast between a liberal who has never served in the military versus a combat-decorated navy SEAL...and it's about more than a liberal Democrat versus a fiscally conservative Republican who still believes in our nation's Judeo-Christian values. It's about the future of America. And it's about the sharp contrast of local family man who was raised here in Rhode Island versus a wealthy, liberal Kennedy who grew up in Washington and Massachusetts. Many people know my father brought our family to Rhode Island because he wanted to serve his country by teaching a course at the worldrenowned U.S. Naval War College in Warick. My family's history of service in the U.S. Armed Forces is something that Patrick Kennedy knows next to nothing about. In fact, neither Patrick Kennedy nor his father Ted have ever served a day in uniform. I'm sure that's at least part of the reason why he votes the wrong way on key defense issues. Patrick Kennedy has never put his life on the line for his country like I have. And he's never had to search deep down in his soul to find out that the meaning of life is not just about the next federal government program a Kennedy can put his name on. That's why I want you to know that as a Congressman, I will always put the interests of our nation first...I have no doubt I'm on the verge of upsetting Patrick Kennedy and winning this race". Dave Rogers, U.S. Navy SEAL, October 25, 2002

Dave Rogers lost, but I couldn't find any information on the results until I received the following letter from Dave dated January 3rd. Here are the non-fundraising excerpts: "Unfortunately we came up short by a swing of only 17,402 votes—but we had a heck of a run...Patrick Kennedy has never faced such a tough reelection campaign...over 40% of the electorate voted against Patrick Kennedy! That's more than seven percent higher than last cycle! Trust me, for a state with only 7% registered Republicans, that's a heck of a result here in Rhode Island...spending less than 10% of what Patrick Kennedy spent on paid advertisements. And yet we convinced 40% of the electorate to vote against him. He is too liberal for Rhode Island, he's weak on defense issues, and he votes against President Bush's common sense agenda for America far too often. Dozens of people have told me that holding Patrick Kennedy to under 60% of the vote was something they never thought anyone would do... I'm being encouraged by friends down in Washington DC and here in Rhode Island to seek a rematch. That's why I am seriously considering running again". But before he can start another campaign he has $91,271 in campaign debts to pay off. That's a lot of money for a man of modest means who had to depend on 13,000 "patriotic individuals" (small contributors) to finance his campaign.

Joe Rogers for Congress (CO-7), c/o Friends of Joe Rogers, P.O. Box 17287, Denver, CO 80217-0287 It appears that what seemed to start out well didn't get too far. Don't know what happened here. http://www.rogersforcongress.com/

Congressman Mike Ferguson, (NJ-7), Friends of Mike Ferguson, 930 Stuyvesant Ave., Suite 17, Union, NJ 07083 Mike Ferguson won, 58%-41%. http://www.fergusonforcongress.com/

Congressman Henry Hyde, although not as vocal as he was in his younger years, has long been a force against abortion. He has been under attack by liberals for prosecuting the Clinton scandal. Henry Hyde, P.O. Box 332, Des Plaines, IL 60016 Henry Hyde won.

"New Jersey Pro-Life PAC Endorses Scott Garrett for Congress in NJ-5 – The director of the New Jersey Right to Life PAC, the independent and leading pro-life organization in New Jersey, Marie Tasy, issued a strong endorsement of Assemblyman Scott Garrett's candidacy for the Congressional seat currently held by pro-abortion Republican Marge Roukema. 'As a Congressman, Scott Garrett will work for laws that promote human dignity and ensure equal protection for all members of the human family, including the right of a child to be born, once conceived,' Mrs. Tasy said. 'Scott is one of those rare individuals in public service who possesses the courage, ability and energy to act on principle rather than succumb to political expediency on matters as fundamental as the right to life.' Congresswoman Roukema is a 20-year incumbent and Dean of the New Jersey delegation. She has consistently opposed pro-life legislation proposed by her Republican colleagues in the House. Scott Garrett will be a welcome change for the pro-life cause." Republican National Coalition for Life FaxNotes-December 7, 2001

"June 5, 2002 BAUER CALLS PRIMARIES 'GREAT NIGHT FOR CONSERVATIVES'

WASHINGTON, D.C. – 'I could not be more pleased by the results of yesterday's primary elections. It was a great night for pro-family conservatives,' said Gary L. Bauer, Chairman of the Campaign for Working Families, on Wednesday following the final tabulations from Tuesday's primaries…'I am also very pleased by the resounding victory of Assemblyman Scott Garrett in New Jersey's 5th Congressional District. The Campaign for Working Families endorsed Assemblyman Garrett in his challenges to liberal incumbent Marge Roukema because she was out of touch with her conservative district. I believe Scott's strong win last night vindicated his challenges…we should not forget that both George Bush and Bret Schundler carried the 5th District in their respective elections. I have no doubt that Scott Garrett will win the 5th District again in November.'" A Campaign For Working Families Press Release http://www.cwfpac.com/press_releases.htm

"New Jersey Group Excited About New Pro-Life Congressman

Trenton, NJ—'New Jersey Right To Life PAC is proud to have delivered the support necessary to help Pro-Life Scott Garret become New Jersey's newest Member of Congress,' said Marie Tasy, Director of Public & Legislative Affairs for NJRL-PAC. 'Today, the voters of the 5th Congressional district wisely chose Pro-Life Scott Garrett over pro-abortion extremist Anne Sumers.'

'Scott Garrett's strong Pro-Life position allowed NJRTL-PAC to build a strong unified base of support which helped Scott win the race,' noted Tasy. 'We are proud of the fact that Scott Garrett will become the 5th Pro-Life Republican Member of Congress from New Jersey backed by NJRTL-PAC.'

Of the six Republicans in New Jersey's congressional delegation, 5 are solidly Pro-Life. NJRTL-PAC undertook an independent, vigorous 'Get Out the Pro-Life Vote' effort which included phone banks and numerous mailings. NJRTL-PAC also directly contributed the maximum $10,000 to Scott Garrett for Congress campaign in 2002.

In addition to the 5th Congressional race, NJRTL-PAC has directly contributed to New Jersey congressional candidates who support President Bush and his Pro-Life agenda. Also, NJRTL-PAC has independently expended funds on 'Get Out the Pro-Life Vote' efforts in the following key races:

2nd District: Pro-Life Republican Frank LoBiondo
3rd District: Pro-Life Republican James Saxton
4th District: Pro-Life Republican Chris Smith
7th District: Pro-Life Republican Mike Ferguson".
From: Steven Ertelt, The Pro-Life Infonet, November 8, 2002
Garrett won 60% to 38%, and Ferguson won 58%-41%.

Shows what can be accomplished, even in a liberal Eastern state.

Republican Bill Simon Jr., for governor of California. "Democratic Gov. Gray Davis...made the unusual decision to spend an estimated $10 million on attack ads targeting...former (Republican) Los Angeles Mayor Richard Riordan...during the GOP primary." "This is not the first time a Democratic gubernatorial candidate maneuvered in a primary election to influence which Republican he would face in the general election. In 1966 Democratic Gov. Edmund 'Pat' Brown worked to ensure that his Republican opponent in November would be a staunch conservative, who he considered unelectable in California. But Ronald Reagan won his party's nomination and then defeated Brown in the autumn vote." I think I see another Reagan/Simon parallel too- charisma.

"...since 1994 more than 1 million Hispanics have registered to vote in California, overwhelmingly as Democrats." Yes, but wouldn't Hispanics be predominately morally conservative Catholics who aren't advocates of abortion? And didn't George Bush carry the Hispanic vote in Texas? The quotes in this paragraph were taken from the Chicago Tribune, Thursday, March 7, 2002. Bill's web site was: http://www.simon2002.com/.

Bill Simon lost, as you probably already know. I just finished reading a very long article in the November 18 issue of the weekly publication Human Events- a paper that usually doesn't run long articles. I'd heard why Simon had lost, but didn't really understand the consensus view that he ran a poor campaign. This article went in to great detail about all the blunders his campaign committed-much more detail than I care to repeat here. In a nutshell, a candidate who seemed appealing from a distance, ran a campaign that was inept and terribly disorganized, and perhaps only explainable by a professional politician or political writer. I'll just give a few excerpts from the article by Arnold Steinberg.

"Simon emerged from the primary unprepared for the general." "On election night, Davis attributed his victory to his pro-choice position on abortion. The fact is that abortion played almost no role in the campaign." "The Times exit polls found that about 60% of the voters had a negative view of both candidates." Ronald Reagan advisor Lyn "Nofziger reacted emotionally, saying Simon was 'too dumb' to win. An exasperated Rep. Tom Davis (no relation to Gray Davis), National Republican Congressional Committee chairman, called Simon's campaign 'the single worst-run race in the country.'"

"Gray Davis was and is one of the most unpopular governors in the nation. His mismanagement of the state is legendary. Most Californians thought the state has been moving in the wrong direction under Davis, they thought he was doing a poor job, and they had/have an unfavorable, even unforgiving, view of him. But he still won."

"Illinois Citizens for Life, PAC has endorsed State Representative James H. 'Jim' Meyer for state representative in the newly drawn 48th House District ...has had a 100% pro-life voting record...cosponsored pro-life legislation... has been a key vote for Life in the House Judiciary—Civil Law Committee... main opponent in the primary...has received financial support from the radical pro-abortion group Personal PAC...support extreme pro-abortion positions...gets some of its money from abortion mills", and opposed a parental notice of abortion bill. Jim won his primary race, despite not having his name printed on some of the ballots.

"Judge Barbara Gilleran Johnson...is running for the 2nd Appellate Court District...is one of us-and she's not afraid to say it. She's a person of deep conviction...has been a judge since 1987...has presided over every type of case...23 years of legal experience...served with the Attorney General's office as Chief of the Crime Victims Division, been in private practice, and is a law professor". Illinois Citizens for Life, PAC, P.O. Box 18132, Chicago, IL 60618.

Jay Dickey, Arkansas 4th Congressional District: "Bill Clinton's hometown Congressman...a conservative Republican...voted...(for). ...impeachment...vowed he would destroy me...(in) the 2000 elections...White House...orchestrated...campaign...demonized me...lost by...1%...only 2,064 votes...his influence...caused me to lose...(but)...I preserved my conscience and my self-respect...and I'm more ready than ever to fight back...My opponent...votes with the...radical Abortion Lobby...I'm proudly pro-life". c/o Dickey for Congress, PO Box 97305, Washington, DC 20090-7305 Jay "...authored legislation banning the exploitation of aborted babies' body parts for profit," when he served before. Quote, NPLA Newsletter Jay Dickey lost, 39%-61%, and I have no idea why he got whipped so badly.

Herbert E. (Herb) Meyer, Former Vice Chairman CIA National Intelligence Council, serving under President Ronald Reagan—c/o Meyer for Congress, PO Box 97302, Washington, DC, 20090-7302 http://www.herbmeyerforcongress.org/

"I served at the top level of America's intelligence community...I know what needs to be done...And I know specific measures that Congress can enact to protect America. I spelled out some of these measures in a 'Wall Street Journal' article titled: 'The CIA Must Learn to Play Offense.'...I'm a conservative Republican who will never back down from a fight. I'm pro-life, pro-tax cuts, pro-Second Amendment, and pro-traditional values...Now, about my opponent...He's a liberal Democrat serving his first term from the 2nd District of Washington. He barely won election last time by a swing vote of just 2%. With your help, I know I can defeat him this November...I...pledge to rebuild America's intelligence...I need you to step up to the plate & help me! Please!!" "It's shocking how one person can do so much damage. The person I'm talking about is Bill Clinton. He's the one person whose...negligence in office crippled the CIA's intelligence gathering capabilities...I'm running for Congress to help President Bush straighten out Clinton's mess...I was not surprised by the tragic events of September 11th...Terrorism had been flourishing around the globe in the last eight years at an unprecedented rate. Yet Clinton and his liberal advisors did nothing about it. Bluntly: he put you and every other American at risk! It is high time to repair the damage Bill Clinton did to our nation's security...before more American lives are lost. Protecting America's national security interests is the sole purpose of the

Central Intelligence Agency. It's a job that every CIA officer and supervisor around the globe has dedicated their lives to. But after decades of assaults by left-wing liberals, the CIA and its Operations Directorate has been gutted by Bill Clinton and the Democrats. Bill Clinton worked for 8 years to destroy America's intelligence-gathering capabilities. It won't be easy, but we must start fixing that damage now. If they're against protecting America to the greatest extent possible, they'll have to deal with me. Liberal Democrats like my opponent, Rick Larsen, support higher taxes, wasteful spending, bigger government, and legalized abortion for any reason whatsoever...we're going to need to win key races like mine to hold onto power."

"As you already know, I lost the primary election in a close race on September 17. Norma Smith will be our Party's candidate in the general election, and I have offered Norma my full support. In addition, I have asked all of my supporters to help Norma as well. Our country is at war, and our economy is fragile. This is no time for sore feelings, or sulking, or for settling scores. Our objective must be to help the President, and in Congress he will have Norma's support. I want you to know that our campaign set the tone for the coming general election in Washington's 2nd district. This reflected in the fact that the incumbent Democrat got only 49% of the total vote." Herb Meyer, Friday Harbor, WA.

From: The Pro-Life Infonet infonet@prolifeinfo.org
Reply-To: Steven Ertelt infonet@prolifeinfo.org
Source: North Carolina Right to Life; April 18, 2002

"North Carolina Pro-Life Day This Saturday

Greensboro, NC—The time is quickly approaching (THIS SATURDAY!!!) for our Annual North Carolina Pro-Life Day.

Due to circumstances beyond everyone's control Armstrong Williams will not be able to attend Saturday's lunch. However, Carol Long Tobias, the PAC Director of National Right to Life, will deliver the keynote address.

In addition, political candidates for statewide elections have been invited to meet you after lunch. To date, Mrs. Elizabeth Dole has confirmed that she will attend. A representative from the Jim Snyder campaign will also attend. We anticipate other candidates will also attend.

The Pro-Life Infonet is a daily compilation of pro-life news and information. To subscribe, send the message "subscribe" to: infonet-request@prolifeinfo.org. Infonet is sponsored by Women and Children First

(http://www.womenandchildrenfirst.org). For more pro-life info visit
http://www.prolifeinfo.org and for questions or additional information email
ertelt@prolifeinfo.org ".

**"NARAL Targets Pro-Life Democrat for Defeat By Christine Hall CNS
News.com Staff Writer May 02, 2002**

(CNSNews.com)-Pennsylvania pro-life Democrat and gubernatorial candidate
Bob Casey, Jr., is taking a drubbing from a national abortion rights group.
The National Abortion & Reproductive Rights Action League launched a new
television ad campaign to tell voters that 'Bob Casey wants to ban abortion,'
and that Casey's Democratic primary opponent Ed Rendell, by contrast,
supports abortion rights. Casey's father, the late Democratic Gov. Bob Casey,
was denied an opportunity to address the 1992 national Democratic convention
due to his pro-life stance on abortion. The two gubernatorial candidates are in
a tight race for the nomination, with Rendell, a popular former Philadelphia
mayor, leading Casey, the state auditor, 45 to 40 percent, according to an April
Mason-Dixon poll. Casey has the endorsement of the state Democratic Party,
which he heads, as well as the major labor unions. 'The public record of these
two men presents starkly different positions on choice,' said NARAL President
Kate Michelman. NARAL is spending approximately $170,000 to run the
initial ad on select cable TV channels in Philadelphia and Pittsburgh through
the May 21 primary." The two are running in the Democratic primary. "Will
he become the last pro-life Democrat ever to be a serious candidate for major
office in a big urban state? Whatever chance State Auditor General Casey had
was wiped out by the abortion lobby's tough campaign against him, conducted
mostly beneath the political radar. Nobody was smiling more broadly on May
22 than NARAL President Kate Michelman. The abortion lobby poured in
$574,000 against Casey, including a blunt television ad...". From "The Last
Pro-Life Democrat?" by Bob Novak in the Chicago SunTimes; June 6, 2002.
Defeated in the primary, and now extinct.

In Oregon, the most prominent pro-life candidates for office are "pro-life U.S.
Sen. Gordon Smith(R-OR) and pro-life GOP gubernatorial nominee Kevin
Mannix." Portland Oregonian; September 6, 2002

**SBA List Candidate Fund 2002 Election Cycle First Round of Endorsed Pro-
Life Candidates for the House:**

Secretary of State Katherine Harris (FL-13), http://www.electharris.org/
Sydney Hay (AZ-1), http://www.sydneyhay.com/
Candice Miller (MI-10)
Marilyn Musgrave (CO-4), http://www.musgrave2002.com/
Lynette Boggs McDonald (NV-1), http://www.lbmforcongress.com/
Barbara Cubin (WY-AL), http://www.house.gov/cubin/

Jo Ann Davis (VA-1), http://www.house.gov/joanndavis/
Jo Ann Emerson (MO-8), http://www.house.gov/emerson/
Melissa Hart (PA-4), http://www.PeopleWithHart.com/
Sue Myrick (NC-9), http://www.house.gov/myrick/
Anne Northup (KY-3), http://www.northupforcongress.com/
Ileana Ros-Lehtinen (FL-18), http://www.house.gov/ros-lehtinen/

Also, Jim Talent (MO-Senate), http://www.talentforsenate.com/
Mary Kiffmeyer (MN-SOS), http://www.kiffmeyer.org/
Marsha Blackburn (TN-07),
Elizabeth Dole (NC-Senate),
Catherine Baker Knoll (PA-Lt. Governor),
Norma Smith (WA-02),
Fran Wendelboe (NH-01),
Terri Lynn Land (MI-Secretary of State).

Added July 25, 2002; some still with primary races:
Lisa Atkins (R) (AZ-02),
Janice Bowling (R) (TN-04),
Randy Forbes (R) (VA-04),
Scott Garrett (R) (NJ-05),
Brose McVey (R) (IN-07),
Jim Nussle (R) (IA-01),
Mike Pence (R) (IN-06).

An interesting aside is that Congressman Nussle was an adopted child.

"So far, 24 of our candidates won their primaries, that's an 89% success rate!"
Jennifer Bingham Executive Director SBA List Candidate Fund, October 17, 2002-
http://www.sba-list.org/index.cfm/section/2002sbacand.html.

More recent endorsements: Marilyn O'Grady (NY-04), Chris Chocola (IN-02), Mario Diaz-Balart (FL-25), and Maria Guadelupe Garcia (CA-51).

"MARILYN O'GRADY Dr. O'Grady is running for New York's 4th Congressional District and faces a Congresswoman who is heavily endorsed by the radical pro-abortion groups including EMILY's List.
O'Grady supports a ban on partial birth abortion, is against taxpayer funded abortions, and believes in parental consent laws. She needs your help today to defeat a pro-abortion Congresswoman.

MARIE GUADELUPE GARCIA Maria is running for the 51st Congressional seat of California. She is challenging a pro-abortion Congressman who has voted against the Ban on Partial Birth Abortion and many other pro-life bills.

338

He has been endorsed by pro-abortion groups including Planned Parenthood and NARAL. Maria needs your help to defeat this pro-abortion Congressman!

MARIO DIAZ-BALART Mario is running for an open seat in the 25th District of Florida. As a Florida State Representative, he voted for numerous pro-life bills. Current polls show him leading his pro-abortion opponent, but he needs your help today to ensure victory in November." Jennifer Bingham, SBA List Candidate Fund Date: 24 October 2002 18:16:51-0400 And he won his race.

"…a political ad being run against Rep. Carolyn McCarthy (D.-N.Y.) by Republican/Conservative candidate Marilyn O'Grady, says in part: 'Barbra Streisand defends Saddam Hussein and then rips George Bush as a frightening dictator. The *Post* calls her Baghdad Babs, but Carolyn McCarthy calls her a contributor.'" From Human Events, The Week of October 28, 2002.

As of the end of April, out of the above group, it seems to me, and this is only my own opinion, that Harris, Northup, and Talent are the candidates most in need of financial assistance now. As of June 6th, I would add Blackburn http://www.sba-list.org/index.cfm/section/ 2002sbacand.html, who is in an August 1st primary. Katherine Harris won her September 10th Republican primary in Florida, but apparently Sydney Hay lost in hers the same day to Rick Renzi. "His insurance company Renzi and Co., insures over 1,200 crisis pregnancy centers and pro-life doctors in the U.S. and Canada." Source: Pro-Life Infonet So I don't think the pro-life cause lost anything there. They all won the general election.

"Arizona Race for New House Seat Appears Dead Even Setting the stage for a tight race, an independent survey taken last week of the new 1st district showed pro-abortion candidate George Cordova (D) and pro-life candidate Rick Renzi (R) tied at 37 percent apiece with 23 percent of voters still undecided. While both sides' primaries were competitive, Cordova's win over Apache County Attorney Steve Udall (D) was particularly surprising. While that result prompted Republicans to crow, the nature of the district suggests the race will likely be extremely close." Source: Pro-Life Infonet; September 19, 2002 Renzi won 49% to 46%.

"From: The Pro-Life Infonet Steven Ertelt infonet@prolifeinfo.org October 25, 2002 Indianapolis, IN—Indiana Right to Life has announced the following candidate endorsements for the 2002 elections: U.S. House Of Representatives Mark Leyva District 1 Chris Chocola District 2 Mark Souder District 3 Steve Buyer District 4 Dan Burton District 5 Mike Pence District 6 Brose McVey District 7 John Hostettler District 8 Mike Sodrel District 9". Chocola won 50%-46%, McVey lost 44%-53%, Hostettler won, Sodrel lost 46%-51%.

"So far, two of our candidates will go head to head with EMILY'S List candidates, a challenge we welcome. All of our candidates have pro-abortion opponents. All of our candidates have been actively involved in different aspects of the pro-life movement for many years. Ten candidates sponsored or helped pass legislation to restrict abortions. One candidate authored a constitutional amendment, protecting the right to life, on the first day of the 105th Congress. Many of our candidates have volunteered or helped raise funds for crisis pregnancy centers and maternity homes that help women facing crisis pregnancies. Three of our candidates, when elected, will be NEW pro-life votes-replacing pro-abortion Members of Congress currently holding these seats!" Jane Abraham, President of SBA List Candidate Fund, April 8, 2002

"In this critical election, the SBA List Candidate Fund, with the help of members like you, was able to make a huge impact on the number of pro-life women in Congress. We increased the percentage by 71%—from 7 to 12! Of the 29 candidates we supported in the General Election, 22 won and one is in a run off.

Here are the results for our endorsed candidates:

OPEN SEATS
WON—Marsha Blackburn (TN-07); LOST—Janice Bowling (TN-04); WON—Chris Chocola (IN-02)—Challenged by pro-abortion woman candidate; WON—Mario Diaz-Balart (FL-25)—Challenged by pro-abortion woman candidate; WON—Elizabeth Dole (NC-Senate); WON—Scott Garrett (NJ-05)—Challenged by pro-abortion woman candidate; WON—Katherine Harris (FL-13)—Challenged by pro-abortion woman candidate; WON—Bill Janklow (SD-AL)—Challenged by pro-abortion woman candidate; WON—Terri Land (MI-Secretary of State); WON—Candice Miller (MI-10); WON—Marilyn Musgrave (CO-04)

INCUMBENTS
WON—Cong. Barbara Cubin (R) (WY-AL); WON—Cong. Jo Ann Davis (VA-01); WON—Cong. Jo Ann Emerson (R) (MO-8); WON—Cong. Randy Forbes (VA-04); WON—Cong. Melissa Hart (PA-04); WON—Secretary of State Mary Kiffmeyer (MN-SOS); WON—Cong. Sue Myrick (R) (NC-9); WON—Cong. Anne Northup (R) (KY-3); WON—Cong. Jim Nussle (IA-01)—Challenged by pro-abortion woman candidate; WON—Cong. Mike Pence (IN-06)—Challenged by pro-abortion woman candidate; WON—Cong. Ileana Ros-Lehtinen (R) (FL-18)

CHALLENGERS
LOST—Maria Guadelupe Garcia (CA-51), Lynette Boggs McDonald (NV-01)—Challenged by pro-abortion woman candidate, Marilyn O'Grady (NY-

04)—Challenged by pro-abortion woman candidate, Brose McVey (IN-07)—
Challenged by pro-abortion woman candidate, Norma Smith (WA-02);
WON—Jim Talent (MO-Senate)-Challenged by pro-abortion woman
candidate; RUN OFF—Suzanne Terrell (LA-Senate)-Challenged by pro-
abortion woman candidate". FROM:
Jennifer Bingham, SBA List Candidate Fund; DATE: November 6, 2002

"Missouri Senate Race May Turn on Abortion Issues...Missouri Right to
Life...the state's largest pro-life group say the U.S. Senate race will figure
prominently in its activities this fall. 'Electing Jim Talent is our top priority,'
said Ellie Dillon, a board member for the group's political-action committee.
As governor, Mel Carnahan was the chief nemesis of the state's pro-life
movement because of his support for abortion. This time, Missouri Right to
Life prepares to challenge his widow, who generally shares her husband's pro-
abortion views on the issue. Several national groups that back abortion,
including Emily's List, already have targeted Carnahan for support. In order
to qualify for the group's support, a candidate must not only favor abortion
but insist on funding it with taxpayer dollars. A spokesman for Talent says
abortion is one issue on which the candidates hold clear differences. 'He thinks
unborn children are human beings and deserve protection under the law,' said
spokesman Rich Chrismer.

Carnahan said in an interview that she also opposes partial-birth abortion, but
that she-unlike Talent-wants any ban to contain exemptions to protect the
health of the mother. Pro-life groups oppose such exceptions because they
allow for all such abortions to remain legal. Meanwhile, the Missouri chapter
of the National Abortion and Reproductive Rights Action League says it
expects to be very active this fall". St. Louis Post-Dispatch-August 18, 2002

"The tide of contributions from Washington, Hollywood and the East Coast
liberals continues without end. Liberal groups like Emily's List and NARAL
who work to defeat Pro-life candidates are lining up to write checks for Jean
Carnahan and to stop my traditional vote from ever reaching the floor of the
United States Senate.

Frankly, many of these Carnahan supporters are frustrated by our growing
strength (the recent poll conducted by KSDK News Channel 5 in St. Louis and
Survey USA showing us up by 6 points was a big blow). They believe the
traditional values you and I share are irrelevant in today's society and they
want the Democrats to keep the Senate so they can continue blocking President
Bush's efforts to create jobs, cut taxes and put traditional judges in our courts.

We can ill afford to show any signs of slowing down...or we will be handing
their friends in the media an excuse to write one negative story after another.
Fortunately, Missouri is the 'Show Me' state and this plays to our advantage

because we have the right message of opportunity, accountability and self-responsibility.

With the stakes so high—we cannot afford to have a single voter without all of the facts...and the facts speak for themselves."

"'Thank you' for all that you are doing to help me spread my message of bringing jobs to Missouri, defending our nation and restoring the timeless values that are central to being an American. Brenda and I can feel the support growing as we travel from corner to corner of Missouri. Momentum is clearly on our side. Our message is resonating with the voters and we have surged forward by gaining 7 points in the recent Zogby poll.

This race has a lot to do with President Bush. When I last met with the President, he made it clear that he is counting on us to win Missouri and return a Republican majority to the U.S. Senate. After 8 years of Clinton/Gore, President Bush has much to do to repair our nation's fabric...

From Hollywood to New York, liberals who would be hard pressed to find Missouri on a map, have opened their pocketbooks to make Jean Carnahan the most well-funded of any Democrat candidate. They have shattered every record by sending her over $8 million and more is on the way. And that DOES NOT include the millions that the National Democrats and special interests are using to saturate the airwaves with attacks...While we will never match them dollar-for-dollar, we must have the resources to continue our momentum.

From the start of this campaign, I have spread the message of my deep-rooted faith in traditional values and reducing the influence of Washington. The polls are proving that when voters have all facts, they choose my message for a better Missouri...

I am the most experienced and qualified candidate in this race: As a State Representative, I served 8 years in the Missouri Legislature in Jefferson City and was the House Minority Leader (the highest ranking Republican office in the State Legislature) for the last 4 of those years. As a United States Congressman, I served the 2nd District of Missouri in the U.S. Congress for 8 years where I was an Assistant Majority Leader, I served on the Armed Services Committee, I was a member of the Education Committee and I chaired the Small Business Committee.

We cannot allow the special interests to buy this election. We have come a long way together, our goal is in sight and we cannot afford to rest...we are surging in the polls because we have the right vision of traditional values and innovative ideas.—I must make sure that I have the resources to counter the special interests' attack ads while continuing to spread my message...Please stay the course with me during the crucial last weeks." Jim Talent

"Approximately 7 to 10 percent of Missouri's voters are still 'undecided'. These are the voters who are just now tuning into the Senate Race. Winning their support is the final piece we need to send Jim Talent to the United States Senate...the Carnahan camp...pay for negative attacks that are designed to shift attention from Jim Talent's positive message by attacking his character. We cannot afford to be silent in the face of attacks that rival what John Ashcroft faced just two years ago. From the start of this campaign, our strategy has been to spread Jim's vision for the future based on the bedrock values of commonsense, compassion, integrity and self-reliance. The Democrats have dodged the debate on issues from the beginning and this bizarre strategy is going backfire on them if we can...keep our message on the air...Jim Talent needs your help to make sure that these crucial undecided voters are given ALL of the facts...We are so close. Let's put Jim's vote in the Senate." Thank you. Lloyd Smith Campaign Manager

"Missouri Senate Candidates Can't be Much Closer The lead here continues to shift back and forth in this top target race. A recent poll showed pro-life candidate Jim Talent with a small lead and a poll over the weekend now shows pro-abortion Senator Jean Carnahan with a 3 point lead (50-47). The race could go down to a few votes in each precinct." The Pro-Life Infonet, Steven Ertelt
infonet@prolifeinfo.org, Oct. 20, 2002

"Republicans are...maneuvering for Sen. Jean Carnahan's immediate removal, should she lose in November. According to Missouri law, if former GOP Rep. Jim Talent should win in November, he could take her seat immediately because she was temporarily appointed two years ago. As a result, control of the Senate would go to Trent Lott and the Republicans in a possible lame duck session.

Republicans have already indicated that they would move for Talent's immediate swearing-in as a way to push through their legislation that has been blocked due to Democratic control (Roll Call, 9/19)." Taken from the Insider News, EMILY's List, Week of September 22, 2002.

I sat quietly in front of the TV, first eating supper, then taking notes and trying to get some other paper work done, until 1:00 AM, the time Jean Carnahan came on to give her concession speech, when I couldn't contain myself any longer and let out a "warhoop". This was the one I wanted most, because of my respect for Jim, and because it would give us control of the lame duck session. As it turned out, it put the Republicans over the top for control of the Senate in 2003, too. "According to FOX News, exit polls showed that about 80 percent of the people who voted for Missouri senate candidate Jim Talent were pro-life. Abortion was the second most important issue for Missouri voters." National Review; November 8, 2002; from an article written by Pia de Solenni, a fellow in life studies at Family Research Council, Washington, D.C.; forwarded by Infonet.

"...in Missouri, the subject of Senator Tom Daschle's last minute fund raising appeal for the National Abortion Rights Action League (NARAL), Senator-elect Jim Talent won his race by 1.2 percent. His winning margin was 22,578 votes. Seventeen percent of the electorate listed abortion as the ONE issue that mattered most. Of these, 80 percent, or 255,000 of the 318,000 votes cast on the abortion issue, went to Talent, more than 10 times his winning margin." Dr. Wanda Franz, the president of National Right to Life

"'Democrats turn heat on Elizabeth Dole.' *The News & Observer*"

"...you can count on every ultraliberal outfit in the country to pour into North Carolina in support of my opponent. The national Democrats have declared North Carolina a battleground state...the chance to pick up a seat in a closely divided U.S. Senate. And expert observers believe that I must win this race in order for Republicans to regain control of the United States Senate!...I need to prepare for the worst...This will be a very difficult, hard fought campaign... the leftwing special interests groups have such deep pockets...And they will spend it to defeat me and elect another liberal Senator from North Carolina. If we can't at least match them, I will lose-because the liberals will be able to get their message to the voters more effectively than my campaign. Elizabeth Dole, August 20, 2002 http://www.elizabethdole.org/home.asp Elizabeth Dole for U.S. Senate

Mrs. Dole (She's the wife of long time Republican Senator Bob Dole, who retired after he lost his bid for the Presidency to Bill Clinton. Regarded as highly intelligent and competent, she held responsible positions in every Republican administration that I can remember, and headed up the Red Cross while Clinton was in office.), won her primary race on September 10th, even though she had to drop her radio and TV ads to try to save funds for the race against her wealthy Democrat opponent.

"Dole supports a constitutional amendment banning abortion and has received the backing of North Carolina Right to Life. Abortion supporters urged support for Democratic candidate Erskine Bowles, because he backs abortion. A recent poll showed Dole ahead of Bowles 47% to 42%." Pro-Life Infonet; October 27, 2002

Elizabeth "Dole, 66...has been the front-runner", Erskine "Bowles, 57, has closed the gap to 6 percentage points in the most recent poll of likely voters, which had an error margin of 4 percentage points." "The narrowing poll numbers reflect the fact that North Carolina, like the country as a whole, is almost evenly split between Democrats and Republicans." Taken from a column by Stevenson Swanson in the Chicago Tribune, on Friday, November 1, 2002. The article also noted that Mrs. Dole was Transportation Secretary in the Reagan administration, and Labor Secretary for President Bush Senior. Dole won easily to become the first woman pro-life Senator.

"Las Vegas City Councilwoman and former Miss American Pageant contestant Lynette Boggs McDonald...an articulate, black Republican woman...is one of our best hopes in years to elect another black Republican to the U.S. Congress. Her victory would be historic...could be the first black conservative woman ever elected to Congress...drawing national press attention...endorsed by six prominent Nevada Democrats...What's more, the political party of Abraham Lincoln would increasingly look like an inviting place for black voters tired of the liberals' divisive racial pandering that traumatized America in the last election...I know from personal experience that many, many black voters hold the same conservative views that you and I do. Lynette...can reach out to black and other minority voters with more authority than the GOP itself can.

In fact, Lynette was recently named the Asian Chamber of Commerce 'Elected Official of the Year'. Lynette is pro-life and...The owner of her own consulting company...Married and proud mother of a six-year-old son...aided the founding of the Andre Agassi Charter School, the first opportunity for school choice in West Las Vegas...six years as a trustee of Catholic Charities of Southern Nevada...helped build the new St. Vincent Plaza. This shelter can house 900 people in need in addition to providing the 500,000 meals already being served each year...Lynette says the best way to help the homeless is to 'help them help themselves.'...sharp and principled Reagan Republican". Alan L. Keyes, Harvard Ph.D. Lynette lost 43% to 54%.

"President Bush stumps in support of Ferguson By Jennifer Potash NEWARK—Extolling Rep. Michael Ferguson's loyalty and hard work in Congress, President George W. Bush urged voters to give the freshman congressman another two-year term. 'If you find an honest person who works hard on behalf of every citizen in the district which he represents, and the person does in office what he said he would do, you need to send him back to Washington, D.C.,' President Bush said of Rep. Ferguson...During the trip back to Washington on Air Force One, Rep. Ferguson...discussed (issues) with President Bush and cabinet officers...the president's visit to New Jersey... illustrates the competitive nature of the race." The Princeton Packet, Tuesday, June 25, 2002

"But as you are aware, the Democrat National Committee has targeted me for defeat in November. They know that it's difficult for freshmen Congressmen running in new districts to get re-elected. They've decided that one of the best chances they have to regain control in Washington is right here in this Congressional District. New Jersey Republican Party Chairman, Joe Kyrillos, put it best when he said, 'If the Republican Party is to maintain its slim majority in Congress, then we must make sure that Mike Ferguson is reelected.' That's one reason why I'm campaigning so hard. I'm proud of my record and believe that in my short time in Congress I have worked to make a difference for America's families. The Democrats are sure they will take this seat. They are looking to the special interests...to win. But I intend to win by running a positive campaign that talks about my record. And I know that with the support of good friends like you, we will be successful in November." Mike Ferguson http://www.fergusonforcongress.com/

"As you may have heard by now, we celebrated a resounding victory in my first reelection campaign! The final numbers were outstanding. We won by a whopping eighteen points, 59% to 41%, over an opponent who was aggressive, hard-working, and who raised and spent over $1 million in his campaign. This was in addition to the hundreds of thousands of dollars the New Jersey Democratic State Committee spent targeting us for defeat. I have been humbled and honored to serve New Jersey in the House of Representatives for the past two years, and I deeply appreciate the opportunity to continue to serve ...public service is a noble calling. It is an opportunity to give new meaning to the values we stand for, and to strengthen our families and communities...". Congressman Mike Ferguson, November 22, 2002 Mike won, see stats above.

"Yet the fact remains, if NPLA-PAC is able to help elect enough Senators and Congressmen who have promised to stand up for the unborn, ending abortion-on-demand may be on the near horizon...with many more competitive House races than normal due to redistricting, experts on both sides agree this year's elections are more crucial to the future of ending abortion-on-demand than ever before in recent memory. That is why pro-lifers must work overtime to make sure their message reaches the American people, and that pro-life Americans know which politicians are on our side. Supporters of abortion-on-demand...know they no longer have a friend in the White House to veto pro-life bills, channel government funds to abortion groups, and appoint radical pro-abortion judges to the federal bench...have made it clear they will spend tens of millions to put both houses of the next Congress in the hands of pro-abortion politicians. NARAL has announced they alone are spending $40 million...collaborating with Hollywood and media elites to villainize pro-life members of Congress and elect their handpicked politicians. Perhaps an even more coveted prize would be control of the House of Representatives, where appropriations bills originate...'The facts must be given to the American people about...the millions of innocent lives destroyed...by doing so, pro-life activists can mute the abortion industry's propaganda machine.' Mary King ". From the Summer 2002 / Newsletter of the National Pro-Life Alliance

"Florida Gov Candidate Picks Pro-Abortion Running Mate Pro-abortion attorney Bill McBride (D), who is running against pro-life Florida Governor Jeb Bush (R), picked Senate Minority Leader Tom Rossin of Royal Palm Beach as his Lt. Gov. running mate. Rossin supports abortion and, as a member of the state legislature, voted against a partial-birth abortion ban and parental notification." Source: Pro-Life Infonet; September 19, 2002

"Florida Poll Shows Dead Heat in Gov Race A new poll says pro-life Gov. Jeb Bush and pro-abortion challenger Bill McBride are in a statistical dead heat three weeks before Election Day. An MSNBC/Zogby Poll released over the weekend showed Bush has the support of 48 percent of voters while McBride has the support of 45 percent. Seven percent of the 500 likely voters who were surveyed between Oct. 8 and Oct. 10 said they were undecided. The survey had a margin of error of 4.5 percentage points, which places the race in a statistical dead heat on the eve of a one-hour radio debate. A survey last month by Zogby International had Bush leading McBride by 10 points." Pro-Life Infonet; October 15, 2002

"Florida Gov Retains Sleight Edge in New Poll Pro-life Florida Gov. Jeb Bush was narrowly leading pro-abortion challenger Bill McBride on the eve of the candidates' last debate in the governor's race before the Nov. 5 election, a poll showed. A poll conducted Oct. 17-20 by the Mason-Dixon Polling & Research Inc. showed Bush ahead of McBride by 49 percent to 44 percent, with 6 percent of the 628 registered voters undecided. The poll, released Monday, had a margin of error of 4 percentage points." Election 2002 News Briefs Pro-Life Infonet; October 22, 2002

"Ten days before the election he went to a church in the Democratic stronghold of Broward County and declared 'life is precious' whether its an 'unborn child or an elder that is frail.' Two days before the election he went to another church, and said: 'I believe in the sanctity of innocent life from the unborn to the end. It's important for people in public life to uphold life." "Jeb...became the first Republican ever re-elected governor of Florida. The Republicans could learn a lesson from his leadership." "Human Events The Week Of November 11, 2002". Jeb won 56% to 43%.

"Terry McAuliffe, Chairman of the DNC, named Jeb Bush his number one target. With the Senate majority in jeopardy, and Jeb's democratic opponent in free fall, McAuliffe sent hundreds of thousands of dollars, as well as President Clinton and Vice President Gore to the Sunshine State in those closing days. He wasted valuable resources: Jeb Bush was reelected by a 13-point margin." Bay Buchanan in The American, November 2002, *Bush Delivers a Wipeout.*

"Democrats also failed to claim a single scalp from the 2000 election dispute. Conservative state House Speaker Tom Feeney won his race for a new congressional seat by 24 points and Katherine Harris, the nemesis of knee-jerk liberals all across the country, cruised to victory in her congressional race. In fact, Democrats in Florida even lost a seat, as veteran House incumbent Karen Thurman was defeated in the newly redrawn 5th District." Gary L. Bauer, CWF *Campaign Watch*, Fall 2002, Issue 17.

"** Governor Bush was the first Republican Governor ever re-elected in Florida history.
** For the first time ever, Republicans hold every seat on our State Cabinet.
** We re-elected every GOP Member of Congress, and added to our majority by gaining three seats.
** And we also increased our Republican majorities in both houses of the Florida Legislature.
...we must also reach out to hundreds of thousands of new Florida voters...and many conservative Democrats who are fed up with their party's ultra-liberal philosophy. If Florida's 27 Electoral Votes will be the deciding factor in the next election, we must make sure it doesn't take 36 days to count the votes... We must also do our part to protect and increase our Republican majority in the United States Senate and House of Representatives." Carole Jean Jordan, State Chairman, Republican Party of Florida-http://www.RPOF.org/

"Maryland Poll Shows Gov. Candidates Even Two polls released Tuesday show the Maryland gubernatorial race remains about even, but for the first time Republican Robert Ehrlich was the choice of more voters than Democrat Kathleen Kennedy Townsend. In the poll 46 percent said they would vote for Ehrlich, a four-term congressman who isn't pro-life but often votes for pro-life legislation, and 43 percent for Townsend, the lieutenant pro-abortion governor. Eleven percent were undecided." Source: Pro-Life Infonet; September 17, 2002

"Maryland Gov Candidate Gets Pro-Abortion Endorsement
The NARAL-PAC announced its endorsement of Kathleen Kennedy Townsend for Governor in Maryland's 2002 electoral race. "Governor Townsend is fully, firmly, unequivocally pro-choice," stated NARAL President Michelman. Michelman cited Townsend's opponent, Bob Ehrlich's voting record on choice, and added, "His record speaks louder than his rhetoric. Since his election to Congress, he has voted against a woman's right to choose more than 55 percent of the time." Source: Pro-Life Infonet; September 19, 2002

"Maryland Gov Race a Tie, Poll Shows Pro-abortion Democratic Lt. Gov. Kathleen Kennedy Townsend and Republican Rep. Robert Ehrlich, who has an 87% pro-life voting record, are in a statistical dead heat in the race for Maryland governor, a poll shows. The Potomac Survey Research Inc. survey released Tuesday showed Townsend leading Ehrlich 45 percent to 43 percent.

Twelve percent said they were undecided. A similar poll two months ago showed Townsend with a 3 point lead over Ehrlich. In January, Townsend had a 15 point lead." Source: Pro-Life Infonet; October 2, 2002 Bob Ehrlich won 51 percent to 48 percent to become the 1st Republican Governor in 34 years.

"Pennsylvania Pro-Life Gov Candidate Gains in Poll
The gubernatorial race between pro-abortion Democrat Edward Rendell and pro-life Republican Mike Fisher has tightened in recent weeks, according to a poll released Wednesday. It showed Rendell is the choice of 47 percent of registered voters and Fisher favored by 39 percent. That compares to 49 percent for Rendell and 36 percent for Fisher in a poll released July 24." Source: Pro-Life Infonet; September 19, 2002 Rendell won 53% to 45%.

"Election 2002: Campaign Updates From Around the Country Alabama Democratic Gov. Don Siegelman and pro-life Republican Rep. Bob Riley are running even in the governor's race less than two months before the Nov. 5 election, a new poll shows. The survey showed 45 percent support for Riley compared to 43 percent for Siegelman. Ten percent of respondents were undecided and 2 percent backed Libertarian John Sophocleus. Riley compiled a 100% pro-life voting record in Congress." Source: Pro-Life Infonet; September 17, 2002-Bob Riley won a cliff-hanger.

"Arizona President Bush will bring his fundraising prowess to Phoenix on Sept. 27 to assist pro-life candidate Matt Salmon's gubernatorial campaign. GOP officials hope to raise $1 million for Salmon and $1 million for the state Republican Party. Salmon emerged from the GOP primary with less than $30,000 on hand." Source: Pro-Life Infonet; September 17, 2002

"Arizona Poll Shows Salmon With Lead in Gov Race The two top candidates in Arizona's governor race are about even after visits by President Bush in support of pro-life Republican hopeful Matt Salmon, a poll released Tuesday found. A statewide poll of 569 likely voters found Salmon with support from 41 percent and pro-abortion Democrat Janet Napolitano with 38 percent. Independent Richard Mahoney was backed by 5 percent and Libertarian Barry Hess by 1 percent, with 15 percent undecided." Pro-Life Infonet; October 2, 2002, Election 2002 Campaign Updates

"Arizona Gov Race has Abortion Advocate Out Front The Arizona Daily Star in Tucson reported that two independent polls released yesterday show pro-abortion candidate Janet Napolitano has taken the lead for governor over pro-life Congressman Matt Salmon. A Behavior Research Center survey puts Napolitano up by 7 points among all voters and a KAET-TV poll shows her up by 9 points." Election 2002 News Briefs Pro-Life Infonet; October 22, 2002

"Arizona Pro-Life Gov Candidate Gains in New Poll

Pro-life gubernatorial candidate Matt Salmon has narrowed the gap in the Arizona governor's race but remains slightly behind pro-abortion candidate Janet Napolitano, according to a poll published Wednesday. Napolitano led the former congressman 42 percent to 37 percent in the telephone poll of 600 registered voters published in The Arizona Republic. A pair of third-party candidates had support from a combined 9 percent of those surveyed, and 11 percent remained undecided. Salmon had a 100% pro-life voting record in Congress." Pro-Life Campaigns 2002-Pro-Life Infonet, 10/30/2002 Janet Napolitano won 47 percent to 44 percent.

"South Dakota Gov Candidates Split on Abortion South Dakota gubernatorial candidates took different sides Thursday when abortion became part of the campaign. Pro-life Republican Mike Rounds and pro-abortion Democrat Jim Abbott debated issues at a forum hosted by KELO-AM in Sioux Falls. When asked what the candidates would do if states were given the power to act on the issue, Rounds said he would support legislation to end it. 'I believe abortion is wrong and would do everything I could to eliminate it,' he said. Abbott says abortion 'is a personal, moral and religious decision that I don't think government should be involved in.'" Election 2002 Updates From Across the US-Pro-Life Infonet; Oct. 15, 2002 Mike Rounds won 57 percent to 42 percent.

There are other Political Action Committees that concentrate on supporting pro-life candidates. Campaign For Working Families is a good example.

Founded by Gary Bauer several years ago, "The CWF Conservative Senate Majority Project...is targeted toward four U.S. Senate campaigns...Lindsey Graham in South Carolina, Jim Thune in South Dakota, Senator Jim Inhofe in Oklahoma and Senator Wayne Allard in Colorado..." to "regain conservative control of the U.S. Senate...every penny...will be used for pro-life, pro-family candidates". More recently they've added Ed Bryant, in the race for the Senate in Tennessee, favoring him over Lamar Alexander. To find out why, go to http://www.cwfpac.com/spotlight_bryant_02.htm. Their web site includes the following categories:

Election Candidates & Information, http://www.cwfpac.com/capwiz/candidates.htm;

CWF Endorsements, http://www.cwfpac.com/spotlight_02.htm;

Congressional Directory, http://www.cwfpac.com/capwiz/officials.htm;

Congressional Scorecard, http://www.cwfpac.com/capwiz/issues.htm;

Candidate Spotlight, http://www.cwfpac.com/spotlight_02.htm, and

Campaign Watch, http://www.cwfpac.com/newsletter.htm.

Ed Bryant lost in the GOP Primary to former presidential candidate Lamar Alexander. "Although Bryant was viewed as the stronger pro-life candidate, some say Alexander will be strong enough and will back pro-life legislative proposals in the Senate." Pro-Life Infonet; August 2, 2002

Rounding out their picks for the Senate as the races near the finish line are: Jeff Sessions-AL, Tim Hutchinson-AR, Saxby Chambliss-GA, Tony Perkins-LA, and Jim Talent-MO.

Campaign For Working Families 2002 Endorsement List, U.S. House: "Races are in order by state. Below is a list of CWF's pro-life, pro-family endorsed candidates. Please check our web site at http://www.cwfpac.com/ for new endorsements.

Dick Monteith	CA-18	Marilyn Musgrave	CO-4	Joe Hefley	CO-5
Tom Tancredo	CO-6	Bob Beauprez	CO-7	Jeff Miller	FL-1
Cliff Stearns	FL-6	Rick Keller	FL-8	Dave Weldon	FL-15
Tom Feeney	FL-24	Calder Clay	GA-3	Charlie Norwood	GA-10
Phil Gingrey	GA-11	Chris Chocola	IN-2	Mike Pence	IN-6
Steve King	IA-5	Geoff Davis	KY-4	Clyde Holloway	LA-5
John Kline	MN-2	Todd Akin	MO-2	Walter Jones	NC-3
Robin Hayes	NC-8	Charles Taylor	NC-11	Scott Garrett	NJ-5
Steve Pearce	NM-2	Joe Finley	NY-2	Mike Turner	OH-3
John Sullivan	OK-1	Melissa Hart	PA-4	Joe Wilson	SC-4
Bill Janklow	SD-AL	John Duncan	TN-2	Jeb Hensarling	TX-5
Rob Bishop	UT-1	John Swallow	UT-2	Jo Ann Davis	VA-1
Eric Cantor	VA-7	Frank Wolf	VA-10	Paul Ryan	WI-1
Ron Greer	WI-2	Mark Green	WI-8"		

So they managed to endorse more candidates than the other conservative PACs, while requiring them to meet more stringent criteria.

"…we improved our winning margin from 51% in 2000 to 65% in 2002!" Rick Keller

There's also a new PAC by Alan Keyes and Colleen Parro called the Life and Liberty PAC, http://www.lifeandlibertypac.org/.

"South Dakota House Candidate Opens Up Lead Pro-life Gov. Bill Janklow (R) has opened up a small but solid lead over pro-abortion challenger Stephanie Herseth (D) in the race for the open seat being vacated by pro-life Rep. John Thune (R). Janklow held a 47 percent to 40 percent advantage in the poll.

"Utah Pro-Life Candidate Gets Keyes' Backing One-time Republican presidential candidate Alan Keyes has endorsed pro-life candidate John Swallow in Utah's 2nd Congressional District. Keyes, a conservative talk-show host, criticized Democratic incumbent Rep. Jim Matheson for voting against a ban on partial-birth abortion. 'His voice is the heart of Utah, but his hands down in Washington are casting votes that are not for Utah or the nation's heart,' said Keyes." Election 2002 Campaign Updates Pro-Life Infonet; October 7, 2002, infonet@prolifeinfo.org. Janklow won 53% to 46%, Swallow lost 106,473 to 108,488.

"Utah Candidate Attacks Congressman's Pro-Abortion Record Pro-life candidate John Swallow, seeking to defeat incumbent pro-abortion congressman Jim Matheson (D) in Utah's second congressional district, is pointing voters to the abortion issue as the reason to make a change. Swallow cites Matheson's 31 percent pro-life voting record and his vote against a ban on partial-birth abortion as being out of step with Utah's strongly pro-life constituents. He said: 'Clearly a vote against this bill is a vote that is not in harmony with the values that we share in Utah.'"
Source: Steven Ertelt, Pro-Life Infonet; October 27, 2002

Alabama Citizens for Life PAC has endorsed endorsed Jeff Sessions (R) for the U.S. Senate. The Pro-Life Infonet, October 9, 2002
Their endorsements for the U.S. House were: 1 Jo Bonner (R), 12 Mitchell BeSheres (R), 2 Terry Everett (R), 13 Tommy Sherer (D), 3 Mike Rogers (R), 14 Ken Guin (D), 4 Robert Aderholt (R), 17 Mike Millican (D), 5 Steve Engel (R), 21 Jerry Dugan (R), 6 Spencer Bachus (R), 22 Sheldon Day (R).

From: The Pro-Life Infonet Steven Ertelt infonet@prolifeinfo.org
Election 2002 Campaign Updates October 11, 2002 Sponsored by
http://www.wevoteprolife.com/

Colorado Pro-Abortion Senate Candidate Gains in Poll

Pro-abortion challenger Tom Strickland has gained on pro-life Senator Wayne Allard in Colorado's Senate race, and the two are now running about even, according to a new poll. The poll, released Thursday, gave Allard 39 percent to 35 percent for Strickland. The margin of error was plus or minus 4.4 percentage points. A similar poll in August showed Allard with an 8-point lead.

New Hampshire Poll Now Shows Pro-Abort Leading

The race for the Senate seat is too close to call. After a summer of playing catch-up in the polls, it appears pro-abortion Democratic candidate, Gov. Jeanne Shaheen, has caught and maybe passed pro-life Republican Rep. John E. Sununu. According to the latest University of New Hampshire poll, Shaheen holds a slight 47 to 44 percent lead over Sununu, with a 4 percent margin of error.

Wyoming Gov Race Too Close to Call Says Magazine

A national magazine is giving Wyoming's race for governor a one-point spread, predicting pro-life Republican Eli Bebout will edge out Democrat Dave Freudenthal next month. According to a feature in the national magazine Campaigns & Elections, odds are 40 to 39 that Bebout will beat Freudenthal in the Nov. 5 general election.

"Colorado Senate Race a Dead Heat As President Bush stumped for incumbent pro-life Senate candidate Wayne Allard in Denver on Monday, and pro-abortion candidate Tom Strickland launched another bus tour on the Plains, the Rocky Mountain News/News4 poll found each candidate with 41 percent of the vote. And that means the election will probably turn on the get-out-the-vote efforts of both political parties, analysts said." Pro-Life Infonet; 10/30/2002 Eli Bebout lost 48% to 50%.

"New Hampshire Senate Race a Dead Heat Pro-abortion Gov. Jeanne Shaheen has pulled about even with pro-life Rep. John Sununu in their race for the Senate, according to a poll released Thursday. The poll showed 48 percent support for Sununu and 46 percent sup port for Shaheen. Six percent were undecided. An American Research Group poll released a week ago put Sununu slightly ahead of Shaheen, 51 percent to 43 percent, with 7 percent undecided. In the gubernatorial race, Craig Benson, supported by New Hampshire Citizens for Life, led Mark Fernald, a state senator, 52-33 percent, with 15 percent undecided." Pro-Life Infonet; October 24, 2002

"DETROIT—As the governor's race approaches its final month, Cardinal Adam Maida next Sunday will tell parishioners that Catholic public officials have 'a special moral obligation' on the abortion issue that supersedes the laws of the land. The advice to Catholic voters follows protests by anti-abortion activists aimed at Attorney General Jennifer Granholm, the Democratic candidate for governor, who is Catholic and pro-choice. Elected leaders who are Catholic, Maida believes, must work actively against laws that allow abortions. Such officeholders can not 'justify inaction with regard to the dignity of human life simply on the grounds that abortion is the law of the land,'...Granholm and her Republican opponent, Lt. Gov. Dick Posthumus, both reacted to Maida's statement in writing. 'Because of my Catholic faith,' Granholm said, 'I believe that life begins at conception and am personally opposed to abortion. However, different faiths believe differently about when life begins and in a pluralistic society, government should respect those differences. 'This matter should be a private decision that a woman makes in consultation with her faith, her family and her physician.' Posthumus, a member of the Church of the Brethren, a Protestant branch, who is pro-life, said his rival can't have it both ways. 'It troubles me when elected officials try to position themselves on both sides of this debate by claiming to be 'personally pro-life,' while promoting a culture which destroys life,' he said. 'I am proud to stand with Cardinal Maida and leaders of faith across this state in defense of life.' 'When it is impossible to overturn or prevent passage of a law which allows or promotes abortion, an elected official should always seek to limit the harm done by such laws,' said Maida". The Detroit News, by Kim Kozlowski From: Colleen Parro rnclife@swbell.net Date: Sun, 29 Sep 2002 20:52:32-0500

"Right to Life of Michigan Supports 2002 Pro-Life Candidates Right to Life of Michigan's PAC has put together several guides to help you find what you need. By going to http://www.rtl.org/html/elections/2002/index.html you can find a listing of pro-life candidates divided by congressional districts. Here you can find pro-life candidates for the national, state and local level. Furthermore, Right to Life of Michigan has put together a web site showing gubernatorial candidate Jennifer Granholm's extreme pro-abortion stance. Visit http://www.granholmgarble.com"The Pro-Life Infonet; 10/29/2002

Jennifer Granholm won. I wasn't real surprised by that. I saved a scrap of a newspaper column on her, but I'm not sure what paper I cut it out of at this late date (01/04/03). This is a woman with impeccable credentials. I don't live in Michigan, so my information on her isn't real thorough, but the only thing I can find wrong with her is that she's pro-abortion. She would be headed for a run for the Presidency-except that she wasn't born in the U.S., and the President of the United States is the only office that the candidate must be born in the U.S. to hold. She's smart, attractive, tough, and an amiable campaigner. "Granholm's story is now the stuff of political legend—in British Columbia where she was born, California where she lived as a child, and now Michigan where she will govern a state. At 21 she became a U.S. Citizen and gave up a fledgling Hollywood career. She studied political science at the University of California-Berkley and law at Harvard. A former federal prosecutor; she became the state's attorney general in 1998." Was that from the Tribune News Service or Human Events? Anyway, considering she went to two of the most liberal schools in the country, it isn't surprising she has a liberal perspective. What intrigues me, is that she's so smart; and really smart adults don't generally push for abortion unless they have ulterior motives. She has a legislature with a strong pro-life philosophy, and I think it's possible she might start to finesse the issue to the benefit of the pro-life movement.

Michigan, apparently, has a very active pro-life movement, although all it's elected candidates don't necessarily reflect that. I guess we'll just have to wait and see what happens, but here's what they're saying in Michigan: "When asked what Michiganders can expect from Granholm's tenure, legislative director for Right to Life of Michigan, Ed Rivet, said 'we're not going to assume anything.' He added that she may be beholden to Emily's List, a political action committee that aggressively supports pro-abortion Democratic women candidates. However, with a pro-life legislature, it will be difficult for the new administration to institute anti-life policies." From: The Pro-Life Infonet, December 17, 2002

"Find Out Who The Pro-Life Candidates Are The RNC/Life 2002 Congressional PAC Report can be viewed on our web site, http://www.rnclife.org. As filing deadlines close in the various states, the RNC/Life Candidate Questionnaire is being mailed to congressional candidates who are competing in contested Republican Primaries. As we receive the candidate's responses, we will list them in the PAC Report. The first primaries are being held in March and the last one will take place in the fall. *Please check the website frequently for additions as they occur.*" From the RNC For Life Report, March/April 2002.

The Madison Project-Information on conservative candidates: http://www.madisonproject.org/

"In 1994, I undertook a task many considered futile. I ran for State Representative against an entrenched, wealthy incumbent. Although I was outspent, my message convinced the voters of the 99th Legislative District that I would better represent them. The voters have continued to have faith in me, re-electing me with substantial victories in 1996, 1998, and 2000. In each of these races my campaign was outspent by a 2-to-1 margin. Nevertheless, many have recognized my qualifications in challenging this 2004 Presidential hopeful: '...neither money nor the redrawn lines has deterred State Rep. Catherine Enz, touted by many as the most experienced politician to ever challenge Gephardt for his job since he was elected congressman in 1976. '...she served eight years and made a name for herself as a staunch conservative who pulls no punches.'-St. Louis Post-Dispatch, July 28, 2002 'She's got some substance. Cathy may give (Gephardt) fits...'-Paul Zemitsch 'We think she's dynamite!'-John Hancock, Missouri Republican Party Executive Director

"On November 5, I will face an adversary-Congressman Richard Gephardt-who some have said is *'undefeatable.'* Yet, we believe he can be *defeated.* He has *abandoned his constituency* and left them behind in his desire for *personal power.* Should we grant Gephardt yet another term to advance his own *agenda* while he ignores the interests of those he purports to represent? I have effectively reached out to voters in the newly redrawn 3rd Congressional District. I am convinced that they truly believe that I would best represent their values-unlike Richard Gephardt! This is a critical election which will affect your future and the direction of our nation for years to come. Seize this *unique opportunity* to eliminate the persistent undermining of our values. I need your help *now* to defeat Dick Gephardt!" Catherine (Cathy) S. Enz For U.S. Congress http://www.enz4congress.com/ "As a pro-life woman, my candidacy will offer the voters an opportunity to cast a ballot for life. The word 'American' ends with the four letters that read, 'I CAN.' That is and will continue to be my motto." From her web site!

Gephardt is one of the most powerful people in Congress-yet he is vulnerable at home. Two years ago, although it was obscured by the Gore theatrics, he barely won election by keeping the polls open late and having his people go door to door to round up voters.

"...there's the potential for voter registration fraud in Missouri—especially in the St. Louis area—where Democrat fraud was rampant in 2000." TVC, Thursday, October 24 @ 21:22:10 EDT

"Facing an opponent who has little chance of winning, Gephardt, who has aspirations of running again for President in 2004, stopped in town last weekend to remind voters that he's up for reelection. The job's a lot easier since he pressed state lawmakers last year to draw him a more Democrat-friendly district." St. Louis Post Dispatch; October 27, 2002, from Pro-Life Infonet. Gephardt won 59% to 39%.

"Michigan Poll Shows Pro-Abortion Gov Candidate Ahead Pro-abortion gubernatorial candidate Jennifer Granholm leads Republican Dick Posthumus by 10 points, according to a poll released Wednesday. The poll by EPIC/MRA found that Granholm, who is state attorney general, was supported by half of the 600 likely voters surveyed. Posthumus, the lieutenant governor, got 40 percent. Nine percent were undecided. A EPIC/MRA poll conducted Oct. 2-3 and 6 found Granholm leading Posthumus 53 percent to 41 percent. In the Senate race, Democratic incumbent Carl Levin led Republican state Rep. Andrew Rocky Raczkowski 57 percent to 30 percent.

New Jersey: Garret and Sumers Clashing on Abortion Republican pro-life House candidate Scott Garrett and his pro-abortion opponent Anne Sumers, who are vying for New Jersey's 5th District House seat, 'differ sharply' on their abortion views, the Newark Star-Ledger reports. Sumers has expressed 'strong support' for abortion, saying, 'We don't need any further laws on abortion. I want it to be safe and legal and rare.' Garrett opposes abortion and would allow it only to save a woman's life.

Pennsylvania Gov Candidate Gets Thumbs Down from Santorum Pro-life Sen. Rick Santorum said Pennsylvanians should oppose pro-abortion Gov. candidate Ed Rendell because of his extreme stance in favor of abortion. Santorum called Rendell an 'advocate of abortion.' He urged pro-life voters to work hard for the pro-life contender, Attorney General Mike Fisher, in the Nov. 5 election. 'Pro-choice doesn't even begin to describe where he is on abortion,' he said of Rendell. 'He will be the first governor in Pennsylvania's history since Roe v. Wade who will be adamantly advocating the pro-choice agenda. This guy is an advocate of abortion. He's not just someone who, you know, just sort of lets it slide. He goes out and runs campaigns about how pro-abortion he is,' Santorum said.

South Carolina Senate Candidates Debate Abortion NBC's 'Meet the Press' on Sunday featured a debate between South Carolina's Senate candidates: pro-life Rep. Lindsey Graham (R-S.C.) and pro-abortion College of Charleston President Alex Sanders (D) about their views on several issues, including abortion. Graham, who has a solid pro-life voting record in Congress and is the sponsor of pro-life legislation protecting unborn children, said he opposes abortion. Sanders said he thinks abortion is 'a legitimate choice' for some women and not 'a decision that the government should make for a woman.'

Maine's Pro-Life Democrat Candidate NPR's 'Weekend All Things Considered' on Sunday reported on the 'unusual' but 'closely watched' race in Maine's 2nd House District, where pro-life Democratic state Senator Mike Michaud is running against Republican Kevin Raye, an abortion supporter. The race is one of the few in the country with a pro-life Democrat running against a pro-abortion Republican." The Pro-Life Infonet Steven Ertelt Oct. 17, 2002

Lindsey Graham won 54%-44%.

"Maine Pro-Life Dem Congressional Candidate Leads The Bangor Daily News reported that pro-abortion candidate Kevin Raye has pulled to within less than a percentage point of pro-life Democrat Mike Michaud in their race for Maine's open 2nd District seat, according to the newspaper's poll released yesterday. The poll shows 36.5 percent for Michaud, 35.8 for Raye and 24 percent undecided." Pro-Life Campaigns 2002 Report Pro-Life Infonet; October 30, 2002

"...on the race for governor between Republican Lt. Gov. Dick Posthumus and Democrat Jennifer Granholm...the contest has tightened up considerably in recent weeks. Posthumus's strong performance in televised debates has been considered a major reason for the tighter-than-expected contest." Human Events, Oct 21, 2002 MI

"Michigan's Gov Race Now Much Closer, New Poll Shows Gubernatorial candidates Jennifer Granholm, who is pro-abortion, and pro-lifer Dick Posthumus are now about even in the latest gubernatorial poll. The poll, released Thursday, showed Granholm had the support of 47 percent of 400 likely voters polled. Posthumus got 39 percent and 12 percent were undecided. 'In the last two nights of polling, Jennifer Granholm led by only four points,' Steve Mitchell of Mitchell Research & Communications told The Detroit News for a Friday story. Posthumus continued to build support among the right-to-life voters. Three times as many pro-lifers now favor him over Granholm, the poll showed. Right to Life of Michigan planned to mail pro-Posthumus literature to as many as 600,000 Michigan households in the final weeks of the campaign. 'We have done and are doing get-out-the-vote calls. We are doing independent mailings for him,' said Larry Galmish, who directs the Right-to-Life political-action committee." Pro-Life Infonet; 10/27/2002

"Carl Levin's main strategy for victory...is to win big in Detroit. As you can imagine, I'm not going to win Detroit where Democrats outnumber Republicans more than 2:1. But in the rest of the state I have a fighting chance. If I can increase the percentage of the rural vote I'm going to get by even 15% because of the work I'm doing in the next two to three weeks, I will have a fighting chance of offsetting my expected losses in Detroit. I need to spend...more in key rural swing counties in these next two weeks to make sure I can ratchet up my victory in my district and elsewhere by the 15% I need to pull off an upset." Andrew "Rocky" Raczkowski, October 16, 2002

From: The Pro-Life Infonet Steven Ertelt infonet@prolifeinfo.org
Subject: Arkansas Right to Life Releases State Voter's Guide
Source: Pro-Life Infonet; October 14, 2002

"Arkansas Right to Life Releases State Voter's Guide

Little Rock, AR—One of the greatest social responsibilities is to elect officials who determine the laws by which our society lives. We are all called to common commitment to protect human life, especially those who are poor and vulnerable. If we vote for candidates who do not respect the sanctity of life, we shouldn't be surprised when they allow nearly born children to be cruelly killed by the partial-birth abortion technique or when they support physician-assisted suicide and euthanasia.

In this voter's guide you will find helpful information that will assist you in determining where the candidates stand on important life issues. Every candidate was given the opportunity to share their views. For your convenience, the phone numbers of those who did not respond to our questionnaire have been provided along with our assessment of the previous voting record of incumbents. Find Arkansas Right to Life's survey of state legislative candidates at: http://www.artl.org/state.shtml Find Arkansas Right to Life's survey of Congressional candidates at: http://www.artl.org/congress.shtml ".

From: The Pro-Life Infonet Steven Ertelt infonet@prolifeinfo.org
Election 2002 Campaign Updates From Across the US; Oct. 20, 2002

"Alaska Gov Candidates Are Close in Poll The Anchorage Daily News reported that gubernatorial candidates Fran Ulmer and Sen. Frank H. Murkowski are even in the polls. Ulmer, an abortion advocate and the current lieutenant governor, trailed pro-life Senator Murkowski by double digits in polls last spring. The latest poll, commissioned by KTUU-TV Channel 2 in Anchorage, showed Ulmer backed by 46 percent to 43 percent for Murkowski, with a 5 percent margin of error.

Minnesota Gov Candidates in Very Tight Race A new poll over the weekend shows pro-abortion State Senate Majority Leader Roger Moe (D) with 29%, pro-life State House Majority Leader Tim Pawlenty (R) with 29%, and pro-abortion ex-Congressman Tim Penny (IP), with 27%. Polls continue to show a virtual three-way tie in this multi-party race.

Oklahoma Pro-Life Candidate for Gov Hold Slim Lead Pro-life Congressman Steve Largent (R) continues to hold a small lead. A recent poll shows him with 43 percent over abortion advocate Brad Henry (38%) and Gary Richardson (16%), who has a mixed position.

Rhode Island Pro-Life Gov Candidate Pulling Closer A new poll shows pro-abortion gubernatorial candidate Myrth York (D) with 48% and pro-life businessman Don Carcieri (R) with 45%. Seven percent remain undecided. York lost her last two attempts to win the gubernatorial race.

South Carolina Poll Shows Pro-Life Candidates Leading Pro-life challenger Mark Sanford has a slight lead over incumbent pro-abortion Gov. Jim Hodges, according to a poll released Friday. The poll, which indicates that

Sanford had 45% of the vote to Hodges' 41 percent, has a margin of error of 4 percentage points.

Tennessee Gov Candidates Tie in New Poll A new poll shows the two nominees for governor of Tennessee running an even race. The poll found Phil Bredesen, a former Nashville mayor, favored by 35.1 percent of the registered voters surveyed, while 34.5 percent favored pro-life candidate Van Hilleary, a congressman. In a similar UT poll conducted Sept. 3-10, Bredesen led by 8 percentage points-37 percent to 29 percent."

"In Alaska, Republican Sen. Frank Murkowski beat Democrat Lt. Gov. Fran Ulmer 56 percent to 41 percent. Republican Tim Pawlenty beat Democratic-Farm-Labor candidate Doug Moe and Independent Party nominee Tim Penny in Minnesota race to succeed Ventura. With 97 percent of the precincts counted, Pawlenty had 45.6 percent, Moe 35.6 percent and Penny 16 percent. Former Clinton administration official Bill Richardson was elected governor of New Mexico, defeating Republican John Sanchez, 57 percent to 38 percent. Of the 10 former Clintonoids who ran for office Tuesday, Richardson is one of only two to win, Fox reported. Republican Donald L. Carcieri, a retired corporate executive, defeated Democrat Myrth York for the open governor's seat in heavily Democrat Rhode Island, 54 percent to 45 percent, with 99 of precincts reporting. Former South Carolina Congressman Mark Sanford unseated incumbent Democrat Gov. Jim Hodges 53 percent to 47 percent. In Tennessee, former Nashville Mayor Phil Bredesen defeated Republican Rep. Van Hilleary, 51 percent to 48 percent." Taken from Republicans Beat Mid-term Election 'Jinx,' Sweep Congress By Jeff Johnson CNSNews.com Congressional Bureau Chief November 06, 2002 Capitol Hill. Steve Largent lost, 441,277 to Henry's 448,143, in Oklahoma.

Republican Mike Cox for Michigan Attorney General, PO Box 532197, Livonia, Michigan, 48153. "...differences between the candidates. Gary Peters, for example, was campaign co-chairman of Proposal B (the losing statewide initiative in 1998 to permit assisted suicide) and has indicated he opposes a ban on state funding of partial birth abortion...Cox...has the strong support of Michigan Right-to-Life.

"Michigan's 11th District (Thad) McCotter vs. (Jack) Kelley

(McCotter) makes no bones about being pro-life and...having the support of Michigan Right-to-Life...Those who have watched him closely...agree that Thad McCotter is a natural for a leadership role in Congress. (McCotter for Congress, 39202 Lyndon St., Livonia, Mich. 48154; 734-524-0834)" Election 2002 Pro-Life Campaign Updates, Pro-Life Infonet; October 24, 2002

360

"Michigan Congressional Candidates Differ on Abortion The New York Times on Friday profiled the race between Thaddeus McCotter (R) and Kevin Kelley (D) for the 11th District in Michigan. McCotter, who opposes abortion, and Kelley, who supports abortion, face 'one of the closest House races in the country,' the Times reports. Although McCotter 'seemed to have the seat sewed up' earlier this year, Kelley has cited recent polls that found the race 'a dead heat.' McCotter, however, said that according to recent polls conducted by his campaign, he leads the race by 10 percentage points." Campaign 2002 News Briefs, Pro-Life Infonet; October 22, 2002 Thaddeus G. McCotter won, 57% to 40%, and is seen as a sort of "rising star".

Hawaii...2nd District...Bob McDermott...A U.S. Marine veteran of Desert Storm and father of three...I'm pro-life, I support the 2nd Amendment, and I support tax cuts...McDermott for Congress, 1509 Piikea St., Honolulu, HA 96818". By John Gizzi, Human Events, The Week of October 21, 2002 McDermott lost to Mink, who was deceased, 40% to 56%, so another election was required. http://www.BobMcDermottforCongress.org/

"Alabama Gov Race a Dead Heat Poll Shows A poll conducted by the Alabama Education Association shows the governor's race is in a dead heat. Gerald Johnson, director of the Capital Survey Research Center, the polling arm of the AEA, said the trend favors pro-abortion Gov. Don Siegelman because pro-life Rep. Bob Riley led 49 percent to 37 in an Oct. 1 poll with about a 5 percent margin of error. The latest poll shows both candidates at 40 percent. Libertarian John Sophocleus is at 3 percent. David Azbell, spokesman for Riley's campaign, said Riley's polls show the congressman with a slight lead with the trend favoring him." Election 2002 ProLife Campaign Updates, Pro-Life Infonet; October 24, 2002

"Oregon Pro-Life Gov Candidate Gaining Significantly in Poll When the Oregon governor's race was taking shape, a sense of inevitability surrounded pro-abortion candidate Ted Kulongoski's campaign. After the primary, the former state legislator and Supreme Court justice held a double-digit lead over pro-life rival Kevin Mannix in an August poll. But with only weeks before the election, Kulongoski has watched his lead in the polls dwindle in the face of an aggressive campaign by Mannix. Kulongoski received 45 percent in a recent poll to Mannix's 41 percent. Mannix has also been criticized for a pro-life stance Kulongoski says is 'too extreme' for Oregon." Pro-Life Infonet; October 24, 2002 Ted Kulongoski 49%, Kevin Mannix 46%, in a liberal state.

"The two candidates for Illinois governor—pro-life candidate Jim Ryan and pro-abortion candidate Rod Blagojevich—hold polar opposite views on abortion. Ryan opposes abortion and supports banning partial-birth abortion procedures, enacting parental notification for minors seeking abortions and

banning public funding of abortions. Blagojevich, as a member of Congress, has voted against the pro-life position on each of these items and holds a 0% pro-life voting record. 'In this election, the difference in candidates on the life issue is pretty stark,' said Carol Wright, a spokeswoman for Illinois Citizens for Life, which distributes a voters guide characterizing Ryan as 'fully pro-life' and Blagojevich as 'totally opposed to pro-life issues.' Meanwhile, Planned Parenthood and Voters For Choice last week began running ads against Ryan. 'My opponent has voted against even that which I think is very reasonable— parental notification,' Ryan said in a debate last week." From: The Pro-Life Infonet Source: Associated Press; October 26, 2002. Steven Ertelt infonet@prolifeinfo.org
Blagojevich won big because of the scandals in the current Republican Governor's (George Ryan) tenure. Whether he would have won against a scandal free and united Republican Party is hard to say.

"Wisconsin Pro-Life Gov Candidate Closes the Gap Pro-abortion candidate Jim Doyle's lead over pro-life Gov. Scott McCallum has dwindled markedly, leaving the race for governor a dead heat, according to a poll released Monday. Of 418 likely voters surveyed by telephone last week, 38 percent said they would vote for Doyle and 36 percent favored McCallum. Sixteen percent were undecided and 10 percent favored third party candidates.

Texas Right to Life Urges Support for Lt Gov Candidate Houston, TX—Most political experts agree that Texas' unique system of government makes the office of Lieutenant Governor the most powerful position in the state Legislature. The Lt. Governor has the ability to single-handedly control the legislative agenda of the legislature and, thus, the power to determine if pro-life legislation gets a chance or dies without a fight. Texas Right to Life recognizes this and is urging pro-life Texans to back pro-life Texas Land Commissioner David Dewhurst. His Democratic opponent, John Sharp, has made very clear his strong opposition to any legislation protecting the unborn.

Wyoming Poll Has Pro-Lifer in Gov Race Lead A snapshot of Wyoming voters two weeks before the general election shows that the gubernatorial race is too close to call, especially given the large number of voters that say they are still undecided. Out of the 400 likely voters that responded to a poll commissioned last week by the Wyoming Tribune-Eagle on behalf of the Wyoming Newspaper Group, 44 percent said they would vote for pro-life candidate Eli Bebout. Another 36 percent said they would vote for Democrat Dave Freudenthal. The remaining 20 percent said they were still undecided." Pro-Life Campaigns Report Pro-Life Infonet; Oct. 30, 2002 Jim Doyle won 45 percent to 42 percent.

"The battle for the Senate is raging all over the United States. Republicans have felt they only needed a one-vote victory for them to regain control of the

Senate, but liberal Republican Lincoln Chafee (R-RI) may leave the party if Republicans gain a one-seat majority this November. Chafee has previously threatened to leave the party if Republicans gain a majority. To be safe, Republicans really need two or three Senate take-overs this November so Chafee's departure won't be missed." TVC, Thursday, October 24, 2002

See the Current Events section for the Doug Forrester, Sen. Robert Torricelli, Frank Lautenberg flap, in the New Jersey Senate race.

Get Out the Vote

I believe pro-life people should know who the pro-life candidates are, and should make the effort to vote. Many of these races are very close, and you have a chance to make a difference by voting.

"The care of human life and happiness, not their destruction, is the first and only legitimate object of good government." Thomas Jefferson

Where Do the Candidates Stand? US Senate, National Right to Life, "These flyers are produced with the intention for you to distribute them via email or printed form." http://www.nrlc.org/Election2002/Senate/

"Click on your state to view a list of Pro-Life candidates." SBA List Election 2002 national map with links to candidates by state: http://www.sba-list.org/index.cfm/section/election2002.html.

"We Vote ProLife.com Launched to Highlight Pro-Life Candidates

A new online pro-life voting guide, http://www.wevoteprolife.com, will point the pro-life community toward pro-life candidates and makes the candidates' positions on life issues crystal clear. Victories in key Senate races in Missouri, Iowa, Minnesota, South Dakota and elsewhere could turn the tide in our favor." From: The Pro-Life Infonet Source: We Vote Pro-Life PAC; October 9, 2002

I found the following opportunity on their web site: "Please also take a moment to sign our Pro-Life Pledge and let the world know that you take candidates' positions on abortion and other life issues seriously and that you will vote first and foremost for candidates who are pro-life! *'As pro-life people, we understand the horrific far-reaching effects of almost 30 years of legalized abortion in the United States. We look forward to the day when our laws protect the sanctity and dignity of human life and truly put women and children first instead of sacrificing one or the other. Although we may feel passionately about other political issues, we know the right to life, as the basic civil and human right, is the cornerstone of the freedoms and liberties we enjoy. Therefore, we will make a candidate's views on pro-life issues our top priority when considering voting for any candidate for any elected office on the national, state, or local level. We will vote for as many pro-life candidates as possible—regardless of political party. We will work within our own political party to advance the pro-life perspective and promote pro-life candidates who seek to change the law and bring about a culture that respects life. We will vote Pro-Life!'*"

From: The Pro-Life Infonet Weekly, Steven Ertelt, November 3, 2002 Reply-To: infonet@prolifeinfo.org

"Pro-Life Guide to Tuesday's Election

Washington, DC (ProLifeInfo.org)—We at the Pro-Life Infonet have compiled a comprehensive guide to finding pro-life candidates for Tuesday's mid-term elections. This guide lists web sites in each state that you can use to find pro-life candidates endorsed by state pro-life groups, voting records, comparison pieces and more.

Please pass this information on to pro-life friends and family.

For a national pro-life voting guide and list of pro-life candidates, visit We Vote Pro-Life at http://www.wevoteprolife.com. For additional information, find your state below:

Alabama-http://www.wevoteprolife.com/alabama.htm
Arizona-http://www.azlifepac.org
Alaska-http://www.akrtl.org/endorsements.html
Arkansas-http://www.artl.org/state.shtml
California-http://www.californiaprolife.org/voter/voter.html
Colorado-http://www.wevoteprolife.com/colorado.htm
Connecticut-http://www.wevoteprolife.com/connecticut.htm
Delaware-http://www.wevoteprolife.com/delaware.htm
Florida-http://www.frtl.org/pac/endorsed%20candidates%20for%20general%20election.htm
Georgia-http://www.wevoteprolife.com/georgia.htm
Hawaii-http://www.hrtl.org/
Idaho-http://www.idahochooseslife.org/endorsements.HTM
Illinois-http://www.ifrl-pac.com
Indiana-http://www.candidatesurveys.com
Iowa-http://www.irlc.org/legislators/index.htm
Kansas-http://www.kfl.org/politics/index.shtml
Kentucky-http://www.krla.org/krla_pac_endorsements.htm
Louisiana-http://www.wevoteprolife.com/louisiana.htm
Maine-http://www.mainerighttolife.com/nws-votguide.html
Maryland-http://www.mdrtl.org/endorsements.htm
Massachusetts–http://www.prolife mcfl.org/About%20Us/candidate%20survey%20data.htm
Michigan-http://www.rtl.org/html/elections/2002/index.html
Minnesota-http://www.mccl.org/votersquide.pdf
Mississippi-http://www.wevoteprolife.com/mississippi.htm

Missouri-http://www.missourilife.org/election.htm
Montana-http://www.wevoteprolife.com/montana.htm
Nebraska-http://www.nebraskartl.org/election2002.htm
Nevada-http://www.wevoteprolife.com/nevada.htm
New Hampshire-http://www.citizensforlife.org/
New Jersey-http://www.wevoteprolife.com/newjersey.htm
New Mexico-http://www.wevoteprolife.com/newmexico.htm
New York-http://www.wevoteprolife.com/newyork.htm
North Carolina-http://www.ncrtlpac.bizland.com
North Dakota-http://www.ndrl.org/
Ohio-http://www.ohiovotesforlife.org/
Oklahoma-http://www.wevoteprolife.com/oklahoma.htm
Oregon-http://www.wevoteprolife.com/oregon.htm
Pennsylvania-http://www.wevoteprolife.com/pennsylvania.htm
Rhode Island-http://www.wevoteprolife.com/rhodeisland.htm
South Carolina-http://www.wevoteprolife.com/southcarolina.htm
South Dakota-http://www.sdrighttolife.org/
Tennessee-http://www.wevoteprolife.com/tennessee.htm
Texas-http://www.texasrighttolife.com/pac/index.html
Utah-http://www.wevoteprolife.com/utah.htm
Vermont-http://www.vrlc.net
Virginia-http://www.vshl.org/elections
Washington-http://www.wevoteprolife.com/washington.htm
West Virginia-http://www.wvforlife.org/pac-endorsements-2002.html
Wisconsin-http://www.wrtl.org/temp.html
Wyoming-http://www.wevoteprolife.com/wyoming.htm

Copy and paste to the Location window at the top of your browser: Highlight
the address you want to go to by placing the cursor at the beginning of the
address and holding down the left button on your mouse as you drag the cursor
over the address. Then click on Edit at the top of your screen, and then Copy
in the drop-down menu. You now have the address on the Clipboard (unseen).

Next click in the Location window to highlight it, then click Edit and Paste and
it will replace the current address with the one you want to go to. Hit Enter,
and it should take you there. For two line addresses you will have to paste the
first line, and then append the second one to it, being careful not to replace
what you already pasted. Of course, if you have the ebook version, and you're
online, you can just click the link.

"The Republican-led House has passed several major pieces of pro-life
legislation. But Tom Daschle has blocked votes on every single one, including
the ban on partial-birth abortion a barbaric procedure that destroys unborn

children in the 7th and 8th months of pregnancy-even though he has voted for the ban in the past. The fact is, our opponents in Congress don't have Bill Clinton's veto to hide behind anymore. That makes Tom Daschle the 'only barrier' to the enactment of pro-family, pro-life legislation. And that's what is at stake this year, my friends. This election is about far more than just control of the United States Senate-it is literally about life and death." Gary L. Bauer, Chairman, Campaign for Working Families, Thursday, October 3, 2002 (Gary apparently forgot we did manage to get the Born Alive Infants Protection Act through the Senate because they wanted to avoid having to debate it.)

From: The Pro-Life Infonet infonet@prolifeinfo.org
Reply-To: Steven Ertelt infonet@prolifeinfo.org
Subject: Democrats Doing Their Worst to Lose the Catholic Vote
Source: Creators Syndicate; July 22, 2002

"Democrats Doing Their Worst to Lose the Catholic Vote
by Marks Sheilds

...in a deliberate act of political bigotry, the Democratic National Committee is daily telling Catholic voters to get lost. Do you think I exaggerate? Then go to the Democratic National Committee website. There you will finds 'links of interest from the Democratic National Committee.'

If your interests include the environment or veterans or Gay and Lesbian or Jewish-American or pro-choice or African-American, the DNC will happily suggest dozens of places for you to spend time. There is under 'Catholic' only one Democratic Party-endorsed site to visit: the absolutely unflinching champions of abortion on demand, 'Catholics for a Free Choice.' How offensive is this? Los Angeles Times national exit poll taken on Election Day 2000, which found that 14 percent of the electorate—that translates into 14.7 million live voters—named abortion as the most important issue in deciding their presidential vote.

Uncritical, unrestricted access to abortion for all has become the litmus test for the national Democratic Party."

To Catholics I would like to say: Abortion on demand is not birth control. It's about killing fellow Catholics. Think about that when you are deciding who to vote for. It's your responsibility.

From: The Pro-Life Infonet, Steven Ertelt infonet@prolifeinfo.org
Subject: Father Frank Pavone: Be There at Election Time
Source: Priests for Life; October 12, 2002

Intecon

Be There at Election Time by Father Frank Pavone

[Pro-Life Infonet Note: Father Frank Pavone is the co-founder of Priests for Life-http://www.priestsforlife.org/. To find more information about pro-life candidates in your state, see http://www.wevoteprolife.com.

"After all is said and done, there is one basic rule for carrying out our duties in the political arena: be there.

Despite who likes which candidate, or what the polls say, or how well the arguments are articulated, elections are decided by the people who actually show up to cast their votes. What gets a candidate into office is that he or she has more voters arriving at the polls on Election Day than the opposing candidate has. There is little time left before this year's elections. Hopefully, we have taken the time to find out who will be on the ballot, and where those candidates stand on the issues. Hopefully, we understand that the most important issue of all is the right to life, and that being 'right' on a whole host of other issues can never justify being wrong on the foundational issue. Now it all comes down to who shows up. That's where you can help at the local level, and you can do it in two ways.

First of all, organize help to get people to the polls. Maybe some people need a ride. Parishes or pro-life groups can organize car pools or vans to accomplish this. Perhaps someone needs assistance to watch the children. You can volunteer to do so, or perhaps organize such a service for a group of parents. You can also simply call friends and relatives to remind them to get out and vote.

Secondly, you can assist those who cannot physically go to the polls to cast their vote by absentee ballot. This is important, for example, in the case of the elderly and homebound, or of people who will be traveling on Election Day. Circumstances of health or travel shouldn't deprive a citizen of his/her voice in the elections.

And let's not forget about the role of priests. We should be hearing from the pulpit during these days about our obligation to go to the polls. Some priests are over-cautious regarding what they may or may not say. But as the memorandum from the Office of the General Counsel of the US Bishops' conference states, 'Both IRS and the Federal Election Commission [11 C.F.R. §114.4(d)] permit Catholic organizations to sponsor voter registration and get-out-the-vote drives, provided that no bias for or against any candidate, political party, or voting position is evidenced.'

368

Throughout the Old Testament, prophets challenged Kings to follow the laws of God. In our day, we not only have the opportunity to challenge government leaders, but to choose them. And the same hands that are lifted up to God in prayer are the hands that pull down the levers in the voting booth. Instead of simply complaining about the moral climate of our nation, let's take action to change it. As our bishops say, 'Every voice matters in the public forum. Every vote counts' (1998: Living the Gospel of Life, n. 34).

This election day, be there."

"Judicial Activism: the Biggest 2002 Election Issue

The most important issue in the election on November 5th is whether or not we elect enough U.S. Senators to confirm constitutionalist judges. It is the Senate's duty to protect America from judicial usurpation and to restore our constitutional balance of powers among the three branches of our government. Since law-abiding citizens can't hold the life-tenured radical judges accountable, grassroots groups everywhere should hold accountable every Senator who fails to act to reign in the Imperial Judiciary.

We have suffered a half century of activist/liberal court decisions that seriously threaten to undermine our Rule of Law. Activist judges have been advancing a liberal agenda that opposes religious values, conventional morality, the separation of powers, our structure of federalism, and even the right of American citizens to govern themselves. The federal courts have been replacing our constitutional system with what we call the Imperial Judiciary.

Bill Clinton appointed almost half of all federal judges now serving, and federal judges serve for life. In addition to the 373 Clinton-appointed judges, federal judges appointed by Presidents Jimmy Carter and Lyndon Johnson are still deciding cases. The federal courts today are precariously balanced between activists and constitutionalists...should galvanize Americans to call a halt to the damage that activists judges have been inflicting on us for decades.

When Justice Clarence Thomas, the Court's strongest voice in behalf of constitutional government, spoke to the Eagle Forum's annual conference several years ago, he explained that when a case is presented to the court, judges can make their decisions in one of two ways. They can look to the United States Constitution and see whether it authorizes or forbids the disputed action, or the judges can impose their own social views on us dressed up with self-serving jargon. Unfortunately, too many judges prefer the latter, rather than accepting the authority of the Constitution. Some activist liberal judges seem to think they are free to write their own views into law. Someone

369

once asked Dwight Eisenhower if he had made any mistakes as President that he later regretted. Ike replied: Yes, two, and they're both on the Supreme Court.

'All' legislative powers are vested in the Congress, according to the U.S. Constitution. That means no legislative power is granted to the courts. Yet, over the past 50 years, judges have become increasingly activist, writing their own ideas into law. The federal courts have invented new 'rights' such as the right to abortion...The federal courts have arbitrarily overturned the votes of the people...who had the old-fashioned belief that they could exercise self-government. The federal courts have set themselves up as a super-legislature and grabbed authority to micromanage...

While the American people typically have the opportunity to correct a bad election result four years later, a bad legal precedent may last forever. The trouble with some judges is that once they are appointed to the federal judiciary, they seem to think they have been anointed to rule over lesser mortals. They just write their own opinions into the law. Some of these activist judges are very arrogant about saying this. Justice William J. Brennan in a 1982 speech revealed the mindset of these liberal activist judges. He praised what he called 'the evolution of constitutional doctrine.' Brennan said that in previous times, 'the function of law was to formalize and preserve (accumulated) wisdom', but 'over the past 40 years Law has come alive as a living process responsive to changing human needs.' He bragged that the law has become 'a moving consensus.' Brennan added, 'our constitutional guarantees and the Bill of Rights are tissue paper bastions if they fail to transcend the printed page.' Justice Brennan made that all up. There is nothing in the U.S. Constitution about evolution, a living process, changing needs, or transcending the printed page. Most Americans, on the other hand, want judges who rely on the United States Constitution as their point of reference, and we desperately need Republican Senators who will confirm Bush's nominees.

Without any authority from the Constitution or citation of any applicable legal precedent...some lower federal courts manifested their disdain for the popular will by arrogantly overturning the wishes of the majority of voters expressed in statewide referenda...in order to maintain the Court's legitimacy, we are told we must not criticize an illegitimate decision!

Congress should limit the jurisdiction of the federal courts, as authorized in Article III of the U.S. Constitution. The federal courts have fundamentally altered our Separation of Powers and effectively changed the definition of 'the supreme law of the land' from 'this Constitution, and the Laws of the United States which shall be made in Pursuance thereof' (Article VI) and substituted 'whatever a federal judge decides this week.' This situation is intolerable, and it is the duty of Congress to use its constitutional powers to restore the balance of power among the three branches.

One of these days, and it could be tomorrow or the day after, a vacancy on the Supreme Court will occur. The result will be as important to America's future as who was elected President. Republicans should...gird for the next judicial nomination that will surely come. In the granddaddy document of limited government, the Magna Carta signed at Runnymede in 1215, King John promised, 'We will appoint as justices, constables, sheriffs, or other officials, only men that know the law of the realm and are minded to keep it well.' You and I expect at least as much from our President and Senators as our forefathers got from King John.

November 5th is our big opportunity to restore our constitutional form of government by electing Senators who will confirm good constitutional judges and Representatives who will curb the power of the federal courts. Phyllis Schlafly, B.A., M.A., J.D., is a member of the Bar in Missouri, Illinois, the District of Columbia, and the U.S. Supreme Court." Excerpted from The Phyllis Schlafly Report, Vol. 36, No. 3, P.O. Box 618, Alton, IL, 62002, Oct. 2002

"I have been reviewing the polls from around the country and there appears to be a record number of races, particularly for the U.S. Senate, that are complete toss-ups. In many cases, the candidates have diametrically opposed views on everything, including the kind of judges who should be on our federal courts, stopping illegal immigration, tax cuts, winning the war on terrorism, the sanctity of life, and protecting the family. In short, there is no excuse for any of us to fail to vote in two weeks. Vote, My Friends! If you have questions about a candidate for Congress, please visit CWF's web site at www.cwfpac.com or call us at (703) 671-8800." Gary L. Bauer, Chairman, CWF, Monday, October 21, 2002

"Be Not Afraid Yet again, the 'religious Left' in America is trying to intimidate pastors, squelch debate and discourage voter participation in the political process. Yesterday, we received a copy of a letter from the Interfaith Alliance urging pastors to reject voter guides from six specifically identified organizations, including the Christian Coalition, Focus on the Family, and the Campaign for Working Families. Evidently, the Interfaith Alliance decided to expand their intimidation campaign this year beyond churches. The letter we received yesterday was sent to a soup kitchen run by a Christian ministry.

To those pastors who are desperately concerned about our growing virtue deficit, you have far more freedom than the Interfaith Alliance would have you believe. You cannot endorse specific candidates by name or party from the pulpit, but you can accept voter guides to help educate your congregations.

And, more importantly, you have every right to preach and teach about moral issues and to exhort your congregations to vote accordingly. This Sunday, 'Be not afraid' and let your pulpits 'flame with righteousness.'" Campaign for Working Families, Gary L. Bauer, Chairman, 11/1/2002

"Pick Your Poll Here we are, less than 24 hours away from Election Day and no one-analysts and pollsters included-can agree on what the trend is, if any, around the country. A Sunday national New York Times poll showed a significant shift to the Republicans, now leading the Democrats 47% to 40%. In contrast, a Zogby poll completed on Saturday showed virtually every close Senate race breaking for the Democrats and previously 'safe' Republican seats, such as Texas, suddenly in play.

My instincts tell me the Republican Party will pick up roughly 5 seats in the House. In the Senate, I believe there could be surprise Republican wins in the Georgia race and in Missouri, perhaps even South Dakota. And, keep in mind, that in several states allegations of voter fraud may delay us knowing the final results for weeks, instead of hours. Stay tuned!" Campaign for Working Families, Gary L. Bauer, Chairman-Monday, November 4, 2002.

"Warning The media will once again be 'calling elections' tonight based on projections before all the votes are counted. Please ignore these calls, which are often wrong, and please go vote!" Gary L. Bauer, Chairman, Campaign for Working Families, 11/5/02.

"...no one should be put in any position of authority who supports who's pro-choice: 'If you agree with a political candidate on every issue except legalizing child abuse, would you vote for him?' He'll say 'no.' The question then is, 'So baby killing is tolerable, but not baby abuse?'" Richard J. Vrabel, in Celebrate Life, May-June 2003, on one issue voting.

Election Recap

It turned out that Gary had a pretty good read on the election, except that computer system problems prevented the usual projections. I took special note of what he had to say about Zogby after the election, because there was a bogus Zogby poll in my area immediately preceding the election, that altered voting patterns, but didn't change who the winners were.

Recap: All the encouragement to vote must have done some good. I remember that a few weeks before the election I received a survey from the RNC about what steps the GOP should take to win the election. I wrote in that President Bush should go on the campaign trail to help the candidates. I'm sure he never saw it, but it is interesting to see that we were on the same wavelength.

When Clinton was in office and the economy was going great I used to like to point out that he had done absolutely nothing about the economy to take credit for. But I never found anybody who disagreed with that. So I don't think it did the Democrats much good to just mention the economy and think people would blame it on Bush. President Bush did more about the economy, by passing his tax cut, in his first year in office, than Clinton did in eight years. I think people admired the way President Bush has handled the war on terror, and didn't blame him for the slowing economy.

The Democrats have seemed to reluctantly concede that the President's campaigning was key to the GOP victory. They prefer that to admitting that their policies and obstructionism might have had something to do with it. There are about 50 pieces of legislation that Daschle had held up in the Senate that should start to move now, along with judicial nominations; some of which have been sitting in committee for over a year. The two judicial nominations they voted down in committee, Pickering and Owen, may make it to the Senate floor now. In the House, the Democrats seem to be moving farther to the left, which will make them even more irrelevant. In the Senate, they can't move much farther left than Daschle. They only seem to speak to each other's misconceptions.

I watched the election news on CNN, which I consider less biased than the major networks (which didn't seem to think the elections were worth covering full time), until 3 A.M., and never once heard the word abortion mentioned, let alone evaluated as a factor in the elections. Yet I know polls show that it is the number one issue for about 16% of the population. I had to wait two days before I got the following information from Gary Bauer: "...in Missouri, the top issue cited by voters was the economy, followed by abortion. And, of those who said abortion, 80% voted Republican!"

I still have some work to do updating the election results above. I hope to eventually account for all the races mentioned (November 15, 2002). That turned out to be a bigger task than I had originally contemplated. It's January 10th, 2003, 4:10 A.M. I don't think it was worth the trouble to update the results. Of course this section was much higher in the document before, then I moved it down here after the election. I may provide a link to it next time, if there is a next time. So if you're reading this, and you found it helpful, send me an email about it. You have a little less than 2 years to vote: intecon@myself.com. Well, it's done now-for the 2002 election cycle.

"NARAL Goes 1-for-20 in Election by David Freddoso Earlier this year, NARAL picked its 20 'key' House and Senate races. In each, it supported its candidate (all of whom were Democrats) with cash and endorsements. Only one 'key' NARAL candidate—Sen. Tom Harkin (D.-Iowa)—won. Ironically, that was over a pro-abortion Republican, outgoing Rep. Greg Ganske. NARAL likely would have gone 1-for-21, but it did not change its web page to endorse Walter Mondale (D.) in Minnesota after the death of Paul Wellstone." "Human Events The Week Of November 18, 2002".

"Pro-abortion PACs: big election losers The Republican National Coalition for Life reports that NARAL's political action committee spent $10 million for pro-abortion candidates in last month's election and lost 10 of 11 contests. The pro-abortion PAC Emily's List, which exclusively backs pro-abortion female Democrats, raised $21 million, yet lost 16 of 21 races. Two of the losses-Missouri and New Hampshire-were seats that made the difference between Republican and Democrat control of the Senate." ALLNews, December 2002, Vol 8 No. 11

"There are always those who contend that the abortion issue is a big loser for Republicans. Republicans will lose suburban women if they take a pro-life stand, according to consultants who supposedly know what they are talking about. Well, the National Right to Life Committee hired pollster John Zogby, a Democrat, to accumulate data on what it meant to take the pro-life position in the 2002 general election. Zogby polled in Arkansas, Colorado, Georgia, Minnesota, Missouri, New Hampshire, North Carolina, South Dakota and Texas. These are states where a pro-life Republican faced a pro-abortion Democrat. What Zogby found, in averaging these races, is the pro-life advantage for the Republican candidates was 7 percent over the pro-abortion candidates. In other words, of those people who listed abortion as their reason for voting in the election, 16 percent of the electorate said that the pro-abortion position was their reason for voting for the Democratic candidates. But 23 percent of the electorate said they voted for the Republican candidates because they took the pro-life position.

This number, by the way, has been consistent over many years. From the time the National Right to Life Committee began doing exit polling in the late 1970s, the pro-life advantage for Republican candidates has been in the 5 percent to 8 percent range in election after election. The higher number usually reflects higher turnout for the Republicans...Similar results can be found in all of the races where a pro-abortion Democrat ran against a pro-life Republican. From "The Pro-Life Advantage At The Polls" By Paul M. Weyrich, chairman and CEO of the Free Congress Foundation, Cybercast News Service and The Pro-Life Infonet, November 18, 2002. He then cites individual races and concludes with the following words: "With more than two decades of proof in Senate, House and presidential races that the pro-life issue helps Republicans when running against a pro-abortion Democrat, one would think the issue would go away. The proof is beyond question. Still every two years pro-abortion Republicans and the media combine to re-create the myth that if Republicans don't take the pro-abortion stance, they will be doomed. How many more elections will it take?"

"CWF won nearly 80% of our races November 5th. What an incredible victory! As I am sure you have heard, our win on November 5th was truly historic. Not only did we take back the Senate, something that has never been done by the party holding the White House in its first mid-term election, but we expanded our control in the House of Representatives and fought the Democrats to a virtual tie among governorships. And beyond that, Republicans went on to pick up 200 state legislative seats." Gary L. Bauer, Chairman CWF

"The November Elections have indeed proved significant in advancing the pro-life cause as new pro-life voices were elected in the House and in the Senate. All of our endorsed incumbents were reelected. This was the best election cycle in the history of the Susan B. Anthony List". Jane Abraham, President SBAList, 12/27/02

"NPLA-PAC supported 39 candidates for the House and Senate in both the primary and general election, 31 of whom defeated their pro-abortion opponents. By contrast, the National Abortion Rights Action League (NARAL) spent $10 million to support their top 11 pro-abortion Congressional candidates. Ten of their eleven candidates were defeated. Emily's List, another radical abortion-on-demand PAC, spent $21 million only to see more than three-quarters of their 21 candidates defeated on election night. The abortion industry clearly did all they could to seize power to promote their radical agenda." *LifeLine*, Newsletter of the National Pro-Life Alliance, Winter 2003

"This past Election Cycle, the pro-abortion groups spent over $50 million!" Jane Abraham, President SBAList, February 4, 2003

"Next year will feature off-year elections in at least four states and, as a result of the losses sustained on November 5th, we are predicting a large number of congressional Democrats will opt to retire in 2004, creating a lot of open seats in the next election." Gary L. Bauer, Campaign for Working Families *Campaign Watch*, Fall 2002, Issue 17.

"There is an old story about a man walking down a road and spotting a turtle sitting atop a fencepost. While the man didn't know exactly how the turtle got there, the one sure observation he could make was that the turtle didn't get there by itself. It's the same way in any successful campaign. Senator Dole would not have won this election without the help of friends like you who lifted her up and carried her through to victory." Back to reality. I took this paragraph from a letter I received from Elizabeth Dole's Campaign Manager, Mark Stephens, dated March 10, 2003. In it he talked about the remaining campaign debt of $400,000, and the urgency of retiring it. He then went on to implore me to send $5, or if I couldn't afford that amount, $3. I know of no better way to make a point. Obviously, my specific $5, or $3, wasn't going to make a dent in the $400,000 campaign debt. But Mark, a savvy campaign manager, thought that this letter would get it down to $150,000 by the end of the month. How so? Because the Dole Campaign had used a small contributors mailing list; and better than that, by now knew which small contributors they could count on to send a contribution and how much was reasonable to ask that person for. It was probably less than 50,000 people they needed a contribution from, because most people would give more than $5. So this demonstrates what I've known for a long time. If you do your part and send in a contribution, you can be assured that a lot of other people are doing their part and sending in a contribution too, and together you can finance a campaign, or a public service organization. Everybody pulling together, and doing their part, not even knowing who the other people are. It's especially important to non-incumbents, who don't have any favors to dispense. One data base I know of is euphemistically called the "Civic Leaders" data base, and consists of over one million names. Even if you send in as little as $5, you'll usually find out it was appreciated and important to them-because down the road you'll get another request for a donation. Not important by itself, but important when it's multiplied 1,000,000 times by other people trying to help out and do their part for something they believe in.

Pregnancy Resources

"'If I knew then, what I know now, my baby would be alive today.'

These are haunting words. Yet they are repeated by thousands of post-abortive women across our country who have made the decision without knowing the truth about abortion…each one of us prays that the words of truth will enlighten someone's heart and that an innocent baby will be rescued from a premature and violent death. And that some young mother will be spared the heartbreak of abortion." Bonnie Quirk, April, 2003

National Campaign to Prevent Teen Pregnancy-(202) 478-8500, http://www.teenpregnancy.org/.

Gravity Teen-http://www.gravityteen.com/ "GravityTeen.com is a place to get inspired, build self esteem, up your personal power and just feel better about yourself. Get teen advice about peer pressure, drugs, and other hard teen challenges and decisions by checking out real life teen stories! And tell your story to help teens, too! There's also a special section in case you or someone you know is pregnant and trying to decide if abortion, adoption or teen parenthood is the answer. It has some very cool prenatal pics and fetal development info to download for school, too! From serious stuff to fun comebacks, gravityteen will have you landing on your feet!"

Unplanned Parenting-"No mother or child left behind 'There are other choices'" Address: P.O. Box 194, CT 06838 Phone: (877) 488-9537 Email:info@unplannedparenting.com http://www.unplannedparenting.com/

"We are advocates for all of those affected by Crisis Pregnancies and totally committed to helping those in need. Unplanned Parenting (UPP) is an international charitable organization providing hope filled alternatives to those who believe the only choice they have is to terminate the pregnancy. UPP is a comprehensive resource and informational website linking known organizations under one umbrella to save lives…by helping women locate support opportunities if their desire is to choose life for their baby. The web site connects counseling, adoption, maternity homes, scholarship and other support agencies around the world and enables a woman to locate support in her geographical area."

"The child, by reason of his physical and mental immaturity, needs special safeguards and care before as well as after birth". Convention on the Rights of the Child, Preamble. "…motherhood and childhood are entitled to special care and assistance." Universal Declaration of Human Rights, Article 25-2. All of the above taken from their web page.

Intecon

LiFE ED-1777 South Bellaire Street, Suite 300, Denver, Colorado Phone: 303.691.6912 Fax: 303.691.9197 Email: director@life-ed.org http://www.life-ed.org/

"Saving thousands of lives Changing thousands minds One at a time The Purpose To promote the value of human life through public education

To counteract the 1.4 million abortions every year in the United States, Life Ed's public education program harnesses the power of mass media to win people's hearts and minds to value human life. Life Ed's messages *for Life* are backed by professional research and evaluation to gently engage the public in a non-confrontational manner on this highly controversial topic. The result is an effective solution to a very difficult problem. Since inception, Life Ed has collaborated with two national, leading producers of dynamic television messages to impact American pregnancy trends *for Life*.

Help for Pregnant Women 'When you're pregnant and scared, no organization can tell you what's right. But the very instant you look into your baby's eye, you'll know—you'll know.'

Help for Post-Abortive Women 'They said you wouldn't be bothered by a voice calling for you in the night. There would be no trail of cereal through the house, no spills or stray toys. The clock ticks; all is calm; and you realize there is still a voice.'" That last spot is called "Night".

"One Woman's Story Tiffany was scheduled for an abortion. The night before, she woke up crying, turned on the TV, and saw the Life Ed message 'Night'. When she called the help line, she talked with a caring counselor at a nearby pregnancy center and scheduled an appointment there instead. At the center she saw her baby waving at her, and she chose life for Jessee!" In other words, she must have seen her child through an ultrasound.

"Since incorporating in 1993, Life Ed is Colorado's most successful life-affirming educational non-profit agency. Babies' lives are saved, women receive help, and everyone is educated *for Life*, from families to public policy makers.

Mass media is powerful and can be used for constructive purposes. Life Ed's success is due in great measure to the unique opportunity for viewers to call a toll-free number. The help line connects to a pregnancy resource center nearest the caller's home where women receive free, confidential, loving assistance, and encouragement to give life to their babies. Spiritual counsel is offered, including support for post-abortive individuals.

378

Life Ed's Colorado Impact since 1997 A dramatic decrease of 57% in the number of abortions reported to the Colorado Division of Vital Statistics (Other factors may be involved, but it is likely the Life Ed TV outreach contributed substantially.) A significant increase of public opinion to pro-life values, as measured by professional polling; 237,000 adults in the general population and 66,000 women ages 18-34 Over 10,400 phone calls into pregnancy resource centers Countless stories of children born, and women, men and families benefiting from the centers". That was all gleaned from a brochure I received from them after making a small donation; which is also why some of the punctuation seems askew.

"Your gift will go directly to our successful effort to promote the value of human life through public education. Over the years, I've had a chance to know many of the women we help. And,...they're good people. Not evil. Just horribly misguided. But what should you and I expect? Just look at the message they hear over and over, day-in and day-out. Those who promote abortion are constantly out there—often backed by government funds – pounding their pro-abortion ideas down the throats of women all across the country. We here at Life Ed don't agree with those people. But we won't fight them. However, we will invest every possible dollar in effective ways to get our message out...A message women respond to well if only they hear it...30-second ads-called spots". Lisa Jacobson, Executive Director, Life Ed National Number: 1-800-395-HELP

I would like to point out here that it took me almost three years to become aware of these people, which demonstrates the value of having so much information in one place so that people can quickly become aware of what's going on in the abortion arena.

Caring Pregnancy Centers in Colorado-http://www.life-ed.org/cpc.html

"Market testing has proven that we can successfully break through the clutter of mass media communications and connect with our audience of young women in a real and relevant way. It also shows that Life Ed can position itself as a viable alternative to organizations like Planned Parenthood and be a voice for truth in our culture." Lisa Jacobson, April 30, 2003, fund raising letter.

"Pregnant and scared? You have options. 1-800-395-HELP Free test. Caring. Confidential." CARE NET http://www.care-net.org / "A Network of Care for Women in Crisis". "Care Net is a network of over 600 faith-based crisis pregnancy centers located in neighborhoods and towns all across the country."

"Last year alone, Care Net centers served women with pregnancy related concerns over 400,000 times. Additionally, we estimate our pro-life network is saving approximately 121 babies every day!" More recent information on Care Net, which also has a new web site called:

PregnantAndScared.com-http://www.PregnantAndScared.com/. "Care Net... assists and promotes the work of our network of 700 pregnancy resource centers located throughout the country. Started in 1975...was influenced by the leadership of Dr. C. Everett Koop and...the late Dr. Francis Schaeffer. Their vision was to move the pro-life movement out of the highly political and increasingly ineffective arena of Congress and the Supreme Court, and to bring it to localities throughout North America. Right now, throughout North America there are nearly 2,000 local pregnancy centers linked to our Toll-Free Help Line. When clients call 1-800-395 HELP, they are automatically patched through the Care Net center nearest them...our website, Pregnant And Scared.com, will show you the pregnancy center closest to you...Care Net has also placed over 22,000 billboards...in 145 cities and 40 states! By the end of the year we hope to have placed 10,000 new billboards."

Their CPCs offer a free pregnancy test, ultrasound, compassionate peer counseling, support in informing family, access to medical services, parenting and life skills training, adoption, maternity clothes and housing; and baby clothes, food, furniture, car seats, and diapers-all at no charge.

"They helped me really think through my options. They gave me clothing, loaned me a crib, and helped with childcare referrals. I don't know what I'd have done if I hadn't made that call that day. That billboard saved my daughter's life."—Anonymous in Tennessee

"The unknown future of a child entering your life is scary. As a teenage Mom myself, I wish I had known the loving counsel and support of Care Net. They can help turn what seemed like a crisis into the most treasured days of your life or heal a broken heart." Hunter Tylo

"The right choice can only be made if all the information is provided. Care Net enables women to make informed decisions for themselves and their babies. Everyone speaks of the right to choose, Care Net makes the right choice possible." Kim Alexis

"Unfortunately many thousands of women don't know all of their options. Statistics tell us some 90% of women who had abortions would have preferred positive alternatives, had they known they were there." Mike Reid, President, Care Net

"And if there is an area of strength for abortion providers, it is their ability, with taxpayer funds, to open centers in...areas, offering thousands of abortions ...unless we have a pro-life pregnancy resource center nearby to help, we will continue to miss opportunities to save lives. We need…to…reach out to women in underserved areas…Care Net provides new centers with highest quality educational and promotional literature, such as our new booklet, *Before You Decide*…Manuals…encouragement and guidance Through our 16 professionally trained, regional consultants, Care Net will provide new local centers with legal and administrative support, advertising help and ongoing training and development, equipping local leaders to meet the needs of thousands of women…great need for new, pro-life pregnancy centers". Care Net, "One Life at a Time". 109 Carpenter Dr., #100, Sterling, VA 20164

There are several messages in the paragraphs above on Care Net-First of all, it's a place to call if you're pregnant. Secondly, there is a need for many more centers, and they're looking for the resources and people to open them. And it raises the question of: Why don't they receive government funds? We should be taking the money that goes to Planned Parenthood under Title X and rerouting it to crisis pregnancy centers along with however much more funding they need; which brings us full circle to the things I proposed when I started this document. And it's an area where pro-life people can get involved, if they have an inclination to do so. In a recent survey I received from them, they asked the following very timely question: "Should Care Net ask Members of Congress to re-direct half of the $200 million designated to pro-abortion organizations to a pro-life ministry like Care Net?" I don't think so. I think they should ask for all of it.

America's Crisis Pregnancy Helpline 1-888-4-OPTIONS
http://www.thehelpline.org/

Crisis Pregnancy Centers Online, http://www.pregnancycenters.org/;
Toll Free numbers, http://www.pregnancycenters.org/hotlines.html; or By State, http://www.pregnancycenters.org/listings.html.

Pregnancy 911-http://www.pregnancy911.com/

U.S. Pregnancy Care Center Listings, by State, and International
http://pregnancycenters.org/listings.html

Directory of Shelters for Pregnant Women by State-(201) 825-7277
http://www.lifecall.org/

Birth Mother-1-800-PREGNANCY-http://www.birthmother.com/

Hidden Choices-National Association of Maternity Homes "Hidden Choices was created out of the need to network 3,000 existing maternity residences in the United States and beyond. The National Association of Maternity Homes (NAMH) was founded to provide linkage for those maternity residences and crisis pregnancy centers. NAMH will provide support in: Guidance and direction Housing Pre-natal care Counseling Adoption alternatives Parenting Financial aid Schooling Career planning" http://www.hiddenchoices.com/. This web site is slated for completion on 04/01/03.

The Women's Center-http://www.womens-center.org/ "Yes, we know that we're up against the marketing powerhouse of Planned Parenthood for the minds of young people...since 1983, we have saved over 24,000 lives from abortion and helped numerous families. We ask for no other reward than to be able to continue saving lives." (Chicago) They also have a video called "Changing Lives and Saving Lives". "These people at the Center truly work miracles. They have hearts of gold and nerves of steel...Nothing is typical or standard for the counselors." Margie Manczko They also make the point that they are rescuing 2 lives-not just one, for each client they assist-for no charge! 5116 North Cicero Avenue, Chicago, Illinois 60630 Phone: 773-794-1313- Email: cwojnar@womens-center.org

"Expectant Mother Care (EMC) http://www.expectantmothercare.org/, is a family-like non-profit counseling service for young girls and women caught in an untimely pregnancy or in a cycle of promiscuity or post-abortion syndrome.

Our calling is to serve the distraught and disadvantaged through life-affirming and pro-chastity education, counseling, on-site contracted medical care, and referrals.

Founded by Chris Slattery in 1984 in Manhattan to provide alternatives-to-abortion support in New York City, EMC now serves over 4,200 young women per year in centers in five locations. EMC is the largest and most effective pregnancy resource center group in the New York metropolitan area.

EMC serves sexually-active young girls or women of any age, pregnant or not, who are in need of pregnancy help or are considering abortion, or are hurting from abortion.

EMC's goals are to encourage expectant moms to choose motherhood, and either marriage, adoption, or self-sufficiency, and to turn toward chaste lifestyles. EMC strives to offer high-quality prenatal care and in the future pediatrics, through physician partnerships, on-site at most of its centers.

Expectant Mother Care (EMC) is New York City's largest alternative-to-abortion organization, with five sites in Manhattan, Brooklyn and the Bronx offering free on-site crisis counseling, pre-natal care, sonograms, maternity and baby clothing, adoption and housing referrals.

Over the coming year, we expect to see over 4,200 new clients, of whom, based on past experience, 2,730 will be pregnant (65%)...
First Pro-Life Center in the World with Medison America's 3-D Ul-trasound... has operational a 3-dimensional ultrasound machine in EMC's contracted medical clinic in the South Bronx."

"As all of us mark this first anniversary of the hideous attacks of September 11th,...It's hard to believe that as we reflect and pray for the over 3,000 victims of that day, NYC abortionists have dispatched another 100,000 unborn victims in the past year. We have so much work to do in this city and country to defend life.

EMC has, through the generosity of many like you, become the first pro-life pregnancy resource operation in the United States to obtain the brand new state-of-the-art GE Voluson 730 4-Dimensional Ultrasound system, which is now in use in our bustling South Bronx pro-life medical clinic. We are in the process of hiring a more experienced sonogram technician...EMC is about to open two new locations to bring us to a total of seven sites! We will be taking under our wing a new crisis pregnancy center location next to a very busy Planned Parenthood in Shrewsbury, New Jersey". 9/4/02 Christopher T. Slattery, Founder and President 210 East 23rd St., 5th Floor, New York, NY 10010 1-(212) 685-3320

Manhattan Right to Life Committee: Pregnant And Need Help?—Call 1-212-243-7119. President: Jeanne E. Head, R. N., 350 Fifth Avenue, New York, NY http://mrlclife.home.att.net/

Sisters of Life, 450 W. 51st St., New York, NY 10019, 212-397-1396, or, St. Paul's Convent, 586 McLean Avenue, Yonkers, New York 10705 http://sistersoflife.org/matsvcs-fr.html

"'Ceci,' appeared at our door...She had a appointment scheduled for an abortion...she asked if we would be able to help her find and view a film she had seen while a student at a Catholic high school. She did not remember the name but by the description, we recognized that she was speaking of *The Silent Scream*. Reminded of the beauty and humanity of the unborn child and the violence of abortion, Ceci's decision was firm. This little one was a child of God; her life was sacred and she, herself, a mother. With great courage and love she received the gift of her child—the gift of a lifetime." Mother Agnes Mary, S.V. "You can reach the Nurturing Network at the Sisters of Life by calling: 718.882.8044 or 1.800.TNN.4MOM". http://www.sistersoflife.org/

Birthright International-http://www.birthright.org/: "Are you pregnant and in need of help?"

"Birthright's Philosophy: Birthright provides caring, non-judgmental support to girls and women who are distressed by an unplanned pregnancy. Using our own resources and those of the community, Birthright provides positive and loving alternatives to abortion. Birthright provides many services, including friendship and emotional support, free pregnancy tests, legal and medical services, financial advice, assistance with housing, referral to social agencies, and maternity and baby clothes. Birthright treats each woman as an individual who deserves kindness and respect, as well as personal attention to her unique situation. And all Birthright services are free, absolutely confidential, and available to any woman regardless of age, race, creed, economic or marital status."

"...the world's first international crisis pregnancy service. In 1993, Birthright International celebrated its 25th anniversary with about 500 chapters world-wide..."

"Birthright is a fully independent organization, not affiliated with any church or public agency."

"An estimated 28,000 women make their first visit to a Birthright centre every month. Birthright also operates a 24-hour North American hotline, at 1-800-550-4900."

"'It is the right of every pregnant woman to give birth, and the right of every child to be born.'"

Westside Pregnancy Resource Center—828 Pico Blvd. #7, Santa Monica, California 90405 Phones: 310-581-1140, 1-800-R-HERE-4-U. http://www.w-cpc.org/ This site offers the most complete array of information of any CPC web site I've seen. I especially liked the pages on:

"What Goes on Inside an Abortion Clinic? http://www.w-cpc.org/abortion/clinic.html ", and

"Choosing an abortion provider—12 considerations http://www.w-cpc.org/abortion/alert.html ";

things I hadn't seen anyplace else. They even have an online pregnancy test.

Liberty Godparent Foundation and national network of homes: Phone (800) 542-4453 or (804) 845-3466 (Liberty Godparent Home) http://www.godparent.org/. "It's a matter of life!"

"As I saw the young pregnant girls in our home busily preparing to celebrate Christmas—I thought of young Mary, the earthly mother of our Lord Jesus

Christ, in the days that preceded the birth of our Savior. I imagine she must have felt alone, burdened and concerned, wondering what the future would hold for her. But God provided what she needed to bring her Child into the world." Interesting to recall that Jesus came into the world under less than ideal circumstances too.

"Our 1-800-54-CHILD national Crisis Pregnancy Hotline provides a counselor for confused, pregnant girls to call to get immediate help...across the nation... to save their babies from the slaughter of abortion...provide...a comfortable, secure place to live...food and clothing...church attendance and Christian counseling...ongoing medical care for mother and baby...education and training and mentoring...and adoption services that place the baby in a loving Christian home." Jerry Falwell

For a small donation they will also send you a video on partial birth abortion, made on the national television talk show "Listen America", called "Jennifer's Story".

Heartbeat International, celebrating 30 years of life-saving ministry. http://www.heartbeatinternational.org/

"Heartbeat International is an interdenominational Christian association of life-affirming pregnancy resource centers, medical clinics, maternity homes and nonprofit adoption agencies. Our mission is to create an environment where every human heart is cherished and protected-within the womb and within strong families. We currently serve 705 affiliates in 46 states, Canada and 17 countries overseas, providing them with the education, training and support they need to serve daily on the front-line of the fight for life." (888) 550-7577

New Beginnings-http://www.HomeforMothers.com/-A Home for Mothers, Denver, Colorado "There is no denying a bond is being formed between mother and child during pregnancy. There is no denying that God created women with not only the ability but also the desirability to raise children and that maternal instinct naturally kicks in. At *New Beginnings* we are advocates neither for parenting the child nor placing the child for adoption. We try to make it clear to each resident facing that decision that it is their decision to make, and we will support them in that decision. The minimum age for a resident at *New Beginnings* is 16. At that age, some residents still need some good, strong mothering themselves, to say nothing of their mothering a child who is totally dependent on them. That is one of the factors to be considered in the heart-wrenching decision residents face on whether to parent their child or to place it for adoption. In some cases, to entrust her child to the loving care of Christian parents might be the only way and the really loving way to go." By

Rev. Douglas and Charlene Bode, Houseparents-New Beginnings "In life what sometimes appears to be the end, is really a new beginning." Toll Free: (800) 720 MOMS Phone: (303) 364 0890

The Mary Weslin Homes-For Pregnant Unwed Mothers-PO Box 5097 Colorado Springs, CO 80931 Maryweslinhomes@catholic.org (719) "Providing a 'Safe Haven' for women in crisis pregnancies" "Our History Many years ago, Mary Lou Weslin and her husband Norman became involved in Pro-Life work. Together they prayed and picketed in front of the abortion mills, and worked hard to save lives of unborn children. Eventually they were involved in starting the Birthright Life Support Centers. Through this work, Mary Lou became aware of a need for 'Safe Haven' homes for women in crisis pregnancy. She dreamed of opening some kind of refuge for these women. However, in 1980 Mary Lou went home to God, dying in a tragic car accident.

Mary Lou's family knew of her dream and after recovering from the shock of her death Norman and their two children decided to follow through with her idea. They all agreed to make the family home in Colorado Springs a 'Safe Haven'. The Mary Weslin Homes For Pregnant Unwed Mothers was founded by Gregory Biltz in 1981. Since then Norman Weslin has become a missionary priest with the Oblates of Wisdom. Through Mary Lou's intercession and the work of her family and friends, over 250 mothers have been cared for and over 150 babies have been born through the home.

Our Mission Our society has become a Culture of Death, providing women in crisis pregnancies with very few options other than to take the life of their baby. Abortion is a permanent solution to a passing hardship. We are here to help these women realize there is a better way. The Mary Weslin Homes assists women in crisis during and after their pregnancy. We provide a safe haven which cares for their basic needs; such as food, shelter, counseling, spiritual guidance and friendship. We are not government or church sponsored institutions. We are average, private, Catholic homes with a Christian family atmosphere. During their stay we assess each woman's individual goals and future needs. Through our love and support we can place the young mother back into a competitive society after her baby is born."

"Abortion Facts: A survey of post-abortive women found that: 28% attempted suicide 31% experienced suicidal feelings 60% commented that the decision to abort made their lives worse 94% regretted the decision to abort". "Abortion is terrorism in the womb." All the above was quoted from the January 2003 Weslin Newsletter.

More "Abortion Facts" from previous issues: "The baby's heartbeat begins 18 days after conception. Brainwaves have been recorded as early as 40 days after conception. Currently a baby can survive outside a mother's womb at 20 weeks. Abortion is legal throughout all nine months (October 2002). The US death rate is now greater than the birth rate. At ten weeks the baby has its own unique fingerprints. Expectant mothers who have had an abortion have a 200% increased risk of miscarriage."

Father Weslin is a man who likes to be where the action is-at the "Tip of the sword". "Fr. Weslin has been imprisoned 70-80 times for non-violent protests against abortion." I know he also walks cross country with the Crossroads walkers in the summer, where he seems to recruit volunteers for the Mary Weslin Homes. Fr. Weslin is available as a speaker (when he's not in jail). One thing he talks about are his experiences in jail.

Choices Medical Clinic (Wichita)-http://www.choicesmc.org/ "For a long time, Wichita has had a doctor specializing in killing babies through the violence of abortion. Now, for the first time, Wichita will have physicians who specialize in saving babies from the violence of abortion. Choices Medical Clinic empowers women to avoid having an abortion by providing prenatal medical care, social services, education, practical support and adoption information-all at no charge!" "Our team of physicians, nurses, social workers and other trained volunteers specialize in offering confidential, individualized care and compassion in assisting mothers and families". 538 S. Bleckly St. in Wichita, Kansas 67218 Phone: 1-800-879-7451

Life Center-(800) 848-LOVE

Nurturing Network-(800) TNN-4MOM

Catholic Charities-(800) CARE-002

Pregnancy Help Now-What Now?
"Experiencing an unplanned pregnancy can be terrifying, you may feel very confused. If you are looking for answers, you've come to the right place! This site is full of helpful information and links to resources. Please take the time to thoroughly investigate your options. In a time when your emotions are running wild, it helps to dig deep for information, advice, and support. So many questions may be going through your mind...What about my education? What about my career? Can I do this alone? How can I afford a child? Give yourself time to seek solutions."
http://www.geocities.com/pregnancyhelpnow/index2.html

"For years, crisis pregnancy centers have served as safe havens for women who want to choose life for their babies. Unlike abortion mills, crisis pregnancy centers offer hope, encouragement and support so women won't feel forced into choosing abortion. CPC's provide pregnancy testing, counseling, clothing, baby supplies, sonograms, medical and financial assistance and/or transportation, all at no charge." Dawn Rizzoni, writing for Celebrate Life.

There are "...more than 3000 centers around the nation that offer women free pregnancy testing, counseling, clothing and baby supplies." Vigil, First Quarter 2002 They will also refer you to an adoption agency, if you so choose, such as the ones listed below.

If you sign up at an adoption agency, they will usually also do whatever is necessary to see that things go well.

"On average, roughly 130,000 adoptions take place in the United States each year." Taken from the September 2002 Growing Branches.

Adoption: Where Families Come Together-http://www.adoption.com/ Very comprehensive and useful web site, but they don't give their geographical location or phone number.

Christian Homes: Maternity Care, Adoption and Foster Care-http://www.christianhomes.com/, **P.O. Box 270 Abilene, TX 79604 Telephone: (915) 677-2205 Toll Free Hot-Line: 800-592-4725 e-mail:** attention@christianhomes.com.

Lifetime Adoption: Facilitation help for birth mothers & families-Our *Exclusive* **Birthparent 24-Hour Hotline is 1-800-923-6784 For more information, Adoptive Families may call 530-271-1740-** http://www.lifetimeadoption.com/. **"Lifetime Adoption is a** *National* **Adoption Facilitation Center. Services are free to birthparents. We offer guidance and encouragement, during and after your pregnancy." Mailing Address: 216 Colfax Avenue, Grass Valley, CA 95945**

Faces of Adoption: America's Waiting Children-http://www.adopt.org/ Email: nac@nationaladoptioncenter.org Phone: 1-800-TO-ADOPT US Mail: National Adoption Center 1500 Walnut Street-Suite 701 Philadelphia, PA 19102

Adoption Services, Inc. -A fully licensed adoption agency – Birthparents call 1-800-943-0400. Adoptive families call 1-717-737-3960. Their web site, http://www.adoptionservices.org/, supplies a lot of information.

Adoption Links-http://www.adoptionlinks.com/. "Linking you to Great Adoption Resources". Web site provides a huge amount of information, a lot of it on one main page of links. Has evolved from prior times I visited it. Comprehensive enough to satisfy the person who wants to learn the technicalities of adoption, and everything else, too. Includes international adoption help. Thorough enough to remind me of my web site on abortion.

Adopting: Assistance, Crisis Pregnancy, Surrogacy, Birthmother-A sister site to the one above, but more homey. Talks more to ordinary folks, and doesn't bury you in information- http://www.adopting.org/.

AMREX Adoption Agencies – "an adoption research and information management firm today with the largest network of adoption professionals worldwide. We provide services to adoption professionals, making it easier for them to locate available children…", addressing "the disproportion between the number of families wishing to adopt and the number of children available". In other words, since Roe v Wade, there have been a lot fewer children to adopt locally in the US, so they fill a need for a central coordinating entity-for international adoptions. But they do help prospective parents select an agency.
AMREX, INC. 3440 Preston Ridge Rd. Ste 400 Alpharetta, GA 30005 USA
PHONE: 678-393-7100 (Mon-Fri 9am-5pm) EMAIL: main@amrex.org
http://www.adoptionagencies.org/

Coleman Adoption Services (Indianapolis)-http://www.colemanadopt.org/
"A not-for-profit agency serving women and building families for 105 years.

It is our mission to provide comprehensive, professional adoption services which support the needs of birth and adoptive parents and promote the innate right of all children to be part of a loving family.

Coleman has helped literally thousands of families become…well… families. Our roots can be traced to the early years of the Civil War. Two civic-minded women gave food, lodging and medical care to women while their husbands were away at war. The need for this assistance grew and by 1894, the agency had become a viable retreat for women. Since our beginning in 1894, Coleman has always placed its priority with children, not with profits." Telephone 317-638-0965 or 800-886-3434 Address: 615 North Alabama, Suite 319 Indianapolis, Indiana 46204 Email General Information:

Intecon

info@colemanadopt.org

Baby Center-http://www.babycenter.com/?CP_bid=-See how your baby develops, step by step. Click on Pregnancy or Baby, then click on "See what YOUR BABY looks like RIGHT NOW", at the bottom of the page. Page down to the images for each month of pregnancy. If you click on the month you are interested in, it will enlarge for a more detailed view. At the bottom of each picture will be links to more extensive explanations. Check out all the neat things on the main page, too. This site won two "Webby Awards"!

1-Pregnancy Directory-http://www.1-pregnancy.com/pregnancy/

American Baby-Your Partner in Parenting-http://www.americanbaby.com/ab/CDA/homepage/

IParenting-http://www.iparenting.com/: Parenting community and resources for parents, by parents. "'As each minute passes, your baby's brain grows 250,000 new cells!'…'The Secret Life of the Brain', a book and upcoming PBS television special".

Healthy Pregnancy-http://www.savonhealth.com/savonhealth/savonmain/preg_intro.asp

Parents Place-Fertility, pregnancy, babies, toddlers. http://www.parentsplace.com/

Christian Life Resources-http://www.christianliferesources.com/cgi-bin/home.pl

Baby Mall-http://www.gatewaytotheinternet.net/#Babies

"There are 40 couples who wait for every baby available for adoption, including children of all races and those with special needs." Dr. William Pierce, Director National Council For Adoption.

"Children from the U.S. and many foreign countries, previously thought 'un-adoptable' have found secure futures with eager adoptive families. Some of these children with 'special needs' were older, mixed-race, emotionally insecure, mentally disabled, or possessing physical challenges such as HIV positive, deafness, blindness, retardation, cleft palates, heart defects, paralysis, polio, epilepsy, etc. Couples eager to adopt wait as long as five, seven and even ten years, depending upon the area they live in. There are also waiting lists of couples wanting to adopt children with 'special needs,' including children with Spina Bifida, Downs Syndrome, congenital, physical, emotional, or mental dis-

390

abilities; proving there is no such thing as an 'unwanted child' but one that is merely misplaced. For national information, write: The National Council for Adoption 1930 17th St. NW Washington, D.C. 20009". From "ADOPTION A LOVING ALTERNATIVE", by Mary Ann Kuharski, for Pro-life Across America, P.O. 18669, Minneapolis, MN 55418, (612) 781-0410-"The Billboard People", http://www.prolifeacrossamerica.org/.

"...Richard and Sue Bergquist of Naperville, Illinois. The Bergquists have a special interest in promoting adoption since they have adopted eight children with special needs. They are keenly aware of what a gift an adopted child is to a family." Choose Life-http://www.choose-life.org/.

"House Passes Adoption Credit Bill On June 4, 2002, the House of Representatives passed H.R. 4800, a bill that will repeal the sunset provisions of the economic Growth and Tax Relief Reconciliation Act of 2001. This legislation deals with the expansion of the adoption credit and adoption assistance program.

This new bill makes the Hope for the Children Act adoption tax credit a permanent one. It passed by a vote of 391-1. It now goes to the Senate for a vote. If this legislation is not passed, beginning in 2011, the adoption tax credit will be cut from a maximum of $10,000 to $5,000; families who adopt special needs children will no longer receive a flat $10,000 credit. They will be limited to $6,000; and the income cap will fall from $150,000 to $75,000 so that fewer families will be eligible for this adoption credit. For added details on adoption tax credits, go to:
http://www.demint.house.gov/Legislation/HopeForChildren.htm
From: 'TVCNews' tvcnewscp@norm.nmailer.com, Vol. 5, Issue 23, Fri, 7 Jun 2002 01:18:08-0400 TRADITIONAL VALUES COALITION NEWS, http://www.traditionalvalues.org/. This email goes out to nearly 500,000 people each week."

Intecon

Post Abortion Stress Syndrome

Safe Haven, "A Place for Healing from the Trauma of Abortion",
http://www.safehavenministries.com/index.html
Email: safehaven@worldvillage.com.

I couldn't help being awed by this site, it's so well done. They deal with "Post-Abortion Syndrome", "Crisis Pregnancy", and "Finding Forgiveness ".

There's a separate page filled with real stories, a page for men, pages for resources and links, and message boards and a chat room. But what touched me the most was their statement of philosophy on the home page. I've copied some of it below. Hopefully they won't sue me. Their approach is to be non-controversial.

"This site is dedicated to my dear friend who, in a moment of panic and fear, for lack of knowledge of a better alternative, took the life of her child through abortion. And to all those like her who have suffered grief, remorse, shame and regret for the children they will never hold or comfort, tickle or tease in this lifetime. For all the mothers and fathers whose arms ache for children they will never hug; for all the bandaged knees they will never kiss; for the college graduations and weddings they will never celebrate, and for the grandchildren that will never be born: this site is dedicated to them."

"Welcome to SafeHaven! SafeHaven is designed to be a safe place for those who have had abortions to find comfort, hope, understanding, and healing in the painful aftermath of abortion. We are a peer support site, meaning that most of those who use this site have had an abortion or have been hurt by abortion. As such, we do not judge nor condemn those who have chosen abortion. On the contrary, you will be fully accepted. We are here to help."

"A Note About The Issue of 'Spirituality' Regardless of what spiritual path you follow-or even if you are not 'spiritual' at all-we want you to know that we accept you. Everyone is welcome at SafeHaven. Although we may disagree on spiritual issues, we are not here to 'convert' you. We believe that it is God who changes hearts, not people. Our main goal is to love you, accept you and help you if you are hurting. We can't help you if you won't allow us to. We invite you to stay whether or not you agree with us spiritually. Regardless of your spiritual beliefs, we have been hurt by abortion just like you. If that is all we have in common, it is enough."

Rachel's Vineyard, 877-HOPE-4-ME; http://www.rachelsvineyard.org/.

The founder of Rachel's, and probably the first person to identify PAS, has published a book-"FORBIDDEN GRIEF: THE UNSPOKEN PAIN OF ABORTION. Hard-cover copies of 'Forbidden Grief' by Theresa Burke, Ph.D. with David Reardon, Ph.D. will be published and available in late March, 2002, at:
http://www.rachelsvineyard.org/book.htm. Copies are $24.95 plus $4.00 S&H. To pre-order copies, please send a check for $28.95 to Rachel's Vineyard Ministries, 743 Roy Road, King of Prussia, Pa. 19406...Here also is a recent comment about the book from an English doctor, Trevor Griffiths...Dr. Griffiths has no involvement in abortion from a policy perspective and prior to reading 'Forbidden Grief,' had never considered the question of post-abortion grief. He is the author of a general work on repressed grief, 'Lost and Then Found.' Dr. Griffiths wrote: 'This book is a masterly, sensitive and thorough opening of a difficult subject that many prefer not to face. I see this deeply quiet suffering re-emerge in some of my patients years after the events. To find my own experience reflected in case after case presented anonymously in this book is a reassurance to me that I am not just conjuring up fantasies. The sensitivity displayed by the authors in presenting this material leaves one in no doubt that their intention is to get proper counseling and support for women who feel trapped with their grief. |Through my practice| I particularly recognize the subjects of lifestyle deterioration and relationship problems covered in the chapters entitled, 'Something Inside has Died,' and 'Paradise Lost'. It is as if for some a dream of self-control has been torn to shreds. But of course, even those who retain high levels of self-control may find that in their quieter moments, and at anniversaries, they still remember.'" So, another free advertisement. "Theresa Karminski Burke, Ph.D., DAPA, NCP Dr. Burke has lectured and trained professionals internationally on the subject of post-abortion trauma and healing. She is the author of several books. Dr. Burke is a nationally certified Psychologist; a diplomat of the American Psychotherapy Association, and a diplomat of the American Board of Forensic Counselors."

The National Office for Post Abortion Reconciliation and Healing- 1-800-5WE-CARE, http://www.marquette.edu/rachel/.

"Founded in 1990, the National Office of Post-Abortion Reconciliation and Healing, Inc. networks researchers and psychotherapeutic professionals working in the field within the U.S. and abroad, consults on the formation of post-abortion support services within secular and religious settings including Project Rachel, provides training for care providers, maintains a national "800" referral line for those seeking assistance in reconciling an abortion experience, publishes the International Post-Abortion Support Services Directory, produces and vends audio, video, and printed materials, maintains an annotated book list, tracks support group models, and sponsors the Healing Vision conference at Marquette University."

After Abortion: Information on the after-effects of abortion and post-abortion healing...The Elliot Institute-http://www.afterabortion.org/.

"This is the web's most complete source of information on the after effects of abortion and post-abortion healing. We have over 500 hundred links to thousands of pages of original research, testimonies, articles, and resources. Most of these are drawn from articles and books published by the Elliot Institute, one of the nation's leading authorities on post-abortion issues."

Post-Abortion Syndrome Healing-http://www.thebridgetolife.org/pas.htm
24-HOUR HOTLINE: (718) 591-7020-Email: thebridgetolife@erols.com
Brooklyn: 718-491-3692-Queens: 718-939-6646 The Bridge to Life Inc.

Healing Hearts Ministries-"Binding Up The Brokenhearted" –
"We provide confidential one to one e-mail and support group counseling to anyone suffering from the affects of an abortion. Our support group materials include a Bible study, "Binding Up the Brokenhearted" written by and for post-abortive women. If you want to talk about it with someone who understands, contact us." PO Box 7890, Bonney Lake, WA 98390-0966 360.897.2711
http://www.healinghearts.org/ heartsinc@healinghearts.org

Researchers: Post Abortion Syndrome A Growing Health Problem-
http://www.r2rministries.com/prolife/X0138_Post-Abortion_Syndro.html
"Post Abortion Syndrome, the negative reactions many women experience after abortion, can be characterized as a form of Post-Traumatic Stress Disorder...a combination of negative reactions to the abortion event, such as flashbacks, nightmares, grief and painful abortion recollections resulting in reduced responsiveness...recognized by the American Psychiatric Association in contexts other than abortion. Secondary symptoms of PAS include depression, substance abuse, sleep disorders and suicidal thoughts...flawed studies on the effects of abortion and political pressure have produced a lack of information, or informational deficit...one study cited...stated that of 80 women who had abortions at a Baltimore area clinic in the mid-1980s, approximately 20 percent had all of the symptoms of Post Traumatic Stress Disorder...45 percent of the women were still having flashbacks of the experience even three to five years later...has been

documented in others who participate in the abortion, such as fathers, siblings and other family members of the child, and abortion clinic staff." You can go to the above url to read the complete study. The site's host seems to specialize in pro-life videos: "Check out Reel to Real Ministries' best-selling pro-life video (over 200 thousand copies distributed!): Hard Truth". For more information, contact: Reel 2 Real Ministries info@r2rministries.com **Call toll free: (877) 701-9279 1925 Fox Quarry Road Cantonment, FL 32533**

The Culture of Life Foundation & Institute-Articles and Sociological Studies On Abortion – Some very interesting articles to peruse. http://www.christianity.com/partner/Article_Display_Page/0,PTID4211|CHID1 02758|CIID276334,00.html

"Long Term Physiological and Psychological Effects of Abortion on Women, both their physical and emotional health including thoughts of suicide and on their ability to be a mother in the future. *An Original Research Paper on Post Abortion Syndrome Disorder By: Jessica Lawlor*" – 160 pages in length: http://www.cirtl.org/syndrome.htm.

Sisters of Life, 450 W. 51st St., New York, NY 10019, 212-397-1396- http://sistersoflife.org/aboraft-fr.html:

"Special retreats are provided for those who suffer the aftermath of abortion and for all those touched by the effects of irreverence toward human life. They take place at Our Lady of New York convent in Bronx, NY. Except in July and August, they are scheduled on Saturdays from 9:00 to 4:30. Open to men and women; reservations are required. Please contact 718-881-8008".

Silent No More-Help after Abortion http://www.HelpAfterAbortion.com/

"This coming January 2003, as our nation recognizes 30 years of legalized abortion, something will take place that has never been done before. Women throughout this country who have had abortions will gather at state capitols and in our nation's capitol to publicly speak out about our abortion experience. This mobilization of women will be the beginning of a national campaign to raise awareness about the after-effects of abortion. The campaign will also seek to reach the many women who are suffering in silence, offering them abortion recovery help and resources. State gatherings are being held in 35-50 states at various times during the week of January 18-26, 2003. The gathering in Washington, D.C. -will take place January 22, 2003 after the March for Life.

Silent No More is inviting women who regret their abortion to join in speaking out by sharing their testimonies during the gatherings.

'We are the voice that hasn't been heard,' says Georgette Forney, Executive Director of NOEL, and one of the co-founders of Silent No More who had an abortion at age 16. 'There is a lot of talk about whether or not abortion should be legal, but very little attention is given to the women who have actually had abortions. I regret having an abortion and I know that there are millions of women who feel the same way.' 'The truth is abortion affects us physically, emotionally and spiritually. It's time to speak honestly about the pain we've lived with and we want to help women who are hurting find healing. After 30 years it's time to listen to the women who have experienced it.' If you are ready to speak out about the pain you experienced after your abortion, please join us. Click below to have information sent to you. Let us know if you are interested in participating in the gathering in Washington or the one in your state.

If you've had an abortion and want to talk with someone who understands how you are feeling either click http://www.pregnancycenters.com/ or call 800-395-HELP for help. The campaign is being sponsored by a partnership between NOEL (the National Organization of Episcopalians for Life), the Justice Foundation and Priests for Life. In addition, we have also developed an ad hoc coalition of abortion recovery programs to provide the support and healing for women who come forward when they learn help is available. Members of the coalition include; Care-Net Pregnancy Centers, Heartbeat International, Ramah International, Rachel's Vineyard, NOPARH (National Office of Post-Abortion Reconciliation and Healing), Hope Alive USA, The Elliot Institute, The Chalfont House, American Victims of Abortion, an outreach program of the National Right to Life Committee and many others."

More about Silent No More: "I have come to know so many women over the years who have been deeply wounded and scarred by abortion. They're determined now to do what they can to make up for what they did, and to warn others not to make the same terrible mistake…the walking wounded of the abortion catastrophe. Their spokeswoman is actress Jennifer O'Neill,…'I was told a lie from the pits of Hell. I had the abortion and paid for it all my life until I healed and am now able to help other women. By age 38 I had mourned 9 miscarriages—certain that they were the result of my agonizing abortion.' For each aborted mother there's an aborted father. In many cases the father pressured the woman and paid to assassinate his own child. Often forgotten are the surviving children of parents who've resorted to abortion. Believe it or not, these children know or *strongly suspect* that a brother or sister is missing-An abortion inevitably impacts the whole family. Make no mistake. Each abortion is an irreversible tragedy of monumental proportions." Excerpted from a February 21, 2003, letter from Joseph M. Scheidler, National Director, Pro-Life Action League.

Post Abortion Syndrome "How to Offer Help to Hurting Hearts"–
http://www.episcopaliansforlife.org/pas%20brochure.htm. There's a lot of
good information in a relatively small space here. It describes what PAS is,
and gives some very interesting statistics. But it seems to be aimed at someone
who knows someone who had an abortion, and wants to help them get past it;
and coaches on how to talk to them about it. At the bottom it has a very good
"List of Post-Abortion Healing Ministries", including some good ones that I
haven't listed here-and how to contact them.

Symptoms and Frequently Asked Questions About Post-Abortion Stress
Syndrome (A "Pro-Choice Site")-http://www.afterabortion.com/faq.html. The
official pro-abortion position on PASS is that it doesn't exist. Therefore, this
web site can't possibly exist, because the gal who runs it is "pro-choice"; unless
she's changed her opinion and didn't notify me. But, even back then this was a
big, packed with information and commentary, message boards, chat rooms,
and, will, you get the idea, web site – and it does very definitely exist.

As I recall, I sent her an email congratulating her on the work she had done,
and she had enough moxie to reply with a very nice email of her own, even
though she knew about my site. Most people wouldn't have bothered to reply.

"This site is owned by 'jilly', a woman who has overcome her own
struggles with PASS." There's even a PASS Foundation. She's put a lot
of work into it, and even though her liberal viewpoint shows through in
some places, there are probably at least several things here you won't
find anyplace else; so if you have a strong interest in the topic, it's
definitely worth a look.

ABORTION-Healing and Forgiveness – A personal site, with a personal
message-http://hometown.aol.com/mark2red/myhomepage/index.html.

"Senate Recognizes Existence of Post-Abortion Syndrome – Senator Bob Smith
(R-NH) successfully attached an amendment to the Labor/ HHS
appropriations bill directing the National Institutes of Health to conduct
research pertaining to post-abortion syndrome. The syndrome is characterized
by severe depression, guilt, eating disorders, anxiety, anger, and low self-
esteem following a woman's abortion. The abortion lobby denies the existence
of post-abortion syndrome, despite massive evidence to the contrary. Common
sense tells us that anyone with even a partially developed conscience who plays
a part in killing her own child is going to be haunted by that memory.
Although the amendment will likely be dropped in the conference committee,
the fact that it passed the Senate is a pro-life victory and a step in the direction
of dealing with important mental health problems faced by millions of women

who have had abortions." Republican National Coalition for Life Fax Notes-November 9, 2001

"...I don't fight to save just the baby but also the baby's mother. A pregnant mother who chooses to abort her baby becomes a ticking time bomb. Although many of these women may feel relieved at first, the full impact of what they've done is likely to hit them sometime later like a ton of bricks. It might happen in 5 or 10 years, or even later than that. Let me tell you what happens to women after they've experienced an abortion. The woman can expect her relationship with the baby's father to turn sour, especially if he pressured her to get the abortion. And her life may go into a sudden and unexplained downward spiral. She might engage in some kind of self-destructive behavior such as promiscuity, alcohol or drug abuse. If she's a student, her grades may suddenly plunge. She may gain weight and then resort to anorexia or bulimia to avoid tummy bulge that reminds her of the pregnancy. She may get so depressed that she contemplates, attempts, or commits suicide. But most of the devastating problems of Post-Abortion Syndrome don't kick in until later. Here are some of the things that aborted women can experience: Disturbing flashbacks of the abortion Vivid nightmares related to the abortion An obsessive-compulsive disorder (for example, repeating a cleaning ritual over and over) Panic attacks Avoidance's (inability to look a baby in the eye, quickly changing the channel when abortion is mentioned or suggested on TV, avoiding the sound of a home vacuum cleaner because of its similarity to the sound of the suction machine, sadness at seeing a pregnant mother, and so on) Amnesia: pathological gaps in memory Hypermnesia: remembering everything about the abortion in heightened detail And then there are the two dates forever etched in the woman's mind: the date of the abortion, and her due date. The aborted woman may become overwhelmed with sadness upon seeing a 12-year-old girl, for example, knowing that her child would have been that age. My heart goes out to these suffering women. I pray that each one will find...peace...I also recommend that they get help form a support group such as Rachel's Vineyard and Women Exploited by Abortion, which have helped so many women...a strange thing happened when she woke up from her third abortion. Carolyn explains that there's a sound you hear when you wake up at an abortion mill: the sound of wailing, like an animal in pain. She had heard it when she woke up from her first two abortions. After her third abortion, *she* was the one wailing. Nurses frantically tried to shush her, telling her, 'It'll be O.K.' But she knew in her heart that it wouldn't be O.K...Then one day it hit her like a ton of bricks. She ran out on her boat dock, literally screaming at God: 'PLEASE FORGIVE ME! I'M SO SORRY! I WANT THEM BACK. GIVE ME ANOTHER CHANCE! JUST LET ME HAVE THOSE BABIES BACK!' She ran into her bedroom and pulled a revolver out of her husband's nightstand. She heard a voice telling her to 'put it to your head and pull the trigger.' She put it to her head,...". Yes, and I had to enter it one character at a time! To hear the full story, and how it turned out, send a contribution of any size to Joe Scheidler, Pro-Life Action League, 6160 N. Cicero Avenue, Chicago, Illinois 60646, and ask them to send you a copy of the Erwin and Carolyn Kolleger audio tape. It should be pretty good-Carolyn was a very successful actress. In case you haven't guessed the quotes were from Joe, too. Joe has been continuously involved in fighting abortion for over 30 years. Probably nobody knows the subject matter better. He is, truly, an expert; and has probably seen it all. He has also written a book called "Closed: 99 Ways to Stop Abortion". "…15 abortion mills have been closed in San Diego County alone since 1986…There used to be 70 abortionists in the San Diego area; now there are 35. We won't rest until it's ZERO!" "'Planned Barrenhood' uses 'deathscorts'-pro-abortion fanatics who try their best to thwart and impede the efforts of our counselors. You might be surprised to know that some people pray before they leave for their abortion appointment. They might pray something like this, 'God, if you don't want me to have this abortion, please show me a sign.' As a sidewalk counselor or prayer warrior, you are that sign. I encourage you to consider becoming a sidewalk counselor or prayer warrior at an abortion mill. I'll gladly send our training materials to anyone who wants them." Joe Scheidler, in a January 20, 2003, letter. http://www.prolifeaction.org/-

I heard a story on the radio today about a woman who had an obsessive-compulsive disorder about germs and cleaning. She spent $200 a week on cleaning supplies. She made her husband undress in the garage before he could come into the house. It was in the news because he had strangled her to death. The gist of the story was that it had apparently pushed him over the edge. I couldn't help wondering if she had had an abortion.

That reminded me of another strange murder story. Some people killed a pregnant girl and cut her open to steal her baby. It was a really stupid thing to do, and they were caught within a couple of days. But, as stupid as they were, at least they understood that there was a baby in there. By the way, the baby's doing just fine.

Not only the mother experiences Post Abortion Stress Syndrome (PASS), and goes for treatment. "Dear Son, The following letter was written by a *Celebrate Life* reader to his aborted son, as part of his healing process…

Your mother told me on Christmas day that she had aborted you. The news struck me like a tidal wave. There was no way to comprehend the information, to assimilate it, to start thinking about the possibility of you and your terrible fate. I couldn't bring myself to discuss it with anyone, so I kept these distant thoughts of you completely to myself for two years before I breathed a word to one of my closest friends. Son, in writing this I just wanted you to know that the rejection was not total. I never had the chance to speak in your defense, and, of course, was never consulted before that awful decision was made and carried out. It is a sad fact that our laws, and a decision known as *Roe v. Wade* made her decision possible. I have no idea, nor could I even begin to speculate, what was on her mind at the time: whether any other alternatives were considered, what else might have been happening, or what ultimately led her to take that fateful action that separates us so completely today. All I know is that I never had a say in the matter, despite having, I believe, every right to, and even today that has been the biggest source of the anger and frustration and pain that has haunted my mind through these many years. She had a choice, and killed you...I wonder why things worked out the way they did, and hope that someday it will all make sense. That's the dilemma I struggle with today; it's my one tenable, tenacious link to your mother and the past that still has any power over me. Perhaps, finally writing this letter will help me take the next step in letting go. I know in my heart that abortion is utterly vile; it...is incredibly damaging to all those involved in it...the deliberate choosing of death over life. And if I feel angry over not having been informed or considered, how must you feel? You, and the millions of others like you, really had no voice, no choice at all; that decision rested solely in the mind and heart of one person, and because of her, we now stand separated by this infinite void...Son, I miss you. I wonder if she ever does. In recent years, I've pondered what life would be like were you here now. Lately I've looked around at families in public places, perhaps in church on days like this, or even watching TV commercials with young children in them, and wondered what you'd be like. Had things not turned out this way, you'd be over four-and-a-half now, and I try to guess by looking at other kids that age how tall you'd be, what clothes you'd wear, what your laugh would sound like, how your hair would drift in the breeze. What kind of food, music and toys would you like? How would you feel if I picked you up, sat in a chair and read to you, held you close and kissed you goodnight? What would your voice sound like if I were able to hear you call me 'Dad'? What would it be like to say bedtime prayers with you? In all these jumbled thoughts I just want to tell you, my son, that you are loved-and are missed from this place. I miss you. Your absence is a very real burden and ache to bear, a longing that will not be fulfilled so long as I walk this earth, and will be with me even when my days are through. But on this particular Father's Day, even though we're apart, I hope you can see the love I have for you written on my heart through all the concerns of my troubled mind. Stay near, my son, and keep the Faith. Love, Dad" Excerpted from the May-June 2002 Celebrate Life, a publication of The American Life League. An incredible depth of feeling for a man, I think, and obviously a very intelligent, caring, and expressive one. But then, I guess I have feelings for the father I can't remember, too. Although I don't always agree with the positions they take on the issues, I consider ALL a totally reliable and rock solid source. And keep in mind that Rachel's Vineyard is a part of ALL, and that they must receive literally thousands and thousands of these letters at their retreats. I'm also aware that men do attend these retreats, sometimes accompanying the woman in their lives. It shows an often overlooked aspect of the harm abortion does.

"Rachel's Vineyard needs to train new leaders to meet an increasing demand for post-abortion retreats...Mental health professionals and clinicians will share a wealth of clinical information on healing post-abortion syndrome, including important presentations on men and abortion, how the abortion wound emerges during the childbearing years and much more...growing need to minister to women and men suffering in the aftermath of abortion...for many people the time of their life during which one or more abortions occurred includes extremely painful memories. Many sustained a traumatic psychological wound in the abortion...the tragedy of choosing to abort changes a mother's life forever...Beverly Hartberg reported on a Rachel's Vineyard retreat she had attended...'I saw a transformation – of broken, hurting, regretful, and pain filled lives'". http://www.rachelsvineyard.org/ Taken from the May 2002 Judie Brown Report.

News, Reference, and Shopping Links

Life News-http://www.lifenews.com/

Abortion Infonet-Legal, Scientific, Moral, and Political Information and Current News-http://www.abortioninfo.net/

Women and Children First-http://www.womenandchildrenfirst.org/

SBA-List Legislative Update Page –
http://www.sba-list.org/index.cfm/section/whatsnew/page/legupdate.html

InterLIFE-http://www.interlife.org/

Ohio Right to Life-http://www.ohiolife.org/

California ProLife Council-http://www.californiaprolife.org/

Life Issues Institute, Dr. J. C. Willke, M.D., President
http://www.lifeissues.org/
Dr. Willke is also president and founder of the International Right to Life Federation. Prior to that "He served for ten years as the president of the National Right to Life Committee." I remember him from 30 years ago when I was briefly involved in the right to life movement at that time. So apparently his involvement has been unflagging. It was through a glossy flyer he produced around that time that I first got the scientific verification of human life in the womb – although I was already pro-life. The source of my conviction before that was a picture of a child in the womb on the cover of Life Magazine; and a question I posed to myself: "Where do you draw the line?" He was one of the big-name speakers at the 2002 Celebrate Life World Family Conference in New Orleans, along with other notables such as Chris Slattery, Dr. Bernard Nathanson, Dr. John R. Diggs, Archbishop Elden Curtiss, Judie Brown, Rev. Johnny Hunter, Congressman David Vitter, Joseph M. Scheidler, Dr. C. Ward Kischer, Mark Crutcher, and former ambassador and presidential candidate Dr. Alan Keyes (Ph.d., Harvard), who gave probably the most inspiring speech I've ever heard.

If you're interested, you can still obtain that Life photo at the following url: http://www.victorywon.com/books.htm. Life Magazine had nothing to do with the pro-life movement, and its inception preceded Roe v. Wade by many years. It was a popular, large circulation magazine built around great photography in the current news category. It folded a number of years ago but appears to have had some reincarnations since then.

Life Corner: Supporting ALL Human Life-http://www.lifecorner.org/

Life Corner-Pro-Life Links-http://www.lifecorner.org/links.html

Pro-Life Net Links-http://www.pro-life.net/links/links.htm

Respect Life Links-http://www.respectlife.org/links.htm

SpeakOut-http://www.speakout.com/activism/abortion/

About.com-http://prolife.about.com/cs/abortion101/

Open Directory-http://www.dmoz.org/Society/Issues/Abortion/Pro-Life/

**Pro-Life Organizations-
http://www.dmoz.org/Society/Issues/Abortion/Pro-Life/Organizations/**

Adoption-http://www.dmoz.org/Home/Family/Adoption/

**National Directory Pro-Life Category-
http://www.nationaldirectory.com/Society/Issues/Abortion/Pro-Life/**

**More Organizations –
http://www.nationaldirectory.com/Society/Issues/Abortion/Pro-
Life/Organizations/**

**Webrings –
http://www.nationaldirectory.com/Society/Issues/Abortion/Pro-Life/Webrings/**

**A list of companies that give support to abortionists-
http://www.stantoninus.net/listab.htm**

Supreme Court Opinions-http://www.findlaw.com/casecode/supreme.html

**The Abortion Law Home Page-
http://hometown.aol.com/abtrbng/index.htm**

**MegaLaw-Legal Research, Case Law, Supreme Court-
http://www.megalaw.com/**

**Roe v Wade. Org: "Read the actual text of the Roe v. Wade Supreme Court
decision and listen to oral arguments; other important abortion-related
Supreme Court Cases are included."
http://www.roevwade.org/index2.html**

STENBERG v. CARHART (99-830) 192 F.3d 1142, affirmed.
http://supct.law.cornell.edu/supct/html/99-830.ZS.html Supreme Court
Collection, The Legal Information Institute-Cornell Law School, Myron Taylor
Hall, Ithaca, NY 14853 lii@lii.law.cornell.edu

United States Senate Committee on the Judiciary-
http://www.senate.gov/~judiciary/

How your tax dollars go to fund abortions: a "PDF" file from the United States
General Accounting Office (GAO)-
http://www.gao.gov/new.items/he00147r.pdf

Selected Internet Resources on Abortion Ethics-
http://ethics.sandiego.edu/Applied/Abortion/index.html

Human Life Alliance-http://www.humanlife.org/

Human Life International-http://www.hli.org/

Family Research Council-http://www.frc.org/

Life Cycle Books-http://www.lifecyclebooks.com/-"North America's foremost
publisher of pro-life and abstinence only educational materials".

Some of the book and brochure titles are: "Dehumanizing the Vulnerable,
When Word Games Take Lives", by William Brennan;

"No One Told Me I Could Cry", by Connie Nykiel, about post-abortive teens;

"Language of Illusion: The Abortion Slogans", by Jean Garton;

"Men and Abortion-A Path to Healing", by C.T. Coyle, Ph.D., "the only pro-
life book ever written specifically for men"; & "Forgotten Fathers", a
brochure.

Additional brochures include: "Adoption: A Loving Choice", "If Someone You
Know Considers Abortion", "Before You Choose", "A Christian Resp-onse to
Abortion", "Secret Sorrow", and "Breast Cancer and Abortion: What's the
Connection?"

Another good, complementary resource, is a book called: "ProLife Answers to
ProChoice Arguments", written by Randy Alcorn. Including appendices, it
runs 455 pages, but you can buy it for just 13 dollars by going to the following
web location: http://www.abortionNO.org/book_01.html.

Victory Won-"If you are searching for pro-life materials, your journey has ended. Choose from our massive selection of bumper stickers, buttons and envelope stickers...visit our books, videos, pins, cards and balloons." http://www.victorywon.com/

A list of some of the "inspirational" slogans you can find on their materials follows. They are the best "one-liners" I've seen anywhere, and would be useful in conversation and debates. I love it!

"The ultimate form of child abuse...ABORTION".

"Abortion is legal. So was slavery."

"If it's not a baby, You're not pregnant!"

"Equal Rights For Unborn Women".

"One Abortion One Dead One Wounded"

"How Much Does an Abortion Cost? One Human Life!"

"Smile! Your Mom Chose Life"

"It's easy to be PRO 'CHOICE' when you're not the one being KILLED."

"Americans Born To Be Free. If only They Were Free To Be Born."

"ABORTION? The Supreme Court also Legalized Slavery"

"Pregnancy is not a Disease!"

"Some Babies Die by Chance. No Baby Should Die By Choice!"

"Choose Life. Your Baby would!"

"ABORTION IS NOT HEALTH CARE"

"Pro-Choice? That's a Lie! 'Babies Don't Choose To Die.'"

"Abortion doesn't make you 'UN' pregnant. It makes you the mother of a dead baby!"

"HOW COME AMERICA??? We Brake for Animals, we Save the Seals, and Protect the Whales, But We Murder Our Unborn Children!!"

"ABORTION? What part of Thou Shalt Not Kill Don't You Understand?"

"Without Life there is no choice".

"ABORTION is it good for the Children?"

"If you can read this YOU WEREN'T ABORTED. Call your MOM today and thank Her!"

"40 Million Aborted Who's Missing from Your Neighborhood?"

"I'm a SURVIVOR of the American Holocaust".

"As a Former Fetus I Oppose Abortion!"

"I think…Therefore I Am Pro-LIFE!"

That alone is worth the price of the book!

Heritage House 76-More Pro-Life materials-
http://www.heritagehouse76.com/

Charity shopping: Shop at these web sites and they will donate a portion of the cost of your purchase to the non-profit pro-life organization of your choice-

Shop & Support-http://www.shopandsupport.com/

Well Spent-http://www.wellspent.org/

Pro Life Communications-http://www.prolifecomm.com/.

Euthanasia, and Some Parting Shots

"Assisted suicide inevitably becomes involuntary euthanasia and every single citizen eventually becomes a candidate." Judie Brown The Judie Brown Report-May 2002 Thanks, Judie, for putting my own thoughts, and fears, into words. I'm not sure that it's inevitable, but I think that it's a very real threat-as is abortion. Once you open the door, even a little, I think it puts everybody at risk.

"Once one category of humanity is declared unfit to live-regardless of the reason-all others become at risk to the whims of society at a given moment." Cal Thomas, Tribune Media Services; January 1, 2003.

"Few people realize that not all 'assisted suicides' are voluntary, which means this is a movement that could one day threaten your own life or the life of a loved one." Wanda Franz, Ph.D., President National Right to Life Committee

"I ask, 'Do you know how much it costs for the drugs used in an assisted suicide?' Answering my own question, I say, 'About forty bucks,' adding 'Since HMOs make money by cutting costs, and it could cost $40,000 (or more) to provide suicidal patients with proper care so they don't want assisted suicide, the economic force of gravity is obvious.' Most people haven't yet made the money connection between assisted suicide and the increasing strains on health-care budgets. Kaiser/Permanente isn't merely permitting doctors to assist in patient suicides, it is *actively soliciting* its doctors to participate in the deadly practice. As revealed by the anti-assisted-suicide medical group Physicians for Compassionate Care, a Kaiser executive recently e-mailed a memo to more than 800 Kaiser doctors soliciting PAS-doctor volunteers. The memo reveals that to the apparent chagrin of Kaiser, to their credit, few plan doctors are willing to participate in the killing of their own patients. Hence, the executive urges any Kaiser doctor…'willing to act as Attending Physician under the law for members who ARE NOT your patients'…Indeed, if assisted suicide ever became nationalized and a routine 'medical treatment,' significant money could be saved—and hence made—by the HMO industry from the hastened deaths of their patients. With the advent of managed care, profits in health care increasingly come from cutting costs. With assisted suicides costing such little money, what 'treatment' could be more effective than assisted suicide?" Taken from "Kaiser Solicits Its Doctors To Kill", by Wesley J. Smith, in Lifeline Winter 2003, a publication of the Life Legal Defense Foundation, P.O. Box 2105, Napa, California 94558 (707) 224-6675, http://www.lldf.org/. So here we see the germ for a new industry, to stand side by side with the abortion industry-doctors who do assisted suicides. It could be even more lucrative than abortion-depending on how big a cut they could demand of the money saved by the HMOs. Or perhaps the abortion doctors would just expand their practice to include euthanasia.

"After speaking for 30 minutes or so, I fielded 1 and 1/2 hours of questioning… As the questions came one after another, they re-enforced a point I had made earlier. Feminism is a totally self-centered, and thoroughly selfish philosophy. It's about 'my rights,' 'my career,' 'having it all,' men not doing 'their fair share,' or the old standby 'we are victims.' I finally was driven to say, 'What could be more singularly selfish than a movement that believes babies should live only if women want them to!' The room fell silent for a noticeable moment. I call that progress." Bay Buchanan, speaking in a hostile environment at the University of Ohio. You can add "It's my body" to that. If you would like to invite Bay to speak on your campus, you can contact her at The American Cause, 115 Rowell Court, Falls Church, VA 22046, phone: (703) 237-2034 http://www.theamericancause.org/. She's the President. Brother Pat is the Chairman.

"ge·net·ics (j…-nμt"¹ks) n. 1. (used with a sing. verb). The branch of biology that deals with heredity, especially the mechanisms of hereditary transmission and the variation of inherited characteristics among similar or related organisms. 2. (used with a pl. verb). The genetic constitution of an individual, a group, or a class."

"human being n. 1. A member of the genus Homo and especially of the species H. sapiens. 2. A person: a fine human being."

"Ho·mo sa·pi·ens (h½"m½ s³"p-…nz,-μnz") n. The modern species of human beings, the only extant species of the primate family Hominidae. [New Latin Hom½ sapi¶ns,: Hom½, genus name + Latin sapins, present participle of sapere, to be wise.]"

"hom·i·cide (h¼m"¹-s°d", h½"m¹-) n. 1. The killing of one person by another." The American Heritage Dictionary, or any dictionary.

ANTIABORTIONISM~The radical notion that unborn humans are people. From Debbie, at the About.com Pro-Life Views Forum, where we debated the abortionists. She also got me started on the string of definitions above.

Any kind of abortion is infanticide; partial-birth abortion is just overtly obvious infanticide.

Abortion-When mothers have their children killed. A homicide. A new form of genocide more massive than the world has ever seen.

Reproductive Health-Generally regarded as a euphemism for abortion.

Choice-Death by dismemberment.

**It's especially important to realize that abortion is *not* "medical treatment".
Both mother and child are almost always healthy and not being treated for any
illness or injury or other medical problem. Abortion is a "hit", an
assassination – by a hired killer; in short, a form of murder, plain and simple-
made legal by our court system and those who profit from it.**

**"Q: How many Americans receive the death penalty each year despite their
innocence? A: Thousands" Taken from a cartoon by Breen via the Asbury
Park Press, Copley News Service, and Celebrate Life, showing a woman
walking into an "Abortion Clinic".**

**"Every abortion involves unspeakable cruelty visited upon an innocent human
being...the slicing and dicing in their mothers' wombs...the act of child killing
is to seek the willful, deliberate, premeditated execution of an innocent human
being." Dr. Thomas A. Droleskey, Oyster Bay, N.Y., May, 2003.**

**Over 3,000 children were murdered in this country yesterday, but because the
media chose not to report it, it's as if it never happened.**

**"Every once in a while my heart just breaks as I view the pain in the world
around me. Last week was one of those times...last Saturday I was at a clinic
with the Survivors and a young girl with us for the first time said to me, 'My
mother was wrong.' She said it with such a pitiful voice I was moved just by
her tone. When I asked her what she meant by that she told me that earlier
that week she had come across some of her mother's old diaries. In one she
found an entry where her mother laments that she is $50 short and can't afford
an abortion. The child she was to abort was none other than the young lady
standing beside me. Tears came to my eyes later as I watched this young girl
singing praises in front of that clinic, she was such a doll. Her mother remains
unconvinced that abortion is wrong. In fact, her mother told her that she does
not mourn for the two children she aborted after her. I prayed with her then,
and I continue to pray for her now. I pray that God will heal the pain she feels
and that she will know love in her life." Your Friend for Life, Jeff White
09/20/02**

**"Signs of Evolution
...if you know anything about science writers in general and Associated Press
science writers in particular, you know there's about a 99.99 percent chance
that they believe a human baby in the womb represents nothing more than
potential life and doesn't become a real person until after it has cleared the
birth canal, taken its first breath and scored at least a 1500 on the SAT tests.
Until all or most of that happens, Associated Press science writers insist that**

potential human life must always be described as a fetus. So, imagine my surprise when I came across an Associated Press article about the discovery of six beautifully preserved tiny dinosaurs still curled up inside their eggshells. Throughout the story, the science writer referred to the dead little creatures inside the eggs as *dinosaur babies*. Not *dinosaur fetuses* or *potential dinosaur life*, but genuine *dinosaur babies*. Wow! An Associated Press science writer actually recognizing a baby when he sees one—that is a major step in journalistic perceptions. And it gives us all hope that the observation skills of science reporters will one day evolve to the point where they can recognize babies higher up on the food chain...by Judie Brown, president, American Life League".

"...we have a system of laws in America that illogically, blindly and arrogantly denies personhood to an entire class of human beings". Judie Brown, in the September-October Celebrate Life

"It's painfully obvious that any battle that lasts for 30 years is going to have extremely heavy losses. Our readers know all-to-well that the casualties in this conflict are innocent babies. Nothing could be more devastating." Elizabeth Daub, Editor Celebrate Life, January-February, 2003, edition.

"The truth is this—that you and I are fighting the deadliest, bloodiest, longest war in history—the war against legalized abortion". Judie Brown, President American Life League, 03/25/03

"The end of abortion is closer than ever. More and more Americans oppose the killing of the unborn. At one time in America there were over 2000 abortion clinics in America. Today there are fewer than 800. The abortion industry cannot find doctors to perform abortions. As abortionists quit, retire, or go to jail no one is willing to take their place." Mark Crutcher, President, Life Dynamics, Incorporated, in a January, 2003, letter.

"Dr. Randall O'Bannon, head of NRL's Education and Research Department, and an expert on statistics involving annual numbers of abortions, reports that there are now about 300,000 fewer abortions each year than there were 10 years ago...due to new pro-life education and new pro-life laws".

"...we're saving more babies than ever before...Meanwhile the abortion industry is in a state of panic because so few young doctors aspire to become abortionists. Older abortionists are dying off, retiring, or converting to the pro-life movement, and the abortion mills are finding it difficult or impossible to replace them. As a consequence, one abortion mill after another is closing ...abortions are at their lowest since 1973, having fallen off 19.3 percent!" Joseph M. Scheidler, National Director, Pro-Life Action League, in a January 20, 2003, letter.

"America, I believe, is on the brink of a new appreciation for the value of human life, especially unborn human life. I believe we are on the cutting edge of a subtle but very clear shift in our attitudes. There is a palpable mood change in the country. Even the secular polls show it. We are winning. Our victory at the Supreme Court is a highly visible proof that we have entered a new phase, but there are also many other indications. One of the most significant is the enthusiasm of young people taking up the pro-life cause in ever-growing numbers." Joe Scheidler, in a February 28, 2003, letter.

"With the replacement of pro-abortion Sen. Tom Daschle as majority leader, pro-life bills will once again be allowed to come up for a vote. New life-saving legislation like a ban on partial-birth abortion should finally be signed into law...our movement is gaining...Whether measured in public opinion polls, November's election results, or a steady drop in the number of abortions... Polls now show that a strong majority of Americans identify themselves as holding a pro-life position; women lead the way in the polls...This change in public opinion came like a tidal wave in last fall's elections. In some U.S. Senate races last year, as many as four times as many voters chose the pro-life candidate because of his or her stance. In states like Minnesota and Missouri, this net pro-life voting increment was easily more than the margin of victory for new pro-life Senators. In other words, the pro-life issue was responsible for removing pro-abortion Tom Daschle from the Senate leadership, sweet justice when you consider that Daschle and his allies blocked almost all pro-life legislation from coming up for a vote...some political consultants have read the election returns, and are now advising their pro-abortion client candidates to drop or downplay their public support for abortion because they now realize it's not a winning issue for them! It's not just in Congress that pro-lifers made important gains in last year's elections, but in state legislatures, as well.

...you are a vital part of the most important movement for justice in our time-the Right to Life movement." Wanda Franz, Ph.D., President, National Right to Life Committee, January 13, 2003.

"In 1973, the U.S. Supreme Court's *Roe v. Wade* ruling overturned 50 state laws regulating abortion and invented the so-called 'right' to kill unborn children. Too many innocent children have already died! Too many women and families have been destroyed by the abortion industry! Now, you and I have a chance to win major, lasting victories in our efforts to limit or halt the barbaric practice of abortion...we have a tremendous obligation...to make the best use of this...groups like Planned Parenthood and NARAL, are extremely well-funded. Abortion is a business...a multi-billion dollar business. Our adversaries will not stand by and let any...bills pass without a massive political and media fight." Beverly LaHaye, Founder and Chairman, Concerned Women For America, February 4, 2003.

"Lives are being saved—and Planned Parenthood is losing money (in Bryan, Texas). 'We thank God for bringing us into contact with STOPP International), because the strategies they taught us are making an incredible impact and saving many lives,' said (David) Bereit. 'If every community that has a Planned Parenthood facility would simply follow STOPP's plan, hundreds of thousands of babies would be saved and Planned Parenthood would cease to be an influential force,' he said." STOPP-http://www.stoppinternational.org/.

From ALL NEWS, January, 2003. American Life League, P.O. Box 1350, Stafford, VA 22555 540-659-4171 Based on this success, and others like it, ALL has developed a plan to shut down all PP abortuaries. They've even established a deadline to meet, just a few years down the road. They have some of the people on staff who have been successful at doing this, so it's not an idle threat. But what worked in one locale, might be much more difficult in someplace like New York City, which has over 80 abortion "facilities", with local government being very supportive, and some of the "facilities" probably located in high crime areas that might be unsettling to picketers and counselors, and a New Yorker mentality that favors abortion, unlike some of the communities that they've been successful in. So I don't think I would want to wait for this to happen. Plus, if PP feels threatened, they will roll out their legal resources, and use their legislative influence, to change the rules of the game. I already see this beginning to happen. But I wish ALL the best of luck, and hope they are successful at it. Besides, they don't really have to shut down every abortuary for it to be a big success in my mind. Every one they shut down, and every community they clean up, will be a big success to me.

I mentioned that I collect books. Well they were piling up on me. I didn't want to be bothered with them, and there was no place to put them. But I couldn't get other things done, because they were in the way. This time it was a problem I had to solve, I couldn't just suggest a plan. Three days later I was finally finishing up my early American history section. It starts out with a book called "The Slave Trade". Then there's a book on the colonists and a couple of books by John Locke, then Thomas Paine and Ben Franklin and books about Thomas Jefferson and the other Founders. It made me think. What we take for granted today, were just ideas then. Nobody really knew whether they would work, and there were many detractors, plus probably a majority that didn't really care. We owe our prosperity, and our nation's success, and greatness, to those ideas, which have since been adopted, at least in part, all over the world. We are a country, and a world, built mostly on those ideals. They haven't come cheap. If George Washington hadn't been there to fight our battles, we probably would never have been. And over the years, other people have stepped up to protect our nation when the need arose. But it's not just on the battlefield that we must defend our country. The underlying ideals that made this country possible, that are its bedrock foundation, must also be defended. And none of those rights is more basic than the one our founders included in The Declaration of Independence, and the 14th Amendment to the Constitution, the "Right to Life", without which it is not possible to enjoy any of the other rights our Constitution guarantees. If we don't defend it, then who will?

"America is great because America is good, and if America ever ceases to be good, America will cease to be great." French historian Alexis de Tocqueville

"The founders of this great country understood that their great experiment in self-government would fall flat on its face if the people were not moral. They said so. Only a moral people are capable of self-government. Immoral people need to be coerced to follow the law, obey the rules and treat one another with respect." Joseph Farah, World Net Daily, January 22, 2003

"I have seen the danger that looms when traditional values become eroded and attacks on our precious heritage go unanswered...the price of freedom is eternal vigilance." Kenneth W. Starr

"As John Whitehead, president of The Rutherford Institute, has written...we are duty-bound to assist those who are oppressed...However, there are those who possess special skills...which can be especially effective in assisting the oppressed. These individuals have a special obligation to act...change begins with the willingness of one person to stand up for what they believe in." Rutherford, Spring 2002 "In America, we have a legacy that has been handed down to us by brave men and women who knew what it was to sacrifice for their beliefs—individuals who, when faced with almost certain defeat, still chose to stand and fight. America now stands at a crossroads, and each of us has a chance to influence the road she will travel in the coming years. It is time that each of us answers the call to stand and defend all we hold dear...what matters most of all is that we contribute in some way to the effort to ensure that America remains a land of the free and a home of the brave. To choose inaction is to give up hope". Rutherford, Spring 2003

If you have thoughtfully and thoroughly read this far, the seed for life now exists within you. I can not go with you or show you how to use it-you must discover that for yourself. Though largely unseen and unreported, this is the Civil War, and World Wars, of your generation. But, like the American Revolution, it must first be a triumph of ideas.

A Forum On About.com

What follows is a dialogue from a forum I started at about.com, http://www.about.com /. My handle here is Intecon.

General Discussion-www.aboutabortions.com
Subscribe

From: INTECON
Oct-13 4:38 am
To: ALL

I would like to offer my web site, http://www.aboutabortions.com/ to the forum as an analysis of the abortion controversy-and how to resolve it. Comments and discussion are of course hoped for and encouraged. I am trying very hard to have an impact on this conflict, and my objective is to have as many people as possible read it.

Edited 10/13/00 4:42:53 AM ET by INTECON

From: Cheesel (RENEEA1)
Oct-13 10:44 am
To: INTECON

Interesting site, but I don't know how many people are going to read that much text. You certainly have a lot to say and I agree that while the Right to Life people are always talking about the baby, the Pro-Choicers always talk about the woman's rights. They don't talk to each other but AT each other. They don't talk about the same subject.

Renee
"Science may have found a cure for most evils; but it has found no remedy for the worst of them all: the apathy of human beings." Hellen Keller

From: INTECON
Oct-13 6:34 pm
To: Cheesel (RENEEA1)

Some very good points. It's good to see what other people's impressions are. You're only the 2nd person to respond to the site content. The other person did read through the entire document, and said that he agreed. He had twins who were delivered at just 24 weeks gestation, and there was no way he would accept that they weren't human beings. I do have some encouraging statistics on my site. Over 1/5 of my visitors return 3 or more times. Over 8% are from educational institutions. And I've had 4 visits from non-profit organizations, who I hope are considering the underlying moral factors. If I can save one life or change one mind or reenforce people's beliefs or influence a vote, then it's worth the effort. But obviously I'm looking at the big picture and trying to hit a home run. I'm hoping my little web site and ideas can initiate societal change. And I'm trying to bridge the gap between pro-life and pro-abortion camps, and encourage unity. Thanks for the insights!

From: INTECON
Oct-13 7:01 pm
To: Cheesel (RENEEA1)

Thanks for the quote, Renee. Hellen Keller was one of my childhood heroes. Jeff White talked about apathy in the last letter I received from him. Jeff has been a consistent pro-life crusader at least since the Roe vs Wade decision. He has spent over a year in jail, and has over a million dollars in fines against him. He also has ten children, and they all help out in the pro-life effort. He can't own anything or have a bank account, because it would just be taken from him to satisfy the judgments. Jeff was one of the founders of The Survivors in California, and his two oldest daughters just started college and have set out to organize their campuses. His family survives financially through donations to his wife, and Jeff continues to fight (non-violently) for the pro-life cause!

From: PESSELL
Oct-20 2:47 pm
To: INTECON

Hi,

I read most of your website, ran out of time so I promise I will come back and finish reading. But I did find a mistake? or misinformation? I do not know where you got your source for saying that at 6 days after implantation all the child's systems are there.

I do not know for sure, but I think this site is unbiased, as it just gives info, both PL and PC people have used it. Go to http://www.visibleembryo.com/baby/stage9.html, this is about 9 days after implantation. This clearly shows that this embryo does not have any system as of yet. I am not sure if yours is a typo and you meant weeks or what.

I am not attacking you, I am just trying to understand this so I understand where you are coming from.

Kristen

EDIT the link I put up does not seem to work, at least not on my computer. You can just type in www.visibleembryo.com and go there.

From: INTECON
6:19 pm
To: PESSELL

Thanks for replying. I thought this thread was dead. I agree it's a lot to read. It was a major undertaking to create too. My statistics show a lot of people do come back multiple times. I've also ended up making frequent additions to the site, although I I hadn't planned to do that. Thanks for the links. I'm going to answer, perhaps partially initially, first; and then check out your links, because I might have difficulty getting back here. I'm not sure whether it matters much at this point, with respect to the arguments I make, whether it's 6 days or 9 days; but it might be important to any final resolution of the problem. It would be significant if I meant weeks. However, I am very concerned about the integrity of my site, and I have tried very hard to give both sides of the controversy, because I would like to encourage a solution. So I welcome any questioning of the information I give. My source for this information was a book called: "The Facts of Life", published by Judie Brown and the American Life League. Judie is a very public, upfront leader of the pro-life movement, and I don't think she'd put out any erroneous information that would damage her credibility. However, if you're looking for hands, arms, legs, and a big smile, I don't think they would be there at this point. Judie starts counting the days at the moment the egg is fertilized. I start counting when the woman becomes pregnant (the moment implantation in the uterus is completed), which would be day 14 by Judie's count. Here's what Judie's book says, and remember the child is still very small and probably indistinguishable visually to the untrained eye as a human being:
"Day 20:-His heart, brain, spinal column, and nervous system are almost complete, and the eyes begin to form."
"Day 22-His heart begins to beat."
The book also includes pictures of the baby at different early stages of development (through the fifth week). If you want to purchase a copy of the book, there is a link to ALL on my website. It's priced very reasonably. So I think our differences are over definitions, and that you can not see the organs in the picture you referred to. But you are right on in trying to determine when human life begins, because that is at the heart of the matter.

From: PESSELL
Oct-21 10:00 pm
To: INTECON

I know that someday we will know when exactly life does begin. It is unfortunate that this debate is so emotionally charged and, at least right now,

the definitions of when life begins and when that life should have rights are so subjective that it is hard to have rational discussions. I am appreciative of those who are trying so hard to make this a rational discussion.
I think the site I refered you to starts counting days past the last period, but I am not sure, I will have to go back and check.

Good luck with your thread.
Kristen

Some Early Comments and Replies

More important than my reply:

COMMENTS: After reading a number of the comments, I was discouraged about the amount of faith put into doctors. They are human, and most certainly NOT God. I have two examples to remain a skeptic of WHATEVER you are told.

1) A couple went for genetic counseling. (which I don't agree with anyway) They found out there was a very high chance (>80%) that their child would be born with a terrible disease (I forget the name of it). Though the disease was not life threatening, the child would be physical inhibited in many manners. They consulted their Priest, who told them the views of the Catholic Church. They prayed intensely, and decided they had to keep the child. Upon birth, they were blessed with a perfectly healthy baby.

2) Even more personal to me, is the story of my Grandmother on my dad's side. She was a great woman, and from the stories I hear a saint, even though she was Lutheran. I kidding, of course. On a serious note, after giving birth to my Aunt Constance, she was told not to have more children for her health would be in great jeopardy. She didn't listen to the doctors. A few years later she gave birth to my Uncle Mike. Again the doctors said not to have any more children as complications could arise that would jeopardize her and her child. Again she refused to listen, and a few years later Grandma gave birth to Aunt Mary. A few years later my Father was born, and a few years later my Aunt Sarah was born. This all from a woman who shouldn't have had children. Thank you Grandma =-)

I'd like a close with a quote from Mother Teresa, "Having too many children in this world is like having too many flowers."

"It does not require a majority to prevail, but rather an irate, tireless minority keen to set brush fires in people's minds."
-Samuels Adams Thank you for your contributions, Andy!

Other comments on abortion:

"I had an abortion. I am not ashamed. You pro-lifers have tried to make me, but I'm stronger than you. I'm strong enough to make a tough decision, and live through it. I'm strong enough to live with the pain, both physical and emotional. You can't break me." Jenn

"I am only thirteen years old and i understand the severity of abortion. I personally think it is murder. The way i see it is you made the baby you should take responsibility for it. there are exceptions, rape, incess, etc. thank you for your time and i hope my comment was worthwhile and has made a difference to someone out there" mallory

"Abortion is wrong. The laws should ban it totally unless you are raped. That is the only case you can get an abortion and you could still have it and give it up for adoption." Rachel

From the Abortion Information Page Guestbook –
http://www.w-cpc.org/abortion/index.htm:

I have always been against abortions, but I never really understood about "partial birth" abortions. My 15 yr old daughter explained them to me. I have spent the last 3 days crying for all the tiny lives that have been murdered. Have people become so evil as to believe it is okay to kill a small helpless baby in the name of "pro choice". There are so many people I know who would love to have the chance to love these little beings. Is there nothing to be done, no way to convince women that these little bodies ARE ALIVE? If it has to be killed it is alive. If it can die it lives. It is inconceiveable to me that one would chose to end a life. No reason is vaild if it means the death of another. How can we stop this from continuing?
Suzanne-Friday, November 10, 2000 at 11:40:38 (EST)

After I wrote the paragraph on the arrest of James Kopp for the murder of Barnett Slepian, I copied it to a forum at About.com
http://prolife.about.com/newsissues/prolife/.

If you missed it on my main page, you might want to go back to read it so you can better understand the exchange that followed. I didn't get permission to reprint this from the individual, and I don't want to embarrass him, so I've shortened the name to S.

From: S. Mar-31 7:58 pm
To: INTECON unread
(82 of 99) 1643.82 in reply to 1643.67

Of course, Dr. Slepian was actually an OB/GYN, who delivered around 200 babies each year, and would perform abortions when it was necessary for his patients, at a rate of around 10 each year. And at the time of the brytal murder of him (maybe you remember this?), there were inetrviews with many of his patients who stated what a wonderful person he was and how he always sought the best for each woman, even to the point of helping them with alternatives if they didn't want to raise a baby. This was NOT a guy who went to the abortion clinic every day, aborting numerous fetuses. This was a physician who gave his everything for each patient, and where it just happened that in rare instances, this meant performing an abortion, but just as often meant setting up adoptions or delivering babies.

(In retrospect, I think he was forgetting about some of his patients, but I didn't think to mention that at the time).

And yet, you think Slepina is a mass murderer, when performing LEGAL medical procedures.

Well, I have assisten in abortions throughout the later years of medical scholls. Are you going to come and shoot me down in front of my wife as well?

(A quote from my main page).

So you are just another supporter of murder. Yes, that is becoming all to clear.

Hey, all you PL who claim that PL is NOT about violence!!! Here they are, crawling out of the dungheap in large numbers excalting murderers at their best ability. care to comment? These slimeballs sure don't seem all that rare anymore.

[I] How many thousands did Doctor Slepian kill?

At best estimate, maybe 50-100, while delivering 100o-2000 babies

S.

Hey S., thanks for the reply and input. Actually, I didn't follow it too closely when it happened. I copied what you wrote, but I won't accept it as fact until I have a chance to delve into it more. However, for the purpose of this discussion, I will accept it, and work from there. If Slepian wasn't full-time into abortion, I would say Kopp didn't pick his target very well, and I would feel a little bit sorry that it happened to him, because he apparently was just misguided. That's the problem when somebody takes the law into his own hands.

My next comment I'm trying to figure out how to say and not sound sarcastic. You'll just have to accept that I mean this in a sincere way. 50-100 abortions would put him in about the same class as John Wayne Gacy. You see, where we differ, is that I consider each of those abortions a murder. Abortion's pretty brutal too. No, I'm not going to come and shoot you; I had hoped I made it clear I didn't approve of that. But I do wonder why a medical student is getting into name calling. If you think I'm a slimeball, I challenge you to visit my website, http://www.aboutabortions. com/, and get my full position on abortion.

Here are some more thoughts for you. Say you are an attorney defending a client accused of murder, and you went into court and said that since your client had brutally, with premeditation, only murdered one person, you didn't think that was so bad, and you think the court should just ignore it and let him go free. That's the rationale I hear when you say Slepian only did 50-100 abortions. I don't think it would fly in court, and I don't think that kind of reasoning will get Kopp off the hook either. On the other hand, given some of the lame brained decisions out of the courts that I have witnessed over the years, beginning with Roe vs. Wade, it wouldn't be impossible.

Also, I wanted to mention that my wife's gynecologists don't do abortions. She says they have a sign right in the waiting room, and the general message is "don't even ask". So gynecologists do have an option, and should be held responsible for their actions just like anyone else.

But as long as we're talking, we can at least learn from the experience, and perhaps sometime in the not too distance future, find common ground.

Intecon at http://www.aboutabortions.com/

From: S. Apr-3 12:28 am
To: INTECON

I frankly don't see much of a chance of common ground with you.
The ONLY common ground I see possible is to focus on the woman's demand for an abortion, and how to provide alternatives. YOu refuse to condemn kopp for being a killer, and you also seem to support restrictions on abortion as your main goal. There is simply no common ground in that basis.

S.

I don't think we're really that far apart, because you just need to take a tiny step and consider the fate of the child. Once you open your mind to that problem, then we'll move closer together. The main difference between us now is that you're primarily concerned with the killing of Slepian, and I'm primarily concerned with the children being killed. I've already moved in your direction by saying I didn't think Kopp was very good at picking his target, and I felt a little sympathy because he was a practicing gynecologist who was just misguided. The implication there is that if Kopp was going to do this anyway he should have picked a fulltime abortionist. Of course, I would probably feel more hostile to Slepian if it had been my child he'd killed.

You're correct, though, about my position on abortions. I'm pretty much against all abortions. But you could probably get me to concede some ground on that, too, for pragmatic reasons.

And I think that we have to assume the child would demand the right to live, if only he could express himself. That's why society protects other children, outside the mother. Just because he's still on the inside doesn't make him any different from you or I or our kids. Just put your hand on your wife's stomach when she gets pregnant. Don't feel anything? Make some noise-he's listening, he recognizes your voice. My son went nuts every time I shaved. Broke his water bag before it was time.

From: WOODWORKE2 Apr-3 12:31 am
To: INTECON

INTECON, Excellent site. thank you. Dave

Thanks for taking the time to visit my web site, Dave. It's not often I get a response of any kind, let alone a complement.
Thanks!

Intecon at http://www.aboutabortions.com/

James Kopp-a soldier in the army of the unborn. I decided not to change what I had written earlier. I thought the generic sense was more important than exactly how the numbers applied to Dr. Slepian. But I wanted to be sure to follow up here so that anyone doing a report based on this site wouldn't be blinded-sided by the numbers thing; and to maintain the integrity of the site.

An Essay And A Poem

You might be put off by the "in your face" approach of the "Abortion is Murder" web site. Here are 2 letters from there:

In December 1977, an 18-year-old woman was faced with the choice of life or death. It began when she met a boy at a hometown IGA grocery store. He was a sacker and she was the checker. A typical small town romance and for both of them—it was love at first sight.

After their first month of dating they spoke of marriage and how they would spend forever with one another. Neither had much money, but they had love which is something money cannot buy.

They also had a future. And, like many young people, they didn't think about the consequences of sex. All of their plans were demolished when the woman discovered she was pregnant. The boy was only 16, in high school and his only income was sacking groceries. The girl had no way of supporting a family and they both were planning to attend college.

Their families could not fund the baby's future, either. So the only solution was an abortion.

Friends of the family and co-workers raised enough money for the operation. The couple, being so young, couldn't face life with a child. They were ready to make a decision which would follow them forever.

To this day, she remembers the hour and a half she spent in the abortion clinic. She and her boyfriend were at the counter and the receptionist smiled as she took her money, treating her as she did all of the other teenagers. The couple waited an hour before the nurse took her to the room.

She says the room was cold and the clasp of the door is a sound that will forever haunt her. The boy says the moments waiting in the lobby seemed like an eternity because the clinic's policy prohibited him being with his girlfriend.

This was not a consultation. She was there for an abortion. No second chances.

This was it.

After each second, the two contemplated their future, individually, wondering what would happen to their relationship.

Fifteen minutes had passed. The doctor was running behind and he still had not visited her. After not being able to bear the time or swallow his conscience, the boyfriend broke the clinics' rules and went into his girlfriend's examination room. He clutched her hand, cried and said, "we don't have to do this. We can make it. I know we can." She balled, hugged him and said, "thank you."

The doctor walked into the room moments later as the two were joined emotionally by their love and physically by their arms wrapped around one another. The couple stormed out of the clinic.

Eight months later, I was born.

Mom and dad could not tell you if they received a refund that day, but they can give you a long 20-minute story on every one of my baby pictures.

Mom chose my life over making things easier on her life. So no matter how prideful my Democratic views are or my liberal beliefs, I could never believe in abortion—regardless of the situation. It's a belief I have more passion for than any other, and I will never change my stance.

Society sugarcoats abortion, calling it pro-choice, saying it's okay to kill a child. I disagree and so should the rest of the world. Not for religious reasons, political beliefs or society's perceptions, but for humanity's sake.

Why not call it pro-death? Because that's what it really is. The fetus has cells, which multiply and grow, thus it's a living organism and it's a person. If life is terminated by another human, shouldn't it be murder? If a pregnant woman is slain, the killer is usually charged with two counts of murder. One count for the woman and one for the child in the womb. Are we saying it's okay to kill the baby as long as he or she is terminated by his or her mother?

One of four pregnant women between the ages 15-44 will have an abortion rather than have a baby. They don't think of abortion as murder. It sounds too bad to think of it that way. Instead, they justify it by saying they don't have enough money or their future is too important.

Money can be earned. A future can be catered to. But an aborted baby can never be brought back to life. Sure going through with the pregnancy would be tough, but life is too precious to give up on, no matter the costs.

Why give the baby up for adoption? The emotional loss is less severe and the woman can feel secure knowing she didn't give up on her baby's life. Stop and think about it. Do you really want to be responsible for his or her death?

Even if the woman is raped, the child should still be born. Regardless of what happened to the woman, the child still has a chance to give back to this society.

For the woman, the burden of rape would be heavy enough. And an abortion would only hurt her more emotionally and physically.

As for the men who fool around and get their girlfriends pregnant, if you're man enough to have sex, you should be man enough to support your girlfriend through a pregnancy. If not, than don't have sex. There's nothing more gutless than a guy who encourages his girlfriend to abort his child.

A lot of people will say, "you don't know until you're in that situation."

I have been. Only I was inside.

Mommy keep me safe, Mommy keep me warm, Handle me with all your love, Mommy keep me from harm. I'm only six weeks old today, This birthday gift to me, A pair of bright blue eyes, That someday you will see. I've barely got ears, A little puppy nose, and at the end of my feet, Little things called toes. Looking forward to my life, toys, teddy bears, snails, and long fairy tales. Where are we going mommy, in a bath, on a bus ride or, perhaps far away. Where are we going being pushed at all force. How funny it feels passing through doors, people dressed in green, if they hurt you mommy just scream. What's happening mommy, I'm starting to cry, Mommy come quickly, they're making me die, Killing me slowly, Pulling me apart, everything inside of me even my heart, Bye mommy, good-bye But how I wanted to see the grass, the trees, hear a sweet song, feel a sweet breeze. Bye mommy good-bye I love You I really do I just wish you could love me too.
It just isn't right to take such an innocent life!

-By Fred Minneck

It's an American tragedy, and I'm a very angry man. I'm angry at the people who have led this country down this road-and I think you should be angry too! It's long overdue to put a stop to it.

Debating On About.com

Christina Dunigan was the person responsible for the Abortion debating on About.com, when I dropped a bomb to start a new thread, unaware that things had gotten pretty nasty since my last visit. Like at the battle of Chancellorsville, our lines got all tangled in the confusion that followed. I couldn't have picked a worse time to post what I posted if I'd tried. Christina is a good person, and an active pro-lifer. The sparks flew. But I decided to start there, anyway, because I think its illustrative of some things. Unfortunately for Christina, she drew my ire-and vice versa. I try to put the other person's posts in quotes. In other cases I saved only my responses, and not the other person's post. It's not a perfect record, and there are gaps, but most people should be able to follow the essence of it if they put their mind to it. Portions that may not seem important, or seem repetitive, are there to support what comes next and are worthy of your attention. The debate for the minds of our young people, mostly those still in school, follows a different tack on the internet than the debate before the general public, often using outrageous arguments and approaches that would never fly with mature adults.

VAAPCON is a database maintained by the FBI on Pro-life people and organizations the Clinton administration thought might be dangerous; like Jerry Falwell, Judie Brown, Pat Robertson, the National Conference of Catholic Bishops, the National Women's Coalition For Life, and so on. It stands for Violence Against Abortion Providers Conspiracy, and it seems to be in the news again. You can read more about it at the following about.com site: http://prolife.about.com/newsissues/prolife/library/weekly/aa071200a.htm What follows is what the website http://www.aboutabortions.com/ has to say about abortion violence. Which side do you agree with?

There is a new Civil War going on in this country, much more violent than the first one, in the 1860's, and the fatalities are much higher. The violence is propagated almost entirely by the side called the "Abortionists", and its savagery is so intense that its defenseless victims are literally pulled apart while still alive, and the remaining pieces then butchered and sold for the highest price. The rules of engagement require that the defenders can only demonstrate at distances too great to save the victims, and if they themselves should in any way engage in violence or intimidation they are immediately arrested and thrown into jail or prison with no certainty that they will ever be released; and by the time you finish reading this I think that you will agree with what I have just said. Worldwide, abortion is the most catastrophic atrocity ever perpetrated by mankind.

What have we become? Is ours a sick society? We have turned on ourselves; we mutilate and murder our own children. Where have our values gone? As we destroy our most precious commodity, we destroy ourselves. Our leaders hide behind slogans and phrases like pro-choice and pro-life and refuse to debate or even discuss what is really going on! Can it be possible this is happening in America? Yes, it is possible, and it is happening, at the rate of 1.5 million abortion-murders each year. Who will be next, if this is allowed to continue?

General Discussion-CRACKDOWN NOTICE Subscribe

From: Christina (AB_PROLIFE) May-28 12:17 pm
To: ALL 1 of 21) 2012.1

This forum, contrary to popular belief, exists to expose people to new information and ideas that I hope will get them thinking about life issues in new ways more conducive to protecting vulnerable people from death.

There seems to be the idea that this forum exists for people to insult, deride, gossip, snipe, fight, backbite, and just be as uncivil as humanly possible.

Well, I'm cracking down on the insulting, deriding, gossiping, sniping, fighting, backbiting, and incivility.

Any post that so much as annoys me on the grounds of incivility will be nuked. Not edited—nuked.

Anybody who is so habitually uncivil that I have to nuke five posts will get ALL posts to or from him or her nuked.

This is a retroactive crackdown, applying to posts that I see regardless of when they were posted.

I am hoping that a few days of a crackdown will improve the tone in this forum.

I am sick of opening my mailbox and finding dozens of complaints. And I am sick of the whole "Y'all are evil!" "No way! Y'ALL are the evil ones!" tone of this forum.

We already know that the prolifers consider abortion evil, and that the prochoicers consider denying abortion evil. So stop repeating what's already assumed. Say something new and constructive.

Since you kids can't fight nice, I'm going to have to be a disciplinarian.

And if you want to get banned or gagged, all you have to do is send me a snotty email telling me I'm being unfair, or unChristian, or a censor, or evil, or what have you. Y'all will learn to be civil if I have to smack civility into you.

To those of you who have been civil all along, thank you for your patience.

The Mom

Well, Christina, I sat dumbfounded looking at your reply to my VAAPCON posting, trying to figure out what you were talking about. After all, my posting got a thumbs-up from whomever else reviewed it. And it was just a simple statement of fact, nothing malicious about it. At first I questioned your intellect, but you've been in this too long and too deeply to be naive. And defending Steen, too. I guess the about.com pro-life site is run by somebody who's pro-abortion, just like the religious tolerance site. I'm curious, too, about whether you're on the Planned Parenthood payroll like some others I've debated in these forums, but I guess I'll never know for sure. Prove me wrong-repost the VAAPCON thing, and this reply. It's the plain, simple, truth; that pro-abortion people like yourself don't want to face up to.

Now I can't find your reply or any reference to my VAAPCON posting. No matter, I screen printed your reply. If you're a Christian, as you claim, then you should be concerned about what you will say to your maker on judgment day. Ah, there it is, I found it again, "VAAPCON threadnuked":http://forums.about.com/n/mb/ message.asp?webtag=ab-prolife&msg=2015.1

Well, that's why I spent nearly a year and a half out of my life creating my own abortion web site: http://www.aboutabortions.com/ so that I could get the truth out about abortion without being censored.

So, Christina, it appears you're not going to reply to my protest about being nuked. You're initial response bore no relationship to what I had posted. What was it I said that you didn't like? I've never been uncivil, or even close to it. The only possible reason I can see for nuking my post is that you didn't agree with what I said, and you wanted to suppress it. I do know it makes pro-abortionists mad to hear the truth. Soon you will achieve nirvana, and only have pro-abortionists and those you can deceive on your forum. Oh, mom, I just turned 60. Intecon, at: http://www.aboutabortions.com/.

I can be booted out of this forum, but I will not be silenced.
Do you agree or disagree? (Original posting reposted)

General Discussion-VAAPCON thread nuked Subscribe

**From: Christina (AB_PROLIFE) May-28 2:05 pm To: ALL
(1 of 2) 2015.1**

I could weep.

Look, folks, I agree 100% that abortion is absolutely and utterly wrong. It's a bunch of grownups ganging up on and killing a young, tiny, defenseless person that they ought to be nurturing and protecting.

But the people doing it don't see it that way, and the constant demonization just sucks those who see abortion for what it is into their own evil.

All the demonization, the "us versus them" mentality, does is bring yet more evil on top of the existing evil.

The way to end evil is to break free of the cycle of evil, not to get sucked into the downward spiral.

You can recognize abortion for the evil that it is, and not demonize those who have been sucked into the lie that it's "sadly necessary".

Those of you who are Christians will do well to remember that we fight not against flesh and blood, but against spiritual forces. If those spiritual forces can sucker us into ignoring them, and attacking their victims, then they've already won.

Fight smarter, not harder.

From: Christina (AB_PROLIFE) May-29 1:50 pm To: INTECON unread (29 of 52) 2012.29 in reply to 2012.27

At a time when we're having trouble even mustering basic civility, we don't need people pouring gasoline on the rhetorcal floor and passing out matchbooks.

Right now I can't afford deliberately imflammatory threads. If you feel an overwhelming need to be inflamatory and provocative rather than persuasive and informative, you can come back in a few days and see if the mood in here is more calm.

Reply to Christina:

My posting was not a "deliberately inflammatory thread". I swear that to you on a bible. It was neither deliberate, or intended to be inflammatory. But I'm beginning to see that it might have been perceived as that in an environment that I am unfamiliar with. My whole purpose was to point out that the overwhelming majority of the violence is performed by abortionists inside the abortion mills.

Since Roe vs. Wade 40,000,000 children have died a horrible death from abortion. But I will not shy from controversy. I question your commitment to the pro-life cause when you equate your concerns of offending the sensibilities of those doing the abortions, and supporting the abortionists; with your concern over the millions of children being killed by abortion. The latter matter is the very serious crimes that are being committed at the rate of 4,000 a day; and I think you have been lured into this sympathy for the former by abortionist rhetoric. There is no sympathy in the abortion clinics for the victims-just death; and you are more worried about offending the people doing and supporting the work? That doesn't make sense.
Intecon at http://www.aboutabortions.com/.

General Discussion-VAAPCON thread nuked Unsubscribe
From: GLEN__19 May-29 8:37 pm To: INTECON unread
(5 of 5) 2015.5 in reply to 2015.3

I think the idea is that you asked a simple question and I answered this with some posts of my opinions as well as those of others who believe it is a war and documented this fact by posting their words.

ABPL does not like such talk of the fact that their are some who believe this to be a war. She also does not like the fact that these same people believe that they did not start this war or that they did not declair this war.

It is a shame to pretend that such ideas and beliefs are not out there.

There is a small but active number of individuals who beleive and live this to be true.

The fact that they are loosely connected and have no formal ties and mostly/mainly disagree on tactics allows them to go under the radar of being caught often.

Did you know that in a ten year period of time 77-87 that there were 17,000 attacks on abortion clinics? (reported by the NAF and the USA Today) 17,000! That sounds more like a war than not.
What do you think?

Did you read the latest on VAAPCRAP?

Thanks for the info and insights, Glen. I saved the stuff on Kopp for possible later use. Actually, though, James Kopp was no place in my thinking when I posted the VAAPCON thing, and it certainly wasn't meant as an encouragement to more violence. It's main message was to point out that the real violence has overwhelmingly been coming from the abortion side-which I consider to be an obvious statement of fact. My purpose is to get people to look at things the way they really are-instead of how they've been indoctrinated to see things by the liberal media, Planned Parenthood, the Clinton administration, radical feminist organizations, and so on. My first reaction to your 17,000 statistic was disbelief, but then I realized I wasn't paying attention to what was going on in the 1977-87 time frame. Did you know that the latest statistics on abortion show that 40,000,000 children have died a horrible death from abortion in the U.S. since Roe vs. Wade? That's the violence I was referring to in my posting. Don't you agree that dwarfs the number of people who chained "themselves together at the doors of abortion facilities", both in numbers, and severity? You can read more about it at my website at: http://www.aboutabortions.com/.

(The gaps in the numbers are due to exchanges between other participants.)

From: IHADSPAM1 May-29 9:26 pm To: INTECON unread (44 of 53)

"'its defenseless victims are literally pulled apart while still alive, and the remaining pieces then butchered and sold for the highest price.'

Tired, old bullspew. It's illegal to sell body parts. The kooky story that aired on Dateline about selling body fetal body parts was debunked over a year ago."

SFinney

Not so. I've seen many accounts of it from many different sources.
There's a loophole in the law that allows this to go on. Partialbirth abortions, especially, are valuable for this because only the brain is missing. In other late term abortions, the baby tends to be dismembered, alive, in the process, so there's more potential for damage to the valuable parts. Also, the organs have to be removed within about 15 minutes of the abortion to still be usable.
There's more information on neat stuff like this at my web site. You can even watch a movie of an abortion; if you happen to like that kind of thing. You say the Dateline story was debunked. I wasn't even aware it had been on Dateline, too. Just more evidence, in my mind. Who do you say debunked it, and how, and where?
Intecon at http://www.aboutabortions.com/.

Listen, Finney, I've got good news. I found out that for 25 dollars you can purchase the book "The Marketing of Aborted Babies" from Life Dynamics, P.O. Box 2226 Denton, TX 76202, or phone 940 380 8800.

From: CRAW7 Jun-1 5:11 pm To: INTECON unread (16 of 23) 2015.16 in reply to 2015.12

Doctors and nurses do not take the life of a baby or child, they LEGALLY abort a zygote, embryo, fetus, regardless of your trying to give a tiny blob the status of a born citizen. Your information is false—there is no brain or heartbeat at that point. Your faantasies help feed your desire to interfere in some strangers choice, which is lawful and never, never any of your business. CRAW PROCHOICE AMERICA'S CHOICE

Aaaah, darnit, I'm going to have to pry my bookcase open again. I got my information from "The Facts of Life", by Judie Brown. I bought a copy because I can never remember the details. There's a lot going on in the early stages. There's someplace on the web you can go, too, but it's not as detailed. However, you can click on the pictures, and they enlarge, and you get a real good closeup. I think it's owned by Johnson and Johnson. There it is. I'll cut and paste the URL, then we'll know it's right:

http://www.babycenter.com/fetaldevelopment?&CP_bid=

You have to page down a couple of times. There's a picture for each of the nine months. Where did you say you got your information?

Intecon at: http://www.aboutabortions.com/

I had some more time, so I went back to the "Baby Center" I told you about:

http://www.babycenter.com/fetaldevelopment?&CP_bid=.

There's more detail than I remembered, when you hunt around a little. There's even enough information at the bottom of the picture for the first month to resolve our dispute. You don't even have to click to enlarge it. It says "By the end of the first month...The heart...has begun beating." So I guess it wasn't a "fantasy" after all. There's a lot more information there if you'd care to take a look.

How, specifically, am I inciting a riot? I'm not aware of it. Please explain yourself.

From: Christina (AB_PROLIFE) 11:28 am To: INTECON unread (63 of 72) 2012.63 in reply to 2012.53

You came in during an intense flame war. And just a few weeks ago I was putting out another flame war started by a post similar to yours.

I've told you I agree with you that abortion is an utterly evil abomination. But demonizing the people involved doesn't address the evil because it doesn't address the SOURCE of the evil, which isn't human.

I very much suggest that you read "Evil: Inside Human Violence and Cruelty" by Roy F. Baumeister. You'll be amazed at how much more clear some Scriptures will be to you after reading this!
There is a lot of very deep truth in this book—truth that Scriptures bear out again and again.

We can start with Proverbs 3:5-7:

"Trust in the Lord with all your heart, and do not rely on your own insight. In all your ways acknowledge him, and he will make straight your paths. Be not wise in your own eyes; fear the Lord, and turn away from evil."

Baumeister points out, with both research and anecdotal evidence, that where there is evil, everybody's perceptions become skewed—not just the perpetrator's (he thinks he has done no wrong, or that he was justified in what he did) but also the victim's (who tends to exaggerate his own innocence and magnify the unjustness of the perpetrator's action). And this is how evil gets into a spiral. Each person leans on his own understanding of the situation— and each person's understanding is skewed—and they proceed from that, which intensifies both the evil and the degree to which everybody's perceptions are skewed. Keep it up, and you end up with Northern Ireland, where nobody is wrong and everybody's just doing what's necessary to keep their people from being stomped by the evil people.

We need to step out of the spiral of evil, and this is a very, very difficult thing to do, because it's human nature to get sucked in.

We fight not against flesh and blood, but against principalities and powers who are decieving people. Once you get your first grasp of this, hold onto it with both hands.

I can see that you have a difficult role to fulfill. I can also see that we approach this in different ways. I agree with you on the danger of a downward spiral of violence, and how that can get started. There is a gap in our thinking that I'm not certain I understand well enough to span. I'm not advocating violence-I'm just pointing to the violence that is already taking place in abortion mills all across this country; at the rate of 3,000-4,000 homicides a day. When you speak of considering people as evil, and demonizing them, I have trouble understanding what you mean because I don't think that way. I don't think there's any hate in me-it's a self destructive emotion-but I am angry about what has been going on in this country, with regard to abortion, for so many years. It's more an issues thing with me-not so much related to individuals. But it's individuals who have been misled, and I'm doing my best to try to straighten that out, and show them how they've been misled. I don't believe legalized abortion can go on forever in this country, and I'm doing as much as I'm able to do as an individual to put an end to it before it can do more harm to our nation. So that's the big picture. I'm thinking you're probably saying who does he think he is, and of course I can't do more than a small part of it by myself, but I'm trying to help, and when I initially put together my web site I didn't realize there were 3,000 other web sites on the internet (over 4,000 now) about abortion, and maybe I wouldn't have done it if I had known. But you can't fully understand where I'm coming from without visiting my web site. I know that's a lot to ask, because you're obviously very busy. Don't try to squeeze it into your coffee break, because it's a very large site. It took me 3 1/2 months working full time to create the initial content, which amounted to about 90,000 bytes (alphanumeric characters) at the time. This doesn't include the three months I spent learning how to build a web site. By the time I finished the original version I had come to believe that I was not doing it by myself. But I thought that would be the end of it. Today it is about 290,000 bytes of text, on two separate pages.

Now back to the point I've been trying to make with you all this week, and that I don't think I've been able to communicate yet. I completely agree with you that there should be no name calling, and that people should try to be as polite as possible in a heated exchange, and that our opponents are not evil-just misguided. But neither must we get caught in a civility "trap". It's a part of the strategy of Planned Parenthood, NOW, and the abortion industry in general-whether or not they understand it as such. Perceptions, subtle use of language to convey their point of view, myths, mind games, are all the stuff they've built their empire on (to completely appreciate and understand this you need to go to my web site). So I guess I'm going to have to sound harsh here, but I have to tell it like it is. To say we're not going to hurt their feelings, talk directly about what's going on, to pretend it's not really bad or even going on, is playing their game, playing into their hands, and lending support and encouragement to the abortion crisis. The people who support abortion politically share responsibility for the massive killing that's going on. The people who run Planned Parenthood, NOW, NARAL, and participate in the abortion industry in general, all know that a child is being killed. Polls show a majority of Americans consider abortion homicide, and only about 37% say no its not. Today only those who subscribe to a radical leftist philosophy, the young and inexperienced, the uninformed, the misinformed, the misled, the desperate, and the ignorant, say differently-no insult is meant. You are invited to add any categories you think I've missed, and I assume that some will, and that's good. It's long overdue time to put an end to the slaughter by providing regulatory guidance to, and support for, people faced with an abortion decision.

You lost me on the message President Bush learned about compassionate conservatism. I would like to respond, but I'm not sure what you were referring to. With regard to Roe vs. Wade, some things have to happen for which I am unable to predict the time table. First, Sandra Day O'connor or John Paul Stevens must retire-an event that I've heard should occur sometime within the current Bush term. Both, I believe, are in their 70's, and reported to have health problems. Rehnquist is also supposed to want to retire, but that will involve replacing a "conservative" with a conservative. Then an appropriate case must make its way to the Supreme Court. I believe there will be a big confirmation battle in the Senate, but I think Bush will be able to get his nominations through-because he was able to get John Ashcroft confirmed. The nominee may even be Ashcroft, although I assume there's a long line of potential candidates already identified. I'm certain that Bush understands the importance of the nomination after what occurred during the election, and he will keep trying until he gets someone acceptable-though it may not be apparent to us. So I see the court thing as more of an intermediate term event. Frankly, I'm more focused on what I think will be happening in the near term. There are other ways to start shutting down the abortion industry.

Intecon at: http://www.aboutabortions.com/

From the American Heritage Dictionary: "zy·gote (z^{o}"g½t") n. 1. The cell formed by the union of two gametes, especially a fertilized ovum before cleavage." Yes, I agree with you, the fertilized egg, or zygote, is not a baby. That stage lasts about 24 hours. By the time the mother learns she is pregnant her child is over 10,000 times the size it was when it attached itself to her uterus, the baby's heart is beating, it's brain waves can be measured, and it looks pretty much like you or I. And the current abortion laws are certainly not safe for the child. I've seen several polls that show a majority of people consider abortion homicide-only 37% say it's not. There are a lot of us working to change the law, as you suggest, and we're not threatening anybody. And the law is going to change. How will your arguments for abortion play when that happens? The true victims of abortion are the children who are aborted-and the women who have the abortions. You can learn more about this at my website: http://www.aboutabortions.com/. I don't see what's brave about nurses and doctors who take the life of a defenseless child, and I don't think the child wants the abortion. Unfortunately, you've been misled.

From: HECK51 Jun-1 7:33 am To: INTECON unread (80 of 80) 2012.80 in reply to 2012.79

You must realize, however, that making abortion illegal will not cause it to go away-it will simply endanger underprivilged or desperate women who will seek out back-alley abortionists or commit self-inflicted mutilations.

Abortion will continue as always, because the bottom line is that women have the right, and the ability to terminate unwanted pregnancies. Enactment of unjust and oppressive laws will not change this.

The public and pregnant women, in particular, will not, and should not comply with any such oppressive legislation. Massive non-compliance and disregard for unjust laws renders them ineffective and meaningless-history provides the following examples ineffective legislation:

Stamp Act
Fugitive Slave Law
Prohibition
VietNam Draft Laws

I think you present a very excellent, rational, and reasonable argument. If Christina is looking for examples of civility, I certainly think it would qualify. I just don't happen to agree, and I guess that's what this forum is partly about, to get people together to talk over what it is they disagree about-and why. Dr. Bernard Nathanson points out, that, before abortion was legalized, there were about 100,000 abortions a year in this country. You can read his entire statement on my web site. At its peak, under legalized abortion, 1,500,000 abortions were performed each year in this country. This doesn't count twins, triplets, etc. I have seen some evidence that pro-life efforts are having an impact and yearly abortions are currently down to 1,200,000. In a letter I recently received from Alan Keyes, he points out that when women don't have convenient access to abortions, they don't get them (of course, I'm sure Alan didn't mean that this was 100% true). And, if abortion were criminalized, don't you think that, in itself, would cut down on the number of abortions? And if public approbation for abortion were removed, this would cut down even more. If pastors and rabbis all across this country were to speak out uniformly against abortion (which is not the case today), this would also help. So I think I've made the point that shutting down abortion mills, rather than being "ineffective and meaningless" would reduce the number of abortions. Would they go back to 100,000? I don't think a shutdown, by itself, would accomplish that. Abortion has become so ingrained in our society, that many people would still see it as their "right", as you pointed out. And Planned Parenthood might still be around preaching that, and holding classes on how to get it done-although their revenues would be substantially reduced without the income from doing abortions. There would be no woman's "right" to abortion once abortion was outlawed. Where would that right come from? Even today,

436

a child's right to live trumps any supposed woman's right to get an abortion. After all, abortion is just a name for a type of murder. At my web site, I don't advocate shutting down abortion mills, anyway. I just teach that abortion should be treated the same as any other type of murder-in the case of the abortionist-retroactive. I don't think that an abortion is generally the fault of the woman; so I propose a mandatory 1 year incarceration for her, as a deterrent-not retroactive; and so that society is crystal clear in the message it sends. But there are a lot more carrots than sticks in my proposals, too numerous to go into now-a whole program of supports, that you can go through at my web site, and that everybody who is pro-abortion should be familiar with, so that they can prepare to lobby Congress for them; because I have seen no signs of the pro-life side picking up on them. I believe my plan would reduce abortions to well below 100,000 a year.

"...it will simply endanger underprivilged or desperate women who will seek out back-alley abortionists or commit self-inflicted mutilations." We must enact programs to prevent this. Alan Keyes also mentions in his letter: "...abortion clinics want the highest possible number of abortions to keep the cash rolling in...the number of abortions skyrocketed after Roe v. Wade... more women are killed, physically injured, raped and psychologically traumatized under 'legal' abortion than before Roe v. Wade in 1973."

Intecon at: http://www.aboutabortions.com/

http://prolife.about.com/newsissues/prolife/library/century/aahxp t2prn.htm

"The Truth of Pre-Roe Abortion Mortality

Just about anybody that's paid attention has heard the claim that 'thousands'—or, more specifically, '5,000 to 10,000' maternal deaths a year in the United States from criminal abortions back in the bad old pre-Roe days. In fact, Planned Parenthood's amicus brief filed with PP v. Casey still cited this bogus 'fact.'

Let's start with the numbers. Where did they come from? Here's an interesting exercise: when you see the 5,000-10,000 claim, check and see who they cite. Odds are it will be Lawrence 'Larry' Lader or some other late 1960's early 1970's abortion guru. This gives the impression that Lader (or whoever) looked at whatever the then-current situation was and wrote up his findings. Nothing could be further from the truth.

The 5,000-10,000 claim is one of the standard abortion promotion tricks: misleading citing. Often you'll see abortion advocates citing some recent (or relatively recent) 'research.' But when you check their source, you'll find that the source cites an even older source. And when you check that source, you'll find that it cites yet another, older source. You'll go round and round. (I've often joked that tracking down pro-choice original source material gives me motion sickness.) Eventually, you'll find the original source. If you're lucky.

Lies, Damn Lies, and Statistics Tricks of the trade abortion advocates use.

In the case of the 5,000-10,000 claims, the original source was a book— Abortion, Spontaneous and Induced—published in 1936 by Dr. Frederick Taussig, a leading proponent of legalization of abortion. Taussig calculated an urban abortion rate based on records of a New York City birth control clinic, and a rural abortion rate based on some numbers given to him by some doctors in Iowa. He took a guess at a mortality rate, multiplied by his strangely generated estimate of how many criminal abortions were taking place, and presto! A myth is born!

Even if Taussig's calculations, by some mathematical miracle, had been correct, they still would have been out of date by the end of WWII. Antibiotics and blood transfusions changed the face of medicine. And you will notice that abortion proponents are all too aware of how dated Taussig's numbers are— why else would they play Musical Cites instead of simply citing Taussig in the first place? But not only are the Taussig numbers dated, they were never accurate to begin with. At a conference in 1942, Taussig himself apologized for using 'the wildest estimates' to generate a bogus number.

Although it took Taussig six years to reject his own faulty calculations, at least he did admit that he'd been wrong. Other abortion enthusiasts lacked Taussig's compunctions. Bernard Nathanson, co-founder of NARAL, admitted that he and his associates knew that the claims of 5,000 to 10,000 criminal abortion deaths were false. They bandied them about anyway, Nathanson confessed, because they were useful. This, too, is old news—Nathanson came clean over twenty years ago.

How many criminal abortion deaths were there, then? An excellent question, and a tricky one to answer. Before the Centers for Disease Control began Abortion Surveillance Activities in 1968, and began looking at abortion mortality in earnest in 1972, all abortion deaths were typically counted together: legal (or 'therapeutic'), illegal, and spontaneous (miscarriage). However, even without the CDC's intervention, public health officials were watching maternal mortality in general, and abortion mortality in particular, very carefully. After all, abortion itself was a crime, and an abortion in which the mother died could well result in a homicide investigation. This was not petty crime; the police, coroners, funeral directors, and hospital administrators were very attentive to possible criminal abortion deaths.

438

Peer-reviewed articles published in the decades before Roe gave varied estimates of the number of abortion deaths annually. One study determined that there were approximately 1.3 criminal abortion deaths per year in Minnesota from 1950 through 1965. Commentary on that study pointed out that if researchers combined known criminal abortion deaths with suspected criminal abortion deaths, 4.4 women were dying from criminal abortions per year in Tennessee from 1955 through 1965. A study in California reported 30 total abortion deaths per year during a period studied from 1957 through 1965, and as many as 87% of those abortion deaths were due to criminal abortions. This meant a maximum death rate in California of 26 women per year during that period.

|Links follow|

What California Found A look at a pre-legalization study of abortion mortality in California.

What Minnesota Found A look at a pre-legalization study of abortion and maternal mortality in Minnesota.

But what can that tell us about mortality nationwide? In 1975 (the first year for which complete numbers are available), Minnesota reported roughly 1.6% of all legal abortions, Tennessee reported about 1.7%, and California about 22%. It is reasonable to assume that the proportion of illegal abortions in each state before legalization would be similar to the proportion of legal abortions in each state after Roe. If each of those states had been representative of the nation at large, that would put the national death rate at 78, 225, and 104, respectively. If we combine the totals, we find 31.7 criminal abortion deaths per year in three states, which represented roughly 26% of abortion deaths. This would mean approximately 123 criminal abortion deaths annually in the decades just before Roe. Are these numbers realistic at all? Mary Calderone, who was then Medical Director of Planned Parenthood, reported on a conference studying abortion in America. She indicated that in 1957, there were 260 abortion deaths nationwide. That number included all abortions: legal, illegal, and spontaneous. The calculations based on state maternal mortality investigations are fairly close to Calderone's numbers based on national data. These numbers were based on alerting doctors, law enforcement, coroners, and hospital administrators, along with public records officials, of their responsibility to report these deaths. Taussig's estimates of 5,000 to 10,000 deaths would have meant that Minnesota authorities should have found 80 to 160 deaths per year when all their efforts could only find one or two. Tennessee should have been finding 85 to 170, rather than 4 or 5. And California should have been finding 1100 to 2200, rather than roughly 26.

Once more, with feeling:

In 1936, Frederick Taussig announced that there were 5,000 to 10,000 maternal deaths from criminal abortion annually in the United States.

In 1942, Taussig admitted that his calculations had been wrong, and that there was no way as many as 5,000 women were dying, much less 10,000.

From 1940 through 1970, abortion mortality fell from nearly 1,500 to a little over 100 (see table).

In 1972, according to the Centers for Disease Control, 39 women died from criminal abortions.

Year Deaths
1940 1,407
1945 744
1950 263
1955 224
1965 251
1965 201
1970 119

Source: 'Induced termination of pregnancy before and after Roe v. Wade' JAMA, 12/9/92, vol. 208, no. 22, p. 3231-3239.

Are we supposed to believe that public health officials in Minnesota, Tennessee, and California, in cooperation with law enforcement, the medical community, coroners, and hospital administrators, were that far off? Are we supposed to believe that among abortion supporters, Planned Parenthood's Medical Director, the AMA, the Alan Guttmacher Institute, and the Centers for Disease Control were all that clueless? Are we to believe that only Taussig's numbers— generated with admittedly faulty calculations over sixty years ago—are the true measure of the cost of criminal abortion in the United States? This is what abortion promoters would have you believe when they cite Taussig's discredited numbers.

You would have to go back to before WWII to find as many as 1000 women dying from criminal abortions annually in the United States. By 1967, when the first states started allowing very limited elective abortions, the number had fallen almost 90%, to 110. Criminal abortion deaths clearly were diminishing dramatically without taking the radical step of legalization. Other strategies, such as liberalizing sterilization laws, providing competent counseling to frightened pregnant women to help them overcome their fears about having their babies, and teaching doctors better diagnostic and treatment strategies for addressing criminal abortion complications, were based on sound research and were likely to reduce criminal abortion deaths to an unavoidable minimum. (As long as some women insist on having abortions, some of them will die, no matter how diligently we try to protect them.) When current strategies are working, it's foolish to throw a monkey wrench into the works. The strategy of improved medical care was solving the problem. Abortion advocates might have done well to listen to the old adage, 'If it ain't broke, don't fix it.'

[Other links]

Practices Before Legalization What was abortion practice like before legalization?

Safe-n-Legal in the 20th Century A look at claims of legal abortion's safety.

Abortionists of the 20th Century Legal, illegal, and quasi-legal.

Sources:
1. Council on Scientific Affairs, American Medical Association, 'Induced termination of Pregnancy Before and After Roe v. Wade: Trends in the Mortality and Morbidity of Women,' Journal of the American Medical Association, December 9, 1992
2. Rachel Benson Gold, Abortion and Women's Health, Alan Guttmacher Institute, 1990
3. Cates, et al, 'Legalized abortion: Effect on national trends of maternal and abortion-related mortality (1940 through 1976)', American Journal of Obstetrics and Gynecology 132:211, 1978
4. Alex Barno, 'Criminal abortion deaths, illegitimate pregnancy deaths, and suicides in pregnancy: Minnesota, 1950-1965,' American Journal of Obstetrics and Gynecology, June 1, 1967.
5. Mary Calderone, 'Illegal abortion as a public health issue,' American Journal of Public Health, July 1960
6. Leon Fox, 'Abortion deaths in California,' American Journal of Obstetrics and Gynecology, July 1, 1967
7. Frederick Taussig, Abortion, Spontaneous and Induced, 1936
8. 'The Abortion Problem,' Proceedings of the conference held under the auspices of the national Committee on Maternal Health, Inc., June 19-20, 1944.
9. Brief for Petitioners and Cross-Respondents, Planned Parenthood v. Casey (1992)

Related Links:

'Confession of an Ex Abortionist'
'More on Illegal Abortion Myths'"

General Discussion-CRACKDOWN NOTICE From: BITSYD
Jun-3 3:50 am To: INTECON (84 of 95)
2012.84 in reply to 2012.79

How would your scenario upset the 5-4 balance in favor of Roe?
(or at least the current flavor of Roe, Planned Parenthood vs.
Casey (1992).

In any case, the Senate is now under control of the Democrats, and there is no Constitutional requirement that there be NINE Justices on the U.S. Supreme Court. It has been mentioned by Democrats on Capitol Hill that they could very easily, and completely with Constitutional support, leave EIGHT justices on the U.S. Supreme Court.

If Chief Justice Rehnquist retires, as he has said he is considering, and the Senate leaves his seat OPEN, the balance of 5-4 in favor of abortion rights shifts...to a 5 to THREE court in favor of abortion rights.

In any case, Rehnquist retiring would be a boon to those who are pro-Roe, but actually a setback to those who are pro-choice. Why?
Because he, like Justices Thomas and Scalia (the prototypes for Bush's selection process for new Justices) has a justification for the right of a woman to have an abortion. He just dislikes the way Roe does it, and has his own justification for a woman's right to an abortion.

You can read where Justices Thomas and Scalia, as well as Chief Justice Rehnquist, all support a woman's right to an abortion (while condemning Roe) by reading the minority opinion they signed in the 1992 decision Planned Parenthood vs. Casey.

Since Thomas and Scalia both support a woman's right to an abortion, and Bush PROMISED during his campaign to appoint only Justices who are "exactly like Thomas and Scalia", one can only hope that Bush KEEPS HIS PROMISE!

Then again, he's broken so many campaign promises so far, how can we believe that he'll uphold another one?

Bits

—In the spirit of FYI, compassionate conservatism means Bush is compassionate to conservatives...

Thanks for passing along the information to me. I'm not really interested in debating it; but I'll be glad to discuss it with you, and give my opinions, for whatever they're worth. I was especially interested in your comment on Rehnquist, because I hadn't examined that possibility, and it made me stop and think about it. I don't think he came up through the judicial ranks, because I remember him from a Republican administration way back whenever. Then I lost track of him, and the next thing I knew he was on the Supreme Court. Maybe it went like this: "Gee Dick, I'd reeeally like to be a Supreme Court justice. Well, Bill, you're certainly well qualified for it. I think you'd make an excellent justice." In other words, although I don't remember any more about him, I think of him as a Republican insider; close to the source of power. Said another way, a "loyal Republican". If that's true, and he's in good health, it's unlikely that he would leave at an "inappropriate" time.

Yes, indeed, the Senate is now under control of the Democrats, which means they will have more say over the order of business. However, that's unlikely to change the way people vote-much.

I found it especially interesting to hear that some Democrats were thinking of leaving the Supreme Court at 8 justices, and I believe you. However, as I said, the vote count should stay about the same. In opposition to John Ashcroft, liberal Democrats were only able to muster 42 votes; and they wouldn't have been able to get that many if they hadn't promised not to filibuster. There's probably nobody they hate more than Ashcroft.

The reason for that is that there are other things that enter into the voting other than just party. For example, some liberal Democrats (like Tom Daschle), are from conservative states. Plus there are friendships and questions of principle and the exchange of favors to get things done for their states. I believe leaving the Supreme Court at just 8 justices would be a very extreme step that could come back to haunt people. For all these reasons I think the Senate will eventually fill empty seats on the Supreme Court.

I looked up the PLANNED PARENTHOOD OF SOUTHEASTERN PA. v. CASEY 505 U.S. 833 (1992) case that you mentioned, "where Justices Thomas and Scalia, as well as Chief Justice Rehnquist, all support a woman's right to an abortion (while condemning Roe) by reading the minority opinion they signed in the 1992 decision Planned Parenthood vs. Casey.

Since Thomas and Scalia both support a woman's right to an abortion, and Bush PROMISED during his campaign to appoint only Justices who are 'exactly like Thomas and Scalia', one can only hope that Bush KEEPS HIS PROMISE!", and I didn't find anything to support that.

It's kind of difficult to wade through all the legalese, so I'll only cut and paste some brief summary lines; but here's an example of what I found. If you can find something I missed, great:

Intecon

"JUSTICE SCALIA, joined by THE CHIEF JUSTICE, JUSTICE WHITE, and JUSTICE THOMAS, concluded that a woman's decision to abort her unborn child is not a constitutionally protected "liberty," because (1) the Constitution says absolutely nothing about it, and (2) the longstanding traditions of American society have permitted it to be legally proscribed. See, e.g., Ohio v. Akron Center for Reproductive Health, 497 U.S. 502, 520 (SCALIA, J., concurring). The Pennsylvania statute should be upheld in its entirety under the rational basis test. Pp. 979-981.

JUSTICE SCALIA urges the Court to 'get out of this area,' post, at 1002, and leave questions regarding abortion entirely to the States, post, at 999-1002.

We believe that Roe was wrongly decided, and that it can and should be overruled consistently with our traditional approach to stare decisis in constitutional cases."

In recognition of the work that I put in to research this, and in the interest of reciprocity, I would really be interested to know where you got your information.

Bits-Bring me up to date on the promises George has broken.

Intecon at: http://www.aboutabortions.com/

From: HECK51 Jun-5 5:14 pm To: Christina (AB_PROLIFE) (99 of 105) 2012.99 in reply to 2012.97

Nathanson fabricated that "Silent Scream/Scam" thing didn't he?? That is hardly credible. the guy's really out of it.

Did you see the Silent Scream? The last I heard he was the director of a pediatrics, or maternity, ward; so he had the access and authority to get it done.

"'The Silent Scream' A first trimester suction abortion shown by ultrasound, with a running explanation of the procedure provided by former abortionist Bernard Nathanson, M.D. This video reveals abortion in all its graphic and gruesome horror. Video, 28 minutes. Order # AB30, $15.00"

"'Eclipse of Reason' Produced by former abortionist Bernard Nathanson, M.D., this film documents the termination of a five-month old boy as seen by a camera placed inside the mother's uterus. Video, 27 minutes. Order # AB31, $25.00" Call 866-LET-LIVE

444

Taken from: http://www.aboutabortions.com/

I think a woman plays the most important role in society-that of childbearing, of replenishing our species, and I think she should take great pride in that role, and accept it as an awesome responsibility. And, after the child is born, the primary caretaker of that child, in many families, is still the mother, and I so admire the job my wife has done with our children.

I made my point that outlawing abortion would reduce the number of abortions in the previous post, and I will refer readers to that to read the reasons and draw their own conclusions.

And I would also like to point out that the "barbaric butchery" you mentioned occurs primarily to the children. However, there are a lot of women who suffer, both psychologically and physically, from an abortion-more so than before abortion was legalized; and you can learn more about this at my web site; and again, in my preceding post. Mr Keyes and Dr. Nathanson are two of the most credible sources of objective information I know of, and I have immense respect for both men. What information do you have that shows that they are not?

You said "Women will always have the right to choose for their own body...". I agree with you 100%. That's one of the reasons I'm against abortion, because about half the kids are girls. And I also think the guys should have that same right. Isn't that only fair?

You said "Any person has the 'right' to receive medical, surgical or dental treatment for any condition that affects them...". Again, I agree, the babies should be able to get all the medical attention they need to stay healthy. But you seem to imply that pregnancy is some kind of illness, and of course it's not; it's a sign of a healthy baby and mother.

There's no right to an abortion in the constitution. Where did you come up with that? In the 2nd paragraph of the Declaration of Independence the founding fathers clearly stated their views on life: "WE hold these Truths to be self-evident, that all Men are created equal, that they are endowed by their Creator with certain inalienable Rights, that among these are Life, Liberty, and the Pursuit of Happiness".

"How can the constitutionally established rights of a person be superseded by the fictious, non-existent 'rights' of a non-person?? They cannot be." Here, again, I agree with you, because a child is a person. Just because a person is inside the mother, instead of outside, doesn't make that person any less a person. To see what that person looks like at the end of each month of pregnancy you can go to:

http://www.babycenter.com/fetaldevelopment?&CP_bid=

To enlarge the pictures and get a better look at what is going on, plus additional facts, just click on the picture.

Just because you call it abortion doesn't alter the fact that you are killing somebody who has done nothing to justify it. How could he (or she) have committed any crime when he is still inside the mother? You have just arbitrarily decided to take his (or her) life. This is capital punishment without cause. Just because you call it by a different name, and because it's legal, doesn't make it any less a murder.

I don't have any problem with you having as much sex, inside or outside marriage, as you want. That's none of my business. But if you happen to get pregnant then there's another person in the world who has the same rights you do. Neither do I want to punish you. I just want to protect that new person who's just come into the world. "By what justification do you deny a person rights to which they are entitled?" I don't want to deny the rights of any person; including the person in the womb.

Intecon at http://www.aboutabortions.com/

We were talking about a woman's right to an abortion. I said:
"Where would that right come from?" You said: "From the constitution itself, of course." I think it's good that we're talking about something concrete, like the constitution. I'm saying, there's nothing in the constitution itself that says "A woman has a right to an abortion." I'm not talking about an interpretation of the constitution. I'm saying wording that refers directly to a woman's right to an abortion. I request that you address that question. Perhaps it's not what you meant in your statement above, but it's what I mean. This doesn't mean you have to abandon your point of view on abortion-perhaps just clarify your meaning. When you make a point that appears to be correct, I will acknowledge that, as I have already done in some cases.

I have my copy of the constitution sitting next to my computer. It sounds to me that you may have one too. If not, I'm sure you can pick one up at the library. I sign on to the internet about six times a week, so I'll still be here. I see only three possibilities: 1. There is language that directly refers to a woman's right to have an abortion. I don't think it's there, so I'm not going to spend time reading it. 2. There is no such language. If you can show me that passage, I will agree that you are right. If you can't show me that passage, then we must conclude that it's not there. In other words, if you are right, it is easy to document. If you mean a woman derives her right to an abortion from an interpretation of the constitution, then we can go on to discuss that and what specific passages she derives it from, or however else you want to make your point.

Continuing on with the constitution, you said: "A born child is a person-an unborn, z/e/f is not a person-specifically excluded-amend #14." "Another obvious falsehood. If it's in the womb, it's not a person. Please read amendment #14, section1".

I read amendment #14. The part that applies to our argument says: "…nor shall any State deprive any person of life…". Same thing as the Declaration of Independence. No place does it say that an "unborn" child (or z/e/f, whatever that is) is not a person. Nor does it define what a person is.

I really like your prohibition analogy. It was a failure. I also agree with Milton Friedman that we should legalize drugs for those same reasons (I've never taken drugs of any kind, I'm not going to debate that with anybody, it's only a personal opinion on a subject I have little knowledge of; and I only cite it to show Heck51 that I agree with her general philosophy).

But we're talking about prohibition of abortion, not prohibition of alcohol. I base my position that the number of abortions would decline if abortion were outlawed on "solid research shows that when abortions become hard to obtain MOST WOMEN DON'T GET ONE!!".I took that passage from the letter I mentioned that I received from Alan Keyes. I took my figure of 100,000 abortions a year prior to Roe vs. Wade from "CONFESSION OF AN EX-ABORTIONIST By Dr. Bernard Nathanson: http://www.mudmap.com/headlines/ex-abort.html. If my plan for outlawing abortion were adopted, doing an abortion would be treated just like any other murder, with maximum sentences of life in prison or the death penalty (for abortion providers, not the women who get the abortions), and it is incomprehensible that anyone would often take that risk just to do an abortion.

So I have given you my sources and reasoning. I know nothing about Poland, how outlawing abortion was implemented, or what the statistics were before or after. I can not accept your assertion of what happened in Poland without knowing your statistics, how they were obtained, where I can go to verify them, and the particulars of the legislation that was enacted there. In a previous post I investigated alleged statements by Justices Scalia and Thomas that proved to be non-existent.

An explanation for why abortion mishaps have increased is that abortionists try to rush through as many abortions as possible to increase their income. Christina has been running a series of articles on that. What is your opinion of those stories? But, beyond that, if you went from 100,000 abortions to 1,500,000 a year, you would have more casualties just because of the larger numbers of women getting abortions-a risk 1,400,000 women could avoid by just not having an abortion! Have you read the book Lime 5? Women are still getting butchered. Do you deny that? There's plenty of evidence. Just recently, there have been awards of 600, 000 and 1,000,000 plus dollars. I know women are suffering psychologically because every month I receive a list of Rachel's Vineyard retreats. "Post-abortion trauma afflicts an estimated 560,000 women in America. Its symptoms are depression, suicidal tendencies, alcoholism, sexual promiscuity and repeat abortions". Judie Brown, American Life League I know you'll deride her, but she doesn't lie, and she has access to the data from Rachel's Vineyard.

Dr. Nathanson was one of the principle proponents of legalized abortion, and a key figure in bringing it about.

"Women will always have the right to choose for their own body". I still agree with you on that, and for the guys, too. Because about half the babies are gals, and about half guys.

"The z/e/f is not a person. Personhood is not attained until birth. the unborn do not have any rights, since they aren't persons."

Excuse my ignorance, but I've never seen the terminology z/e/f used anyplace before. Did you get that from a medical textbook, or learn it in a class? Are you talking about one thing or three? Do the letters stand for something? It seems to be related to personhood, and that's something I'd really like to discuss, but I'm hesitant to start that conversation until you clarify what it means. If the letters stand for something, how do you define that something, and what are the timelines? Those are perhaps the most important factors.

You're tough, Heck51.

Intecon at: http://www.aboutabortions.com/

If a right isn't specifically addressed in the constitution, then it's not a constitutional right. Sure, everybody has lots of rights, but they're not constitutional rights. I was taught way back in grade school, and it wasn't a religious school, it was a public school; that we all have lots of rights, just so long as they don't infringe on the rights of others. Perhaps you were home sick that day.

Here are the rights you mentioned in a previous post:

"The 'right' to eat scrambled eggs the 'right' to purchase a new car the right to log onto the internet by personal computer-no constitutional mention, surely

The right to have heart surgery the right to have a gall bladder removed the right to have a fracture reduced the right to have a tooth extracted, a cyst or tumor removed the right to receive treatment for an infection, and so on, and on."

I realize you're not a constitutional lawyer, but most people would see all those things as having no relation to anything legal, let alone the constitution. There's no right necessary to do any of those things-you just go and do them. It only becomes a question of whether you have a right to do something if it infringes on another person's rights or violates some ordinance. The real question here is whether you're infringing on another person's rights when you get an abortion.

I do see, however, that there are areas where we agree. You aren't claiming that a right to have an abortion was included in the Constitution. However, you are claiming that it exists in the 14th amendment; and if that is true, then it has the same force as if it had been included in the original document. You said:

"The amendment 14 specifies that persons may not be deprived of life, liberty or property without diue process. All persons are entitled to equal protection under the law. If a guy can have a tooth extracted-then a woman may terminate a pregnancy."

However, you didn't show me a specific passage that said a woman had a right to an abortion, and I couldn't find one either, so the only conclusion to come to is that those specific words aren't there-section 1 isn't very long. However, this doesn't mean that you're not entitled to an abortion-just that it wasn't included specifically. If you can find that language later on, I'll accept it.

Now then, Amendment 14 does define citizens as being people born in this country or naturalized, you are very correct on that point, I'm glad that you read the amendment, and I concede that point to you. Personally, I believe that a person is born when a woman becomes pregnant, and that the person's age should be calculated from that point. Isn't that the craziest thing you've ever heard? How absurd! So now that I've said it, you don't have to, and I won't pursue it further-but everybody is entitled to believe whatever they want in a free country just so long as it isn't acted upon in a way that harms someone else. I never claimed to be politically correct.

Amendment 14 says "nor shall any State deprive any person of life, liberty, or property, without due process of law; nor deny to any person within its jurisdiction the equal protection of the laws."

Writing an amendment to the Constitution must be a very big deal; it probably gets debated for a long time, it has to be approved by the states, it takes years to complete the process, and doesn't happen very often. I think it's safe to say that the exact language is given a lot of thought and discussion. The above quote says "person", not "citizen". "…any person within its jurisdiction". To make the argument that it is alright to kill a baby in the womb because it is not considered a citizen would be equivalent to saying it is alright to kill immigrants who are not citizens if we decide we have too many of them. We could just start a policy of rounding them up and shooting them as they sneak across the border-no charges and no trial required.

You used Amendment 14 to justify your rights. My contention is that a baby in the womb is a person who has those same exact rights, and if you abort it, then you've violated the right to life it is given in Section 1, Amendment 14, of our Constitution; in some very precise language. Our basic disagreement is over whether that child is a person. Said another way, I think having an abortion is a much more serious event than having a tooth extracted.

Whether or not what you call a Z/e/f is a person is a rather complex subject. It's 3 a.m. here, and I've been so engrossed in this that I still have work to do on the computer I use for business; so I'm going to shut this one down now and get back to this discussion, hopefully, later today.

Intecon, at: http://www.aboutabortions.com/

Hey Heck, I'mmm back. But I'm still on 2012.107. Like I said before, you're tough.

Well, Mr. Keyes has a lot of credibility with me; and the 1 million people who voted for him in the last presidential election. How many votes did you say you got? Did you know Keyes has a Phd from Harvard? Do you know how difficult it is just to get in there? I've learned a lot from Alan; most notably about the importance of religion in society. I think there might even be some reciprocity. Jess seems to have a history background-maybe she could tell us more about the role religion played in the formation of our government. Keyes based the statements I attributed to him on survey information.

What basis do you have for calling "The Silent Scream" a scam? Do you have information I'm unaware of, besides someone's opinion? I explained to you in a previous post how he was able to do it. Substantiate your statements, because at this point it appears that you're labeling it a scam just to divert people from seeing it. Have you even seen it, or the second movie he made on an abortion at 5 months, which I listed in another post? On Poland, you said:

"There was a news article on it not too long ago-Steen G. posted up the link-basically it asserted that the illegalization of abortion in Poland had led to a thriving, underground, overpriced abortion industry in this country. Illegal abortion was rampant."

O'k, I'd be interested in reading it, where's the link? If you'll recall the main interest was whether outlawing abortion had decreased the number of incidents, and we'd need reliable statistics to determine that. Will I find that information in the article? It would seem to me to be difficult to get reliable numbers from an illegal industry. It's also rather disturbing to imagine what would happen in that environment if something went wrong-say, as I have read about in some cases, the abortionist poked a hole in the woman's uterus, and she's going to bleed to death unless she receives immediate surgery. Does he call 911 and say I was doing an illegal abortion, or does he just drop her body in the Danube? An argument for not getting an illegal abortion. The other critical question was what the abortion law that was passed looked like. I would assume that exactly what you described above would occur if there were no teeth in the law; that is, severe penalties. That's a big part of the reason I advocate making abortion punishable as any other murder. Plus infants should receive the same protection under the law as everybody else. Note, again, I don't advocate charging the mothers with murder-just the providers.

"post-abortion syndrome is in no way accepted by the medical community-its very existence is dubious."

It's a fairly recent development. There's a woman psychiatrist or psychologist, with a Phd, that kept encountering women with similar problems.

Finally she realized that what they all had in common was an abortion, and the result was the establishment of Rachel's Vineyard. They're up to about 100 retreats a year now, all over the country. If anyone would like for me to look up her name and contact information, I'd be glad to do so.

Whether or not it's received official recognition, there's lots of evidence it exists.

Safe Haven was established by a woman whose good friend shared her grief with her.

Intecon at: http://www.aboutabortions.com/

"I'm not talking about an interpretation of the constitution. I'm saying wording that refers directly to a woman's right to an abortion."

I've already addressed this-most of our rights are not specifically addressed in the constitution. If you believe that a woman hasn't the right of bodily choice, then you must also agree that no person has any right to receive medical, surgical or dental treatment for any condition. this is absurd, of course.

The amendment 14 specifies that persons may not be deprived of life, liberty or property without diue process. All persons are entitled to equal protection under the law. If a guy can have a tooth extracted-then a woman may terminate a pregnancy.

"If you can't show me that passage, then we must conclude that it's not there."

Read amendment 14-section 1. case made and closed."

Case reopened!

I see another area of agreement, that most of our rights are not specifically addressed in the Constitution. The Bill of Rights and Amendments just focused on the rights deemed most important and fundamental, like freedom of speech, the right to bear arms, freedom of religion, the right to life (Section 1, Amendment XIV), and so on, upon which a free society should be based. So, of course, a woman's right to an abortion would not be stated explicitly, but would be derived from some other basic right.

Intecon, at: http://www.aboutabortions.com/

I've got to hand it to you, Heck, you've really made me think deeply about this. After all, I don't want to deny anyone medical or surgical treatment. Now you need to think deeply too, to follow what's next, or it will go right past you. I want to get us out of familiar circumstances with an example. Say a young woman, just graduated from high school, takes her savings, just enough to get her started in a new life, and moves to the big city, far from her little farm town. She finds an apartment, makes the down payment and the first month's rent, and then goes to work for a small travel agency, starting out as a secretary. She doesn't have much money left, but enough to buy food until payday. And being from a small town, she still looks a little frumpy. Then she discovers a large growth under her arm. Is it just a big cyst, an infection, or cancer? She's really worried about it, so she takes time off work to have it taken care of. She goes to a doctor's office, or a hospital's emergency ward. She holds up her arm and says "see this big ugly thing, I think I might need some surgery." And the receptionist says "Oh my! Can I see your insurance card?" "I don't have insurance yet, I just moved here." "Well, then, can I see your credit card?" "Aa, I don't have any credit cards yet either." "Well, dear, why don't you come back when you get something that covers pre-existing conditions." She can stand there and argue she has a "right" to surgery as long as she wants to, but they aren't going take her as a patient. So, you see, there is no right to surgery at all, only an implied economic agreement, or contract; where the patient pays, or demonstrates the ability to pay. It's the same way if you walk into McDonald's- you don't have a right to have that Big Mac unless you pay for it.

So, my point is, nobody has a right to surgery, let alone a constitutional right. Once the doctor accepts you as a patient you certainly acquire that right, in an implied business agreement to pay for services. On the other hand, the baby does have a right to life, as set forth in Section 1, Amendment XIV, and you would be violating that right by having the baby killed.

Intecon, at: http://www.aboutabortions.com/

Like I said before, I'm certainly not against someone receiving medical treatment. But abortion isn't medical treatment-it's murder. You can call it abortion, but the fact remains, it's murder. Someone dies, undeservedly. Like the person at this web site:

http://www.babycenter.com/general/3284.html?CP_bid=

You don't have to buy your right to life; it exists just because you exist. You don't have to buy your liberty; you have it just because you're an American. But the Constitution says nothing about a right to medical attention: you acquire that right through an implied contract. The Constitution does give you the right to enter into an agreement to buy property; but I can't think of any other commercial contract, off hand, that it gives you the right to. Perhaps you can. But it's not medical treatment.

Intecon, at: http://www.aboutabortions.com/

"Once born, yes the born baby has rights under the constitution-prior to birth, it has no rights, and is specifically excluded. There is no "right to life" for fetuses. Totally imaginary."

O'k, where is it "specifically excluded"? Show me.

You're telling me that prior to birth the baby has no rights, so we seem to agree that we're talking about the same baby in both instances. I don't think we're talking about an imaginary baby-there has to be a baby there to be aborted, or there could be no reason to have an abortion.

What is this thing you call a fetus? If you'll show me you have enough medical knowledge to define what a fetus is, then I can discuss it with you. I can't discuss something with you when I'm not sure what you're referring to. What does "fetus" mean to you?

In a prior discussion, we were able to establish that Section 1 of the Fourteenth Amendment to the Constitution states:

"...nor shall any State deprive any person of life, liberty, or property, without due process of law; nor deny to any person within its jurisdiction the equal protection of the law."

Intecon, at: http://www.aboutabortions.com/

"Are frogs snakes, and lizards persons??"

Obviously, persons would have to have human parents, and the human genetic code, which exists from the moment of fertilization.

Going back to The American Heritage Dictionary:

"per·son (pûr"s...n) n. Abbr. per., pers. 1. A living human being." Since we've already established that the object of this discussion has to be alive, or it wouldn't be necessary to kill it, and it has the human genetic code, it must be a person. And "human being n. 1. A member of the genus Homo and especially of the species H. sapiens. 2. A person: a fine human being." In other words, definitely not "frogs snakes, and lizards". "genetic code n. The sequence of nucleotides in the DNA molecule of a chromosome that specifies the amino acid sequence in the synthesis of proteins. It is the basis of heredity.—genetic coding n." "Ho·mo sa·pi·ens (h½"m½ s"'p¶-...nz,-µnz") n. The modern species of human beings, the only extant species of the primate family Hominidae."

Intecon, at: http://www.aboutabortions.com/

"Sounds like Nathanson was a great asset to your side at one time." Apparently. What happened, did he fall off the wagon??"

"Nathanson fabricated that "Silent Scream/Scam" thing didn't he?? That is hardly credible. the guy's really out of it."

"Credible source?? "The Silent Scream/Scam"?? oh please..."

"the silent scream"? Don't you mean, "The Silent Scam"?

"This was shown to be a complete travesty, filled with misrepresentation and incorrect information. Emotional hyperbole in the extreme, probably the most discredited "document" in the whole abortion issue."

"We must assume that Nathanson's fabrication of the "Silent Scam" was done knowingly, with his approval of the contents. As a physician, he must have been aware of the deliberate falsehoods included-how are we to take him seriously re abortion??"

Well, maybe there's even more like this, but I've got plenty to make my point. For the casual passerby, or "guest", this is a great example of a technique called labeling. Repeating denunciations and labels over and over again to discredit someone or something until a lot of people come to believe they're true. It's sometimes difficult to tell whether someone is doing it deliberately, or just unknowingly propagating it. Always ask yourself, where is the supporting evidence? Of course, it might be inaccurate too. There is nothing at all given to substantiate the above claims. I don't doubt that the radical left may have made statements like this, but, still, where is the supporting evidence?

Here are some of the things Doctor Nathanson had to say about the techniques used by the pro-abortion people:

"We persuaded the media that the cause of permissive abortion was a liberal enlightened, sophisticated one. Knowing that if a true poll were taken, we would be soundly defeated, we simply fabricated the results of fictional polls. We announced to the media that we had taken polls and that 60% of Americans were in favour of permissive abortion. This is the tactic of the self-fulfilling lie. Few people care to be in the minority. We aroused enough sympathy to sell our program of permissive abortion by fabricating the number of illegal abortions done annually in the U.S. The actual figure was approaching 100,000 but the figure we gave to the media repeatedly was 1,000,000. Repeating the big lie often enough convinces the public. The number of women dying from illegal abortions was around 200-250 annually. The figure we constantly fed to the media was 10,000. These false figures took root in the consciousness of Americans convincing many that we needed to crack the abortion law. Another myth we fed to the public through the media was that legalising abortion would only mean that the abortions taking place illegally would then be done legally. In fact, of course, abortion is now being used as a primary method of birth control in the U.S. and the annual number of abortions has increased by 1500% since legalisation."

Taken from "CONFESSION OF AN EX-ABORTIONIST",
By Dr. Bernard Nathanson

http://www.teachlife.org.au/abortion/NA.htm

The above is just a sampling of the lying that was done-there's more there. I had a link to it on my web-site that was no longer good, so I entered the above title into Google. Suddenly I realized why my site had never gotten a hit on my link. This thing is posted all over the internet. So there's my source. Where's there's? And like I've said before, it's still going on today-because there's big money to be made doing abortions!

Intecon at: http://www.aboutabortions.com/

http://www.iwhc.org/poland.html

I went to the Poland link, but I didn't find a news article.
Here's what I found:

"Wanda Nowicka, Director of the Federation for Women and Family Planning in Warsaw, spoke recently in New York at an informal breakfast sponsored by the International Women's Health Coalition."

"Background information from the World Population Foundation's April 1996 Newsletter".

To me this is Planned Parenthood talking at a Planned Parenthood banquet. I'm not going to debate that this is exactly true, but that's the type of situation. I just got through giving my low regard for Planned Parenthood, and that applies here.

"Doctors perform an estimated 50,000 underground abortions a year."

This is the sole statistic given on the number of abortions being performed before or after criminalization. There is no reason to believe it is true, no supporting evidence, and given the source, totally unreliable. And there's nothing about penalties in the law.

"Although 95% of Poland's population is Roman Catholic, less than 75% are practicing, and an estimated 50-60% of the population is pro-choice. In the face of these divided loyalties, the Roman Catholic Church in Poland has waged an all-out war against legalized abortion."

These are the same tactics Dr. Nathanson described in his confession:

"THE SECOND KEY TACTIC WAS TO PLAY THE CATHOLIC CARD

We systematically vilified the Catholic Church and its "socially backward ideas" and picked on the Catholic hierarchy as the villain in opposing abortion. This theme was played endlessly. We fed the media such lies as "we all know that opposition to abortion comes from the hierarchy and not from most Catholics" and "Polls prove time and again that most Catholics want abortion law reform". And the media drum-fired all this into the American people, persuading them that anyone opposing permissive abortion must be under the influence of the Catholic hierarchy and that Catholics in favour of abortion are enlightened and forward-looking."

A glimmer of truth:

"Publicly, women have been strong supporters of abortion restrictions and ardent followers of the Roman Catholic Church."

Steen, are you starting to see the light yet?

Intecon at: http://www.aboutabortions.com/

"Also, if done correctly by a good doctor, the risk of anything like infertility is extremely low."

How low do your statistics show it to be, and what is your source? Some people would say that "a good abortion doctor" is a contradiction in terms. That is, that good doctors don't do abortions. As a matter of fact that is essentially what former presidential candidate Alan Keyes is stating below:

"…more women are killed, physically injured, raped and psychologically traumatized under 'legal' abortion than before Roe v. Wade in 1973." "The truth is, abortion clinics want the highest possible number of abortions to keep the cash rolling in."

"…if you survey physicians on what they think about abortionists, virtually all of them—even 'pro-abortion' doctors—regard abortionists as losers—the dregs of the medical profession. Legalized abortion keeps them out of jail, but they're still regarded as scum by their fellow doctors!"

Taken from http://www.aboutabortions.com/

"But with pregnancy, however, there are risks of many things…way more risks than abortion."

Could you elaborate on the risks, and what data you have? If you're having an abortion and there's a problem, like they've poked a hole in your uterus and they can't stop the bleeding, what do you think they do? They call 911-the paramedics-to take you to the hospital. Then it's a matter of whether they can get you there in time to keep you from bleeding to death. On the other hand, if you're having your baby delivered normally, you're already in the hospital. If any complications should arise, you have the full resources of the hospital, and for all practical purposes, a limitless supply of blood plasma, to come to your aid. I would think it would be very difficult for an otherwise healthy mother to die in the hospital. An added benefit would be that your baby survives too.

Christina, our guide, has started a list of women who have died from their abortions. You can read their stories by clicking on the link below; or maybe you'll have to cut and paste:

Intecon, at http://www.aboutabortions.com/

http://prolife.about.com/newsissues/prolife/library/deaths/bldeaths.htm?terms =abortion+deaths

From: Christina (AB_PROLIFE) Jun-29 10:13 pm To: JINX50 (363 of 452) 2012.363 in reply to 2012.201

The CDC gets its stuff from "state reporting agencies," as you put it, via the National Center for Health Statistics, which gets it from SAMPLES of death certificates.

Don't lecture me on how abortion morbidity and mortality data is collected. I did extensive research on it. The morbidity data ("Oh, complications are ever so low!") comes from abortion facilities, most notably Reproductive Health Services in St. Louis, a facility so shoddy that the abortionists went on strike after running out of supplies in the middle of an abortion. The mortality data comes mostly from the NCHS (and is based on samples, not full reporting), and from anybody who voluntarily reports an abortion death that doesn't make it through the NCHS gauntlet.

From: Christina (AB_PROLIFE) Jun-29 10:16 pm To: JINX50 (364 of 452) 2012.364 in reply to 2012.203

Seems to me they got caught often enough. I have a file full of newspaper clippings about raids on abortion mills.

After all, SOMEBODY is going to know where she went. Even in cases where the body was dismembered and dumped, the culprit was often tracked down.

Less accountability? Like it's easier to dispose of a body when you killed the person during the commission of a crime than it is to just fill out a death certificate and let it all blow over?

That was such a nice, friendly, reply, that I have to try to do just as well.

"I'm betting that we'd both agree that the base issue-the real goal-ought to be the prevention of unwanted pregnancies. That would greatly reduce the number of abortions, for certain, without endangering anyone, denying rights to anyone…".

Ya, how can anyone say no to that. President Bush and what I call the Christian Right are especially big on pushing abstinence, and Catholics have gotten very good at training and supervising for marriage.

However, I can tell you still haven't visited my web page. While working toward abstinence, and using birth control methods, are good goals-I give them a 0% chance of solving the problem; though they may help some. If you'd like to discuss this further, I'd be glad to.

The American Life League has a branch of their organization that has done nothing but follow the activities of Planned Parenthood for, I think, 16 years, called STOPP. Now, I'm not against family planning, or birth control. My wife and I used birth control pills to space our kids, and it worked out well, except sometimes I wish we'd had another one-they're all so different. She didn't want to take the chance of having any more past the age of 35, because the chances of having complications are so much higher, so she had what I think is called a tubal ligation. However, STOPPs information shows that sex education is the principle tool used by Planned Parenthood to generate business for their abortion mills. It's probably not just the sex education itself, but how Planned Parenthood teaches it. They budget $30,000,000 a year for it. Pretty outrageous idea? Well, my life experience tells me that teach somebody something they had little or no knowledge of before, and it increases the likelihood that they will go out and do it. It also tells me that condoms aren't the best way to have sex. And why spoil the moment while you go look for one. So I tend to accept the results, especially because I regard Planned Parenthood as a very scheming and untrustworthy organization, based on my knowledge of what they've done in the past. Those are just my personal opinions, that I pass along to you, as a forum friend, and I don't see any point in my defending or debating them.

As I argued before, and anyone can go back in this dialogue to see my reasons, more women are being maimed and killed by abortionists now, than before Roe vs. Wade; because of production line approaches to make as much money as possible, and because there has been a 1500% increase in abortions-as pointed out by an expert on the subject-Dr. Nathanson. I invite anybody following this discussion to go to the start page of the pro-life forum and page down two times to Christina's link to the list of the mother's who died from their abortions in June. Not only does the abortion kill the child, it is also very risky for the mother. Here's the link:

http://prolife.about.com/newsissues/prolife/

Another very significant risk is the increase in the likelihood of the woman getting breast cancer. Would you like to see the studies and statistics? I had to have them, because it seemed pretty farfetched to me at first.

Intecon, at: http://www.aboutabortions.com/

Hi Jess!

"Your credibility might be a bit higher if you knew your American history and did not attempt to persuade with misinformation."

Aww, Jess, that's not fair-I haven't even had a chance to respond yet. I'm sitting here facing four bookshelves of books on American history, from before independence to after the Civil War, and it picks up again in the next room. So if you want me to look up anything on American history for you, let me know.

My point was only that there was no right to an abortion mentioned "in" the Constitution, and that was in my reply to Heck51.

I understand what the court's decision was in Roe vs. Wade, but it doesn't have any basis in the Constitution. The fact that the Court made the wrong decision is the heart of the problem, and please let's not debate the word "fact"-I just couldn't find a better word to use. So that's my contention.

I understand the D of I isn't a governing document, and that it's not a statement on life. But they did state their views, in the process of explaining their quest for independence, and one of those views stated, unquestionably, was that "Life" was an "inalienable Right". They said it, it's there, in capital letters. Agreed, they didn't find it necessary to include it in the Constitution too. But, as I pointed out to Heck51, it made it in there afterwards. And I think it's a good thing to have there.

Intecon, at: http://www.aboutabortions.com/

"a woman…is of course entitled to abort a pregnancy, and her right to do so is protected by the constitution-indisputable, undeniable-and no pompous decree by yourself is going to change it"

There's no need to deny it, or dispute it, or make a decree, because it's simply not there, and we've shown that in this forum.

"her right to abort a pregnancy is protected by the constitution-persons may not be deprived of life liberty or property"

That's what happens to the child when you have an abortion; not what happens to you. The child is deprived of life, and any chance of attaining liberty or property. You've got it exactly backwards.

"Now for the kicker-from Roe v. Wade-

3. State criminal abortion laws, like those involved here, that except from criminality only a life-saving procedure on the mother's behalf without regard to the stage of her pregnancy and other interests involved violate the Due Process Clause of the Fourteenth Amendment, which protects against state action the right to privacy, including a woman's qualified right to terminate her pregnancy.

Like it or lump it-learn to love it, and memorize it."

Finally, something concrete, at least, Roe vs. Wade. That goes to the heart of the issue, was that opinion correct? Nobody denies that that was the decision the majority of the court made. The question then, is was the majority right, and did the decision have a basis in the Constitution? Because the decision represents only an interpretation of the constitution-it is not a part of the Constitution itself.

The same arguments I have made in this forum that the decision was not based on the Constitution still apply completely when debating Roe v. Wade. There's no need for me to change anything I've said up to now, but I will elaborate.

Sections 2-5 have nothing to do with this discussion, they are mainly about issues of governmental organization. I'll copy and paste section I below:

AMENDMENT XIV

Passed by Congress June 13, 1866. Ratified July 9, 1868.

Note: Article I, section 2, of the Constitution was modified by section 2 of the 14th amendment.

Section 1.
All persons born or naturalized in the United States, and subject to the jurisdiction thereof, are citizens of the United States and of the State wherein they reside. No State shall make or enforce any law which shall abridge the privileges or immunities of citizens of the United States; nor shall any State deprive any person of life, liberty, or property, without due process of law; nor deny to any person within its jurisdiction the equal protection of the laws.

461

The first thing that strikes me is that there isn't anything "which protects against state action the right to privacy". Where does this come from? They don't give any explanation. Have they created a right just for this case? Well, I can't say, I'm not a legal expert, but it certainly isn't stated specifically in Amendment XIV. And if it was, it should apply to everyone equally-in this instance, mother and child. Can you give an explanation of where this right to privacy comes from; since the court didn't make a case for it in their decision? It seems like I've heard of it-but from where does it come? It can't come from Amendment XIV directly; it would have to come from an interpretation, or another part of the Constitution. Otherwise Roe v. Wade would be built on another right not specifically granted by the constitution or it's amendments. And how would her privacy be violated by not having an abortion? The abortion clinic is certainly going to know about it and have a record of it. So already it looks like a big stretch just on the "Due Process Clause" and "privacy" issues, and we haven't even gotten to the heavier legal issues or the rights of the child. Justice William Rehnquist comments on these same concerns below.

Here are some of the statements on Roe v. Wade by people much more legally knowledgeable than I am:

"Make no mistake, abortion-on-demand is not a right granted by the Constitution. No serious scholar, including one disposed to agree with the Court's result, has argued that the framers of the Constitution intended to create such a right. Shortly after the Roe v. Wade decision, Professor John Hart Ely, now Dean of Stanford Law School, wrote that the opinion "is not constitutional law and gives almost no sense of an obligation to try to be." Nowhere do the plain words of the Constitution even hint at a "right" so sweeping as to permit abortion up to the time the child is ready to be born.

This is not the first time our country has been divided by a Supreme Court decision that denied the value of certain human lives. The Dred Scott decision of 1857 was not overturned in a day, or a year, or even a decade."

President Reagan

"I have difficulty in concluding, as the Court does, that the right of "privacy" is involved in this case. Texas, by the statute here challenged, bars the performance of a medical abortion by a licensed physician on a plaintiff such as Roe. A transaction resulting in an operation such as this is not "private" in the ordinary usage of that word. Nor is the "privacy" that the Court finds here even a distant relative of the freedom from searches and seizures protected by the Fourth Amendment to the Constitution, which the Court has referred to as embodying a right to privacy. Katz v. United States, 389 U. S. 347 (1967).

"The Court eschews the history of the Fourteenth Amendment in its reliance on the "compelling state interest" test. See Weber v. Aetna Casualty & Surety Co., 406 U. S. 164, 179 (1972) (dissenting opinion). But the Court adds a new wrinkle to this test by transposing it from the legal considerations associated with the Equal Protection Clause of the Fourteenth Amendment to this case arising under the Due Process Clause of the Fourteenth Amendment. Unless I misapprehend the consequences of this transplanting of the "compelling state interest test," the Court's opinion will accomplish the seemingly impossible feat of leaving this area of the law more confused than it found it.

...partakes more of judicial legislation than it does of a determination of the intent of the drafters of the Fourteenth Amendment.

The fact that a majority of the States reflecting, after all, the majority sentiment in those States, have had restrictions on abortions for at least a century is a strong indication, it seems to me, that the asserted right to an abortion is not "so rooted in the traditions and conscience of our people as to be ranked as fundamental," Snyder v. Massachusetts, 291 U. S. 97, 105 (1934). Even today, when society's views on abortion are changing, the very existence of the debate is evidence that the "right" to an abortion is not so universally accepted as the appellant would have us believe.

To reach its result the Court necessarily has had to find within the scope of the Fourteenth Amendment a right that was apparently completely unknown to the drafters of the Amendment.

The only conclusion possible from this history is that the drafters did not intend to have the Fourteenth Amendment withdraw from the States the power to legislate with respect to this matter."

JUSTICE WILLIAM REHNQUIST

"With all due respect, I dissent. I find nothing in the language or history of the Constitution to support the Court's judgment. The Court simply fashions and announces a new constitutional right for pregnant mothers and, with scarcely any reason or authority for its action, invests that right with sufficient substance to override most existing state abortion statutes...As an exercise of raw judicial power, the Court perhaps has authority to do what it does today; but, in my view, its judgment is an improvident and extravagant exercise of the power of judicial review that the Constitution extends to this Court."

JUSTICE BYRON WHITE

The point I am remaking here, and that you have no way to avoid, is that the Constitution in no place says "a woman has a right to an abortion". Rather, this is an interpretation of the meaning of the Constitution that many people disagree with, among them many legal scholars.

Here is another example of that disagreement:

"Philadelphia, PA—The plaintiffs in the two landmark Supreme Court cases of Roe v. Wade and Doe v. Bolton, the two companion cases decided on January 22, 1973 which compelled legalized abortion throughout the nation, are appearing in Philadelphia on Thursday, May 31, 2001, to personally file Friend of the Court briefs with the United States Court of Appeals. In their briefs they tell the Courts why the decisions in their own landmark cases have proven to be harmful to the rights of women and why the decisions in their own cases should be overturned.

Norma McCorvey (Jane Roe in Roe v. Wade) and Sandra Cano (Mary Doe of Doe v. Bolton) are filing their Friend of the Court briefs in the case of Donna Santa Marie, et al v. Christine Todd Whitman, et al. The Santa Marie case is a federal class action suit brought by five women (three of whom had abortions that were performed without voluntary or informed consent) who argue that New Jersey's abortion laws violate the most important constitutional rights of women."

Taken from the About.com web site.

There are many other efforts being made today to overturn that Judicial opinion. For example:

"The Life at Conception Act, which takes the Roe decision's own instructions to Congress to define exactly when constitutionally-protected life begins".

The change of just one Justice on the Supreme Court would result in a reversal of Roe v. Wade. Today polls show a majority of people consider abortion murder, and 80% want partial-birth abortion outlawed. The country's top cop, Attorney General John Ashcroft, is a staunch opponent of abortion, and could probably shut down most of the abortion mills in the country just by enforcing current laws. Today, more and more people, partly through scientific advances, like ultrasound, are becoming aware of the personhood of the child in the womb; and you have been unable to refute it in this debate forum-irregardless of what you claim. And that is the key-that the child in the womb is a person with equal rights under God and the 14th Amendment-especially the right to life.

"The promises of our Declaration of Independence are not just for the strong, the independent or the healthy. They are for everyone, including unborn children...We share a great goal, to work toward a day when every child is welcomed in life and protected in law…to build a culture of life, affirming that every person at every stage and season of life, is created equal in God's image."

President George W. Bush

I believe there is a tide change going on in this country, and that the law on abortion is going to change in the not too distant future; and then, as you said, you will be the person who has to "Like it or lump it-learn to love it, and memorize it." So hold your tongue.

Have a nice 4th-I will be catching up on other things.

Intecon, at http://www.aboutabortions.com/

Duh-I find it really difficult to believe you're still debating the following points. I guess you figure that if you just keep repeating the big lie, that people will believe you. I happen to believe that most people, when presented with both sides of an argument, and with no "axe to grind", are capable of sorting out the obvious lies and determining the truth. Here's what President Reagan had to say about that; note that more, very moving material, has been added to a previous, similar post:

"Despite the formidable obstacles before us, we must not lose heart. This is not the first time our country has been divided by a Supreme Court decision that denied the value of certain human lives. The Dred Scott decision of 1857 was not overturned in a day, or a year, or even a decade. At first, only a minority of Americans recognized and deplored the moral crisis brought about by denying the full humanity of our black brothers and sisters; but that minority persisted in their vision and finally prevailed. They did it by appealing to the hearts and minds of their countrymen, to the truth of human dignity under God. From their example, we know that respect for the sacred value of human life is too deeply engrained in the hearts of our people to remain forever suppressed. But the great majority of the American people have not yet made their voices heard, and we cannot expect them to—any more than the public voice arose against slavery—until the issue is clearly framed and presented. What, then, is the real issue? I have often said that when we talk about abortion, we are talking about two lives—the life of the mother and the life of the unborn child. Why else do we call a pregnant woman a mother? I have also said that anyone who doesn't feel sure whether we are talking about a second human life should clearly give life the benefit of the doubt. If you don't know whether a body is alive or dead, you would never bury it. I think this consideration itself should be enough for all of us to insist on protecting the unborn. The case against abortion does not rest here, however, for medical practice confirms at every step the correctness of these moral sensibilities. Modern medicine treats the unborn child as a patient. Medical pioneers have made great breakthroughs in treating the unborn for genetic problems, vitamin deficiencies, irregular heart rhythms, and other medical conditions. Who can forget George Will's moving account of the little boy who underwent brain surgery six times during the nine weeks before he was born? Who is the patient if not that tiny unborn human being who can feel pain when he or she is approached by doctors who come to kill rather than to cure?

The real question today is not when human life begins, but, What is the value of human life? The abortionist who reassembles the arms and legs of a tiny baby to make sure all its parts have been torn from its mother's body can hardly doubt whether it is a human being."

You might want to modify your posts to be more rational, rather than just repeating prior posts that have already been shot down. At least, I hope so-so that we can make some headway in this discussion. On the other hand, I do appreciate you providing me with a platform to present my position and ideas, and those of others, on abortion and when human life begins. I certainly hope everyone took the time to read the excerpts from Ronald Reagan's "Abortion and the Conscience of the Nation". He's such a wise man; much more so than I had realized when he was president. You can read the entire document at:

https://www.humanlifereview.com/reagan/reagan_conscience.html

Intecon, at web site: http://www.aboutabortions.com/

"You've learned nothing which is disappointing-the constitution most certainly protects a woman's right to abort-persons may not be deprived of life liberty or property, without due process.

I will accept your concession of this point, that we don't continue to clutter up cyber-space confirming the obvious-that women indeed have the constitutional right to abort an unwanted pregnancy, as cited above."

No concession necessary. The obvious, when you look at Roe v. Wade and the 14th Amendment, is that there's no support for Roe v. Wade in the Constitution, even though Roe v. Wade refers to Amendment 14.

But I kind of understand where you're coming from now; you've been told that "life, liberty or property" is what gives a woman a right to an abortion, and you're taking it on faith, and sticking to your guns. And then they gave you that excerpt from Roe v. Wade, that says the same thing. So maybe I've been too tough on you.

What I would like to get you to do, is to use your own intellectual powers to make a determination of your own. Just open your mind, and read those words that you have been reposting, "life, liberty or property", and ask yourself how a woman's right to an abortion could possibly be embodied in them. A woman in America today has her life, unchallenged, her liberty, and the right to own property (which, unfortunately, wasn't always the case).

It is really the child's right to these things that is at stake now. Their right to life itself, their right to do what they want within the law, that has the same right to be respected as anyone else.

Just as we Americans had to fight first to give African Americans their rights, and then women theirs, today we are fighting to give children still in the womb theirs; and it is just as great a cause as those that went before; and more urgent. Given modern day science, the child's existence can no longer be denied, as you probably found out from that link I gave you that you've avoided discussing. Roe v. Wade points us to the 14th Amendment and says: "which protects against state action the right to privacy", but we go to the 14th Amendment and find nothing about it. Roe v Wade says: "interests involved violate the Due Process Clause". Some time ago, when I was debating Heck51, I asked my daughter, who is an attorney, to explain to me what that meant, and I framed the question several different ways. Basically, it refers to when someone commits a crime, they have a right to a jury trial, and all that goes along with that. But a woman who has become pregnant has committed no crime, and has not been charged with one, and so this would not apply to her case.

So, although there was some attempt by the court to tie the decision to the Constitution, it doesn't really work. I believe that a majority on the court simply wanted to make abortion legal-I can understand that sentiment, and I talk quite a bit about it at my web site. But it was a big, big mistake, because they neglected to take into account the rights of the child. As a result, 40,000,000 have died a horrible death in this country, and we're still counting.

Intecon, at http://www.aboutabortions.com/

"How does a woman's pro-choice position regarding abortion in any way equate with the oppression of Born children???"

One way to answer this is to say that a child exists long before it exits what should be the safe confines of its mother's womb, and should be protected from the oppression of its life and liberty even when it can only be seen thru ultrasound. In other words, not being able to see it is certainly not proof most people would accept that it doesn't exist; after all, everybody knows a woman is pregnant for about 9 months. But there is also another way to look at this.

A lot of people, actually just about everybody, have the misconception that children are born when when they're delivered at the hospital. For pro-lifers, its like they're in a race with a ball and chain around their ankle, and have to keep dragging that darned old thing, that old idea, along with them. They talk about the pre-born, the unborn, and the fetus, thereby giving away the race; apparently oblivious to the fact that they don't have to drag that ball and chain, that baggage around. The idea that the child is born when it miraculously appears at the foot of the bed "is an archaic notion superseded by modern science." Let me quote to you further from my website:

"In other words they are telling people that they still subscribe to the antiquated idea that a child is born, or comes into the world, when the doctor delivers it at the hospital. This might have seemed to make sense in the Dark Ages, but we live in the 21st century, where they open people up, take out their defective heart, and put in a healthier model. We know what happens inside a woman every step of the way; how the child grows, develops, and matures. It should be obvious that a child is born when a woman becomes pregnant... Again, the pro-lifers are defeated by linguistics; they unwittingly accept the language of their opposition."

So I say to you, that children are born, or "come into existence", as I quoted to you from the dictionary in a previous post, when a woman becomes pregnant, and you are violating that person's rights, which equates "with the oppression of Born children", to use your words, when you deny that born child's right to live by killing him.

Now I know that people have trouble comprehending new ideas. For example, Gregor Mendel had been dead for many years before they were able to understand that his work formed the basis for modern day genetics; and there are many other examples of people's ideas which weren't understood until after their death. I understand that to think this way people must change some very ingrained habits; but I hope it won't take so long that I won't be here to see it.

Hey, alright, you did your homework on abortion and breast cancer! Or at least someone gave you something on it. Great!

But when I went to the end, as you asked me to, to look at the sources, what I found is that it had been written by Planned Parenthood, the biggest provider and promoter of abortions. On the other hand, my information came from the Chicago Tribune, hardly a pro-life publication. The other thing I noticed was that the most recent information was dated 1999-two years ago. And another was that they confirmed a lot of the information I gave you-they just tried to discredit it.

From my web site:

"Dr. Janet Daling and colleagues at the Fred Hutchinson Cancer Research Center, in a study commissioned by the National Cancer Institute, found that 'among women who had been pregnant at least once, the risk of breast cancer in those who had…an induced abortion was 50 percent higher than among other women.' The risk of breast cancer for women under 18 or over 29 who had induced abortions was more than twofold. Women who abort and have a family history of breast cancer increase their risk 80 percent. The increased risk of women under 18 with that family history was incalculably high… 'I would have loved to have found no association between breast cancer and abortion, but our research is rock solid, and our data is accurate. It's not a matter of believing, it's a matter of what is.'"

Since "the National Cancer Institute" mentioned above by the PP paper "commissioned" the study, it is hard for me to imagine that they wouldn't support the conclusions of their own research. But if that's not what they wanted to find, I guess they might not; they might just ignore it.

Although the National Cancer Institute's 2001 annual report chooses not to take a position on the causes, it does point out that: "breast cancer incidence rates have increased by more than 40 percent from 1973 to 1998." 1973 was the year of Roe v Wade. Why do you suppose the NCI chose that year as their benchmark?

"The questions that irrevocably cement the woman's right to abort an unwanted pregnancy are the following:

1) The pregnant woman is indisputably a person, entitled to the same right s as all other persons. On what basis is she denied these rights?? (none)

2) The z/e/f is indisputably a non-person, it has no rights, not until it is born. On what basis do you grant a non-person rights, that would supersede those real rights of a person, the pregnant woman??? (again, none)"

We don't want to deny a woman her rights. There's isn't any basis for it. But nobody has the right to have an innocent person killed-even that person's mother. The child inside the mother is an individual just as much a person as the mother herself, with the same God given and Constitutional rights as anybody else in this country. The problem is getting people to realize this-and most Americans do. The goal of the people you work for, and you yourself, is to define children as non-persons so that you can keep on doing abortions. And let me remind you again that you lost the argument on personhood because you would not recognize and debate web page:

http://www.babycenter.com/general/3284.html?CP_bid=

3) what is it about pregnancy that reduces a woman to sub-citizen, sub-person status, in which she is not entitled to the same rights as other persons?? (nothing)"

Gee, I don't know why you feel that way, or have this attitude toward women who are pregnant. Perhaps you're prejudiced, or need to go in for a psychiatric check up. Maybe you've just taken some propaganda too literally. I hope you can work through it. A pregnant woman in our society has a special status, because she's responsible not only for herself, but also for the well-being of her child. She's allowed to take time off from work, she's encouraged to get the best prenatal care possible, there's a whole world of literature, people stop to talk to her about it, people go out of there way to do things for her, and she has every right to be proud. Who can say, perhaps her child will grow up to be President or some other famous person-many of our presidents have come from poor or disadvantaged families-and in this country, a free and open society, people believe any achievement is possible, and all her family and friends have great hopes. Perhaps the child will just be there to comfort her and take care of her in her old age. Yes, a pregnant woman holds a position of respect in our country-whether she realizes it or not; and, really, for most good people, the circumstances of that pregnancy are not too important. There are literally hundreds of agencies all over this country to help women who are pregnant regardless of their circumstances-people who believe their assistance will make their own lives, and the mother's, richer.

You can find many of them at my web site:

http://www.aboutabortions.com/

Regards,

Intecon

"Tell me, tho-

In the US, we practice freedom of religious choice. correct??

Each individual has the right to choose his/her own religion, or choose none at all. correct??

But no government is allowed to dictate religious choice to anyone, and no group may enact legislation that would restrict religious choice. correct??

Choice regarding one's own life and body follow them same principle, and rightfully so.

Any woman may choose to abort, or to not abort a pregnancy, this is her own choice to make, just as religious choice is hers to make. Correct??

Nobody else, government or special interest group may dictate her choice regarding pregnancy, just as they may not do so regarding her religious choice.

Therefore, the doctrine of choice is firmly founded in the American system of government and it's principles of individual liberties.

How can somebody defend religious choice as a basic American value, and then oppose a pregnant woman's right of choice regarding her own body???

Remember-the unborn is not a person, so let's not even waste time with it."

Hogwash. Religious freedom is guaranteed by the Constitution-because it was deemed fundamentally important enough to be there:

"Congress shall make no law respecting an establishment of religion, or prohibiting the free exercise thereof". That's Amendment I.

But nowhere does the constitution give you the right to kill someone else; which is the choice you're talking about. And rightfully so, or society would be engulfed in people killing each other. Plus the child's body is a separate body from the mother's-not even connected to hers. The child is connected through the umbilical cord to the placenta-a separate entity also, that is attached to the wall of the mother's uterus: "A hollow muscular organ located in the pelvic cavity", specifically designed to carry a child.

Remember, I established that a child inside its mother is indeed a person, by referring you to the following picture and scientific discussion:

http://www.babycenter.com/general/3284.html?CP_bid=

I must have done that at least a dozen times now; but still no response. Obviously, you prefer to ignore it, and any scientific information-because you know that that type of discussion will establish beyond any doubt that the child inside the mother is indeed a child. And common sense tells you this too; how could the child inside the mother not be a person one minute, and the next minute be one, just because it's physical location has changed from inside to outside. What you are being paid to do is to perpetuate this fallacy for the abortion industry; because once the child is acknowledged to be a person you can no longer kill it for your convenience and profit. This is what is at the heart of your movement-don't acknowledge that the child inside the mother is a person; and frame it as "a woman's right to choose", when it is really a woman's right to have her child murdered; as if it was a piece of property with no rights of its own-just like the slaves were regarded prior to the Civil War. That's at least part of the reason I have said that this country is engaged in "a new Civil War".

Intecon, at http://www.aboutabortions.com/

"No-the unborn is not a person, not a separate being-I already stipulated this... I know that you think that a z/e/f is a person, but let's disregard this for a time, since it is a false contention."

You can stipulate all you want, but that doesn't make it true. You surrendered that point long ago in our discussion, because you were unable to defend whether a person existed at this stage:

http://www.babycenter.com/general/3284.html?CP_bid=

I've proven my point, you haven't. K-lynn may be nice enough to let you slide on this, but I'm not; I'm personally offended when you call a person a z/e/f-I consider it derogatory and demeaning terminology. And I understand why you do it: it's hard to think of a "z/e/f" as a person, and you need to establish that it's not a person in order to be able to kill a child legally. It's an insult to a fellow human being, and I'll never get tired of pointing that out to you; or that the person inside the mother is still the same person outside the mother; and the emphasis is on person-because you are unable to prove otherwise, and never will be able to, nor will anyone else. As a matter of fact, you haven't even attempted to debate it with me since I posted that link; but that hasn't prevented you from continuing to make the claim-which you know is not true, but is essential to your position. Without it, everything falls apart for you.

Intecon, at http://www.aboutabortions.com/

"'there is a pro-life plot to deny women the right to kill their children;' women do not have the right to kill born children-this is meaningless and irrelevant."

It's not meaningless and irrelevant to me when somebody is being killed through no fault of their own.

"Abortion concerns not just the unborn child, it concerns every one of us. The English poet, John Donne, wrote: '...any man's death diminishes me, because I am involved in mankind; and therefore never send to know for whom the bell tolls; it tolls for thee.' We cannot diminish the value of one category of human life—the unborn—without diminishing the value of all human life."

"We will never recognize the true value of our own lives until we affirm the value in the life of others, a value of which Malcolm Muggeridge says: '...however low it flickers or fiercely burns, it is still a Divine flame which no man dare presume to put out, be his motives ever so humane and enlightened.'"

"Abraham Lincoln recognized that we could not survive as a free land when some men could decide that others were not fit to be free and should therefore be slaves. Likewise, we cannot survive as a free nation when some men decide that others are not fit to live and should be abandoned to abortion or infanticide. My Administration is dedicated to the preservation of America as a free land, and there is no cause more important for preserving that freedom than affirming the transcendent right to life of all human beings, the right without which no other rights have any meaning." President Ronald Reagan

These words of wisdom echo my feelings exactly. I could expound further on this, but I realize it would be wasted on you. I was stunned when I read it, because our views were so nearly identical. Only, he says it much better than I ever could. However, if you would like me to copy and paste to the forum his entire "Abortion and the Conscience of the Nation"; go ahead, insult me about this; go ahead, and insult Ronald Reagan; a man I learned to respect, admire, and appreciate most, long after he was gone from public life.

Intecon, at: http://www.aboutabortions.com/

"If you wish to regard the unborn as a child, and not abort it, that's your choice-but you cannot expect to dictate your own personal beliefs onto all of society. If you don't like abortion, then don't have one."

It's not me alone, there are a lot of other people who believe pretty much the same as I do. And we're right, and when you're right, it doesn't really matter whether you're one voice, or 200,000,000.

The kids you're killing wouldn't regard it as right either-if they had a choice in the matter. Almost no one likes being killed. Hemingway said it, too, in one of his books, in the very last sentence: "no matter for whom the bell tolls, it tolls for you", or something almost identical.

Some of us understand that; others don't. It's not just eloquent rhetoric-it's underlaid by truth. There are a lot of things that go one in society that I don't really care about. Abortion I care a lot about. If you stand aside and let other people's ideas shape society, you may end up with a result you don't like, and that's not good for the country. So some of us feel a responsibility to get involved in some matters, depending on how important we think they are to society-and ourselves-and our families.

Actually, as a matter of practicality, what happens in society affects each of us, so it also becomes a matter of self-interest. I don't want to find out some day that one of my daughters, or granddaughters, or daughter-in-laws, had my grandchild killed, because some shallow person, or persons, or propaganda made it seem like it was an o'k thing to do. I have a keen sense of continuity and connectivity with my offspring. As a matter of fact, I decided to marry and have children, in large part, because I realized that I was going to die someday, and that then that would be it-the end-unless I had children. And I believe that you live on through your children, in a sense, hopefully better than you were yourself. So, when you mess with my kids, even through propaganda, I get very concerned, because I feel you're messing directly with me; and the kind of world they will live in. And, I ask myself, if it's acceptable to kill one group of people, surely then a rationalization to kill another group of people could be devised, too. I don't want to be ninety-five years old, and still enjoying life (there's longevity in my family, this is not unreasonable), and have it decided by my government that in order to balance the social security budget people my age will be exterminated because "they have no value to society". And I could go on with similar scenarios, that you would understand no better if you have no knowledge or sense of history.

Our country has it good now, but there's no guarantee that that will continue, if we are not good stewards. In terms of human history, we haven't even been around very long, when you compare us to the British, or Roman, empires, for example. I see it as worth preserving, and I want it to go on, together with my descendents, after I'm gone. I doubt that can continue if some of the things that are going on in our country now go on unchecked-especially abortion. When we start singling out certain groups for extermination, I don't think we have too far to go as a society unless we put a stop to it. I suppose most of this will go right over your head, but maybe someone else will get some good out of it.

Of course, I'll expect a point by point rebuttal; since you have yet to agree with anything I've said.

Intecon, at: http://www.aboutabortions.com/

"For instance-'The problem arises because when a woman terminates an unwanted pregnancy she is also terminating the life of her child' simple perusal of the constitution and amendments will reveal that the pregnant woman is indeed a person, entitled to the same rights as all other persons. There is no basis for denial of these rights. The unborn, OTOH, is not a person, and has no rights-there is no justification for granting it any rights that supersede those of the mother."

It's not necessary for the Constitution to define a woman as being a person. Everyone can see that she obviously is one. In 1973 it might have been difficult to make the point that a pregnant woman carries a child who is also a person; but today, with the advances of modern science, it is overwhelmingly obvious that it is. You seek to deny the child his rights by denying that he is a person-defining him out of his personhood-so that you can legally kill him for reason to profit from the abortion, and for the convenience of the mother. And that's what you get paid to do; to keep making the arguments for abortion, no matter what. There's no way you would spend so much time and effort doing what you're doing out of conviction unless you were being paid by the abortion industry. I would never believe otherwise. That is not an insult; just a statement of the obvious.

Nobody wants to grant the child "rights that supersede those of the mother." Just equal rights, under the Constitution-the right to life, "without which none of the other rights have any meaning".

"'Nobody has deemed medical treatment to be against the law.'

Thank you, your concession is graciously accepted. Of course it's not against the law-people have the right to protect and provide for their own health and welfare-(rights of life, liberty, remember?? it's in the constitution!!)"

I don't see how that is a concession. I never claimed medical treatment should be against the law. Abortion is not medical treatment for an illness or health condition; it's medical murder. People also have a right to provide for their own health and welfare; but it's not a right that's included in "rights of life, liberty"-H E A L T H is not spelled L I F E.

Intecon at http://aboutabortions.com/

"you've fallen back on the anti-choicers most hopeless, unsupportable position:

<the woman shouldn't terminate an unwanted pregnancy, because I don't want her to>

<the z/e/f is a person, because I think it should be>

Neither of these pseudo-arguments is particularly persuasive, unless you are recruiting people for the PRO-CHOICE SIDE!!"

I have? I don't remember saying that. And I'm not anti-choice. I believe that everybody can do what they choose, within the law, and if it doesn't harm someone else. Abortion doesn't fit that last criteria.

I can't respond to your statement about the z/e/f/, because no such thing exists. So how could I have an opinion on what a z/e/f is? Are you through making up positions for me yet? I certainly hope so. Your "pseudo-arguments" that you are putting me down for I never made; you made them up yourself.

Intecon, at http://www.aboutabortions.com/

"<the woman shouldn't terminate an unwanted pregnancy, because I don't want her to>

<the z/e/f is a person, because I think it should be>

Neither of these pseudo-arguments is particularly persuasive"

You said that-I certainly didn't. Are you reduced to making up arguments for me, and then shooting them down? I think I've made it abundantly clear that I'm against abortion because it kills the child; a person just like you or me; as evidenced by the image and information on this web page:

http://www.babycenter.com/general/3284.html?CP_bid=

"H: <what is it about pregnancy that reduces a woman to sub-citizen, sub-person status, in which she is not entitled to the same rights as other persons?? (nothing)>

I: 'I don't know why you feel that way, or have this attitude toward women who are pregnant.'

I don't. anti-choicers do-they want to deny them rights to which they are entitled, as are all persons."

Wrong. People of pro-life beliefs don't want to deny anybody rights which they are entitled to. Fundamentally, this is what their whole position on life is based on: That everybody should have equal rights, especially the right to life. Your philosophy, on the other hand, is built around denying all rights to a certain group of individuals, including the right to life. For your convenience and profit, you seek to define them out of existence-to treat them as property, just like African Americans were once treated as property, and women were denied the right to own property and vote; except you have gone far beyond that, by killing them at will.

"rights to which they are entitled, as are all persons." That's the part I agree with, with the emphasis on "all persons".

"You've already conceded that there is no basis for this denial."

Yes, rights that don't harm other people. Rights that don't kill other people, like abortion does.

"to deny them rights to which they are entitled, as are all persons." This is basically a figment of your imagination.

Intecon, at http://www.aboutabortions.com/

"You wrote: ***Nonsense. Pure and utter nonsense. I think you're finding what you want to find.***"

I'm glad you responded to that, because I want to pursue it further. If you'll recall, I was referring to your "secret handshake" statement to, I believe, France, about how you understand that everything pro-lifers say is lies; like you just assumed everybody knew that.

Rather than the implication, I would like to see the things you think I've lied about in the last several weeks that I've been on the forum-since you seem to be following the discussion. And if you can't come up with that, I'd still be curious to see a list of things that you think other pro-life people have lied about-specific instances; since I can't argue implications and vague generalities. I certainly can't vouch for what other pro-lifers say; but personally I've never run across any pro-life lies. Deeply held religious beliefs I would classify as opinions. And please don't make up positions for us like Heck01 does. And I think you have to distinguish between when someone is just stating an opinion, or is insisting it is factual, too. Having different opinions isn't lying-if it's clear they are opinions. Intentionally trying to mislead is what I would classify as a lie. I would also very much like to hear what you think the motive would be for prolifers to lie-I still haven't gotten a clear statement about that from anyone. You certainly seem to be a mature and intelligent person; so we should be able to find common ground-unless you have a hidden agenda; instead of just mindlessly defending a pre-set position, with pre-set arguments.

"I am reasonably confident in my research skills and my ability to discern which sources are authoritative and credible after I read them. If I'm not certain, then I contact experts in the field to learn more."

O'k, you're up to bat. Like Sgt. Friday used to say, "We just want the facts, ma'am". Show me. And let's see who your experts are.

"Before you say, "nonsense," please remember that it is you, not I, who has a web site strictly devoted to promoting pro-life propaganda and anti-choice attitudes."

My web site offers facts, information, ideas, solutions, and opinions. I consider it a very valuable resource for people who oppose abortion or are just learning about it. It also has some limited influence in the controversy. I can discern that from some of the indirect feedback I get; and by following where my visitors come from. As I state in my lead paragraph: "it is an excellent place to start a study of abortion. It has also evolved into a center for the best current thinking on the topic of abortion, including evaluations of the health risks." There are no lies. It just presents a point of view, and expands on it. A lot of the ideas there you can't find elsewhere. I am very meticulous in being certain there is nothing there that is incorrect. If you should happen to find anything that I've overlooked, please let me know so that I can change it. And as I've explained before, I am not anti-choice. Do you understand the distinction I make there? Please don't force an untrue and misrepresentative label on me.

Intecon, at web site: http://www.aboutabortions.com/

"You know, I'm just gonna assume you two were civil to each other, at least until someone complains of a violation. Thirty posts of you two going in circles just wasn't readable."

Yea, ain't it the truth. But on each round I try to add new things and expand further on the topic. I just wish we could break some new ground. It sounds like you're sitting in for Christina to police the discussions. Heck01 isn't going to say anything that offends me-I just consider the source. You don't have to delete his posts for fear I'll be offended. I try really hard not to say anything that will be deleted, because I put a lot of effort and thought into my responses. If you ever feel you have to delete something I've posted, would you please notify me, and, hopefully, email the offending post to me so that I can reword it and repost it?

Intecon, at http://www.aboutabortions.com/

"'But nowhere does the constitution give you the right to kill someone else;'

Actually it does-a person may not be denied life or liberty without due process-if your life/liberty is threatened you may be within your rights to kill to protect it."

Well, I guess your statement, made above, could be used to justify attacking abortion clinics and abortion doctors. Is that what you had in mind, or did you have something else in mind? Somebody else to kill? We probably shouldn't be talking about killing abortion doctors-it's not politically correct, you know. But it's o'k to talk about killing children, so I think we'd best stick to that.

Intecon

"'Plus the child's body is a separate body from the mother's-not even connected directly to hers.'

ROFL-that's hilarious!! you ARE joking, of course??

Pray tell, if the z/e/f is not connected to the mother, how does it receive oxygen and nourishment from her?? 'divine intervention'??

Without one of the silliest statements we've seen, on a board that simply abounds in silly statements-truly outstanding!!!

'I established that a child inside its mother is indeed a person, by referring you to the following picture and scientific discussion:'"

http://www.babycenter.com/fetaldevelopment?&CP_bid=

Finally, perhaps we're getting somewhere. It seems the problem may be a lack of medical and scientific knowledge. Yes, it is true, the child is always a separate entity from the mother, and is never, ever, a physical part of her; or any other kind of part, for that matter; from what you refer to as conception, until birth. Neither is the child connected directly to her. What actually occurs, is that the blastocyst splits, at about the time implantation is imminent, into the placenta and the child. It is the placenta that attaches itself to the mother's uterus, and the child is attached to the placenta by the umbilical cord; kind of like an astronaut floating in space. The placenta, I would suppose, is at least part of what becomes the afterbirth; and is certainly always separate from the child after they split. This is especially apparent, in the pictures above, from the 1st through 4th months of pregnancy, because the child is not yet big enough to obstruct a clear view of the placenta and umbilical cord. The link I entered above is not exactly the same one I gave you before; it the previous page that shows pictures of all nine months of pregnancy; the address I gave you before only shows the enlarged picture of a child inside its mother during the ninth month of pregnancy, because it is so abundantly clear that the child is a person in the ninth month. Of course, it's pretty clear in the preceding months, also. But you can click on any of the monthly pictures and they will enlarge to give you a clearer view-sort of like my photography web site. There's information on each stage given under each monthly picture. When, for instance, the fourth month is enlarged, there are arrows pointing to the placenta and umbilical cord directly, the baby looks just like you or I, and you can click on any one of five weeks listed below to read an article on the baby's development during that week. Pretty cool, and definitely not a pro-life web site. As a matter of fact, an award winning site. It's especially important to understand that the child is not a part of the mother's body; thus when she decides to make a decision to have an abortion she is not making a decision about what to do about her own body-she is making a decision about what to do about the child's body-to kill it, in a word. I know this is all pretty new, but when we've been through it 8-10 times I think you'll get it. At least you admitted that a child gets "oxygen and nourishment from her".

Intecon, at web site http://www.aboutabortions.com/

The Final Word On Lying

"What has any of this to do with the z/e/f' status as a non-person??-which is confirmed conclusively in the constitution. You've already conceded this, along with the point that there is no basis for denying a pregnant woman rights to which she is entitled."

Two very big, very obvious, lies about what I said. This person is a L I A R!! This is not meant as an insult-just as a simple statement of fact. He apparently has nothing better to say.

It is also a gross distortion of what I said when he states: "You've already... conceded there is no basis for denying a pregnant woman rights to which she is entitled", because he knows that I did not include the right to an abortion; that is, to have her child killed, as a right she was entitled to.

In addition, as I've pointed out before, no such thing as a z/e/f exists. If he was serious about this discussion, he could discuss any one of those abbreviations separately; for example the, "f", as represented here:

http://www.babycenter.com/general/3284.html?CP_bid=

He has steadfastly refused to discuss this for several weeks now. Hopefully, I will find a change of heart further down in this forum.

"non-person??-which is confirmed conclusively in the constitution." We've been over this several times-he knows that's not in the Constitution. He could easily take a different tack on this, but doesn't. A B I G L I E!

I have conceded nothing of the sort mentioned above; and I refuse to leave the field of battle with him claiming victory, irregardless of how ridiculous that claim is.

Intecon, at http://www.aboutabortions.com/

"Any attempt to equate slavery with pro-choice regarding abortion must be instantly discarded as meaningless and false.

There is no parallel, the correct equation is Slavery with antichoice."

The parallel, for anyone else who completely missed it, as Heck01 did, is that both decisions were very wrong and totally unjust. So much so, that it's difficult to believe people appointed to the Supreme Court could come up with them. What should be "discarded as meaningless and false" is the decisions themselves. One down, one to go.

Intecon, at http://www.aboutabortions.com/

"You, yourself, have conceded that there is no basis for perpetrating this injustice."

Another big lie, or at least a big distortion. First of all, there's no injustice. Therefore, secondly, there was nothing to be conceded.

Intecon, at http://www.aboutabortions.com/

"I established that a child inside its mother is indeed a person, by referring you to the following picture and scientific discussion:"

http://www.babycenter.com/general/3284.html?CP_bid=

"More nonsense-we've proven again and again-the z/e/f is not a person-medically, biologically, physically, legally, socially-your futile repetitions will not change reality-unborn =/= person."

The idea is to actually look at the picture. What does it look like to you? It certainly looks like a person to me. It definitely bears no resemblance to a frog or snake. In essence, it proves, to anyone who chooses to look at it, that it is a person. You can tell it's a person just by looking at it. And you can get the specific information on it by clicking on one of the four weekly articles below it.

"we've proven again and again-the z/e/f is not a person-medically, biologically, physically, legally, socially-your futile repetitions will not change reality-unborn =/= person."

You know, I can't come right out and say this is a lie, because there is no such thing as a z/e/f. But it really is a lie, because you're using it to represent a child inside it's mother. You've proven nothing. If so, where's your proof? My proof is that web page above, that anybody can look at. Where's your proof? It also shows that a child within its mother is a person. Look at it. Where's your proof that it's not? It's not too late to come up with something. Would you like to see some more pictures, some more data? But first you've got to discuss that one.

"lie2 (lº) n. 1. A false statement deliberately presented as being true; a falsehood. 2. Something meant to deceive or give a wrong impression.—lie v. lied, ly·ing (lº"'ng), lies.—intr. 1. To present false information with the intention of deceiving. 2. To convey a false image or impression"

Well, according to the above dictionary definition, I think it qualifies as a lie. All of it. If not all of it, certainly parts of that statement. But if we go with the dictionary-all of it.

So I'm trying hard not to convey a false impression myself, but the dictionary is pretty clear on it. The reason this is important is because it's about which side lies. Are you listening, Jess. Are you prepared to defend this person as being truthful? And this is not the first time. It re-emphasizes, as Dr. Nathanson pointed out, that the pro-abortion side lies; and is still lying. They attach little importance to being truthful. They'll say anything to try to support their side. The mole pregnancy is another good example of that.

Since I save all this stuff, we can discuss it, if you wish, Jess. I think I can be especially authoritative on what I did and didn't say.

"'because once the child is acknowledged to be a person'

It won't happen-it's unconstitutional, and it's completely unsupportable-biologically, medically, physically, legally, socially, all ways..."

If we hadn't discussed this before, I'd consider it opinion. But I know Heck01 knows better now, so I'd classify it as another lie. He's just defending his position-no matter what.

And it is going to happen, probably some of it this year, and some of it next year. Not a complete ban on abortion yet, but the start of restrictions. The born alive act should pass, and the ban on partial-birth abortions probably will too. And it should become a homicide to kill a pregnant woman's child while committing a crime.

"because you may not wrongly persecute pregnant women and wrongly deny them rights to which they are entitled."

Well, I've touched on this before. Why would a majority of women be interested in persecuting themselves? Why would a majority of the pro-life leaders be interested in persecuting themselves? Why would famous feminists over the years be against abortion if they thought they were denying themselves rights they were entitled to? Why would so many women get on this forum to defend life (note that I'm excluding you this time Jay). If you'd like to challenge me on any of those statements, I will gladly go into a lot more detail.

Intecon, at http://www.aboutabortions.com/

In this case it is true, as I've shown repeatedly-the z/e/f is not a person-OBJECTION OVER-RULED. Next..."

That's a blatant lie.

"Deal with it-the unborn is a z/e/f, and most certainly not a person, as I've proven time after time. You are, of course, unable to present any proof that it is."

By my count 4 more lies.

"The rest of your rant is not worth my attention-so lacking any cogent proof to the contrary-the unborn, z/e/f remains, as it has always been, a non-person."

Two more obvious lies.

And so it's also very obvious which side lies. Whether it's you or somebody else presenting the lies for the pro-abortion side, so that you can claim that the child inside the mother is not a person; so that you can treat it as a piece of property, deny it any rights, and have it killed if you choose-just like in the Dred Scott era. Except that slaves usually weren't killed, because they were worth a lot of money. As anyone can see from the following picture, which you have so far refused to discuss with me, the child inside its mother is just as much a person as the child outside:

http://www.babycenter.com/general/3284.html?CP_bid=

What do you call your theory of humanity? Perhaps the "Inside, outside" theory? Or just "inside out"? Or "upside down"? Because that's about as scientific as you get.

Have sex, and then kill the evidence to avoid embarrassment, seems to be the prevailing morality on your liberal side of the political spectrum. You quote to me from Roe v Wade as if it proved something. Roe v Wade is the problem, not the solution. It's a reflection of the liberal morality above. It's a Supreme Court decision at least as poor as Dred Scott; plus it's resulted in 40,000,000 deaths. Only 621,000, on both sides, died during the 1st Civil War. Unlike that first Civil War, those 40,000,000, brutally killed, have all been on one side. And Roe v Wade will be overturned. Today it serves only as a convincing example of the faulty reasoning on your side, and of a court ignoring what the Constitution says in favor of fabricating a decision to reflect their own personal contorted political views.

You, and the Supreme Court, attempt to define out of existence something that it is obvious to almost everyone does exist-and which in fact does exist-the child inside its mother; in favor of your personal convenience. As a result, 40,000,000 people have been murdered, because the court has defined abortion as not being murder. But this ballgame is far from being over. Injustices such as this eventually get redressed-just as the Dred Scott decision was. Just one Supreme Court justice needs to change to relegate this sordid chapter in history to the scrap heap, along with the holocaust in Nazis Germany, and the "Rape of Nanking". Of course, it will surpass all other such similar events by its magnitude. Neither you, or the Supreme Court, have offered any scientific or medical evidence that the child inside its mother is not a person-for a simple reason-because you know you can not win that argument. Dred Scott, meet Roe v Wade.

Let me present the convoluted reasoning that you bolded in Roe v Wade: "no case could be cited that holds that a fetus is a person within the meaning of the Fourteenth Amendment." "None indicates, with any assurance, that it (person) has any possible pre-natal application." "...persuades us that the word "person," as used in the Fourteenth Amendment, does not include the unborn." "There has always been strong support for the view that life does not begin until live birth." "Perfection of the interests involved, again, has generally been contingent upon live birth. In short, the unborn have never been recognized in the law as persons in the whole sense."

They're giving their opinions that nothing can be found in the law that says a child inside its mother is a "person". Whether the child has been previously defined as a person in the law. What they're omitting, in their rush to judgment, is that there haven't been any decisions based on medical and scientific grounds that held that a child inside its mother is not a human human being-is not a person. Just like in the Dred Scott decision, they sought to define a group of people out of their personhood, even though everybody can see with their own two eyes that a person does in fact exist, as supported by all the scientific evidence. It's called a prejudiced decision; a decision based on the prejudiced opinions of the justices, rather than on the facts and evidence available. A decision that has had deplorable, disastrous, and catastrophic consequences.

"That's the ballgame, folks, rant and rave to your heart's content-the z/e/f is NOT a person, never has been...", and the z/e/f has never existed, or ever will, or ever can, at one time.

Intecon, at http://www.aboutabortions.com/

(As I copied this from my hard drive, I was reminded that Phyllis Schlafly in a recent letter made the point that the Constitution nowhere mentions "men" or "women". It uses terms like persons, citizens, etc.; and I would assume that it doesn't use words like child or adult either. So anyone trying to base their human rights on sex, or adulthood, or age, or being born, would find that the Constitution isn't supportive of those specific criteria; although things like the right to vote would of course be age contingent.)

"That's the ballgame, folks, rant and rave…"

Listen Heck, everybody's heard about Roe v Wade by now, and the unique way the Supreme Court uses global positioning as the determinant factor in defining whether human life exists; you needn't keep ranting and raving about it. As for the ballgame, the score's pro-infanticide 5, anti-infanticide 4, with anti-infanticide at bat, bottom of the ninth, bases loaded, no outs.

Intecon, at website:

http://www.aboutabortions.com/

"No-the unborn is not a person, not a separate being-I already stipulated this…".

What if you had a woman 9 months pregnant, and you took a knife and cut her stomach open? This actually happened not too long ago. They did it to steal her baby. It was a pretty dumb thing to do, and it didn't take the police long to catch them. The mother's very dead, but the baby's doing fine. Dumb as they were, they did at least understand that they'd find a baby in there. Dumb, dumber…

Intecon, at website:

http://www.aboutabortions.com/

P.S. Watch out for that sucker punch.

"'The Constitution does not give a woman the right to have an abortion.

There is no place the Constitution says a woman has a right to an abortion.'

The constitution most certainly does provide this right-the right to life, liberty-which includes the right to protect and provide for one's own health, and treat those conditons which affect it."

"Try as you will, you cannot deny that the right to life and liberty most certainly includes protecting one's own health, and receiving medical treatment for those conditions affecting it."

Nope, just "the right to life, liberty", which includes-"the right to life, liberty"; not anything anybody happens to dream up. Besides, a pregnancy doesn't have an adverse affect on a woman's health, or any affect on her health, for that matter. It's a very natural state of health to be in for a woman. Most women eventually become pregnant; and with no adverse effects on them. When women stop becoming pregnant, the whole human race is in really big trouble. Nobody's against a woman receiving medical treatment that she really needs. She can get it by entering into an agreement with a provider. Some young ladies even receive medical treatment while they are still in the womb- for example, to correct a condition known as spina bifida. You can see a picture of such an operation, one of two such pictures I know of, at the following address:

http://www.aboutabortions.com/Baby.html

There's even a musical accompaniment, courtesy of the web site.

This is becoming too easy. It's not really a challenge anymore.
Do you think you could come up with something new?

Intecon, at: http://www.aboutabortions.com/

"The constitution does not stipulate that you have the right to eat scrambled eggs, or drive a red car, or hook up to the internet, or have an appendectomy- yet these rights are enjoyed by Americans."

Yes they are. But they're not in the Constitution. They don't need to be. You get all these things by buying them; by entering into an explicit or implicit contract to pay for them. You can't buy a red car if you don't enter into an agreement to pay for it; and you couldn't even get an attorney to file a case otherwise.

"(Read amendments 9, 10)"

Everybody has a right to enter into a contract for services or merchandise that are legal. But nobody has a right to enter into a contract for services that violate the rights of another guaranteed by the Constitution; especially the right to life which is guaranteed in Amendment 14, and is fundamental to all rights. The other rights don't do you any good if you're dead. The rights guaranteed by the Constitution don't apply only to pregnant women; they apply equally to everybody, not just some special classification. And the rights specifically mentioned in the Constitution take precedence over those rights people assume that are not specifically mentioned in the Constitution.

Intecon, at web site http://www.aboutabortions.com/

"'Since modern day science makes it abundantly clear that the child inside the mother is a person,'

Complete nonsense. Since any day science makes it abundantly clear that the z/e/f is in no way a person, the constitution is completely correct in its exclusion of the unborn from protection as persons."

First of all there's no exclusion of any group of people who haven't committed a crime from protection by the Constitution. You're incorrect about that.

Secondly, there's no such thing as a z/e/f, except in your own vocabulary. Where's there a reference? None exists.

My scientific proof exists at this award winning web site:

http://www.babycenter.com/general/3284.html?CP_bid=

The science at pharmaceutical companies is generally regarded as being very good.

I don't think I can dumb it down any more than that for you.

Where's your scientific proof? You don't have any to offer, because it doesn't exist.

Have you ever seen a woman nine months pregnant? Why do you think her stomach is so big? Bad Gas? If you were a doctor, what would you prescribe for her condition-Imodium? Or would you still prefer abortion?

Intecon, at web site:

http://www.aboutabortions.com/

"But remember-that it will make no difference, women will continue to abort unwanted pregnancies as is their right and ability to do so. There is nothing you can do to stop it. simply learn to live with it and accept it. Ranting and raving will change nothing…"

It seems to me that you're the one doing the ranting and raving.

I don't accept it, and I'm not going to live with it. I'm going to help to change it. It's nobody's right to kill another person not possibly guilty of any crime or provocation. And I am making a difference, whether you like it or not. We are going to stop it.

Under my plan of treating abortion just like any other murder, which it is, some abortionists, depending on the courtroom verdict, would be sentenced to prison terms, including life in prison, and capital punishment. Any woman who had an abortion would be sentenced to one year in a special facility-assuming any women were able to actually obtain abortions. Under threat of these severe penalties, abortion in this country would become insignificant. Then the question would also arise as to whether people needed to be prosecuted for conspiracy in promoting abortion. I think they should be.

Intecon, at web site: http://www.aboutabortions.com/

"it's a picture of a z/e/f, a potential person-inside its mother. (potential actuated at birth.)"

(Criticism of the Supreme Court after their election decision.)

"'and now you're telling me I should respect their abortion decisions.'

Different court-different people-the wise justices who correctly freed women from wrongful oppression have been replaced by partisan politicos out to promote personal agendas.

Your poll statistics are crap"

The same court that ruled just months ago to uphold partial birth abortion, a procedure every poll shows 80% of Americans oppose.
Are you saying that you don't support the court that made that decision? I would certainly suppose that you do, and that you're part of the other 20%.

My statistics aren't crap. I quoted you directly form my web site which states:

"According to the LA Times Poll published on June 18, 2000, 67% of Americans believe abortion is murder."

That's a fact. If you don't believe it, go to that back issue of the LA Times and prove that I'm wrong. And the LA Times is not considered a pro-life paper.

The people who are being oppressed are the children being murdered.

Intecon, at web site http://www.aboutabortions.com/

"Face it-anti-choicers are an intolerant vocal minority trying to force their oppression on all of society."

We should begin by defining the terms being used here, and "choice" as you've used it here means a woman's right to have her child murdered.

People who oppose abortion are the majority-you are the minority, part of the 20% minority who support infanticide even after the baby is delivered. Part of the minority that supports overall abortion.

Pro-life people are intolerant of murder, as everyone else should be. They are trying to defend those who can not defend themselves.

The people being oppressed are the people being killed-41,000,000 is the latest figure I've seen.

As for tolerance, here's an interesting quote from my web site:

I wonder if a statement of tolerance for the views that slavery should be permitted, or that racism is O.K., or that handicapped people can be discriminated against, or that America should disarm, or that taxes should be raised, would be acceptable to those who want our Party to go on record as respecting the views of those who justify killing babies." Phyllis Schlafly

Here's another:

"America, it is said, is suffering from intolerance. It is not. It is suffering from tolerance of right and wrong, truth and error, virtue and evil, Christ and chaos. Our country is not nearly so much overrun with the bigoted as it is overrun with the broadminded...In the face of this broadmindness, what the world needs is intolerance." Archbishop Fulton J. Sheen

You can find more of the same at my web site:

http://www.aboutabortions.com/

"'She's not receiving medical treatment for an illness'

Irrelevant-a traumatic injury, a broken limb is not an illness. Pregnancy is most certainly a condition that affects the woman's life and health, as such she has every right to have it treated. Or are you saying that pregnant women cannot receive treatment from a physician??;)"

So what's broken when a woman's pregnant? That doesn't make sense.

O'k, I'll change my wording. She's not receiving medical treatment for an injury or illness. So that fixes that. Pregnancy is a natural condition that's doesn't adversely affect a woman's health.

Abortion is a procedure that adversely affects the health of the child by dismembering and killing it, certainly a much more serious prospect than pregnancy. I'm saying pregnant women can receive treatment from a physician as long as it doesn't kill the other person inside her-her child. Relevant.

Intecon, at web site: http://www.aboutabortions.com/

"Time to remind you of the insurmountable obstacles that defeat anti-choicers every time:"

I don't consider myself an anti-choicer, but I'm not aware of any obstacles in this debate that I haven't surmounted.

"A pregnant woman is a person, by what justification do you deny her rights to which she is entitled??"

The only right I deny to a pregnant woman is her non-right to kill another woman-or man-based on the excuse that she's pregnant; to which she is not entitled.

"A z/e/f is not a person. by what justification do you grant it fictitious rights that would supersede the real rights of the mother, who is undeniably, a person??"

A z/e/f is a fictitious creation of your imagination that never exists, never can exist, and never will exist.

"What is it about pregnancy that reduces a woman to sub-person, sub-citizen status??"

I still don't understand why you feel this way about women.
Personally, I think it's a little warped, to say the least.
I hold pregnant women in especially high regard and respect.

This is sooo easy. Why don't you come up with some new arguments or topics? Listen, I realize this isn't really a fair exchange.

Where you're always stuck with defending flawed arguments, I just have to figure out what's wrong with them. It's tough having to defend the losing side of an argument. I remember once when I had to do it in school. What I did was I gave the losing side, then right after it I gave the winning side. The person I was supposed to debate didn't even have to get up to give his side of it. I think you would be just about unbeatable on this side-such tenacity!

Intecon, at http://www.aboutabortions.com/

"'But it is not guaranteed by the Constitution,'

We have already covered this-a person has the right to life and liberty, and with it the right to provide for and protect his /her health."

This right applies to all people, not just pregnant women, including their children.

Intecon

"Your feeble argument <a woman shouldn't have the right to terminate an unwanted pregnancy because I don't think she should> is laughably pathetic"

That's a lie. I never said that. Shows you which side makes up things, because they don't have any solid arguments to offer.

"you've not offered anything concrete in the last 20 posts…"

Well, I shouldn't be too critical of that, you probably don't have the capacity to understand them. But other people do.

Intecon

"Complete nonsense-you're obviously desperate and frantic, just grasping at anything no matter how ridiculous."

I think you're saying that because that's what you're doing.
Where's the cane?

Intecon

"Actually you do have the right to take someone's life, if you are acting in self-defense. But that's another issue-your statement is totally irrelevant to abortion, because as we all know by now-the unborn is not 'someone', it is not 'someone else'. It's not a person, it has no rights."

That's a position you've been coached in because abortionists like to take it so that they can profit from killing the child by claiming it's not a person.

Perhaps you could follow up by explaining why self-defense is necessary against a child in the womb.

Intecon

"'<Abortion is not medical treatment because I don't want it to be>'"
"'I don't think it's a good argument either;'"

"Then why do you persist in using it??"

That's another obvious lie. I've never used that argument.

Intecon

"All you've done is offer up flimsy personal opinion-

<A woman should not abort because I think she shouldn't>

<A z/e/f is a person because I want it to be>

<Abortion is not medical treatment because I don't want it to be>
type opinions that are hopelessly out of synch with reality.

you're going to have to engineer some substantial constitutional amendments
to have your pipe-dream opinions become reality."

Five lies. This is even easier. There's no reason to reply to things I never said.

Intecon

"What is it about pregnancy that reduces a woman to sub-person, sub-citizen
status??"

Perhaps your feelings about pregnant women, which you express above, are
the root cause of your support for abortion. Is it that you want to punish them
for becoming pregnant by having them get an abortion??

(I had been informed via email that the person who I was debating had said
that his wife had had several miscarriages. It puzzled me. Why would
someone who was trying to have children be so staunchly pro-abortion? So as I
pondered I was probing. In retrospect, I can see that, given their attitude
toward abortion, her miscarriages might have been caused by her former
abortions.)

"'Just because something is legal, doesn't make it right.'

Doesn't make it wrong, either. Roe v. Wade is without doubt one of the
greatest decisions issued by the USSC."

Roe v Wade, Stenberg v Carhart, and Dred Scott are the three most horrendously and obviously wrong decisions the Court has ever made. Dred Scott had to be reversed by the Civil War, which took 621,000 lives; Roe v Wade and Stenberg v Carhart have caused the brutal murder of 41,000,000 people. If you don't think there's any doubt about Roe v Wade why do you think so many people are trying to undo it? "Without doubt one of the greatest decisions" is without a doubt an erroneous statement. I won't call it a lie-just a misrepresentation. So you think that a decision that resulted in the murder of 41,000,000 people is a great decision. I think that's a monumental blunder.

Intecon, at the updated web site http://www.aboutabortions.com/

"'It's not meaningless and irrelevant to me when somebody is being killed through no fault of their own.'

Right-the killing of born beings is wrong, and should be the concern of society no doubt. What possible application does this have to abortion?? the z/e/f is an unborn, non-person."

There is no such thing as a z/e/f, never has been, never will be, and never can be. The application to abortion is that during an abortion you're killing a person, just like you or I except for size and age and physical position, who has actually come into existence, or been born, inside it's mother; a person just like the one in this picture:

http://www.babycenter.com/general/3284.html?CP_bid=

Planned Parenthood wants to be able to kill this category of person to be able to profit from it financially. Other organizations want to be able to kill it for their convenience. Just like in the case of Dred Scott, they are saying that they have rights superior to those of the child-that the child is their property to do with whatever they choose, and this person has no rights of it's own. In other words, they want to define this person as a non-person so that they can be free to kill it-just like you do. Am I making myself clear enough yet? You're really not fooling anybody anymore with your approach.

Intecon, at http://www.aboutabortions.com/

"'We cannot diminish the value of one category of human life—' 'without diminishing the value of all human life.'

I agree-The category of pregnant women must not be wrongly oppressed-women are persons, entitled to the same rights as others."

Also, the category of people still inside their mothers "must not be wrongly oppressed-" children in the womb are just as much persons as anyone else, and are "entitled to the same rights as others."

Do we see eye to eye on this yet?

Intecon, at http://www.aboutabortions.com/

Intecon

Abortion and the Conscience of the Nation

"RR<we cannot survive as a free nation when some men decide that others [pregnant women] are not fit>...to enjoy the same rights as all other persons".

Pregnant women already have the same rights as others. What we need to be concerned with here is that the rights of the child inside its mother are being denied so that it can be medically murdered.

"'Only, he says it much better than I ever could.'

And he's totally full of crap. where's that leave you??"

"'if you would like me to copy and paste to the forum his entire'Abortion and the Conscience of the Nation'; go ahead, insult me about this;'

Oooooooo!!!! is that supposed to be some big threat or something??-gracing the forum with the senile babblings of a pre-natal Alzheimer's victim??

'Ronald Reagan; a man I learned to respect, admire, and appreciate most,'

You don't hold American statesmen to a very high standard, do you??"

Ronald Reagan is obviously a man of much greater intellect and character than you are. His achievements include two times President of the United States, and two times Governor of California. Obviously a lot of people had a lot of respect and admiration for him.

Alzheimer's is a disease of old age, which many people eventually get. It doesn't mean they've had it all their lives, as you implied in your sick and unfeeling comment. The big threat was because I thought you'd have enough sense not to want to have it posted to the forum-obviously you didn't. So here it is for everybody to read and draw their own conclusions; and it's something everybody should read:

http://www.humanlifereview.com/reagan/reagan_conscience.html "The Human Life Review", 215 Lexington Avenue, 4th Floor, New York, NY 10016

"Ronald Reagan, while sitting as the fortieth president of the United States, sent us this article shortly after the tenth anniversary of Roe v. Wade; we printed it with pride in our Spring, 1983 issue, and reprint it now, after Roe's twentieth anniversary, just as proudly.

Abortion and the Conscience of the Nation

Ronald Reagan

The 10th anniversary of the Supreme Court decision in Roe v. Wade is a good time for us to pause and reflect. Our nationwide policy of abortion-on-demand through all nine months of pregnancy was neither voted for by our people nor enacted by our legislators—not a single state had such unrestricted abortion before the Supreme Court decreed it to be national policy in 1973. But the consequences of this judicial decision are now obvious: since 1973, more than 15 million unborn children have had their lives snuffed out by legalized abortions. That is over ten times the number of Americans lost in all our nation's wars.

Make no mistake, abortion-on-demand is not a right granted by the Constitution. No serious scholar, including one disposed to agree with the Court's result, has argued that the framers of the Constitution intended to create such a right. Shortly after the Roe v. Wade decision, Professor John Hart Ely, now Dean of Stanford Law School, wrote that the opinion "is not constitutional law and gives almost no sense of an obligation to try to be." Nowhere do the plain words of the Constitution even hint at a "right" so sweeping as to permit abortion up to the time the child is ready to be born. Yet that is what the Court ruled.

As an act of "raw judicial power" (to use Justice White's biting phrase), the decision by the seven-man majority in Roe v. Wade has so far been made to stick. But the Court's decision has by no means settled the debate. Instead, Roe v. Wade has become a continuing prod to the conscience of the nation.

Abortion concerns not just the unborn child, it concerns every one of us. The English poet, John Donne, wrote: "...any man's death diminishes me, because I am involved in mankind; and therefore never send to know for whom the bell tolls; it tolls for thee."

We cannot diminish the value of one category of human life—the unborn—without diminishing the value of all human life. Wesaw tragic proof of this truism last year when the Indiana courts allowed the starvation death of "Baby Doe" in Bloomington because the child had Down's Syndrome.

Many of our fellow citizens grieve over the loss of life that has followed Roe v. Wade. Margaret Heckler, soon after being nominated to head the largest department of our government, Health and Human Services, told an audience that she believed abortion to be the greatest moral crisis facing our country today. And the revered Mother Teresa, who works in the streets of Calcutta ministering to dying people in her world-famous mission of mercy, has said that "the greatest misery of our time is the generalized abortion of children."

Over the first two years of my Administration I have closely followed and assisted efforts in Congress to reverse the tide of abortion—efforts of Congressmen, Senators and citizens responding to an urgent moral crisis. Regrettably, I have also seen the massive efforts of those who, under the banner of "freedom of choice," have so far blocked every effort to reverse nationwide abortion-on-demand.

Despite the formidable obstacles before us, we must not lose heart. This is not the first time our country has been divided by a Supreme Court decision that denied the value of certain human lives. The Dred Scott decision of 1857 was not overturned in a day, or a year, or even a decade. At first, only a minority of Americans recognized and deplored the moral crisis brought about by denying the full humanity of our black brothers and sisters; but that minority persisted in their vision and finally prevailed. They did it by appealing to the hearts and minds of their countrymen, to the truth of human dignity under God. From their example, we know that respect for the sacred value of human life is too deeply engrained in the hearts of our people to remain forever suppressed. But the great majority of the American people have not yet made their voices heard, and we cannot expect them to—any more than the public voice arose against slavery—until the issue is clearly framed and presented.

What, then, is the real issue? I have often said that when we talk about abortion, we are talking about two lives—the life of the mother and the life of the unborn child. Why else do we call a pregnant woman a mother? I have also said that anyone who doesn't feel sure whether we are talking about a second human life should clearly give life the benefit of the doubt. If you don't know whether a body is alive or dead, you would never bury it. I think this consideration itself should be enough for all of us to insist on protecting the unborn.

The case against abortion does not rest here, however, for medical practice confirms at every step the correctness of these moral sensibilities. Modern medicine treats the unborn child as a patient. Medical pioneers have made great breakthroughs in treating the unborn—for genetic problems, vitamin deficiencies, irregular heart rhythms, and other medical conditions. Who can forget George Will's moving account of the little boy who underwent brain surgery six times during the nine weeks before he was born? Who is the patient if not that tiny unborn human being who can feel pain when he or she is approached by doctors who come to kill rather than to cure?

The real question today is not when human life begins, but, What is the value of human life? The abortionist who reassembles the arms and legs of a tiny baby to make sure all its parts have been torn from its mother's body can hardly doubt whether it is a human being. The real question for him and for all of us is whether that tiny human life has a God-given right to be protected by the law—the same right we have.

What more dramatic confirmation could we have of the real issue than the Baby Doe case in Bloomington, Indiana? The death of that tiny infant tore at the hearts of all Americans because the child was undeniably a live human being—one lying helpless before the eyes of the doctors and the eyes of the nation. The real issue for the courts was not whether Baby Doe was a human being. The real issue was whether to protect the life of a human being who had Down's Syndrome, who would probably be mentally handicapped, but who needed a routine surgical procedure to unblock his esophagus and allow him to eat. A doctor testified to the presiding judge that, even with his physical problem corrected, Baby Doe would have a "non-existent" possibility for "a minimally adequate quality of life"—in other words, that retardation was the equivalent of a crime deserving the death penalty. The judge let Baby Doe starve and die, and the Indiana Supreme Court sanctioned his decision.

Federal law does not allow federally-assisted hospitals to decide that Down's Syndrome infants are not worth treating, much less to decide to starve them to death. Accordingly, I have directed the Departments of Justice and HHS to apply civil rights regulations to protect handicapped newborns. All hospitals receiving federal funds must post notices which will clearly state that failure to feed handicapped babies is prohibited by federal law. The basic issue is whether to value and protect the lives of the handicapped, whether to recognize the sanctity of human life. This is the same basic issue that underlies the question of abortion.

The 1981 Senate hearings on the beginning of human life brought out the basic issue more clearly than ever before. The many medical and scientific witnesses who testified disagreed on many things, but not on the scientific evidence that the unborn child is alive, is a distinct individual, or is a member of the human species. They did disagree over the value question, whether to give value to a human life at its early and most vulnerable stages of existence.

Regrettably, we live at a time when some persons do not value all human life. They want to pick and choose which individuals have value. Some have said that only those individuals with "consciousness of self" are human beings. One such writer has followed this deadly logic and concluded that "shocking as it may seem, a newly born infant is not a human being."

A Nobel Prize winning scientist has suggested that if a handicapped child "were not declared fully human until three days after birth, then all parents could be allowed the choice." In other words, "quality control" to see if newly born human beings are up to snuff.

Obviously, some influential people want to deny that every human life has intrinsic, sacred worth. They insist that a member of the human race must have certain qualities before they accord him or her status as a "human being."

Events have borne out the editorial in a California medical journal which explained three years before Roe v. Wade that the social acceptance of abortion is a "defiance of the long-held Western ethic of intrinsic and equal value for every human life regardless of its stage, condition, or status."

Every legislator, every doctor, and every citizen needs to recognize that the real issue is whether to affirm and protect the sanctity of all human life, or to embrace a social ethic where some human lives are valued and others are not. As a nation, we must choose between the sanctity of life ethic and the "quality of life" ethic.

I have no trouble identifying the answer our nation has always given to this basic question, and the answer that I hope and pray it will give in the future. America was founded by men and women who shared a vision of the value of each and every individual. They stated this vision clearly from the very start in the Declaration of Independence, using words that every schoolboy and schoolgirl can recite:

We hold these truths to be self-evident, that all men are created equal, that they are endowed by their Creator with certain unalienable rights, that among these are life, liberty, and the pursuit of happiness.

We fought a terrible war to guarantee that one category of mankind—black people in America—could not be denied the inalienable rights with which their Creator endowed them. The great champion of the sanctity of all human life in that day, Abraham Lincoln, gave us his assessment of the Declaration's purpose. Speaking of the framers of that noble document, he said:

This was their majestic interpretation of the economy of the Universe. This was their lofty, and wise, and noble understanding of the justice of the Creator to His creatures. Yes, gentlemen, to all his creatures, to the whole great family of man. In their enlightened belief, nothing stamped with the divine image and likeness was sent into the world to be trodden on...They grasped not only the whole race of man then living, but they reached forward and seized upon the farthest posterity. They erected a beacon to guide their children and their children's children, and the countless myriads who should inhabit the earth in other ages.

He warned also of the danger we would face if we closed our eyes to the value of life in any category of human beings:

I should like to know if taking this old Declaration of Independence, which declares that all men are equal upon principle and making exceptions to it where will it stop. If one man says it does not mean a Negro, why not another say it does not mean some other man?

When Congressman John A. Bingham of Ohio drafted the Fourteenth Amendment to guarantee the rights of life, liberty, and property to all human beings, he explained that all are "entitled to the protection of American law, because its divine spirit of equality declares that all men are created equal." He said the right guaranteed by the amendment would therefore apply to "any human being." Justice William Brennan, writing in another case decided only the year before Roe v. Wade, referred to our society as one that "strongly affirms the sanctity of life."

Another William Brennan—not the Justice—has reminded us of the terrible consequences that can follow when a nation rejects the sanctity of life ethic:

The cultural environment for a human holocaust is present whenever any society can be misled into defining individuals as less than human and therefore devoid of value and respect.

As a nation today, we have not rejected the sanctity of human life. The American people have not had an opportunity to express their view on the sanctity of human life in the unborn. I am convinced that Americans do not want to play God with the value of human life. It is not for us to decide who is worthy to live and who is not. Even the Supreme Court's opinion in Roe v. Wade did not explicitly reject the traditional American idea of intrinsic worth and value in all human life; it simply dodged this issue.

The Congress has before it several measures that would enable our people to reaffirm the sanctity of human life, even the smallest and the youngest and the most defenseless. The Human Life Bill expressly recognizes the unborn as human beings and accordingly protects them as persons under our Constitution. This bill, first introduced by Senator Jesse Helms, provided the vehicle for the Senate hearings in 1981 which contributed so much to our understanding of the real issue of abortion.

The Respect Human Life Act, just introduced in the 98th Congress, states in its first section that the policy of the United States is "to protect innocent life, both before and after birth." This bill, sponsored by Congressman Henry Hyde and Senator Roger Jepsen, prohibits the federal government from performing abortions or assisting those who do so, except to save the life of the mother. It also addresses the pressing issue of infanticide which, as we have seen, flows inevitably from permissive abortion as another step in the denial of the inviolability of innocent human life.

I have endorsed each of these measures, as well as the more difficult route of constitutional amendment, and I will give these initiatives my full support. Each of them, in different ways, attempts to reverse the tragic policy of abortion-on-demand imposed by the Supreme Court ten years ago. Each of them is a decisive way to affirm the sanctity of human life.

We must all educate ourselves to the reality of the horrors taking place. Doctors today know that unborn children can feel a touch within the womb and that they respond to pain. But how many Americans are aware that abortion techniques are allowed today, in all 50 states, that burn the skin of a baby with a salt solution, in an agonizing death that can last for hours?

Another example: two years ago, the Philadelphia Inquirer ran a Sunday special supplement on "The Dreaded Complication." The "dreaded complication" referred to in the article-the complication feared by doctors who perform abortions-is the survival of the child despite all the painful attacks during the abortion procedure. Some unborn children do survive the late-term abortions the Supreme Court has made legal. Is there any question that these victims of abortion deserve our attention and protection? Is there any question that those who don't survive were living human beings before they were killed?

Late-term abortions, especially when the baby survives, but is then killed by starvation, neglect, or suffocation, show once again the link between abortion and infanticide. The time to stop both is now. As my Administration acts to stop infanticide, we will be fully aware of the real issue that underlies the death of babies before and soon after birth.

Our society has, fortunately, become sensitive to the rights and special needs of the handicapped, but I am shocked that physical or mental handicaps of newborns are still used to justify their extinction. This Administration has a Surgeon General, Dr. C. Everett Koop, who has done perhaps more than any other American for handicapped children, by pioneering surgical techniques to help them, by speaking out on the value of their lives, and by working with them in the context of loving families. You will not find his former patients advocating the so-called "quality-of-life" ethic.

I know that when the true issue of infanticide is placed before the American people, with all the facts openly aired, we will have no trouble deciding that a mentally or physically handicapped baby has the same intrinsic worth and right to life as the rest of us. As the New Jersey Supreme Court said two decades ago, in a decision upholding the sanctity of human life, "a child need not be perfect to have a worthwhile life."

Whether we are talking about pain suffered by unborn children, or about late-term abortions, or about infanticide, we inevitably focus on the humanity of the unborn child. Each of these issues is a potential rallying point for the sanctity of life ethic. Once we as a nation rally around any one of these issues to affirm the sanctity of life, we will see the importance of affirming this principle across the board.

Malcolm Muggeridge, the English writer, goes right to the heart of the matter: "Either life is always and in all circumstances sacred, or intrinsically of no account; it is inconceivable that it should be in some cases the one, and in some the other." The sanctity of innocent human life is a principle that Congress should proclaim at every opportunity.

It is possible that the Supreme Court itself may overturn its abortion rulings. We need only recall that in Brown v. Board of Education the court reversed its own earlier "separate-but-equal" decision. I believe if the Supreme Court took another look at Roe v. Wade, and considered the real issue between the sanctity of life ethic and the quality of life ethic, it would change its mind once again.

As we continue to work to overturn Roe v. Wade, we must also continue to lay the groundwork for a society in which abortion is not the accepted answer to unwanted pregnancy. Pro-life people have already taken heroic steps, often at great personal sacrifice, to provide for unwed mothers. I recently spoke about a young pregnant woman named Victoria, who said, "In this society we save whales, we save timber wolves and bald eagles and Coke bottles. Yet, everyone wanted me to throw away my baby." She has been helped by Save-a-Life, a group in Dallas, which provides a way for unwed mothers to preserve the human life within them when they might otherwise be tempted to resort to abortion. I think also of House of His Creation in Catesville, Pennsylvania, where a loving couple has taken in almost 200 young women in the past ten years. They have seen, as a fact of life, that the girls are not better off having abortions than saving their babies. I am also reminded of the remarkable Rossow family of Ellington, Connecticut, who have opened their hearts and their home to nine handicapped adopted and foster children.

The Adolescent Family Life Program, adopted by Congress at the request of Senator Jeremiah Denton, has opened new opportunities for unwed mothers to give their children life. We should not rest until our entire society echoes the tone of John Powell in the dedication of his book, Abortion: The Silent Holocaust, a dedication to every woman carrying an unwanted child: "Please believe that you are not alone. There are many of us that truly love you, who want to stand at your side, and help in any way we can." And we can echo the always-practical woman of faith, Mother Teresa, when she says, "If you don't want the little child, that unborn child, give him to me." We have so many families in America seeking to adopt children that the slogan "every child a wanted child" is now the emptiest of all reasons to tolerate abortion.

I have often said we need to join in prayer to bring protection to the unborn. Prayer and action are needed to uphold the sanctity of human life. I believe it will not be possible to accomplish our work, the work of saving lives, "without being a soul of prayer." The famous British Member of Parliament, William Wilberforce, prayed with his small group of influential friends, the "Clapham Sect," for decades to see an end to slavery in the British empire. Wilberforce led that struggle in Parliament, unflaggingly, because he believed in the sanctity of human life. He saw the fulfillment of his impossible dream when Parliament outlawed slavery just before his death.

Let his faith and perseverance be our guide. We will never recognize the true value of our own lives until we affirm the value in the life of others, a value of which Malcolm Muggeridge says:…however low it flickers or fiercely burns, it is still a Divine flame which no man dare presume to put out, be his motives ever so humane and enlightened."

Abraham Lincoln recognized that we could not survive as a free land when some men could decide that others were not fit to be free and should therefore be slaves. Likewise, we cannot survive as a free nation when some men decide that others are not fit to live and should be abandoned to abortion or infanticide. My Administration is dedicated to the preservation of America as a free land, and there is no cause more important for preserving that freedom than affirming the transcendent right to life of all human beings, the right without which no other rights have any meaning."

Published by: The Human Life Foundation, Inc.
215 Lexington Avenue, New York, New York 10016

"And he's totally full of crap. where's that leave you?? You don't hold American statesmen to a very high standard, do you??"

A much more erudite document than you ever could have produced. Where does that leave you? Probably unable to appreciate the man's greatness.

Intecon, at web site http://www.aboutabortions.com/

"'And as soon as the language in the Constitution is strictly adhered to'…then the abortion question will be settled once and for all in favor of pro-choice, just as it is now."

504

I don't think anybody is against choice. A lot of people are against what you mean by choice, which is the right to choose to have a child killed. That violates their right to choose to go on living.

This is the part of the Constitution that needs to be adhered to, which protects the child's right to live:

"...nor shall any State deprive any person of life...nor deny to any person... equal protection of the laws", which both the Roe v Wade and Stenberg v Carhart decisions violated.

President Reagan pointed out the intent of the Congressman who drafted the 14th Amendment.

Plus, the Declaration of Independence further clarifies the intent of the Founders:

"...certain unalienable Rights, that among these are Life".

So your imagination and historical revisionism about the intent and content of the Constitution doesn't hold water.

Intecon, at http://www.aboutabortions.com/

Z/E/F's and Slavery

"This equates exactly with the ANTI-CHOICE attitude towards pregnant women, that women may be unjustly denied rights to which they are entitled."

B.S., a majority of women are opposed to abortion, a large percent of women head anti-abortion organizations, many leading feminists have opposed abortion, and it just so happens that the traditional families that oppose abortion include women. The women in my family outnumber the men and certainly wouldn't claim that I was denying them rights. Are you trying to tell us that all these women are for oppressing women? That would mean that they were for being oppressed themselves.

Intecon, at web site: http://www.aboutabortions.com/

"'Besides, I was replying to a claim that you made about women being treated as sub-humans'

Which is exactly the gross injustice that anti-choicers are trying to perpetrate against pregnant women. It's undeniable-your goal is to wrongly oppress pregnant women."

A majority of women oppose abortion, a majority of pro-life leaders are women, prominent feminists throughout history have opposed abortion, and a majority in this forum who debate for the prolife cause are women.

Knowing this, no rational person without a hidden agenda would believe that these women are struggling to have themselves oppressed. Plus anyone who's a member of our society has only to look around them to see that it's total nonsense. So it's really quite deniable that the goal of pro-lifers is to oppress women. Again, obviously, you're dead wrong, and it's plain for everybody to see. You should be embarrassed to even make such a ridiculous and unfounded claim.

Intecon, at http://www.aboutabortions.com/

"'Well, polls show 80% of the population think partial-birth abortion is infanticide.'

This is a totally meaningless statement-95% of the population can call the z/e/f a chocolate cream pie if they want-this does not make it so. An infant is a person-therefore aborting a fetus cannot, by definition, be infanticide; since, as we all, know, the z/e/f is not a person."

506

Maybe it is 95% by now-because it's difficult to imagine anyone, except for you, believing that partial-birth abortion is not infanticide, once the procedure has been explained to them.

And I don't think poll results, that strongly against something, can be dismissed as meaningless. You just want to ignore everything that doesn't support your position.

About the chocolate cream pie-I've only heard two people use the terminology z/e/f, and they may be the same person.

You're right that an infant is a person-that's why almost everybody thinks partial-birth abortion, or killing a child when it is clearly outside the mother, except for its head, is infanticide.

I'll remind you, again, that because you continue to ignore, or even mention, the following web site, that you lost the debate on personhood a long time ago. I understand it's impossible for you to defend your position when scientific facts are presented, and that's why you just skip over them, and rely on slogans and language manipulation instead. Science shows us that a child does exist inside the mother, but nobody needs to really dig into the data, because the child can be seen clearly through an ultrasound. However, I'll be glad to recite some of the scientific data if you would like for me to.

On the other hand, no such thing ever exists that is a z/e/f. It's only a figment of your imagination. It has to be one or the other of those things it is supposed to be an abbreviation for; it can't be all those things at the same time. Here's that link, again:

http://www.babycenter.com/general/3284.html?CP_bid=

"'she means she believes that a woman has the right to choose to have her child killed.'

Meaningless hyperbole. nobody favors killing born children, do they?? Abortion does not involve killing born children, so this is irrelevant."

Not meaningless. Not hyperbole. Not irrelevant. The child inside the mother is just as much a person as the child outside the mother. You seem to think that you can convince me that the child inside the mother is not a child, but a minute later becomes a child when it appears outside the mother. You will never convince me of that; you're wasting your time trying. Abortion does involve killing children, not possibly guilty of any crime. And on a grand scale-40,000,000 so far, just in this country alone, just since Roe v Wade.

And you're not current on the thinking in your circle, or maybe you just prefer to not mention that the people you work with believe a woman who goes in for an abortion is entitled to a dead child-or should have a certain period of time to make up her mind-after, or whether or not, the child is "born"; as you define it. Well, you can stop hoping for that, because there is a bill moving through the Congress, as we speak, that will put an end to that kind of thinking; and I predict it will pass.

If you don't believe that look at the following picture. It's not a picture of a dead baby; it's a picture of a live baby-inside its mother!

http://www.babycenter.com/general/3284.html?CP_bid=

Intecon, at: http://www.aboutabortions.com/

"'I'm certainly not against someone receiving medical treatment.'

Then you have no objection to a woman aborting an unwanted pregnancy??"

She's not receiving medical treatment for an illness. Pregnancy is not an illness. She's having another person-her child-murdered. It's the unpleasant truth. I realize that you would rather I called it something different-like abortion. But most people would agree with my murder statement; as I just proved with the poll in the preceding post. I believe that it also needs to be said, instead of just being polite so as to not hurt anyone's feelings; so that we can go about putting an end to it, instead of ignoring it as you would prefer.

Intecon, at: http://www.aboutabortions.com/

"'You don't have to buy your right to life; it exists just because you exist.'

Once you exist as a person-the z/e/f is not a person

'You don't have to buy your liberty; you have it just because you're an American.'

Once you are born, and are considered a person. the z/e/f is not a person"

As I just pointed out, there is no such thing as a z/e/f. It's the shorthand you use so that you can say a z/e/f is not a person.

Tell me, then, what is this, you are so steadfastly ignoring:

http://www.babycenter.com/general/3284.html?CP_bid=

I'll tell you what it is, it's a person inside a person, and you can see it with your own two eyes; two separate people, not one; that which you deny exists. You can not define it into non-existence, because the reality that everyone can see for themselves is that it does exist.

Intecon, at http://www.aboutabortions.com/

"'But the Constitution says nothing about a right to medical attention:'

But you have every right to life and liberty, therefore you and society may take measures to preserve these. Medical treatment is undeniably applicable to protection of life and liberty."

Certainly society takes measures to provide medical treatment. But it is not guaranteed by the Constitution, and you can not go from that to say you have a constitutional right to take someone else's life, which you do in abortion. Abortion is not even a form of medical treatment-it's a form of murder.

Intecon, at: http://www.aboutabortions.com/

"'<Abortion is not medical treatment because I don't want it to be>' is hardly a persuasive argument against a woman's right to receive medical treatment."

It's not anything I said, so I don't know why you put it in <>.
It's something else you made up. I don't think it's a good argument either; and that's why I never said it.

But as this discussion develops, it helps me see through things that I might have accepted before without questioning them. And today I've seen that abortion is not a medical treatment for any of a woman's health conditions-it's a guy with a vacuum, or a knife, who might be a doctor, killing somebody else, plain and simple. Perhaps we should coin a term here: Medical Murder.

Intecon, at: http://www.aboutabortions.com/

"Alas, abortion is legal. No 'argument' is necessary."

Alas, it won't be forever. And, I hope, not for too much longer. Just because something is legal, doesn't make it right. There are things being done to change that. Roe v Wade is no more a correct decision than Dred Scott. Don't you agree?

Intecon, At; http://www.aboutabortions.com/

"'instead of being treated as sub-humans, and denied their rights under the Constitution-Amendment XIV, Section 1-and then exterminated.'

What a ridiculous statement!!-born children are persons, and are protected under the constitution and its laws."

What a ridiculous statement. Children are just as much persons whether they are inside or outside the mother. Everybody should be able to understand that-even you. And as soon as the language in the Constitution is strictly adhered to, they will be. Besides, I was replying to a claim that you made about women "being treated as sub-humans", which obviously wasn't true. Look at this:

http://www.babycenter.com/general/3284.html?CP_bid=

Intecon, at: http://www.aboutabortions.com/

"'Just because a child is still inside its mother doesn't make it any less a child.'

but it makes it a non-person in the eyes of society and its laws-and rightfully so."

Wrongly so. What is important here is the reality, not what people think. The reality is that a child inside its mother is just as much a person there as it is a minute later when it's outside. And most people realize that, or polls wouldn't show that a majority of people believe abortion is murder. You think that by simply defining it as a non-person you can make its extermination acceptable. It's not acceptable, and I'm not the only one saying that-I just happen to be a proxy today for a lot of people who are probably out doing other things; and, a proxy for, as you like to say, the "unborn"-a volunteer, a soldier, a marine, in the army of the unborn; my computer is my weapon, and I don't intend to give up any more than we did on Iwo Jima, or Guadalcanal, or at the Chosen Reservoir; because we have something here in America worth fighting for, worth preserving.

Intecon, at: http://www.aboutabortions.com/

"'that children are born, or 'come into existence',…when a woman becomes pregnant'

Unsupported opinion-and of course, you run aground on the shoals of the pesky mole pregnancy-it's a product of conception-is it a person?-a BORN person?"

That's strange, I thought I presented a lot of support for it. I guess you didn't get it. But like I said before, you've never agreed with anything I've said-so I shouldn't expect you to agree with a new concept like that.

Your mole pregnancy theory never got off the ground. I guess you didn't even notice that. It's not pesky, and it's not something anybody should ever run aground on again-whose followed this debate. The mole pregnancy isn't really a pregnancy at all, in terms of conception. It's a genetic error-a mole. It never even has the potential for human life. However, I find it very interesting that you called it a product of conception, because conception implies that a human being is conceived, and it seems that you understand that process after all. Thanks; finally a concession!

Intecon, at: http://www.aboutabortions.com/

"From Webster's New collegiate:

Unborn-not yet brought into life

(Human) Being-a LIVING person"

From Webster's New collegiate:

"unborn: existing without birth"

"born 1 a: brought into existence"

There is no "human being" in Webster's. Nor would I expect there to be-it's two words. Here's what is in Webster's:

"human: having human form or attributes"

Say, this all sounds very familiar. Do you remember anything that went before? Have you learned anything, or progressed at all?

Intecon, at http://www.aboutabortions.com/

"Obviously, the unborn does not qualify as a person, and as such, does not have any rights."

But that's what I just explained to you! A child in the womb is a person, and does have rights. Look at this-see with your own two eyes!

http://www.babycenter.com/general/3284.html?CP_bid=

Isn't life wonderful! We should all be so grateful to be blessed with it-ours and our children's! Can't you feel the excitement of a "newborn" about to arrive!

Intecon, at http://www.aboutabortions.com/

"'and you are violating that person's rights; which equates with your 'oppression of Born children'; when you deny that born child's right to live by killing him.'

Oh, please-this is hopelessly garbled. The unborn are not persons-they are specifically excluded in the constitution. A mother's aborting an unwanted pregnancy in no way affects a born being, a person."

It just seems garbled now! I know you can get it if you just keep trying-then we can have some really great discussions-instead of just opposing everything each of us says! I think I'm getting the missionary fervor!

And, oh, by the way, children in the womb are included in the Constitution, because they are definitely persons, just like this one!

http://www.babycenter.com/general/3284.html?CP_bid=

Intecon, at http://www.aboutabortions.com/!

"'Gregor Mendel had been dead for many years before they were able to understand that his work formed the basis for modern day genetics;'

I'm afraid your 'wishful thinking' gibberish is not remotely of the same caliber and quality as the good monk's worthy contributions."

Ya, ain't it the truth. Anybody who can turn peas into genetic theory is really special. I've gotta get around to reading that book so I can find out how he did it. Can you imagine that: peas form the whole basis for today's most modern theories of genetics But I am encouraged to hear that you've heard of Gregor-maybe there's hope for you after all!

And I'd like to talk to you sometime about some of the most recent genetic discoveries-that support the assertion that a person begins to exist the moment a woman becomes pregnant.

But not now.

Intecon, at http://www.aboutabortions.com/

"the z/e/f is not a person, it is not protected by the Constitution. The argument is thus, convincingly, made."

I would imagine that by now you're the only one convinced of that; except that I don't believe that you believe it either-other than to define it (him or her) out of existence so that you can kill it (him or her), legally. However, I do understand that you can make that statement without really lying, in a technical sense, because no such thing as a z/e/f ever exists, or ever could.

This is probably a good place to explain this further to anyone else who may be following this discussion, because I assume that Heck01 already understands it:

First of all, to really get down to basics, "z" stands for zygote, "e" stands for embryo, and "f" stands for fetus in Heck01's universe; even though some stages are missing.

No such thing as a z/e/f can ever exist in one person at one time, because the terms are, by definition, mutually exclusive; and they don't even represent the complete developmental cycle that a person goes through inside the mother. Said another way, you can have a "z" or "e" or "f", but you can never have a "z" and "e" and "f" in one person, at one time. This is an important distinction, and whoever devised this strategy understands that: that's why they keep using the "z/e/f/" terminology. It's also a way to keep from having to discuss the scientific detail, facts, and data, of each stage in a child's development; because you can't discuss the facts about something that doesn't exist. And that's what the pro-abortionists want to avoid at all costs; discussing the medical facts about a child's development inside the mother. Instead they want to define it out of existence by saying it's not a person. I must have posted the following link a dozen times by now:

http://www.babycenter.com/general/3284.html?CP_bid=

and Heck01 has never discussed it himself. If you only read Heck01's posts you would probably never even guess what had been posted. Actually, Heck01 has never discussed any scientific facts about abortion at all; and that can probably be said for the other abortionists on this forum, too; although I haven't been trying to follow all the other discussions going on at the same time-I seem to have trouble keeping up even without doing that. They just want to say that the child doesn't become a person until it is "born", without having to give any scientific analysis or evidence. They don't want to discuss the scientific facts about when human life begins, because they want to be able to kill at all levels. If a person is not a person until they say it is then they can even kill after the child is born; by saying, it's not really a person until it can rollover, or crawl, or walk, or talk, or any other characteristics they want to include before they will define somebody as a person. Will I find a discussion by Heck01 about this web page further down in the posts:

http://www.babycenter.com/general/3284.html?CP_bid=

I doubt it, because it is almost impossible to discuss it and claim it's not a person without looking incredibly stupid. Plus, then you would have to discuss the medical facts that are there, too.

It's not a dead baby. It's a picture of a child inside its mother. How very radical is the view that it's alright to kill it. And it's not a pro-life site. The last time I checked it was owned by a large pharmaceutical/medical products company. Before being acquired, it won two Webby Awards; one in 1998, and one in 1999. I think Heck01 will look more and more foolish by avoiding to discuss any facts about the development of the child inside its mother. Let's take a vote. Everybody click on the following link:

http://www.babycenter.com/general/3284.html?CP_bid=

then post a vote; yes it is a person, or no it's not a person; and a short explanation of whether you think this child is a person. Then you can battle it out as to who's right, or wait until I come along in a couple of weeks to analyze the results.

Right Steen?

Flashback:

"'you've lost that point, of whether a child is a person, because you have been unable to come up with any defense against the proof at web site:'

LOL!! that is too funny-I've utterly demolished your premise and you've already conceded that the z/e/f is not a person. Additionally, your site provides nothing even resembling proof that the z/e/f is a person. Everyone knows that it isn't, as we've already established."

You have? I have? If so, you're probably the only one that still believes that, despite any supporting posts that may follow from your partners in crime. Haven't you figured out yet that you're losing this debate? It takes more than a victory statement, you know. If you want to continue to debate, let's move on to some new topic, instead of you making up conclusions about what's taken place.

"person-an individual entity, or (connected entities), physically separate from and biologically independent of the host-mother, capable of sentience, autonomy, homeostasis and independent existence.

The unborn z/e/f obviously does not exhibit these characteristics, therefore, can not be regarded as a person."

"host-mother"? Did you get that out of Marx, or what. You never did explain where you got that definition from. It looks like somebody just made it up to suit their purposes-killing children. Even then it has holes in it. A child in the womb is an individual entity-which would be evident if you went to that link I posted. A child in the womb is physically separate-which would be evident if you went to that link I posted. I suppose you're referring to the umbilical cord, which is attached to the placenta, when you say biologically independent. Independent existence certainly can't be a required condition, unless you want to still be able to kill the child after it is "born"; because the child is not going to be able to live independently for a long time after you take it home from the hospital. As for sentience, the child is certainly conscious and capable of feeling while it is still in the womb. Would you like to discuss the scientific findings on this? And although it doesn't have much room in the womb to move around, it certainly does do so, so that covers homeostasis. We've already covered autonomy. So it sounds like you need to come up with a new definition.

Doesn't it bother you at all that you're killing a fellow human being when you do an abortion? Don't B.S. me, you know. Have you no conscience?

Intecon, at web site http://www.aboutabortions.com/

"This has no application whatsoever to abortion, however, because, as has been shown over and over-the z/e/f is not 'someone', or 'someone else', it's not a person."

No such thing as a z/e/f ever has existed, or ever will. It can be a "z" or an "e" or a "f", but it can never be all those things at the same time. Which suits your purpose, because you don't want to discuss an "f" separately, so you stick to something that doesn't exist. However, a child does exist inside it's mother, as demonstrated at the web page below, which so far you have refused to discuss, or even acknowledge:

http://www.babycenter.com/general/3284.html?CP_bid=

The above child, inside its mother, is obviously a person. A person due the same full rights as any other person. Being inside the mother instead of outside the mother doesn't make it a nonperson. Your whole purpose in trying to say it's not a person is to deprive the child of its rights so that you can kill it for the convenience of the parents and the profit of the abortion industry who you are employed by. First they make a profit off doing the abortion, and then they make money by cutting the child up and selling any undamaged pieces. For example, there is a set price for a brain, a liver, a spleen, and so on. I've seen several price lists-it's generally accepted that this goes on. You denying it won't change it. It's a person that's being aborted-not a z/e/f that never exists.

Intecon, at http://www.aboutabortions.com/

"'But nowhere does the constitution give you the right to kill someone else;'

Actually it does-a person may not be denied life or liberty without due process-if your life/liberty is threatened you may be within your rights to kill to protect it."

Well, I guess your statement, made above, could be used to justify attacking abortion clinics and abortion doctors. Is that what you had in mind, or did you have something else in mind? Somebody else to kill?

Intecon

"Here we go again, more nonsense:

<a z/e/f is a person because I think it should be>

unsupported personal opinion-Just as meaningless now as the last 10 times..."

Well, you've said it so many times, repeated it so many times by rote, without actually bothering to think about what you were saying, that you finally got it turned around to where it's correctly stated.

Intecon, at http://www.aboutabortions.com/

"'The child inside the mother is just as much a person as the child outside the mother.'

Nope-and simply repeating this endlessly will not make it so. The unborn are excluded from protection as persons by the US Constitution."

Still going with the "inside/outside" theory of human existence, I see. Or perhaps we could call it the popcorn theory. Which constitution are you talking about? It's certainly not in the U.S. Constitution. You might at least give me a hint about where to look.

Here's a related opinion from my "Replies to Comments" web page:

"I am only thirteen years old and i understand the severity of abortion. I personally think it is murder. The way i see it is you made the baby you should take responsibility for it. there are exceptions, rape, incess, etc. thank you for your time and i hope my comment was worthwhile and has made a difference to someone out there" mallory

"Abortion is wrong. The laws should ban it totally unless you are raped. That is the only case you can get an abortion and you could still have it and give it up for adoption." Rachel

Savvy kids.

Here's a quote from my main page:

"My Silent Scream: My silent scream, My plea for life. This world unseen Sentences me to die. You say 'it's my body...It's my choice.' But I have no voice! So cry for me. And pray for me. Because humanity Has forgotten me. The love I have Is pure and true. This beating heart Cries out to you. You ignore my cries. You ignore the truth. Please God forgive them For they know not what they do." Joel Messener, 16. Joel understands, do you?

Even children understand.

"By article VI, which is adopted by all states, that's the supreme law of the land. You don't like it?? amend the constitution..."

Article VI says: "All Debts contracted and Engagements entered into, before the Adoption of this Constitution, shall be as valid against the United States under this Constitution, as under the Confederation". Say, are we talking about the same constitution? I think you'd better change your sources.

So here's that web site again so you can see for yourself what's going on:

http://www.babycenter.com/general/3284.html?CP_bid=

Or are you going to continue to say "I'm putting my hands over my eyes and I'm not even going to look or even discuss it, so there?
Like the three little monkeys-see no evil, hear no evil, speak no evil?"

Intecon, at web site:

http://www.aboutabortions.com/

Intecon

"'Look at this:

http://www.babycenter.com/general/3284.html?CP_bid='

I have-once it's born, it will be a person.;)"

Finally! That demolishes the popcorn theory of human development!
Or would you like to pursue that further?

Well, it certainly looks like a person to me. I remember when my wife was
pregnant with our first child, the doctor wanted to induce it on Friday so he
would not have to come in on the weekend. I called him personally and said
"no way"! But since he wasn't an abortion doctor, I assume he thought she
could live outside my wife. As a matter of fact I've heard of babies of just 24
weeks gestation who survived even though they had to be delivered
prematurely. Or was it 21 weeks? What's the earliest you've heard? What do
you think is different about this child that makes him non-human, other than
being inside instead of outside-an argument I don't have much patience with. I
know he's not breathing on his own, but he'll start doing so once he (or she)
pops out.
What else is there?

Intecon, at http://www.aboutabortions.com/

"it's a picture of a z/e/f, a potential person-inside its mother. (potential
actuated at birth.)"

So that allows you to kill it. I'm sorry, my two eyes do not deceive me-that's a
person. To say otherwise is totally absurd. It's your inside/outside theory of
humanity again; or we should call it inside-out, because that's pretty much
what you're trying to do to make it make sense. Where is the medical and
scientific evidence to support your contention? It doesn't exist.

Intecon, at web site http://www.aboutabortions.com/

"'What is important here is the reality, not what people think.'

Oh-so you are self-appointed determiner of reality!!! LOL!!!"

The reality is that a child inside its mother is just as much a person there as it
is a minute later when it's outside.

This is reality:

http://www.babycenter.com/general/3284.html?CP_bid=

Yours is a make believe world, a house of cards. A fantasy world created by the abortion industry to keep the dollars rolling in.

Intecon, at http://www.aboutabortions.com/

Intecon, at http://www.aboutabortions.com/

"If you would deny a woman the right of reproductive choice-then you are most certainly against her right to choose!!"

Hey, I'm not against your "right of reproductive choice"! Reproduce all you want to.

"What happens in a woman's womb is her own business-not yours, mine or anyone else's."

I agree. Everyone should keep hands off-including abortionists.

"'We're anti-infanticide.'

So am I, and every other pro-choicer I know. infants are born-what has this to do with a woman's undeniable right to abort??"

Well, polls show 80% of the population think partial-birth abortion is infanticide. That's when a baby, being delivered, is turned around so that it comes out feet first. Then, with just it's head still inside the mother, a sharp instrument is used to punch a hole at the base of it's skull, a hose is attached to the opening, and its brains are sucked out. So I'm glad to hear that at least you're against partial-birth abortion.

Also, a lot of people deny that a woman has a right to abort. So I guess it is "deniable", after all.

Also, some of us think that when a woman says she is "pro-choice", she means she believes that a woman has the right to choose to have her child killed.

Intecon, at web site: http://www.aboutabortions.com/

"PRO-CHOICE, AMERICA'S CHOICE, THE ONLY CHOICE!"

Translation: PRO-INFANTICIDE, THE CHOICE OF PLANNED PARENTHOOD AND THE RADICAL LEFT, THEIR ONLY CHOICE, AND NO CONCESSIONS!

Intecon, at http://www.aboutabortions.com/

"You're not right about anything-you're just sanctimoniuos and intolerant, which guarantees that you turn people off to your point of view-"

I don't know how much more sanctimonious a person can be than to say "You're not right about anything", as you just did. As usual, you're guilty of what you accuse others of.

Perhaps you've forgotten this is the pro-life forum. I'm pretty sure I'm not turning off the pro-lifers, because I know we share a lot of the same beliefs. I just happen to be doing the grunt work of dealing with you because nobody else can stand or tolerate you. I certainly hope people appreciate it. If you want to turn people on to your view, high-tail it over to the pro-abortion forum where I assume you'll be more appreciated.

Intecon, at http://www.aboutabortions.com/

"These are the facts-learn to love them and live with them-it's how it is, and will always be:

a person has the right to life and liberty, and with it the right to provide for and protect his/her health."

I won't quarrel with that so long as it includes all people and not just certain groups; for example, it should definitely include the child inside it's mother, irregardless of age, size, or physical positioning. And so long as it's clearly a health problem, rather than killing another person.

Intecon, at http://www.aboutabortions.com/

"While your ranting and raving away, spewing forth your unsupported personal opinions, how about some answers:"

I've presented a plethora of evidence and facts to support my positions. You've come up with zero, zip, because you have nothing to support the arguments you've chosen to advance.

"A pregnant woman is a person, by what justification do you deny her rights to which she is entitled??"

I don't deny rights to a woman to which she is entitled, but that doesn't include killing somebody else. That she's not entitled to.

"A z/e/f is not a person. by what justification do you grant it fictitious rights that would supersede the real rights of the mother, who is undeniably, a person??"

A z/e/f is a fictitious creation of somebody's imagination. Nothing, or nobody, can be all those things concurrently.

"What is it about pregnancy that reduces a woman to sub-person, sub-citizen status??"

Like I've said before, I have no idea why you feel this way about women, or why you want to kill their children. Like Birthright says: "It is the right of every pregnant woman to give birth, and the right of every child to be born." I still think it's imperative that you see a psychiatrist, rather than continuing to repeatedly spew forth this rote vituperation.

Intecon, at web sit http://www.aboutabortions.com/

From: alegria (JFISHER60) Jul-16 10:29 pm
To: INTECON (518 of 1162) 2012.518 in reply to 2012.516

"Nearly all injustices stem from one evil: the blatant disregard for the value of human life. This evil acts using human beings as agents, infecting them with the belief that it is acceptable to degrade or destroy another human being in order to enhance their own condition. From it surges discrimination, hatred, and slaughter—the very elements that are responsible for the most inhumane of acts. American slavery was a prime example of this evil at work. Human beings were enslaved, tortured, and killed at the hands of those who profited from their pain and anguish. However, after time and a war, society eliminated this horror of history—but the evil from which slavery was born lives on. It lives on in the hearts and the minds of many American people, where there remains the mentality that it is appropriate to destroy another human for the well-being of the self. Now, however, the target is the unborn child. The political, societal, and moral parallels of the inhumanities of abortion and slavery are unmistakable and direct; yet, even though slavery rains down on present day society as being an indisputable crime against mankind, abortion exists today in the exact circumstances as did slavery. The very same mentality that allowed for slavery in the past allows for abortion in the present. The evil and destructive characteristics of American slavery are born again in abortion; thus, to correct society and to save millions of unborn children, abortion must be abolished.

Both slavery and abortion exist in cultures that do not appreciate the value of human life. Today, it is commonplace for people to deem acceptable the action of hurting fellow humans in order to better their own condition. Any society that not only allows for but even encourages a woman to end the life of her unborn child so that her own life may be better is a society that does not value human life. It is a culture that inappropriately acts with the belief that mothers and children cannot coexist; thus, it is a culture that pits mothers against their own children. In a society where this concept runs rampant, the most natural relationship, that of mother and child, is defiled and destroyed. This condition exists because society stresses selfishness over selflessness. In criticism of American society and the problem of abortion, Mother Teresa noted that 'it is a poverty to decide that a child must die so that you may live as you wish' and that 'any country that accepts abortion, is not teaching its people to love, but to use any violence to get what it wants.' Never has the truth of the matter been stated so clearly. However, the truth of the injustice of the whole situation is revealed vividly through a parallel to slavery. The culture that allowed for slavery did not value human life. Humans were enslaved and tortured so that their tormentors could reap the benefits of their labor and pain. Although the actual crimes against the slaves were different from the current crimes against unborn children, the mentality that allows for each is the same. Just like abortion terminates the natural relationship between mother and child, slavery terminated the natural relationship of brotherhood and sisterhood between human beings. In both situations, the victimizer damages or destroys the victim so that he or she may live better. Both slavery and abortion stem from the same selfish principle.

The final parallel to be drawn here is that concerning legality, showing how the law-based elements in both slavery and abortion consist of similarities that are entirely uncanny. The primary legal parallels exist in the form of landmark Supreme Court decisions. In slavery, a decision was made, Dred Scott v. Sandford, which clarified that slaves were not to be considered United States citizens and were, in fact, protected property of their owners. Regarding this decision, Lincoln remarked, 'I believe the decision was improperly made, and I go for reversing it.' Of course, this decision was indeed overturned by the Thirteenth Amendment. In abortion, too, there has been a legal decision made in Roe v. Wade that does the very same as Dred Scott v. Sanford. Roe v. Wade denied the right to citizenship and even personhood to unborn children, claiming that they are only 'potential life' and thus subservient to their mothers. In both institutions, slavery and abortion, legal decisions were made that denied citizenship and natural rights to humans and placed them below their victimizers. The decision pertaining to slavery was overturned, and so will, in time, the decision pertaining to abortion.

The consistencies between abortion and slavery are major and many. Just as the causes and circumstances between the two crimes against humanity are parallel, so too shall be the resolve to each. Slavery has been undermined and overthrown, and the forces which instituted it have been shut down. Their descendants, the proponents of abortion, will receive a similar fate, and their victims will achieve something as basic as the freedom granted to the slaves: life. Society and history have their ways of eventually weeding out the evils visited upon mankind; thus, it is only time that stands between now and a time where unborn children will be treated as the humans they are.

Abortion: Slavery Reincarnate
http://rlbm.home.tripod.com/lincoln.html" (Similar arguments were used to justify ethnic cleansing in Bosnia and Kosovo).

"What has any of this to do with the z/e/f' status as a non-person?"

Two very poor Supreme Court decisions that denied people their rights-by denying that they were equal people (persons). The parallel is very clear and obvious here. You want to deny that a class of people are persons so that you can legally kill them. In other words, you want to treat them like property-just like the slaves were once treated; as demonstrated by the Dred Scott decision.

Intecon

"No one may wrongly oppress a born person. Persons may not be deprived of life and liberty without due process-whether they be black slaves, or pregnant women."

No one may wrongly oppress a person. Persons may not be deprived of life and liberty without due process-whether they be black slaves, or pregnant women, or children who just happen to still be inside their mothers. Physical location does not determine personhood.

Intecon, at http://www.aboutabortions.com/

From: alegria (JFISHER60) Jul-16 11:46 pm
To: HECK01 (529 of 1220) 2012.529 in reply to 2012.525

(The above essay was reposted, in part, to Heck01, then:)

"Your misinterpretation of Roe v. Wade is staggering in its inaccuracy. The SC did not deny the unborn citizenship or personhood-it simply agreed with and upheld the constitutional provisions that exclude the unborn."

The SC ignored the personhood of the child in order to make the decision it wanted to make. It's an outrageous misrepresentation that there are Constitutional provisions that exclude the unborn. Where does it say "the unborn are excluded"? It doesn't. Show me. You can't, because it's not there.

We've been over what the Constitution says a number of times now-the exact language.

"The SC did confirm the pregnant woman's rights however-which is, of course, the real issue. The pregnant woman is the person-her rights are paramount. The z/e/f is not a person, it has no rights."

There is no such thing as a z/e/f. You seek to deny the rights of the child inside the mother. Out of sight, out of mind, is, I guess, your philosophy; so that you can kill that person at your discretion. In other words, treat it like property, like a nonperson; just like a slave.

"violate the Due Process Clause of the Fourteenth Amendment, which protects against state action the right to privacy, including a woman's qualified right to terminate her pregnancy."

An error of the court. There's no "right to privacy" in the 14th Amendment. They couldn't even get the language of the Constitution right, they were so ignorant of it. Besides that, she violates her own right to privacy by going to an abortion clinic and making it a matter of record. They made up these things to serve their own purposes-legalizing abortion-just like you make up things to justify your arguments. Unfortunately, the mentality is the same. And "due process" applies to someone who is accused of a crime. Being pregnant isn't a crime. Nobody is ever accused of a crime for being pregnant; so the right to due process isn't applicable here. The Supreme Court Justices made up arguments to justify the Roe v Wade decision, just like a previous Supreme Court made up arguments to justify slavery in the Dred Scott decision. That's why the two decisions are related. What this is basically all about is that the Supreme Court Judges made the wrong decision in Roe v Wade-just like in Dred Scott. And there's no "right to terminate her pregnancy" in the Constitution either. That's another thing they made up.

Intecon, at http://www.aboutabortions.com/

The slaves had one big advantage over today's oppressed. They could be sold for money; they had economic value. That's one of the things that I think is wrong in how our society handles unwanted pregnancies. People should be able to pay for undelivered, unwanted children. It would provide a free enterprise solution to the problem. Instead of having to pay for an abortion, girls could get paid for having their child.

"As I said-any attempt to equate slavery wrongly with pro-choice will be instantly dismissed."

It's not dismissed with me. It's the right equation.

Intecon

"The injustice is of course, the wrongful oppression directed against pregnant women".

You're talking oppression of women, by women; because a majority of women oppose abortion. Now that doesn't make sense, does it?
Or why do you think a majority of women want to oppress other women; and themselves? Your oppression argument makes no sense.

"identical to slavery" Slavery was outlawed by the 13th Amendment to the Constitution, so you should be able to take that to court; if you can find an actual example of it.

Intecon, at http://www.aboutabortions.com/

"The wrongful oppression of born persons-whether they be black slaves or pregnant women is a toxic hate-virus that must be defeated always."

You didn't get that quite right, but maybe it's a typo. That's o'k, I'll correct it for you, because we don't want to leave any people out; don't want to let them fall through the cracks.

The wrongful oppression of all persons-whether they be black slaves or pregnant women or children, is a toxic hate-virus that must be defeated always.

There, that's much better. Now let's do another one right too.

"a society, country, government cannot consider itself free or civilized if it tolerates the wrongful oppression of its citizens, or born persons living within its jurisdiction."

A society, country, government cannot consider itself free or civilized if it tolerates the wrongful oppression of its citizens, or persons living within its jurisdiction.

"This is clearly outlined in the US Constitution." Yea, I think we've got it right now. Let's see, there's one more:

"The injustice of anti-choice will always be unacceptable, and will always be defeated by the forces of liberty and personal freedom."

Intecon

The wording "anti-choice" doesn't really convey any meaning. I mean, everybody's for choice. Let's change that, too, and I think it will be more meaningful.

The injustice of abortion will always be unacceptable, and will soon be defeated by the forces of liberty and personal freedom.

Now I think we've got it right! Let's go to press!

Intecon

Mole Pregnancies, Politics, and The Future

Here's what I was able to find on a "mole pregnancy".

"A molar pregnancy, or hydatidiform mole, is a pregnancy gone awry, resulting in a tumor of the placenta. The chorionic villi of the placenta grow into a grape-like bunch of cysts within the uterus.

Most molar pregnancies are unable to support a fetus a fetal heartbeat is not heard

An ultrasound examination can confirm the diagnosis.

The hormone level is then checked every few months for up to a year, to be certain that the disease is in remission and that no malignant changes have occurred.

Molar Pregnancy (Hydatidiform Mole):

Molar pregnancy is very rare. It is also called "a mole". A molar pregnancy is the result of a (purely chance) genetic error during the fertilisation process that in turn causes the growth of abnormal tissue (which is not an embryo) within the uterus.

The growth of this material is very rapid compared to normal foetal growth. It has the appearance of a large and random collection of grape-like cell clusters.

There are two types of hydatidiform molar pregnancy, 'complete' and 'partial'.

In a 'complete mole' the mass of tissue is completely made up of abnormal cells that would have become the placenta in a normal pregnancy. There is no foetus and nothing can be found at the time of the first scan.

In a 'partial mole', the mass may contain both these abnormal cells and often a foetus that has severe defects. In this case the foetus will be consumed by the growing abnormal mass very quickly.

For the more scientifically minded amongst you:

Complete moles often have a diploid (double) karyotype (chromosome analysis) 46,XX due to fertilisation of an empty egg by a single sperm followed by reduplication of the haploid (single) chromosome.

Partial moles have a triploid (triple) karyotype (69,XXX or 69,XXY) due to the fertilisation of a single egg with two sperm."

So, it sounds like a mole pregnancy is more like a disease, and doesn't have the genetic makeup of a human being; e.g., 23 chromosomes. As a "genetic error", it could not be said to ever be a genetic human being, or to have "the human genetic code". So I think my definition of a human, or person, as being someone who has the human genetic code, still stands correct.

Intecon, at: http://www.aboutabortions.com/

"'Conception of a human being never occurred.'

But the mole pregnancy is a product of conception. Is it human life?? conception is inadequate to determine whether human life was produced.

also-the identical twin is not present at conception-is it not human life?? It doesn't appear until later with subsequent cell division.

Follow-up observations or tests are required, which eliminates conception as the deciding event.

Here's the problem-sperm unites with egg-has a human life been initiated?? or is it a mole, or a flawed ovum? twin or whatever??

You cannot tell-therefore conception is not adequate as the defining marker of human life."

Well, you started off wrong with your first sentence. I decided that if I was going to talk about conception I had better understand exactly what it meant, so I looked it up in the dictionary I have on my computer. Here's what it said:

"con·cep·tion (k…n-sμp"sh…n) n. 1.a. Formation of a viable zygote by the union of the male sperm and the female ovum".

A "viable" zygote is not formed in a mole pregnancy, so conception has not occurred. Here's what is formed: "a tumor of the placenta. The chorionic villi of the placenta grow into a grape-like bunch of cysts within the uterus." Sounds to me like you're trying to work a play on words again.

"The hormone level is then checked every few months for up to a year, to be certain that the disease is in remission and that no malignant changes have occurred."

Note that in the medical source I used it referred to it as a "disease".

It also called it "very rare", so I have to wonder somewhat about why you want to keep discussing something that so seldom happens.

And I don't understand where you come up with this identical twin stuff. I would have to put it in the lie category, unless you can come up with a reference to supporting literature. I'm not necessarily accusing you of lying, it could very well be where you're getting your information from. I don't accept it. It would have to be something I could personally verify, without having to travel to John Hopkins, etc.; or even South Dakota. But I'll assume you really meant fraternal twins. As I see it, that would be a partial mole:

"In a 'partial mole', the mass may contain both these abnormal cells and often a foetus that has severe defects. In this case the foetus will be consumed by the growing abnormal mass very quickly." You would have two genetic errors; one more severe than the other. Even if they were identical twins, it's not inconceivable that you could have one blastocyst that turned into a mole, and another blastocyst with severe defects that would have eventually resulted in a miscarriage; but instead was consumed by the mole. But I don't see much point in probing the frontiers of science, or the freaks of nature, when abortion is such a simple matter to understand that even you should be able to get it eventually. Is this to confuse us so that we are distracted from the real issue? None of this changes the fact that a healthy child in the womb is a person that you can easily see and identify through an ultrasound, or that is depicted on this web page:

http://www.babycenter.com/general/3284.html?CP_bid=

So I've already wasted too much time on something that's pretty irrelevant. After all, I'm not a doctor. Right Steen? But if you're still not satisfied, and can come up with some new, more worthwhile issues, I'll look into it further for you.

Intecon, at http://www.aboutabortions.com/

"Conception certainly did take place. If you want to hold on tight to that 'it's a person/human being from the moment of conception' argument, you have to concede that hyditaform moles are persons/ human beings. And you still have to contend with identical twins, fraternal twins that merge to become *one* embryo and parthenogenetic embryos. Or you could concede that the biology that is at work here simply won't let you play the 'person/human being at conception' card."

SOME_GUY1 enters the fray! We're back to tag team debating!

I'm not sure who you're debating, though. Maybe it's partly my fault; maybe I didn't say something with sufficient clarity. But from my end I can tell you that I've never been debating when a person, or a human being, comes to exist. That's an entirely different argument, so far as I'm concerned. Let's keep things relatively simple when we can. A mole pregnancy is difficult enough to understand by itself, because it's so rare that there's very little literature on it (which is a situation that I would expect PP to exploit); without mixing in other topics, too. My concern is: exactly what is a molar pregnancy, and what does it prove, if anything; that is, what conclusions can we draw from it?

You wanted me, you've got me. First of all you didn't spell it right. If you were an expert in mole pregnancies, instead of just mimicking, I would think you could at least spell it right. You spelled it "hyditaform". It's actually spelled "hydatidiform". It's so rare it's not even in any of the dictionaries I checked out.

A hydatidiform mole is never a person; it's, a, well, hydatidiform mole. Pretty surprising, isn't it? I don't know where you guys hung out during school, but if you had just listened to me before you would have gotten some clues. I wasn't just making that stuff up. I was quoting from internet sources. I didn't record exactly where the information came from, but if you call me a liar I'll go back and make you look like a fool by finding them. So let me repeat myself:

"A molar pregnancy, or hydatidiform mole, is a pregnancy gone awry, resulting in a tumor of the placenta. The chorionic villi of the placenta grow into a grape-like bunch of cysts within the uterus."

I think that's a very distinct summation. It's never a person, or even a potential person. It might start out as a placenta, that then mutates out of control. A placenta is a separate entity from a person, or even a potential person, if you prefer, for the sake of this argument. It attaches itself to the uterus, and the child is attached to the placenta by the umbilical cord. If the placenta doesn't develop properly it can't provide proper nourishment to the child. "Most molar pregnancies are unable to support a fetus…a fetal heartbeat is not heard". So the part that split off from the placenta never makes it to 22 days after fertilization when the heart would start to beat.

"Molar pregnancy is very rare. It is also called "a mole". A molar pregnancy is the result of a (purely chance) genetic error during the fertilisation process that in turn causes the growth of abnormal tissue (which is not an embryo) within the uterus."

If it's not ever an embryo it certainly can't go on to become a person, or even a potential person. Am I making myself clear? "you have to concede that hyditaform moles are persons/human beings." B.S. Rubbish.

"The growth of this material is very rapid compared to normal foetal growth. It has the appearance of a large and random collection of grape-like cell clusters.

There are two types of hydatidiform molar pregnancy, 'complete' and 'partial'.

In a 'complete mole' the mass of tissue is completely made up of abnormal cells that would have become the placenta in a normal pregnancy. There is no foetus and nothing can be found at the time of the first scan.

In a 'partial mole', the mass may contain both these abnormal cells and often a foetus that has severe defects. In this case the foetus will be consumed by the growing abnormal mass very quickly."

"And you still have to contend with identical twins".

No I don't.

"A type of twins derived from a single egg. Identical twins form when a single fertilized egg splits into two embryos. Because the twins share the same DNA set, they tend to have similar features."

"Complete moles often have a diploid (double) karyotype (chromosome analysis) 46,XX due to fertilisation of an empty egg by a single sperm followed by reduplication of the haploid (single) chromosome.

Partial moles have a triploid (triple) karyotype (69,XXX or 69,XXY) due to the fertilisation of a single egg with two sperm."

It should be obvious to everyone that an empty egg can't produce a person. The single chromosome has nothing to combine with so it just keeps replicating itself and becomes a mole-not a person or even a potential person.

"fertilisation of a single egg with two sperm." So what do you get when this happens? I wasn't sure, so I spent a couple of hours at Barnes and Noble going through everything they had that was even remotely related to the subject. I ended up getting one book that seemed to be the most helpful. I can tell you with a high degree of certainty that you wouldn't get identical twins. Common sense tells you that too; something that's missing at PP. If the sperm were to cause the egg to split in two, each half containing one of the sperm, obviously they couldn't be identical. How are identical twins formed? "...monozygotic, or identical, in which a single fertilized egg divides into two or more individuals ...Monozygotic pregnancy involves a single sperm and egg". That's taken from: "The New A to Z Women's Health Fourth Edition A Concise Encyclopedia" A single sperm and egg. Every book I looked at, at Barnes and Noble, that had anything to say about twins said the same thing-one sperm, one egg. And it's hereditary-certain families have a stronger history of multiple births.

No place i've looked said anything about two sperms entering one egg; except that statement on molar pregnancies. Usually when a sperm enters an egg the egg immediately slams the door shut; shields up!, so that no other sperm can get in. In other words there is a change in the egg's surface that prevents the other 250 sperm that made it that far, out of the original 250,000,000, from penetrating the wall of the egg. Of course, if you had an empty egg, it might not be able to do this. Two sperm, one egg, only seems to result in a molar pregnancy. Unless you can show me some verifiable evidence otherwise. What it doesn't result in is identical twins. So it seems that your source of information isn't very reliable. Are you being lied to? You figure it out.

I don't understand at all why you threw in fraternal twins. Do you? One egg, one sperm, multiple times. If one of the placentas turned into a molar pregnancy it would probably consume the separate, healthy one. I don't know, there was nothing in the literature I looked at about it. Does it matter? Perhaps you should go to Barnes and Noble and stand shoulder to shoulder with the pregnant women going through the books looking for them. After you've been there for awhile they start to accept you as one of them.

"fraternal twins that merge to become *one* embryo"

I don't know what you think this is going to prove. I haven't seen anything that refers to it. Does it happen, or is it another figment of your imagination? Redeem yourself, and tell me where I can go to learn about it, and what bearing you think it might have on this discussion.

"and parthenogenetic embryos."

"par·the·no·gen·e·sis (pär"th…-n½-jμn"'-s's) n. A form of reproduction in which an unfertilized egg develops into a new individual, occurring commonly among insects and certain other arthropods. [New Latin: Greek parthenos, virgin + genesis.]
—par"the·no·ge·net"ic" (-j…-nμt"'k) adj.
—par"the·no·ge·net"i·cal·ly adv."

I'm not even going to touch that one. It sounds like a step down from the "frogs and snakes" Heck01 uses to prove his theories on human reproduction.

Just stop and think about it for a moment: Every child is the best of 250,000,000 possible choices.

Intecon, at web site:

http://www.aboutabortions.com/

">>It should be obvious that a child is born when a woman becomes pregnant...etc<<

Let's say for the sake of this individual post that it is. What then? How is society supposed to direct that concept towards protecting these children?

Let's say for example that a particular child is three weeks old (3 weeks post-conception) and is lined up for the chop but no one other than the woman is aware of this. How can you rationalise the idea that you are looking to save something that you don't even know exists?

In fact, the woman could be the only person aware of the presence of the child right up until the time the pregnancy is visibly apparent and even then you'd still have problems. How would you know whether a woman who is visibly pregnant one week but not the next week has given birth, aborted or miscarried?

How would you go about protecting these children from the moment of their 'birth' onwards? Do you not think that if there is no realistic and cost-effective way in which this these children can be protected then your comment serves no purpose whatsoever?

One of the reasons women have been using abortion since time-immemorial is because pregnancy is such a personal issue that abortion goes on unnoticed and therefore can have no detrimental effect on society. Nothing has changed in this department, and until the act of conception automatically tattoos a person's forehead with the information then it is unlikely to ever do so."

Well, I don't agree with you that aborting a child has no detrimental effect on society. Perhaps this child would have been hopelessly crippled by a terrible neurological disease, unable to care for himself, and little hope for him even to live to adulthood. In a word, Stephen Hawking, the man who explained the origins of the universe. What a terrible loss it would have been to society, science, and our whole world to lose Stephen. The last I heard, Stephen had divorced his wife and married his nurse; while his former wife married his doctor. So, it seems to me, Stephen is enjoying his life quite a bit, and has made his parents proud. And please don't hit me up along side the head if I didn't get something quite right in this example-what I didn't get right could have been true in an example I entirely made up instead; but Stephen Hawking himself is reality; not a figment of my runaway imagination.

Well, now that I've caught up with your post, you should have read the other reasons I gave about why I thought abortion was detrimental to society, so I hope I don't have to keep repeating them like I do with Heck01-they're history-right?

I'll take your example of a child three weeks post-conception. Let's define conception as the moment of fertilization, because I think that's the way most people think of it, and I think that's what you probably meant. Fertilization occurred a week before her period is due. A week goes by. She has her period. Why? Because she's not pregnant. You stop having your period after you become pregnant. Next day that fertilized egg, a little bit more developed than when fertilization occurred (and we don't need to get into that much detail for the purposes of this discussion, which I would have to take five or ten minutes to look up anyway), collides with the woman's uterus. It then breaks in two, or divides, into two parts. One part is the placenta. The placenta begins to attach itself to the wall of the uterus. I don't know exactly how it does that-but somehow it gets very close without actually becoming a part of the woman; like if I shook your hand, I would get very close to you without actually becoming a part of you; if your hand was sweaty, you would transfer some of that sweat to my hand; if we both had cuts on our hands and they came into contact we might actually exchange blood. Of course the placenta doesn't have cuts; it is pre-programmed to attach itself in a way that allows an exchange of fluids between placenta and mother. And it takes about a week to do that. Someplace within that week, a message is sent to the mother-ping, your pregnant, I guess. But, in our example, and we can do another example later if you want to, she isn't due to have her period for another three weeks, so she doesn't get the message. But her body knows. Five weeks after "conception" her ovaries fail to release an egg, and she doesn't have a period. Does she say, "oh, I've missed my period, on day 1"? Probably not. She probably doesn't even notice.

But after several days she'll probably notice that her period's late. Does she say, "oh, I'm pregnant"? Probably not; she probably says "I hope I'm not pregnant!". But she has definitely started to worry about, or hope, that she's pregnant. So I think it's reasonable to assume that it takes at least a week after she misses her period before alarm bells, or church bells, start to go off in her head. Now, it's six full weeks since fertilization occurred.

But wait, what happened to the kid! There's been no mention of the kid! Let's go back and see what happened to the kid! There he is, floating attached to the umbilical cord like a spacewalker, and we can see that the umbilical cord is attached to the placenta, which has somehow anchored itself to the uterus.

Wow! He's over 10,000 times larger than he was when he split off from the placenta! We can actually see his heart beating! We can see his face! We can measure his brain waves!

But now mom wants to find out whether she's really pregnant, so she calls the doctor's office. "Is it an emergency?" "Well, no, not exactly". So they make an appointment for her one week from today. How many women would self-test? I don't think we can say for sure. Let's assume she wants to make absolutely certain she's pregnant, so she's going to go to a gynecologist, or her family doctor. She can't go to an abortion mill, because abortion has been outlawed, and is now treated just like any other murder; and they just sent an abortion doctor up the river to spend life in prison with no possibility of parole; and everybody's afraid to roll the dice and take that risk. So, she goes to her doctor, and finds out that, yes, she is pregnant. So now seven weeks have gone by since "conception". She goes home to ponder what she should do.

Meanwhile, the doctor fills out a report, and estimates the date of conception. He then sends the report to an agency set up especially for that purpose. The agency assigns the child a social security number, and enters the information into the central computer. I know this sounds Orwellian at this point, but please bear with me anyway-it all works out in the end.

At home, mom is going over her options. She has been taught in sex education class that if she doesn't produce a baby in nine months, or evidence from a hospital of a miscarriage, she will have to spend a year of incarceration (three more months than she would have been pregnant) in a facility set up specifically for women who have aborted. She knows of no place she can go to get an abortion anyway, and she's not certain she could find someone to do it even if she tried. However, her situation isn't desperate at all. Actually, a world of opportunity opens up to her.

There is a long list of people waiting to adopt her baby, and she can pick whomever she wants, if she so desires, and be able to see the child sometime in the future, too, if she wishes. Moreover, they will pay her to adopt her baby. Or, if she prefers, she can get a college scholarship that is worth a lot more than the cash. If desired, all her prenatal and delivery costs will be covered for her-no charge. If there are problems at home, she is free to move in with other women in a home for pregnant mothers without support-at no cost. Or maybe she'll be required to help out somehow-do her part, so to speak.

There will be a special school for mothers to go to if she wants to attend. And if she decides to keep her child and raise it herself, there will be programs to help her get established. And this is only the beginning, because there are many people who are much more creative than I am, who can, I am sure, come up with many more ideas about how to run this support program. This is my vision for an America where abortion has fallen well below the level it was at before Roe v Wade (about 100, 000 in 1972), where it is only a distant rumor out of a dark past; and every child is welcomed into a life of opportunity limited only by his or her own abilities; and every pregnant mother is given all the respect and assistance she needs, to bring to life, hopefully, the next Stephen Hawking.

Intecon, at web site http://www.aboutabortions.com/

The slaves had one big advantage over today's oppressed. They could be sold for money; they had economic value. That's one of the things that I think is wrong in how our society handles unwanted pregnancies. People should be able to pay for undelivered, unwanted children. It would provide a free enterprise solution to the problem. Instead of having to pay for an abortion, girls could get paid for having their child. This is something most people would recoil from in disgust. Well, the old way is resulting in 3,000-4,000 kids being killed every day in the U.S. That's even more disgusting. I don't mean a bidding war-it would need to be regulated. With 1.2-1.5 million unwanted pregnancies per year there should be enough supply to keep the price down. After all, we wouldn't want to encourage girls to get pregnant just to get the money. Today, a lot of people who can't have children of their own have to go overseas to adopt from places like China and Russia.

If there turned out to be an oversupply, government could pay for the surplus, kind of like Boy's Town. I'd much rather be someplace like that than be dead.

Unconventional thinking? Yes. But that seems to be my niche. And I've been thinking about this probably longer than a lot of you have been alive.

"You know, when you haven't studied history in a while, it can be shocking and sad to read these words...

I am sometimes still amazed by the evil that people are capable of...I guess I shouldn't be...

Don't you wonder how such opinions could ever have been expressed by members of the Supreme Court? How educated, intelligent people could ever have considered these ideas acceptable? Yet they did. Society accepted these ideas. They weren't shocked by them."

Yes, I agree with you, it is pretty amazing. It certainly doesn't reflect the way I was brought up, and we weren't even very religious; although abortion wasn't an issue in those days. I've spent a lot of time pondering this. When I was planning my web site, I decided a pre-requisite was going to be that I would start out by examining the other side; I didn't want to just rant, as Heck01 just accused me of doing. I wanted to be constructive, and offer solutions. This was the hardest part of my website to do, because it didn't really come from conviction, from the heart. But I think I did pretty good at it considering my strong feelings against abortion. It's about the difficult situation an unplanned pregnancy can present. I think that if you read it it may help you to better understand the problem, although a lot of people have come up with the wrong solution. Beyond that, I think people aren't as independent minded as they like to think. They're prone to herd behavior, and being manipulated. Not everybody, but a large number. Most young people are especially vulnerable to being misled. Because they don't have the life experience to make sound judgements on their own they can be easily misled by others, and apparently are often being misled even where they go to school. We are also a product of the ideological environments we grow up in, and those things are very hard to separate out. I've also noticed that a lot of people have been brainwashed into believing that being a liberal shows that they are intelligent, and they always walk in lockstep with any professed liberal viewpoints. My own daughter told me not too long ago that she wasn't a conservative. She's the most conservative person I've ever met, and I know her pretty well. And I know she does her own thinking; that's where I get it from. So I'm not too worried about that case. But to me, in most cases, to say you're a liberal is the same as saying you're a fool. Which brings us back to the Supreme Court; are they fools? Do they believe that they're shown to be more intelligent by holding liberal views? Do they only show very poor judgement? And in the case of the women on the court, do they misguidedly believe they are defending women's rights and upholding feminists ideals? Does their decision derive from a concern about the problem of unplanned pregnancies, without giving equal concern to the fate of the child; or is it an ignorance of basic human reproductive and developmental biology? I personally think that these people, far from being wise and erudite, have absorbed the culture around them and are a product of their own ideological environments, incapable of making good independent judgements in this instance. Then where do these ideological beliefs originate? Dr. Bernard Nathanson answers this question for us, in his Confession Of An Ex-Abortionist:

http://www.aboutabortions.com/DrNathan.html

This is why this document is so important, and why abortionists so want to discredit him. I've read more about him, and he is obviously a man of superior intellect and integrity, who realized the error in judgement he had made with the advent of ultra-sound in 1973; the same year of the Roe v Wade decision, and has since been doing all he can to undo the damage he participated in bringing about. I'm not a person of superior intellect, and I can't say it nearly as well as he did, so you owe it to yourself to click on that link and read what he had to say.

But I can summarize it in my own way. I see Planned Parenthood as a huge, evil corporation, interested only in amassing huge profits from performing abortions-sort of like a cigarette company, except that what they are marketing kills much more quickly than cigarettes. Now I'm not saying I think all corporations are evil, or that cigarette companies are anywhere near as evil as the abortion industry-after all, my views basically are conservative; but it helps to understand what's going on if you use this model.

In order to keep the money rolling in they defend and promote their product constantly, intertwining it with peoples' fears of the difficult circumstances of unwanted pregnancies, liberalism, feminism, women's rights, and so on. They spend huge sums to train people in the availability of their service and encourage and promote its use. They brainstorm to come up with new ideas to defend it, and hire people to defend it in forums like this one. They put other abortionists out of business whenever possible, and get referral fees otherwise. They burrow into philanthropic and government organizations to get more revenue from that source. And as Dr. Nathanson pointed out, they have no compunction against lying. They are a cancer on the morality of this once great nation. They contribute huge sums to elect officials who favor abortion, and to defeat those that don't. They work closely with other organizations like NOW and NARAL and Emily's List in the actual political campaigns. And all this spending and propaganda doesn't go unnoticed by the politicians-they see the chance to ride it to political power. Jesse Jackson said: "What happens…to the moral fabric of a nation that accepts the aborting of the life of a baby without a pang of conscience?" That was in 1977. Since then he's "seen the light". But notice that he didn't have his own illegitimate child aborted. That's for other folks. Senator Dick Durbin was a devout Catholic opposed to abortion until he got the message. So we have a failure of leadership to lead here, possessed instead by what they see as self-interest, and they pander to it to get elected.

Perhaps what stuns me the most is that whole religions have embraced abortion. To the best of my knowledge it's still condoned by Methodists, Evangelical Lutherans, and at least accepted by Reform Jews, and probably Conservative Jews. Orthodox Jews oppose it, as far as I know-they ex-communicated Joseph Lieberman because of it (that's a fact, it's on my web page), and the Missouri Synod of Lutherans are against abortion. I think the Evangelical Lutherans have tried to modify their position somewhat. But I'm far from being an expert on religion, and I would welcome any input on this. So some of the blame has to be placed at the doorstep of churches that don't condemn it, because they're supposed to provide moral leadership, and haven't; instead of going with a consensus of their membership. They've failed in their leadership role also.

Intecon, at website:

http://www.aboutabortions.com/

"We look back now, and the evil is clear, but somehow it was not clear to them."

"Do you ever wonder what 'side' we would have all been on had we lived back then?"

I can bear witness to the fact that there was considerable opposition to abortion, as Dr. Nathanson says, prior to Roe v Wade.

I've tried to determine, by going back through my memory, when I first became opposed to abortion. I can remember taking a sex education class in 1968, where, during the first class session, the instructor asked for us to fill out a card stating, as I remember it, what we would like to learn from the class. I was one of the last to hand in my card, so I could follow its progress. What I had written was about abortion being murder. When the instructor read my card (visually), it was as if someone had stabbed him with a knife, and he said he would get back to that one. He did, after he had had a little time to think it over, but I don't remember how he finessed it, except that it didn't make an impression on me. So if I was calling it murder way back then, it must have had time to form in my mind. I believe my opposition to abortion must have commenced when Life magazine published a picture of a child, in peaceful repose, in utero, on its cover. It was an amazing technical feat for its time; I didn't realize it was possible to do something like that, at a time when my main camera experience was with a Kodak Brownie my mother let me use. So if that predates 1968, that's probably the point at which I became opposed to abortion. I was also involved in anti-abortion activities in the early 70s, although I can't remember whether that was pre-Roe or afterwards. But there was a lot of that type of activity going on.

"Are we so naive to think that there are not similar evils in our society today that the large numbers of people cannot see for what they really are?"

I've always had an interest in history. I took a lot of it in school, and I collect books on history. This is unprecedented in human history in its magnitude, either now or in the past. There's nothing else going on in this country that even comes close to rivaling it, although there are some pretty strange things going on; and yes, there are evils "that the large numbers of people cannot see for what they really are". But I just stick to abortion, because I think it is the most serious threat, and I don't want to try to be knowledgeable about everything. However, I do try to do my part and complete opinion polls and make small contributions to other causes.

Intecon

Intecon, at: http://www.aboutabortions.com/

"It sometimes pains me to realize that organizations like ours struggle against so many obstacles, while evil empires like Planned Parenthood receive ridiculously large support from government, foundations and wealthy benefactors. But God chooses the weak and the lowly to do His work, so that all the honor and glory go to Him, as it should. He often provides just enough for our needs, and so helps us to grow…".

Conrad Wojnar
The Women's Center
5116 North Cicero Avenue
Chicago, Illinois 60630

http://www.womens-center.org/

It's amazing how much timely information you can get for a small contribution.

Intecon, at: http://www.aboutabortions.com/

Thanks for that update on Florida politics. I may be able to use that someday. Do you happen to remember the number of illegal voters, and why nothing was done about it? I know I probably wouldn't remember the numbers. I find it rather sad about the Democratic party. It used to be that both parties would try to command the middle ground. For example, I voted for Lyndon Johnson, when I usually vote for Republicans; and a lot of Democrats voted for Ronald Reagan (are you listening, Heck01). I don't consider myself a Republican, but I can see no place I would fit into the Democratic party today. Our representative to Congress is a Republican who is staunchly pro-abortion. If a Democrat were to run on an anti-abortion platform I would vote for him (or her); and I've never voted for our current representative. As a matter of fact, I frequently don't vote for any candidate for a specific office; so in Florida I guess my ballot would be eligible for the "guess" procedure; even though I am capable of punching the holes. Did the state get new voting machines for all the precincts?

Intecon, at http://www.aboutabortions.com/

Pretty surprising they would deride him when his brother is Governor of the state. In a state so closely divided, I wonder if it hurts their circulation any. I think I've heard they're considering going nationwide with identical voting systems, but don't know whether it will come to pass. I think President Bush's committee sent him that recommendation (Ford, Carter, etc.). I believe it's a good idea. Plus, if voting standards were set nationally, it could eliminate illegal voters without stepping on anyone's toes.

Intecon

There seems to be a lot of dislike between the appeals court and Penfield Jackson. I have no idea why. Of course, Microsoft is still guilty of monopolistic practices; it's just the remedy that's been overturned. I thought the appeals court might overturn everything, given their enmity towards Jackson. It's a sad state of affairs when courts' decisions have to be framed against a background of their prejudices-instead of the merits of the case. I've come to the conclusion that our system of justice doesn't work very well, and needs a thorough overhaul. How judges are chosen, how juries are chosen, etc. I don't really have any strong feeling of antipathy toward David Boies, even though he is one of the Democrat's top guns; because I see his role as basically just representing a client. But I do feel a lot of dislike towards Bill Gates because of the way they use their market power to cut out competitors; and because he's a very large contributor to Planned Parenthood through his foundations.

Intecon, at: http://www.aboutabortions.com/

"Does this distaste mean that you will stop using Mr. Gates' products???"

No. The products his company makes are omnipresent, essential to the things I do, necessities not options, and often times only available thru Microsoft. If I made a really big effort I could probably eventually work around them, but I would be hurting myself much more than Mr. Gates. However, where there is a worthwhile choice, I often go with that. For example, I use Netscape Navigator. But there are other ways to fight Mr. Gates. For example, I've participated, in a very modest way, in running ads in his home town newspaper about his position on abortion. This hasn't changed his mind, because, for one thing, his company is a monopoly. However, similar tactics have been successful with companies like Wal-Mart, Target, and, I think, K-mart; plus the New York Transit Authority. The Transit Authority doesn't have any competition either; but they were educated on the meaning of free speech. And the people in this forum who were not aware of his position on abortion, and his contributions to Planned Parenthood, are now informed.

Or is it the New York Port Authority? Well, whatever agency runs the subways in New York.

Intecon, at web site http://www.aboutabortions.com/

Steen, you're still here? Why? Don't you have anything else to do? No, the real terrorist acts have been the brutal murder of 40 million children in the U.S. since Roe vs. Wade, and those who supported those acts. Isn't this where we left off? Still no concern for the kids? Intecon at http://www.aboutabortions.com/. No offense meant.

My "lies" statement wasn't aimed specifically at you, although I understand why you took it that way.

With regard to post-abortion syndrome, I agree that a majority of women who get abortions apparently don't have that problem. Maybe they never understand what they did. But the 560,000 number that I cited is a pretty big number. I also gave a reliable source for it; plus the fact that Rachel's Vineyard hosts 100 retreats a year for these women, another source you could check. So this is not a bogus claim. Maybe you missed that information in my previous post to someone else. I also mentioned Safe Haven, a third source you could check. You could also check with The Elliot Institute, or The National Office for Post Abortion Reconciliation and Healing. All the contact information is on my web site. Do your own study. So that's my answer to your challenge. What information do you have to contradict it?

Intecon at: http://www.aboutabortions.com/

From: INTECON May-30 10:19 pm To: GLEN__19 unread (8 of 9) 2015.8 in reply to 2015.7

Ouch! It's kind of scary when you think of what could logically happen. But in a democracy, we're supposed to be able to work these things out-if the democracy is working like it should. A strength of a democracy is being able to change to address injustices. A weakness is when that process can be corrupted to prevent that change from occurring.

From: Steen Goddik (SGODDIK) May-30 11:57 pm To: INTECON unread (9 of 9) 2015.9 in reply to 2015.8

[I] Ouch! It's kind of scary when you think of what could logically happen.

Indeed. Especially when you realize that when people are systematically being attacked with violence, they will fight back at whomever they can identify as a target. So the continued violence agaoinst clinics, staff and physicians, not to

542

mention the vruel harranguing of women, might well lead to similar tactics against anybody voicing opposition against abortion as well.

As you might have read in TIME magazine, there is an organization called Medical Students for Choice. Our local president here in South dakota received death treats when she started our chapter, which prompted all of us to compile lists of people to watch out for. This, of course is more defensive as in never to be alone with any of them or exposing yourself in their territory.

But the step to a potential target list, of course, is not that great. If she was to get shot at and if similar attacks happened to the rest of us members, then the likelyhood of some kind of defensive action will become likely.

So it is really up to the PL whether they will accept violence' with anything else than "but I personally think it is wrong" with what the future might bring as well.

Steen

Gee, Steen, maybe I should study it more carefully, but I really don't see anything there to disagree with. This is no fun. But let me add that since the victims of abortion can't stand up for themselves; are, in fact, defenseless-we, you and I, need to stand up for them. Not just for them but for ourselves, too-lest we become a target for extermination some day because we belong to the wrong group of people-say the aged, which isn't too far in the future for me-and who can say what maladies I might come down with between now and then that would mark me as expendable.

I think it's good to take precautions, but then again it sounds like you're overreacting when you talk about "defensive actions". I don't think there's a "conspiracy" going on "to get you", but there must be something going on for you to be so concerned; and it's probably individuals or small groups that are doing it. Don't judge the whole pro-life movement based on what a few individuals are taking upon themselves to do-the pro-life organizations I follow aren't that way.

There's some anxiety on our side, too, and if you read what's on my web site you'd notice that. I had a bunker mentality too when I was getting ready to put up my web site, before I found out there were thousands of other web sites on abortion, some with names like abortionismurder; and while the Clinton administration was still in office. One reason I was so apprehensive was my familiarity with what had happened at Ruby Ridge, Waco, and to the man who wrote the book on TWA Flight 800. I was also a little concerned about what the fanatical abortion rights people might do to retaliate; but my primary fear was the federal government. So before I put my website online, I distributed copies to several different sources, in case something should happen to me. I had a security system installed in my home, and held a discussion with my family about how to keep the house secure. Then, enduring considerable ridicule, I put them through a drill on how to get out of the house and call the local police if we should be raided like the person who wrote TWA 800 was. I didn't really think it likely that we would have a problem, but I was going to cover the bases, just in case. I placed a loaded gun next to my computer, and resolved that if federal agents were going to confiscate my computer, like they did to the Flight 800 author, they would have to go through me to do it, and we would sort it out in court afterwards. So I'm very committed here.

But Steen, you're studying to be a doctor. Doctor's are supposed to help sick people get well, and save lives-not kill people. Why are you championing a woman's right to kill her child? It's not your battle. Let me read something to you from a letter I received from Alan Keyes today-a man for whom I have the utmost respect. "…if you survey physicians on what they think about abortionists, virtually all of them—even 'pro-abortion' doctors—regard abortionists as losers—the dregs of the medical profession. Legalized abortion keeps them out of jail, but they're still regarded as scum by their fellow doctors!" "Abortionists themselves testify that being an abortionist is a miserable way to spend your life."

Personally, I believe you're being used-manipulated.

I don't think anybody is going to start shooting medical students at your school, and risk spending the rest of their lives in prison or getting the death penalty-although today a shooting can happen at any school. But people are very mad about what's going on, myself included. There's a simple way for you to avoid the harassment and threats that seem to be going on. Don't do abortions, and don't support doing them.

Intecon at http://www.aboutabortions.com/

From: Steen Goddik (SGODDIK) Jun-1 10:24 am To: INTECON
(14 of 23) 2015.14 in reply to 2015.13

[I] I think it's good to take precautions, but then again it sounds like you're overreacting when you talk about "defensive actions".

Not if some loon from AoG truly seeks to get me or put me on the nuremberg site.

BTW, did you read the article on Salon.com? Our host is promonently featured along with info on some of her associations.

|I| but there must be something going on for you to be so concerned; and it's probably individuals or small groups that are doing it

----

I am only concerned if the loons are allowed free reign.

|I| Don't judge the whole pro-life movement based on what a few individuals are taking upon themselves to do

----

I am not. On the other hand, it now seems that just by posting here, I might get on the fanatics' radarscreen according to Salon.com

----

|I| One reason I was so apprehensive was my familiarity with what had happened at Ruby Ridge, Waco,

----

LOL. ALl you have to do to avoid that is to not stuff your house with illegal automatic weapons.

|I| and to the man who wrote the book on TWA Flight 800.

??? You are not talking about those missile conspiracy crazies, are you?

|I| I was also a little concerned about what the fanatical abortion rights people might do to retaliate;

That is why I am puzzled that the PL here are not more vocal against glen, c541, spitz or coffeegoddess. When you stand among them and they shoot at us, exactly what do you think will happen?
Do you trust our aim? We are not the ones with paranoid "government is out to get me" fantasies, militia and domestic terrorist connections or the stockpile of automatic weapons, weekend survival training and all that anti-democracy nonsense.

|I| but my primary fear was the federal government.

Here is a hint for you: ***YOU*** are the federal Government. We all are. You vote, don't you?

|I| Then, enduring considerable ridicule, I put them through a drill on how to get out of the house and call the local police if we should be raided like the person who wrote TWA 800 was.

Oh? are you perpetuating illegal activity? Is your house a hotbed of illegal activity? Are you perpetuating interstate illegal anti-abortion activities? Otherwise why worry? I am always struck by how, sooner or later, so many PL turns out to be paranoid and convinced that "the government" is out to get them. Is that something inherent in the more radical part of the movement?

|I| I didn't really think it likely that we would have a problem, but I was going to cover the bases, just in case. I placed a loaded gun next to my computer, and resolved that if federal agents were going to confiscate my computer, like they did to the Flight 800 author, they would have to go through me to do it, and we would sort it out in court afterwards. So I'm very committed here.

If the federa; agents have a warrant for your copmputer and you try to stop them with a gun, then you would indeed be guilty of a serious crime and would deserve imprisonment. That, and you would run the risk of being shot. You could claim that it would be Waco all over again, but then remember that Waco also arose from somebody trying to obstruct legal activity of the federal government and tried to shoot at them. Waco, Ruby Ridge, McVeight, Eric Rudolph and all those types are CRIMINALS. And they deserve the law to get them. That is the JOB of the law, to protect the rest of us from these gun-toting hate mongers. And if you start swinging guns around, then you are part of that crowd.

|I| But Steen, you're studying to be a doctor. Doctor's are supposed to help sick people get well, and save lives-not kill people

----

I am VERY committed to helping people. Oh, did you forget that women are people?

|I| Why are you championing a woman's right to kill her child?

I am not. Killing a child is very illegal.

|I| It' not your battle.

But you have made it yours. You have decided that you somehow knows better than the woman who is pregnant. And thus, your frantic desire to impose your morality on her MAKES it my business. I have a wife, sisters, nieces etc., and I have NO intention of letting others inflict their twisted morals onto my family.

|I| Alan Keyes today-a man for whom I have the utmost respect.

547

Well, I see Keyes as one of the major scumbags of all times. frankly, if he has any kind of opinion, I would find it likely that I will disagree.

[I].if you survey physicians on what they think about abortionists, virtually all of them—even 'pro-abortion' doctors—regard abortionists as losers—the dregs of the medical profession. Legalized abortion keeps them out of jail, but they're still regarded as scum by their fellow doctors!"

As I know MANY physicians and as none of them have EVER voices such a sentiment, it is obvious that Keyes is BLATANTLY lying. And that does not suprise me one bit. Facists rarely pay heed to fairness and truthfullness.

And more to this point, MANY OB/GYN physicians perform abortions as well. And they are certainly HIGHLY repsected members of the medical profession. maybe you ought to talk to physicians yourself instead of listening to Keyes who obviously don't know truth if it hit him on the head.

[I] "Abortionists themselves testify that being an abortionist is a miserable way to spend your life."

Oh? What happened to all the claims that abortion providers are so hip on the money and that they are really happy with their job as it provides them with untold riches? Can I presume that you then disagree with the fundies who make that particular claim?

[I] Personally, I believe you're being used-manipulated.

Yeah, whatever. Do you care to hear what I think about you lapping up the propaganda of the right-wing fundamentalist fundraisers?

|I|I don't think anybody is going to start shooting medical students at your school,

----

Several med students have received death treats for voicing their support for abortion. Not to mention the stuff they get sent in the mail.

|I| But people are very mad about what's going on, myself included

----

Guess what. So am I. I am furious at the anti-abortion loons and their supporters. I am furious at the violence-apologists. I am severely p.o.'d at those who think that attacking, belittling, lying and so on is a justifiable method to deal with medical science.

And guess what. That is DIRECTLY the reason why I have decided to learn how to perform abortions. Your radical friends are the SOLE reason for that. I'll be dmaned if I will let fanatic right-wingers tell me what to do EVER. I will ALWAYS fight the right-wing fanatics, whether they are facists, latin-american death squads or anti-abortion fundie loons. The more they push, and the more they get 'excused' by the rest of PL, the more I get determined to fight back.

|I| There's a simple way for you to avoid the harassment and threats that seem to be going on. Don't do...|Message truncated|

Boy, I've got a lot of material to cover. Thanks for not deleting it, Christina. O'k, Steen, let's say somebody does take a shot at one of you-it's certainly possible. Or shoots one of you. Or shoots and kills one of you. Are you going to go out and take a shot at one of them; or shoot one of them; or shoot and kill one of them? And then what? You're on the run, or in jail. Maybe you didn't shoot the right person. You're locked up, but they may never figure out who took the first shot. What happens to your medical career? What happens to your marriage? Will she wait for you to get out or move on? Will you get out in time to have a family of your own? Would you look good in an orange jumpsuit? Does South Dakota have a death penalty? If you get caught up in a cycle of violence, you could find yourself in this kind of a situation. Don't be pulled down to their level by the people who are threatening you. Besides, I'm a little familiar with how they get things done in rural areas, and it's more likely they would run you off the road when you were driving your car-then you're dead and it looks like an accident. Don't you see what you're getting yourself into? I'm just trying to be your friend, and you're putting me down. I was really surprised to see you giving out details on your location; there are violent people on both sides of this thing; and I try to be careful not to give out that kind of information. That's just being realistic. I have no illegal weapons. I have a .22 long rifle, and a .38 caliber revolver. They're both registered. I got both of them at times I thought they would be banned. I know how to use the revolver, but I'm not so sure about how to load the .22. My only rifle experience has been with an M1 and a BAR. I'm not real brave guy. If you break into my house and the alarm goes off, you'd better hope the police get here quick, because I'm not going to mess around. I don't mean you specifically, but anybody who breaks into my house-badge or no badge. The people who broke into the man's apartment who wrote the book about TWA 800, roughed him up, handcuffed him and his wife, confiscated his computer, and locked them up; were federal agents who had no search warrant and no arrest warrant, and that was what I was going on. What other reason would they have to do that, except to try to shut him up? The book he was writing pretty much paralleled what I had seen on TV. There were a lot of witnesses on the ground who saw a missile hit the plane. They saw a missile hit the plane on radar. I saw the recovered missile on the TV news (minus the warhead, of course. It would be armor piercing and the explosion would be directed forward). I wasn't interested enough to read the book, but I've seen accounts of what's in it. Right or wrong, what I knew was enough to cause me concern. "You are not talking about those missile conspiracy crazies, are you?" O'k, you tell me what your understanding of what happened is, and what you base it on. I also have never belonged to a militia. I'm not paranoid about the government being out to get me; but I was concerned about what the Clinton administration might do-remember the armed raid on the Cuban family in Miami who were sheltering the little boy? Would you like to discuss Ruby Ridge? There is no illegal activity going on at my house. I first read about Ruby Ridge and Randy Weaver in a national news magazine; Newsweek, I'm pretty sure. I hadn't paid much attention at the time it was going on, and this was after the trials were over. What caught my interest was why would a news magazine I perceived as liberal be running a cover story on Randy Weaver? Then, when I was building my website, I ended up doing online research on it. Let me quote to you from Reason Online, October 1993: http://www.reason.com/9310/fe.bock.html "The eight-week trial of Randy Weaver and Kevin Harrison grew out of such a bizarre set of circumstances that it's not surprising it took a while for the jurors to sort things out. It probably also took them a while to come to grips with the idea that government agencies could so blatantly engage in entrapment, lying, cover-ups, and the killing of innocent people. As one alternate juror, excused before deliberations were completed, put it: 'I felt like a little kid that finds out there is no Santa Clause' On July 8, 1993, in what The New York Times called 'a strong rebuke of the Government's use of force during an armed siege,' a jury in Boise found Randy Weaver, 45 and almost always described in the media as a 'white separatist,' and family friend Kevin Harris, 25, not guilty on six of eight counts, including murder of a U.S. marshal, conspiracy to provoke a confrontation with the government, aiding and abetting murder, and harboring a fugitive. Weaver was found guilty on two minor counts: failure to appear on an earlier firearms charge and violating conditions of bail on the same count." This is followed by a very long and detailed account of what happened, which pretty much was the same story I read in Newsweek. There's another account at http://www.cableaz.com/users/mcharmor/randyweaver.htm; at least I hope it's still there. There was another account at: http://users.netonecom.net/~gwood/TLPref/weaver.htm. But there's nothing that I can find there about how it finally turned out. So I'll just have to relate it from memory. Randy Weaver, was, of course, set free in short order. Then it was the government's turn to go on trial. For the killing of his wife and 15 year old son, who hadn't even reached puberty, he was awarded a million dollar judgment. I'm not sure about the exact amount, but it was between 1 and 3 million dollars. Randy moved back to Iowa with the remainder of his family, and remarried, to the secretary of his attorney. Well, I'm going to quit now, because my eyes are starting to mist up. Some of us in the pro-life movement are that way, you know. Now you're much better informed than the crowd you're hanging out with. End of lesson.

Intecon at: http://www.aboutabortions.com/

Boy oh boy, are you in luck, too, Steen; because the highly respected Dr. Nathanson has made a sequel to Silent Scream, probably because the first one was soooo popular:

"'Eclipse of Reason' Produced by former abortionist Bernard Nathanson, M.D., this film documents the termination of a five-monthold boy as seen by a camera placed inside the mother's uterus. Video, 27 minutes. Order # AB31, $25.00" Call 866-LET-LIVE

Taken from: http://www.aboutabortions.com/

Better yet, you can here him speak, in person, at:
Celebration of Life World Family Conference, June 20-24, in Minneapolis, Radisson Hotel South, Bloomington, 1-888-546-2580

That's right there in your neck of the woods, Mr. Goddick.

You can read CONFESSION OF AN EX-ABORTIONIST at:

http://www.teachlife.org.au/abortion/NA.htm

and the strategy of the "Big Lies" they used to sell abortion to the country-which is still going on full force today.

In that confession he says:

"In 1973, I became director of obstetrics of a large hospital in New York City and had to set up a prenatal research unit, just at the start of a great new technology which we now use every day to study the foetus in the womb." "Foetology makes it undeniably evident that life begins at conception and requires all the protection and safeguards that any of us enjoy."

"...1.55 million abortions means an industry generating $500,000,000 annually."

"It is clear that permissive abortion is purposeful destruction of what is undeniably human life. It is an impermissible act of deadly violence."

"Although I am not a formal religionist, I believe with all my heart that there is a divinity of existence which commands us to declare a final and irreversible halt to this infinitely sad and shameful crime against humanity."

Obviously a man of high intelligence and conscience, trying to make amends for the crimes he committed. He has accomplished more than any of us ever will, and you try to discredit him by telling lies? Many women have problems after just one abortion-think of what he has to live with. I think it's a positive thing to have our heroes; and Dr. Nathanson is one of mine.

Intecon at: http://www.aboutabortions.com/

I was pretty nutty about that TWA Flight 800 thing, wasn't I? Feature this:

"World Net Daily Exclusive WorldNetDaily.com 2003
Flight 800 book sales flying high 'First Strike' ranked at 21 on Amazon best-seller list Posted: March 17, 2003 2:33 p.m. Eastern

A new title from WND Books that strongly suggests terrorism was behind the downing of TWA Flight 800 in 1996 is striking a chord among the nation's book buyers as it soars to No. 21 on Amazon's list of best sellers.

'First Strike: TWA Flight 800 and the Attack on America' was catapulted by the recent vindication of co-author James Sanders, a police officer-turned-investigative reporter who was arrested and jailed because his investigation into the mysterious crash exposed flaws in the government's official probe.

Sanders, who battled the government in court for five years, wrote the book with Jack Cashill.

In December 1997, Sanders and his wife, Elizabeth, a TWA flight attendant and trainer who knew Flight 800's pilots and had trained many of its flight attendants, were arrested for conspiracy to steal government property after receiving material from a whistleblower within the Flight 800 investigation.

Although Sanders and Cashill have always maintained the charges were trumped up by the government so as to chill and discredit Sanders' investigation into what really happened to Flight 800, it has taken years for official vindication to come.

The authors maintain the Clinton Justice Department 'used its considerable powers to thwart Sanders' by denying his standing as a journalist. But the Bush administration Justice Department now admits its predecessors 'conspired to print factually false information in a Justice Department letter to deprive James Sanders of his civil rights...' The current Justice Department also now concedes it 'fabricated a defense where none existed' in earlier opposing the Sanderses' civil action, writes Cashill. 'It also concedes there is no defense for the 32-counts of federal lawlessness committed in pursuit of destroying a journalist and his wife.'

Cashill, who has created documentaries for regional PBS and national cable channels, and who hosted daily talk radio shows for five years, sums up the importance of the Sanders case: 'In so conceding' its previous railroading of Sanders, 'the Justice Department tacitly acknowledges that yes, the TWA Flight 800 investigation has been corrupted, and no, we are not prepared to contest this fact.'

Sanders tells WND the government's time to respond actually ran out in early February – after two warnings.

'The big thing that forced the government to stop responding,' Sanders told WND, 'was that they got caught fabricating a defense. Once that happened, there are rules in civil court that say if they don't cease and desist, they are in big trouble. They knew it was coming again, and they had nothing to say.'

Cashill calls the case 'among the most egregious violations of a reporter's constitutional rights in the history of American journalism.'

What comes next in the case? Sanders tells what should happen next in his view: 'The judge should make a summary judgment ruling in my favor.'

In their groundbreaking expose 'First Strike,' Sanders and Cashill uncover substantial new information – including a terrorist connection – about the fate of TWA Flight 800.

Sept. 11, 2001, they claim, did not represent the first aerial assault against the American mainland. The first came July 17, 1996, with the downing of TWA Flight 800. Their book looks in detail at what people saw and heard on that fateful night.

The book also shows the relationship between events in July 1996 and Sept. 2001, and proclaims how and why the American government attempted to cover up the truth.

'TWA Flight 800 and the Attack on America' is available from WorldNetDaily's online store, ShopNetDaily.

© 2003 WorldNetDaily.com, Inc. Contact WND Co-Located at Fiber Internet Center" http://www.worldnetdaily.com/

And, lest I sound like a right wing gun nut to you, here's what President Clinton told the Cleveland *Plain Dealer* about gun control: "The fight for the assault-weapons ban cost 20 members their seats in Congress," and is "the reason the Republicans control the House". And at a press conference he remarked: "There are some [Democrats] who would be on this platform today, who lost their seats in 1994 because they voted for the Brady Bill and they voted for the assault weapons ban."

Abortion in Poland and India, and Depopulation

From: Colleen Parro rnclife@swbell.net
Subject: Republican National Coalition for Life FaxNotes
Date: Wed, 26 Feb 2003 15:46:50-0600

"What Happens If You Make Abortion Illegal??? – Poland did it!!!
– That is the title of a new brochure from Jack and Barbara Willke's
Life Issues Institute. It points out the fallacy of the argument that
making abortion illegal will just 'drive women into the hands of illegal
abortionists and there will be blood running from the back alleys.' But
Poland did make abortion illegal, and with spectacular pro-life results!

Poland, a nation of 40 million people in which abortion was legal during
44 years of Communist rule, averaged around 150,000 abortions per
year. In 1993 abortion was outlawed. By 2000 the annual number of
abortions had dropped to 138! To read about these and other exciting
statistics you can order the brochure by contacting Hayes Publishing
Co., Inc – Phone: 513/681-7559; Fax: 513/681-9298; e-mail:
hayespub@aol.com."

I ordered the brochure. Here is more information from it: "None of the
dire predictions of back alley abortions materialized. The actual effects
were almost no abortions, healthier women and greater infant survival.

Are Statistics Accurate? The 1993 Polish law requires annual reports
from three separate federal agencies, hence these numbers. All of these
reports have been challenged by pro-abortion groups and all have been
shown to be accurate.

Number of abortions	1968 = 168,000	2000 = 138
Miscarriages	1955 = 59,000	1999 = 41,000
Deaths due to Pregnancy and Birth	1990 = 70	1996 = 21
Neonatal deaths/1000 live births*	1990 = 19	1998 = 9
Illegal abortions (not deaths)	1999 = 99	

* Note that abortions often tear the cervix, weakening it. The result is
more premature births. Preemies die more often.
Therefore, this is an indirect measure of frequency of abortions." (Jack
Willke is a MD)

why?

On the other hand, "Romania currently has the highest abortion rate in the world—3 out of every 4 pregnancies there end in abortion!" Father Thomas Euteneuer, president of Human Life International, speaking at The Women's Center Annual Life Banquet, February 2003.

"*The San Francisco Chronicle* recently reported that abortionists in India are exploiting that culture's strong preference for males. Female feticide has become rampant. 'In the states of Punjab, Madhya Pradesh, Hariyana and Rajistan, the ratio of girls to boys in the 6-and-younger age group is steadily dropping and is now less than 800 girls for every 1,000 boys, official records show. A normal global ratio shows about 1,003 females to 1,000 boys.'1 The article goes on to disclose that, 'Health workers worry that the steady drop in female population will not only lead to a shortage of available wives, but spur an increase in the trafficking of women for the sex trade.' Abortion kills unborn girls and magnifies the misery of many of their born sisters. What a 'woman's right.'

World magazine recently reported on the real problem of *depopulation*, brought on in part by abortion. 'The president of Estonia goes on national TV to urge his countrymen to have more children. Russian President Vladimir Putin warns his parliament about 'a serious crisis threatening Russia's survival': the nation's low birth rate. The government of Singapore is trying to reverse that country's birth dearth by sponsoring a massive taxpayer-funded matchmaking service.'2

The U.S. Centers For Disease Control and other observers of 'abortion medicine' variously estimate that about 1.3 million 'pregnancy terminations' occur each year in this country. The World Health Organization, however, reports that some 55 million abortions are committed globally each year. This stupefying number is made all the more problematic by the fact that virtually no country outside of the United States has a truly proactive pro-life movement." Center for Bio-Ethical Reform, Gregg Cunningham, March 2003. However, opposition to abortion is gathering momentum in countries like Canada and the UK. My web site gets visitors from all over the world. Little Singapore ranks 6th in the number of visitors.

1 "Indian Women trapped in culture of contempt," *The San Francisco Chronicle*, Dec 6, 2002
2 "Population Implosion," *World*, Feb. 15, 2003.

PostScript

I promised I would tell you how to use the website to get the scoop on the latest developments. As you probably realize by now this book is a work in progress.

As events unfold, the web site will continue to grow, although I can't guarantee how far into the future I'll be able to keep it up to date. If it's a big success, I could be doing this for a number of years yet – until the abortion crisis has disappeared in this country, as it eventually must. Or I might go back to making a living doing computer work; or I might be dead, given the stage of life I'm entering. So if there's a new abortion related development you want to get my interpretation on, just go to my document web site:

http://www.aboutabortions.com/, click on Edit at the top of your browser, then click on Find, and enter a search literal. If you were doing this today you might want to enter Laci Peterson to find out what my take is on that homicide event.

If that doesn't find anything, you could try just Peterson, or Laci. If that doesn't work, you might want to come back later, and try again, maybe even on a different topic. Because on my web site almost everything is on one main web page, you can also use this technique as a quick way to use the links you find in the book. In that case, you could right click on the link with your mouse to open the new destination in it's own window, leaving the main document still open so that when you close the new window the old one will still be loaded. You can visit a number of links quickly using this approach: Find, Open in New Window, Close, and repeat for each link you are interested in visiting. In bringing yourself up to date through the companion web site, remember that it is more chronological than the book, so that when you find a good starting point on a new development, you may be able to just keep reading to bring yourself up to date on what's been happening. At least stop by for the 2004 pro-life candidates links.

As enough new material accumulates on the web site to warrant it, there may be later editions of the book. Any future editions would probably include pictures of the major players, and major events, that I have taken.

I hope I didn't fool anybody into thinking my real name is Intecon, although I imagine there will be someone. Intecon is the unique internet handle I chose when I set up the email account related to my web document. It is an acronym for Intellectual Conservative. Conintel wasn't available, probably because of the telecommunications industry. Due to the controversial nature of the subject matter, and how it might affect my professional life, I chose anonymity over self–promotion. I'm not really interested in any personal recognition. I just want to do what I can to help stop the killing, before it can undermine our society any more than it already has. It allows me to segment the controversy out of my everyday life – though it is never far from my thoughts. On the other hand, I am available for speaking engagements, if you know a group that is interested in discussing the topic. I can be contacted through that internet email address, at: intecon@myself.com.

One thing everybody can do to help is to get on the mailing lists of these organizations. They will keep you up to date on what is being done, and give you a chance to support their efforts financially from time to time. I'm always very grateful for the opportunity to contribute that their mailings give me. I've learned I can't do it all by myself, but I always send something when the subject is abortion, and hope that everybody else does, too. I've developed a system for doing it that works well for me, because I get a lot of mail, but don't have a lot of time. I open my mail as I eat supper, and right next to me I have my stamps and return address labels. I open the bills first, and write on them when they are due. Then I open the mail from pro-life organizations. In my wallet I have bills in the denominations I want to use. If there is a request for a donation, I wrap the correspondence around a bill, at least two sheets, put it in their return envelope, apply the address label and a stamp and perhaps some scotch tape to the envelope flap, and it's ready to go. Well, I told you I was strange, remember? If I think a request requires a larger contribution it goes with the bills. If you have a problem with sending cash through the mail, and most people would, you might keep a checkbook with the stamps and labels, or just put the prolife correspondence in with the bills. If you go out to eat, take a flashlight…

Some Conclusions

As you've viewed each of the "trees", I would suppose you've grown to see and understand the "forest"; that is, the pieces in the puzzle have come together to show you the "big picture". Consequently, I'm not going to elaborate too much on that, except to say that some people compare how abortionists use language to George Orwell's book "1984". Today, we need to bypass "oldspeak", and "newspeak", and get on to truespeak. We need to speak plain English instead of Latin, and perhaps place a child's birth at the time of implantation instead of delivery, and call that instead the child's "coming out", although I realize it has some negative connotations in today's society. But if the "peaceniks" could replace the victory sign with the peace sign, I think we could do it, and have "comingout" parties; if we want to celebrate that point in an individual's development-instead of birthday parties. Spanish Foreign Minister Ana Palacio, speaking at the UN on March 7, 2003, about a different topic, used words that I believe best describe what organizations like Planned Parenthood and NOW and NARAL and Emily's List have been doing: "a continuous and systematic misrepresentation of the facts."

As I've followed events these past few years, I've come to some political conclusions about how our system of government works, that may not all be innovative, but for which I'd like to add my voice. Eighty percent of the country can be for a particular piece of legislation, and it can still die in our U.S. Senate.

This is not how democracy, or even a republic, should function. A few special interests should not be able to frustrate the will of the vast majority of an educated electorate. Our supposedly democratic system of government fails to the extent that it does not respond to this kind of obvious consensus, and we need to fix it. This is most apparent in the U.S. Senate, where a number of the members seem to see themselves as unassailable princes. They are completely out of touch with, and unresponsive to the people. That's why I've gone over to favoring term limits. If the President can only serve two terms, why then are senators allowed to serve indefinitely? They acquire this longevity simply because of the greater resources available to the incumbent and the stature of the office and campaign coffers filled by special interests wanting influence. I don't know how we get there, but I think two four year terms should be the limit. Then, at election time, you would have two candidates competing on an equal basis and elected based on their stands on the issues. Also, the filibuster has no place in a democracy. It is a procedural rule that we should be able to eliminate with an up or down vote. There has been a breakdown in our system of democracy that allows small groups to frustrate the will of the majority.

Likewise, there should be term limits for the House. Probably four two year terms should be the maximum before new candidates square off on an equal footing.

No industry should be able to control a political party the way the abortion industry controls the Democratic Party. I don't know what is necessary to put an end to this kind of thing, but it has to be found.

They promote prostitution, sex trafficking, child murder, forced abortion and sterilization worldwide. Their committee on human rights is made up mostly of human rights violators, and the only newsworthy event they've produced lately is to condemn Israel of human rights violations. Their committee on terrorism recently voted that suicide bombing wasn't an act of terrorism. Their membership is dominated by dictatorships and socialists. They are racked by an accounting scandal, where they can't account for where their money goes. We provide 25% (approximately) of their funds and a place for their head-quarters. Yet,

France, a country whose leader was elected with 17% of the vote, defies and tries to dominate us through it and use it to its own ends. Since at least the end of World War II, which is as far back as I can remember, their government has determined its foreign policy mostly by figuring out what ours is and then opposing it. 17%, which is the number I've seen for the ruling party in their parliament, is not, in my mind, democracy-is certainly not majority rule, but minority rule, and closer to anarchy, which is what they ended up having during their French revolution where they went around killing each other until Napoleon put a stop to it and went off to conquer the world. But yet they have grandiose dreams of dominating the UN, probably much like they run their own government back home, where they advocate abortion through the decadent and socialist dominated European Union. And, as one of our legislators remarked, if it wasn't for us they'd all be speaking German.

The United Nations has become a caricature of what it was once meant to be.

Spineless, conniving, decadent, opportunistic. They want to control us through an international court, an army that we supply but they command, a world tax on each of us, set our moral standards, tell us how to raise our children so that they can provide them with abortions, set up a network of legal prostitution and sex trafficking as our newest industry, and on and on. President Bush isn't going to let that happen. But a President like Bill Clinton or Jimmy Carter might. Change, is one of the hardest things to predict or to produce. But the League of Nations outlived its usefulness, and the UN has outlived its – in my opinion. As a matter of fact, I think it may have become a moral imperative that we take action. When they start dragging American leaders down the UN steps, in the U.S., it is time for them to go and for us to get out. They're out of control; and acting like the dictators and backward, undemocratic countries they represent. Let the debate begin.

I'm not against labor unions. I'm still a card carrying member of the Teamster Union. But, according to what I hear, many of the unions are controlled by socialists, where their rank and file members are blue collar, and good, Americans. Again, it distorts our Democratic system when a philosophy alien to our form of government is able to extort funds from these working people and use it for basically subversive purposes. Funds used for political purposes by the unions should come only from voluntary political contributions by its membership for that purpose.

Laws against vote fraud should carry stiffer penalties. Currently, when Democrats hold power, they just ignore them.

And, of course, the courts. Oftentimes they can't convict the guilty in the most obvious of cases, or even show a basic understanding of our constitution. A jury of one's peers, I think, needs to be replaced by juries of legal experts, who need to pass written examinations to serve as professional jurists. The lawyers have too big an advantage over the run of the mill citizen juries selected. If this requires a constitutional amendment, we should get on it, to protect the innocent, and convict the guilty. There have been far too many wrongful and overturned convictions in recent years. The present system fails us way too often.

The Supreme Court is perhaps the most vexing problem, and how we can get it to work right, and not experience any more Dred Scotts or Roe v Wades. I think we need to appoint a selection committee of Constitutional experts who devise and administer an examination that all nominees must pass in order to complete the appointment process. I think the committee should be comprised of scholars from major universities and legal organizations who have specialized in constitutional law, and have a dedication to it rather than to any political party or process. Preparing for this examination, hopefully, would instill an understanding of the constitution in prospective judicial appointees. And, at the very least, judicial nominations should not be subject to filibuster, or a committee majority. All judicial nominees, who have passed the examination, should be sent to the Senate floor, with, of course, the committee's majority, and, if present, minority, recommendations.

Last, but certainly not least, the importance of electing pro-life candidates can not be overemphasized. If everyone works toward that goal and does their part we can get it done. Then, not only can we get the necessary legislation passed, but judges who will uphold it can be appointed.

INDEX

call this curious notion the, 148
call upon all Americans, 146
calling elections, 372
calling the police, 274
callous, 296
calls girls' homes, 260
Cambodia, 15, 21
Cambridge, 61
campaign contributions, 157
campaign debt, 331, 376
Campaign for Working Families,
   159, 165, 172, 194, 205, 219, 225,
   231, 242, 243, 244, 251, 320, 332,
   367, 371, 372, 376
campaign issue, 227
Campaign Updates, 316, 349, 352,
   359, 360, 361
Campaign Watch, 201, 348, 351, 376
campaigning was key, 373
campaigns, 132, 191, 196, 327, 350,
   357, 538
Campaigns & Elections, 353
Campbell, 170
Campfire Girls, 275
Campus Life Tours, 41, 71
campus pro-life club, 44
campuses, 41, 44, 136, 415
can be defended in the courts, 161
can feel pain, 466, 498
CAN get an abortion, 264
can no longer hide, 134
can not defend themselves, 490
can not win, 485
Canada, 114, 116, 209, 215, 339,
   385, 556
Canadian woman dies, 80
cancer, 77, 79, 87, 88, 89, 90, 91, 92,
   93, 94, 101, 102, 221, 288, 300,
   452, 538
cancer attributable, 87
cancer incidence has risen, 89
cancer link, 90
cancer research, 91
Candice Miller, 337, 340

Candidate Fund, 319, 320, 337, 338,
   339, 340, 341
Candidate Profiles, 329
Candidate Questionnaire, 355
Candidate Spotlight, 350
Candidates & Information, 350
candlelight vigil, 230
candor, 249
candy-apple baby, 293
cannot consider itself free, 525
cannot get a tattoo, 264
Cano, 221, 222, 223
Canon Law, 284
Canonical Petition, 130
Cantonment, FL, 395
Cantor Fitzgerald, 265
capable of feeling, 515
capacity, 55, 193, 199, 492
capacity for honesty, 193
capital punishment, 15, 446, 489
Capital Survey, 361
capitalize, 112
Capitol Hill, 82, 123, 231, 247, 250,
   253, 360, 442
Capitol Switchboard number, 174
capped, 129
capricious, 83
capsules, 77
captain, 41
caption, 29, 101, 136, 137
captive, 108
capture, 69, 116
captured, 70, 113, 321
car seats, 380
Carbone, 207
carcinogenicity, 79, 80
carcinogens, 89
Cardinal Newman Society, 288, 289,
   291
Cardinals, 25
cards, 105, 139, 262, 263, 405, 452,
   519
care, 1, 2, 55, 68, 81, 84, 133, 134,
   139, 140, 145, 146, 149, 190, 210,
   230, 236, 273, 276, 287, 288, 292,

627

investigative report, 213, 553
investigative work, 267
invests that right, 463
inviolability, 502
invisible, 143
invited, 44, 290, 291, 336, 434
invoke cloture, 246, 253
involuntary euthanasia, 407
involuntary sterilization, 192
involuntary tubal ligation, 207
involved in, xiv, xvii, 2, 38, 40, 45,
    47, 64, 77, 108, 109, 151, 182,
    189, 192, 198, 206, 275, 283, 285,
    295, 330, 340, 350, 386, 399, 400,
    402, 462, 472, 474, 497, 539
involved in abortion, 189, 192, 206
involved in mankind, 472, 497
involvement, 132, 196, 208, 214,
    267, 271, 275, 319, 393, 402
IORG, 215, 216
IORP, 213
Iowa, 139, 254, 255, 316, 364, 365,
    374, 438, 551
IParenting, 390
IPPF, 110, 211
IQ, 16
Iran, 314
Iranians, 108
Iraq, 246, 274, 315
ire of the EC, 216
Ireland, 116, 215
Irish, 129
Ironically, 62, 103, 179, 222, 255,
    374
irony, 177
irreducible minimum, 195
irregular, 141, 466, 498
irregular heart, 466, 498
irresponsible judges, 52
irreversible, 69, 552
irrevocably cement, 469
is not constitutional law, 462, 497
Islamic terrorists, 309
Israel, 294, 317, 561
issue of abortion, 50, 103, 300, 306

issue was decisive, 315
Issues, 80, 89, 126, 157, 215, 256,
    341, 403
issues raised, 33, 159
Issues Update, 80, 89, 126, 157
Item 2272, 130
Ithaca, NY, 404
Ivy League, 250
J Epidemiol, 95
J.D.'s, 283
Jack Cashill, 553
Jack Conway, 328
Jack Kevorkian, 47
Jack Lemmon, 323
Jack Reed, 282, 327
Jackson, 60, 538, 541
Jaclyn Kurr, 201, 202
Jacob, 294
Jacques Chirac, 247
jail, 32, 96, 97, 112, 124, 158, 387,
    410, 415, 426, 457, 544, 548, 549
Jakki Jeffs, 114
JAMA, 440
James Dobson, 196, 318
James Gerstenzang, 203
James Inhofe, 327
James Kennedy, 44
James Kopp, vii, 112, 113, 115, 116,
    419, 422, 431
James McGovern, 285
James Moran, 285
James Sanders, 552, 553
James Saxton, 333
Jane Abraham, 26, 194, 265, 319,
    340, 375
Jane Chastain, 41, 100
Jane Roe, 60, 62, 64, 70, 221, 464
Janet Daling, 87, 88, 90, 469
Janet Despain, 141
Janet Folger, 226, 227
Janet Napolitano, 349, 350
Janet Reno, 19, 38, 105
Janet Woodcock, 85
Janice Bowling, 338, 340
Janice Crouse, 62, 65